FOR YOUR OWN GOOD

ABOUT THE MERCATUS CENTER AT GEORGE MASON UNIVERSITY

The Mercatus Center at George Mason University is the world's premier university source for market-oriented ideas—bridging the gap between academic ideas and real-world problems.

A university-based research center, Mercatus advances knowledge about how markets work to improve people's lives by training graduate students, conducting research, and applying economics to offer solutions to society's most pressing problems.

Our mission is to generate knowledge and understanding of the institutions that affect the freedom to prosper and to find sustainable solutions that overcome the barriers preventing individuals from living free, prosperous, and peaceful lives.

Founded in 1980, the Mercatus Center is located on George Mason University's Arlington and Fairfax campuses.

FOR YOUR OWN GOOD

Taxes, Paternalism, and Fiscal Discrimination in the Twenty-First Century

EDITED BY ADAM J. HOFFER AND TODD NESBIT

MERCATUS CENTER
George Mason University

Arlington, Virginia

Printed in the United States of America

Mercatus Center at George Mason University
3434 Washington Blvd., 4th Floor
Arlington, VA 22201
www.mercatus.org
703-993-4930

Cover design by Studio Gearbox, Sisters, OR
Editing and composition by Westchester Publishing Services, Danbury, CT
Index by Connie Binder

Library of Congress Cataloging-in-Publication Data

Names: Hoffer, Adam J., editor. | Nesbit, Todd, editor.
Title: For your own good : taxes, paternalism, and fiscal discrimination
    in the twenty-first century / edited by Adam J. Hoffer and Todd Nesbit.
Description: Arlington, VA : Mercatus Center at George Mason University,
    [2018] | Includes index.
Identifiers: LCCN 2017040140 | ISBN 9781942951384 (pbk.)
Subjects: LCSH: Fiscal policy—United States. | Taxation—United States.
Classification: LCC HJ257.3 .F67 2017 | DDC 336.200973—dc23
LC record available at https://lccn.loc.gov/2017040140

CONTENTS

Part III: Fiscal Federalism and Selective Taxation

Part IV: The Economics of the Failing Nanny State

I n this book we have compiled essays that collectively scrutinize selective taxation through the lens of institutional economics and public choice theory—or, as some have referenced it, the economics of interest-group politics. The focus of this book is threefold. We first describe why taxes of various types and on specific commodities are enacted in the institutional structure of our government. We then consider how those policies impact outcomes, devoting specific attention to the undesirable secondary and unintended effects of such policies. Finally, we return our attention to the institutional rules and how they can be better formed to improve policy outcomes.

For instance, broadening the list of items subject to sin taxation and escalating existing sin taxes have become commonplace. The definition of a sin good is no longer limited to alcohol, tobacco, and gambling. Policymakers now use selective taxation to discourage innumerable consumer purchases, including selected foods and drinks, entertainment, automobiles, clothing, and the bags used to carry home our purchases. Further, many sin taxes have grown far beyond modest inconveniences: total federal, state, and local taxes paid on a pack of cigarettes are now $7.17 and $6.86 in Chicago and New York City, respectively.[1] This is more than the after-tax price of a pack of cigarettes in much of the country.

To question whether the government should be involved in discouraging the consumption of sin goods is a worthwhile endeavor, and one that we partially pursue in this book. However, even supposing that consumption modification is an acceptable role for government, the ineffectiveness of taxation to discourage consumption (not just the legal purchase) of sin goods and the resulting list of undesirable secondary outcomes suggest that alternative public policy may be more appropriate. We document these outcomes and offer policy guidelines that can produce better results.

The approach and broad subject of this book is not new. The public choice analysis of selective taxation was undertaken in the 1997 volume edited by William F. Shughart II, *Taxing Choice: The Predatory Politics of Fiscal Discrimination* (hereafter, *Taxing Choice*). Indeed, *Taxing Choice* greatly influenced the research interests of both editors of this book and served as inspiration for compiling the present volume.

Todd Nesbit read *Taxing Choice* as an undergraduate student; it was through that reading that he first began to understand how seemingly simple excise taxes could invoke complex and unintended consequences. Largely inspired by the arguments presented in *Taxing Choice* related to the nanny state, the historical evolution of excise tax policy, earmarking, prohibition, social costs of taxation, and rent-seeking, Nesbit wrote his dissertation in 2005, titled "Essays on the Secondary Impacts of Excise Taxation: Quality Substitution, Tax Earmarking, and Cross-Border Effects." He has since published numerous peer-reviewed articles related to selective taxation, specifically on the topics of tax-induced cross-border shopping, quality substitution, and illicit behavior.

Adam J. Hoffer read *Taxing Choice* as a graduate student. In his public economics courses, he found that most of the empirical research on public policy was single directional. A policy would be enacted, and researchers would flock to study the policy's effects. *Taxing Choice* was a rare example of research that investigated public policy from the other direction—putting policy outcomes on the left-hand side of the regression equation, so to speak. *Taxing Choice* asked whether we could explain and predict the observed policy outcomes using standard economic techniques. The basic answer was yes, we could. Politicians are individuals who respond to incentives and follow their own self-interests in the same way we expect everyone else to behave. Hoffer followed this logic in his 2012 dissertation, "Three Essays on the Political Economy of Public Finance." He continues to write and publish peer-reviewed research following the examples put forth in *Taxing Choice*.

While the basic techniques of interest-group politics involving selective taxation have largely remained unchanged—rent-seeking, coalition-building, earmarking, and the like—in the 20 years since the publication of *Taxing Choice*, political entrepreneurs have continued to expand the application of such tools in terms of both the number of items subject to tax and the magnitude of the taxes imposed. Inflation-adjusted state and local government revenue from selective taxation from fiscal years 1997 to 2014, the most recent fiscal year for which data are available at the time of this writing, has increased by 105 percent.[2] Reliance on nontraditional excise taxes—selective taxes on items other than motor fuel, alcoholic beverages, tobacco products, and public utilities—has particularly accelerated, with such revenues increasing by nearly 178 percent (inflation adjusted).[3] This indicates a growing and increasingly intrusive government fulfilling its revenue requirement partially through selective taxes on politically disfavored consumption that is justified on the basis of being for our own good. This trend is, to say the least, of concern and warrants additional thoughtful consideration.

The arguments presented in *Taxing Choice* remain relevant today, and those arguments set the stage for the present volume. In fact, we started with the table of contents from *Taxing Choice* when first sketching the preliminary outline of this book to determine which discussions require a fresh look due to substantial policy changes over the past 20 years and which topics are more deserving of consideration today that were marginal issues in 1997. Our list of contributors includes five authors from *Taxing Choice*, including that book's editor, William F. Shughart II. We believe that our organization of the topics covered and the mix of contributing authors uphold the intellectual contribution of *Taxing Choice* and further advance the discussion of appropriate tax policy.

We thank the publications team at the Mercatus Center not only for supporting this project but also for providing guidance throughout the publication process. We are truly grateful for their assistance. We also thank each of our contributing authors who, despite each being engaged in an already overwhelming research agenda, made the time to contribute valuable essays to this project and to hold to our submission and revision deadlines.

Last, and most importantly, we thank our wives, Chelsea (Adam) and Julie (Todd). This book was a rewarding project that developed at an immensely busy time for both of us. We each welcomed a new child to our respective families during this multiyear project. Our wives deserve much credit for taking on increased responsibilities with our young children and dealing with the added stress during times when this project required additional attention in the evenings and on weekends.

NOTES

1.   Campaign for Tobacco Free Kids, https://www.tobaccofreekids.org/research/factsheets/pdf /0267.pdf.

2.   US Census Bureau, Annual Surveys of State and Local Government Finances, 1997 and 2014, https://www.census.gov/govs/local/historical_data.html.

3.   Ibid.

An Introduction to Selective Taxation

ADAM J. HOFFER

Department of Economics, University of Wisconsin–La Crosse

TODD NESBIT

Department of Economics, Ball State University

S elective taxation of "sin" is one of the oldest and most persistent forms of tax collection. It was such an early component of US history that "Congress—on the recommendation of Treasury Secretary Alexander Hamilton—imposed a tax on whiskey before the ink on the U.S. Constitution was dry" (Hoffer et al. 2014, 50). In recent years, proposals to collect additional tax revenue from selective taxation have garnered broad political support, from cigarette tax increases in Alabama to new soda taxes in Philadelphia.

As explored in detail throughout this book, the motivations for increased selective taxation are manyfold. But basically, selective taxes generate two outcomes: they marginally deter consumption, and they create revenue for the government. These outcomes are very attractive for any politician searching for government revenue and, strangely enough, given sometimes conflicting goals, any individual wishing to decrease social consumption of some disfavored good or activity.

Because a minority of the population consumes any single target of selective taxation,[1] selective tax proposals muster little resistance. The result has been a steady increase of existing selective tax rates and an expansion of which items are selectively taxed. The average state cigarette tax increased from 40.8 cents to 164.9 cents (a 304 percent increase) per pack from 2000 to 2017. In addition, the nominal federal tax rate on cigarettes has increased by nearly 200 percent (34 cents to 101 cents per pack) since 2000.[2]

US federal, state, and local governments have also been creative in the development of new selective taxes. Depending on where you live, you may have to pay a selective tax—in addition to any existing sales tax—on the purchase of a deck of playing cards, fur clothing, marijuana (both legally and illegally purchased), sex-related or nude services, candy, soda, chewing gum, potato chips, pretzels, milkshakes, baked goods, ice cream, popsicles, bagel slicing, sporting or entertainment tickets, parking, a hotel room, medical devices, an electric car, health insurance, and even *not* purchasing health insurance (Hoffer et al. 2014).

Support for new and increased selective taxes has come from both sides of the political aisle. Selective tax rates have increased in every state, with support coming from the most conservative and the most liberal legislatures. In Michigan, for example, Democrats proposed sixty-nine selective state tax increases from 2001 and 2015.[3] While Republicans proposed fewer tax increases, they were responsible for introducing two-thirds of the twenty-one tax increase proposals that were eventually enacted by the state government. On average, Republicans were more supportive of the enacted selective tax increases: 68 percent of Republicans voted in favor of the twenty-one enacted tax increases, while 58 percent of Democrats voted in favor.

THE PROBLEMS WITH SELECTIVE TAXATION

Selective taxation seems to be one of the areas in which Democrats and Republicans agree. Unfortunately, selective taxes often represent inefficient, lazy public policy.

The problem with selective taxes is that they fail most of the metrics by which economists evaluate tax policy. Selective taxes disproportionately affect low-income households, they lack transparency and consistency, they promote inefficient practices by consumers and firms, and they decrease well-being more than other forms of taxation. In addition, selective taxes are among the least-effective ways to discourage "undesirable consumption," and empirical research shows that the revenue generated by selective taxes does not result in increased government expenditures on programs desired by some of the tax proponents. In other words, we can achieve more desirable outcomes at lower costs by using better policy tools than selective taxes.

Employing selective taxation to modify the social and economic outcomes is neither simple nor straightforward. The taxes certainly generate revenue, but they also generate a whole host of undesirable outcomes, detailed throughout this book. The ability (or inability, as it may be) to employ these selective taxes to improve the well-being of American citizens and solve the United States' ballooning public expenditures and debt problem serves as motivation for this volume. Specifically, this book is intended to advance the discussion of the many impacts of tax policy choices—direct and indirect, intended and unintended—so that voters and elected officials can better understand and determine what is and is not good tax policy.

ANALYZING PATERNALISM, TAXES, AND FISCAL DISCRIMINATION

Our analysis is conducted through the lens of public choice theory and institutional economics. Public choice economics insists that all individuals—consumers, producers, voters, bureaucrats, and elected officials—are guided in their decision-making by their own self-interests. Nobel Prize laureate James Buchanan (1979, 359) emphasized the quality of institutional rules in determining the desirability of both private and public outcomes:

> Modern public choice, which has only been developed within the decades since World War II, now allows us to understand more about the way governments work. This understanding in turn suggests that governments, like markets, work effectively only if they are constrained by constitutional rules, by laws and institutions that serve to keep various natural proclivities to excess within bounds or limits.

Public policy is not enacted in a vacuum. Instead it is developed and enacted in a specific institutional structure and by self-interested individuals. As such, a proper study of public policy must move the discussion away from an idealistic conception of optimal policy and instead focus on the process of policy making under specific laws and institutional rules, how such rules influence the outcomes of that policy making process, and the observed outcomes of such polices.

Paternalistic observers typically assume that participants in the political system are benevolent and that this benevolence leads to public policy that maximizes some murky concept of social welfare. This assumption is severely flawed.

Even if all political participants were benevolent, elected and appointed officials do not possess enough information to enact social welfare–maximizing public policy. This need not indicate that attempts will not be made to maximize social welfare; instead it indicates that information constraints—particularly among a relatively small number of so-called elites—generally prevent such outcomes from being realized. Understanding this point is crucial in order to conduct accurate assessments of public policies as they are, rather than as we might hope they would perform.

Informational constraints can also pose problems for the private sector. However, each individual error made in the private sector due to a lack of information is dispersed and impacts only a small number of individuals. Such errors in the public sector are more severe, since a whole town, county, state, or nation of people incur the costs of poor public policy decisions. In short, the limits of centralized knowledge add greatly to the difficulties facing policymakers.

Democracies are also messy and far from perfect. Given the diverse conditions, interests, perceptions, and circumstances of every individual, the preferences of individual constituents vary. A majority of the population often cannot agree on a combination of several policies. Even if a majority of the population did agree on particular policies, allowing any group of individuals—majority or minority—to make choices for others will decrease the well-being of those unable to choose for themselves.

Donald Trump was elected president of the United States in 2016. He received 46.1 percent of the popular vote.[4] He defeated Hillary Clinton, who received 48.2 percent of the popular vote. Their last-to-be-defeated primary opponents were Senators Ted Cruz (R, Texas) and Bernie Sanders (I/D, Vermont), both of whom carried significant support from voters in their respective parties. Many Americans express displeasure at President Trump's policies. However, many Americans would have expressed displeasure at the policies enacted by any of the other three finalists.

Further complicating matters in a democracy, it is quite reasonable to expect that a majority of the population will never agree to a *stable* definition of what is desirable. Kenneth Arrow's (1963) Impossibility theorem states in part that no voting rule exists for making group decisions that leads to consistent outcomes reflecting the preferences of individual voters. The theorem thus implies that the task of maximizing social welfare proves fruitless, because there is no unambiguous way to translate individual desires into a single group decision. That is, any collectively determined concept of social welfare is in constant flux, even if every individual voter's preferences remain unchanged.

Even benevolent policymakers are destined to enact suboptimal policy, since the collectively agreed-on vision of what is optimal—that which is to guide the benevolent policymaker—likely changes before a bill even makes its way out of committee.

Finally, political participants simply are not benevolent. Putting aside a few dark examples making the case for Hayek's (1944, 138–56) "Why the Worst Get on Top [in Politics]" and Matt Ridley's (2017) succinct summary, "It Takes a Government to Do an Auschwitz," we believe that most of the elected policymakers in the United States are generally well-meaning individuals who are arguably not much different from other citizens. What separates policymakers from those they govern is primarily the power granted to them to direct others through threat of coercion. For many politicians, it was the opportunity to use this power to make a positive difference that drew them to their chosen career.

However, to maintain that opportunity and maintain job security, politics must be played, and that involves tradeoffs. Given the institutional rules governing elections and appointments, granting concentrated benefits to organized special interests at the expense of dispersed costs on the many (or on a minority who engage in socially undesirable activities) is often the winning strategy in politics. This process generally involves discriminatory taxation through selective sales and excise taxes, which result in numerous undesirable outcomes. The chapters to follow in this book discuss these processes and outcomes.

OUTLINE OF THE BOOK

For Your Own Good is organized into five parts.

Part I. Public Finance and Public Choice: Establishing the Foundation

In chapter 1, William F. Shughart II explores why selective taxation has persisted throughout US history. Four themes recur. First, Shughart explains that proposals to tax a particular good or activity almost always elicit less opposition than proposals to levy taxes on a broad base. Second, opposition to excise taxes is muted by war and other national emergencies. Third, selective tax policies create tremendous advantages for certain producers and consumers, who, in turn, levy political pressure to get such policies passed. Last but not least, selective tax proposals often are combined with appeals to a higher moral purpose, such as improving the public health.

The next two chapters examine a variety of margins on which tax policy is evaluated. In chapter 2, Justin M. Ross presents the prima facie economic case against selective taxation and in favor of uniform tax principles. Ross examines three philosophical arguments—utilitarian, beneficiarian, and contractarian—each of which favors uniform tax principles over selective taxation along the margins of efficiency and neutrality. He illustrates the arguments through three examples: the 2012 Kansas exemption of pass-through income, per unit taxation, and sales tax holidays. While individuals and groups may differ in the value placed on other evaluative margins, Ross explains that there is little demonstrative difference across the three philosophies as they relate to selective taxation. This lack of disagreement concerning the opposition to selective taxation contrasts with the realized persistence of such taxes, which may be an indication of the effectiveness of special interest groups' tactics.

In chapter 3, Adam J. Hoffer and William F. Shughart II continue the assessment of selective taxation by examining performance in relation to six common areas of interest. Many public finance scholars and practitioners have focused on the analysis of selective taxation as a revenue source. Such analysis regularly concludes that selective consumption taxation of sins is a relatively efficient tool for raising revenue, since consumers tend to be highly resistant to price changes. More recently, however, selective sales and excise taxes have been imposed not only to raise revenue but also to paternalistically encourage individuals to avoid "bad" choices, such as food high in calories.

Unfortunately, paternalists either overlook or ignore that policymakers may be subject to the same cognitive failures as consumers and that the public policy process is largely driven by the influence of special interest groups rather than by the actions of public-spirited politicians and bureaucrats. Hoffer and Shughart reevaluate selective taxes according to popular metrics used to compare different kinds of tax methods, including efficiency, neutrality, horizontal and vertical equity, unproductive consequences, and consumer information and paternalism.

In chapter 4, Richard E. Wagner closes part I with a discussion of how normative economic analysis has potentially tarnished positive (scientific) economic analysis. Economists can contribute to both strands of research; however, they cannot do so at the same time. Yet, as Wagner suggests, researchers can and do permit a confounding of scientific conclusions with various and conflicting ideological presuppositions. All these presuppositions are based on the idea that taxation reflects the acts of benevolent, well-informed leaders who use their power to tax to do good for the people they tax. However, tax policy is not crafted in such an idealistic environment.

When such ideological smokescreens are removed, the actual tax policies that are implemented arise through competition among interest groups, for whom the best tax is always one that someone else pays. Thus, the tax system resides in a political system and is not independent of or autonomous from that political system. Hence, the scope for effective (as opposed to cosmetic) tax reform is limited without reform of the political system that generates the tax system.

Part II. The Political Economy of Public Budgeting

Part II explores the political economy of public budgeting. In chapter 5, Randall G. Holcombe examines the Affordable Care Act (ACA) of 2010, more commonly referred to as Obamacare. The ACA contained a number of new taxes, providing clear illustrations of common political strategies used to minimize opposition to selective taxation. The new taxes were designed so that the burden of those taxes appeared to fall on someone other than an individual healthcare consumer and so that the taxes appeared to not be taxes at all. A Supreme Court decision (in a five-to-four vote) was needed to confirm that the health insurance mandate was actually a tax.

This disguising of the taxes to finance ACA was done in several ways. One strategy was to place taxes on groups who were a clear minority of the population, and often a minority that many people felt could afford the taxes and maybe even deserved to be taxed. Another strategy was to place taxes on the less visible and understood supply side of the market. And, as already noted, yet another strategy was to deny that the taxes were taxes. Holcombe's chapter explores the ACA taxes and the political strategy that intentionally designed the taxes to hide the policy's costs.

Another popular mechanism to generate support and reduce opposition for a new or increased selective tax is to promise to spend the newly generated tax revenue on a politically popular cause. Such promises can be informal—unofficial statements of the intended use of the future revenues but not codified in the tax code—or formally written into law. In chapter 6, George R. Crowley and Adam J. Hoffer consider the case of formal promises, generally referenced as tax earmarking.

The publically stated argument for an earmarked tax is to increase spending on the politically popular program. However, Crowley and Hoffer suggest that because tax revenues can be perfectly substituted for one another, there is no reason to expect an earmarked dollar to have any more of an impact on expenditures than a general fund, undedicated dollar. In the extreme case, policymakers can use an additional earmarked dollar in place of a previously used general fund dollar, freeing that general fund dollar to be used elsewhere and so resulting in no spending change in the targeted expenditure category. Given the complexity of the public budget, voters generally are unaware of such fund reallocations and continue to support future similar earmarked tax proposals.

In chapter 7, Todd Nesbit examines the potential for selective taxation to lead to quality substitution and explains why such substitution matters. Quantity substitution is commonly recognized and is often the intended outcome of a tax: a tax is imposed on a good to increase its price and thus cause consumers to substitute away from the product, reducing the quantity consumed. This substitution in quantity will occur whether the tax is imposed on a per unit or ad valorem (percentage of the price) basis. However, when the taxed good varies in quality level, the per unit taxes can also lead to substitution across quality grades in the product itself, whereas ad valorem taxes do not. That is, per unit taxes can lead consumers who continue to purchase the taxed item to substitute higher quality and more potent versions of the good.

Quality substitution can matter for two reasons. First, it is an unintended consequence of taxation that is often mistakenly ignored. For instance, if per unit taxes lead to the consumption of fewer total units of a good deemed unhealthy but also to an increase in the average potency—a measure of quality—of the good, it is possible that the policy worsens the health of some consumers. Second, the potential for quality substitution may help explain why per unit taxation of sin goods is more common than ad valorem taxation. While no firm actively seeks to be taxed, large established producers of higher quality versions of a good will prefer per unit taxes to minimize the damage to their profits, often at the expense of smaller, upstart firms in the industry.

In chapter 8, Bruce Benson and Brian Meehan examine the evolution of drug policy in the United States from a predatory revenue-seeking perspective. As William Niskanen (1971) first theorized and many other public choice researchers have since expounded on, bureaus can best be described as pursuing a goal of budget maximization. Benson and Meehan's account of the evolution of drug policy—from the imposition of sin taxes and prohibition to the various state policies in effect today—indicates that drug enforcement bureaus are no exception to the pursuit of budget maximization.

With the prohibition of narcotics and marijuana, drug enforcement bureaus acquire revenues through two primary sources: (1) interbureaucratic competition for funds arising from direct taxation and (2) asset seizures. The stiff competition for budgets led to much budgetary entrepreneurship; relevant to this case is state and federal policy to permit civil asset forfeiture and expand its use to both the guilty and the innocent. These asset seizures serve as implicit earmarked taxes for the enforcement bureaus in which the tax rate and base is determined by the bureau itself. Given the independence of this revenue source from the traditional budgetary process, civil asset forfeiture presents a unique case to contrast with the standard earmarks discussed by Crowley and Hoffer in chapter 6.

Robert Lawson concludes part II with a look at gross receipts taxes in chapter 9. Specifically, the chapter distinguishes between the effects of a gross receipts tax and a conventional sales or excise tax. The impact of a tax is not dependent on the statutory (legal) incidence; instead, it is the economic incidence that matters. Lawson shows that, after tax shifting, the gross receipts tax is no different from a sales tax. Recent political support for newly imposed or expanded gross receipts taxes is yet another example of manipulating voter perception—good politics but poor policy. Pitting citizens against one another—households versus corporations, for instance—is not only questionable on moral grounds, but it also leads to poor policy choices.

When considering any tax proposal, the public needs to understand that taxes are ultimately paid by people and that those who pay may not be obvious due to tax shifting. An honest public discussion of these ideas is needed when considering any tax proposal. Lawson illustrates this by detailing a legal challenge to Ohio's commercial activity tax (CAT) on the grounds that it violates the state constitution's ban on sales taxation of food. Given that the CAT and a sales tax impose the same economic incidence on individuals, Lawson suggests that the CAT is an illegal tax under the state's constitution, an argument that the Ohio Supreme Court did not share in 2009.

Part III. Fiscal Federalism and Selective Taxation

Part III takes a closer look at the role of selective taxation in a system where multiple levels of government—federal, state, and local—each have the power to implement tax and expenditure policy. In chapter 10, Peter T. Calcagno and Frank Hefner begin the section with an examination of the effects of using targeted tax incentives as an economic development tool. Targeted tax incentives—various tax credits, tax abatements, infrastructure financing, and grants and loans of public funds—have become a fixture of modern economic development policy. They are often offered to attract or retain private companies to a local community with the promise of increasing economic growth and local jobs.

Calcagno and Hefner assess the consequences of targeted tax incentives on state and local economic development. Specifically, the authors examine whether targeted tax incentives actually deliver on their promise to create jobs and economic growth and to what extent such policies create economic distortions and unintended consequences. After summarizing the efficacy of targeted tax incentives as described by academic research findings, the authors explore specific cases in South Carolina, in which targeted tax incentives were employed. They discuss how the resulting perverse incentives led to various unintended consequences and, ultimately, ineffective policy.

While not the only recipients of targeted tax incentives and subsidies, professional sports franchises receive significant incentives to relocate or stay in their host cities. Like other recipients of targeted incentives, proponents of public financing for professional sports facilities regularly promise regional job growth, economic growth, and increased tax revenue as a result of the stadium and events that take place there. Despite the lack of support for such claims in the academic literature, as discussed by Dennis Coates and Craig A. Depken II in chapter 11, public financing of professional sports facilities remains undeterred, with substantial subsidies in many cases. These subsidies must be funded, and Coates and Depken highlight the range and prevalence of various taxes—typically selective excise taxes—employed to finance stadium and arena construction. The authors offer some insight as to who ultimately pays these taxes, suggesting that more of the tax burden remains with the local community than is generally promised.

In chapter 12, Thad Calabrese examines the financing options for the growing pension shortfall. The primary form of retirement benefit for public employees is a defined benefit pension system, in which all employer and employee contributions are aggregated and deposited into a pension fund for investing purposes. Unfortunately, states have been dramatically underfunding their pension obligations. As of 2013, state pensions were underfunded by more than $1.1 trillion. Calabrese notes that it would currently require devoting nearly 35 percent of total annual state and local government spending to return these pensions to full funding.

State governments recognize the pending fiscal disaster and are experimenting with options to mitigate the problem. Pension benefits are extraordinarily difficult to decrease; therefore, a more common approach has been to increase revenue to close the pension gap. Calabrese details many of the selective taxes that states have implemented to increase revenue, providing case studies from Pennsylvania and Illinois to illustrate some common approaches and their respective impacts.

Part III concludes in chapter 13 with a radical proposal by J. R. Clark and Dwight R. Lee to change the tax system. The largest single source of tax revenue in the United States is the federal income tax. No matter in which state an individual resides, they pay taxes according to the same federal income tax schedule. This model of taxation leaves little room for tax policy experimentation and greatly limits the incentive for voters to "vote with their feet," because no matter where they move, the federal income tax follows them.

Clark and Lee examine what would happen if the federal income tax and all other current federal taxes were abolished and replaced with a system that limited the federal government to collecting a percentage of the total tax collected by each state. The result may better encourage the benefits of a federal system of government.

While it would be presumptuous to claim to completely forecast the results of such a large shift, Clark and Lee point out the resultant significant changes to political and constituent incentives. Different tax regimes would dramatically increase the rewards to individuals voting with their feet. State and local governments would have an incentive to reduce expenditures, reduce taxation, and improve efficiency. But perhaps most importantly, competition and experimentation among state governments would thrive, promoting the development of new and better ideas. Their radical proposal is intriguing and offers much potential. While it may or may not be politically feasible, it offers considerable insight into continued tax reform.

Part IV. The Economics of the Failing Nanny State

Part IV focuses on the failed attempts to employ selective taxation as a means to eliminate or even discourage the consumption of disfavored products and services. This section addresses the failed nanny state with respect to obesity, cigarettes, gambling, and plastic shopping bags. Paternalists argue that the lessons from behavioral economics justify extending government intervention to correct individual failure rather than limiting it to cases of clear market failure. They argue that policymakers can exploit individuals' departures from rationality in ways that correct what paternalists see as irrational individual mistakes. The paternalists aim to fix individual failure by introducing "nudges" (soft paternalism) or "shoves" (hard paternalism) devised by better-informed, benevolent policymakers.

Michael Marlow and Sherzod Abdukadirov argue in chapter 14 that the growing use of paternalism to justify government intervention is often misguided and that policies are too easily justified by assuming that government officials are better informed than the individuals they seek to guide. The benefits of (need for) paternalism are systematically overestimated, while the costs of such actions are consistently underestimated. An examination of the obesity issue demonstrates that government intervention is often ineffective in remedying individual failures and that, in some cases, its actions are counterproductive.

The publicly announced goal of sin taxes, such as the soda tax discussed by Marlow and Abdukadirov, is to reduce consumption of the taxed item by increasing its price. In chapter 15, Michael LaFaive coins the phrase "prohibition by price" to describe the implications of such tax policy. Proponents of paternalistic taxation point to reduced legal sales as a sign of success. However, legal sales and consumption are not one and the same. While consumption likely does decline at least modestly as a result of the tax, there is also a shift at the margin from purchases made in the legal sector to those made in the underground economy.

The larger the sin tax is, the stronger the similarities become between the impacts of the sin tax and prohibition. At modest levels of taxation, much of the consumer response is tax avoidance as consumers reduce consumption and, for those located near a lower-taxing jurisdiction, engage in cross-border shopping (casual smuggling). However, as taxes rise to prohibitive levels, the incentive to engage in arbitrage—buying in bulk in low-taxing states and illegally reselling in high-taxing states (commercial smuggling)—also grows. These are essentially the same criminal operations as those brought about by prohibition, and they bring with them the same negative consequences: violence against person and property, turf wars, public corruption, and distrust between citizens and enforcement officers, among others. LaFaive provides estimates of the size of casual and commercial smuggling of cigarettes in US states and details many of the related unintended consequences due to the taxation of cigarettes.

In chapter 16, E. Frank Stephenson reviews the impacts of public policy targeting plastic shopping bags. Like other paternalist policies, proponents of taxes and bans on disposable, single-use shopping bags overestimate the net benefits of their policies by not properly assessing the costs and benefits and by not anticipating changing consumer behavior in response to their prescriptions. Many of the policies intended to reduce the usage of disposable, single-use plastic shopping bags and thereby mitigate the resulting environmental damage are, like the anti-obesity policies discussed by Marlow and Abdukadirov, shown to be counterproductive. Furthermore, to the extent that local attempts to encourage reusable bags, such as the modestly popular burlap bags, have been successful, they have also led to increased health risks related to salmonella and *E. coli* outbreaks. Stephenson explains that plastic bag taxes and bans better represent symbolic attempts to reduce environmental damage than they do effective or sound public policy.

Part IV concludes in chapter 17 with Doug Walker and Collin D. Hodges's discussion of the evolution of policy related to legal gambling in the United States. In most states, gambling is specifically banned either through the state constitution or long-standing legislation. Requiring a state act to permit the industry to function creates an environment rife with rent-seeking, in which the state extracts large sums from the industry. Despite substantial controversy, nearly all states have legalized lotteries and many have legalized brick-and-mortar gambling. Authorization of these industries often comes with large take-out rates for the state, and this revenue is often earmarked for politically correct causes, such as public education and college scholarships. The evolution of gambling policy thus serves as an excellent case study that applies many of the concepts discussed in earlier chapters.

Part V. Evaluating and Prescribing Better Tax Policy

Part V, the final section of this book, is dedicated to evaluating and prescribing better tax policy. The section starts with a first-of-its-kind paternalism index presented by Russell S. Sobel and Joshua C. Hall in chapter 18. Sobel and Hall measure the extent to which each state tries to replace the judgment of individuals with those preferred by, and enacted through, the state political processes. The paternalism index is constructed using a similar methodology to the Economic Freedom of the World Index (Gwartney et al. 2016).

The index contains four separate categories in addition to the aggregate paternalism ranking. States are ranked according to (1) relative use of selective taxes, (2) extensive use of "sin" taxes, (3) use of "saint" subsidies, and (4) miscellaneous bans and restrictions. Overall, Wyoming is identified as the most free from paternalism, while New York was the least free in 2013. Broader regional differences are also apparent, with the Northeast and the West Coast being the least free from paternalism. This index should be useful for future empirical studies explaining how paternalistic policy impacts local economies and social outcomes and why some states are more paternalistic than others.

In chapter 19, Matthew Mitchell suggests that the complex and often counterproductive, unjust, and inefficient tax code observed at the state and federal levels is not accidental. Each provision, imposition, and complexity was purposefully enacted largely at the behest of special interests. Mitchell offers the following eight common explanations for the development and stability of such policy: (1) rent-seeking; (2) concentrated benefits and diffused costs; (3) increasing returns to political activity; (4) logrolling; (5) bootleggers and Baptists; (6) agenda control; (7) rational ignorance and rational irrationality; and (8) the transitional gains trap.

But as Mitchell notes, special interests do not always win, and from such circumstances we can learn important lessons concerning how we might overcome special interests for the development of future public policy. While the detail of each lesson is left to Mitchell to describe in his chapter, we list them here: (1) ideas matter, especially in the long run; (2) institutions matter, too; (3) go for the "grand bargain"; (4) reform requires good leaders; (5) sometimes it takes a special interest to beat a special interest; (6) never let a crisis go to waste; and (7) embrace permissionless innovation. Of course, voters must remain diligent, as each of these lessons can just as easily be used to benefit special interests as they can be to hold them at bay.

In the final chapter of this book, we attempt to summarize the common themes and major policy prescriptions offered throughout the book, as identified by the editors, Adam J. Hoffer and Todd Nesbit. Every chapter of this book discusses one, if not both, of the following themes: (1) selective taxation is discriminatory, and (2) selective taxation fails as a society-improving tool. We then present a range of policy guidelines, ranging from first-best solutions involving constitutional constraints to other marginal improvements that may be less than ideal policy but offer the benefit of being more politically palatable. As should be expected of any concise summary, we most certainly do not capture all policy prescriptions suggested by the contributors, and an omission should not be interpreted as indicative of the worthiness of the author's contribution.

CONCLUSION

We hope to provide readers of this book with analyses on multiple dimensions of selective taxation. Too often, we believe, selective taxes are advertised as easy and politically palatable solutions to societal problems. The high costs of these taxes are rarely considered and thus are hidden from public view. This book highlights the often-hidden costs of these policies.

We also hope to highlight the fact that selective taxes and the revenue they generate fall under the control of politicians, not benevolent social planners. Those politicians are individuals who respond to incentives and harbor their own personal objectives. To become law, taxes pass through a political process plagued by imperfect information and unchecked self-interest. As a result, the realized impact of a given public policy is generally far from its idealized and promised impact. It is important to evaluate, as we do in this book, public policy outcomes as they are rather than as proponents might wish them to be.

Americans deserve better public policy. This book provides the thorough analysis of selective taxation needed to motivate better policy.

NOTES

1. For example, only 15.1 percent of US adults smoked cigarettes in 2015, according to the Centers for Disease Control. https://www.cdc.gov/tobacco/data_statistics/fact_sheets/adult _data/cig_smoking/index.htm.

2. Orzechowski and Walker (2015), https://www.tobaccofreekids.org/research/factsheets/pdf /0275.pdf.

3. This excludes income tax proposals. The full data can be downloaded from michiganvotes. org. The targets of the tax increases introduced in the Michigan legislature during the 2001–2015 fiscal years include airplane fuel, alcohol, bottled water, businesses, casinos, couriers, dentures, fast food, gas, gross receipts, liquor, luxury homes, pornography, sales, services, severance payments, soft drinks, tobacco, transfer payments, televisions, use (tax on personal property and purchases, usually purchased out of state, on which the state sales tax was not paid), and vapes.

4. The Electoral College votes determine presidential election outcomes, enabling a participant with less than a majority of the popular vote to become president. This was the fourth time that the winner of the Electoral College lost the popular vote (1876, 1888, 2000, and 2016).

REFERENCES

Arrow, Kenneth. 1963. *Social Choice and Individual Values*, 2nd ed. New York: Wiley.

Buchanan, James M. 1979. "Constitutional Constraints on Governmental Taxing Power." *ORDO: Jahrbuch für die Ordnung von Wirtschaft und Gesellschaft* 30: 349–59.

Gwartney, James, Robert Lawson, and Joshua Hall. 2016. *Economic Freedom of the World 2016 Annual Report*. Toronto: Frasier Institute. http://www.fraserinstitute.org/.

Hayek, Friedrich August. 1944. *The Road to Serfdom*. London and New York: Routledge.

Hoffer, Adam J., William F. Shughart, and Michael D. Thomas. 2014. "Sin Taxes and Sindustry: Revenue, Paternalism, and Political Interest." *Independent Review* 19 (1): 47–64.

Niskanen, William. 1971. *Bureaucracy and Representative Government*. London: Transaction Publishers.

Orzechowski, William, and Robert Walker. 2015. *The Tax Burden on Tobacco,* Historical Compilation, volume 50. Fairfax, VA: Orzechowski and Walker.

Ridley, Matt. 2017. "It Takes a Government to Do an Auschwitz." Plenary address. Presented at the Association of Private Enterprise meeting, April 11, Lahaina, HI.

PART I

PUBLIC FINANCE AND PUBLIC CHOICE
Establishing the Foundation

CHAPTER 1
Selective Consumption Taxes in Historical Perspective

WILLIAM F. SHUGHART II
Jon M. Huntsman School of Business, Utah State University

Imposts, excises, and, in general, all duties upon articles of consumption, may be compared to a fluid, which will, in time, find its level with the means of paying them. The amount to be contributed by each citizen will in a degree be at his own option, and can be regulated by an attention to his resources. The rich may be extravagant, the poor can be frugal; and private oppression may always be avoided by a judicious selection of objects proper for such impositions. . . .

It is a signal advantage of taxes on articles of consumption, that they contain in their own nature a security against excess. They prescribe their own limit; which cannot be exceeded without defeating the end proposed, that is, an extension of the revenue. When applied to this object, the saying is as just as it is witty, that, "in political arithmetic, two and two do not always make four."

If duties are too high, they lessen the consumption; the collection is eluded; and the product to the treasury is not so great as when they are confined within proper and moderate bounds.

—*Alexander Hamilton, Federalist No. 21*

Until the ratification of the Sixteenth Amendment to the US Constitution in 1913, which authorized the collection of taxes on incomes, the federal government of the United States relied heavily on indirect taxes (import duties and selective excises) to generate revenue.[1] In 1912, for example, internal tax receipts (90.4 percent of which were generated by various excise taxes) represented just over half (50.8 percent) of all federal revenues; customs duties accounted for most of the rest (40.8 percent of the total) (Yelvington 1997, 44, 47). As a matter of fact, until 1862, following the outbreak of the War between the States in April 1861 and the disruption of the nation's international trade triggered by the secession of the Confederacy's thirteen member states, import duties comprised all or nearly all of the US government's revenues (Yelvington 1997, 45–46).

That source of revenue began drying up from 1914 onward as the income tax rose in importance and two global wars, the Great Depression, and protectionist trade policies (e.g., the Smoot-Hawley tariff and international retaliation to it) caused customs duties to fall off the fiscal cliff.[2] Taxes on foreign goods imported into the United States nowadays produce only about 2 percent of the federal government's total revenues; excise taxes account for roughly twice that percentage. Except for intermittent one-off proceeds from sales of federal lands and auctions of parts of the radio spectrum and of drilling rights to energy producers both offshore and on, taxes on individual and corporate incomes combined are responsible for the bulk of current federal gross receipts.

The fiscal stances of the US states differ markedly on the revenue side of the ledger from that of the federal government. In 2014, the latest year for which data on tax receipts are available from the US Census Bureau's *Annual Survey of State Government Finances*, the fifty states collected more than $865.8 billion in total taxes altogether, of which "general sales and gross receipts taxes" accounted for 31.3 percent and "selective sales and gross receipts taxes" accounted for 16.2 percent.[3] Individual income and corporate net income taxes accounted for another 41.2 percent of total state tax revenues, with license fees and all other taxes (e.g., severance taxes, property taxes, death and gift taxes, documentary and stock transfer taxes) completing the picture.

Those revenue sources vary considerably both across states and over time. Some states do not tax individual incomes at all, and some do not levy general sales taxes. Some states run lottery games or tax land- or water-based casinos; gambling is illegal in others. Taxes imposed at the wholesale level or retail markups on wholesale prices brought in just under $7.5 billion in revenue in the 15 states that operate state liquor store monopolies. Taxes levied at local (city and county) levels of government also vary a great deal, defying efforts to summarize neatly the extent to which subnational governments in the United States rely on selective consumption taxes. For that reason, this chapter focuses on tax policies at the federal level. In the sections that follow, I supply a thumbnail sketch of the evolution of the selective sales and excise taxes from colonial times to the present day.

COLONIAL EXCISES

Americans have paid selective excise taxes since colonial times.[4] Such taxes initially were imposed on the colonists by Great Britain's King George III as a means of helping defray the costs of the British troops deployed to America. These troops were used to protect his subjects from the death and destruction wreaked by Native American tribes in response to the pressures on their customary ways of life inflicted by colonists inexorably moving west to occupy and settle Indian homelands.[5] Although the excise tax on tea (and the Boston Tea Party in reaction to it) is perhaps better known, the Stamp Act of April 1765— the first internal, indirect tax levied on the colonies by Westminster—was in fact the flashpoint that eventually triggered the American Revolution (Watkins 2016, 47). That law required the colonists to buy special paper embossed or imprinted with an official symbol for documenting legal and commercial transactions (e.g., marriage licenses, bonds, contracts, deeds, and bills of sale) in order for them to be recognized and enforceable in a British colonial court; it in essence imposed a tax on paper goods, including newspapers and playing cards (Smith 2011a).[6]

The colonists' reaction to the Stamp Act echoed Samuel Johnson's definition of *excise* in his justly famous *Dictionary of the English Language* as "a hateful tax levied upon commodities, and adjudged not by common judges of property, but by wretches hired by those to whom the excise is paid" (quoted in Yelvington 1997, 33).[7] Witnessing the same heavy-handed tax-law enforcement some colonists had seen before emigrating from England, mob violence erupted in Boston seven months before the Stamp Act was scheduled to go into effect; it soon spread to the 12 other colonies. The mobs targeted the local officials granted authority to distribute stamped paper, pressuring them to resign their offices to avoid a hangman's noose (Smith 2011a). The mobs destroyed property, including warehouses and the home of Thomas Hutchinson, Massachusetts's lieutenant governor and chief justice. By the time the law went into effect on November 1, 1765, only Georgia's stamped paper distributor remained in place; he resigned just two weeks later (Smith 2011b).

Excises were hated in England and in its American colonies owing to the system used to collect them. Tax collectors were supplied with incentives to collect as much revenue as possible;[8] they had authority to enter private homes, cargo ships, and warehouses to search for and seize contraband goods for non-payment of taxes. Britain's colonial revenue agents, sometimes accompanied by armed British soldiers, predictably abused that authority. In the words of the Declaration of Independence, besides imposing taxes on the colonies without colonial representation in Parliament or their representatives' consent, King George had "erected a multitude of New Offices, and sent hither swarms of Officers to [harass] our people, and eat out their substance."

Their victory eventually won at Yorktown with General Charles Cornwallis's surrender to troops led by the Marquis de Lafayette on October 19, 1781,[9] the citizens of the newly independent United States of America might have felt considerable relief and satisfaction from throwing off the yoke of the hated British excise tax. If so, subsequent history was not very kind to US taxpayers. The original thirteen colonies, now the thirteen states, ended the Revolutionary War with massive debts incurred to mobilize and provision the troops that General, now President, George Washington had enlisted to defeat George III's army. That accumulated debt was a key concern of Alexander Hamilton, the new nation's first treasury secretary. To prevent unraveling of the Constitution agreed to at Philadelphia in 1786—a document he, in collaboration with James Madison and John Jay, had supported strongly in contributions to the Federalist Papers—Hamilton lobbied vigorously for the new federal government to take responsibility for paying them. But from whence was the revenue to be raised?

Under the Articles of Confederation that prior to 1787 governed the thirteen states, the central government had no taxing authority; it could only requisition funds from the Confederation's members to support general spending requirements, with no power to compel payment of what essentially were voluntary contributions (Watkins 2016). Seen as one of the Articles' major defects, taxing authority was granted to the US Congress in Article I, Section 2, of the Constitution, which provides for the collection of "direct taxes . . . apportioned among the several States" on the basis of their respective populations. That constitutional provision meant that any direct taxes levied by the national government had to be "uniform," a restriction that "was taken seriously" at the time (Gifford 1997, 61).

THE FEDERAL EXCISE TAX ON DISTILLED SPIRITS AND THE WHISKEY REBELLION

Treasury Secretary Hamilton's first measure to raise the revenue required to pay off the states' Revolutionary War debts was to impose a selective federal excise tax on whiskey. Submitted to Congress in June 1790, the whiskey tax bill elicited vigorous opposition, not only because the hated excise had returned to America when the Constitution's ink barely was dry, but also because the tax had consequences that were perhaps unintended, although foreseeable.

The tax collection system became a particular source of grievance after the whiskey tax's implementation in 1791. As in ancien régime France, authority to collect the tax on whiskey was placed in private hands—those of tax farmers who paid lump sums into the federal treasury in return for the right to assess and gather tax payments owed by the distillers operating within defined taxing jurisdictions. The office of tax farmer was valuable to the extent that the tax collectors were able to keep any payments collected from taxpayers over and above the amounts paid for tax collection rights. Not surprisingly, the tax farmers worked assiduously, often abusively violating private property rights by entering barns and cellars to harvest as much tax revenue as humanly possible, including a 4 percent take on any bootleg whiskey they uncovered and seized. The tax farmers were hated, and some were tarred and feathered (Adams [1993] 2001, 321–26; Yelvington 1997, 34) as had been done to colonial sympathizers of the British Crown by the rebels prior to Independence (Roberts [1940] 1999).

The tax redistributed wealth interregionally (from the South and West to the East) and within the whiskey distilling industry itself (from distillers of relatively low-quality spirits, which tended to be small, to larger distillers producing and marketing higher quality whiskey). Grain farmers located on the western borders of Pennsylvania, Virginia, and North Carolina were especially hard hit by Hamilton's whiskey tax. Prior to its implementation in 1791, the farmers there had concluded that distilling whiskey locally and shipping spirits to markets in the East was more profitable than bearing the cost of transporting bulky, low-value-to-weight grains to those same markets over the Allegheny Mountains on poor roads. Paying the new whiskey tax ate substantially into those profits. The distillers in the West and South also produced whiskey of lower quality and in smaller batches than did the larger distillers located in the eastern United States. A uniform tax levied per gallon of whiskey, regardless of quality, effectively reduced the relative prices of Eastern spirits (Gifford 1997, 61, citing Barzel 1976; also see Razzolini et al. 2003).[10]

The sectional grievances created by the first federal excise tax ignited what has since been called the Whiskey Rebellion, which erupted in 1794, when grain farmers in western Pennsylvania refused to pay it. The uprising was quelled by militia units dispatched there by President Washington, fortunately without bloodshed, after the rebels agreed in the face of guns pointed at their heads to comply with the federal tax collectors' demands. A federal excise tax on whiskey and other alcoholic beverages has been in effect since 1791, except during Prohibition, which began in January 1920, following ratification of the Eighteenth Amendment to the US Constitution, and ended in 1933 with repeal of that constitutional provision by the Twenty-First Amendment.[11]

In addition to Hamilton's revenue-raising aims, the nation's first Treasury secretary seized the moral high ground to justify the federal levy on whiskey, as many proponents of selective sales and excise taxes frequently have done both before and since. Hamilton argued that whiskey constituted a "luxury" good and, moreover, that

> the consumption of ardent spirits particularly, no doubt
> very much on account [of] their cheapness, is carried out
> to an extreme, which is truly to be regretted, as well as in
> regard to the health and the morals, as to the economy of
> the community. (Cooke 1964, 64; quoted in Yelvington
> 1997, 33)

We thus see here three recurring themes in the history of selective sales and excise taxes in the United States. The first is a politician's or policy-maker's claim of needing additional revenue to finance an essential public spending program, such as extinguishing Revolutionary War debts incurred by the states. Second, selective tax policies almost always create winners and losers, each affected group therefore having strong interests in the outcome of a tax policy debate, either so as to capture financial benefits for themselves or to avoid higher tax bills by shifting the burden onto the shoulders of other, less politically effective groups. Last, but not least, are appeals to higher moral purposes (the public health or other social benefits claimed to flow from the imposition of a new tax or from increasing an existing one) joined with the more parochial interests of groups who stand to gain from a particular selective tax, either by capturing shares of the tax revenue collected from disfavored constituencies and then redistributing it to favored ones or by bringing political influence to bear so that the tax differentially burdens competitors. This last justification applies the "Bootleggers and

Baptists" model of regulation (Smith and Yandle 2014) to the realm of selective tax policy.[12]

MAY THE EXCISE BE WITH YOU ALWAYS

Despite igniting the Whiskey Rebellion in 1794, a new federal excise tax was imposed on horse-drawn carriages, a more plausible luxury good, that same year. The federal excise tax regime soon was extended to include "certain liquors," snuff, salt, and the proceeds from auction sales. Owing to the high cost of collecting those levies, though, Thomas Jefferson campaigned for the presidency on a platform plank pledging to repeal all the nation's internal taxes. Except for the tax on salt, which was not rescinded until 1802, Jefferson kept his campaign promise soon after being sworn into office in 1801 (Yelvington 1997, 34–35).

The War of 1812

Wars and other national emergencies supply cover for politicians seizing opportunities to impose new taxes to finance the expenses of mobilizing troops and equipping and deploying them to the battlefield. New federal excise taxes were enacted during the War of 1812, but were short lived; they were temporary revenue measures and passed under a law promising they would expire—and actually did lapse—the next year. Those excise taxes did not elicit strong opposition for two reasons: the war was popular on the home front, and the treasury's tax farmers had been replaced with a professional tax-collecting federal bureau, a predecessor to today's Internal Revenue Service (Yelvington 1997, 35; Adams 1998, 81).

The War between the States

From then on, as mentioned previously, taxes on foreign trade—tariffs—returned and remained the national government's chief source of revenue. Moreover, from 1817 until 1857, the federal government's budget usually was in the black; those budget surpluses meant that proposals for new sources of tax revenue from internal sources would go unheeded (Yelvington 1997, 37). Washington's fiscal stance changed dramatically as sectional differences over tariff policy and the issue of slavery boiled over into war in April 1861, when President Abraham Lincoln ordered federal reinforcements to Ft. Sumter (in Charleston, South Carolina's harbor), which had been encircled onshore and subsequently bombarded by rebel artillery units commanded by General P. G. T. Beauregard.

Because war interrupted international trade once again, the Union's customs duties declined precipitously, and new sources of revenue were needed to finance President Lincoln's decision not to let secession succeed. The Internal Revenue Act of 1862, signed by the president on the same day (July 1) Congress passed it, imposed the first income tax in US history, although that tax was of doubtful constitutionality and would be repealed 10 years later.[13] The 1862 law also created an inheritance tax and resurrected "all of the excise taxes, license fees and stamp duties levied by the federal government during the War of 1812" (Yelvington 1997, 37). The stamp duties of 1862 covered a larger set of legal documents and financial transactions than had been taxed in 1813. Every manufactured item was taxed. Ad valorem rates of between 0.3 percent and 1.5 percent were imposed on the gross receipts of various transportation companies (including railroads, ferries, and steamships), of toll bridges, and of advertisers (Yelvington 1997).

As the budgetary cost of the War between the States continued to mount, the Internal Revenue Act of 1864 raised existing federal excise taxes sharply. Tax rates on distilled spirits rose from $0.20 per proof gallon to $1.50 (and climbed further to a top rate of $2 per gallon the next year). The federal tax on loose tobacco more than doubled, and the tax on cigars went from $3.50 per thousand to $40 per thousand (Yelvington 1997).

The First World War

All but the 1864 federal liquor and tobacco taxes were repealed either in 1867 or 1870 (Yelvington 1997, 37). But, in any case, as had been true in 1813, raising revenue to finance war spending (rather than social control) was the primary justification for the new federal taxes enacted earlier in the decade. The same reasoning lay behind proposals for imposing new taxes, resurrecting old ones, or increasing existing tax rates in every major conflict the United States later entered as a belligerent. The War Revenue Tax Act of 1913 reauthorized all federal excise taxes of the Civil War period and expanded the list to include theater admissions, jewelry, toilet articles, luggage, and chewing gum. The selective taxes enacted the year before the outbreak of the First World War in August 1914—2 years before the American Expeditionary Force was dispatched to bleed and die in the mud of Belgium and France—eventually were repealed by laws passed in 1924 and 1928. The tobacco, liquor, and stamp duties remained in effect, though (Yelvington 1997, 38).

The Great Depression and the Second World War

Selective sales and excise taxes also were important sources of revenue during the Second World War and then the Korean War, as we shall see later. But before Japanese aircraft bombed the US naval base at Pearl Harbor, Hawaii, on December 7, 1941, President Franklin Delano Roosevelt oversaw the return to discriminatory consumption taxation as part of his policy agenda rushed through Congress in response to the Great Depression, during which the US economy collapsed, hitting bottom in 1933, and did not return to normalcy until after the Second World War had ended in 1945.[14] The economy's collapse also meant that federal income tax receipts had declined sharply, along with the revenues from all other taxes linked to economic activity. Prohibition likewise had driven selective taxes on alcohol down to zero as thirsty consumers switched to homemade "bathtub" gin or to the booze supplied illegally by the bootleggers who smuggled Canadian whiskey into the United States.

FDR campaigned for election to the White House in 1932 on a platform that promised in part to support repeal of the Constitution's Eighteenth Amendment, thereby allowing beer, wine, and whiskey to be produced and sold legally in the United States—and then of course taxed again by the federal government as it was before passage of the National Prohibition (Volstead) Act on October 28, 1919. The Twenty-First Amendment, repealing the Eighteenth, was ratified on December 5, 1933, just 8 months after FDR had been inaugurated, and the pre-Prohibition alcohol tax rate of $1.10 per proof gallon was raised soon thereafter to $2 (Yelvington 1997, 40).[15]

FDR's New Deal imposed federal excise taxes on the manufacturers of "automobiles, trucks, buses, [household] appliances, and other consumer durables" (Yelvington 1997, 40). For the first time, selective consumption taxes were imposed on telephone calls and gasoline. Both of those taxes were passed as temporary revenue measures, but the federal excise tax on long-distance telephone calls—reauthorized by Congress twenty-nine times and eventually applied to local calls—was not repealed until mid-2006, and then only in part.[16] Excise taxes on motor fuels at both the state and federal levels, along with those on alcoholic beverages and tobacco, have, of course, become permanent parts of Americans' daily lives.

Yelvington (1997, 42–49) supplies information on various components of US federal tax receipts from 1791 through 1993, including the totals and percentages accounted for by customs duties and excise taxes. Similar, but not fully comparable, data are reported here in figure 1 for each year running from 1934 through 2020 (the latter of which is estimated).[17] Nevertheless,

Figure 1. Composition of US Federal Receipts by Source

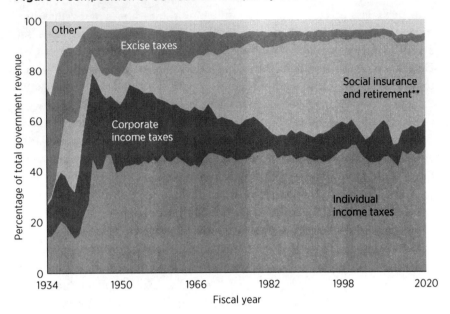

Source: US Office of Management and Budget (n.d.), Historical Table 2.2.
* "Other" comprises principally estate and gift taxes, customs duties and fees, and miscellaneous receipts; for details, see US Office of Management and Budget (n.d.), Historical Table 2.2.
** Payroll tax receipts funding Old Age, Survivors and Disability Insurance plus Medicare. The percentages shown are based on the total amounts generated by payroll taxes, which since 1937 have been divided into "on-budget" and "off-budget" percentages, the latter supposedly being redirected to so-called trust funds. Also see table 1 in this chapter.

the importance of excise tax receipts and the relative unimportance of income taxes to the federal budget during the Depression years of 1934 through 1946 or 1947 stand out clearly.[18]

The modern high-water mark of selective federal sales and excise taxes was reached during the New Deal. Such taxes generated between 30 percent and 45 percent of total federal revenues then, a share that fell to 20 percent during the Second World War. The relative contributions of the selective taxation of various goods and services waned, owing primarily to federal income tax increases enacted in response to December 7, 1941 (Yelvington 1997, 41).

After America entered the Second World War (with FDR's New Deal excise taxes still in effect), many existing tax rates were raised, and new ones were introduced. The federal excise tax on alcohol was increased from $2 to $9 per proof gallon mainly because the wartime conversion of distilleries to the production of grain alcohol had created a shortage of drinkable spirits on the home front; upward pressures on their market prices may have been seen by Washington as an opportunity to disguise a major increase in the tax. The rationing of many consumer goods—automobiles (which no longer were being produced at all), gasoline, tires, tubes, leather goods, and refrigerators—was combined with new excise taxation to shift more such products and the inputs used to manufacture them to the war effort. Taxes on admissions and organizational dues also were enacted; "luxuries," such as "furs, toilet preparations, jewelry, and luggage" were added to the federal excise tax base (Yelvington 1997, 38, quoting Anderson 1951, 409).

Korea and More Modern Times

Consistent with explaining them as temporary war measures, Congress planned to reduce the Second World War's excise taxes dramatically in the Revenue Act of 1950, thereby reducing federal revenues by $910 million. But President Truman's launching of a "police action" in Korea prompted Congress to replace the law's excise tax cuts by tax increases amounting to $55 million. Televisions, deep freezers, and diesel fuel were taxed for the first time. Although the existing federal taxes on alcohol and tobacco generated nearly half (47 percent) of Washington's total excise tax receipts, at least one commentator observed that excise taxpayers had become so comfortable with such levies that considering eliminating them "is not worthwhile. . . . [C]onsumption of . . . particular commodities warrant[s] the payment of a high tax penalty" (Yelvington 1997, 39, quoting Due 1956, 206–7). Put differently, taxpayers then and in more recent times have become "state-broken," that is, accustomed to a strong government hand (McGraw 2007, 365).[19]

The Korean War's excise tax regime was scaled back and returned to pre-war levels in April 1956. A few years later (in 1965), liquor, tobacco, and gasoline were the major sources of Washington's excise tax receipts. The justification for collecting the last of those "Big Three" federal excise taxes (on gasoline) was reinvigorated in 1956 when the revenue generated by it, along with the taxes on diesel and other motor fuels, were earmarked for the Highway Trust Fund, created to finance construction and maintenance of the interstate highway system (launched during the Eisenhower administration) and other federal roads. (Federal excise tax revenue from tires and the operations of heavy trucks and buses on federal highways and byways were dedicated to the same fund.) An Airport and Airway Trust Fund was created for similar purposes in 1970, to be financed by federal excise taxes on aviation fuel; commercial airline passengers; and, more recently, by taxes on domestic and international airport departures and arrivals. (Table 1 shows total receipts for all

Table 1. Composition of Social Insurance and Retirement Receipts and of Excise Taxes, Millions of Current Dollars, 2014 (Actual), 2015 (Estimated), and 2018 (Estimated)

	2014	2015	2018
Federal funds			
Alcohol	9,815	9,589	10,547
Tobacco	15,562	15,257	29,019
Crude oil windfall profit[a]	—	—	—
Telephone	611	586	—
Ozone-depleting chemicals/products[b]	—	—	—
Transportation fuels	-3,509	-3,398	-1,026
High-cost health insurance coverage	—	—	736
Health insurance providers	7,987	11,125	14,300
Indoor tanning services	92	95	106
Medical devices	1,977	2,068	2,310
Other	1,705	2,439	2,444
Subtotal	32,240	37,761	58,436
Trust funds			
Transportation	39,049	39,261	39.882
Airports and airways	13,513	13,138	15,987
Black lung disability	579	568	577
Inland waterways	82	97	109
Hazardous substance superfund	—	—	1,064
Post-closure liability (hazardous waste)[c]	—	—	—
Oil spill liability	436	501	770
Aquatic resources	569	534	545
Leaking underground storage tanks	173	205	206
Tobacco assessments	1,140	278	—
Vaccine injury compensation	243	242	262
Supplementary medical insurance	3,209	2,940	4,098
Patient-centered outcomes research	135	373	443
Subtotal	59,128	58,137	63,943
Total Excise Taxes	93,368	95,898	122,379

Source: US Office of Management and Budget (n.d.), Historical Table 2.4.
[a] In effect from 1980 through 1986.
[b] In effect from 1990 through 2001.
[c] In effect from 1981; the fund ran deficits beginning in 1986, which continued through 1990.

major federal excise taxes as of 2014, along with estimated excise tax revenues for 2015 and 2018.)[20]

The earmarking or dedication of excise tax revenues for specific spending programs like the two trust funds mentioned above is a relatively recent justification for imposing such taxes in the first place. Tax revenue earmarking, especially if the spending program it helps finance is deemed worthy, tends to overcome resistance to a new tax or to an increase in an existing one (Lee 1997). What driver, after all, can complain about paying a tax to finance the building or repairing of the roads on which he or she travels, thereby adding to the wear and tear on the roads' asphalt or concrete surface? Earmarking seemingly transforms the tax into a user fee, one that imposes heavier charges on people who drive more miles per day, per month, or per year. Similar arguments have been advanced for taxing cigarettes, whose consumers access more public healthcare services for treating smoking-related diseases (but see Viscusi 1994), and for drinkers of alcoholic beverages, who are responsible for disproportionate numbers of highway injuries and deaths.

It turns out, though, that trust funds and other spending programs financed by dedicated excise tax revenues frequently are raided by the politicians who have created them (Hoffer et al. 2014, 2015). The accumulated balances in state and federal highway trust funds have in large part been reallocated to financing public transit systems, including high-speed rail transportation initiatives in California and Florida, thereby breaking the link between taxes paid by motorists and road quality. An overwhelming majority of the payments received by the states in their Master Settlement Agreement with the nation's major tobacco companies has been spent, not as intended to help off-set the public sector's costs of treating smoking-related diseases, especially those incurred by Medicaid-eligible patients, but rather to fund more pressing budget priorities (Stevenson and Shughart 2006). Such political redeployment of tax revenues means that tax earmarking rarely results in increases in revenue for the programs to which tax receipts have been dedicated (Crowley and Hoffer, chapter 6, this volume).

Some of the newer federal excise taxes listed in table 1, such as the levies on health insurers, high-cost (so-called Cadillac) health insurance policies, medical devices, and indoor tanning services, were enacted by Congress in 2010 to help pay the Affordable Care Act's estimated $940 billion price tag (though 2019). (Table 2 reports information on the selective tax rates in effect for selected years from 1944 through 2008.) In 2010, the selective ad valorem tax (10 percent) on the bills of tanning salon customers was projected to raise $3 billion in new revenue over the next decade. It will raise barely one-third of that amount because, by 2014, more than half (52 percent) of the tanning salons operating in 2010 had gone out of business. The lingering effects of the Great Recession and rising public concerns about skin cancer surely help explain the carnage visited on tanning salon owner/operators (70 percent of whom are women), but the negative effects of a 10 percent tax on the gross revenues of those small businesses was one of the key factors (Faler 2015).[21]

The foregoing summary of the history of selective sales and excise taxation in the United States teaches several lessons. First, combined with customs duties,

Table 2. Federal Selective Tax Rates, Selected Years, 1944–2008

	1944	1954	1964	1990	1995	2000	2002	2003	2008
Liquor									
Spirits[a]	$9	$10.50	$12.50	$13.50	$13.50	$13.50	$13.50	$13.50	$13.50
Still wines[b]									
≤ 14%	15¢	17¢	17¢	17¢	$1.07	$1.07	$1.07	$1.07	$1.07
> 14%–21%	60¢	67¢	67¢	$1.57	$1.57	$1.57	$1.57	$1.57	$1.57
> 21%–24%	$2	$2.25	$2.25	$2.25	$3.15	$3.15	$3.15	$3.15	$3.15
Beer[c]	$6	$9	$9	$9	$18	$18	$18	$18	$18
Tobacco[d]									
Small cigars	75¢	75¢	75¢	75¢	$1.125	$1.594	$1.828	$1.828	$1.828
Large cigars[e]	$2.50–$20	$2.50–$20	$2.50–$20	8.5% up to $20	$30	$42.50	$48.75	$48.75	$48.75
Cigarettes	$3.50	$4	$4	$8	$12	$17	$19.50–$40.95	$19.50–$40.95	$19.50–$40.95
Pipe tobacco[f]	10¢	10¢	10¢	–	–	95.67¢	$1.10	$1.10	$1.10
Manufacturers									
Gasoline[g]	1.5¢	2¢	2¢	9.1¢	18.4¢	18.4¢	18.4¢	18.4¢	18.4¢
Tires		5¢	10¢	15¢–50¢	15¢–50¢	15¢–50¢	15¢–50¢	15¢–50¢	(h)
Trucks	7%	10%	10%	12%	12%	12%	12%	12%	12%
Firearms[i]	11%	11%	11%	11%	11%	11%	11%	11%	11%
Handguns	11%	11%	10%	10%	10%	10%	10%	10%	10%
Bows	–	–	–	11%	11%	11%	11%	11%	11%
Arrow shafts	–	–	–	–	–	–	–	–	42%
Fishing gear	–	10%	10%	10%	10%	10%	10%	10%	10%
Gas guzzlers[j]				$1,000–$7,700					
Miscellaneous									
Local calls	15%	10%	10%	3%	3%	3%	3%	3%	3%
Long distance	25%	10%	10%	3%	3%	3%	3%	3%	–
Air passengers	15%	10%	5%	8%	10%	(k)	(l)	(m)	(n)
International departure	–	–	–	$6	$6	$12.40°	$13.20°	$13.40°	$15.10°
Air freight	–	–	–	5%	6.25%	10%	6.25%	6.25%	6.25%
Wagers[p]	10%	10%	10%	2%	0.25%	0.25%	0.25%	0.25%	0.25%
Accepting bets[q]	–	$50	$50	$50	$50	$50	$50	$50	$50
Foreign insurance									
Life insurance	1%	1%	1%	1%	1%	–	–	–	–
Other insurance	4%	4%	4%	4%	4%	–	–	–	–

						$1.10 per ton (underground mines) or 55¢ per ton (surface mines)
Coal	—	—	—	—	—	
Superfund						
Crude oil[r]	9.7¢	9.7¢	—	—	—	—
Chemicals[s]	22¢–$4.87	—	—	"Varies"	—	5¢
Retailers						
Jewelry	20%	10%	10%	—	—	—
Furs	20%	10%	10%	—	—	—
Diesel fuel	15.1¢	24.4¢	24.4¢	24.4¢	24.4¢	24.4¢
Non-gasoline[t]	9.1¢	—	—	—	—	—
Other gasoline[u]	12.1¢	19.4¢	19.4¢	19.4¢	19.4¢	19.4¢
Aviation fuel[v]	14.1¢	21.9¢	21.9¢	21.9¢	21.9¢	21.9¢
Inland water[w]	11.1¢	24.4¢	24.4¢	24.4¢	24.4¢	24.4¢
Gasohol[x]	3.1¢	14.4¢–18.4¢	13¢–15.3¢	13.2¢–15.4¢	13.2¢–15.4¢	12.25¢–13.25¢

Source: Tax Foundation. 2008. "Federal Excise Tax Rates, 1944–2008. Selected Years." Updated November 9, 2008. http://taxfoundation.org/article/federal-excise-tax-rates-1944-2008-selected-years.

a Per proof gallon.
b Per gallon by alcohol content.
c Per 31-gallon barrel.
d Per thousand except pipe tobacco.
e In 1990, 8.5% of wholesale price up to $20.
f Per gallon.
g Per pound.
h 8.5% of wholesale price up to $20.
i Includes shells and cartridges.
j Fuel-inefficient automobiles.
k 7.5% plus $2.50 for each flight segment from January 1, 2000 to December 31, 2000.
l 7.5% plus $3 for each flight segment from January 1, 2002 to December 31, 2002.
m 7.5% plus $3.40 for each flight segment from January 1, 2007 to December 31, 2007.
n 7.5% plus $3.70 for each flight segment.
o Per person, per arrival, and per departure.
p Amount wagered (except pari-mutuel bets).
q Occupation of accepting wagers.
r Per barrel.
s Per ton.
t Gasoline substitute fuels for highway vehicles and motor boats (per gallon).
u Gasoline used in noncommercial aviation (per gallon).
v Noncommercial aviation fuel other than gasoline (per gallon).
w Inland waterways users' fuel (per gallon).
x Per gallon.

such taxes generated the bulk of Washington's revenue until the authorization of federal taxes on individual (and, later, corporate) incomes in 1913. Second, war and other national emergencies, such as the Great Depression, frequently have afforded opportunities for imposing new federal taxes on the consumption of particular goods and services and raising the rates of existing ones. Third, although selective excise taxes on the traditional "sins" of drinking, smoking, and gambling have been in place since colonial times, the collection of gasoline and motor fuel taxes received a fresh justification in 1956, when their proceeds were earmarked for the Highway Trust Fund, morphing those taxes into so-called user fees, whereby the consumers of the nation's federal road network supposedly pay for the benefits they receive and, moreover, are charged for the environmental damage caused by their tailpipe emissions. Policies dedicating tax revenue for specified spending programs, such as healthcare, expanded thereafter. More recently, however, consumers' own choices have become matters of public policy concern following the publication of evidence (and the emergence of political lobbying) by groups claiming that purchasing certain goods and services, such as sugar-sweetened soft drinks and tanning salons, not only harms third parties but also compromises the well-being of consumers themselves. Those new justifications for selective sales and excise taxes are discussed next.

CONCLUSION

Selective consumption taxes are age-old. Customarily levied on the so-called sins of smoking, drinking, and gambling, such taxes mainly are justified on two heads: first, as correctives for the market's "failure" (Bator 1958) to price the external costs (or benefits) of consumption not borne (or captured) by consumers themselves (Pigou [1920] 1952), thereby forcing them to internalize the externalities. Second, they are justified by observing that the demands for those goods tend to be inelastic (meaning that increases in their after-tax prices cause the quantities consumers are willing and able to buy to decline less than proportionately). Such taxes are more efficient (create smaller excess burdens) than those imposed on goods for which consumers are more sensitive to changes in price (Ramsey 1927). Selective taxes on the purchases of sin goods therefore are revenue engines for the public sector because, by their very nature, such taxes do not reduce the consumption of the taxed goods and services very much.

More recently, though, selective sales and excise taxes have been imposed at the US state and federal levels of government not to reduce the purchases of goods and services plausibly generating negative externalities—that is, harm to innocent third parties (battered spouses and the victims of drunk drivers, for example)—but instead with the aim of protecting the health and welfare of consumers themselves, or what might be called "internalities" (Hoffer and Shughart, chapter 3, this volume). We therefore see taxes imposed on sugar-sweetened beverages and junk food so as to reduce the incidences of obesity-related diabetes and heart disease for consumers' own good. But, if the demands for such goods also tend to be inelastic, as the econometric evidence suggests they are, taxing those food items will not achieve public health professionals' stated goal of reducing consumption significantly. Moreover, because all consumption taxes are regressive, the tax burden will fall most heavily on low-income households (Novak 2012; Hoffer et al. 2017; Hoffer and Shughart, chapter 3, this volume).

The elasticity of demand for any taxed good hinges on the availability of substitutes for that good. The substitution possibilities available to consumers, in turn, depend largely on income (which supplies another reason poorer people tend to bear the burden of selective consumption taxes), and on how broadly or narrowly the selective tax base is defined. Berkeley, California's first-in-the-nation excise tax on sugary soft drinks apparently is being widely avoided by cross-border shoppers, as was Denmark's first-on-the-planet "fat tax" (also see Shughart 1997; Vedder 1997; Kliff 2012; and Coons and Weber 2013).

Support for selective sales and excise taxation has been reinforced in recent times by the findings reported by behavioral economists and psychologists who claim that consumers' decision-making is beset by cognitive anomalies inconsistent with the models and predictions of neoclassical economic theory. A fatal flaw in the new behavioral approach to taxation and other governmental interventions in private markets is that the behaviorists neither ascribe those same cognitive failures to public policymakers (Mannix and Dudley 2015; Viscusi and Gayer 2015), nor do they recognize that even if politicians and bureaucrats somehow were immune to such failures, the public policy process is by and large driven by special-interest group influence and not by vague notions of the public's interest.

NOTES

1. According to one textbook definition, "direct taxes are levied in factor [i.e., input] markets, indirect taxes are levied in [final] product markets" (Hillman 2009, 252).

2. Four years earlier (1910), liquor taxes had accounted for 30 percent of federal revenues (McGirr 2016, 23).

3. Available at http://www.census.gov/govs/statetax/. According to the Census Bureau's definitions, selective sales and gross receipt taxes include taxes on alcoholic beverages, tickets or charges for admission to "amusement businesses," insurance companies, motor fuels, pari-mutuel betting, public utilities, tobacco products, and other selective levies (e.g., on margarine and lubricating oils).

4. As defined by Hoffer and Shughart (chap. 4, this volume), sales taxes are levied ad valorem, that is, as percentages of a good's pre-tax retail or wholesale price. Excise taxes, by contrast, are levied as so many cents or dollars per unit purchased. Obviously, the consumer's sales tax bill rises in absolute dollar terms as the taxed good's pre-tax price rises—7 percent of $1 is less than 7 percent of $10, for example. An excise tax rate, say 48 cents per gallon of gasoline, is the same on every unit purchased.

5. The bloodshed in North America was called the French and Indian War in the colonies and the Seven Years' War, involving England, France, and Spain, elsewhere.

6. Gifford (2007, 72–74) contends that the excise tax on newspapers was meant to suppress criticism of King George III and that newspaper publishers predictably led opposition to the tax. Such a tax had been imposed in England as early as 1756, was increased several times afterward, up to four pence in 1815, and was not repealed until 1861.

7. Excise taxes also had been imposed in England on liquor; coffee; soap; salt; and, predictably, tea (Yelvington 1997, 33; Adams [1993] 2001, 261–62). For more on the importance of Samuel Johnson's dictionary to the development of the English language, see Reksulak et al. (2004).

8. See more on tax farming in the next section.

9. The victory was formalized by the Treaty of Paris, signed on September 3, 1783.

10. Gifford (1997, 61) notes that if Hamilton's whiskey tax had been levied ad valorem rather than per gallon, distillers in the West would have been favored, because the pre-tax prices of Eastern distilled spirits were roughly twice those of the Western distillers. Assuming that the tax fully had been passed on to consumers, applying the same percentage tax markup uniformly to all whiskey thus would have made Eastern whiskey relatively more expensive.

11. For relevant historical details, see Okrent (2010) and McGirr (2016).

12. Bruce Yandle (1983) coined the phrase "Bootleggers and Baptists" to signify the coalition succeeding in convincing many jurisdictions in the American South to ban alcohol sales on Sunday. Both interest groups gained from such regulations—Baptist preachers from making the Lord's Day "dry" and bootleggers from selling booze illegally to thirsty parishioners. "Methodists and Moonshiners" might be more accurate in the case of national Prohibition (McGirr 2016).

13. Fast forward to the mid-1890s: members of President Grover Cleveland's own Democratic Party introduced and passed legislation resurrecting Lincoln's income tax to offset tariff revenues that were shrinking, not because of war but rather because of domestic economic crisis (the Depression of 1893). The president opposed the measure but allowed the law to take effect without his signature; the income tax was declared unconstitutional in 1895 (Higgs [1987] 2012, 98, 102).

14. It is a (Keynesian) mistake to think that the Great Depression ended in 1941 as America mobilized for the Second World War. The unemployment rate did then decline quickly from double to single digits, but that was only because 8–12 million men eventually were drafted to serve on the front lines and thus no longer stood in soup-kitchen lines. The period from 1941 until 1945 was a command economy ("war socialism") rather than a consumer economy; comparisons with the postwar years thus largely are meaningless (see Shughart 2011, with special attention to the work of Robert Higgs cited therein).

15. During his first weeks in the White House, FDR instructed his advisors to do "something about beer." The "beer bill" the new administration formulated moved swiftly through Congress; beer sales were "relegalized on April 6 [1933]" (McGirr 2016, xiii).

16. Local telephone calls continue to be subject to federal tax, provided that the consumer's tax bill is computed based on the call's length, but not on its distance (see IRS Notice 2006-50, 2006 I.R.B. 25, dated May 25, 2006).

17. Customs duties and fees, for example, are included in "Other," which also includes revenue from estate and gift taxes along with miscellaneous tax receipts. Also shown in figure 1 are payroll tax receipts, levied and collected to finance transfers to social-insurance-eligible recipients—the Old Age, Survivors and Disability Insurance and Medicare programs—which nowadays account for roughly 30 percent of the federal government's total revenue, a fraction that has been rising for a decade and will continue to rise as the population ages and more of the members of the so-called baby boom generation retire from the nation's workforce. As the number of payroll taxpayers per retiree falls, pressures for reforms—such as higher payroll tax rates, cuts in pension benefits, and delays in the ages at which full retirement benefits can be claimed—will mount.

18. Yelvington's (1997, table 2.2, 43) numbers indicate that excise tax receipts represented the following percentages of total "federal internal tax collections" in the 5 years preceding 1934: 15.6 (1929), 15.4 (1930), 18.8 (1931), 26.3 (1932) and 44.4 (1933). Customs duties ranged from 17 percent of total internal tax receipts in 1929 to 13.4 percent in 1933 (Yelvington 1997, table 2.3, 48).

19. Due (1956, 307) writes that Congress would have supported the "retention of an excise on bread and milk if one had been levied during the war" (quoted by Yelvington 1997, 39).

20. Some of the excise taxes listed in table 2, such as the tax imposed in 1980 to clean up hazardous waste disposal sites (the Hazardous Substance Superfund), the tax on ozone-depleting chemicals and the Crude Oil Windfall Profits Tax, are no longer in place. Newer federal excise taxes like the 10 percent federal ad valorem tax levied on the bills of the customers of tanning salons are discussed further below.

21. Former Congressional Budget Office Director Douglas Holtz-Eakin likened the effects of the tanning salon tax to a luxury tax on yachts, imposed as part of a 1990 budget-cutting deal between Congress and President George H. W. Bush, which ended up destroying the US yacht industry (Faler 2015).

REFERENCES

Adams, Charles. [1993] 2001. *For Good and Evil: The Impact of Taxes on the Course of Civilization*, 2nd ed. New York: Madison Books.

———. 1998. *Those Dirty Rotten Taxes: The Tax Revolts That Built America*. New York: Simon and Schuster.

Anderson, William H. 1951. *Taxation and the American Economy: An Economic, Legal, and Administrative Analysis*. New York: Prentice-Hall.

Barzel, Yoram. 1976. "An Alternative Approach to the Analysis of Taxation." *Journal of Political Economy* 84: 1177–97.

Bator, Francis M. 1958. "The Anatomy of Market Failure." *Quarterly Journal of Economics* 72: 351–79.

Cooke, Jacob E. 1964. *The Reports of Alexander Hamilton*. New York: Harper & Row.

Coons, Christian, and Michael Weber (eds.). 2013. *Paternalism: Theory and Practice*. Cambridge: Cambridge University Press.

Due, John F. 1956. "The Role of Sales and Excise Taxation in the Overall Tax Structure." *Journal of Finance* 11: 205–20.

Faler, Brian. 2015. "No Fist Bump for Obamacare Snooki Tax." *Politico*, April 25. http://www.politico.com/story/2014/04/obamacares-snooki-tax-disappoints-106026.html?hp=l7.

Gifford, Adam Jr. 1997. "Whiskey, Margarine, and Newspapers: A Tale of Three Taxes." In *Taxing Choice: The Predatory Politics of Fiscal Discrimination*, edited by William F. Shughart II, 57–77. New Brunswick, NJ: Transaction.

Higgs, Robert. [1987] 2012. *Crisis and Leviathan: Critical Episodes in the Growth of American Government*. Oakland, CA: Independent Institute.

Hillman, Arye L. 2009. *Public Finance and Public Policy: Responsibilities and Limitations of Government*, 2nd ed. Cambridge and New York: Cambridge University Press.

Hoffer, Adam J., Rejeana M. Gvillo, William F. Shughart II, and Michael D. Thomas. 2015. "Regressive Effects: Causes and Consequences of Selective Consumption Taxation." Working Paper, Mercatus Center at George Mason University, Arlington, VA.

Hoffer, Adam J., William F. Shughart II, and Michael D. Thomas. 2014. "Sin Taxes and Sindustry: Revenue, Paternalism and Political Interest." *Independent Review* 19 (1): 47–64.

Kliff, Sarah. 2012. "Denmark Scraps World's First Fat Tax." *Washington Post*, November 13. http://www.washingtonpost.com/news/wonkblog/wp/2012/11/13/denmark-scraps-worlds-first-fat-tax/.

Lee, Dwight R. 1997. "Overcoming Taxpayer Resistance by Taxing Choice and Earmarking Revenues." In *Taxing Choice: The Predatory Politics of Fiscal Discrimination*, edited by William F. Shughart II, 105–16. New Brunswick, NJ: Transaction.

Mannix, Brian F., and Susan E. Dudley. 2015. "The Limits of Irrationality as a Rationale for Regulation." *Journal of Policy Analysis and Management* 34 (3): 705–12.

McCraw, Thomas K. 2007. *Prophet of Innovation: Joseph Schumpeter and Creative Destruction*. Cambridge and London: Harvard University Press.

McGirr, Lisa. 2016. *The War on Alcohol: Prohibition and the Rise of the American State*. New York and London: W. W. Norton.

Novak, Julie. 2012. *Nanny State Taxes: Soaking the Poor in 2012*. Melbourne, Australia: Institute of Public Affairs.

Okrent, Daniel. 2010. *Last Call: The Rise and Fall of Prohibition*. New York: Scribner.

Pigou, Arthur C. [1920] 1952. *The Economics of Welfare*. New Brunswick, NJ: Transaction.

Ramsey, Frank P. 1927. "A Contribution to the Theory of Taxation." *Economic Journal* 37 (145): 47–61.

Razzolini, Laura, William F. Shughart II, and Robert D. Tollison. 2003. "On the Third Law of Demand." *Economic Inquiry* 41: 292–98.

Reksulak, Michael, William F. Shughart II, and Robert D. Tollison. 2004. "Economics and English: Language Growth in Economic Perspective." *Southern Economic Journal* 71: 232–59.

Roberts, Kenneth L. [1940] 1999. *Oliver Wiswell*. Lanham, MD: Rowman & Littlefield (Down East Books).

Shughart, William F. II (ed.). 1997. *Taxing Choice: The Predatory Politics of Fiscal Discrimination*. New Brunswick, NJ: Transaction.

———. 2011. "The New Deal and Modern Memory." *Southern Economic Journal* 77 (3): 515–42.

Smith, Adam, and Bruce Yandle. 2014. *Bootleggers and Baptists: How Economic Forces and Moral Persuasion Interact to Shape Regulatory Politics*. Washington, DC: Cato Institute.

Smith, George H. 2011a. "'Liberty and Prosperity!' The Sons of Liberty and Resistance to the Stamp Act, Part 1." http://www.libertarianism.org/publications/essays/excursions/liberty -property-sons-liberty-resistance-stamp-act-part-1.

———. 2011b. "The Sons of Liberty and Resistance to the Stamp Act, Part Two." http://www .libertarianism.org/publications/essays/excursions/sons-liberty-resistance-stamp-act -part-two.

Stevenson, Taylor P., and William F. Shughart II. 2006. "Smoke and Mirrors: The Political Economy of the Tobacco Settlements." *Public Finance Review* 34: 712–30.

US Office of Management and Budget. N.d. Historical Tables. https://www.whitehouse.gov/omb/budget/Historicals.

Vedder, Richard K. 1997. "Bordering on Chaos: Fiscal Federalism and Excise Taxes." In *Taxing Choice: The Predatory Politics of Fiscal Discrimination*, edited by William F. Shughart II, 271–85. New Brunswick, NJ: Transaction.

Viscusi, W. Kip. 1994. "Cigarette Taxation and the Social Consequences of Smoking." In *Tax Policy and the Economy*, Volume 27, edited by James M. Poterba, 51–102. Cambridge, MA: MIT Press.

Viscusi, W. Kip, and Ted Gayer. 2015. "Behavioral Public Choice: The Behavioral Paradox of Government Policy." *Harvard Journal of Law and Public Policy* 38 (3): 973–1007.

Watkins, William J., Jr. 2016. *Crossroads for Liberty: Recovering the Anti-Federalist Values of America's First Constitution*. Oakland, CA: Independent Institute.

Yandle, Bruce. 1983. "Bootleggers and Baptists: The Education of a Regulatory Economist." *Regulation* 7 (3): 12–16.

Yelvington, Brenda. 1997. "Excise Taxes in Historical Perspective." In *Taxing Choice: The Predatory Politics of Fiscal Discrimination*, edited by William F. Shughart II, 31–56. New Brunswick, NJ: Transaction.

CHAPTER 2
Welfare Effects of Selective Taxation: Economic Efficiency as a Normative Principle

JUSTIN M. ROSS
Indiana University

My dean once lightheartedly complained that, for all the numerous occasions in which controversial tax policies were proposed and debated, he struggled to find among his own public finance faculty any significant level of disagreement. This was not for a lack of ideological diversity, as we spanned the usual range of Democrats and Republicans along with libertarian interlopers. Certainly, we disagreed about the appropriate levels of taxation and the degree to which the government should intervene in the economy. Yet he was entirely correct that we seldom disagreed on specific proposals that appeared in tax policy debates, at least not to the degree that allowed the dean to hold an exciting forum.

This chapter seeks to explain why there seems to be considerable opposition to selective taxation despite many substantive philosophical differences. The next section overviews how economic efficiency provides the prima facie case for uniformity principles in taxation. The third section provides labels for the major "tax philosophies" and employs some examples of actual tax policies considered in these perspectives. The major takeaway is that while each philosophy might allow for selective taxes under specific conditions, actual tax policy frequently caters to special interests, and as a result policies take on features of selective taxation that meet widespread objections. The consequence is that a broad deference to uniform tax principles exists even when economic efficiency is not the dominant concern.

SELECTIVE TAXATION AND EFFICIENCY IN CONTEMPORARY ECONOMIC THEORY

The first part of this chapter seeks to provide the reader with a background on how taxation is considered in terms of economic theory. Uniform ad valorem taxation (i.e., taxing all goods and services at identical percentage rates) reproduces the efficiency outcomes otherwise observed under a poll tax.[1] As the conditions that uphold this conclusion erode, so strengthens the case to be made for selective taxation (i.e., taxing selected goods and services at nonuniform rates), albeit as a less than ideal solution.

Efficiency and the Prima Facie Case against Selective Taxation

Economics attributes special significance to the choices made by households in their purchases of goods and services. The default perspective is that consumer choices reflect their own value judgments within a budget constraint, and that to coerce them into choosing differently would be to make them worse off. When households are producers, it is similarly regarded that their choices reflect their own assessment of the most efficient means of producing a good or service in the face of many competing constraints. These inferences are important components of what is referred to as the First Fundamental Theorem of Welfare Economics, which is frequently taken to mean that these choices are "allocative efficient," so a policymaker cannot improve the standing of one household without leaving others worse off. Selective taxation of particular goods and services therefore induces special harm to people by disturbing the allocations of resources across households.

The significance of allocative efficiency can be illustrated by a pair of numerical examples. Suppose we observed a consumer at a baseball game with $7 to spend on beer, pretzels, and nachos. Each of these goods provides satisfaction, or "utility," that is measured in units called "utils." The buyer experiences utility with each purchase, but at a diminishing rate. For example, beer in its first serving increases the consumer's happiness (i.e., marginal utility) by 120 utils, whereas the second serving increases it by only 100 utils. Nachos,

Table 1. Marginal Utility by Unit of Consumption

	Marginal Utility per Dollar		
Item (Price)	Beer ($1)	Pretzels ($1)	Nacho ($1)
First	120	90	70
Second	100	75	60
Third	80	60	50
Fourth	60	55	40
Fifth	40	40	30

by comparison, increase happiness by 70 utils in their first serving and 60 utils in their second. For simplicity, start from the assumption that the consumer can buy any of these goods for $1 per piece, so that marginal utility per dollar is the same as marginal utility, and this pattern of positive but diminishing returns is presented in table 1.

A consumer who seeks to maximize their total utility with the preferences in table 1 subject to a budget of $7 will choose a mix of goods that can be understood if one thinks about spending down the budget $1 at a time. Based on table 1, the consumer should spend their first dollar on a serving of beer, which yields the highest marginal utility (120 is greater than 90 or 70). In spending their second dollar, they could have their second beer, their first pretzel, or their first nacho. The second beer yields greater marginal utility (100) than either the first pretzel (90) or first nacho (70), so they should again buy another beer. In the third dollar, it is the first pretzel that offers the highest marginal utility (90) rather than either the third beer (80) or first nacho (70). We can proceed in this fashion through the $7 budget. Table 2 summarizes the consumer's expenditures dollar by dollar through $7, at which point the consumer could buy any of the three goods and receive 60 additional utils. The final allocation of the budget results in this consumer having purchased three beers, two pretzels, one nacho, plus any one extra of the three offerings, which results in total utility of 595. Indeed, there is no alternative way to spend $7 that yields a greater level of utility for this consumer.

Now imagine that a 100 percent tax was levied on beer, raising the consumer's effective price from $1 to $2, while the other goods go untaxed. Marginal utility per dollar is halved for beer but unchanged for the others. Table 3 updates these calculations of marginal utility per dollar, and we can repeat the exercise of sequentially determining each dollar of spending so long as the items are within the budget constraint. The first pretzel offers the highest marginal utility per dollar, increasing the consumer's satisfaction by 90 utils. The second pretzel also offers more marginal utility per dollar (75) than the

Table 2. Consumer's Optimal Choice

Dollar Spent	Choice	Utility Gain
First	Beer	120
Second	Beer	100
Third	Pretzel	90
Fourth	Beer	80
Fifth	Pretzel	75
Sixth	Nacho	70
Seventh	Any/Indifferent	60

Bundle: three beers, two pretzels, one nacho, plus one of any choice.
Total utils: 595

Table 3. Marginal Utility by Unit of Consumption

	Marginal Utility per Dollar		
Item (Price)	Beer ($2)	Pretzels ($1)	Nacho ($1)
First	60	90	70
Second	50	75	60
Third	40	60	50
Fourth	30	55	40
Fifth	20	40	30

Table 4. Consumer's Optimal Choice

Dollar Spent	Choice	Utility Gain
First	Pretzel	90
Second	Pretzel	75
Third	Nacho	70
Fourth to seventh	One beer, one pretzel, and one nacho	240

Bundle: one beer, three pretzels, and two nachos.
Total utils: 475

first beer (60) or first nacho (70). The first nacho yields the highest marginal utility for the third dollar spent. At this point, all items have the same marginal utility (60), and acquiring them will spend out the remainder of the $7 budget. As demonstrated in table 4, the consumer's bundle under the 100 percent beer tax is one beer, three pretzels, and two nachos that in sum yield 475 total utils of satisfaction. Note also that, since the consumer purchased one beer, tax revenue to the government is $1.

Comparing these two bundles is quite revealing in how the patterns of consumption have changed—notably, as beer becomes the least acquired good instead of the most. The $1 of tax revenue has resulted in utility losses of $595 - 475 = 120$ utils. This is a significant loss of utility compared to a simple $1 tax on the individual (also known as a poll tax), which would have left the consumer's prices unchanged and allowed the consumer to maximize on the marginal utility per dollar values that appeared in table 1. Under a $1 poll tax, the consumer would have the same pattern of consumption as in table 2, except that the seventh dollar would be lost to tax revenue and the consumer's utility would be reduced by just 60 utils to 535. By selectively applying the tax to a single good, the selective tax lost an additional $535 - 475 = 60$ utils beyond what would have been lost under a poll tax with the same revenue. These additional utility losses beyond the poll tax are regarded as the excess burden of the selective tax structure.

Importantly, it can be shown that a uniform ad valorem tax is equivalent to the poll tax. With a little bit of algebra, an ad valorem tax that increased the price of all goods to approximately $1.167 will result in the consumer purchasing the same pattern as the no-tax scenario in table 2 before running out of money on the sixth purchase.[2] The tax revenue after buying three beers, two pretzels, and one nacho would be $1, and the total consumer utility would be 535, the same as in the case of the poll tax. As a result, the uniform ad valorem tax structure has no excess burden, because the utility losses are identical to those of a poll tax. This realization that uniform tax rates are equivalent to poll taxes provides the prima facie case against selective taxation in economics.

Taxation on Business-to-Business Sales Violates Uniformity

Economic theory recognizes household consumption as the basis for selecting what should and should not be taxed under a system of uniform taxation. In the practice of tax administration, many taxes are collected at point of sale (i.e., where ownership of the good is transferred). Certain sales, however, do not reflect household consumption and are instead business-to-business (B2B) sales. Purchases of energy, fuel, machinery, and equipment are all examples of potential B2B sales. B2B sales should not be taxed, as they do not represent a point of final consumption; instead they are goods or services that will be used to some other end. A sales tax that includes these B2B exchanges results in what is commonly referred to as "tax pyramiding" or "tax cascades." That is, the tax on a B2B sale of inputs that are used to produce a good sold to a household embeds the earlier tax into the apparent pre-tax price. This creates further distortions as producers seek to make their goods with a greater proportion of untaxed inputs. Furthermore, B2B taxation incentivizes vertical integration of the production process, as a firm that makes rather than buys its inputs can gain a competitive cost advantage because of an artifact of the tax code. Through tax pyramiding in the pre-tax prices and distorting the firm's make-or-buy choices, the incorporation of B2B into the tax base represents a violation of uniformity in taxation.

Extensions That Weaken the Case for Uniform Taxation

The First Fundamental Theorem of Welfare Economics implies a presumptive case against selective taxation. It is also the starting point for the majority of normative theories on tax policy. Broadly speaking, these considerations come in three strands: (1) equity concerns, (2) market failure violations of the First Fundamental Theorem, and (3) government failure in applying uniform tax administration.

Resource distribution and equity concerns are absent from the First Fundamental Theorem, and as a result, theory justified on its basis is subject to criticisms for this neglect. Progressive income taxation is sometimes motivated, for example, by considering that higher income consumers may have lower marginal utility of income. The arguments for progressive taxation also support the proposition that income-inelastic goods that occupy a large fraction of low-income households' budgets relative to those of high-income households might justify lower rates of taxation on equity grounds.[3] This proposition is obviously antithetical to uniform ad valorem taxation (which, as mentioned before, is mathematically equivalent to a single flat rate on the flow of income and other net gains in wealth).[4] To dodge this efficiency-equity tradeoff, a small cottage industry of academic research known as "tagging" has emerged. Tagging consists of identifying features of the population that are strongly correlated with the ability to pay but do not affect the choice to earn.[5] If the circumference of the skull, for example, were a strong indicator of intelligence and ability, a tax based on skull circumference would likely be progressive but free of the excess burden associated with the distortion of choice.

As stated before, the First Fundamental Theorem of Welfare provides the framework for regarding undistorted choices as determining the optimal allocation of resources. Relaxing assumptions that go into this theorem, however, open the possibility that individual choices do not represent optimal outcomes and thereby increase the prospect for interventions. These assumptions include the following:

1. Perfectly competitive markets, so that prices reflect true consumer valuations and resource costs;

2. Externalities, or third-party spillover effects, in consumption or production of the good or service;

3. Complete, perfect, and symmetric information about the goods and services exchanged; and

4. Rational consumers in the sense that they are capable of making utility-maximizing choices in the face of budget constraints.

Examples where selective taxation is motivated by the violation of one or more of these assumptions are commonplace throughout this book and so will not be extensively addressed here. The main takeaway is that certain goods might be selectively targeted for taxation on the grounds that the tax will lead consumers to behave as if they were satisfying the conditions of the assumptions. For example, if beef is more pollutive than other types of meat, then a well-structured tax would cause consumers to adjust the amount of their budget allocated to meat consumption in a manner that would mimic their accounting for the harm caused by the pollution.

Another argument for selective taxes arises when the government fails to appropriately define the tax base by either ignoring services or taxing business inputs. In the United States, for example, state legislation governing taxation generally applies to finished goods rather than to final household consumption. Consider the case where a retailer acquires a cash register in furtherance of their profit, so while the cash register is "finished," it is also a business input. Likewise, many household services go untaxed. It is estimated that states apply the retail sales tax to about 40 percent of household consumption and that business purchases represent a little more than 40 percent of taxable sales.[6] An approach known as "Ramsey Rule taxation" can motivate a selective taxation approach to partially compensate for leaving services untaxed, and it can also motivate the taxation of B2B sales.[7] A haircut at a barbershop may go untaxed, but the business inputs like scissors, chairs, and creams could be taxed under the general sales tax and ultimately lead to a condition more strongly resembling conditions described in the First Fundamental Theorem of Welfare than if the business inputs were left untaxed.[8]

Although selective taxation is seldom considered a first-best approach, theory provides ample support for giving it serious consideration in the messy real world. It also highlights the need for substantive theories of public choice to determine what kind of tax system might be delivered in different political systems. As Winer and Hettich (1998) argue, allowing for deviations from uniform taxation might incentivize self-interested politicians in a representative democracy to equalize the marginal political cost rather than the marginal excess burden implied by the optimal selective taxation models provided by the Ramsey (1927) rule. It also highlights the need for carefully performed empirical studies to weigh in on the sizes and magnitudes of the various distortions of selective tax systems.

OPTIMAL TAX SYSTEMS BY MAJOR PHILOSOPHIES

The remainder of this chapter advances a more challenging thesis, which is that there is frequently strong agreement against selective taxes. The selective excises explored elsewhere in this book tend to emphasize the more popular and defensible forms of selective taxation. However, a larger spectrum of proposed and existing selective taxes lack such support. Although the motivation and rationale for objecting to these taxes differ, they implicitly or explicitly accept efficiency arguments against tax systems that distort choices. The chapter appendix provides an illustrative sampling of these criteria,[9] and a similar perspective is summarized by Mirrlees et al. (2011) in an overview of the variety of tax design features observed around the world that they believe to command near-universal support:

> *for a given distributional outcome*, what matters are:
> - the negative effects of the tax system on welfare and economic efficiency—they should be minimized;
> - administration and compliance costs—all things equal, a system that costs less to operate is preferable;
> - fairness other than in the distributional sense—for example, fairness of procedure, avoidance of discrimination, and fairness with respect to legitimate expectations;
> - transparency—a tax system that people can understand is preferable to one that taxes by "stealth."
>
> As we shall see below, simple, neutral, and stable tax systems are more likely to achieve these outcomes than are complex, non-neutral, and frequently changing systems. But simplicity, neutrality, and stability are desirable

because they promote these ultimate outcomes, not in
their own right. (Mirrlees et al. 2011, 22–23)

Selective taxes add complexity and violate neutrality and, as Mirrlees et al.
(2011) note, come into conflict with other transparency and nondistributional
fairness concerns. For this reason, most tax ideologies tend to oppose choice-
distorting taxes even when economic efficiency is of little or no concern. To
begin, I identify three tax philosophies for the strict purpose of providing a
useful taxonomy for evaluating tax policies from these different perspectives.
Few people likely identify according to tax philosophies in the way they do
with political ideologies, but specific tax policy proposals tend to reflect at least
one of the following views:

1. Utilitarians: Taxes should be allocated in a manner that maximizes social
   welfare according to some notion of collective well-being. Mainstream
   welfare economics follows in this tradition, which was outlined in the previous section, and is often associated with Paul Samuelson and A. C. Pigou.

2. Beneficiarians: Tax burdens should fall on those who benefit from the
   spending, with public services levied on a willingness-to-pay principle.
   A perfectly developed benefit principle system is one where taxes function like prices in the allocation of resources across markets. User fees
   for government services, property taxes for local schools, and gasoline
   taxes to fund highway maintenance are all common examples of public
   revenues raised according to the benefit principle. The related academic
   literature in this field frequently cites Erik Lindahl for its origins.

3. Contractarians: In this chapter, "contractarians" will be used to refer
   to those who prefer tax systems that would be acceptable or otherwise emerge from a socially acceptable process that respects individual
   rights. A Rawlesian tax system would be a tax system that everyone
   would agree to if they stood behind a "veil of ignorance" of their actual
   social position, which is a popular criterion among many progressives.
   Buchanan (1976) advocated a tax system whose evolution is governed
   by a democratic procedure in which improvements are made through
   negotiation and agreement in a fashion that avoids undue fiscal exploitation. Buchanan's view of a strict "fiscal constitution" has been widely
   adopted in libertarian circles.

The root of agreement across these perspectives lies in the likely role of special interests in formulating actual tax policy. The dominant theory of special

interest groups in economic policy is that they seek to create concentrated benefits for their relatively small group at a cost that is diffused across a large group of actors. Tax policies formulated under such pressure likely result in outcomes that deviate from what anyone operating under these perspectives would adopt. Selective taxes can benefit a special interest by either exempting them from the broader tax or by creating disproportionate taxes on their competitors (Holcombe 1998). Allocating tax rates according to political cost rather than efficiency cost will deviate from most designs preferred by utilitarians. By diffusing costs and concentrating benefits, special interest objectives are diametrically opposite those favoring benefit principles. By circumventing broadly democratic processes for fiscal exploitation, tax policy for special interests violates the tendency to favor uniformity seen among contractarians.

To illustrate the application of this process, I use three examples of actual tax policies. The cases are chosen specifically because they are relatively easy to argue against under any of the ideologies, presuming that everyone agrees on the empirical facts.

Example: Kansas 2012 Exemption of Pass-through Income

Even before President Trump's administration began proposing similar elements in its 2017 tax plans, the Kansas 2012 tax reform was widely regarded as one of the most controversial state tax reforms of recent decades.[10] The plans attracted attention because of their proposed reduction of personal income tax rates and consolidations of tax brackets that aimed to considerably reduce the state's general tax revenues and require spending cuts. The argument over progressivity and scope of government is predictably divisive on ideological grounds, but another major component of the reform included the complete exemption of pass-through income from the personal income tax base. The exemption of pass-through income was in stark contrast to arguments over rates and progressivity, as this element was broadly condemned by the major tax analysis think tanks.[11]

The widespread criticism of the reform is based on its selectivity. Many "small businesses" (e.g. sole proprietorship, partnerships, certain S-corporations) have owners who must report their own salaries as a business expense in calculating profits. Typically, the profits are then passed through (added to) the salary of the owners for the purpose of calculating personal income taxes. Prior to the reform, the personal income tax did not treat differently that portion of business owners' incomes derived from pass-through and that portion attributable to their salaries. After the reform, the effective personal income tax rate on the pass-through portion was zero in Kansas, and was a significant windfall of tax savings to taxpayers who filed for income taxes on Schedule C or E. It also offered a competitive advantage to individuals payed by contractor income (1099-MISC) or as employees (W-2). That is, the tax code began providing a cost advantage to firms that hired a janitorial services LLC to replace an in-house custodian staff, and to law and accounting firms that promoted employees to partners.

From a utilitarian prospective, these incentives imply investment and business decisions being redirected for advantages in the tax code (i.e., an inefficient distortion of economic activity). A process- or rights-oriented perspective might ask whether this approach to the tax system would be considered acceptable to someone uncertain as to whether they would be paid by W-2 or 1099-MISC. Nor does there appear to be any expectation that the beneficiaries of the tax exemption are reconciling some better alignment with their imposed costs in the public sector. Indeed, the tax selectively targets relatively wealthy taxpayers with organized business activities.[12]

Example: Per Unit Taxes

A common alternative to ad valorem sales taxes is to levy a tax on a per unit basis.[13] At first blush, it might appear as if this would be an efficient tax if implemented in a uniform manner. However, it is widely believed that doing so distorts choice along the dimension of quality. For example, high-quality coffee may be regarded as a distinct good from low-quality coffee, and consequently the pre-tax prices differ. If a coffee tax of $1 per cup were levied, those lower end brands that sold for $0.25 pre-tax are more likely to be declined by consumers than are the coffee brands that originally sold for $5.

While the distortion of choice explains the utilitarian efficiency argument against per unit taxes, per unit taxes are also sometimes regarded as an implicit form of protectionism that caters to specialized interests or the wealthy. An interesting historical example is described by John Nye (2007) in *War, Wine, and Taxes*, which explores the political economy of British-French trade in the eighteenth century. Nye argues that producers of low-quality wine out of Portugal, to which the British had exclusive export rights, were threatened by expanding trade with France following the conclusion of the War of the Spanish Succession in 1713. To protect these producers, Britain erected a large, volume import tariff on French wine that effectively wiped out the availability of low-end French wine for the British masses and did comparatively less harm for the higher end wine consumption of the wealthy British elites.

Once again, there is no corresponding service for which the payers of this tariff can be regarded as beneficiaries. It is also difficult to see how a tax that so disproportionately harms a large group of consumers in favor of a small group of wealthy elites would find support among the social contract or process-oriented contractarian tax philosophies. Replacing the per unit tax with an ad valorem rate would enhance efficiency and would adhere to a principle of uniformity that would be more likely to find supporters among tax philosophies.

Example: Sales Tax Holidays

Some states have specific days of the year in which the sale of particular items (e.g., clothing, energy, computers, or guns) is exempt from taxation (figure 1). The motivation for these policies is typically some mix of providing welfare assistance and encouraging consumption. Although these sales tax holidays are popular among retailers and their customers, it is difficult to find a tax expert who thinks they represent good public policy. In fact, special reports from both the left-leaning Institute on Taxation and Economic Policy and the right-leaning Tax Foundation have heavily criticized these policies.

Figure 1. Sales Tax Holidays in 2016

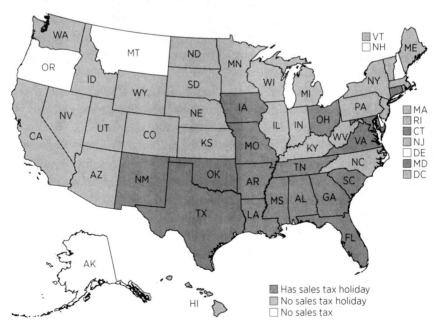

Source: Federation of Tax Administrators. 2016. "2016 Sales Tax Holidays." Updated July 25, 2016 (http://www.taxadmin.org/2016-sales-tax-holidays).

Like any selective tax, sales tax holidays imply that the revenue raised could have been achieved with lower rates on a base that was neutral to the consumer's choices on goods and timing of purchases. If sales taxes are general funds, as they typically are, for public services, then there is little relationship to ability to pay or benefit principles of this temporary tax relief. It is also poorly targeted welfare, whose gains are possibly captured by a narrow set of retailers.[14] As a tax policy, it resembles a government taking an active role in encouraging the consumption of very specific goods. Once again, this practice appears more consistent with a political process conferring specialized favors and is therefore antithetical to contractarian concerns.

CONCLUSION

This chapter demonstrated the prima facie economic case against selective taxation in favor of uniformity. The economic efficiency gains from uniform taxation are widely accepted as being close to the first-best structure of a tax in the sense that a uniform tax produces no burdens in excess of what would be realized under a poll tax. The concept that taxes should be neutral with respect to economic choices is one that reaches broadly across different tax philosophies, even though efficiency/neutrality is just a single dimension of a broader and more diverse set of policy criteria. Although certain groups may explicitly value other dimensions as being of more substantive concern, in practice, actual tax policies and proposals that advance selective taxation are often roundly criticized. In other words, the various perspectives on how taxes should be structured seldom demonstrate much disagreement over the failings of existing or proposed tax policy. This broad criticism is plausibly due to the effectiveness of special interests using selective taxation as an opportunity to create concentrated benefits with widespread costs, resulting in policies that lack a rationale that is supported in these different tax philosophies.

NOTES

1. On hearing the term "poll tax," many American readers may immediately think of the Jim Crow South, where some states required that voters make a payment known as a poll tax before they were allowed to vote. However, in economics a poll tax (also known as a head tax) is a uniform tax that is imposed on every individual.

2. More specifically, the ad valorem tax rate would actually be $100 \times (1/6)$ percent for the arithmetic to be equal.

3. See Diamond (1975) for an example of such a model.

4. See Haig (1921), Simons (1938), and Kaldor (1955) for discussion.

5. See Akerlof (1978) and Cremer et al. (2010) for the origins of and recent contributions to tagging.

6. For discussions of these estimates, see Ring (1999) and Mikesell (2012).

7. The "Ramsey Rule" is in reference to a theory of optimal commodity taxation by Ramsey (1927), which has resulted in a substantive literature of variations on this original model. The so-called rule is generally known as levying taxes inversely to the consumer's price elasticity. That is, the more price sensitive consumers are to a good, the lower the tax on that good if one seeks to minimize excess burden for a given public revenue requirement.

8. This insight falls in the general domain known in economics as "the theory of the second best" (Lipsey and Lancaster, 1956–1957), the main principles of which demonstrates that distortions may offset one another under the correct circumstances.

9. A sampling of other examples of tax policy criteria offers support for the universality of these principles. The appendix includes such a sampling from well-known progressive economist Joseph Stiglitz, the right-leaning Tax Foundation, the left-leaning Institute on Taxation and Economic Policy, and the classically liberal Adam Smith.

10. For example, see the news story about the contrasts between the Trump and Kansas plans in Weissmann (2017).

11. The Tax Foundation produced numerous blog posts, reports, and other statements against the pass-through exemption. A recent summary of their views can be found in testimony by Drenkard and Henchman (2017) to the Kansas House Committee on Taxation, in which they contrast the exemption against their tax policy criteria. The Institute on Taxation and Economic Policy similarly produced many such documents, albeit focusing mostly on the regressivity of the reform. Nevertheless, they frequently targeted the pass-through exemption (e.g., see Gardner 2017) as violating their "tax neutrality" standard for uniformity in taxation.

12. See Leachman and Mai (2014) for a revenue and distributional impact analysis.

13. Per unit taxes are less common in general sales taxation because they raise difficulties in administratively defining the unit of the different goods and services.

14. For empirical work on this aspect of sales tax holidays, see Ross and Lozano-Rojas (2017).

REFERENCES

Akerlof, George A. 1978. "The Economics of 'Tagging' as Applied to the Optimal Income Tax, Welfare Programs, and Manpower Planning." *American Economic Review* 68 (1): 8–19.

Buchanan, James M. 1976. "Taxation in Fiscal Exchange." *Journal of Public Economics* 6: 17–29.

Cremer, Helmuth, Firouz Gahvari, and Jean-Marie Lozachmeur. 2010. "Tagging and Income Taxation: Theory and an Application." *American Economic Journal: Economic Policy* 2 (1): 31–50.

Diamond, P. 1975. "A Many-Person Ramsey Tax Rule." *Journal of Public Economics* 4: 335–42.

Drenkard, Scott, and Joseph Henchman. 2017. "Testimony: Reexamining Kansas' Pass-through Carve-Out." Presentation to the Kansas House Committee on Taxation, January 19. https://taxfoundation.org/testimony-reexamining-kansas-pass-through-carve-out/.

Gardner, Matthew. 2017. "Testimony before the Alaska House Labor & Commerce Committee on House Bill 36." April 1. http://itep.org/itep_reports/2017/04/testimony-before-the-alaska-house-labor-commerce-committee-on-house-bill-36.php#.WRStz1X1Bpg.

Haig, Robert M. 1921. "The Concept of Income—Economic and Legal Aspects." In *The Federal Income Tax*, edited by Robert Murray Haig, Thomas Sewall Adams, and Thomas Powell Reed, 1–28. New York: Columbia University Press.

Holcombe, Randall G. 1998. "Tax Policy from a Public Choice Perspective." *National Tax Journal* 51 (2): 359–71.

Institute on Taxation and Economic Policy. 2011. *The ITEP Guide to Fair State and Local Taxes.* www.itep.org/pdf/guide.pdf.

Kaldor, Nicholas. 1955. *An Expenditure Tax.* London: George Allen & Unwin.

Leachman, Michael, and Chris Mai. 2014. "Lessons for Other States from Kansas' Massive Tax Cuts." Research Report by the Center on Budget and Policy Priorities. March 27. http://www .cbpp.org/research/lessons-for-other-states-from-kansas-massive-tax-cuts?fa=view&id=4110.

Lipsey, R. G., and Kelvin Lancaster. 1956–1957. "The General Theory of Second Best." *Review of Economic Studies* 24 (1): 11–32.

Mikesell, John L. 2011. *Fiscal Administration: Analysis and Applications for the Public Sector*, 8th ed. Boston: Wadsworth Cengage Learning.

———. 2012. "State Retail Sales Taxes in 2011." *State Tax Notes* 66 (December 24): 961–65.

Mirrlees, James, Stuart Adam, Tim Besley, Richard Blundell, Steve Bond, Robert Chote, Malcolm Gammie, Paul Johnson, Gareth Myles, and James Poterba. 2011. *Taxes by Design.* Oxford: Oxford University Press.

Nye, John V. C. 2007. *War, Wine, and Taxes: The Political Economy of Anglo-French Trade, 1689–1900.* Princeton, NJ: Princeton University Press.

Ramsey, Frank. 1927. "A Contribution to the Theory of Taxation." *The Economic Journal* 37 (145): 47–61.

Ring, Raymond J., Jr. 1999. "Consumers' Share and Producers' Share of the General Sales Tax." *National Tax Journal* 52, n1 : 79–90.

Ross, Justin M., and Felipe Lozano-Rojas. 2017. "Sales Tax Holidays: Evidence on Incidence." SSRN Working Paper 2986456. https://papers.ssrn.com/sol3/papers.cfm?abstract_id=2986456.

Simons, Henry. 1938. *Personal Income Taxation: The Definition of Income as a Problem of Fiscal Policy.* Chicago: University of Chicago Press.

Smith, Adam. [1776] 1904. *An Inquiry into the Nature and Causes of the Wealth of Nations*, edited by Edwin Cannan. Library of Economics and Liberty. www.econlib.org/library/Smith/smWN.html.

Stiglitz, Joseph E. 2000. *Economics of the Public Sector.* New York: W. W. Norton.

Tax Foundation. 2015. "Principles of Sound Tax Policy." http://taxfoundation.org/principles -sound-tax-policy.

Weissmann, Jordan. 2017. "Donald Trump's Tax Plan Would Turn the Whole U.S. into Kansas." *Slate.com*, April 26. http://www.slate.com/blogs/moneybox/2017/04/26/donald_trump_s _tax_plan_would_turn_the_whole_u_s_into_kansas.html.

Winer, Stanley L., and Walter Hettich. 1998. "What Is Missed if We Leave Out Collective Choice in the Analysis of Taxation." *National Tax Journal* 51 (2): 373–89.

APPENDIX

Sampling of Tax Policy Criteria

In the following samples, the criteria against selective taxation appear in italics.

Joseph Stiglitz (2000, 458)

1. *Efficiency: The tax system should not be distortionary; if possible, it should be used to enhance economic efficiency.*

2. Administrative simplicity: The tax system should have low costs of administration and compliance.

3. Flexibility: The tax system should allow easy adaptation to changed circumstances.

4. Political responsibility: The tax system should be transparent.

5. *Fairness: The tax system should be, and should be seen to be, fair—treating those in similar circumstances similarly, and imposing higher taxes on those who can better bear the burden of taxation.*

John L. Mikesell (2011, 350–53)

1. Revenue adequacy: The ability of the tax to raise revenues at socially acceptable rates.

2. *Equity (horizontal and vertical): Equity in taxation arises from similar taxpayers receiving similar tax bills (horizontal), and whether the amount of the tax changes with the ability of the taxpayer to bear the burden of taxation (vertical).*

3. *Economic effects: Minimizing the distortion of choices made by households and firms in the economy.*

4. Collectability: Minimizing the burden of public and private resources devoted to administering the tax and collecting the revenue.

5. Transparency: There should be consistency in the design of the tax so that the rules applied the government provide clear guidance to tax authorities, taxpayers, and third parties in defining how a tax will be calculated.

Adam Smith ([1776] 1904, V.2.24–28)

1. The subjects of every state ought to contribute towards the support of the government, as nearly as possible, in proportion to their respective abilities; that is, in proportion to the revenue which they respectively enjoy under the protection of the state.

2. The tax which each individual is bound to pay ought to be certain, and not arbitrary. The time of payment, the manner of payment, the quantity to be paid, ought all to be clear and plain to the contributor, and to every other person.

3. Every tax ought to be levied at the time, or in the manner, in which it is most likely to be convenient for the contributor to pay it.

4. *Every tax ought to be so contrived as both to take out and to keep out of the pockets of the people as little as possible over and above what it brings into the public treasury of the state.*

Tax Foundation's (2015) "Principles of Sound Tax Policy"

1. Simplicity: Administrative costs are a loss to society, and complicated taxation undermines voluntary compliance by creating incentives to shelter and disguise income.

2. Transparency: Tax legislation should be based on sound legislative procedures and careful analysis. A good tax system requires that taxpayers be informed and understand how tax assessment, collection, and compliance works. There should be open hearings, and revenue estimates should be fully explained and replicable.

3. *Neutrality: Taxes should not encourage or discourage certain economic decisions. The purpose of taxes is to raise needed revenue, not to favor or punish specific industries, activities, and products.*

4. Stability: When tax laws are in constant flux, long-range financial planning is difficult. Lawmakers should avoid enacting temporary tax laws, including tax holidays and amnesties.

5. No retroactivity: As a corollary to the principle of stability, taxpayers should be able to rely with confidence on the law as it exists when contracts are signed and transactions are completed.

6. *Broad bases and low rates: As a corollary to the principle of neutrality, lawmakers should avoid enacting targeted deductions, credits, and exclusions. If tax preferences are kept to a minimum, substantial revenue can be raised with low tax rates. Broad-based taxes also produce relatively stable tax revenues from year to year.*

Institute on Taxation and Economic Policy's (2011, 5) "Important Tax Policy Principles"

1. *Equity: Does your tax system treat people at different income levels, and people at the same income level, fairly?*

57

2. Adequacy: Does the tax system raise enough money, in the short run and the long run, to finance public services?

3. Simplicity: Does the tax system allow confusing tax loopholes? Is it easy to understand how your state's taxes work?

4. Exportability: Individuals and companies based in other states benefit from your state's public services. Do they pay their fair share?

5. *Neutrality: Does the tax system interfere with the investments and spending decisions of businesses and workers?*

CHAPTER 3
The Theory and Practice of Selective Consumption Taxation

ADAM J. HOFFER
Department of Economics, University of Wisconsin–La Crosse

WILLIAM F. SHUGHART II
Jon M. Huntsman School of Business, Utah State University

Selective sales and excise taxes are perhaps the oldest tools of public finance known to humankind (Adams [1993] 2001).[1] And for nearly as long as selective taxes have been in place, economists have debated their merits.

Economic analyses of the effects of selective sales and excise taxes have become all the more important for two reasons: (1) Proposals to impose or to raise existing tax rates have garnered renewed support from dieticians and other health professionals arguing that they are justified to counteract a new "epidemic" of obesity associated with the consumption of sugary soft drinks, fast food, and so-called junk food. Such items are termed calorie-dense and high in (trans-) fats, sugar, and salt, ingredients that have been implicated as contributors to excessive body mass indexes, type II diabetes, cardiovascular disease, and other poor health outcomes. (2) Contributions to a recent literature in the relatively new field of behavioral economics (e.g., Kahneman 2011) have supplied additional justifications for governmental intervention in private markets in ways that offset alleged cognitive biases in consumers' decision-making processes, thereby channeling them toward better choices— "better," that is, from the perspective of social science experts and political elites (Thaler and Sunstein [2008] 2009; Sunstein 2013; Thaler 2015).

In chapter 2 of this volume, Justin Ross outlined the variety of margins on which tax policies are evaluated. In this chapter, we assess selective taxes in the context of six issues of interest to public finance scholars and practitioners: (1) efficiency (defined below), (2) neutrality, (3) horizontal equity, (4) vertical equity, (5) rent-seeking and tax avoidance, and (6) information and paternalism.

EFFICIENCY

Efficiency is the metric by which most economists judge market outcomes. A market is efficient if it maximizes the gains from trade (allocative efficiency)[2] or if it utilizes resources in the best possible manner, that is, goods and services are produced at the lowest achievable average cost (productive efficiency).

One way to measure the efficiency of a tax system is to determine whether (and by how much) the imposition of a tax on a market reduces the aggregate gains from trade; a second important issue is tax incidence, that is, how the losses are distributed among the buyers and sellers of the taxed product. All other things being equal, a tax that lessens gains from trade to a smaller degree would be preferred to a tax that lowers them more substantially.

Two justifications are commonly advanced to support selective taxes in terms of efficiency. First, selective taxes can be imposed on goods that generate negative externalities—that is, those for which consumption decisions harm others not directly participating in the markets in which buyers and sellers interact. The traditional "sins" of smoking, drinking, and gambling are textbook examples of activities that impose costs on third parties. Selective taxes on such goods, which reduce market transactions in them, thus may actually be efficiency enhancing.[3] Second, consumers of sinful goods and some other targets of taxation tend to be very unresponsive to after-tax price increases. The quantities demanded of such goods decline in percentage terms by less than the corresponding percentage increase in the tax-ridden price. That unresponsiveness is the chief reason selective taxes generate relatively small reductions in market gains from trade compared to other possible tax targets. But as we shall see, the simple models used to support selective taxes unfortunately often overlook more complex factors that ultimately undermine their attractiveness from an efficiency standpoint.

Negative Externalities

Taxes on tobacco, alcoholic beverages, and gambling customarily are known as sin taxes, because those consumption choices generally have been—and still are—thought to be activities the public sector should discourage. Smoking not only impairs the health and shortens the lives of smokers themselves (adverse outcomes that have been known for a long time: when first introduced in the United States in the late nineteenth century, cigarettes were called "coffin nails"), but it also can harm nonsmoking bystanders who are exposed to secondhand ("environmental") tobacco smoke.[4] Orthodox public finance arguments contend that immoderate gamblers and drinkers of beer, wine, and distilled spirits squander their wages, batter their spouses and children, often miss work or are less productive on the job, and lead lives of dissipation that compromise the sanctity of family home life. Intoxicated riders of horses and, later, drivers of automobiles sometimes damage public or private property and injure or kill pedestrians, passengers, and fellow users of the nation's byways and highways.

Viewed as a category of activities whose effects potentially spill over onto nonconsuming third parties, economists began classifying smoking, drinking, and gambling as a type of market failure (Bator 1958)—a "negative externality" caused by the inability of the consumers to take account of the full (social) costs of their choices. In other words, the private costs of smoking, drinking, and gambling are less than their social costs, which include the value of the harm imposed on others. Imposing sales (ad valorem) or excise (or per unit) taxes on purchases of the goods in question equal to the difference between the private costs and social costs of consumption can in principle close that gap (Pigou [1920] 1952). Scaling the tax rate appropriately, which of course requires a fairly precise estimate of the social costs generated per unit of the good consumed,[5] forces buyers to internalize the externality and to respond to the higher after-tax price by reducing their purchases. Private costs (including the tax paid) thereby are in theory brought into alignment with social costs, and market outcomes approximate those that would prevail in an ideal world where the decisions made by producers and consumers were optimal (i.e., included all relevant costs and benefits) from society's point of view.

Pigouvian taxes on goods or activities producing negative externalities (and the public subsidies Pigou recommended for private activities generating positive externalities, such as education or immunization against communicable diseases) carry the whiff of a normative, social engineering perspective on fiscal policy. But it is important even in that world to keep in mind that government intervention to correct perceived market failures is justified only when externalities are Pareto relevant—namely, when the social cost of intervening is less than the expected social benefits of shifting responsibility for acting to the public sector. And it may well be that the scope of Pareto-relevant externalities, both positive and negative, is much narrower than commonly assumed.[6]

Minimizing Excess Burden

A more positive economic analysis of selective sales and excise taxes can be found in the theoretical work of Frank Ramsey (1927).[7] Ramsey's model begins by assuming that the public sector aims to raise a predetermined (and fixed) amount of revenue at the lowest possible social welfare cost. As is known (or at least should be known) by every principles of economics student, selective taxes in general drive a wedge between the after-tax price of the taxed good to buyers and its cost of production. That wedge creates a deadweight loss of pretax producer and consumer surplus (Harberger 1954), which in the parlance of public finance is called the tax's "excess burden," measured as the amount by which the surpluses lost by consumers and producers exceed the revenue received by the taxing authority.[8]

According to Frank Ramsey, a tax is efficient if its excess burden is small, which will be so if the demand for the taxed good is inelastic, meaning that a 1 percent increase in the taxed good's price, other things being equal, leads to a less than 1 percent reduction in quantity demanded. So, a benevolent dictator ("social planner") who wants to use selective taxes to raise a targeted amount of revenue efficiently will set tax rates inversely proportional to the elasticities of demand for the goods on which taxes are levied. Imposing the highest tax rates on those goods for which demands are most inelastic and then moving down the list to goods having less inelastic (i.e., more elastic) demands until the revenue target is achieved thus minimizes the social welfare cost of a selective tax regime.

It turns out that the demands for cigarettes and alcohol are very inelastic—the median estimates from meta-analyses of multiple empirical studies of the own-price elasticities for both types of goods hover around –0.5 (Hoffer et al. 2015), implying that, other determinants of demand being the same, a 10 percent increase in price leads to about a 5 percent reduction in the quantities consumers are willing and able to buy.[9] Singling out those two categories of sin goods for selective taxation therefore is consistent with Ramsey's rule: the excess burdens of those taxes are relatively small and, for that reason (quantity demanded does not decline very much after the taxes are imposed), they generate considerable revenue for the public sector.

Three points must be kept in mind, though. First, the Ramsey rule applies only when government starts with a revenue target and then asks how that revenue target can be reached most efficiently. The fiscal policy implications of the rule become less relevant if the public sector's objective instead is to raise as much revenue as possible without regard to social welfare considerations.[10] Other factors then come into play, such as (as we shall see) the political costs and benefits of singling out particular goods or services for discriminatory taxation.

Second, the Ramsey rule is not designed to reduce purchases of the goods subject to selective taxation per se, but to generate tax revenue at the lowest possible social welfare cost. If the public sector relies on the Ramsey rule to curtail the consumption of the goods it taxes selectively for public health benefits or any other reason, the results will be disappointing precisely because Ramsey taxes are efficient: quantities demanded decline in percentage terms less—sometimes much less—than the corresponding percentage increases in after-tax prices.

Third, the Ramsey rule assumes that taxation carries no political costs. Holcombe (1997) emphasizes that this is certainly not the case. Tax rates are generated in a political process, wherein electoral goals are paramount and outcomes are determined by legislative vote trading (logrolling). "Interest groups, not social welfare criteria, determine the structure of excise taxes" (Holcombe 1997, 81). Hoffer (2016), for example, finds that the sizable variation observed in state tax rates on cigarettes is explained largely by the influence of tobacco special interests in tobacco-producing states.

Holcombe explains how the political costs of selective taxation increase as politicians become abler tax-rate discriminators. A basic implication of the Ramsey rule is that a different tax rate is applied to every single taxable good and service, which is inversely proportional to the elasticity of demand for it. The political costs of such a tax regime would be massive. Every company in every product-differentiated industry would have incentive to allocate resources, inefficiently from a social welfare perspective, in an attempt to obtain a more favorable tax rate. Holcombe suggests that political costs would be minimized if all goods were instead taxed at the same rate.

NEUTRALITY

Because they distort taxpayers' behavior to far lesser extents, taxes imposed on and collected from broad taxable bases (e.g., income or general sales taxes) raise revenue for the public sector more efficiently (i.e., at a smaller excess burden) than taxes imposed discriminatorily on narrow bases. When a tax base is defined broadly, the ability of individuals to take advantage of untaxed or more favorably taxed substitutes for the good or activity in question necessarily is constrained. A broad-based tax cannot easily be avoided; tax bills cannot be reduced significantly by modifying one's behavior.[11] Such taxes are said to be neutral.

Neutrality is one of the holy grails of tax policy, because taxpayers' choices among the available alternatives are unaffected (or only modestly so) by the levying of a broad-based tax.[12] In an ideal, hypothetical world of public finance, taxes do not change taxpayers' allocations of time between work and leisure, of income between consumption and saving, or of spending across myriad goods and services.

Selective sales and excise taxes obviously fail the neutrality test. Tax bills vary depending on whether an individual chooses to buy a selectively taxed good and, if so, how much of it is purchased per week, per month, or per year. Although excise tax rates are the same per unit, smokers pay more tobacco taxes in total than nonsmokers do, drivers are taxed more heavily than nondrivers when buying motor fuels and vehicle tires, and the tax bills of consumers in some states who purchase beverages sweetened by sugar or high-fructose corn syrup are larger than those of buyers of artificially sweetened diet soft drinks.

HORIZONTAL EQUITY

The normative principle of tax neutrality is closely related to the standard of horizontal tax equity. Horizontal tax equity says that households earning similar incomes ought to face similar tax bills. That roughly would be true for personal income taxes, but for the tax code's many exemptions, deductions, and credits that, for example, allow homeowners (but not renters) to deduct mortgage interest payments or working low-income families with children (but not childless households) to claim the widely abused earned income tax credit.

Selective sales and excise taxes also violate that norm, because household tax bills vary according to consumption choices. A household choosing to consume alcohol or tobacco, for example, will pay more in taxes than one choosing not to consume those goods. Unless every selectively taxed item is purchased by everyone in a given income bracket, it cannot be true that the taxes are horizontally equitable.

VERTICAL EQUITY

A tax is said to be vertically equitable if it is progressive, that is, rises as the ability to pay taxes rises. Under this normative principle of public finance, the tax bills paid by high-income households will be larger as percentages of income than those faced by low-income households.

Selective sales and excise taxes are inconsistent with the norm of vertical tax equity, because it turns out that low-income households typically spend larger fractions of their incomes on goods subject to such taxes than do their high-income counterparts. Like consumption taxes in general, selective taxes therefore are regressive, meaning that, as proportions of income, their burdens fall most heavily on households at the lower end of the income distribution, thereby reinforcing pre-tax income inequality.

One explanation for this observation is that the quantities consumed of selectively taxed goods do not rise proportionately with income: a doubling of a household's income almost never will cause the members of that household to double the number of packs of cigarettes, cases of beer, or six-packs of sugary soft drinks they buy per day, week, or month. While it is true that high-income households may choose to buy upscale taxed goods of higher quality (finer wines or cigars, for instance, or premium rather than regular or mid-grades of gasoline), selective tax rates do not vary with product quality—the same per unit or ad valorem tax rate is applied to every unit purchased. The members of upper income households who do buy more selectively taxed goods than their lower income counterparts will of course pay absolutely larger tax bills, but the tax rate per unit, which influences purchases at the margin, remains the same.

In contrast, for reasons explained more fully below, because the burdens of such taxes typically fall on identifiable minorities of taxpayers and purchases of most selectively taxed goods do not decline substantially in response to tax-caused increases in their prices (the demands for them tend to be inelastic)[13], selective sales and excise taxes are robust revenue engines for the governments that impose them. But that characteristic of consumer demand introduces a policy contradiction. The traditional justification for taxing some goods and not others—initially applied to the so-called sins of drinking, smoking, and gambling—is that such taxes reduce the purchases of goods deemed harmful to the health or welfare of buyers themselves or of third parties affected negatively by an individual's consumption choices. But if such taxes are meant to force consumers to internalize the externality imposed on others, they fail that test: evidence adduced by Viscusi (1994), for example, suggests that the excise tax rates on cigarettes imposed by state and federal governments already exceeded plausible scientific estimates of the social costs of smoking per pack more than a generation ago.

However, if, as the evidence shows, the quantities demanded of alcoholic beverages, tobacco, and most other selectively taxed goods decline only modestly in the face of tax-induced increases in their prices, the behavioral modification justification for selective tax policy is weakened. In such cases, the stated public policy aim of imposing or raising such taxes to regulate socially undesirable or unhealthful consumption behavior simply is a smokescreen misdirecting attention from policymakers' actual purposes, namely, to generate tax revenue at comparatively low political cost. In other cases, for instance, when a tax is conceived as a user fee (e.g., motor fuel taxes to pay for road construction and repair, or tobacco taxes to pay for the public healthcare costs of treating smoking-related diseases), the main question to be addressed is whether the tax revenue actually is spent as intended. The answer typically is "no."[14]

RENT-SEEKING AND TAX AVOIDANCE

Selective tax policies create winners and losers. Those groups and the agents representing them therefore have strong incentives to participate actively in the political process that determines tax bases and tax rates (Holcombe 1997). The outcome of that process, in turn, determines how much the winners stand to win (in the form of the shares of the tax revenue redistributed to them) and how much the losers stand to lose (in the form of higher tax bills).[15] Each potentially affected group thus will engage in rent-seeking activities (Tullock 1967) to shape the legislation in ways that maximize its own collective benefits net of lobbying costs.[16]

In that sense, proponents of government intervention aimed at correcting perceived behavioral anomalies are like Adam Smith's "man of system," who

> is apt to be very wise in his own conceit; and is often so
> enamoured with the supposed beauty of his own ideal plan
> of government, that he cannot suffer the smallest deviation
> from any part of it. He goes on to establish it completely
> and in all its parts, without any regard either to the great
> interests, or to the strong prejudices which may oppose
> it. He seems to imagine that he can arrange the different
> members of a great society with as much ease as the hand
> arranges the different pieces upon a chess-board. He does
> not consider that the pieces upon the chess-board have

> no other principle of motion besides that which the hand
> impresses upon them; but that, in the great chess-board of
> human society, every single piece has a principle of motion
> of its own, altogether different from that which the legisla-
> ture might chuse to impress upon it. If those two principles
> coincide and act in the same direction, the game of human
> society will go on easily and harmoniously, and is very
> likely to be happy and successful. If they are opposite or
> different, the game will go on miserably, and the society
> must be at all times in the highest degree of disorder.
> (Smith [1761] 1982, 233–34)

Among other things, Adam Smith's "man of system" ignores the substitution opportunities available by cross-border shopping in neighboring jurisdictions where tax rates are lower (Vedder 1997) as well as those created by differential tax rates on items in broader product categories (Gant and Ekelund 1997). Insofar as they impose the same tax rate on every unit purchased, selective consumption taxes are blunt instruments for pricing the external costs suppos- edly associated the commission of sin (Wagner 1997). A policy's unintended consequences emerge either because supporters are not good economists (Bastiat [1850] 1964) or because most effects beyond the immediately fore- seeable ones were in fact known and therefore intended (Stigler 1971).

In early 2015, paternalistic impulses were on display in northern California. A ballot measure in the city of Berkeley asked voters to approve or reject an ordinance proposing to levy an excise tax of 1 cent per ounce on carbonated soft drinks and other sugar-sweetened beverages (SSBs) as a way of counter- ing a perceived epidemic of obesity-related type II diabetes and other health problems linked in part to excessive consumption of sugar and high-fructose corn syrup.[17] The referendum passed by a margin of 60 percent to 40 percent. Some months later, San Francisco approved an ordinance requiring health warnings on billboards and other advertising messages for SSBs, advising that "Drinking beverages with added sugar(s) contributes to obesity, diabetes, and tooth decay" (Esterl 2015). Although educational campaigns are a form of soft paternalism, the American Beverage Association joined the California Retailers Association and the California Outdoor Advertising Association to sue San Francisco on First Amendment grounds.

Berkeley's referendum recommending levying a selective excise tax on sugar-sweetened soft drinks triggered the expenditure of $3 million— $2.5 million spent by its opponents and $0.5 million by its supporters—or roughly $30 per vote cast. Such lobbying outlays (both to seek rents and to defend them) add to the social cost or excess burden of the tax initiative (Tullock 1967). Given that Berkeley's selective excise tax on SSBs at the time it was proposed was anticipated to generate about $1 million in new revenue for the city's coffers in each of the following years, that extra revenue will not begin to offset its deadweight social cost until 2018 at the earliest.[18] This first-in-the-nation selective excise tax on sugary soft drinks is a poster-child for modern uses of taxes to generate revenue over and above the practice in most jurisdictions to include those consumer goods in their existing sales tax bases.

Evidence is accumulating, though, that artificially sweetened beverages contribute as much to the supposed ongoing obesity epidemic—and perhaps more so—than does consumption of SSBs (e.g., Imamura et al. 2015; Shughart 2015). If those findings are supported by additional evidence, Berkeley's and San Francisco's recent policy initiatives will turn out to have been counter-productive. Hard and soft paternalism relying on preliminary, incomplete, or flawed scientific evidence may be worse than not taking any action at all.

INFORMATION AND PATERNALISM

Imagine that during one week, you hand a neighbor your grocery money to do all your shopping at a local grocery store. The only food you have available to eat is selected by someone else. He or she would most likely be able to buy items for meals that are nutritional, but dollar for dollar, you almost certainly could have bought food that would have pleased you more. Maybe you neighbor drinks skim milk, but you prefer 2 percent; your neighbor buys canned corn, but you prefer frozen; your neighbor buys fresh salmon, but you do not eat much fish; your neighbor likes "organic" food, but you want to minimize your grocery bill for the week. Having someone else buy your groceries is apt to lead to disappointment.

At the societal level, delegating to any central organization authority to allocate goods and services means that alignment of such decisions with individual preferences is impossible:[19]

> The economic problem of society is thus not merely a
> problem of how to allocate "given" resources—if "given" is
> taken to mean given to a single mind which deliberately
> solves the problem set by these "data." It is rather a problem
> of how to secure the best use of resources known to any of
> the members of society, for ends whose relative importance

only these individuals know. Or, to put it briefly, it is a
problem of the utilization of knowledge which is not given
to anyone in its totality. (Hayek 1945, 519–20)

Modern policymaking elites use findings from behavioral economics to collapse all individual preferences or goals into the one preference or goal arrived
at somehow by others.[20] These paternalists blur the distinction between tax
policies ostensibly designed to address negative externalities, such as the injuries and deaths associated with drunk driving, and what might be called "internalities;" internalities represent harm caused to one's (future) self, plausibly
arising from informational deficiencies or time-inconsistent preferences that
lead some individuals to be intemperate drinkers, smokers, or eaters of high-
fat or salt-heavy foods today, because they discount heavily the future consequences of those consumption choices.[21] Many modern selective tax regimes
are proposed and enacted for the express purpose of reducing consumption for
consumers' own good. We might call such policies "meddlesome preferences"
(Sen 1970; Buchanan 1986)—with teeth.

Proposals to impose a new selective tax or to raise an existing one for purely
fiscal reasons often are combined with appeals to a higher moral purpose
(improving public health, correcting pervasive biases in consumers' decision-
making processes or producing other benefits for society as a whole). Such
appeals join with the more parochial financial interests of the individuals and
groups who stand to gain from imposing a selective sales or excise tax to form
decisive political coalitions similar to the the "Bootleggers and Baptists" model
of regulation (Smith and Yandle 2014).

CONCLUSION

Selective consumption taxes are age-old. Customarily levied on the "sins" of
smoking, drinking, and gambling, such taxes are justified by observing that
they are relatively efficient means of generating revenue for the government.
Most sin goods have relatively few substitutes, meaning that increases in their
after-tax prices cause the quantities consumers are willing and able to buy to
decline less than proportionately. Such taxes are more efficient (create smaller
excess burdens) than those imposed on goods for which consumers are more
sensitive to changes in price (Ramsey 1927). Selective taxes on the purchases of
sin goods therefore are revenue engines for the public sector because, by their
very natures, such taxes do not reduce the consumption of the taxed goods
and services very much.

More recently, though, selective sales and excise taxes have been imposed at the US state and federal levels of government not to reduce the purchases of goods and services plausibly generating negative externalities—that is, harm to innocent third parties (e.g., battered spouses and the victims of drunk drivers) or as so-called user fees (e.g., motor fuel taxes)—but instead to protect the health and welfare of consumers themselves, or what we have called internalities. We therefore see taxes imposed on sugar-sweetened beverages and junk food so as to reduce the incidences of obesity-related diabetes and heart disease for consumers' own good mainly to disguise their revenue-raising prowess. But if the demands for such goods also tend to be inelastic, as the econometric evidence suggests, taxing those food items will not achieve public health professionals' stated goal of reducing consumption significantly. Moreover, because rates of smoking, drinking, and gambling as well as the more modern sins (eating fast food and junk food) are higher among poor than rich people, the burden of selective sales and excise taxes falls most heavily on low-income households.

Support for selective sales and excise taxation has been reinforced recently by the findings of behavioral economists and psychologists, who report that consumers' decision-making is beset by cognitive anomalies inconsistent with the models and predictions of neoclassical economic theory.

Unfortunately, the paternalists either overlook or ignore critics of their models who argue that, because they, too, are flawed human beings, policymakers themselves are subject to those same cognitive failures and, moreover, that the public policy process largely is driven by special-interest groups rather than by public-spirited health professionals, politicians, and bureaucrats.

Placing individual consumption choices further under the control of public policymakers and special-interest groups makes individuals and society worse off. The US government tried Prohibition (of alcohol production and sales) between 1920 and 1933 (Shughart 2016). Most people did not stop drinking; black markets in booze, violent crimes, and political corruption were rampant. Modern tax regimes assuredly are less onerous than banning the consumption of politically incorrect goods and services outright, but both policy approaches have been justified by the same political rhetoric supposedly aimed at promoting the interests of society and each member of it. We know that such arguments are flawed. Taxes distort consumption choices, by definition, creating excess burdens (deadweight social welfare losses), and making both producers and consumers worse off and poorer (especially those at the lower end of the income distribution). Selective consumption taxes transfer money from the pockets of American consumers and businesses into the public treasury, where it will be spent mostly to buy the votes of people who think (erroneously) that government officials are wiser and less self-interested than ordinary citizens. Ever since Treasury Secretary Alexander Hamilton first imposed a federal excise tax on whiskey in the late 1780s, selective taxation of traditional and more modern sins has been the means by which revenue for the public sector can be raised by targeting the paths of least political resistance to expanding the state rather than a means to help otherwise autonomous individuals to avoid supposedly bad consumption choices.

At bottom, optimal tax policies are a chimera, grounded in the recommen-dations of so-called public finance experts, who see ways of raising revenue for the public sector at the lowest possible excess burden (deadweight social costs). But those recommendations necessarily must be filtered through a political process, the actors in which are motivated, not by notions of tax efficiency but by more parochial goals, such as maximizing probabilities of election or reelection. In the end, selective tax policies in practice target the consumers of products who can be portrayed as imposing costs on themselves or on innocent third parties, even if those costs do not stand up to dispassion-ate scientific examination. Markets may fail to achieve optimal results, but gov-ernment failure in the context of tax policy is a much more serious problem.

Determined by political processes, selective sales and excise tax rates plainly are inconsistent with normative public finance principles of efficiency, neutrality, and equity. Because the politicians who enact them lack accurate information about consumers' preferences, are influenced by lobbying by special-interest groups supporting or opposing tax policy changes, and some-times compete to raise revenue from the same tax base (e.g., selective local, state, and federal taxes on tobacco, alcohol, and motor fuel), it should not be too surprising that tax rates often exceed the level that maximizes tax revenue (Shughart and Tollison 1991) or any credible estimate of the social costs of consuming certain goods.

NOTES

1. A sales tax is levied ad valorem (i.e., as a percentage of the taxed good's retail price). An excise tax, in contrast, is levied as so many cents or dollars per unit purchased. Examples of the latter include Berkeley, California's penny per ounce tax on sugary soft drinks, and state and federal excise taxes on cigarettes and gasoline. Selective sales taxes on one good are rarer than selective excise taxes, although, for example, moist smokeless tobacco (snuff) is subject to a selective ad valorem tax in some jurisdictions. Many jurisdictions "tax the tax": local and state sales taxes often are applied to retail prices on top of any selective excise tax.

2. The hallmark of allocative efficiency is a situation in which a good's market price is equal to the marginal cost of producing it. Allocative efficiency is achieved only in a market that satisfies the strict textbook assumptions of perfect or pure competition, namely, (1) perfect

information on the part of both buyers and sellers, (2) product homogeneity (i.e., no spatial or quality differentiation among sellers), and (3) costless entry and exit by all market participants.

3. Such taxes are corrective in the sense of A. C. Pigou ([1920] 1952), who was the first economist cum sociologist to recommend them as ways of aligning private costs with the social costs of consumption. The chief problem associated with Pigouvian taxes is that policymakers rarely have access to the information required to measure social costs accurately or the incentives to act on that information in ways that improve social welfare. On that insuperable problem, see Hayek (1945) and the discussion below.

4. Cigarette smoking became a serious public health issue following the publication of the US surgeon general's report on smoking and health in 1964 (Hoffer et al. 2015, 32). The surgeon general was concerned at the time with establishing a direct link between cigarette smoking and the incidences of lung cancer and heart disease in tobacco users. It was not until 15 years later (1979) that worries about the adverse health impacts of smoking on others, then known as involuntary or passive smoking, began to be raised (Aviado 1986).

5. Distinguishing carefully between the social costs of consumption (those imposed on third parties) from the corresponding private costs (those borne by the consumer personally) is critical in computing the optimal tax rate. If, for instance, cigarette smokers are absent more often from workplaces than nonsmokers, smokers themselves will bear the majority of those costs in the forms of, for example, lower wages, smaller pay raises, and slower promotions. Conflating social costs and private costs leads to excise tax rates on cigarettes that are much too high for the purpose of forcing smokers to internalize the externality (e.g., Viscusi 1994). Virtually all estimates of the social costs of consuming particular goods, including tobacco, also ignore (and therefore fail to net out) consumption's individual benefits or ways in which consumption reduces burdens on the public treasury, the latter including early death, which lowers taxpayer-financed healthcare and pension expenditures.

6. See, for example, King (2007) on K–12 public education, Holcombe and Sobel (1995) on state legislatures, and McAndrew (2012) on crime labs, all of which find private benefits but few public benefits flowing from the provision of such services. The externalites in these cases thus seem to be infra-marginal, not marginal ones that would justify government intervention.

7. The economics literature that followed Ramsey on the effects of selective excise taxes is both broad and rich; see, for example Shughart et al. (1987) as well as the contributions both to theory and to policy practice cited in Shughart (1997).

8. The size of the excess burden depends mainly on the tax rate and the elasticities of the demand for and the supply of the taxed good. In the simple case of linear demand and constant marginal cost (perfectly elastic supply), it can be shown (see, e.g., Hillman 2009, 252) that the excess burden of an excise tax is computed as $(\frac{1}{2})(pq)\eta_D t^2$, where p and q are respectively the price and quantity prevailing in the market before a tax of t dollars (or cents) per unit is levied on the good, and η_D is the elasticity of demand at the pre-tax price and quantity. The excess burden thus rises as demand becomes more elastic (η_D increases in absolute value) and as the tax rate increases. (As a matter of fact, all else equal, the excess burden rises by the square of the tax rate.) No excess burden materializes in the very special case of perfectly inelastic demand $\eta_D = \infty$ since in that case consumers are completely unresponsive to a tax-ridden increase in price; the quantity of the good they are willing and able to buy does not change. The tax in that case is paid fully by the individuals on the demand side of the market, as it is when supply is perfectly elastic. If demand is perfectly elastic ($\eta_D = \infty$), a selective tax raises no revenue whatsoever, because the after-tax market price does not change; producer surplus will be lower, though, creating an excess burden without any offsetting benefit.

9. The elasticity of the demand for any good, including tobacco and alcohol, largely depends on the number of substitutes available to the consumers of the taxed good. Other things being equal, demand elasticity increases with the number of substitutes on offer currently and that become available over time, as buyers are given opportunities to search for and take advantage

of them. Demand elasticity thus hinges in part on how broadly or narrowly the tax base is defined. The demand for Camel cigarettes is more elastic, for instance, than the demand for all brands of cigarettes taken together. The substitution possibilities help explain why electronic cigarettes, the exhaled vapors from which are not now known to impose adverse health effects on nearby nonsmokers, are in the process of being added to the tobacco tax base in many jurisdictions.

10. See Brennan and Buchanan ([1980] 2000, chap. 4), for an analysis demonstrating the critical importance of Ramsey's assumption about an overall revenue target and explaining why neither his nor Pigou's normative conclusions hold for a Leviathan government's selective commodity tax regime.

11. Poll or head taxes, which are levied lump sum on every man, woman, and child, are for that reason the most economically efficient means of raising revenue for the public sector. Such taxes can be escaped only by moving out of the jurisdiction imposing them or by dying. Because a poll tax of $1,000 imposes a heavier burden on someone with an annual income of $10,000 than on someone else who earns $100,000 per year, such taxes also are regressive, which explains the fairly widespread opposition to them.

12. Tax neutrality is a goal advanced frequently to justify the collection of state sales taxes from remote (out-of-state) sellers. But cross-border shopping is a key contributor to consumer-friendly interjurisdictional tax-rate competition (Vedder 1997; Shughart 2000).

13. The (own-price) elasticity of demand for any good is computed as the ratio of the percentage change in quantity demanded to a 1 percent change in the good's own price, holding all other determinants of demand, such as the prices of related goods (i.e., substitutes and complements for the good in question), the consumer's income, and his or her tastes and preferences, constant. Demand is said to be inelastic, unit elastic, or elastic according to whether that ratio is less than, equal to or more than one in absolute value.

14. Owing to the familiar equi-marginal principle of neoclassical economic theory, no politician ever will allocate all revenue raised by an earmarked tax to spending by the program to which the taxes ostensibly are dedicated. Well-known examples include the diversion of monies away from healthcare and smoking-cessation programs under the Master Settlement Agreement with the tobacco industry (Stevenson and Shughart 2006), legislative raiding of motor fuel tax receipts deposited into highway trust funds, and the reallocation of lottery and casino tax revenues earmarked for public education. See Lee (1997) and Crowley and Hoffer (chap. 6, this volume) for discussions of the earmarking of tax receipts as a way of overcoming political resistance to new selective taxes or increases in existing ones.

15. When selective taxation prompts consumers to reduce their purchases of taxed goods or services, they also suffer utility losses. Tobacco and alcohol deliver satisfaction to consumers; gambling is fun for casino patrons and lottery players. Taxes also reduce the income available for spending on goods not subject to tax.

16. Rent-seeking by groups supporting and opposing selective sales or excise taxes raises problems of organizing and mobilizing collective action not addressed explicitly here (see Olson 1965).

17. High-fructose corn syrup is the sweetener of choice for many food manufacturers owing to US import quotas on cane sugar—trade restrictions that have raised sugar's domestic price to twice that prevailing on world markets—and subsidies for corn growers to support ethanol production.

18. Six months after implementation, the tax's effects on soft drink prices were falling short of proponents' projections. Only about 22 percent of the penny per ounce SSB tax (levied on distributors) is being shifted forward to consumers, likely because of opportunities for shopping beyond Berkeley's city limits and substitution of (untaxed) diet drinks for their sugar-sweetened versions (Cawley and Frisvold 2015). Berkeley's voters could have taken the lesson learned by Denmark, which was forced to repeal a tax on foods with a saturated fat content of 2.3 percent or more, because many Danes crossed the border into Germany or Sweden to buy cheese and other high-fat items (Kliff 2012).

19. Policymakers' information sets also must account for consumers' attitudes toward risk, which play significant roles in behavior leading to obesity, especially among low-income African-Americans (de Oliveria et al. 2015).

20. We have adapted here one of James Buchanan's (1986) objections to the Kaldor-Hicks test judging public policies that create winners and losers (as all surely do) to be Pareto superior to the status quo if it is possible for the former (as a group) to compensate the latter (also as a group), even if no compensation occurs.

21. Our definition differs from that of Charles Wolf. According to Wolf, "internalities are the private goals that apply within non-market organizations to guide, regulate, and evaluate the performance of agencies and their personnel" (quoted in Levy and Peart 2015, 3).

REFERENCES

Adams, Charles. [1993] 2001. *For Good and Evil: The Impact of Taxes on the Course of Civilization*, 2nd ed. New York: Madison Books.

Aviado, Domingo M. 1986. "Health Issues Relating to 'Passive' Smoking." In *Smoking and Society: Toward a More Balanced Assessment*, edited by Robert D. Tollison, 139–65. Lexington, MA: Lexington Books.

Bastiat, Frederic [1850] 1964. "What Is Seen and What Is Not Seen." In *Selected Essays on Political Economy*, edited by Frederic Bastiat, 1–50. Irvington-on-Hudson, NY: Foundation for Economic Education.

Bator, Francis M. 1958. "The Anatomy of Market Failure." *Quarterly Journal of Economics* 72: 351–79.

Brennan, Geoffrey, and James M. Buchanan. [1980] 2000. *The Power to Tax: Analytical Foundations of a Fiscal Constitution*. In *The Collected Works of James M. Buchanan*, vol. 9. Indianapolis, IN: Liberty Fund.

Buchanan, James M. 1986. "Politics and Meddlesome Preferences." In *Smoking and Society: Toward a More Balanced Assessment*, edited by Robert D. Tollison, 335–42. Lexington, MA: Lexington Books.

Cawley, John, and David Frisvold. 2015. "Incidence of Taxes on Sugar-Sweetened Beverages: The Case of Berkeley, California." NBER Working Paper 21465. National Bureau of Economic Research, Cambridge, MA. http://www.nber.org/papers/w21465.

Esterl, Mike. 2015. "Beverage Industry Sues to Stop San Francisco Health Warnings on Sugary Drinks." *Wall Street Journal*, July 24. http://www.wsj.com/articles/beverage-industry-sues-to-stop-san-francisco-health-warnings-on-sugary-drinks-1437779307/.

Gant, Paula A., and Robert B. Ekelund Jr. 1997. "Excise Taxes, Social Costs, and the Consumption of Wine." In *Taxing Choice: The Predatory Politics of Fiscal Discrimination*, edited by William F. Shughart II, 247–69. New Brunswick, NJ: Transaction.

Harberger, Arnold C. 1954. "Monopoly and Resource Allocation." *American Economic Review Papers and Proceedings* 44: 77–87.

Hayek, Frederick A. 1945. "The Use of Knowledge in Society." *American Economic Review* 35 (4): 519–30.

Hillman, Arye L. 2009. *Public Finance and Public Policy: Responsibilities and Limitations of Government*, 2nd ed. Cambridge and New York: Cambridge University Press.

Hoffer, Adam J. 2016. "Special-Interest Spillovers and Tobacco Taxation." *Contemporary Economic Policy* 34 (1): 146–57.

Hoffer, Adam J., Rejeana M. Gvillo, William F. Shughart II, and Michael D. Thomas. 2015. "Regressive Effects: Causes and Consequences of Selective Consumption Taxation." Working Paper, Mercatus Center at George Mason University, Arlington, VA.

Holcombe, Randall G. 1997. "Selective Excise Taxation from an Interest-Group Perspective." In *Taxing Choice: The Predatory Politics of Fiscal Discrimination*, edited by William F. Shughart II, 81–103. New Brunswick, NJ: Transaction.

Holcombe, Randall G., and Russell S. Sobel. 1995. "Empirical Evidence on the Publicness of State Legislative Activities." *Public Choice* 83 (1–2): 47–58.

Imamura, Fumiaki, Laura O'Connor, Zheng Ye, Jaakko Mursu, Yasuaki Hayashino, Shilpa N. Bhupathiraju, and Nita G. Forouhi. 2015. "Consumption of Sugar Sweetened Beverages, Artificially Sweetened Beverages, and Fruit Juice and Incidence of Type 2 Diabetes: Systematic Review, Meta-Analysis, and Estimation of Population Attributable Fraction." *British Medical Journal* 351: h3576. http://www.bmj.com/content/351/bmj.h3576.full.

Kahneman, Daniel. 2011. *Thinking Fast and Slow*. New York: Farrar, Straus and Giroux.

King, Kerry A. 2007. "Do Spillover Benefits Create a Market Inefficiency in K–12 Public Education?" *Cato Journal* 27 (1): 447–58.

Kliff, Sarah. 2012. "Denmark Scraps World's First Fat Tax." *Washington Post*, November 13. http://www.washingtonpost.com/news/wonkblog/wp/2012/11/13/denmark-scraps-worlds-first-fat-tax/.

Lee, Dwight R. 1997. "Overcoming Taxpayer Resistance by Taxing Choice and Earmarking Revenues." In *Taxing Choice: The Predatory Politics of Fiscal Discrimination*, edited by William F. Shughart II, 105–16. New Brunswick, NJ: Transaction.

Levy, David M., and Sandra J. Peart. 2015. "Learning from Failure: A Review of Peter Schuck's *Why Government Fails So Often: And How It Can Do Better*." *Journal of Economic Literature* 53 (3): 1–8.

McAndrew, William P. 2012. "Are Forensic Science Services Club Goods? An Analysis of the Optimal Forensic Science Service Delivery Model." *Forensic Science Policy and Management* 3 (4): 151–58.

de Oliveira, Angela C. M., Tammy C. M. Leonard, Kerem Shuval, Celette S. Skinner, Catherine Eckel, and James C. Murdoch. 2015. "Economic Preferences and Obesity among a Low-Income African American Community." *Journal of Economic Behavior and Organization*. http://dx.doi.org/10.1016/j.jebo.2015.11.002.

Olson, Mancur. 1965. *The Logic of Collective Action: Public Goods and the Theory of Groups*. Cambridge, MA: Harvard University Press.

Pigou, Arthur C. [1920] 1952. *The Economics of Welfare*. New Brunswick, NJ: Transaction.

Ramsey, Frank P. 1927. "A Contribution to the Theory of Taxation". *Economic Journal* 37: 47–61.

Sen, Amarta K. 1970. "The Impossibility of a Paretian Liberal." *Journal of Political Economy* 78: 152–157.

Shughart, William F. II (ed.). 1997. *Taxing Choice: The Predatory Politics of Fiscal Discrimination*. An Independent Institute Book. New Brunswick, NJ: Transaction.

——. 2000. "E-taxes: A Public-Choice Perspective." *Quarterly Journal of Electronic Commerce* 1: 151–60.

——. 2015. "Should There Be a Tax on Soda and Other Sugary Drinks? NO: The Health Benefits Are Far Less than Claimed." *Wall Street Journal*, July 13, p. R2. http://www.wsj.com/articles/should-there-be-a-tax-on-soda-and-other-sugary-drinks-1436757039.

——. 2016. "Jan. 16, 1920: Another Day that Should Live in Infamy." *The Hill*. http://thehill.com/blogs/congress-blog/politics/265912-jan-16-1920-another-day-that-should-live-in-infamy/.

Shughart, William F. II, and Robert D. Tollison. 1991. "Fiscal Federalism and the Laffer Curve." *Economia Delle Scelte Pubbliche [Journal of Public Finance and Public Choice]* (1) (1991): 21–28.

Shughart, William F. II, Robert D. Tollison, and Richard S. Higgins. 1987. "Rational Self-Taxation: Complementary Inputs and Excise Taxation." *Canadian Journal of Economics* 20 (3): 527–32.

Smith, Adam. [1761] 1982. *The Theory of Moral Sentiments*. Glasgow Edition of the Works and Correspondence of Adam Smith, vol. 1, edited by D. T. Raphael and A. L. Macfie. Indianapolis, IN: Liberty Fund.

Smith, Adam, and Bruce Yandle. 2014. *Bootleggers and Baptists: How Economic Forces and Moral Persuasion Interact to Shape Regulatory Politics*. Washington, DC: Cato Institute.

Stevenson, Taylor P., and William F. Shughart II. 2006. "Smoke and Mirrors: The Political Economy of the Tobacco Settlements." *Public Finance Review* 34: 712–30.

Stigler, George J. 1971. "The Theory of Regulation." *Bell Journal of Economics and Management Science* 2 (1): 3–21.

Sunstein, Cass R. 2013. *Simpler: The Future of Government*. New York: Simon and Schuster.

Thaler, Richard H. 2015. *Misbehaving: The Making of Behavioral Economics*. New York: W. W. Norton.

Thaler, Richard H., and Cass R. Sunstein. [2008] 2009. *Nudge: Improving Decisions about Health, Wealth, and Happiness*, revised and expanded ed. New York: Penguin.

Tullock, Gordon. 1967. "The Welfare Costs of Tariffs, Monopolies, and Theft." *Western Economic Journal* 5: 224–32.

Vedder, Richard K. 1997. "Bordering on Chaos: Fiscal Federalism and Excise Taxes." In *Taxing Choice: The Predatory Politics of Fiscal Discrimination*, edited by William F. Shughart II, 271–85. New Brunswick, NJ: Transaction.

Viscusi, W. Kip. 1994. "Cigarette Taxation and the Social Consequences of Smoking." In *Tax Policy and the Economy*, Volume 27, edited by James M. Poterba, 51–102. Cambridge, MA: MIT Press.

Wagner, Richard E. 1997. "The Taxation of Alcohol and the Control of Social Costs." In *Taxing Choice: The Predatory Politics of Fiscal Discrimination*, edited by William F. Shughart II, 227–46. New Brunswick, NJ: Transaction.

CHAPTER 4
The Language of Taxation:
Ideology Masquerading as Science

RICHARD E. WAGNER

Department of Economics, George Mason University

T he economics of taxation is part of the economic theory of public finance. However, economists have thought about matters pertaining to public finance along two distinct paths. The more prominent path today treats public finance as a servant of practical statecraft. Along this path, theorists seek to develop ideological articulations that facilitate the marshaling of support for particular political programs. The less prominent path treats public finance as part of the science of economics. The science of economics seeks to explain how it is that societies exhibit generally orderly patterns of economic activity even though no one is in charge of creating that order. Similarly, a science of public finance would seek to study the observed organizational patterns that emerge out of political activity once it is recognized that such patterns are far too complex to be simple products of choice by some political figure. Somewhere on the order of 40 to 50 percent of economic activity these days is organized through political and not commercial activity. No person or office can truly direct that much activity. On the contrary, that volume of activity can only be an emergent quality of some process of democratic competition. The explanatory challenge along this analytical path is to explain how generally orderly patterns of fiscal activity arise without embracing what

Mitchel Resnick (1994) calls the centralized mindset, by which he means the tendency to attribute orderly patterns to some ordering agent when there is no such agent who creates that order. Just as the orderliness of a market economy arises through a competitive process, so too do fiscal patterns emerge through complex processes of democratic competition.

These distinct orientations for public finance were contrasted cogently by the Italian economist Antonio de Viti de Marco in his preface to the 1936 English edition of his *First Principles of Public Finance*. There, de Viti (1936, 15) notes that for the more popular conception of public finance "the phenomena of Public Finance give rise to problems, not of theory, but of practical statecraft . . . [about which] each writer has recourse to his personal ideals of social justice, on the basis of which he offers gratuitous advice to the politician, often without noticing that the latter accepts the advice and follows it only in so far as the precepts . . . happen to coincide with the interests that the politician is defending." In contrast to this normative path, de Viti set forth his scientific vision: "I treat Public Finance as a theoretical science, assigning to it the task of explaining the phenomena of Public Finance as they appear in their historical setting." With respect to de Viti's contrast between normative and scientific orientations, it is worth noting that de Viti spent some 20 years as a member of the Italian Parliament in addition to serving as a professor of public finance, as Giuseppe Eusepi and Richard Wagner (2013) note in their explanation of the contemporary relevance of de Viti to the theory of public finance, as Manuela Mosca (2011) sets forth in her synopsis of de Viti's life and work, and as Michele Giuranno and Manuela Mosca (2016) amplify in their examination of de Viti's (1930) explicitly political writings.

The material of public finance thus occupies an equivocal position in the framework of economic theory. An explanatory science of public finance seeks to explain fiscal outcomes and patterns as emerging out of complex processes of political competition, as Buchanan (1967, 1968) exemplifies and which Wagner (2007) explores. For this explanatory science of public finance, fiscal phenomena are to be explained along the same lines as economists explain market phenomena as arising through competition among producers to satisfy consumer demands. An explanatory theory of public finance, however, is not useful to participants in the fiscal process. For participants, the central task is persuasive and not explanatory: it is to gain support for their favored programs in competition with others who favor different programs. Such participants need a scientific-sounding language that is able to resonate more effectively with voter sentiments than the language used by supporters of other programs.

A language that seeks to explain or characterize the outcome of a competitive process is not suitable for strategic use by participants in that process. The contemporary theory of public finance is thus an amalgamation of two distinct dialects. A scientific dialect is suitable for a posture of detached or disinterested observation, where the analytical challenge is to explain how observed patterns of taxing and spending reflect institutionally governed processes of fiscal competition. In contrast, an ideological dialect seeks to create images that resonate with the sentiments of the population and use that resonance to lead voters to support particular political programs. This admixture of scientific and ideological dialects leads the economic analysis of taxation to tuck a variety of ideological presuppositions behind a facade of science, as Louis Eisenstein ([1961] 2010) explains masterfully in his examination of the rhetoric of tax analysis. An Italian economist from a century ago, Amilcare Puviani (1903) developed an explanatory theory of public finance based on the twin presumptions that supporters of political programs seek systematically to exaggerate the benefits from those programs while understating the costs. The vehicle for doing this entailed the creation of ideological smokescreens that operated to soften the opposition to taxation. Puviani has not been translated into English, but Buchanan (1967, 126–43) provides a short introduction to Puviani's thought. Furthermore, Puviani has been translated into German (Puviani 1960). In his foreword to Puviani's book, Schmölders explained that "over the past century *Italian public finance has had an essentially political science character. . . .* This work [Puviani's book] is a *typical product of Italian public finance,* especially a typical product at the end of the nineteenth century. Above all, it is the science of *public finance combined with fiscal politics,* in many cases giving a good fit with reality" (Puviani 1960, 8; my translation and italics).

I start this chapter by describing some of the efforts of economists acting through the years as fiscal philosophers to set forth maxims for a good tax system. These writings are then contrasted with fiscal practice, finding that the practice of taxation bears but faint resemblance to the philosophical writings. Subsequently, the paper examines two specific contexts where the writings of fiscal philosophers create ideological images that obscure the activities of political realists. These two contexts are (1) so-called redistributive taxation and (2) so-called corrective taxation. As Wagner (2012) illustrates with particular regard to macroeconomics and public finance, it is possible to bring economic theory to bear on the construction of economic theories. In part, economic theories are generated in response to curiosity about how generally orderly patterns of economic activity are able to emerge in societies even though those societies are not directed by some master puppeteer. Economic theories also arise from desires some people have to shape and control societies, with those desires typically manifested through political action. A good deal of economic analysis explains why programs of political control can have at most modest success accompanied by myriad consequences that were neither desired nor intended, because those questions cannot be answered scientifically in the first place. Such programs lead to ideologies masquerading as science along the lines that Eisenstein ([1961] 2010) recognized.

IDEOLOGY, SCIENCE, AND TAXATION

Above the entrance to the headquarters of the Internal Revenue Service in Washington, DC, is chiseled a quotation from Oliver Wendell Holmes: "Taxation is the price we pay for civilization." This quotation contains a significant truth, though one whose reach is limited and is also easily corrupted. The truth resides in the quote's recognition of the wisdom reflected in the Declaration of Independence's assertion that a free people establish governments to preserve and protect their prior rights of person and property. Governments do not truly create or grant such rights, contrary to the effort by Murphy and Nagel (2002) to treat governments as the source of individual rights. Instead, the Declaration of Independence recognizes that governments are instituted to fend off predators, both foreign and domestic, though the possession of such power also enables governments to become predators themselves.

Experience through many millennia has shown that political power is easily abused, both through evil and through kindness. By "evil," I mean any intentional usurpation of political power by someone who has the ability to do so. Carl Schmitt ([1932] 1996) argued that holders of political power always have some range of autonomy in conducting their offices. While political power can be constrained to some degree through the construction of suitable constitutional arrangements, such products of construction will always be incomplete. Among other things, exceptional circumstances will always arise that are not covered by constitutional constraints or legal principles. In these circumstances, the holder of political power possesses some range of autonomous action. In such circumstances, the holders of political power can act arbitrarily in doing what he or she regards as advantageous, regardless of the abuse this might wreak on other people. This form of abusing power receives the bulk of historical attention and conforms to the arbitrariness against which the tea partiers in Boston reacted in December 1773.

While this commonly perceived form of abuse corresponds to widely held notions of the evil side of power, abuse can also arise through acts of kindness, or at least what are widely considered actions that stem from kindness (even if some might think such kindness is misguided). Charles Warren's (1932) treatment of *Congress as Santa Claus* illustrates lucidly how power can be abused through kindness, leading in turn to constitutional erosion through the years. Warren traced the changing interpretation of the general welfare class throughout the nineteenth century until early in the twentieth century, which Runst and Wagner (2011) examined in their effort to develop an explanatory rather than normative theory of constitutional process. Originally, the general welfare clause of the American Constitution was interpreted to limit Congress to restricting appropriations to projects that promoted the general welfare as distinct from promoting the welfare of particular people in the nation. As Warren explains, a suggestion that Congress make an appropriation to aid some drought-stricken residents of Ohio was overwhelmingly rejected, because doing that would violate the general welfare clause. In pointing out this unconstitutionality while also recognizing the dire straits of those farmers in Ohio, Representative David Crockett of Kentucky recommended that the members of Congress collect contributions among themselves to distribute to those stricken farmers.

Throughout the nineteenth century, similar situations arose that invariably fueled sentiments in Congress to offer aid despite recognition of the Constitution's prohibition on making such appropriations. During this period, suggestions for awarding such aid increasingly were accompanied by ideological claims that such aid actually conformed to the general welfare limit on appropriation, as against being for the welfare of a small subset of the nation's population. Support for such measures increased in Congress throughout the century, eventually passing near the end of the century with an appropriation to aid drought-stricken farmers in Texas. This measure was vetoed by President Grover Cleveland. By the 1930s, such measures no longer received presidential vetoes, and the general welfare clause had effectively been transformed to mean that the general welfare was whatever Congress declared it to be.

The general welfare clause, as it was originally understood, supported nondiscrimination in congressional budgeting. An appropriation for the construction of roads that facilitated transit among the states could be reasonably reconciled with the general welfare clause in light of the Constitution's establishment of a free-trade zone among the states. The construction of the interstate highway system that started in the 1950s would surely be congruent with that free-trade basis, though in this case President Dwight

Eisenhower supported the program based on the defense power of the federal government. In contrast, an appropriation to construct roads in a particular state or a subset of states paid for by federal appropriations would not pass a reasonable test of constitutionality, because it would represent a discriminatory taxation of citizens of some states for the advantage of citizens in other states. Eventually, however, the general welfare clause was reinterpreted to mean that any appropriation would fit the general welfare requirement should Congress declare that this was its intention. This transformation from relatively nondiscriminatory to relatively discriminatory taxation and appropriation was accompanied by ideological articulation that enabled willing listeners to believe that the discriminatory measures being supported were consistent with the generality principles asserted in the Constitution.

The writings of the fiscal philosophers provide tools to enable this transformation. With taxation recognized to be the price we pay for civilization and with Congress as a representative body that determines what constitutes the general welfare, the ideological stage is set for fiscal discrimination according to the logic of interest group politics along the lines that Warren (1932) explained. With taxation as the price we pay for civilization, whatever taxes are imposed and however they are imposed is better—according to the dominant ideological framework—than the alternative that would result if they were not imposed. The ideological sentiment that the aforementioned quotation chiseled into the IRS headquarters building elicits holds no room for the possibility that taxation beyond some point can become destructive of civilization. Nor does it hold room for recognition that people can generate significant civilization with little governmental involvement along the lines that Edward Stringham (2015) examines in showing how good social order can be generated without the use of force by governments.

In his 1776 masterpiece, *The Wealth of Nations*, Adam Smith advanced four maxims for a good system of taxation. Those maxims were that (1) a good tax should be levied in proportion to a taxpayer's ability to pay, (2) individual liabilities should be certain and not arbitrary, (3) taxes should be convenient to pay, and (4) taxes should be limited to what is necessary to cover the expenses of the state. These maxims have been carried forward to this day in public finance textbooks, even though they also contain significant ambiguity, which can be illustrated by considering Smith's first maxim.

To levy a tax in proportion to ability to pay is inherently ambiguous, in contrast to taxation based, say, on height or weight, because the notion of an ability to pay tax has no established meaning. That notion can acquire meaning only as a reader supplies that meaning. Different readers, and speakers, can easily supply different meanings, as the historical record shows. The ability to pay tax could be defined as based on income, pure and simple. In this interpretation of Smith's maxim, someone who has twice the income of another would be judged to have twice the ability to pay tax. Under this interpretation, Smith's maxim would yield a flat rate of tax on all income. Surely a good number of people would find this form of taxation intuitively or ideologically reasonable.

Just as surely, many people's intuition and ideology might hold that the ability to pay tax starts only after a taxpayer has attained some base level of income that is thought necessary to keep that person materially comfortable. This interpretation of Smith's maxim would yield a flat rate of tax coupled with some tax-exempt level of income. Just what that exempt level of income might be is not covered by Smith's maxim, and instead can only be determined by political power as abetted by ideology (de Jouvenel 1948). It would be easy to arrive at a tax-exempt level of income whereby half the voting age population is exempt from tax, which is approximately the case for the American federal income tax today. For people in this position, there is no limit to the size of government they might support when financed through income taxation, because the activities that government undertakes are free to people who have tax-exempt status. Once an exempt level of income is brought into play, the clarity of Smith's maxim vanishes, because that maxim is incapable of determining the level of tax-exempt income.

The situation becomes even murkier once the principle of a flat rate of tax is left behind and replaced by the principle of progressive taxation. A flat rate tax imposes the same rate of tax on all taxpayers, even though the presence of an exempt level of income will affect the share of the population that pays tax. In this case, tax discrimination is limited to the selection of the level of income to exempt from tax. Progressive taxation injects an indefinitely large number of points of discrimination into the tax system. Moreover, income is not some natural object that exists in a society. On the contrary, income is defined by acts of legislation in conjunction with rules issued by the Internal Revenue Service. It is easily possible to imagine a combination of progressive rate structure and a wide variety of exclusions and exemptions from income that lead to each taxpayer being assigned a unique tax liability. This situation would represent the fiscal equivalent of the perfect price discrimination that appears in textbook illustrations of monopoly. The actual extent of such tax discrimination will be a product of political power and the ideological belief that supports it, even if fiscal philosophers curtsey to Smith's maxim, which is silent on such matters.

Smith's maxims allow a speaker to feel good about his or her speech supporting one form of taxation over another. One can invoke a principle of ability to pay to support a flat tax on a comprehensive income base. One can do the same while allowing small exemptions for very low income. One can also do this while increasing the tax-exempt level of income. Similarly, one can readily support exclusions and exemptions from the comprehensive base by adducing ideological formulations about the general public welfare, along the lines that Charles Warren (1932) set forth. It is likewise easy to develop ideological arguments to explain that a progressive rate structure does not entail tax discrimination, because progressive rates are warranted by some principle of equity that everyone would support from behind some imagined or hypothesized veil of ignorance. Smith's maxims provide a grammatical framework in which a supporter of one tax measure over another can feel good about his or her proposal for reform, because that proposal can invariably be reconciled with one of those maxims. This is the virtue of ambiguity, which Smith's popular maxims have in spades: almost any tax scheme can be portrayed as consistent with Smith's maxims, for there is very little that those maxims exclude, due to the linguistic elasticity that the notion of ability to pay entails.

REASON, RATIONALIZATION, AND POLITICAL PRICING

Vilfredo Pareto ([1916] 1935) explained that rationality plays out differently in market settings than in political settings, and Patrick and Wagner (2015) illuminated the resonance between Pareto's thought and public choice theory. In market settings, consumer action follows an if-then pattern, which Pareto described as "logical action." Consumers can compare options and make choices based on their evaluations of those options. Those options, moreover, can be tested by consumers and compared against other options. In some cases, this testing and comparing is a simple matter of direct physical examination, as when flashlights might be examined to compare the strengths of their beams of light. In other cases, evaluation must follow some preceding experience with the good or service, as in buying cars. Furthermore, competition among sellers also generates a variety of error-reducing measures. Among other things, sellers realize that they must overcome consumer hesitancy to make purchases in advance of experience with such goods, especially relatively expensive ones. Sellers can mitigate such hesitancy by doing such things as offering warranties, being willing to accept returns in some specified period of time, and offering free samples. Moreover, consumers can do such things as compare television sets as a by-product of staying in hotels during their travels and also renting different makes of car during those travels. Consumer action in market settings conforms to that of a scientific experiment: a consumer forms an if-then hypothesis and then tests that hypothesis by paying for and using that product. This situation led Pareto to describe such behavior as logical action.

In contrast, Pareto described action in democratic polities as nonlogical. This description does not assert that such action is irrational or chaotic, as opposed to action that is intelligible. Instead, it recognizes that the substance of rational action depends on the environment in which action occurs, similar to Gerd Gigerenzer's (2008) treatment of rationality as entailing interaction between a person and the particular environment in which the person acts. To treat political action as nonlogical simply recognizes that such action does not conform to the if-then framework of consumer action in market transactions. With political action, no immediate and observable connection exists between action taken and the resulting consequence that the person experiences and can evaluate. Furthermore, political competitors are aware that no such connection exists, which gives political rationality a different substantive content than market rationality. Political competition revolves around candidates competing largely by creating images that resonate better with the ideological sentiments rooted deeply in voters than do the images crafted by other candidates.

While taxes have been described as the price we pay for civilization, taxes are not prices in the ordinary sense of the term. Tax revenues are not derived directly from the supply of services by governments. Rather, those revenues are derived by governments making parasitical attachments to market transactions, as Maffeo Pantaleoni (1911) explained and as Richard Wagner (1997) elaborated. Market prices serve as instruments of commercial navigation that direct producers toward some lines of activity and away from other lines. Taxes serve no similar purpose. For instance, an income tax is a parasitical attachment to transactions that yield income. Similarly, excise taxes are parasitical attachments to transactions in which particular products are bought and sold. Where market transactions offer guidance for the organization of production through the prices those transactions generate, the parasitical attachments to market transactions that taxes represent offer no such direct guidance, because the resulting revenues are not direct reflections of the demands for political activities.

In markets, businesses must sell their products in a setting where consumers can test producer claims, both by inspection and by experience, and producers must work with the selling costs that this environment holds. In politics, candidates must likewise sell their programs and also themselves, only the environment is not one where rival claims can be tested through inspection or experience. In a political environment, competition occurs through the creation of ideological images that resonate more strongly with a larger number of voters than the images offered by other candidates. Those images, moreover, must connect with voter sentiments or beliefs about themselves and the world. Pareto described these sentiments as "residues." These are the foundational beliefs and values, unobservable at that, from which particular sentiments and judgments spring. A common axiom of market theory is that consumers prefer more of what they value to less. This is not an empirical and disputable proposition; instead it is a prime quality of human nature that is necessary for speech to be meaningful. With regard to political competition, the relevant axiom is that people prefer to feel better about themselves and their actions than to feel worse. This elemental fact of human nature gives a different character to political competition than it gives to market competition.

Several ideologies regarding taxation can be observed. The claim that taxation is the price we pay to maintain good civil order, as represented by the notion that taxation is something we do to ourselves (as set forth clearly by Slemrod and Bakija 1996), is one such ideology. The claim that public debt is something that we owe to ourselves is another example. There is no way that voters can subject these claims to some if-then test grounded in experience. Taxes as the price of civilization or public debt as something we owe to ourselves is not a conclusion that people can reach from personal choice and experience. The causal arrow points in the other direction: from belief to action and not from action to evaluation of that action. Someone who is inclined to support particular political programs and candidates can always invoke reasons or rationalizations for doing so. Doing this gives a veneer of logicality to what is necessarily a nonlogical action.

Another form of ideology, articulated crisply by Vincent Ostrom (1984, 1996), treats taxation as a form of Faustian bargain. In this formulation, taxes are inherently instruments of evil in that they inject force into human affairs. It might be hoped that the bargain will bring more good than evil, but taxation is a Faustian bargain all the same. Richard Epstein (1985) advanced a similar formulation in describing taxes as "forced exchanges." Faustian bargains and forced exchanges are not wholly contrary to claims that taxation is something we do to ourselves to derive the advantages of civilization, but the two claims do point in divergent directions. The image of taxation being the price of civilization relegates to the remote background the possibility that taxation might reach destructive heights. The Faustian claim brings that possibility to the foreground, especially in light of the peculiar qualities of political competition relative to commercial competition (Wagner 2016).

The tea party in Boston that led to the founding of the United States recognized explicitly that taxation can become destructive. That founding was grounded on the recognition that individual rights of person and property took precedence over the claims of government. Government was not a source of those rights but rather was established to protect and preserve them. This simple principle provides guidance for taxation and tax policy. While the term "forced exchange" might appear a bit oxymoronic, it conveys an important truth. Government must possess some power to tax as a matter of necessity in light of the inability to fund governments wholly through voluntary contributions. Yet that power can be easily abused by using political power to confer advantage on favored groups while imposing disadvantages on others.

The central feature that enables governments to abridge rights of person and property through taxation is the ability to practice tax discrimination. To speak of "taxing ourselves" is surely to speak of a nondiscriminatory pattern of taxation, save to the extent that some people volunteer to pay taxes for other people. Yet taxation often rewards or punishes specific persons and forms of activity, as illustrated profusely in the essays collected in Shughart (1997). For instance, some people are punished for driving heavy cars, smoking cigarettes, and drinking alcoholic beverages. Other people are rewarded for having more children, home mortgages, or low incomes. Controversy surrounds these discriminatory activities, with supporters claiming they are socially beneficial, though such claims cannot be tested by voters directly through experience regarding the use to which their tax monies are put.

A tax code that reflects the principles of nondiscrimination might contain ten pages and would result in tax returns that could be filed on postcards (Hall and Rabushka 1985, 1995). The difference between that type of tax code and our present multivolume code testifies to the fecund ability of democratic competition to generate tax discrimination, as Hebert and Wagner (2013) explain. While fiscal philosophers give many arguments supporting nondiscrimination, political realists are continually promoting fiscal discrimination—and advancing scientific-sounding arguments to justify their desires to promote their favored forms of discrimination. Any instance of discrimination can be justified by claiming that it serves some greater public good. Typically, such claims cannot be tested directly by inspection or experience, which leads to a situation where ideology masquerades as science. For instance, it could be claimed that home ownership provides civic advantages that renting does not provide. Consequently, it could be argued that a city composed of homeowners would exhibit greater civic mindedness than would a city composed largely of tenants. Based on this claim, someone could reconcile support for nondiscrimination with support for giving a tax advantage to homeowners by allowing an income tax deduction for mortgage interest.

Voters have no way to determine the truth of this claim. Civic mindedness is ambiguous to its core, as is ability to pay. Civic mindedness is not subject to any kind of direct measurement that would allow voters to determine how much of it they are receiving. As a scientific matter, seeking to treat civic mindedness as something that can be elicited to a greater or lesser degree through tax policy is surely impossible, because the political process does not accommodate the if-then form of logical action. But why should or must voters judge their actions against their experiences? Doing this is possible only in settings where logical action is possible. In nonlogical settings, the desires piqued by successful ideological articulations carry the day. People either support or oppose a deduction for mortgage interest, and then they embrace those rationalizations that support their position.

INCOME REDISTRIBUTION AND IDEOLOGIES OF LEVELING

There would seem to be little room for doubting that from an individual's point of view, the best tax is always one that someone else pays. A principle of generality or nondiscrimination operates to resist fiscal discrimination (Buchanan and Congleton 1998). But it does not prevent it. After all, principles are not acting entities. Only people can act, and if they want to act in a discriminatory fashion, they will. To be sure, the human mind has a highly elastic ability to see what it chooses to see by the judicious use of names and labels. A system of income taxation where all income is taxed at the same rate would seem clearly to be nondiscriminatory as a simple matter of definition. Through relabeling, however, this form of income tax could be branded as discriminatory, because it subjects poor persons to higher real tax burdens than it subjects rich persons. The trick in achieving this relabeling is to transform income from a measure of what someone receives by multiplying that measure by some scheme of weighting by utility derived from income.

Francis Edgeworth ([1897] 1958) posed the problem of a ruler who wanted to raise a specified amount of revenue from his subjects in a manner that caused the least total sacrifice to those subjects. Paying tax reduced the income the subjects had for their personal purposes. Edgeworth posited that subjects received utility from their incomes, but with the marginal utility received from that income declining as income increased. In this setting, Edgeworth explained how a ruler could increase the total satisfaction of his subjects by transferring some income from people with high incomes who had low marginal utility to people with low incomes who had high marginal utility. By approaching income taxation in this manner, Edgeworth inspired what eventually became known as the theory of optimal taxation, an early version of which is given in Ramsey (1927). Atkinson and Stiglitz (1980) provide a wide-ranging survey, and Diamond and Saez (2011) provide strong support for progressive taxation in this analytical framework.

Edgeworth also recognized that such confiscatory taxation would reduce the incentive of people with high incomes to earn income. The receipt of transfers by people with low incomes would likewise reduce their incentives to earn income. The subsequent development of the notion of optimal income taxation formalized this recognition. Government became treated as the entity in society that would redistribute income so as to maximize aggregate societal welfare as this is defined by the income-utility construction. Government was no longer construed as having been established by citizens to preserve and protect their prior rights of person and property. It was now construed as a lord of the manor that was in charge of the happiness of its subjects, to which it tended by selecting a scheme of redistributive taxes and transfers that maximized aggregate utility. The relevant analogy for government was now of a benevolent parent who would choose how evenly or unevenly to slice the pieces of a cake when the size of that cake shrank as the pieces were sliced more evenly.

Optimal taxation is surely the predominant framework of tax analysis by economists today, but it is a peculiar framework: in its vision of the relationship between people and their governments, it treats governments as rearranging property rights to fit someone's notion of social welfare. Individual liberty evaporates in the ideology of optimal taxation, because it conceives the central task of government as optimizing some collective notion of happiness. The alternative is that people would attend to their particular notions of happiness in the framework of private property and freedom of contract.

If income below some base level is exempted from tax, then discrimination will have been introduced into the tax system. Additional discrimination will be introduced if marginal rates of tax vary with taxable income. To be sure, progressive tax rates are typically advocated based on some claim that such rates promote equitable taxation. What is equitable or fair, however, surely depends on what the speaker wants to say and listeners want to hear. We are operating in Pareto's world of derivations, where the speaker gives a logical-sounding reason to justify what has determined to be desirable on other grounds. Such a speaker can support redistributive taxation while embracing the principle of nondiscrimination, because nondiscrimination is defined as pertaining not to actual income but to some equity-weighted measure of income.

It is easy enough to understand why people whose incomes are exempt from tax would favor their tax exemption. It is equally easy to understand why people in neighboring income levels might like to see that exemption extended to them. It is furthermore easy to understand why politicians looking for votes would support tax exemptions that would favor significant numbers of potential supporters. No political figure, however, is going to announce support for discriminatory tax exemption as a strategy for securing support. The claims advanced through the use of income-utility functions are ideological constructions that employ a scientific-sounding vocabulary to support such measures. With roughly half the American population of voting age free of liability from the federal income tax, it is easy enough to see why such tax exemption commands strong political support. The ideological justification makes it possible to avoid claims of supporting tax discrimination by changing the baseline along which discrimination is measured; what was once an observable measure of income becomes an imaginary construction of a hypothesized utility from income.

CORRECTIVE TAXATION AS IDEOLOGICAL CONSTRUCTION

Tax theory has two main branches. One supports broad-based taxation; the other supports narrow-based taxation. Most fiscal philosophers treat the two branches as complementary. The narrow-based branch is often described by the term "corrective taxation." Where broad-based taxation is advocated as a means of supporting general governmental activities, narrow-based taxation is advocated as a means of overcoming what are claimed to be market failures of one form or another. Corrective tax claims mostly involve claims that market prices do not fully reflect the cost associated with the use of particular products. For instance, in choosing to drink alcoholic beverages, a consumer will pay for the ingredients used in making the product but not for the damage that sometimes is inflicted on other people by drunk driving. Alternatively, someone who drinks sugary beverages or eats fatty foods might pay for those ingredients but not for the higher medical expenses associated with a greater incidence of coronary problems associated with sugar and fat. Yet again, someone might pay for the materials required to make a computer without paying for the disposal of that computer in a nontoxic manner.

It is easy to claim that the consumption of distilled spirits entails the use of resources that are not reflected in the cost of producing those spirits. For the most part, such usage takes the form of damages done to third parties through automobile-related accidents. Such injury and property damage could be regarded as a cost associated with the consumption of distilled spirits. If one were to perform the "what if" exercise of imagining what would happen to the price of distilled spirits if producers were required somehow to buy permission to injure or even kill people and damage their property, the cost of producing distilled spirits would rise to reflect the cost of those inputs associated with the consumption of distilled spirits that are not reflected in ordinary market prices. This increase is typically described as a corrective tax to indicate that it is imposed to correct what are alleged to be market failures and not to raise revenue.

The ability to conjure up instances where a tax might be claimed to be necessary to correct incomplete market pricing is almost limitless. For instance, the use of throwaway bottles for beer and soft drinks might lead to an increase in litter strewn along highways and in parks. Such litter degrades the aesthetic value of the landscape, however this might be valued, and such a tax could always be advocated as a form of market correction. Alternatively, motorized lawn mowers disturb the peacefulness of the neighboring environment. Lawn mowers can be produced with various degrees of noisiness in their operation, with lower noisiness coming always at a higher cost of direct production. In this instance, it could be claimed that putting a tax on gas lawn mowers according to their decibel ratings would be a means of pricing the environmental degradation that these mowers unavoidably create. The result might be heavier lawn mowers that consume more gas but make less noise.

To argue that producers will produce more of something when there are inputs that they can use for free than if they had to purchase permission from the owners of those inputs is a truism. It does not follow, however, that the actual imposition of a tax will conform to the principle of corrective taxation. It is a simple blackboard exercise to show how a so-called corrective tax can overcome a postulated market failure. This exercise creates a fantasy world that bears little resemblance to reality. For instance, it assumes that the taxing authority has the knowledge necessary to replicate and correct actual market outcomes. Yet not even market participants possess such knowledge, and they know much more about their businesses and the markets in which they operate than do tax officials or politicians. The central thrust of the theory of markets is to explain how a socially coherent pattern of market activity emerges, even though no participant in that process knows how to produce that outcome. To presume that a politician has the necessary knowledge of relevant consumer preferences and firm production functions, and can compute an appropriate corrective tax, is fantasy: the relevant knowledge is never available in its totality. Rather it is distributed among producers and consumers, and only the operation of the market process itself makes it possible to summarize observed outcomes through simple blackboard exercises. There is no way to determine some "correct" market outcome independently of observing that process at work.

Corrective taxation does not describe some technique of market correction, for no such technique exists. Rather, it is an ideological construction that allows a speaker to advocate discriminatory taxation while claiming that it is a form of market correction and not a form of tax discrimination. Corrective tax claims strengthen the willingness of politicians to increase excise taxes by allowing them to make logical-sounding arguments that superficially appear to have nondiscriminatory character. This oft-repeated scene fits nicely Puviani's (1903) treatment of how the imposition of taxes conforms to some principles of fiscal perception and illusion. Rather than truly trying to offset market failures (if, indeed, such failures can be identified), perhaps the tax is supported because of a desire to increase public revenue, and some kind of rational-sounding argument is necessary to marshal support for the added tax.

Moreover, such tax measures are not reasonable approximations to the market transactions that the corrective tax claim presumes to be missing. The so-called corrective tax increases governmental revenue, but it does not compensate for the damages suffered by resource owners whose resources were used without their permission. For one thing, tax revenues accrue to the taxing governments and do not accrue to people who are damaged or who claim to be damaged by the taxed product. Furthermore, to the extent that uncompensated damage arises from consumption of a product, it arises from particular instances of consumption and not with production of the product per se. For instance, the consumption of distilled spirits at home is not a plausible source of external costs. Such costs are conceivable when people consume away from home and then drive home. But even in this case, most consumption is surely modest, so external costs would arise only in a subset of cases. In short, excise taxation cannot effectively distinguish among such attributes as the location of consumption or the drinking proclivities of consumers. The corrective tax idea, however, seems plausible, which makes such taxes easy for politicians to sell to voters. With respect to the selling of taxes to the public, no excise tax hits all products equally. Excise taxes can modify price relationships among products being subject to the tax. For instance, a tax increase of $10 per gallon on distilled spirits would lower the relative price of higher priced products, thereby reducing the ability of producers of less expensive whiskeys to compete with those making more expensive whiskeys.

DEMOCRACY AND TAXATION: A CONSTITUTIONAL QUANDARY

As tax codes grow increasingly complex, cries to reform the code some-times become sufficiently intense to lead to significant reform, with some tax reforms occurring nearly annually in any case. For instance in 1986, the code was simplified by reducing rate brackets from fourteen to two and by reduc-ing marginal rates from a high of 50 percent to one of 28 percent. Soon after that legislation was signed, the process of increasing discrimination through crafting particular tax provisions began anew, resulting now in seven brackets and a top marginal rate of 39.6 percent. In recent years, calls for significant tax reform have again surfaced in the political arena. This ebb and flow of calls for tax reform is a readily understandable feature of democratic political economy. If we start from a position of a generally nondiscriminatory tax system, the receipt of special tax revisions will offer high gains to recipients by imposing modest costs on those who provide those gains through paying higher taxes. As discriminatory provisions are piled onto a previous stock of discriminatory provisions, it becomes increasingly costly to continue to expand discrimina-tion. A point can be reached where large-scale tax reform becomes possible, as happened in 1986 and might be gaining momentum again. Any such reform, however, will not be the reform that ends future reforms, but rather will herald the start of a new sequence of an increasing quantity of discriminatory provi-sions, followed eventually by growing calls for yet another round of reform.

A tax system is the creation of a political system, and the imperatives pres-ent in the political system will be infused in the tax system. A political system whose constitutional arrangements give wide scope for political majorities to determine what constitutes a legitimate use of political power will be open to tax discrimination. In this setting, theorists can be counted on to develop complementary ideological constructions that will help sell that discrimina-tion in the relevant forums where most people have little incentive to peer behind ideological smokescreens, because they cannot change the situation even if they were to try. To the extent taxation takes on a greater measure of nondiscrimination, it will be because the political system gives less scope to the rent-seeking and rent extraction that are the common currency of modern political economy.

CONCLUSION

Much has been made of the high cost of political campaigns. Criticisms of that high cost are misdirected. It is not the high cost of political campaigns that expands the scope for venality in politics. Rather it is the wide scope for venality that governs the amount that people contribute to political campaigns. Our large, interfering government in its present form is able to affect people's earnings in all industries throughout the land simply through changes in taxes and regulations. It is no wonder that so many trade associations have relocated to Washington, DC. Nor is it any wonder that so many corporate executives pass through Washington regularly on business. No products are produced in Washington, but political decisions significantly impact the fortunes of particular enterprises. A large interfering government that can fine-tune specific tax provisions as it chooses will elicit larger campaign contributions than a government that is bound by principles of nondiscrimination among people, groups, and types of business.

A government that is subject to relatively strong constitutional limits on its ability to discriminate among taxpayers will have limited ability to affect the commercial value of particular enterprises. With election outcomes thus having less impact on the value of particular enterprises and activities, fewer or smaller campaign contributions will be made. The stronger the constitutional limits placed on government, the narrower will be the scope for venality. Elections are becoming more expensive because government has acquired an ever larger presence in our lives, and naturally has used that presence to confer privileges on supporters and impose liabilities on others. It is relatively unlimited government and its ability to change people's fortunes for good or bad that cause costly battles for political office. Restrict the ability of government to affect people's fortunes, and elections naturally will become less costly; maintain that ability and taxation unavoidably will be a discriminatory instrument for conferring advantages and disadvantages according to political calculation.

REFERENCES

Atkinson, Anthony B., and Joseph E. Stiglitz. 1980. *Lectures on Public Economics*. New York: McGraw-Hill.

Buchanan, James M. 1967. *Public Finance in Democratic Process*. Chapel Hill: University of North Carolina Press.

———. 1968. *The Demand and Supply of Public Goods*. Chicago: Rand McNally.

Buchanan, James M., and Roger D. Congleton. 1998. *Politics by Principle, Not Interest: Toward Nondiscriminatory Democracy*. Cambridge: Cambridge University Press.

de Jouvenel, Bertrand. 1948. *On Power: Its Nature and the History of Its Growth*. London: Hutchinson.

de Viti de Marco, Antonio. 1930. *Un trentennio di lotte politiche*. Rome: Collezione Meridionale Editrice.

———. 1936. *First Principles of Public Finance*. London: Jonathan Cape.

Diamond, Peter, and Emmanuel Saez. 2011. "The Case for a Progressive Tax." *Journal of Economic Perspectives* 25 (4): 165–90.

Edgeworth, F. A. [1897] 1958. "The Pure Theory of Taxation." In *Classics in the Theory of Public Finance*, edited by R. A. Musgrave and A. T. Peacock, 119–36. London: Macmillan.

Eisenstein, Louis. [1961] 2010. *The Ideologies of Taxation*. New York: Ronald Press.

Epstein, Richard A. 1985. *Takings· Private Property and the Power of Eminent Domain*. Cambridge, MA: Harvard University Press.

Eusepi, Giuseppe, and Richard E. Wagner. 2013. "Tax Prices in a Democratic Polity: The Continuing Relevance of Antonio de Viti de Marco." *History of Political Economy* 45: 99–121.

Gigerenzer, Gerd. 2008. *Rationality for Mortals*. Oxford: Oxford University Press.

Giuranno, Michele, and Manuela Mosca. 2016. *Political Realism and Models of the State: Antonio de Viti de Marco and the Origins of Public Choice*. Lecce, Italy: University of Salento.

Hall, Robert E., and Alvin Rabushka. 1985. *Low Tax, Simple Tax, Flat Tax*. Stanford, CA: Hoover Institution.

———. 1995. *The Flat Tax*. Stanford, CA: Hoover Institution.

Hebert, David, and Richard E. Wagner. 2013. "Taxation as a Quasi-Market Process: Explanation, Exhortation, and the Choice of Analytical Windows." *Journal of Public Finance and Public Choice* 31: 163–77.

Mosca, Manuela. 2011. *Antonio de Viti de Marco: Una Storia degna di Memoria*. Milan: Bruno Mondadori.

Murphy, Liam, and Thomas Nagel. 2002. *The Myth of Ownership*. Oxford: Oxford University Press.

Ostrom, Vincent. 1984. 'Why Governments Fail: An Inquiry into the Use of Instruments of Evil to Do Good." In *Theory of Public Choice II*, edited by J. M. Buchanan and R. D. Tollison. Ann Arbor: University of Michigan Press, 422–35.

———. 1996. "Faustian Bargains." *Constitutional Political Economy* 7: 303–8.

Pareto, Vilfredo. [1916] 1935. *The Mind and Society*. New York: Harcourt Brace.

Pantaleoni, Maffeo. 1911. "Considerazioni sulle proprieta di un sistema di prezzi politici." *Giornale degli Economisti* 42: 9–29, 114–33.

Patrick, Meg, and Richard E. Wagner. 2015. "From Mixed Economy to Entangled Political Economy: A Paretian Social-Theoretic Orientation." *Public Choice* 164: 103–16.

Puviani, Amilcare. 1903. *Teoria della Illusione Fianziaria*. Palermo, Italy: Sandron.

———. 1960. *Die Illusionen in der öffentlichen Finanzwirtschaft*. Translation of *Teoria della Illusione Fianziaria* into the German and Foreword by Gunter Schmölders. Berlin: Dunker & Humbolt.

Ramsey, Frank P. 1927. "A Contribution to the Theory of Taxation." *Economic Journal* 37: 47–61.

Resnick, Mitchel. 1994. *Turtles, Termites, and Traffic Jams*. Cambridge, MA: MIT Press.

Runst, Petrik, and Richard E. Wagner. 2011. "Choice, Emergence, and Constitutional Process: A Framework for Positive Analysis." *Journal of Institutional Economics* 7: 131–45.

Schmitt, Carl. [1932] 1996. *The Concept of the Political*. Chicago: University of Chicago Press.

Shughart II, William F. (ed.). 1997. *Taxing Choice: The Predatory Politics of Fiscal Discrimination*. New Brunswick, NJ: Transaction.

Slemrod, Joel, and Jon Bakija. 1996. *Taxing Ourselves: A Citizen's Guide to the Great Debate over Tax Reform*. Cambridge, MA: MIT Press.

Stringham, Edward P. 2015. *Private Governance*. Cambridge: Cambridge University Press.

Wagner, Richard E. 1997. "Parasitical Political Pricing, Economic Calculation, and the Size of Government." *Journal of Public Finance and Public Choice* 15: 135–46.

———. 2007. *Fiscal Sociology and the Theory of Public Finance*. Cheltenham, UK: Edward Elgar.

———. 2012. "The Social Construction of Theoretical Landscapes: Some Economics of Economic Theories." *American Journal of Economics and Sociology* 71: 1185–1204.

———. 2016. *Politics as a Peculiar Business: Insights from a Theory of Entangled Political Economy*. Cheltenham, UK: Edward Elgar.

Warren, Charles. 1932. *Congress as Santa Claus: National Donations and the General Welfare Clause of the Constitution*. Charlottesville, VA: Michie.

PART II

THE POLITICAL ECONOMY OF PUBLIC BUDGETING

CHAPTER 5
The Politics of Taxes
in the Affordable Care Act

RANDALL G. HOLCOMBE
Department of Economics, Florida State University

I n 2010, Congress passed the Patient Protection and Affordable Care Act (ACA), often referred to (with President Obama's approval) as Obamacare. The stated intention of the law was to extend health insurance coverage to more uninsured individuals and to lower healthcare costs for everyone. This twofold goal presents an obvious challenge, because if more people have health insurance coverage, this by itself should cause healthcare costs to rise. Health insurers are third-party payers. If people pay their own healthcare costs out-of-pocket, they have an incentive to economize on their use of the healthcare system. If a third party pays, the marginal cost to the user goes down, so the user would be expected to demand more. Similar incentives exist on the supply side. If a doctor is deliberating about a treatment for a patient, the doctor and patient have an incentive to discuss the costs that would be imposed on the patient, but with a third-party payer, someone else bears the cost, so both patients and healthcare professionals have less of an incentive to control costs.

The author gratefully acknowledges research assistance from Robert Gmeiner and helpful comments from Adam Hoffer, William Shughart, two anonymous reviewers, and participants at the 2015 annual meeting of the Public Choice Society.

The ACA's goal of broadening coverage requires an increase in revenues to fund it, regardless of the rhetoric of cost reduction, and the fact that the ACA includes new taxes appears to acknowledge that it will cost more.

Some provisions in the ACA might work to offset these supply and demand effects and to control prices, but the ACA does mandate new taxes and does not lower or remove any existing taxes. The ACA was controversial to begin with, and taxes are always unpopular. Thus, the architects of the ACA had every incentive to design the taxes to finance it in such a way as to minimize political opposition. They did this by designing the taxes in the Act so that it would appear to most people as if others would pay those taxes, and sometimes by claiming that taxes to finance the ACA were not actually taxes. This disguising of the taxes to finance ACA was done in several ways. One strategy, which Holcombe (1997) notes is frequently used, was to place taxes on groups who were a clear minority of the population, and often a minority that many people would say could afford the taxes and maybe even deserved to be taxed. Another strategy was to place taxes on the least visible, and least resistant, side of the market. And, as already noted, another strategy was to deny that the taxes were taxes.

The ACA was a very prominent and controversial piece of legislation, but the lessons in its passage are more generally applicable to the design of taxes to finance all government programs. When costs of programs are designed to be less transparent, political opposition from those who bear the costs can be reduced, which raises the chances of passing the programs. This chapter looks at the politics behind the design of the taxes that are used to finance the ACA. Many other aspects of the ACA have provoked controversy and discussion, including its mandated benefits and the fact that many people who had health insurance prior to the ACA had their policies canceled as a result of the Act's provisions. This chapter is more narrowly focused on how the taxes in the ACA were designed to maximize political support for the passage of the Act.

EXPERT COMMENTARY

While economists have developed an extensive framework for designing optimal tax policies, economists do not actually design taxes. Taxes are a product of the political process, so the taxes that actually exist are those that are most politically palatable rather than those that are the most equitable or economically efficient. The ACA was controversial enough that its designers did not want the tax cost of the program to stand in the way of its adoption.

They wanted the Act's tax provisions to be as inconspicuous as possible and to appear as benign as possible. The idea of hiding the costs of the ACA from those who are paying them was not lost on the designers of the Act. MIT Professor Jonathan Gruber, one of the architects of ACA,[1] was quoted extensively in the news media in November 2014, giving lectures in which he makes this clear.[2] In one talk, Gruber said,

> This bill was written in a tortured way to make sure CBO [Congressional Budget Office] did not score the mandate as taxes. If CBO scored the mandate as taxes, the bill dies. Okay, so it's written to do that. In terms of risk rates subsidies, if you had a law which said that healthy people are going to pay in—you made explicit healthy people pay in and sick people get money, it would not have passed. . . . Lack of transparency is a huge political advantage. And basically, call it the stupidity of the American voter or whatever, but basically that was really really critical for the thing to pass. And it's the second-best argument. Look, I wish Mark was right that we could make it all transparent, but I'd rather have this law than not.[3]

Look at Gruber's statement sentence by sentence to see what he is saying about the design of ACA. The first sentence discusses the individual mandate—the requirement that everyone have health insurance or pay a penalty for not being insured. The penalty is the higher of $695 per uninsured person or 2.5 percent of annual household income.[4] The penalty is collected by the IRS, paid at the time that individuals file their tax returns. But note that even though the IRS is collecting the money along with income taxes, Gruber makes it clear that calling the mandate a tax would mean the political death of the ACA.

However, when the ACA was challenged on constitutional grounds, the Supreme Court upheld the law, with Chief Justice Roberts writing in his opinion, "The Affordable Care Act's requirement that certain individuals pay a financial penalty for not obtaining health insurance may reasonably be characterized as a tax. . . . Because the Constitution permits such a tax, it is not our role to forbid it, or pass upon its wisdom or fairness."[5] The Supreme Court says that for the ACA to be constitutional, the individual mandate must be interpreted as a tax, whereas Gruber says that if it were presented to the public that way, the Act would not have passed.

The next sentence refers to the rate structure that overcharges young poli-cyholders, who tend to have lower healthcare costs, in order to undercharge older policyholders, who tend to have higher healthcare costs. The Act also prevents insurers from taking into account preexisting conditions when deter-mining premiums. Again, Gruber says that if this subsidizing of policies for the old and sick by overcharging the young and healthy were made transparent, the ACA would never have passed. He notes, "Lack of transparency is a huge political advantage." Gruber makes it clear that hiding the true costs of ACA was instrumental to its passage. He then goes on to call the American voter stupid.

In another presentation, Gruber said, "We have experimented with choice in public insurance: Medicare Part D. . . . Typical senior has 50 PDPs [Prescription Drug Plans] to choose from. . . . Seniors do a terrible job choos-ing [the best one]."[6] In this case, Gruber is going further than calling voters stupid; he is calling consumers stupid. While the same physical people play the roles of voters and consumers, those people face very different incentives when they vote and when they buy things with their own money.

Referring to the tax the ACA places on so-called Cadillac insurance plans, Gruber said that part of the legislation was made more palatable "first, by mislabeling it, calling it a tax on insurance plans rather than a tax on people and we all know it's really a tax on people who hold those insurance plans."[7] People are more sympathetic to taxing insurance companies, which they view as impersonal and profitable corporations, than they are to taxing people who are trying to buy health insurance. But, as noted below, there is more to this Cadillac tax than most voters realize.

SELLING THE ACA TO VOTERS

Economic models of taxes and public expenditures are heavily oriented toward deriving optimal policies and often ignore the political challenges that impede getting optimal policies designed and passed. Models of optimal taxation, like Ramsey (1927), Diamond and Mirrlees (1971a, b), and Mirrlees (1971, 1976), are oriented toward designing a tax system that minimizes the excess burden of taxation or that maximizes the well-being of society. In fact, real-world tax systems are not designed by economists who are trying to implement efficient or equitable optimal tax policies. They are designed by politicians who are trying to implement tax systems that will minimize political opposition so they can be approved through the political decision-making process, and that will not negatively impact those politicians' brand name capital. Politicians avoid politically unpopular taxes, and the economic efficiency of taxes is at best a secondary consideration. Politicians will not support taxes that will harm their chances to advance their political careers. Taxes are designed through the political process to maximize political support, not to maximize social welfare.

Thinking about the design of tax systems in a supply and demand framework, policymakers supply and voters demand public policy measures that contain tax provisions, like the ACA. Economic models are prone to derive optimal policies and implicitly assume that government is an omniscient benevolent dictator that will do what is optimal. But as Holcombe (2012) notes, government is not omniscient, it is not benevolent, and it is not a dictator. Government is a group that makes collective decisions by designing policies that maximize political support. As Jonathan Gruber noted, lack of transparency enabled the passage of the ACA, which would not have garnered political support had voters actually understood it. The ACA provides a good case study to see why, in general, economic models that depict government as an omniscient benevolent dictator are inappropriate for understanding public policy outcomes.

In most cases, policymakers cannot obtain all the information necessary to design an optimal policy, as Holcombe (1998, 2002) notes, so government is not omniscient. One reason, especially applicable to the ACA, is that the value of goods and services (e.g., health insurance provided under the Act) cannot be calculated in the absence of market prices, an argument that goes back to Mises ([1922] 1951) and Hayek (1945). With insurance companies acting as third-party payers, consumers do not face the full cost of their health care, and so they will demand a larger quantity than if they had to pay the full cost themselves. By the very design of the program, government cannot obtain sufficient information to design an optimal health insurance market.

Government is not benevolent. Policymakers often face incentives that go against the public interest, and policymakers, like everyone else, respond to incentives. Elected officials face the challenges of retaining political support and getting reelected. Bureaucrats are not residual claimants in the programs they oversee, so they do not have incentives to make them operate efficiently, and, as Tullock (1965) and Niskanen (1971) suggest, often have incentives to make them operate inefficiently. Applied to the ACA, the taxes incorporated into the Act were designed to enable it to get political support, as Jonathan Gruber noted, rather than to be economically efficient or optimal. The taxes were designed to be politically optimal, which is different from being economically optimal. The political realities were an explicit part of Gruber's second-best argument.

Government is not a dictator. This goes to the heart of the preceding discussion. To implement the ACA, its supporters needed to design it so that it would win the approval of the American public and get the support of a majority in Congress. As Professor Gruber's comments above indicate, the designers of the Act realized that they could not just write it as they thought was best—and most transparent—but had to disguise what the Act actually contained to make it politically palatable. The lack of transparency was an intentional trait of the Act's construction, to allow it to garner the support it needed to pass. If government was a dictator, it would just pass the Act it wanted, but because it is not, the Act had to be designed to get the political support of a number of groups, including a majority of those in Congress, and the general public.

Professor Gruber referred to the stupidity of the American voter, but a public choice approach to voter behavior might give a more charitable interpretation to voter behavior. Downs (1957) notes the incentive for voters to be rationally ignorant because the probability that they will cast a decisive vote is so small. Brennan and Lomasky (1993) note that because voters realize their individual votes will not be decisive, they tend to vote expressively. In this case, they might support the ACA not because of its specific provisions but rather because they want to express support for the general idea of providing more healthcare security to Americans. This might be a significant factor in the design and passage of the ACA. The Act was sold as a way to extend health insurance coverage to those who did not have it, who could not afford it, and who had preexisting conditions that made it unobtainable for them. These all sound like desirable goals, so voters might feel good about supporting those goals without having to consider whether the ACA could actually accomplish them, because they know they will not cast decisive votes. They can support candidates who campaign on desirable outcomes without having to consider whether they can implement policies that would actually accomplish those goals.

Caplan (2007) goes a step further to argue that because no election is decided by a single vote, so one voter will not change the election outcome, voters bear no costs from supporting policies that impose costs on them or are not in the public interest. Because they bear no personal cost from voting irrationally, they can and do vote to support irrational policies and those that can make everyone worse off. The idea that Congress can pass a law that will provide health insurance to more people and mandate an expansion on what insurance must cover while lowering healthcare costs would seem to be irrational. That is not intended to pass judgment on the overall desirability of the

ACA, but merely to note that it may be irrational to expect the ACA to both provide more coverage and do so at lower cost.

Perhaps voters are stupid, as Gruber suggests, but models of rational economic behavior indicate why voters have little incentive to understand the true costs of any legislation and why they can be easily deceived by architects of legislation. They have little incentive to be informed, they will often vote expressively, and they pay no price for voting irrationally. It makes sense, from a policymaker's perspective, to design legislation so that it hides the costs of legislation from those who will bear those costs. A more detailed analysis of the tax provisions of the ACA will illustrate how this was done.

TAX SHIFTING

A well-known principle of taxation is that the people who end up bearing the burden of a tax are not necessarily the people on whom the tax is initially placed. When a tax is placed on producers or consumers in a market, the tax is shifted toward the more inelastic side of the market. Furthermore, it does not matter whether the same tax (say, a 5 percent excise tax) is placed on the suppliers in a market or the demanders. The ultimate burden on suppliers is the same in either case, and the ultimate burden on demanders is the same in either case. If the elasticity of supply is the same as the elasticity of demand, the ultimate burden of the tax will be shared equally between suppliers and demanders. If the elasticities are different, the burden is shifted toward the more inelastic side of the market, and in extreme cases, a perfectly inelastic supply or demand would shift the entire tax to that side of the market while a perfectly elastic supply or demand would shift the entire tax to the other side of the market.

For political purposes, these principles of tax shifting suggest placing the taxes to help finance the ACA on the supply side of the market. One reason is that the typical voter does not understand the concept of tax shifting, so placing taxes on insurers and healthcare providers appears to them as taxing the people who are making all the money from healthcare provision. The insurance companies, doctors, and hospitals can afford the taxes; often, the healthcare consumers cannot. Thus the strategy is to design taxes so that it appears to most people that someone else is being taxed.

In fact, the demand for health care is inelastic, partly because when people have health issues, they are very inclined to address them, and partly because, as already noted, when third-party providers are paying for the health care so there is little out-of-pocket cost to the consumer, consumers will not be very price conscious.[8] Inelastic demand means that consumers will end up bearing the burden of those taxes. For this reason, even though the tax appears to be placed on the suppliers of health care, suppliers have less reason to put up political opposition than demanders would, because the taxes will be shifted away from the suppliers in any event. Consumers will have a hard time seeing this because it is not their out-of-pocket costs that will increase; it is the cost of their insurance. Ultimately, insurance companies must cover the cost of the payments they make with the premiums they collect. These principles of tax shifting and public choice can help illuminate the reasoning behind the tax provisions in the ACA. The next several sections examine some of the ACA's taxes using this framework.[9]

The Individual Mandate

The individual mandate was discussed above as having been deliberately designed to disguise its being a tax. Jonathan Gruber is quoted as saying that the Act would not pass if the individual mandate were called a tax, so the ACA's architects constructed the law so it would not appear so. Also, as noted above, the Supreme Court determined that the individual mandate was constitutional only if the charges that were to be levied on the uninsured were construed as a tax. This creates the curious situation (pointed out by critics) that the ACA's supporters claimed the individual mandate was not a tax to pass the legislation but claimed it was a tax to keep it from being ruled unconstitutional. In an interview prior to the Supreme Court's upholding the mandate, George Stephanopoulos asks President Obama, "But do you reject that it's a tax increase?" to which the president answers, "I absolutely reject that notion."[10]

On the healthcare.gov website, the mandate is referred to as a fee, and the site answers the question "What happens if I don't pay the fee?" by saying "The IRS will hold back the amount of the fee from any future tax refunds. There are no liens, levies, or criminal penalties for failing to pay the fee."[11] The fee is collected by the IRS, and if not paid, the government will collect it only by increasing one's future taxes (reducing a tax refund). Does this make it a tax?

Reference to the public choice literature on voter behavior explains how the ACA's supporters can have it both ways. Voters are rationally ignorant, so many may be unaware of the dual claims of the ACA's supporters that the individual mandate is, for some purposes, not a tax, and for other purposes, it is. Voters vote expressively, so those who favor the ACA's coverage will support it regardless of inconsistent claims. That support in the face of inconsistent claims is a good example of Caplan's (2007) rational irrationality.

The individual mandate requires that individuals obtain health insurance, or pay a tax (according to the Supreme Court) of $695 or 2.5 percent of their household's income to the IRS.[12] For many young healthy low-income individuals it may be less costly to pay the tax than to obtain health insurance, although these individuals may also be eligible for subsidized policies from government healthcare exchanges. The political appeal of the tax is apparent: most Americans have health insurance, and realize that the minority who do not impose costs on those with insurance if, as is often the case, they do not pay their medical bills in full. So most Americans will see this as a justified tax that will be paid by other people as a consequence of making an irresponsible choice.

The Employer Mandate

The ACA requires that employers of more than fifty employees provide health insurance to employees working 30 hours or more a week, or pay a tax of $2,000 per worker. The most obvious effect of this tax is that employers will shift employees from full-time to part-time work. For low-wage full-time workers, employers will find it less costly to pay the tax than to provide them with health insurance.[13] As with the individual mandate, this will push those who want health insurance toward government-subsidized health insurance exchanges to buy their insurance. The employer mandate and individual mandate are both designed to provide incentives to use the government exchanges.

Because employer-provided health insurance is not taxed (it is an expense to the employer and a nontaxable benefit to the employee), most health insurance is provided by employers, creating an expectation of employer-provided health insurance and making those employers who do not provide it appear to be stingy toward their employees. The same motivations that provide general support for minimum wage laws, sick leave, and paid vacation time make employer-provided health insurance look like something an employer that treats employees fairly would do. People who do not understand the marginal productivity theory of wages often conclude that employers are profitable and can afford to pay for health insurance for their employees. Even if this is true, employers still will not pay more to hire an employee—including the cost of health insurance—than the employee can produce in income for the employer. Whether employers can afford to pay for health insurance for their employees is an irrelevant economic argument, but a relevant political one.

If many people see things this way, the tax, which appears to be paid by someone else (the stingy employer), will be politically popular. Many voters will not perceive the secondary effects, such as that mandated benefits will tend to lower wages and will cause part-time employment to be substituted for full-time employment.[14] The tax is fairly well hidden, and it appears to most people to be paid by someone else, making it a politically viable policy.

Annual Fee on Health Insurance Providers

The ACA specifies that health insurance providers pay an annual fee, determined by the share of total policies they write divided into the total amount of fees to be collected as specified in the Act. The Act has a fee schedule specifying the total dollar amounts to be collected through 2018; after 2018, the current year's fee total will be last year's total adjusted for the rate of premium growth. For example, the total amount of fees collected in 2014 was $8 billion, scheduled to increase to $14.3 billion in 2018 and adjusted by premium growth after that. For 2018, an insurer's fee will be $14.3 billion times by the fraction of total policies issued by that insurer. Thus, in 2018, an insurer that issued 10 percent of health insurance policies would pay a fee of $1.43 billion ($14.3b $\times$ .1).

One issue insurers could have with this fee is that they will not know what their fee is until the end of the year. Because the fee is a cost to the insurers, they will have to estimate this cost as they price their policies. One might say that any insurer is always facing unknown costs, because they do not know what losses their policyholders will have in the upcoming year. Still, this fee adds another layer of financial risk to writing health insurance policies, so could be expected to drive up the cost of a policy by more than the fee associated with the policy.

Because purchasers of health insurance policies will have very inelastic demands for coverage, tax shifting theory suggests that this tax will be passed on to policyholders in the form of higher premiums, as Gruber noted in his comments on the ACA. The individual mandate makes the demand for health insurance even more inelastic, because people who do not buy it are subject to the tax. Placing the tax on insurers rather than on policyholders means the tax is less visible—likely invisible—to most policyholders. The tax lowers the political cost of financing the ACA, because buyers of health insurance will not mind a tax being put on insurers (and some will even favor taxing that profitable industry). Most buyers will not realize that the tax is shifted to themselves. Meanwhile, insurers will offer less political resistance to the tax, because they can pass it on in their premiums. One thing they cannot pass along, however, is the uncertainty about how much they will have to pay, because of the way the tax is calculated. The big advantage here goes to the federal government, which knows exactly how much in tax revenues it will collect.

Medical Device Excise Tax

The ACA specifies a 2.3 percent medical device excise tax on "certain medical devices." The tax was scheduled to begin being collected in 2013 but was postponed and is now scheduled to begin in 2018.[15] This tax, like any excise tax, will be shifted at least partly to the purchasers of those medical devices, and because many medical devices are paid for by insurance, the consumers of these devices will often bear no direct cost as a result of the tax. Insurance rates will have to rise to cover the increased cost, but that cost increase is indirect and is spread among all policyholders rather than applied to just those who use the taxed devices. As a result, most people will be unaware of how much they are paying for this tax.

The tax has a "retail exemption" that offers further evidence that the tax was designed to be hidden from those who ultimately pay it. The retail exemption specifically exempts eyeglasses, contact lenses, hearing aids, and "the sale of any other devices that are of a type generally purchased by the general public at retail for individual use."[16] If consumers could see that they are directly paying the tax, then the device is exempt. The tax is only placed on devices for which the consumer cannot tell how much, if any, tax they are paying, and because insurance will pay for most of the devices, even the ultimate user will not bear the cost of the tax directly. Ultimately, this is a tax on insurance policies, which few policyholders will recognize. It would be difficult to design a tax that is better hidden from those who ultimately will pay it.

Excise Tax on Indoor Tanning Services

The ACA provides for a 10 percent excise tax on indoor tanning facilities that went into effect in 2010. This excise tax appears completely unrelated to health care. It was included as an excise tax on a consumer service that would face relatively little opposition. The provision excludes from taxation "phototherapy services performed by a licensed medical professional on his or her premises," so medical use of such services escapes taxation, while nonmedical use is taxed. The tax also exempts "physical fitness facilities that offer tanning as an incidental service to members without a separately identifiable fee." The obvious motivation for this exemption is to avoid levying a tax on a large number of people who might object to it. Many more people have memberships at gyms and fitness facilities than patronize indoor tanning facilities, so the exemption keeps those gym members from being taxed and therefore eliminates one reason for them to have a direct objection to ACA.

This tax is unusual among ACA taxes in that it is levied directly on the consumers who will bear the burden of the tax. This speaks to the low level of political clout that the ACA's designers perceived could be wielded by those who provide or use indoor tanning facilities, perhaps because they were unaware of that provision in such an extensive piece of legislation. The Tax Foundation reports that revenues from the tax were slightly more than one-third of the revenues projected when the ACA was passed, likely from a combination of tanning salons going out of business and noncompliance from those in business.[17]

Patient-Centered Outcomes Research Trust Fund Fee

Provision 6301 in the ACA established a Patient-Centered Outcomes Research Institute (PCORI) that will undertake research to help clinicians and policy-makers make informed health decisions. PCORI is funded by an excise tax on insurance policies and self-insured health plans. The amount of the tax is calculated by multiplying the number of people covered by a plan times the applicable dollar amount for that year. For 2015, the amount was $2.08 per person covered, and the fee increases by the "inflation in National Health Expenditures, as determined by the Secretary of Health and Human Services."[18] Because healthcare expenditures rise more rapidly than the general level of prices, this provision means that PCORI tax revenues will rise faster than inflation.

The tax is placed on insurers, providing yet another case in which the tax is hidden from the people who will ultimately pay it. If healthcare expenditures increase by an average of 5.5 percent a year and inflation is 2 percent a year (the Federal Reserve's target rate), this tax, per policy, would increase by 3.5 percentage points more than the rate of inflation. The inflation-adjusted tax per policy would double in about 20 years (using that modest assumption of increases in healthcare costs), and because of population growth, funding for PCORI would much more than double.

This back-of-the-envelope calculation illustrates what is likely a conservative estimate of the real increase in tax revenues for PCORI, but the larger point is that the program is designed so that the revenues funding PCORI will grow every year. The initial tax appears to be modest, and few observers will calculate the future growth that is built into it. The tax is designed to take advantage of the rational ignorance of voters.

Annual Fee on Branded Prescription Pharmaceutical Manufacturers and Importers

This tax is very complicated. It is calculated by dividing the aggregate amount to be collected under this provision by each taxpayer's share of prescription pharmaceuticals sold. The aggregate amount to be collected varies by year; for 2015 it is $3 billion, rising to $4.1 billion in 2018, and then falling to $2.8 billion for 2019 and thereafter. Like the fee on health insurance providers, the ACA specifies the total revenue to be collected by the tax, which is then divided among the taxpayers.

A complicated formula determines each seller's covered sales during the year, and then a progressive rate schedule determines the percentage of these sales that is counted in calculating the seller's tax liability. Sales below $5 million carry no tax liability. Sales between $5 million and $125 million mean that 10 percent of the seller's sales are covered by the tax. Sellers with sales between $125 million and $225 million count 40 percent of their sales; those with between $225 million and $400 million count 75 percent of their sales; and those with more than $400 million count 100 percent of their sales. The total amount of sales subject to tax is summed, and each firm pays the percentage of the aggregate amount to be collected that corresponds with that firm's sales subject to tax.

For example, assume that for a year after 2019, a firm calculates that it has made $200 million in covered sales. Its sales taken into account for tax purposes is 40 percent of $200 million, or $80 million. Now assume that its $80 million is 10 percent of the total for all firms. The aggregate amount of collections for the year is $2.8 billion, so this firm would owe a fee of $280 million.[19] Note that the progressive tax schedule does not adjust for inflation, so the longer-run effects of inflation alone will push these taxpayers into higher tax brackets over the years.

As with the fee on healthcare providers described above, the firms paying the fee cannot predict what their tax liability will be, because the ACA specifies only the total amount to be collected. Each taxpayer's liability is determined by its share of that total amount, which is determined by its share of total sales and cannot be calculated ahead of time.

Ultimately, consumers will end up paying this tax, because demand for prescription drugs is very inelastic. One reason this is true is that the people who consume the drugs are not the ones who pay for them, because a large share of prescription drugs are covered by insurance. That also means that the consumers of the drugs are the demanders, while it is the consumers of health insurance who pay the costs, further diluting any incentive for drug users to be price sensitive. The demanders of the drugs are not the ones who pay for them. One can see how a tax like this will face relatively little opposition from either suppliers or demanders. On the supply side, two factors weigh in: the ability to shift the tax to demanders, and the fact that there are few sellers of pharmaceuticals, so only a small group of firms would object to the tax. On the demand side, the tax is hidden as a component of everyone's health insurance, and because demanders are unlikely to perceive that the tax is shifted to them, they do not object to taxing the sellers of pharmaceuticals, which are highly profitable corporations.[20]

Excise Tax on "Cadillac" Health Plans

Beginning in 2020, a 40 percent excise tax will be levied on high-priced health-care plans, which the ACA defines as costing more than $10,200 for an individual plan or $27,500 for family coverage.[21] This tax was originally scheduled to go into effect in 2018 but has been delayed by Congress. The excise tax applies to any amount of the premium that exceeds those limits. The stated idea behind this tax is that excessively generous insurance plans insulate policyholders from the true cost of health care and so encourage overuse of healthcare services. (Of course, the purpose of any insurance is to insulate the policyholders against the costs for which they have purchased insurance.) The individual mandate in the ACA requires everyone to have a minimum amount of coverage, and this excise tax on high-cost plans would appear to be an attempt to also limit the maximum amount of coverage. The designers of the ACA appear to have in mind some correct amount of insurance coverage and do not want people to have too much or too little. In anticipation of this tax, some employers are already raising deductibles and co-pays for their plans, and limiting coverage to the extent that the law allows such limits.

Another argument supporting this tax is that the people most likely to have high-priced health insurance are upper-income people who get this coverage through their employers. Because employer-provided health care is not taxable, this amounts to a tax subsidy to the (employed) rich, which is not available to lower-income workers who are more likely to have less generous insurance plans. A "tax the rich because they can afford it" argument tends to receive political support, because many voters question whether the rich pay their fair share in taxes, and because the rich are a small percentage of voters. With regard to the ACA, many of those who would oppose the tax would not be supporters of the Act anyway, so this provision causes little change at the margin with regard to voters who would support it.

The limit that determines high-cost plans adjusts for inflation. The ACA specifies that in 2018 and 2019, the limit will rise by the increase in the Consumer Price Index (CPI) plus 1 percent; in 2020 and beyond, the limit will increase only by the same percentage as the CPI. Because healthcare expenditures tend to rise faster than the CPI, over time, more and more plans will fall into the high-cost category. It is not much of a stretch to see that if this Cadillac tax remains as currently designed, almost every health insurance policy eventually will be taxed by it. But it is also not much of a stretch to foresee that as more plans are taxed, there will be a political backlash leading to a modification of the tax. Politically, it works if it appears to be a "tax the rich" tax, but does not if it appears to be a tax on the median voter's health insurance.

The obvious popular appeal of this excise tax is that for most taxpayers, it will appear to apply to other people, not to themselves. As an increasing number of plans are covered, it will be interesting to see whether a political backlash will require a redefinition of high-priced, or whether the provision will stick and bring in tax revenue. A public choice viewpoint would suggest the former.

As the tax is currently designed, it amounts to a simple income tax on plans costing more than the limit. Employer-provided health insurance is not taxable, but the 40 percent tax rate on Cadillac plans is very close to the 39.6 percent highest marginal income tax bracket. In effect, for people in that bracket, an employer-provided plan is not taxed up to the limit, and after that the cost of the plan is taxed as ordinary income.

CONCLUSION

The taxes incorporated into the Affordable Care Act provide a good example for illustrating how taxes are designed more generally. The economics of taxation rests largely on models of optimal taxation, where theoretical models are developed to illustrate how to minimize the burden of taxes or to maximize some definition of social welfare. The implied policy implication of optimal tax models is that policymakers should design tax structures so that they conform with those models. The reality is that taxes are a product of the political process, and policymakers actually design taxes to minimize the political resistance to getting them approved—not to meet some economists' standards of optimal taxation.

Whereas optimal tax models deal with efficiency and equity in taxation, the more important application of tax theory to the politics of taxation is tax shifting. The key insight behind tax shifting is that the ultimate burden of a tax does not necessarily fall on the people initially targeted by the tax but can be shifted to others. Tax shifting is relevant to the politics of taxation, because knowledgeable taxpayers will resist a tax less if they perceive that the burden of the tax will be shifted to others and will resist more if they realize the burden of the tax will be shifted to them. Most voters, however, are rationally ignorant of the effects of taxes. Rationally ignorant constituents may resist taxes that are placed directly on them, because the taxes are visible, but will offer less resistance—and perhaps will even support—taxes that are levied on others. In short, knowledgeable taxpayers will offer more political resistance to a tax when they are on the more elastic side of the market, while less knowledgeable taxpayers will offer more political resistance when a tax is placed directly on them rather than on the other side of the market. The taxes embodied in the ACA provide good examples of this fact.

Suppliers in the markets for health insurance and healthcare products have a concentrated interest in the healthcare market, and so will be knowledgeable taxpayers. Demanders in those markets have inelastic supply schedules, partly because the demand for health care is, in general, inelastic, and partly because third-party payers shift the cost away from those who directly demand the services. Because demand is more inelastic than supply, the bulk of the burden of taxes in these markets will be shifted away from knowledgeable suppliers, toward rationally ignorant demanders. Thus, to minimize political resistance, taxes in the ACA were deliberately put on suppliers, who resist less because they can shift those taxes to demanders, and were not placed directly on demanders.

A review of the taxes in the ACA shows that almost all are taxes on providers, who the general public views as profitable businesses that can afford to pay those taxes. More than just limiting opposition to the taxes, this placement even leads to a degree of public support, because it appears that the taxes are being paid by others who are profiting from healthcare provision, who can afford to pay them, and who are impersonal corporations rather than real people. Opposition from those who ultimately bear the burden of the taxes is minimized in this way. Meanwhile, the more knowledgeable corporations, while they are not necessarily in favor of the taxes, offered less of a political roadblock to the passage of the ACA because, first, they understand that ultimately most of the burden of the taxes levied on them will be shifted toward others, and second, because corporations represent fewer voters than the healthcare consumers on the demand side of the market.

The taxes in the ACA offer an interesting case study into the politics of taxation. The generally applicable lesson is that taxes are designed to minimize political opposition. They are not designed to minimize the welfare losses from taxation, promote equity, or maximize some characterization of social welfare, as is so often implied in economic models of taxation.

NOTES

1. After Professor Gruber made comments like those quoted below, members of the Obama administration were quick to distance themselves from both Professor Gruber and the statements he made.

2. Professor Gruber gave at least five public talks in which he was recorded delivering a message similar to the one that follows, and the recordings were shown on television news programs and were available on many websites. The talks were addressed to academic audiences and not intended for the general public, so the comments ought to be viewed as Gruber's explanation to his academic peers about the political decisions that were behind the selling of the ACA to the general public. One reviewer thought I was being too hard on Gruber and that Gruber had backed off of some of the comments he made, but he did make similar comments repeatedly and only sought to "clarify" what he meant after substantial public criticism.

3. A video containing this quotation can be found at www.forbes.com /sites/theabothecary/2014/11/10/aca-architect-the-stupidity-of-the-american-voter-led-us-to-hide-obamacares-tax-hikes-and-subsidies-from-the-public/#d008d52779b.

4. See www.healthcare.gov/fees-exemptions/. The fee listed is for 2016 and is adjusted for inflation in years after 2016.

5. National Federation of Independent Business et al. v. Sebelius, Secretary of Health and Human Services, et al., 567 U.S. (2012).

6. This quotation can be found at www.dailycaller.com/2014/11/16/gruber-seniors-do-a -terrible-job-choosing-health-plans/.

7. This quotation can be found at www.cnn.com/2014/11/18/politics/gruber-obamacare -promises/.

8. Ringel et al. (2002) review the literature and find that the price elasticity of demand for health care is very inelastic—less than -0.2—but the larger point is that when healthcare costs are paid for by third-party payers, consumers will be very insensitive to the real cost of their health care.

9. A summary of the ACA's tax provisions is given at www.irs.gov/uac/Affordable-Care-Act -Tax-Provisions, and the individual descriptions of those provisions have links to more detailed explanations. Unless otherwise noted, the facts about the ACA's tax provisions come from that website.

10. See www.abcnews.com/blogs/politics/2012/06/obama-in-2009-its-not-a.tax/ for this statement and additional statements by President Obama arguing that the individual mandate is not a tax.

11. See www.healthcare.gov/fees/fee-for-not-being-covered/.

12. This is the 2016 amount, which will be adjusted for inflation in future years.

13. For some evidence on this, see www.fivethirtyeight.com/features/yes-some-companies -are-cutting-hours-in-response-to-oabamacare/. Because the ACA is relatively new and academic studies take some time to complete and go through a review process, one would expect more academic studies on the subject in the future.

14. Leibowitz (1983) and Baughman et al. (2003) provide statistical analyses showing that higher levels of fringe benefits are offset by lower wages.

15. See www.irs.gov/uac/Medical-Device-Excise-Tax-Frequently-Asked-Questions.

16. The quote is from www.irs.gov/uac/Newsroom/Medical-Device-Excise-Tax.

17. See www.taxfoundation.org/blog/five-years-later-indoor-tanning-excise-tax-revenues-are -below-2010-aca-projections.

18. See https://www.irs.gov/uac/patient-centered-outcomes-research-trust-fund-fee-questions -and-answers, accessed June 27, 2017.

19. The description of the calculation comes from Department of the Treasury, IRS memorandum RIN 1545-BJ39, Final Regulations, Temporary Regulations, and Removal of Temporary Regulations, published in the Federal Register, July 28, 2014. The memorandum explaining the fee is sixty-one pages long.

20. The arguments of Caplan (2007) about irrational voters come into play here.

21. See "Excise Tax on 'Cadillac' Plans," *Health Policy Briefs*, September 12, 2013, found at www .healthaffairs.org/healthpolicybriefs/brief.php?brief_id=99.

REFERENCES

Baughman, Reagan, Daniela DiNardi, and Douglas Holtz-Eakin. 2003. "Productivity and Wage Effects of 'Family-Friendly' Fringe Benefits." *International Journal of Manpower* 24 (3): 247–59.

Brennan, Geoffrey, and Loren Lomasky. 1993. *Democracy and Decision: The Pure Theory of Electoral Preference*. Cambridge: Cambridge University Press.

Caplan, Bryan. 2007. *The Myth of the Rational Voter: Why Democracies Choose Bad Policies*. Princeton, NJ: Princeton University Press.

Diamond, Peter A., and James A. Mirrlees. 1971a. "Optimal Taxation and Public Production: I." *American Economic Review* 61 (March): 8–27.

———. 1971b. "Optimal Taxation and Public Production: II." *American Economic Review* 61 (June): 261–78.

Downs, Anthony. 1957. *An Economic Analysis of Democracy*. New York: Harper & Row.

Hayek, Friedrich A. 1945. "The Use of Knowledge in Society." *American Economic Review* 35 (4): 519–30.

Holcombe, Randall G. 1997. "Selective Excise Taxes from an Interest-Group Perspective." In *Taxing Choice: The Predatory Politics of Fiscal Discrimination*, edited by William F. Shughart II, 81–103. New Brunswick, NJ: Transaction.

———. 1998. "Tax Policy from a Public Choice Perspective." *National Tax Journal* 51 (2): 359–71.

———. 2002. "The Ramsey Rule Reconsidered." *Public Finance Review* 30 (6): 562–578.

———. 2012. "Make Economics Policy-Relevant: Depose the Omniscient Benevolent Dictator." *Independent Review* 17 (2): 165–76.

Leibowitz, Arleen. 1983. "Fringe Benefits in Employee Compensation." In *The Measurement of Labor Cost*, edited by Jack E. Triplett, 371–94. Chicago: University of Chicago Press.

Mirrlees, James A. 1971. "An Exploration in the Theory of Optimum Income Taxation." *Review of Economic Studies* 38: 175–208.

———. 1976. "Optimal Tax Theory—A Synthesis." *Journal of Public Economics* 6 (4): 327–58.

Mises, Ludwig von. [1922] 1951. *Socialism.* New Haven, CT: Yale University Press.

Niskanen, William A. 1971. *Bureaucracy and Representative Government.* Chicago: Aldine-Atherton.

Ramsey, Frank P. 1927. "A Contribution to the Theory of Taxation." *Economic Journal* 37: 47–61.

Ringel, Jeanne S., Susan D. Hosek, Ben A. Vollaard, and Sergej Mahnovski. 2002. "The Elasticity of Demand for Health Care: A Review of the Literature and Its Application to the Military Health System." Santa Monica, CA: Rand.

Tullock, Gordon. 1965. *The Politics of Bureaucracy.* Washington, DC: Public Affairs.

CHAPTER 6
Earmarking Tax Revenues:
Leviathan's Secret Weapon?

GEORGE R. CROWLEY

Department of Economics and Finance,
Sorrell College of Business, Troy University

ADAM J. HOFFER

Department of Economics, University of Wisconsin–La Crosse

T he practice of dedicating a portion of tax revenue to a specific expenditure category is a popular fiscal tool for state governments. Despite its widespread use, this practice, also known as earmarking, has ambiguous theoretical effects in terms of how it should affect the amount or composition of expenditures. Empirical studies have found evidence that some portion of earmarked revenue does "stick" to its intended target, though the majority of the earmarked revenue goes elsewhere. In this chapter, we outline a political economy theory of earmarking that seeks to explain its widespread use in the face of these apparent shortcomings.

The authors gratefully acknowledge the financial support of the Mercatus Center at George Mason University. An earlier version of this chapter, titled "How Earmarking Tax Revenue Impacts Government Spending," was released as part of the Mercatus Center Working Paper series.

The fundamental theoretical issue with earmarking tax revenue is fungibility. So long as expenditures from the general fund are at least as large as the amount of the earmarked revenue, there is no reason to expect an earmarked dollar to have any more of an impact on expenditures than an undedicated dollar—in other words, tax revenues (like all dollars) can be perfectly substituted for one another. In the extreme case, policymakers can use an additional earmarked dollar in place of a previously used general fund dollar, freeing that general fund dollar to be used elsewhere. The result would be no change in spending on the targeted expenditure category. In the event that the earmarked revenue exceeds previously used general fund monies, however, an increase in expenditures would be expected.

Despite this potential meaninglessness of the practice, several arguments favor the earmarking of revenue, such as guaranteeing funding for important programs or constraining politicians' choices on budgetary matters. However, by applying the "Leviathan" model of government, which assumes government seeks to maximize its size, a possible use of earmarking that runs contrary to these arguments is uncovered. Since earmarked funds may be used (in theory) to increase spending in other areas through the fungibility of revenues, policymakers in government may turn to tax increases earmarked to politically popular programs (e.g., education) or highly visible public goods (e.g., highways) when more general tax increases are not feasible politically. In other words, the potential theoretical shortcomings of earmarking tax revenue may be viewed by some policymakers as an attractive feature allowing for an increase in total government size through an increase in revenue purportedly dedicated to some popular program.

In this chapter, we present evidence from forty-nine states (as is common in the state fiscal-policy literature, we drop Alaska from the analysis). Unlike previous studies of earmarking, which rely on some aggregate measure of total dollars earmarked to a specific program, we separate specific taxes and other revenue sources to determine any differences in the relative stickiness (and thus ability of government to use the funds elsewhere) across earmarks. Our results indicate that the majority of earmarks fail to increase spending in their target expenditure category. These same earmarks, however, are quite effective at increasing spending on other expenditure categories. In general, the practice of earmarking tax revenue leads to larger government overall. In other words, we find evidence that policymakers may use earmarking to mask increases in government spending.

EARMARKING TAX REVENUE: THEORY, PRACTICE, AND EMPIRICAL EVIDENCE

Earmarking tax revenue is a budgetary practice that involves dedicating a percentage of the tax revenue from a specific source to a specific expenditure. Every US state earmarks a percentage of its revenue for a certain purpose, but the percentage of total state revenue that is earmarked varies widely. In 2005, Alabama earmarked 84 percent of its total state revenue, the largest percentage in the United States, while Rhode Island earmarked only 4 percent of its revenue, the lowest among US states.[1]

Table 1 presents a summary of popular earmarked revenue sources and their most common destination in 2005. The tax revenue sources earmarked the most frequently were the motor fuels tax and the general sales tax. The most popular expenditure categories to receive earmarked funding were education, state highways, and local governments. Overwhelmingly, the most common earmark across the fifty states is gasoline tax revenues targeted to highway expenditures.

Earmarking practices not only vary across states, but they also have changed substantially over time. The National Conference of State Legislatures first collected and reported data on state earmarking practices in 1954. That year, 54 percent of all state revenue was specifically dedicated to some expenditure category. Its recent survey of fiscal year 2005 shows that only 24 percent of state revenues were earmarked.[2]

Given the differences in earmarking practices through time and across states, it is necessary to discuss why earmarks are implemented in the first place. Earmarked tax revenues are typically justified by legislators for several reasons. An earmark may be assigned to a source of tax revenue as a means for guaranteeing funding for a particular government expenditure category. This is often used to gain popular support for the creation of a new source of government revenue. A popular example of this has been governments' justifying the implementation of lotteries, the proceeds of which are to be used to fund such programs as education.[3]

This use of earmarking may be implemented as an attractive marketing strategy. Governments may be able to encourage additional consumption of a taxed good by promoting the advertised expenditure destination. In the case of lottery revenue earmarked for education expenditures, politicians can politicize the need for additional education revenue to sell more lottery tickets—not unlike the use of small-scale lotteries (e.g., 50/50 raffles) as fundraisers for nonprofit organizations. Participants are often willing to purchase tickets, not

Table 1. Earmarking in the United States, 2005

	Revenue Source												
	General Sales	Tobacco	Alcohol	Insurance	Utilities	Pari-mutuel	Personal Income	Corporate Income	Motor Fuel	Motor Vehicle Registration	Gaming	State Property	Severance
States levying tax	45	50	50	50	50	37	43	45	50	50	20	37	39
States earmarking tax	35	26	23	26	10	9	20	14	49	12	14	9	26
Expenditure Targeted by Earmark													
Local government	17	14	10	7	4	1	7	4	22	5	6	n/a	24
Education	11	10	4	4	3	2	8	5	2	1	4	3	6
State highways	7	1	n/a	n/a	1	n/a	n/a	n/a	45	8	1	n/a	n/a
Health/Welfare/Human services	2	23	13	3	2	n/a	2	1	n/a	n/a	1	1	n/a
Pensions	2	1	1	7	n/a	n/a	2	1	n/a	n/a	1	1	n/a
Parks/Natural resources	4	2	1	n/a	n/a	n/a	n/a	n/a	12	1	1	2	6
Debt service	5	4	1	n/a	n/a	1	4	1	10	3	4	2	4
Environmental programs	4	2	n/a	n/a	n/a	n/a	n/a	n/a	3	n/a	n/a	n/a	6
Other	14	7	13	11	3	8	5	3	19	5	5	3	8

Source: Pérez (2008).
Note: n/a = nonapplicable.

only at the hope of winning, but also because they know their money goes to an organization they support.

Another popular argument in favor of earmarks is that they act as the transfer medium of a Pigouvian tax; that is, when a tax is placed on a good that creates a negative externality in an effort to deter consumption, the earmark ensures transfer of the revenue to government programs that are designed to alleviate the burden of the externality. A related justification is tied to the principle of benefits-received taxation and the provision of public goods.[4] In this case, the tax acts as a mechanism to help mitigate the free-rider problem, and the revenues are dedicated to the provision of the public good. A popular example of this type of earmark is state gasoline excise tax revenues that fund state highway and road expenditures, which are generally considered to have public-good characteristics. Gasoline tax revenues can be used to maintain roads, which incur wear and tear due to drivers' use. In a sense, a gasoline tax "charges" drivers in direct proportion to their contribution to the need for road maintenance: those who drive more will purchase more gasoline and therefore pay more in taxes used to fund repairs.

Stratmann and Bruntrager (2011) describe why this use of earmarks is unjustified, primarily from the perspective that excise taxes fail to fully capture any externalities (1) created by the product being taxed or (2) created by the public good. In describing the gasoline excise tax, they argue that charging tolls and a broader tax on all carbon emissions would be a more accurate way to match benefits received to expenses paid.[5] Nevertheless, several of these earmarks remain in place today. In 2005, every state earmarked a percentage of its gasoline tax to spending on roads, with the median percentage of revenue earmarked at 95.9 percent.[6]

Looking at how states choose to earmark revenues, this logic is clearly incomplete; many earmarks exist that are entirely unrelated to the Pigouvian argument. For example, in 2005, Alabama earmarked 40 percent of its beer tax revenue to public schools and higher education. While many argue that education provides positive externalities enjoyed by all citizens of a state, it is difficult to justify why individuals who purchase alcohol reap any higher proportion of the positive spillovers. Thus, while the Pigouvian argument is a popular one for the justification of earmarked tax revenues, other motivations for the practice clearly exist.

The formal theoretical discussion of the practice of earmarking begins with Buchanan (1963). Buchanan argued from a position of methodological individualism that viewed the distinction of earmarked versus general fund revenues as analogous to consumer choice over individual goods versus a "tie-in-sale" or "bundle." For Buchanan, the unbundling of expenditure programs inherent in the practice of earmarking revenues allowed a median voter greater control over the taxing and spending activities of government and could serve as a constraint on policymakers; conversely, financing government out of a general fund distorted the median voter's choice calculus. The extent to which overall spending would be affected by using general fund versus earmarked revenue would depend on the relative elasticity of the publicly provided goods and services being discussed. Specifically, if a move was made from a system of strict earmarking toward a new general fund financing scheme that favored spending on a good or service for which demand was relatively elastic, Buchanan expected overall government expenditure to increase—a situation that would indicate earmarking acted as a constraint. Should the new general fund financing scheme favor spending on goods for which demand was relatively inelastic, however, the move away from earmarking would result in smaller government—in other words, general fund financing was more effective at limiting the size of government. In short, the extent to which earmarking affects total government size is left as an empirical question.

Further complicating the practice of earmarking is the issue of fungibility: because governments allocate much of their spending through a general fund, the revenue they receive from any source is easily transferred to any expenditure. Thus additional earmarked revenue dedicated to a specific expenditure can be used as a substitute for previous funding that had been coming from the general fund, so long as this previous level of spending was at least as large as the earmarked revenue. This characteristic was identified by Buchanan (1963), who showed that under some specific circumstances, earmarking tax revenue to a specific expenditure category should have, by itself, no theoretical effect on the amount of spending on the targeted program.[7] This issue of fungibility is crucial to our hypothesis of earmarking as a tool used to increase general fund revenues and the overall size of government, presented in a later section of this chapter.

Despite earmarking's theoretical shortcomings and occasionally dubious economic justifications, state governments have widely adopted the practice. Furthermore, empirical studies have shown that despite the issue of fungibility, some percentage of revenue (typically in the form of intergovernmental grants or revenues from special sources, such as lotteries) will tend to stick to its targeted expenditure. This phenomenon, known as the "flypaper effect," is discussed in the following section. We then turn our discussion to a political economy framework of why the practice of earmarking remains popular.

THE FLYPAPER EFFECT

The concept of fungible revenue is central to a separate but related literature concerning the so-called flypaper effect. Inman (2008) claims there may be as many as 3,500 studies that investigate the flypaper effect. These papers investigate whether fungible revenue sticks to its intended expenditure destination. Theoretically, because revenues are fungible, there is no reason that an increase in revenue from a new source—say, a federal grant to a state—should have an impact on expenditures different from any other increase in income in the state. Taken a step further, economic theory predicts that in most scenarios, governments receiving revenue from a new source will increase expenditure by the same amount they would have had the new revenue come simply from an increase in income. In other words, government would be expected to treat this new income (which may very well be earmarked for a specific expenditure program) in the same way it did the revenue it had previously been using, and therefore relatively little of the new revenue will reach its intended destination—just as an increase in income would be expected to result in only a relatively small increase in demand for government expenditures.[8] Counter to theory, however, the common theme among empirical studies is that a higher than expected portion of such revenue sticks where it hits.

Estimates of how much sticks vary widely. Gramlich (1977), Hines and Thaler (1995), and Bailey and Connolly (1998) provide summaries of empirical studies that investigate the effects of lump-sum grants. Like earmarked tax revenue, grant revenue is a new source of fungible funding that can be used as a substitute for previously used general fund revenue. The most popular of these investigated grants have been intergovernmental grants (federal to state and local governments, and state to local governments). Gramlich and Galper (1973) find a flypaper effect of 0.25 (indicating that 25 cents of every dollar sticks), while Inman (1971) finds a unitary increase in spending from a $1 increase in revenue. Generally, however, the flypaper estimates tend to range from 0.30 to 0.70, with a median of around 0.45 (Sobel and Crowley 2014). This suggests that an extra dollar in federal grants to a state will result in increased spending of about 45 cents and a potential tax reduction of approximately 55 cents.

More recently, the flypaper effect has been estimated for own sources of revenue that are earmarked for specific expenditures—a strand of the literature more in line with our current topic. Dye and McGuire (1992) show very limited effects on expenditures of earmarks targeting education, highways, or local governments. Other studies have focused on state lottery revenues earmarked for education. Evans and Zhang (2003) investigate sixteen states that earmark lottery revenues for K–12 education. They find that an extra dollar in lottery revenue leads to an increase in education expenditures between 60 and 80 cents. This increased expenditure on education is 30–50 cents more than a similar increase in lottery revenue in states that earmark lottery revenue for other purposes and 20–30 cents more than a similar increase in revenue in states that do not earmark lottery revenue whatsoever. Similarly, Novarro (2002) finds that earmarked revenues increase K–12 spending 60 cents more than revenue earmarked for other sources and 36 cents more than revenue that was not earmarked.

Other researchers have found less consistent results, indicating a possible substitution of earmarked lottery revenues for previously used general fund revenue. Pantuosco et al. (2007) find no evidence that earmarking lottery revenue for education expenditure increases spending—though, strangely, lottery revenues not earmarked for education (i.e., revenues that enter a state's general fund) have a positive impact on spending. Garrett (2001) found little evidence that Ohio's earmarked lottery revenues led to increases in spending on education. Erekson et al. (2002) find significant evidence of fungible lottery revenues substituting for general fund expenditures on education, resulting in no net increase in spending.

Other work has examined the flypaper effect for state highway spending. Nesbit and Kreft (2009) find that a $1 increase in revenues earmarked for highway expenditures increases expenditure by approximately $1. Goel and Nelson (2003) find states that earmark their gasoline tax revenue for general funds (rather than for highway expenditures) spend $2.54 less on highways for each $1 diverted to the general fund.

Among all these studies, the issue of flypaper-effect asymmetry (i.e., possible differences in response to increases vs. decreases in grant income) remains relatively unexplored. The few studies that have investigated symmetry have found mixed results. Gamkhar and Oates (1996) examine federal grants to state and local governments from 1953 to 1991, finding symmetry effects. Similarly, Gamkhar (2000) and Goodspeed (1998) find symmetry in state and local government responses to changes in aid. Heyndels's (2001) study of Flemish municipalities, Volden's (1999) analysis of US states, and Levaggi's and Zanola's (2003) study of Italian healthcare expenditures all find asymmetries in the replacement of local government funds. Using Wisconsin municipalities, Deller and Maher (2009) find that the treatment of intergovernmental aid is asymmetric, depending on service. Specifically, local governments are more likely to respond to decreases in intergovernmental aid by substituting local revenue in the case of vital services (e.g., waste disposal services and road expenditures) than for less vital services (quality of life expenditures, which include spending on libraries, parks, and cultural services).

Thus, although theory predicts that earmarking revenues should have little effect on the size or composition of expenditures, the flypaper literature has shown some effects. Given its limitations, the question remains why states continue to rely on earmarking tax revenues for specific expenditure categories. We propose a hypothesis in the following section.

MASKING INCREASES IN GOVERNMENT SPENDING

The Brennan and Buchanan (1977, 1978, 1980) Leviathan model of government can help explain the disconnect between theory, empirical evidence, and the underlying practice of earmarking. According to this theory, government seeks to maximize its power and size. Barring some strict fiscal constitutional rules, government continues to increase the level of taxation and expenditure.

In this context, the fungibility of the different sources of funds available for expenditure provides policymakers with a way to increase government size without highly unpopular increases in rates on general fund taxation sources. Specifically, by earmarking tax revenues for a specific expenditure, policymakers are able to advocate for increases in the earmarked tax on the basis of benefiting the targeted expenditure category. Should the tax increase be approved, the earmarked revenues may be used in place of previously used general fund revenues, allowing those monies to be spent elsewhere. The result is little to no net effect on the targeted expenditure and an increase in total government size.

An example will help clarify this theory. Assume that a state government spends $100 from the general fund on education. Suppose the legislature is able to pass a new special sales tax on the basis of its revenue being earmarked for education spending. Further, suppose this new tax brings in $50 in revenue. Although it may seem natural to assume education spending will increase by $50 as a result of the earmarked revenue (to $150), policymakers actually have the option to decrease spending on education out of the general fund. Even if the entire $50 earmarked to education spending is actually spent on education, total education expenditures may remain unchanged if the legislature decides to decrease general fund spending from $100 to $50. This allows policymakers to spend elsewhere $50 of revenue previously dedicated to education, and the earmark is functionally equivalent to a $50 increase in unspecified general fund revenue. Importantly (for interpretation of our empirical results), this substitution would have an observed effect: the earmark would have no impact on education spending.

Thus, politicians may use the earmarking of tax revenues to specific expenditure categories to covertly raise revenue and expand total government size. This option becomes especially attractive when the public resists general increases in taxes. Instead, policymakers may choose to enact new taxes earmarked for spending on politically popular programs (e.g., education) or obviously visible public goods (e.g., highways) as a way to expand total government size by exploiting tax revenue fungibility. In other words, politicians may actually view the theoretical and empirical shortcomings of earmarking as attractive features of the practice.

The degree to which earmarking is used in this manner is an empirical question. Although previous studies have looked at how earmarked revenues affect expenditures in the targeted category (the flypaper-effect literature), we are equally interested in how earmarked revenues affect other expenditures. To be clear, we investigate two effects: (1) whether earmarked revenue is used for the intended purpose and (2) whether overall spending and spending on categories other than the intended destination increase as the amount of earmarked revenues grows. Certain earmarks are more likely to stick than others; therefore, we focus on specific taxes earmarked to specific expenditures and not some broader measure of total earmarked revenue as used in previous studies. The following section outlines our empirical test of the hypothesis that earmarking can increase the overall size of government.

EMPIRICAL APPROACH AND DATA

To test the degree to which specific earmarked tax revenues affect their targeted expenditure, we estimate the following equation:

$$EXP_{it} = \beta_1 EAR\ REV_{it} + \beta_2 OTH\ REV_{it} + \beta_3 X_{it} + \mu_t + \theta_i + \varepsilon_{it}, \tag{1}$$

where for state i in year t, EXP_{it} is real per capita expenditure in the targeted category; $EAR\ REV_{it}$ is a collection of real per capita revenue sources earmarked to the expenditure; $OTH\ REV_{it}$ is real per capita, own-source revenue from sources other than the earmarked taxes; X_{it} is a collection of other demographic and economic control variables; μ_t and θ_i are year and census region fixed effects; and ε_{it} represents the regression model's error term. The primary coefficient of interest is β_1, which represents how much of each additional dollar of earmarked revenue is spent on its intended expenditure.

If the earmark increases targeted expenditures, β_1 will be positive and statistically significant. The magnitude is also crucially important: if β_1 takes a value less than 1, it indicates some portion of the earmarked revenue is not sticking to its intended expenditure.

Following Dye and McGuire (1992), we focus our analysis on the three major expenditure categories for which tax revenues are earmarked: education, local governments, and highways. To capture potential differences in the stickiness of earmarks, we focus on the individual revenue sources that are earmarked and not on some aggregate measure of earmarked funds as has been used in the previous literature. We analyze revenues from the general sales tax, tobacco tax, alcoholic beverage tax, personal income tax, corporate income tax, gambling tax, gasoline tax, and motor vehicle registration. We then calculate the specific revenue earmarked by multiplying the total revenue from each source by the percentage earmarked for the expenditure category.

As discussed above, many states earmark a variety of taxes for the same expenditure category. Thus, in our specifications, the $EAR\ REV_{it}$ variable is actually a collection of several variables, accounting for each earmarked revenue source. This approach differs from those previously seen in the literature and allows us to test differences in the degree to which certain earmarked revenue sources may stick to their intended expenditures. In our estimates of education expenditures, $EAR\ REV_{it}$ comprises real per capita general sales tax revenue, tobacco tax revenue, alcohol tax revenue, personal income tax revenue, and corporate income tax revenue multiplied by the percentage of such revenue specifically earmarked for education spending. For example, if a state earmarks 50 percent of tobacco tax revenue for education spending, our regression includes total tobacco tax revenue multiplied by .5, yielding the total dollars of tobacco tax revenue designated for education. For the estimates of local government spending, $EAR\ REV_{it}$ contains real per capita general sales tax revenue, tobacco tax revenue, alcohol tax revenue, personal income tax revenue, corporate income tax revenue, gasoline tax revenue, and motor vehicle registration tax revenue, multiplied by the percentage of such revenue specifically earmarked for local government spending. Finally, $EAR\ REV_{it}$ comprises real per capita gasoline tax revenue and motor vehicle registration tax revenue earmarked for highways in our estimates of highway expenditures.

The $OTH\ REV_{it}$ variable is total real per capita own-source revenue minus that revenue contained in the $EAR\ REV_{it}$ variables. The inclusion of this variable allows us to interpret the effect of an earmarked dollar relative to all other sources of revenue. We also estimate our models using a collection of nonearmarked revenues in place of the $OTH\ REV_{it}$ variable. This specification allows for an interpretation of a difference in effects between an earmarked dollar of revenue versus a nonearmarked dollar of revenue from the same source. More specifically, it allows for a direct test of the flypaper effect for these revenues, as we can statistically test for any difference between the estimated coefficients on the earmarked and nonearmarked revenues. The group of variables that make up X_{it} includes demographic and economic controls that may influence expenditures. Specifically, these controls include the percentage of the population that is white, the percentage of the population that is under the age of 15, the percentage older than 65, the percentage older than 25 with a high school education, real per capita personal income, real per capita federal grants to the state, and an indicator variable for the political party of the state's governor.[9]

To fully test our hypothesis, we also estimate the effect of earmarking on both nontargeted expenditures ($NON\ EXP_{it}$),

$$NON\ EXP_{it} = \beta_1 EAR\ REV_{it} + \beta_2 OTH\ REV_{it} + \beta_3 X_{it} + \mu_t + \theta_i + \varepsilon_{it}, \tag{2}$$

and total state government spending ($TOT\ EXP_{it}$),

$$TOT\ EXP_{it} = \beta_1 EAR\ REV_{it} + \beta_2 OTH\ REV_{it} + \beta_3 X_{it} + \mu_t + \theta_i + \varepsilon_{it}. \tag{3}$$

Again, the variable of interest in these specifications is β_1, which measures the effect of the marginal earmarked dollar, this time on expenditures other than those for which the earmark is dedicated. If our hypothesis is correct and earmarked dollars are used to increase general fund revenues and thus the size of government, we would expect positive, statistically significant values for β_1.

Our data span forty-nine states (dropping Alaska, as is common practice in state-level revenue/expenditure studies) and 3 years (1988, 1993, and 2005).[10] Our rather eclectic collection of years is due to the publication dates of the most comprehensive study of state government earmarking practices, the *Earmarking State Taxes* report by the National Conference of State Legislatures, from which we obtain the percentages of specific tax revenues earmarked for specific expenditures (Fabricius and Snell 1990; Pérez and Snell 1995; Pérez 2008). Our data on state expenditures, revenues, personal income, and federal grants come from the Census Bureau's *State Government Finances* report. Data on governors' political affiliation come from the Council of State Governments' *Book of the States*. Finally, our measures of the percentage of the state population that is white and the age and education breakdowns come from the Census Bureau. All fiscal variables are expressed in real per capita terms (2005 dollars) to control for inflation and state population.

RESULTS

Table 2 presents our results for revenues earmarked for spending on education. The first column shows our estimation of equation 1, the effects of earmarked revenues on the targeted expenditure category (in other words, the extent of the flypaper effect). Earmarked general sales tax revenue has no effect on education spending. Roughly 56 cents of every dollar of earmarked personal income tax revenue is spent on education, while earmarked alcohol and tobacco tax revenue also have a positive effect on education spending. The coefficient on earmarked alcohol tax revenue is quite large, implying a complementarity between the earmarked revenue and additional expenditures funded out of the general fund—this result is unsurprising, however, given the relatively small amount of revenue generated by the alcohol tax.[11] Earmarked corporate income tax revenue has a negative effect on education spending, implying that when these revenues are earmarked for education, general fund spending is reduced by an amount larger than the earmark. Finally, expendi-

Table 2. Effect on Spending of Revenue Earmarked for Education

	Dependent Variable		
	Education Expenditure	Noneducation Expenditure	Total Expenditure
Earmarked general sales tax revenue per capita	0.232 (0.166)	0.727*** (0.171)	0.958*** (0.144)
Earmarked tobacco tax revenue per capita	1.683* (0.999)	−0.483 (1.536)	1.201 (1.582)
Earmarked alcohol tax revenue per capita	15.269*** (4.642)	−11.628* (6.118)	3.641 (6.313)
Earmarked personal income tax revenue per capita	0.564*** (0.088)	0.113 (0.129)	0.677*** (0.130)
Earmarked corporate income tax revenue per capita	−1.833* (1.070)	4.362*** (1.372)	2.529** (1.065)
Real own-source revenue per capita from other sources	0.295*** (0.035)	0.560*** (0.042)	0.855*** (0.054)
Observations	146	146	146
R-squared	0.78	0.94	0.96

Source: Authors' estimates based on data from Fabricius and Snell 1990; Pérez and Snell 1995; Pérez 2008; US Census Bureau, *Annual Survey of State Government Finances* (https://www.census.gov/econ/overview/go1500.html) and other data; and Council of State Governments, *Book of the States* (http://knowledgecenter.csg.org/kc/category/content-type /bos-archive).

Note: All specifications include the following controls: the percentage of the state's population that is white, the percentage that is under the age of 15, the percentage over 65, the percentage over 25 with a high school education, real personal income per capita, real federal grants per capita, an indicator variable for the political party of the state's governor, and year and census region fixed effects. Coefficient estimates for these variables are available on request. Robust standard errors in parentheses: *** indicates statistical significance at the 1 percent level, ** at the 5 percent level, and * at the 10 percent level.

tures on education are increased by approximately 30 cents of every dollar of own-source revenue from other sources.

The second column of table 2 shows the results from the first of our tests of the hypothesis that earmarked revenues are used to increase total government size. Here we test equation 2, in which the dependent variable in these specifications is total expenditures less those in the category to which the revenue source is earmarked (i.e., education). Notably, general sales tax revenue and corporate income tax revenue earmarked for education have a positive effect on noneducation expenditures. This result lends credence to our hypothesis, as these earmarks had either no effect or a negative effect on education spending, implying that the revenues were transferred instead to the general fund. Earmarked alcohol tax revenue (which had the largest positive effect on education spending) has a similarly large negative effect on other expenditures, suggesting a complementarity between this particular earmark and expenditures from the general fund. Predictably, earmarked personal income tax and tobacco tax revenue, which each had a positive effect on education spending, have no effect on noneducation expenditures. Notably, an F-test on the education-earmarked revenues in this specification yields evidence that earmarked dollars are indeed associated with increases in spending in areas other than education. Specifically, we are able to reject the hypothesis that the earmarked dollars collectively have no effect on noneducation spending, indicating that together, these earmarked revenues do in fact affect spending in areas outside what was targeted.[12]

Finally, the results from our estimation of equation 3, the effects of earmarked revenue on total government expenditure, are shown in the third column. General sales tax revenue, personal income tax revenue, and corporate income tax revenue earmarked for education all increase the overall size of government spending by amounts approaching one full dollar per dollar earmarked. This result provides some evidence of the flypaper effect generally, in that nearly all revenue in these earmarked tax revenues is associated with increases in spending (though not necessarily in the targeted area).

The first column of table 3 shows the estimation of earmark effects on local government expenditures. Nearly all (83 cents) of an additional dollar of general sales tax revenue earmarked for local government expenditures is spent on local governments—the strongest flypaper effect we observe. Earmarked vehicle registration revenue also has a positive impact on expenditures on local governments, with a very large magnitude (though again, the amount of revenue collected by the average state for this tax is relatively small). Earmarked tobacco tax, alcohol tax, personal or corporate income tax, and gambling tax

Table 3. Effect on Spending of Revenue Earmarked for Local Governments

	Dependent Variable		
	Local Government Expenditure	Nonlocal Government Expenditure	Total Expenditure
Earmarked general sales tax revenue per capita	0.830*** (0.315)	0.371 (0.419)	1.201*** (0.195)
Earmarked tobacco tax revenue per capita	−0.972 (0.827)	2.573*** (0.736)	1.601** (0.735)
Earmarked alcohol tax revenue per capita	−0.536 (6.401)	−6.331 (6.669)	−6.867 (4.614)
Earmarked personal income tax revenue per capita	−0.038 (0.172)	0.656*** (0.206)	0.618*** (0.171)
Earmarked corporate income tax revenue per capita	−3.073 (1.913)	5.048*** (1.740)	1.974 (1.339)
Earmarked gambling tax revenue per capita	33.979 (36.044)	−80.095 (55.936)	−46.116 (42.9930)
Earmarked gasoline tax revenue per capita	−2.564** (1.279)	2.256 (1.693)	−0.308 (1.464)
Earmarked vehicle registration revenue per capita	8.562*** (2.489)	−8.111*** (2.378)	0.451 (2.374)
Real own-source revenue per capita from other sources	0.134*** (0.050)	0.708*** (0.076)	0.841*** (0.054)
Observations	146	146	146
R-squared	0.52	0.89	0.96

Source: Authors' estimates based on data from Fabricius and Snell 1990; Pérez and Snell 1995; Pérez 2008; US Census Bureau, *Annual Survey of State Government Finances* (https://www.census.gov/econ/overview/go1500.html) and other data; and Council of State Governments, *Book of the States* (http://knowledgecenter.csg.org/kc/category/content-type /bos-archive).

Note: All specifications include the following controls: the percentage of the state's population that is white, the percentage that is under the age of 15, the percentage over 65, the percentage over 25 with a high school education, real personal income per capita, real federal grants per capita, an indicator variable for the political party of the state's governor, and year and census region fixed effects. Coefficient estimates for these variables are available on request. Robust standard errors in parentheses: *** indicates statistical significance at the 1 percent level, ** at the 5 percent level, and * at the 10 percent level.

revenues have no effect on spending on local governments, yet earmarked gasoline tax revenue has a negative effect on spending. An additional dollar of own-source revenue from other sources increases expenditures on local government by approximately 13 cents.

The second column of table 3 shows the effects on nonlocal government spending of revenue earmarked for local governments. Earmarked tobacco tax revenue, personal income tax revenue, and corporate income tax revenue (all of which had no effect on expenditures on local government) have a positive effect on all other categories of expenditure, again implying that the earmarks

Table 4. Effect on Spending of Revenue Earmarked for Highways

	Dependent Variable		
	Highway Expenditure	Nonhighway Expenditure	Total Expenditure
Earmarked gasoline tax revenue per capita	0.259 (0.198)	−0.238 (0.499)	0.022 (0.466)
Earmarked vehicle registration revenue per capita	0.304 (0.253)	1.729*** (0.640)	2.033*** (0.612)
Real own-source revenue per capita from other sources	0.041*** (0.016)	0.809*** (0.047)	0.850*** (0.052)
Observations	146	146	146
R-squared	0.55	0.95	0.96

Source: Authors' estimates based on data from Fabricius and Snell 1990; Pérez and Snell 1995; Pérez 2008; US Census Bureau, *Annual Survey of State Government Finances* (https://www.census.gov/econ/overview/go1500.html) and other data; and Council of State Governments, *Book of the States* (http://knowledgecenter.csg.org/kc/category/content-type /bos-archive).
Note: All specifications include the following controls: the percentage of the state's population that is white, the percentage that is under the age of 15, the percentage over 65, the percentage over 25 with a high school education, real personal income per capita, real federal grants per capita, an indicator variable for the political party of the state's governor, and year and census region fixed effects. Coefficient estimates for these variables are available on request. Robust standard errors in parentheses: *** indicates statistical significance at the 1 percent level, ** at the 5 percent level, and * at the 10 percent level.

were used to effectually increase general fund revenue. Vehicle registration revenue has a predictably negative effect on nonlocal government spending, given its very large positive effect in the previous model. The general sales tax revenue earmarked for local governments, almost all of which was shown to be spent on local governments in the previous results, unsurprisingly has no effect on other expenditures. As before, an *F*-test demonstrates a significant relationship between the earmarked revenues and nontargeted expenditure.[13] The results of our test of the relationship between revenues earmarked for local governments and total government size are shown in the final column of table 3. Earmarked general sales tax revenue, tobacco tax revenue, and personal income tax revenue all lead to increases in the overall size of government.

Table 4 shows results for the models of revenues earmarked for highway expenditures. The results in the first column show that neither gasoline tax revenue nor vehicle registration revenue earmarked for this category have any effect on highway spending. The second and third columns, however, show that earmarking vehicle registration revenue for highways does lead to increases in nonhighway spending as well as in the overall size of government.

Taken together, these results indicate that the majority of these earmarks (eight out of fifteen) have no effect on their targeted expenditures, while two actually have a negative effect, implying that spending from the general fund is reduced by an amount greater than the earmarked revenue. Furthermore, the results presented in tables 2, 3, and 4 provide evidence that earmarked revenues do increase expenditures in categories other than those targeted, as well as the overall amount of government spending. Specifically, sales tax revenue earmarked for education has no effect on education expenditures, but nearly 73 cents of every earmarked dollar is used to increase expenditures in categories other than education, and total government expenditure increases by 96 cents for every dollar earmarked. The result is compounded for education-earmarked corporate income tax revenues, for which the earmark allows general fund expenditures on education to be reduced by roughly $1.83 for every $1 of earmarked revenue, leading to an associated increase in expenditures on noneducation programs. Other notable results include tobacco tax revenue, personal income tax revenue, and corporate income tax revenue earmarked for local government spending, none of which has any statistically significant effect on the targeted expenditure category. Each of these, however, is associated with increases in nonlocal government spending, and earmarking tobacco and personal income tax revenue leads to increases in the overall size of government. A similar result is found with vehicle registration revenue earmarked for highway spending, which does nothing for spending on highways but increases nonhighway expenditure and overall government spending. Even in some cases where the earmark partially sticks, the portion that does not get spent on the targeted category is spent on other programs (e.g., see the table entries for personal income tax revenues earmarked for education).

The results in tables 5–7 show our specifications with the $OTH\ REV_{it}$ variable replaced by individual nonearmarked revenue from each of the earmarked revenue sources, allowing us to test for differences in earmarked and nonearmarked revenues from the same sources. The results are largely identical. Table 5 shows revenue sources earmarked for education expenditure. As before, sales tax revenue earmarked for education has no significant effect on the level of education expenditures. Nonearmarked sales tax revenue, however, does increase education spending, further illustrating the ineffectiveness of the earmark. Earmarked alcohol tax revenue has lost its significance from the previous specification, though earmarked personal income tax revenue is associated with increases in education expenditure. Nonearmarked personal and corporate income tax revenue positively affect education expenditures. Turning to a comparison of earmarked and nonearmarked revenues' effect on education spending, we observe no statistically significant difference in the effects of sales, tobacco, or alcohol taxes; the effect of earmarked personal income tax revenue is statistically significantly

Table 5. Effect on Spending of Earmarked and Nonearmarked Revenue (Education)

	Dependent Variable		
	Education Expenditure	Noneducation Expenditure	Total Expenditure
Earmarked general sales tax revenue per capita	0.181 (0.193)	0.364* (0.191)	0.545** (0.274)
Nonearmarked general sales tax revenue per capita	0.347*** (0.102)	0.210 (0.138)	0.557*** (0.214)
Earmarked tobacco tax revenue per capita	2.999* (1.678)	−1.853 (2.636)	1.146 (3.428)
Nonearmarked tobacco tax revenue per capita	2.563 (1.993)	5.563** (2.390)	8.126** (3.790)
Earmarked alcohol tax revenue per capita	8.384 (8.163)	−25.779*** (8.820)	−17.395 (13.517)
Nonearmarked alcohol tax revenue per capita	0.660 (1.400)	−3.100** (1.260)	−2.439 (1.993)
Earmarked personal income tax revenue per capita	0.757*** (0.121)	0.231 (0.179)	0.988*** (0.241)
Nonearmarked personal income tax revenue per capita	0.249*** (0.058)	0.335*** (0.081)	0.583*** (0.112)
Earmarked corporate income tax revenue per capita	−2.721** (1.264)	2.890* (1.501)	0.168 (1.520)
Nonearmarked corporate income tax revenue per capita	0.636* (0.343)	1.457*** (0.536)	2.093*** (0.768)
Observations	146	146	146
R-squared	0.70	0.89	0.88

Source: Authors' estimates based on data from Fabricius and Snell 1990; Pérez and Snell 1995; Pérez 2008; US Census Bureau, *Annual Survey of State Government Finances* (https://www.census.gov/econ/overview/go1500.html) and other data; and Council of State Governments, *Book of the States* (http://knowledgecenter.csg.org/kc/category/content-type/bos-archive).

Note: All specifications include the following controls: the percentage of the state's population that is white, the percentage that is under the age of 15, the percentage over 65, the percentage over 25 with a high school education, real personal income per capita, real federal grants per capita, an indicator variable for the political party of the state's governor, and year and census region fixed effects. Coefficient estimates for these variables are available on request. Robust standard errors in parentheses: *** indicates statistical significance at the 1 percent level, ** at the 5 percent level, and * at the 10 percent level.

larger than the effect of nonearmarked personal income tax revenue. Also as before, earmarked general sales tax revenue has a positive and significant effect on noneducation spending and total government size. The results for all other earmarks remain similar as well, the only exception being earmarked corporate income tax revenue, which now has a positive and significant effect on total government spending.

Results from our second look at local government earmarks are shown in table 6. The results are nearly identical to the previous specification (shown

Table 6. Effect on Spending of Earmarked and Nonearmarked Revenue (Local Governments)

	Dependent Variable		
	Local Government Expenditure	Nonlocal Government Expenditure	Total Expenditure
Earmarked general sales tax revenue per capita	0.795** (0.331)	−0.020 (0.508)	0.775** (0.390)
Nonearmarked general sales tax revenue per capita	0.296** (0.130)	0.286 (0.265)	0.582** (0.253)
Earmarked tobacco tax revenue per capita	−0.036 (2.350)	6.968* (4.256)	6.932* (3.985)
Nonearmarked tobacco tax revenue per capita	0.290 (2.064)	5.680 (3.847)	5.970* (3.531)
Earmarked alcohol tax revenue per capita	−0.387 (6.692)	−12.334 (10.131)	−12.721 (9.480)
Nonearmarked alcohol tax revenue per capita	−3.299* (1.998)	1.832 (2.653)	−1.466 (2.221)
Earmarked personal income tax revenue per capita	0.106 (0.222)	0.836*** (0.303)	0.942*** (0.246)
Nonearmarked personal income tax revenue per capita	0.154* (0.089)	0.494*** (0.122)	0.647*** (0.111)
Earmarked corporate income tax revenue per capita	−2.360 (1.886)	2.409 (2.592)	0.049 (2.167)
Nonearmarked corporate income tax revenue per capita	0.812* (0.428)	1.107 (0.775)	1.918*** (0.696)
Earmarked gambling tax revenue per capita	35.777 (40.112)	−83.492 (66.979)	−47.715 (55.171)
Nonearmarked gambling tax revenue per capita	−7.975 (5.889)	−0.022 (11.051)	−7.997 (8.905)
Earmarked gasoline tax revenue per capita	−5.632*** (1.716)	1.907 (3.019)	−3.725 (3.033)
Nonearmarked gasoline tax revenue per capita	−3.271*** (1.130)	3.321** (1.645)	0.050 (1.564)
Earmarked vehicle registration revenue per capita	8.836*** (2.591)	−4.034 (5.132)	4.802 (4.868)
Nonearmarked vehicle registration revenue per capita	2.058** (0.980)	1.532 (1.537)	3.590** (1.726)
Observations	146	146	146
R-squared	0.59	0.81	0.88

Source: Authors' estimates based on data from Fabricius and Snell 1990; Pérez and Snell 1995; Pérez 2008; US Census Bureau, *Annual Survey of State Government Finances* (https://www.census.gov/econ/overview/go1500.html) and other data; and Council of State Governments, *Book of the States* (http://knowledgecenter.csg.org/kc/category/content-type /bos-archive).

Note: All specifications include the following controls: the percentage of the state's population that is white, the percentage that is under the age of 15, the percentage over 65, the percentage over 25 with a high school education, real personal income per capita, real federal grants per capita, an indicator variable for the political party of the state's governor, and year and census region fixed effects. Coefficient estimates for these variables are available on request. Robust standard errors in parentheses: *** indicates statistical significance at the 1 percent level, ** at the 5 percent level, and * at the 10 percent level.

Table 7. Effect on Spending of Earmarked and Nonearmarked Revenue (Highways)

	Dependent Variable		
	Highway Expenditure	Nonhighway Expenditure	Total Expenditure
Earmarked gasoline tax revenue per capita	1.198*** (0.307)	−1.009 (1.546)	0.189 (1.577)
Nonearmarked gasoline tax revenue per capita	1.435*** (0.321)	−0.518 (2.178)	0.917 (2.227)
Earmarked vehicle registration revenue per capita	0.803** (0.362)	1.873 (1.920)	2.676 (2.015)
Nonearmarked vehicle registration revenue per capita	0.794** (0.346)	1.890 (1.516)	2.685 (1.644)
Observations	146	146	146
R-squared	0.61	0.82	0.82

Source: Authors' estimates based on data from Fabricius and Snell 1990; Pérez and Snell 1995; Pérez 2008; US Census Bureau, *Annual Survey of State Government Finances* (https://www.census.gov/econ/overview/go1500.html) and other data; and Council of State Governments, *Book of the States* (http://knowledgecenter.csg.org/kc/category/content-type /bos-archive).
Note: All specifications include the following controls: the percentage of the state's population that is white, the percentage that is under the age of 15, the percentage over 65, the percentage over 25 with a high school education, real personal income per capita, real federal grants per capita, an indicator variable for the political party of the state's governor, and year and census region fixed effects. Coefficient estimates for these variables are available on request. Robust standard errors in parentheses: *** indicates statistical significance at the 1 percent level, ** at the 5 percent level, and * at the 10 percent level.

in table 3). Nonearmarked sales tax, personal income tax, corporate income tax, and motor vehicle registration revenue all positively affect expenditures on local governments. Statistical tests for differences in the coefficients on the earmarked and nonearmarked revenue sources once again show there is little evidence of earmarked revenue having any different impact on spending.[14] In contrast, non-earmarked alcohol tax and gasoline tax revenues have a negative effect on expenditures on local governments. Our results for the statistical tests also remain largely unchanged. Earmarked tobacco tax revenue and personal income tax revenue both increase nonlocal government spending and the overall size of government, while earmarked sales tax revenue increases total spending as well.

Table 7 displays results for the expanded model of earmarks targeting highway expenditures. In this case, gasoline taxes and vehicle registration revenue earmarked for highway spending have a positive and significant effect on expenditures—a result contrary to our previous look at highway spending, perhaps driven by controlling for only these specific sources of revenue in this specification. The same is true for nonearmarked revenue from these sources. Importantly, we observe no statistically significant difference in the effect on highway spending between an earmarked and nonearmarked dollar for these revenue sources—unsurprising, given the similarity in their coefficients. The magnitude also indicates that nearly the entire earmarked dollar sticks to highway expenditures. To the extent gasoline taxes are justified under the Pigouvian criteria discussed previously, this result is not unsurprising, though it does differ from the findings presented in table 4. The final two columns of table 7 show no evidence that these earmarks increase nonhighway spending, which is to be expected, given the results shown in the first column, though again different from the previous findings. Unlike earmarks for education or local governments, specifically controlling for nonearmarked taxes is important for the analysis of highway expenditures.

In general, these estimates show that earmarking is not an effective method of increasing expenditures on specific programs, and typically some (or all) of the increase in revenues dedicated to a program is compensated for by associated decreases in spending from the general fund (resulting in a statistically insignificant effect of the earmark). Of the fifteen earmarks explored, only tobacco tax revenue and personal income tax revenue earmarked for education and sales tax revenue and vehicle registration revenue earmarked for local governments unambiguously lead to increases in expenditures on the targeted category. In some cases, such as the corporate income tax revenue earmarked for education, our results suggest that the associated decrease in general fund spending overcompensates, and the earmark has a negative effect on spending in the targeted category. Furthermore, when we compare the effects of earmarked and nonearmarked revenue from the same sources, we find very little statistical evidence that an earmark is any more effective at increasing spending.

In nearly every case where an earmark failed to stick (either partially or at all) to its targeted expenditure, however, nontargeted spending increased, suggesting that earmarks make for an effective means of indirectly increasing general fund revenue. General sales tax revenue and corporate income tax revenue earmarked for education spending; tobacco tax revenue, personal income tax revenue, and corporate income tax revenue earmarked for local governments; and vehicle registration revenue earmarked for highway spending all lead to increases in nontargeted expenditures in at least one of the specifications considered here. Furthermore, in seven of the fifteen cases analyzed, earmarks led to increases in total government expenditure. These results lend credence to the hypothesis presented above; they provide evidence that the fungible nature of earmarks is used to increase general fund revenue and the overall size of government and not solely to increase spending in the targeted expenditure category. At the very least, the results call into question the effectiveness of using earmarked revenue to meaningfully influence the composition of spending.

CONCLUSION

The practice of earmarking tax revenues for specific expenditure categories remains popular with state governments, despite its lack of firm theoretical justification and empirical evidence showing that only cents on the dollar actually stick to intended expenditures. In this chapter, we propose that Leviathan governments are aware of earmarked revenues' fungibility and they exploit it to increase total government size.

Our empirical analysis provides two main results: (1) most earmarks are ineffective at increasing spending on their targeted expenditure category, and (2) most earmarks that fail to stick are in fact very effective at increasing overall government size and spending on other categories unrelated to their intended target. These results are consistent with a theory of Leviathan government and imply that policymakers use tax revenues dedicated to politically popular programs (e.g., education) or prominent public goods (e.g., roads) to increase overall government size.

The policy implications of this research are straightforward. As our hypothesis suggests, the practice of earmarking can be used to increase the total size of government without the implementation of unpopular general tax rate increases. Our findings show that with some exceptions, the revenue raised from earmarks primarily does not go to its intended expenditure category, but rather it is used as fungible revenue to be spent at the government's discretion. From a voter's perspective, these increases in total expenditures may be inefficient, and therefore the elimination of earmarking—at the very least in those cases where it cannot be shown to benefit its intended target— would likely be in the public interest. While it may seem counterintuitive to give more discretion to policymakers, the research presented here shows that dedicating tax revenues already gives them that discretion but does so covertly. If policymakers choose to raise taxes to increase the overall size of government, it must be done as transparently as possible so that voters can respond as necessary.

NOTES

1.   This does not include the state of New Jersey. These data are from a National Conference of State Legislatures survey, to which New Jersey did not respond. See Pérez (2008). In 1993, New Jersey earmarked 37.6 percent of its gasoline tax revenue to spending on roads.

2.   A discussion of possible explanations for this downward trend in the amount of revenue earmarked on average across states—especially given our findings in this chapter—remains an area ripe for future research.

3.   Doug Walker (chap. 17, this volume) provides additional discussion of the tax treatment of gambling and of lotteries in particular.

4. Justin Ross (chap. 2, this volume) discusses several tax principles, including benefits-received taxation.

5. While the gas tax does not perfectly match costs and benefits, one of its primary justifications is its simplicity. The administrative costs associated with the implementation of a perfectly monitored and executed toll system could easily exceed the welfare gain.

6. See Pérez (2008). The median state (at 95.9 percent) in 2005 was North Dakota.

7. Buchanan (1963) refers to this circumstance as "full equilibrium," where the proposed general fund composition of spending matches the mix that would be preferred by a median voter if he or she were able to vote on spending programs separately.

8. Technically, the size of this expected increase in government can be thought of as the average citizen-voter's marginal propensity to consume government, which reflects the percentage of an additional dollar in income that would be used to purchase additional government goods and services.

9. Educational attainment may be endogenous especially to the specifications including spending on education. Dropping the educational attainment control did not meaningfully affect the results.

10. New Jersey did not provide data for 2005, so our panel is made up of 146 observations.

11. Specifically, states in our sample on average collected roughly $19 per capita (real 2005 dollars) in alcoholic beverage tax revenue, compared to more than $600 per capita in general sales tax revenue.

12. The F-test statistic is 10.28, associated with a p-value of 0.00.

13. Specifically, the F-test statistic is 10.44 (p-value of 0.00).

14. The only statistically significant difference observed was for corporate income tax revenue, where nonearmarked revenue had a larger effect on spending than did earmarked revenue. In all other tests, we were unable to reject the null hypothesis that the coefficients on each earmarked and nonearmarked revenue source were equivalent.

REFERENCES

Bailey, Stephen J., and Stephen Connolly. 1998. "The Flypaper Effect: Identifying Areas for Further Research." *Public Choice* 95 (3/4): 335–61.

Brennan, Geoffrey, and James M. Buchanan. 1977. "Towards a Tax Constitution for Leviathan." *Journal of Public Economics* 8: 255–74.

———. 1978. "Tax Instruments as Constraints on the Disposition of Public Revenues." *Journal of Public Economics* 9: 301–18.

———. 1980. *The Power to Tax: Analytical Foundations of a Fiscal Constitution.* Cambridge: Cambridge University Press.

Buchanan, James M. 1963. "The Economics of Earmarked Taxes." *Journal of Political Economy* 71 (5): 457–569.

Deller, Steven C., and Craig Maher. 2009. "Is the Treatment of Intergovernmental Aid Symmetric?" *Applied Economics Letters* 16: 331–35.

Dye, Richard F., and Therese J. McGuire. 1992. "The Effect of Earmarked Revenues on the Level and Composition of Expenditures." *Public Finance Quarterly* 20 (4): 543–56.

Erekson, O. Homer, Kimberly M. Deshano, Glenn Platt, and Andrea L. Ziegert. 2002. "Fungibility of Lottery Revenues and Support of Public Education." *Journal of Education Finance* 28: 301–12.

Evans, William, and Ping Zhang. 2003. "The Impact of Earmarked Lottery Revenue on State Educational Expenditures." University of Maryland mimeo, July.

Fabricius, Martha A., and Ronald K. Snell. 1990. *Earmarking State Taxes*, 2nd ed. Washington, DC: National Conference of State Legislatures.

Gamkhar, S. 2000. "Is the Response of State and Local Highway Spending Symmetric to Increases and Decreases in Federal Highway Grants?" *Public Finance Review* 28: 3–25.

Gamkhar, S., and W. Oates. 1996. "Asymmetries in the Response to Increases and Decreases in Intergovernmental Grants: Some Empirical Findings." *National Tax Journal* 49: 501–12.

Garrett, Thomas A. 2001. "Earmarked Lottery Revenues for Education: A New Test of Fungibility." *Journal of Education Finance* 26: 219–38.

Goel, R. K., and M. A. Nelson. 2003. "Use or Abuse of Highway Tax Revenues? An Economic Analysis of Highway Spending." *Applied Economics Letters* 10: 813–19.

Goodspeed, T. J. 1998. "The Relationship between State Income Taxes and Local Property Taxes: Education Finance in New Jersey." *National Tax Journal* 51: 219–38.

Gramlich, Edward M. 1977. "Intergovernmental Grants: A Review of the Empirical Literature." In *The Political Economy of Fiscal Federalism*, edited by Wallace E. Oates, 219–40. Lexington, MA: D.C. Heath.

Gramlich, Edward M., and Harvey Galper. 1973. "State and Local Fiscal Behavior and Federal Grant Policy." *Brookings Papers on Fiscal Activity* 1: 15–58.

Heyndels, B. 2001. "Asymmetries in the Flypaper Effect: Empirical Evidence for the Flemish Municipalities." *Applied Economics* 33: 1329–34.

Hines, James R., Jr., and Richard H. Thaler. 1995. "Anomalies: The Flypaper Effect." *Journal of Economic Perspectives* 9 (4): 217–26.

Inman, Robert P. 1971. "Toward an Econometric Model of Local Budgeting." In *Proceedings of the 64th Annual Conference on Taxation*, 699–719. Lexington, KY: National Tax Association.

———. 2008. "The Flypaper Effect." NBER Working Paper 14579, National Bureau of Economic Research, Cambridge, MA.

Levaggi, R., and R. Zanola. 2003. "Flypaper Effect and Sluggishness: Evidence from Regional Health Expenditures in Italy." *International Tax and Public Finance* 10: 535–47.

Nesbit, Todd M., and Steven F. Kreft. 2009. "Federal Grants, Earmarked Revenues, and Budget Crowd-Out: State Highway Funding." *Public Budgeting and Finance* 29 (2): 94–110.

Novarro, Neva Kerbeshian. 2002. "Does Earmarking Matter? The Case of State Lottery Profits and Educational Spending." Discussion Paper 02-19. Stanford Institute for Economic Policy Research, Stanford, CA.

Pantuosco, Louis, William Seyfried, and Robert Stonebraker. 2007. "The Impact of Lotteries on State Education: Does Earmarking Matter?" *Review of Regional Studies* 37 (2): 169–85.

Pérez, Arturo. 2008. *Earmarking State Taxes*, 4th ed. Washington, DC: National Conference of State Legislatures.

Pérez, Arturo, and Ronald Snell. 1995. *Earmarking State Taxes*, 3rd ed. Washington, DC: National Conference of State Legislatures.

Sobel, Russell S., and George R. Crowley. 2014. "Do Intergovernmental Grants Create Ratchets in State and Local Taxes?" *Public Choice* 158 (1): 167–87.

Stratmann, Thomas, and William Bruntrager. 2011. "Excise Taxes in the States." Working Paper 11–27. Mercatus Center at George Mason University, Arlington, VA.

Volden, C. 1999. "Asymmetric Effects of Intergovernmental Grants: Analysis and Implications for U.S. Welfare Policy." *Publius* 29 (3): 51–73.

CHAPTER 7
Excise Taxation and Product Quality Substitution

TODD NESBIT
Department of Economics, Ball Sate University

Commodity taxes come in two forms: per unit and ad valorem. Per unit taxes are taxes imposed as a fixed amount per unit of a good sold or purchased. For example, the current federal gasoline tax is levied at 18.4¢ per gallon of gasoline purchased. Ad valorem taxes, such as the general sales tax and the tax on distilled spirits in many states, are taxes levied as a percentage of the value of the commodity. The choice between the two forms of taxation may be influenced by convenience, collection and enforcement costs, and the incentives introduced for market participants to change their behavior. It is this latter relationship—how the behavioral responses differ in response to the two types of commodity taxes—that is the topic of this chapter.

Commodity taxes lead to behavioral responses on many margins. For instance, consumers may, in response to a new or increased tax, choose to purchase less of the taxed good or adjust the timing (Drenkard and Henchman 2016) and location (Kaplan 2017) of purchase. While both ad valorem and per unit taxes can induce these behavioral responses, only per unit taxes are theorized to potentially lead to a shift in purchases across product quality grades. Specifically, per unit taxes are argued to cause consumers to purchase less of a particular good (quantity substitution) and to cause a subset of other consumers choosing to continue consuming the good to purchase higher quality versions of the good (quality substitution). This quality substitution can be explained by two theorems. The Alchian-Allen theorem suggests quality substitution results from a reduction in the relative price of higher quality versions of the good. The Barzel theorem suggests that the quality substitution is due to quality going untaxed under per unit taxation, so that consumers substitute from the taxed attribute—quantity—and toward the untaxed attribute—quality. These two theorems will be explored further in the second section of this chapter.

Quality substitution is important for two primary policy reasons. First, the quality substitution response to taxes designed to reduce consumption of addictive and habit-forming substances can at least partially offset the direct benefits of a reduction in consumption. For instance, consumers may choose to imbibe fewer alcoholic drinks in light of an increased per unit tax on alcohol; however, the alcohol content of each drink consumed could rise, possibly to the point where the resulting health problems linked to alcohol consumption are worsened. Given the addictive and habit-forming nature of many so-called sin goods (i.e., cigarettes, alcohol, and gambling), quality substitution is an important aspect to consider when evaluating the appropriateness and effectiveness of sin taxes in encouraging desirable outcomes. Second, the effects of quality substitution on firm revenues may invite further rent-seeking, particularly in sin good industries, in which the expectation is generally that taxes will be imposed or increased.

This chapter proceeds as follows. The two relevant theorems—the Barzel theorem and the Alchian-Allen theorem—are explained in the next section before discussing the empirical evidence supporting these theorems in light of various fixed charges, including the per unit tax. I conclude with a discussion of the policy implications, detailing the importance of understanding and considering quality substitution when developing tax policy.

WHY QUALITY SUBSTITUTION OCCURS

An individual adjusts her behavior in response to changes in prices and other factors in an effort to maximize her individual utility. Standard tax theory, as it is typically covered in a classroom setting, focuses on the individual's substitution away from the taxed good and toward greater consumption of untaxed alternative goods. However, the quantity of a good that is consumed is not the only margin on which consumers can adjust. Barzel (1976) acknowledges that quantity is just one attribute of consumption. The quality—taste, texture, durability, among many other characteristics—of a good consumed represents another primary attribute of consumption. Instead of only considering which goods are taxed, Barzel shifted the discussion to which attributes of taxed goods are taxed, specifically considering whether quality attributes are taxed in addition to the quantity attribute. He theorized that consumers substitute away from taxed attributes of a good and toward untaxed attributes.

Applying Barzel's logic to selective goods taxation, Barzel indicates that per unit taxes, which only tax the quantity attribute of a good, will cause a substitution away from the taxed attribute (quantity) and toward the untaxed attribute (quality). Consider a tax imposed on consumers of $10 per bottle of wine purchased and assume the full burden of the tax is on consumers. Regardless of the choice between a higher quality and lower quality wine, the consumer pays the same $10 tax. As a percentage of price, the per bottle tax is smaller for higher priced items. Consider a $40 bottle of higher quality wine and a lower quality $10 bottle of wine. The $10 per bottle tax represents a 100 percent tax for the lower quality wine, while it is only a 25 percent tax on the higher quality wine. So, while the $10 tax is likely to lead some consumers to reduce their consumption of wine (quantity substitution), there will be others who continue to purchase wine, and some of those individuals will choose to substitute higher quality wine (quality substitution) due to a lower effective tax rate on the higher quality wine.

In contrast, ad valorem taxes tax both attributes of the good and therefore cause no substitution between quantity and quality. This is because quality attributes of a good are capitalized in the price of the good. The absolute tax paid on a 100 percent ad valorem tax will be a larger sum if a consumer purchases a higher quality $40 bottle of wine than if she purchases a lower quality $10 bottle. Maintaining the assumption of full tax shifting to the consumer, the absolute tax paid on the high-quality wine is four times as much as that paid on the lower quality wine ($40 relative to $10). Thus, under the ad valorem tax, the absolute tax paid adjusts in accordance with quality such that the tax paid as a percentage of the price remains constant across all quality grades. As such, the only behavioral response expected is a reduction in consumption of wine generally (i.e., quantity substitution).

An alternative explanation of the incentives leading to quality substitution can be drawn from Armen Alchian and William Allen (1964, 74–75) in their classic and influential textbook. Alchian and Allen explain that the imposition of a "fixed charge" causes the price of the higher quality version of a good to fall relative to the lower quality version. A fixed charge can be described as any type of cost that is the same regardless of the choice of the quality version of the good.

These two theorems—the Barzel and the Alchian-Allen theorems—can be viewed as special applications of the First Law of Demand. Most textbook discussions of tax-induced quantity substitution consider only the substitution from the taxed commodity and toward untaxed alternatives, ignoring quality variation altogether. However, Barzel and Alchian and Allen suggest the proper market definition is not (in this case) wine generally but is, for example, lower quality wine. The full range of substitutes for lower quality wine necessarily includes higher quality wine in addition to the traditionally included list of alternatives of distilled spirits, beer, soda, and so forth. Consumers naturally economize, seeking out options that provide the highest value per dollar spent on a commodity. In other words, consumers modify their purchases in an attempt to maximize the ratio of product value to after-tax price.

For some, the per unit tax will lead consumers to purchase less lower quality wine and more higher quality wine, as explained by both Barzel and Alchian and Allen; other consumers may instead purchase less higher quality wine and more lower quality wine, the opposite of the result theorized above. What will ultimately determine the direction of this quality substitution for a given consumer is the relative dominance of the income and substitution effects. The substitution effect is the result of changes in the relative price of alternative goods; this is consistent with the Alchian-Allen theorem. Per unit taxes reduce the relative price of higher quality versions of the good, leading consumers to substitute toward higher quality. However, the income effect will generally work in the opposite direction. The increased tax reduces the consumer's real income—because of higher after-tax prices, she can no long purchase the same consumption bundle on a fixed income—leading consumers to substitute lower priced (lower quality) options. A priori, we cannot theoretically predict whether the substitution effect or the income effect will dominate, making this question empirical. In cases where the substitution effect is larger in magnitude than the income effect, we will observe outcomes consistent with the predictions of the Barzel and Alchian-Allen theorems.

Some common applications of the theorems include shipping costs, travel costs, payment of a babysitter, and, of importance for this chapter, per unit taxation (additional examples are detailed in the next section). Parents who must pay for a babysitter to enjoy a date night are (1) likely to consume fewer date nights (First Law of Demand) and (2) more likely to go to a fancier restaurant and the opera or play rather than to a sit-down chain restaurant and a movie. The latter holds only if the substitution effect dominates the income effect, an observation that is less likely to occur for less wealthy households. When shipping costs are incurred, consumers in distant markets are likely to prefer higher quality versions of the good more than do consumers who are more local. Bertonazzi et al. (1993) explain that the implications of the theorem do not depend on whether the goods travel to the consumer or the consumer travels to the goods; travel costs are expected to produce similar results as shipping charges. One must be careful when attempting to apply the theorem to travel costs. The logic applies only to a scenario in which the location of travel has been determined (e.g., a vacation to Charleston, SC) and the cost of travel varies, such as when a household observes airfares and begins to plan their vacation activities only to find out that airfares have increased by the time they begin booking the vacation. Some households may respond by canceling vacation plans or opting for a lower travel cost destination. Others, according to the Barzel and Alchian-Allen theorems, short of strong income effects, are expected to change some of the vacation plans in favor of an even higher quality experience. The theorem specifically does not apply to quality of vacation when comparing airfares across two destinations.

For the sake of discussion of the theorems' application to taxation, consider the 100 percent ad valorem and $10 per unit taxes on wine discussed above. Given the initial prices ($40 and $10), the higher quality wine is four times as expensive as the lower quality wine, as depicted in panel (a) of figure 1; an individual could purchase four bottles of low-quality wine for the same price as the high-quality wine. With the imposition of a $10 per bottle tax, the prices increase to $50 and $20, respectively, for a ratio of 2.5 to 1; see figure 1, panel (b). An individual can now only purchase 2.5 bottles of the low-quality wine for the same price of the high-quality wine. While the absolute difference in price has remained constant at $30, the relative price of high-quality wine has been reduced, and consumers are expected to substitute accordingly by purchasing less wine and, for those who continue to purchase wine, higher quality wine.

Now consider the 100 percent ad valorem tax on wine. After the tax—still assuming the full burden is shifted to consumers—the price of high-quality wine is $80 and the price of low-quality wine is $20; see figure 1, panel (c). High-quality wine is still four times more expensive than low-quality wine; an individual can still purchase four bottles of low-quality wine for the same price as one bottle of high-quality wine. Provided that price- and income-elasticity are roughly equal across the two quality grades, we should not observe any sizable shift in consumption across quality grades. Consumers purchase less of each quality grade of wine in roughly equal proportions.

Figure 1. Hypothetical Taxation of Wine

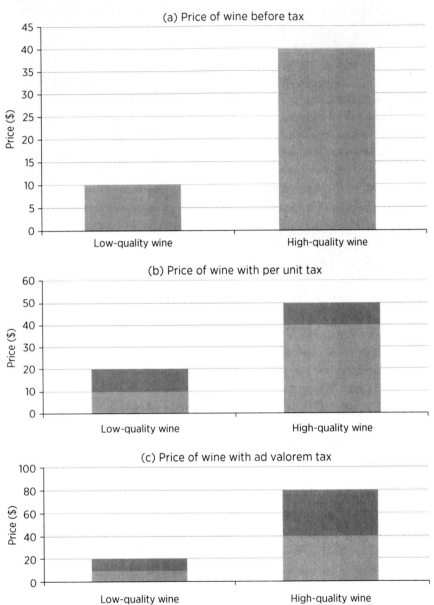

Note: Lighter shading indicates base price; darker shading indicates amount of tax.

Given the breadth of empirical validations of the theorem, some researchers, such as Bertonazzi et al. (1993), have elevated the status of the Alchian-Allen theorem to the Third Law of Demand. However, others claim that the theorem is much more limited in its application, largely due to ignored income effects. John Umbeck (1980), while admitting that Alchian and Allen were generally correct regarding the effect of shipping charges, argues that the theorem is little more than an interesting application of the First Law of Demand under strict restrictions regarding the nature of the fixed charge. According to Umbeck (1980), the theorem only applies when the common fixed charge does not reflect a change in the good itself. For instance, an increase in the airfare for a given seat on the flight to a vacation destination does not directly change the value characteristics of any possible vacation activities. However, paying a higher airfare to be upgraded to first class on the flight does change the value characteristics of the flight, which is part of the vacation experience. Along these lines, Umbeck states that Thomas Borcherding's and Eugene Silberberg's (1978) explanation of the service charge at a restaurant as a relevant fixed charge is misplaced, because it reflects a difference in the good being purchased: in addition to the physical meal, diners also consume the ambiance, friendly service, food preparation, and clean-up service on the completion of the meal. As such, the experience of dining at a restaurant is not equivalent to dining at home. Therefore, the Alchian-Allen theorem is not applicable in explaining the difference in the quality of meat consumed at home versus that consumed at a restaurant. Umbeck's (1980) argument is similar to that of Tyler Cowen and Alexander Tabarrok (1995), who conclude that the theorem is not supported when a third good is bundled with two similar goods of different quality. However, Umbeck (1980) argues that shipping offers no inherent value to the consumer, does nothing to change the good itself, and thus is a suitable application for the theorem. Likewise, Umbeck (1980) explicitly states that per unit taxes present an ideal application for the Alchian-Allen theorem.

Anderson and Kjar (2008), analyzing the issue of travel costs and product quality choices, present a criticism of Bertonazzi et al. (1993) and an alternative explanation for the Alchian-Allen theorem. They first acknowledge that, regardless of distance, some individuals do not value the good enough to incur any costs of travel or shipping and therefore will not purchase the good, and travel costs will only be imposed on consumers who decide to purchase the good. Thus, each consumer, before purchasing the good, first decides whether the benefit of the good available at a greater distance is worth the additional travel cost over options available to them locally. This decision can ultimately lead to a selection bias. The local consumers will consist of a greater percentage of less wealthy and lower-demand individuals than will the long-distance consumers: only those who are wealthy enough and who highly value the good will be willing to incur the large travel cost. Given these self-selection issues, it is likely that those consumers with larger travel costs will opt to purchase higher quality versions of the good for reasons unrelated to relative prices. At a minimum, Anderson's and Kjar's (2008) criticisms suggest that economists conducting empirical tests of the Alchian-Allen theorem must specifically control for income and latent demand for the good generally. Some of these empirical issues may be lessened when, say, examining the consumption differences of individuals who travel similar distances but face dissimilar travel costs.

The final limitation discussed here regarding the appropriate application of the Alchian-Allen theorem is offered by Laura Razzolini, William Shughart, and Robert Tollison (2003). The authors admit that the Alchian-Allen theorem is rich in empirical implications. However, when "placed in the context of a market model, its range of applications is narrower than has been acknowledged in the literature heretofore" (Razzolini et al. 2003, 292). Razzolini et al. (2003) present a theoretical model indicating that the theorem's conclusions are correct only under the assumptions of perfect competition and a constant cost industry. Under alternative market assumptions, it is possible that relative prices (and therefore the choice of quality versions) will be unchanged or for the price of the lower quality version of the good to become relatively cheaper. Indeed, as noted by the authors, outlet malls offer a counterexample to the conclusions of the Alchian-Allen theorem. Customers of outlet malls drive nonnegligible distances—a fixed cost of shopping—to buy lower quality (out-of-season, blemished, etc.), lower priced items.

The above criticisms and limitations should not be viewed as arguments that the logic of the Alchian-Allen theorem is wrong. Rather, at worst, the theorem should be viewed as a special case rather than a law of demand. Given these concerns, the occurrence of quality substitution in response to various fixed charges largely becomes an empirical question. I address the empirical evidence in the next section, starting first with broader applications that are relevant only to the Alchian-Allen theorem. I then discuss the empirical findings regarding per unit excise taxes as tests of both the Alchian-Allen and the Barzel theorems.

EMPIRICAL EVIDENCE

Many intriguing empirical confirmations and theoretical proofs have been presented to support the implications of the Alchian-Allen theorem in various markets. For space considerations, I choose not to provide detailed discussions of any of the theoretical proofs, opting instead to focus attention on select empirical studies. Some of those applications not discussed here include wages and the leisure-childcare tradeoff (Minagawa and Upmann 2013), the use of the contraceptive pill and the preference between masculine or sensitive men in sexual activity (Cuellar 2005), labor market opportunity costs and the choice of college (Caudill et al. 2008), and college tuition and the number of registered credits per semester (Caudill et al. 2008). Their exclusion is purely for space considerations and in no way is a reflection of the quality of the work or importance of its implications.

Nontax Applications

While the primary interest of this chapter in the Alchian-Allen theorem is with regard to its application to excise taxation, I do want to briefly highlight some nontax applications as an indication of the large number of areas to which the theory can be applied. The discussion in this section of the chapter is not an exhaustive coverage of the literature concerning the Alchian-Allen theorem.

Sports offers numerous cases to which the Alchian-Allen theorem can be applied. Bertonazzi et al. (1993) examine the choice of seat at Clemson University football games based on variation in travel distance to attend the game. The authors do, indeed, find that fans who travel the farthest tend to purchase the highest quality seats, as measured by seats purchased across the six seat-quality categories established by the university. Matthew Brown et al. (2007) use a survey of Ohio golf course patrons to test whether golf tourists treat travel costs as a sunk cost or as a bundled cost in planning their golf outings. Their results indicate a strong correlation between distance traveled and expenditures on greens fees, suggesting that tourists treat travel costs as a bundled expense and offering support for the Alchian-Allen theorem. Steven Cobb and Douglas Olberding (2010) conduct a similar test of sports tourists in Ohio who participated in the 2008 Flying Pig half and full marathons. They show that runners who spend more time traveling to Cincinnati enjoyed a higher quality visit, as measured by discretionary expenditures.

The Alchian-Allen theorem also exhibits strong explanatory power in underground markets. For those engaging in the consumption of illegal goods, the threat of detection and arrest by police can be viewed as a unit charge for consuming such goods. This is particularly true of marijuana, where weight and packaging of the product in possession of the accused influences the extent of legal action, and tetrahydrocannabinol (THC) levels specifically play no role in the enforcement of the law. In most cases, the THC levels of confiscated marijuana—the measure of its potency (i.e., quality)—is never tested. In a coauthored paper, Robert Lawson and I examine whether the Alchian-Allen theorem helps explain the observed average marijuana price differences across the states (Lawson and Nesbit 2013). Employing user-reported data on the website PriceOfWeed.com, we determined that the price of user-identified high-quality marijuana is higher in states with a higher perceived level of law enforcement. However, the price of user-identified low-quality marijuana is lower in these states. These findings suggest that consumers in states with greater perceived law enforcement are switching from lower quality to higher quality marijuana, consistent with the Alchian-Allen theorem.

Along these lines, the Alchian-Allen theorem may be useful in explaining the consumption trends of prohibited goods, such as alcohol during the Prohibition era and many narcotics today. Mark Thornton (1991) explains the fixed charge nature of prohibitions as follows:

> Prohibition establishes a gambling environment rather than an explicit tax. Participants who are actually caught face huge losses from lost revenue, fines, confiscations, and jail terms. Those not caught reap large monetary profits. All market participants, however, incur large costs of risk bearing. The tax is evaluated as a function of the penalties and the likelihood of capture and conviction. (Thornton 1991, 96)

Given imperfect enforcement of Prohibition, concealment becomes desirable. To better conceal the product from authorities, the potency is generally increased, allowing for smaller packages. As such, there are multiple margins of quality—taste, quality of the "high," and concealment, among others—in these examples that could confound an analysis. Despite these potential confounding issues, it is a reasonable hypothesis to expect the quality substitution to take the form of a shift from kegs of beer to quart jars of moonshine or other distilled spirits. Based on estimates by Clark Warburton (1932), the price ratio of spirits to beer in the absence of Prohibition would have been 15.42 to 1; the actual estimated ratio in 1929–1930 was 11.78 to 1. Irving Fisher (1927) produced an alcohol price index indicating that the price of beer rose by approximately 700 percent during Prohibition, while the price of rye whiskey increased by only 312 percent. It should be noted that it is not clear what share of these price effects are due to supply-side adjustments to risk and what is due to demand-side quality substitution. With that said, Warburton (1932, 170) estimates changes in alcohol expenditures that are at least consistent with the Alchian-Allen theorem: "Prohibition has raised the amount spent for spirits to three and a half billion dollars, and reduced that for beer to less than a billion dollars."

Finally, as a transition back to a discussion of excise taxation, I explore the empirical literature applying the Barzel and Alchian-Allen theorems to the shipping industry, specifically with regard to transportation costs, import quotas, and tariffs. Yoram Barzel and Christopher Hall (1977, 65–71) present evidence of quality substitution in response to import quotas on crude oil. David Hummels and Alexandre Skiba (2004) hypothesize that shipping costs lead firms to ship high-quality goods abroad while leaving lower quality goods for consumption domestically, extending the "shipping the good apples out" argument to a broad case. Using detailed shipping data for every three-digit commodity classification covered in the Harmonized System, they find strong evidence in support of their hypothesis. Specifically, the authors estimate that a doubling of freight costs increases average free on board prices (exclusive of shipping prices) by 80–141 percent, suggesting in most cases a substitution to higher value commodities.

Additionally, Hummels and Skiba (2004) examine the potential for ad valorem tariffs to cause quality substitution. Ad valorem costs are generally argued to have no effect on quality substitution. However, Hummels and Skiba suggest that in the presence of a second cost in the form of a per unit cost (shipping charges), an increase in the ad valorem cost dampens the effect of the per unit cost. As such, they argue, the ad valorem tariff is expected to reduce average product quality as measured by free on board prices. Their results are consistent with their logic. They find that a doubling of ad valorem tariffs reduces average free on board prices by 146–256 percent. Their argument that ad valorem charges work to dampen the Alchian-Allen quality substitution is also supported by the results of Pramesti Resiandini (2012), who investigates Japanese and Korean automobile exports. Resiandini finds that insurance and other charges, which are ad valorem in nature, tend to reduce or eliminate the Alchian-Allen effect expected from per unit freight charges.

Excise Tax Applications

Barzel (1976) originally tested his hypothesis in three markets: cigarettes, gasoline, and alcohol. His empirical results were only weakly supportive of his theory, as only the cigarette market generated statistically significant results.

Terry Johnson (1978) and Michael Sumner and Robert Ward (1981) made improvements to Barzel's (1976) model to better account for ad valorem taxes, adding state fixed effects and adjusting for backlogged inflation, but both still rely on tests concerning the change in price. Johnson's (1978) results offer support of the expected quality substitution, while Sumner and Ward (1981) found no evidence of such substitution. Although the findings of these three studies offer, at best, mixed evidence in favor of Barzel's theorem, when interpreted in the context of a modeling bias, the results may be more supportive than they initially seem.

Each of the three papers discussed above suffered from data limitations that prevented their authors from conducting a direct test of the theory. Without data on market shares, the researchers relied on a test involving whether the average price increased by more than the tax. They interpret a price change exceeding the tax as an indication that consumers bought a higher percentage of higher quality and higher priced versions of the good. This method, which assumes the full burden of the tax falls on consumers, biases the results against finding supportive evidence of the theory. Consider a scenario with a $1 unit tax where only $0.80 of the tax burden falls on consumers. In such a scenario, had the researcher found evidence that the price increased by $0.95, he would have concluded that there is insufficient evidence to support quality substitution, since the price did not increase by more than $1. This conclusion would be mistaken, as the proper test is whether the price increased by more than $0.80, the share of the tax shifted to consumers: in this example, the price did indeed increase by more than the consumers' share of the tax burden. Each of these studies also are based on a pure cross-section of state-level data such that the results rely on the quality of cigarettes differing from state to state, something that even Barzel (1976) mentions as a potential limitation.

Russell Sobel and Thomas Garrett (1997) avoid the modeling issues faced by Barzel (1976) and others by using data on the quantities of premium and generic brand cigarettes sold—data not previously available. Generic brand cigarettes were introduced and began to acquire a sizable market share in 1982. Sobel and Garrett (1997) explain that generic cigarettes are of a lower quality relative to premium brands on several margins: taste, quality of tobacco, and freshness, to name a few. As Sobel and Garrett (1997) suggest, the timing of the arrival of generic cigarettes to the market offers support for Barzel's theorem. The authors explain that the theory indicates that the introduction of generic cigarettes should coincide with a period of low unit taxes preceded by a period of relatively high per unit taxes that initially supported high-quality versions of the good. At the time of their writing (1997), Sobel and Garrett explain that 1972 represented the highest historical real value of cigarette taxation, and the taxes of 1982 represented the lowest historical real cigarette taxation after the high inflation rates of the 1970s eroded the real value of unit taxation. Thus, it appears that the theorem may apply symmetrically. That is, the imposition of a fixed charge (e.g., a unit tax) leads to a substitution toward higher quality, while the removal or reduction of a fixed charge provides incentives to substitute toward lower quality. I discuss this symmetry in greater detail below.

Given the modern availability of market share data, Sobel and Garrett (1997) are able to test the Barzel and Alchian-Allen theorems directly for the period 1990–1994. Specifically, they look for systematic changes in the market share of premium-brand cigarettes that can be explained by variation in state tax rates. Their results indicate that for every 3¢ increase in a state's per pack cigarette tax, the market share of premium-brand cigarettes increases by one percentage point. Given the average per pack cigarette tax ($0.54) in their sample, their results imply that the market share of premium-brand cigarettes was, on average, 17 percentage points larger than it otherwise would have been, solely due to the taxation of cigarettes. Sobel and Garrett (1997) also test for the impact of ad valorem taxes. While no state imposed an ad valorem excise tax on cigarettes—New Hampshire switched to the per unit tax prior to the introduction of generic cigarettes in 1982—forty-four states applied the state sales tax to cigarettes, and a handful of those states also applied the sales tax to the excise tax on cigarettes. Ultimately, sales taxes were found to have a negative but statistically insignificant impact on the market share of premium cigarettes. The direction of this estimated relationship may be consistent with the Hummels and Skiba (2004) argument that ad valorem costs work to dampen the effects of per unit charges, leading to a potential reduction in average quality. Ultimately, as Hummels and Skiba (2004) argue, the magnitude of this effect will depend on the size of the ad valorem charge relative to the per unit charge. In this case, the ad valorem taxes are not very large relative to the per unit taxes, suggesting that the quality substitution effect attributed to the sales tax may be statistically weak.

In a more recent study of the Barzel theorem in the cigarette industry, Javier Espinosa and William Evans (2013) employ high-frequency price and quantity data available from supermarket scanners in 812 stores across twenty-nine states during 2001–2006. Their sample includes thirty-two state tax increases and one tax reduction. They present three interesting and relevant results. First, they find a pass-through rate of roughly 100 percent for both premium-brand

and generic cigarettes; that is, for every $1.00 tax increase, retail prices increase by $0.99. The estimated pass-through rate is nearly identical to that found by Lesley Chiou and Erich Muehlegger (2010), who also use scanner data. Thus, it appears that consumers bear the full burden of the excise tax on cigarettes. This finding at least suggests that any bias in the empirical models of Barzel (1976), Johnson (1978), and Sumner and Ward (1981) is minimal.

Espinosa and Evans (2013) also test the Barzel theorem, allowing for the substitution in quality to be revealed in two fashions. The first test is the standard substitution across brands, similar to that of Sobel and Garrett (1997). They find no tax-induced shift toward premium-brand cigarettes, despite a reduction in the relative price of such brands. The authors thus conclude that there is no flight to higher quality in response to per pack cigarette taxes, as is suggested by the Barzel theorem. While this result differs substantially from that of Sobel and Garrett (1997), the authors note that circumstances are substantially different in the two time periods examined. Specifically, Espinosa and Evans note the greater industry concentration, substantially higher taxes, and increased restrictions on advertising during the period studied relative to the 1990–1994 sample of Sobel and Garrett (1997).

Espinosa and Evans do offer support for the Barzel theorem when accounting for convenience as a measure of quality. Specifically, they hypothesize that if "the convenience of purchasing single packs (e.g., easier to store, more convenient to carry around) is an untaxed quality dimension, we should see a shift to single pack purchases" (Espinosa and Evans 2013, 149). This is, in fact, what the authors observe. A $1.00 increase in the per pack cigarette tax rate is shown to reduce the carton market share by about 6.2 percentage points, a nearly 14 percent reduction from the mean market share.

This shift toward individual packs of cigarettes may also lead to shifts in the location of purchase, as consumers will visit stores more frequently to purchase cigarettes, albeit buying a smaller quantity each trip. It may be a reasonable assumption, then, that these consumers will attempt to minimize the inconvenience of such purchases and favor convenience stores/gas stations over grocery stores and supermarkets. As such, the earlier discussion of consumers shifting their preference of location for purchases may be an outcome that is at least partially explained by the Barzel and Alchian-Allen theorems. For instance, according to industry interviews summarized by Bloomberg writer Jennifer Kaplan (2017), the tax of 1.5¢ per ounce of sugary drink tax imposed in January 2017 in Philadelphia is "hurting grocery stores and bodegas in poor neighborhoods, where shoppers tend to buy in bulk, more than [it hurts] convenience stores." After little more than a month into the new Philadelphia sugary drink tax, retailers are also observing a shift toward smaller, single-serve containers of soda.

I earlier mentioned the possible symmetric nature of the Alchian-Allen theorem. Critics of the theorem often attempt to use narratives involving the removal of or reduction in fixed charges to suggest the nonuniversal nature of the Alchian-Allen theorem. For instance, in their critique of Bertonazzi et al. (1993), Anderson and Kjar state:

> If a fan living a long distance away were able to find a less expensive . . . mode of travel to the games, then he or she would be more likely to stay in a Motel 6 or a KOA camp-ground instead of the usual luxury accommodations. Although this seems to be a ridiculous example, nevertheless, if the theory were to hold one way (adding a fixed cost drives consumers to the higher-quality good), then it also would have to hold in the other direction (subtracting a fixed cost drives consumers to the lower-quality good). (Anderson and Kjar 2008, 655–56)

Although the authors use an unrealistic and extreme substitution—luxury hotels to KOA campgrounds—to make their point (substitutions occur at the margin, not in the extremes), their message is correct. If the Alchian-Allen theorem is to be considered a law of demand, it must hold in both directions.

Philip DeCicca, Donald Kenkel, and Feng Liu (2015) provide such a test of the Alchian-Allen theorem in the reverse direction. New York State excise taxes historically need not be collected on sales of cigarettes on Indian reservations. Although taxes on sales to nontribal members are to be collected, this has been difficult to enforce, given that the state has relied on voluntary reporting by the tribes of such sales. The tax advantage to nontribal members traveling to tribal land to purchase cigarettes is thus substantial and effectively represents the removal of a unit tax.[1] DeCicca et al. (2015) find that nontribal members purchasing cigarettes on New York Indian Reservations are nearly 20 percentage points more likely to purchase low-quality cigarettes and are about 15 percentage points less likely to purchase high-quality, premium-brand cigarettes. Their results thus offer some empirical evidence that the Alchian-Allen theorem does, indeed, hold in the other direction: subtracting a fixed cost does appear to drive consumers to purchase more of the lower quality versions of a good. The remainder of my discussion returns to the

Alchian-Allen theorem in its original direction, the imposition or increase of a fixed charge leading to increased product quality.

Empirical tests of the Barzel and Alchian-Allen theorems extend beyond the cigarette industry. In a 2007 publication, I test for tax-induced quality substitution in the gasoline industry, measuring quality not by brand but by octane rating (Nesbit 2007). This particular test of the Alchian-Allen theorem is interesting, as the predictions of the theoretical literature have thus far not arrived at a consensus regarding the applicability of the theorem in a world of three or more quality grades of a good. John Gould and Joel Segall (1968) suggest that the introduction of a third quality option leads to conclusions that violate the Alchian-Allen theorem. In contrast, Borcherding and Silberberg (1978) show that the introduction of the third good will not violate the theorem as long as the other two goods are close substitutes. Liquin Liu (2011) presents a theoretical model generalizing the Alchian-Allen theorem to a commodity group with three quality-differentiable versions. My empirical analysis (Nesbit 2007), in which I conclude that per gallon gasoline taxes tend to lead to proportionately more consumption of premium-grade gasoline, proportionately less consumption of regular-grade gasoline, and no net effect on the consumption of mid-grade gasoline, ultimately appears to be more consistent with the theoretical modeling of Liu (2011). A 10¢ increase in the gasoline tax rate is shown to increase the market share of premium-grade gasoline by 1.6 percentage points (a 9.4 percent increase) and reduce the market share of regular-grade gasoline by roughly 1.6 percentage points (a 2.2 percent decrease).[2]

Using an empirical model similar to that of Sobel and Garrett (1997) and Nesbit (2007), Martin Ljunge (2011) finds that the market share of high-quality wine increases in response to unit taxes on wine, while ad valorem taxes have no significant effects. The sample covers 1995–2000 and is restricted to thirty-two US states plus the District of Columbia, because the remaining eighteen states are control states, where the sale of wine is directly controlled by the government such that it is difficult to separate a markup from any sort of effective tax. Per unit excise taxes on wine are levied on a per gallon basis and range from 10¢ to $2.46 with an average of 71¢ during the sample period. Ljunge (2011) finds that the effect of the average per gallon tax on wine is to increase the market share of high-quality, imported wine by 1.35 percentage points, an 8 percent increase from the mean market share. These results are qualitatively consistent with estimates by Christian Rojas and Tianji Shi (2011) of an increase in the sales of high-quality beer in response to higher transportation costs.

THE POLICY RELEVANCE OF TAX-INDUCED QUALITY SUBSTITUTION

The implications of the Barzel theorem and Alchian-Allen theorem must be understood and taken into account by policymakers to develop appropriate tax policy. In this chapter, I focus the discussion on two primary concerns: (1) the use of unit taxation as a nudge to reduce the consumption of addictive and habit-forming goods can backfire, and (2) an understanding of tax-induced quality substitution offers another margin on which firms engage in active and reactive rent-seeking. I discuss each concern and offer appropriate policy responses below.

Selective Taxation, Nudges, and Addictive and Habit-Forming Consumption

The use of excise taxes to discourage the consumption of socially undesirable, addictive, and habit-forming goods has been common throughout US history. Taxes on alcohol, cigarettes, gambling, and—before their prohibition—opium and cocaine all gained at least some public support, because the proponents promised that the tax would reduce the consumption of the respective good. Whether this support for reduced consumption has its origins in religious, moral, health, or other arguments is irrelevant to this discussion. If per unit taxes are employed in an attempt to reduce the consumption of such goods, we should observe consumers buy fewer units while also substituting toward higher quality versions of the good. In other words, we should observe consumers shift toward more potent versions of the good. According to Adam Gifford (1999), to determine whether such an outcome is desirable, we must also examine the biological and behavioral aspects of addiction and habit formation.

Gifford (1999) presents two biological mechanisms of addiction that ultimately will have policy consequences. First, he argues that addictive substances activate the motivational area of the brain, establishing cues that develop into a desirable complementary component of consuming the good. The complementary associations, say, between smoking and drinking can make it difficult to quit one without quitting the other (Gulliver et al. 1995). The sight of a needle can reinforce the effects of heroin such that seeing a needle stimulates the craving of the drug. Similarly, the sight of a particular person with whom an individual regularly consumed an addictive substance can stimulate a desire for the good.

Second, Gifford (1999) discusses how addictive goods tend to lead to set-point behavior: individuals will seek to maintain the set-point level of blood or brain concentrations of the active drug. The set point is established based on the blood or brain concentrations resulting from the initial consumption of the good and then is updated as longer term consumption patterns change. For example, in response to a mandate to reduce nicotine levels in each cigarette, the set-point response by an individual would be simply increase "the volume and depth of inhalations or the number of cigarettes smoked in a given period of time" (Gifford 1999, 304). Such a response ultimately increases the health dangers caused by tars and other harmful substances in cigarettes.

Both biological mechanisms, particularly when taken combined with the implications of the Barzel and Alchian-Allen theorems, can be problematic for designing excise taxes intended to reduce the prevalence of a particular addictive good. Premium-brand cigarettes generally are more flavorful, but it is the tars that give cigarettes their taste (Gifford 1999). When consumers respond to increased unit taxes on cigarettes by substituting premium brands, they expose themselves to greater concentrations of tars and other substances. The taste of the cigarettes can serve as the complementary good that ultimately reinforces the effects of nicotine. Furthermore, given that consumers are also purchasing fewer packs of cigarettes (First Law of Demand), it is quite possible that many consumers do increase the volume and depth of inhalations of the higher quality cigarettes, which already have increased tar content. William Evans and Matthew Farrelly (1998) find that, in response to per unit cigarette taxes, consumers do substitute toward cigarettes with greater concentrations of tar and nicotine. Furthermore, while adults consume fewer cigarettes, their nicotine and tar intake is unaffected. This is in contrast to teenagers, whose demand is more elastic. According to Evans and Farrelly (1998), teenagers' average daily tar and nicotine intake is estimated to rise after a tax hike.

Following from Gifford (1999), prohibition—whether through outright bans or via prohibitions by price (see chapter 15, this volume, by Michael LaFaive)—ultimately "results in substitutions along several margins, most of which, when coupled with biological effects, work in the opposite direction of the goal of reducing harmful outcomes" (Gifford 1999, 306). The preceding discussion of tax-induced quality substitution alongside the biological mechanisms may lead some readers to conclude that ad valorem taxation might be preferable to per unit taxation. This would be misguided. Ad valorem taxation that is large enough to overcome the complementary characteristic of addictive goods and substantially reduce the legal consumption of the commodity will still fall prey to the same set-point behavioral response discussed above. Furthermore, such a tax also will not avoid the incentives of many consumers to instead purchase the product in underground markets with questionable quality and content and with increased health risks. A better policy might be one of not employing taxes to nudge consumers. This does not necessarily eliminate the role of the government in reducing the occurrence of addictions. For instance, the government could still provide funding for educational campaigns concerning the harmful effects of addictive substances, but it may be wiser to raise the tax revenue to fund such a program via a broad-based tax.

Tax-Induced Quality Substitution and Rent-Seeking

In 2010, California's Proposition 19, which proposed to legalize marijuana for recreational purposes for individuals aged 21 and older, was opposed by the majority of residents of the tri-county region known as the "Emerald Triangle," a region known to be highly dependent on the marijuana crop for medicinal purposes.[3] At first thought, this might be a surprising outcome. Legalization would arguably bring about additional demand, and those in the Emerald Triangle have the experience and know-how to accommodate a significant expansion of that demand. However, legalization would also bring about additional competition, particularly from to-be growers of lower quality marijuana that would not require the complex hydroponic grow systems common in the Emerald Triangle. Many of the marijuana growers of the Emerald Triangle, then, appear to have voted against legalization in an effort to protect their market share and their past investments in complex growing systems. Prohibition of recreational marijuana also benefits law enforcement bureaus who maintain a level demand for their services and those skilled in the production and distribution of marijuana in the underground economy who profit from the demand left unfulfilled in legal markets. This is a classic case of Bruce Yandle's (1983) "Bootleggers and Baptists" theory in which individuals who otherwise are on opposite sides of a broader issue find themselves benefiting from the same policy but for entirely different reasons.

I introduce Yandle's "Bootleggers and Baptists" because the implications of the Barzel and Alchian-Allen theorems can make for some strange bedfellows in other cases involving excise tax policy. For instance, if the cigarette industry is confident that new taxes on the industry are forthcoming, the health lobby may find themselves on the same side with premium-brand cigarette manufacturers arguing in favor of unit taxation. Premium-brand manufacturers would want to minimize the damage to their profits. If the choice is between an ad valorem tax (which does nothing more than reduce demand generally) and a per unit tax (which reduces demand generally but shifts a portion of the remaining demand toward premium-brand cigarettes), it should be obvious that the premium-brand manufacturers would favor the latter and might go to considerable expense to promote that option. Generic-brand manufacturers likely would not sit idly by, as they stand to lose in two respects: reduced sales following from the First Law of Demand (quantity substitution) and reduced sales following from the Barzel and Alchian-Allen theorems (quality substitution). Lobbying expenditures on one side begets additional lobbying expenditures on the other.

Consider other examples. The health lobby and convenience store owners likely share common interests in supporting the 1.5¢ per ounce sugary drink tax in Philadelphia. It is possible that convenience stores may lose some revenue due to an overall reduction in the consumption of sugary drinks; however, if consumers are responsive enough on the quality (convenience) margin, it is possible, although not likely on a large scale, that some individual convenience stores would experience an increase in net sales.

Finally, environmental activists favoring an increase in the federal gasoline tax may not face strong opposition from gasoline retailers. Profits of gasoline retailers could feasibly remain largely unchanged if (1) the markup on premium-grade gas is sufficiently higher than on regular-grade gas, and (2) if the substitution between quality grades is sizable enough to offset the loss in total sales. In regards to the first condition, *The Chicago Tribune* (Zwahlen 1990) reported that the typical markup for premium-grade gasoline is 7 percent while it is only 3 percent for other grades. Determining whether the quality substitution is large enough to fully offset the loss in sales generally is an empirical question that is beyond the scope of this chapter. However, it is feasible that gasoline retailer profits could remain largely unaffected by modest gasoline tax increases such that the industry would expend few resources opposing proposed tax increases.

The primary point I am making here is that firms are likely adjusting their lobbying efforts in light of their own observations of outcomes consistent with the Barzel and Alchian-Allen theorems. While it is highly unlikely that firms lobby in favor of new or increased taxation on their own industry, it would not be surprising to observe producers of higher quality, name-brand commodities lobbying in favor of per unit taxes over ad valorem taxes when new taxes are eminent. This lobbying can lead to costly and inefficient policy outcomes that come at the expense of consumers or smaller, less politically connected firms.

CONCLUSION

Yoram Barzel (1976) and Armen Alchian and William Allen (1964) have both theorized that the imposition of per unit taxes, while reducing the overall quantity of a good consumed, can create incentives for those consumers who choose to still purchase the good to substitute, on average, toward higher quality versions of the good. The quality substitution theorems are not without their detractors. Ultimately, in light of the various concerns brought forward since its introduction, the question of whether the Alchian-Allen theorem applies in various circumstances must be resolved empirically. The empirical evidence with respect to unit taxation has been generally supportive of the Alchian-Allen and Barzel theorems. As such, it may be reasonable to expect that the imposition of per unit taxes is likely to systematically lead to a shift from lower quality and newer brands of a good toward higher quality and well-established brands. As such, per unit taxes can potentially serve as additional obstacles to new market entrants, further protecting the already entrenched firms.

This chapter leads to one primary policy implication: to minimize the impact that tax policy has on changing consumer choices, it may be preferable to impose ad valorem taxes rather than per unit taxes when commodity taxation is to be employed as a means to fulfill a revenue requirement. Ad valorem taxes have been argued and empirically shown not to alter relative prices or the choice between different quality grades of the taxed commodity. This is not to suggest that a universal sales tax is preferable; indeed, the ad valorem tax rate could vary by commodity in line with other theories, such as the Ramsey Rule, regarding efficient commodity taxation. My argument here is simply that by favoring ad valorem taxation as opposed to per unit taxation, the efficiency of the tax code can be improved and the potential for political favoritism toward select firms is reduced.

NOTES

1. While the unit tax is removed, it is replaced by a smaller fixed charge in the form of transportation costs. As such, a more accurate description of this scenario may be a reduction in the aggregated fixed charge of purchasing cigarettes.

2. Coats et al. (2005) also find modest evidence in the gasoline market in support of the Barzel theorem.

3. See http://www.allgov.com/news/unusual-news/marijuana-growers-voted-against-legalization?news=841715.

REFERENCES

Alchian, Armen, and William Allen. 1964. *University Economics: Elements of Inquiry.* Belmont, CA: Wadsworth.

Anderson, William, and Scott Kjar. 2008. "Can Good Apples Be Mixed with Bad Economics? A Mengerian Critique of the Alchian and Allen Theorem." *American Journal of Economics and Sociology* 67 (4): 645–60.

Barzel, Yoram. 1976. "An Alternative Approach to the Analysis of Taxation." *Journal of Political Economy* 84: 1177–97.

Barzel, Yoram, and Christopher Hall. 1977. *The Political Economy of the Oil Import Quota.* Stanford, CA: Hoover Institution.

Bertonazzi, Eric, Michael Maloney, and Robert McCormick. 1993. "Some Evidence on the Alchian and Allen Theorem: The Third Law of Demand?" *Economic Inquiry* 31 (3): 383–93.

Borcherding, Thomas, and Eugene Silberberg. 1978. "Shipping the Good Apples Out: The Alchian and Allen Theorem Reconsidered." *Journal of Political Economy* 86 (1): 131–38.

Brown, Matthew, Daniel Rascher, Chad McEvoy, and Mark Nagel. 2007. "Treatment of Travel Expenses by Golf Course Patrons: Sunk or Bundled Costs and the First and Third Laws of Demand." *International Journal of Sport Finance* 2: 45–53.

Caudill, Steven, Franklin Mixon Jr., and Kamal Upadhyaya. 2008. "Shipping the Good Anecdotes In: Illustrations of the Alchian-Allen Effect from American Culture and History." *Perspectives on Economic Education Research* 9 (2): 18–38.

Chiou, Lesley, and Erich Muehlegger. 2010. "Consumer Response to Cigarette Tax Changes." Research Working Paper RWP10-020. John F. Kennedy School of Government, Harvard University, Cambridge, MA. https://research.hks.harvard.edu/publications/getFile.aspx?Id =559.

Coats, R. Morris, Gary Pecquet, and Leon Taylor. 2005. "The Pricing of Gasoline Grades and the Third Law of Demand." Microeconomics 0506006, EconWPA.

Cobb, Steven, and Douglas Olberding. 2010. "Shipping the Runners to the Race: A Sport Tourism Interpretation of the Alchian-Allen Theorem." *International Journal of Sport Finance* 5: 268–79.

Cowen, Tyler, and Alexander Tabarrok. 1995. "Good Grapes and Bad Lobsters: Applying the Alchian and Allen Theorem." *Economic Inquiry* 33 (2): 253–56.

Cuellar, Steven. 2005. "Sex, Drugs and the Alchian-Allen Theorem." Unpublished paper. https:// www.sonoma.edu/users/c/cuellar/research/Sex-Drugs.pdf.

DeCicca, Philip, Donald Kenkel, and Feng Liu. 2015. "Reservation Prices: An Economic Analysis of Cigarette Purchases on Indian Reservations." *National Tax Journal* 68 (1): 93–118.

Drenkard, Scott, and Joseph Henchman. 2016. "Sales Tax Holidays: Politically Expedient but Poor Tax Policy 2016." *Tax Foundation Special Report* 233. July 25. Washington, DC. https://files .taxfoundation.org/legacy/docs/TaxFoundation_SR233%5BFINAL%5D.pdf.

Espinosa, Javier, and William Evans. 2013. "Excise Taxes, Tax Incidence, and the Flight to Quality: Evidence from Scanner Data." *Public Finance Review* 41 (2): 147–76.

Evans, William, and Matthew Farrelly. 1998. "The Compensating Behavior of Smokers: Taxes, Tar and Nicotine." *RAND Journal of Economics* 29 (3): 578–95.

Fisher, Irving. 1927. "The Economics of Prohibition." *American Economic Review* 17 (1): 5–10.

Gifford, Adam, Jr. 1999. "The Unintended Consequences of Regulating Addictive Substances." *Cato Journal* 19 (2): 301–11.

Gould, John, and Joel Segall. 1968. "The Substitution Effects of Transportation Costs." *Journal of Political Economy* 77 (1): 130–37.

Gulliver, Suzy, Damaris Rohsenow, Suzanne Colby, Achintya Dey, David Abrams, Raymond Niaura, and Peter Monti. 1995. "Interrelationship of Smoking and Alcohol Dependence, Use and Urges to Use." *Journal of Studies on Alcohol* 56: 202–6.

Hummels, David, and Alexandre Skiba. 2004. "Shipping the Good Apples Out? An Empirical Confirmation of the Alchian-Allen Conjecture." *Journal of Political Economy* 12 (6): 1384–1402.

Johnson, Terry. 1978. "Additional Evidence of the Effects of Alternative Taxes on Cigarette Prices." *Journal of Political Economy* 86 (2): 325–28.

Kaplan, Jennifer. 2017. "Philadelphia's Soda Sellers Say Tax Has Reduced Sales by as Much as 50%." *Bloomberg*, February 17. https://www.bloomberg.com/news/articles/2017-02-17/philly-soda -sellers-say-tax-has-reduced-sales-by-as-much-as-50.

Lawson, Robert, and Todd Nesbit. 2013. "Alchian and Allen Revisited: Law Enforcement and the Price of Weed." *Atlantic Economic Journal* 41 (4): 363–70.

Liu, Liqun. 2011. "The Alchian-Allen Theorem and the Law of Relative Demand: The Case of Multiple Quality-Differentiable Brands." *Mathematical Social Sciences* 61: 52–57.

Ljunge, Martin. 2011. "Do Taxes Produce Better Wine?" *Journal of Agricultural & Food Industrial Organization* 9 (1): Article 12.

Minagawa, Junichi, and Thorsten Upmann. 2013. "A Note on Parental Time Allocation." *Labour Economics* 25: 153–57.

Nesbit, Todd. 2007. "Excise Taxation and Product Quality: The Gasoline Market." *Economic Issues* 12, Part 2. 1–14. http://www.economicissues.org.uk/Files/207Nesbit.pdf.

Razzolini, Laura, William F. Shughart II, and Robert Tollison. 2003. "On the Third Law of Demand." *Economic Inquiry* 41 (2): 292–98.

Resiandini, Pramesti. 2012. "Japanese and Korean Automobile Exports and the Alchian-Allen Theorem." *Munich Personal RePEc Archive*, No. 41928. https://mpra.ub.uni-muenchen.de /41928/.

Rojas, Christian, and Tianji Shi. 2011. "Tax Incidence When Quality Matters: Evidence from the Beer Market." *Journal of Agricultural & Food Industrial Organization* 9 (1): Article 10.

Sobel, Russell, and Thomas Garrett. 1997. "Taxation and Product Quality: New Evidence from Generic Cigarettes." *Journal of Political Economy* 105 (4): 880–87.

Sumner, Michael, and Robert Ward. 1981. "Tax Changes and Cigarette Prices." *Journal of Political Economy* 89 (6): 1261–65.

Thornton, Mark. 1991. *The Economics of Prohibition.* Salt Lake City: University of Utah Press.

Umbeck, John. 1980. "Shipping the Good Apples Out: Some Ambiguities in the Interpretation of 'Fixed Charge.'" *Journal of Political Economy* 88 (1): 199–208.

Warburton, Clark. 1932. *The Economic Results of Prohibition.* New York: Columbia University Press.

Yandle, Bruce. 1983. "Bootleggers and Baptists: The Education of a Regulatory Economist." *Regulation* 7 (12): 12–16.

Zwahlen, Cyndia. 1990. "Regular, Premium Gasolines Keep Fueling High-Octane Debate." *Chicago Tribune*, June 17.

CHAPTER 8
Predatory Public Finance and the Evolution of the War on Drugs

BRUCE BENSON
Economics Department, Florida State University

BRIAN MEEHAN
Campbell School of Business, Berry College

S ubstances that alter perceptions, feelings, behavior, or decision-making (e.g., narcotics, marijuana, alcohol, and tobacco) are widely targeted sources of government revenue (taxes), in part because demand is inelastic over a substantial range, so consumers' total expenditures rise with price increases, and moral/paternalistic arguments can be used to justify revenue-extraction policy. Revenues obviously can be generated through sales or excise taxes on (or licensing fees for) production, distribution, or consumption. This approach is used to generate revenue from tobacco policy and from alcohol policy in non-liquor monopoly US states. However, there are other ways to tax markets for such substances, including some that are not explicitly labeled as taxes. Revenues can be obtained through direct control (monopolization) of distribution in legal markets, thereby hiding the implicit tax in the price (essentially, the rents arising because the quantity supplied is limited, minus any increased production costs as labor or other resources capture part of the rents, serves as an implicit tax for government sales), as several US states do in alcohol wholesaling, retailing, or both (Benson et al. 2003). Implicit taxes can also be generated through various kinds of regulation that involve fees, fines, or both for violations. Various direct and implicit tax policies are widely used to generate revenues. Executive agencies that collect direct or implicit taxes often do not have authority to retain the revenues they collect. However, they should still pursue collection activities aggressively, since they must compete for a portion of those and other revenues when the latter are allocated by legislatures. This ongoing competition for budgets occurs at all levels of government and often between levels of government.[1] Horizontal and vertical interjurisdiction competition for control of such revenue sources can be intense. Agencies, supported by their political allies (e.g., interest groups and politicians representing those groups) are also motivated to obtain direct control of the tax revenues they collect in order to enhance their budgets without going through the competitive budgetary process. Earmarked taxes are common for highways, for instance, but they can also apply to taxes on the various substances discussed here (e.g., a portion of a tax on tobacco might be earmarked for addiction treatment).

Regulations can be very strict, including full prohibition of production, sales, and consumption, as the alcohol prohibition episode in the United States illustrates. The dominant policy in the United States for narcotics and marijuana over the past century also has been prohibition. This policy may appear to undermine the suggestion that revenue-seeking is a policy determinant. However, understanding the evolution of this policy choice requires recognition of both the attractiveness of these substances as targets for revenue extraction and of the importance of competition among executive bureaucracies/agencies for the control over spending of these and other revenues. Furthermore, while most enforcement agencies dealing with narcotics and marijuana do not have the authority to retain taxes, fees, fines, or other revenues they collect, they have gained such authority for one source of revenue (they still must compete for the attention of those who have budget allocation powers in order to obtain revenues from taxes for substantial portions of their budgets). Prohibition of the production and use of these substances can be a very attractive revenue-seeking policy in the general interbureau competition for budgets, at least for some executive agencies. Since complete prohibition is essentially impossible to achieve, this policy provides a never-ending justification for agency existence (job security) and expanding budgets. Enforcement-related budgets can be pursued by propagating information, both accurate and misleading, about successful enforcement (arrests, seizures), the costs of enforcement, and more importantly, the alleged negative consequences for individuals and society without prohibition (costs that cannot be measured when prohibition is in place). This predatory public financing is widely practiced by enforcement agencies.

Prohibition drives narcotic and marijuana markets underground, but it does not come close to eliminating these markets. In fact, the resulting illicit markets involve substantial cash flow, large profits, and significant investments in capital (and in some cases, land) used in producing, processing, transporting, and distributing the illegal products. Seizures of cash, land, and capital used in or generated by illegal markets has a long history. Legislators may control such seizures, just as they control monopoly profits, taxes, and licensing fees. If prohibition enforcers can convince legislators to allow them to keep seized assets, however, prohibition becomes even more attractive for the bureaucrats.[2] Congress responded to these demands more than four decades ago. The result is another kind of implicit tax. The ability of enforcement agencies to keep the proceeds from forfeiture means that this source of revenue is much like an earmarked tax, with a key difference being that there is no established tax rate. The recipient bureaucracies effectively dictate the tax rates themselves. We examine the evolution of drug policy in the United States from a predatory revenue-seeking perspective by considering both this earmarked tax (asset seizures) and the interbureaucratic competition for budgets arising from other tax revenues.

PUBLIC FINANCE, BUREAUCRATIC INTERESTS, AND FEDERAL DRUG PROHIBITION

That the primary federal drug-policy enforcement agency in the United States was in the Treasury Department from passage of the Harrison Act in 1914 until 1968 suggests that revenue-seeking significantly influences drug policy. Indeed, the Harrison Act, often seen as the source of federal drug criminalization, was actually a regulatory and tax statute involving "a special tax on all persons who produce, import, manufacture, compound, deal in, dispense, sell, distribute, or give away opium or coca leaves, their salts, derivatives, or preparations, and for other purposes" (Harrison Narcotics Tax Act of 1914, Ch. 1, 38 Stat. 785). In essence, this act established very modest "sin taxes" on the sale of narcotics, such as opiates. What apparently became illegal as a result of the act was possessing or selling untaxed narcotics. The bureau in the Treasury Department that was put in charge of enforcement expanded its jurisdiction, however, by interpreting the Harrison Act expansively and policing aggressively.

BRUCE BENSON AND BRIAN MEEHAN

The Act recognized physicians' right to prescribe narcotics, but they were required to register with the Bureau of Internal Revenue in the Treasury Department, pay taxes, and keep records of dispensed drugs. Doctors largely complied with these regulations, and for several years after its passage, the Harrison Act served as a limited source of taxes and regulatory measures (Reinarman 1983, 21). At the federal level, opiate use began to be criminalized with the bureau's decision to interpret the Act as if it allowed them to pursue criminal charges against physicians who prescribed narcotics to addicts. The Federal Bureau of Narcotics instigated raids on morphine treatment clinics in 1919 (King 1957; Lindesmith 1965; Klein 1983, 32). These raids led to a series of court decisions that reinterpret the Harrison Act and became the pretext for criminalizing drug sales and use (Reinarman 1983, 21). The federal court accepted the bureau's contention that, while the Act allowed physicians to prescribe narcotics for normal medical problems, it did not allow them to do so for treatment of addicts (*Webb v. United States*, 249 U.S. 96, 99 (1919)). King (1957, 122) explains that "the Narcotics Division launched a reign of terror. Doctors were bullied and threatened, and those who were adamant [about treating addicts] went to prison." Drug addicts and doctors or pharmacists selling to them were turned into criminals, the black market for drugs quickly developed, and criminal organizations entered as suppliers. As a result, enforcement became much more costly, demanding an ever-growing bureaucracy and budget to pursue enforcement. The creation of the Narcotics Division in the Bureau of Internal Revenue in 1921 and of a standalone Bureau of Prohibition in 1927, still in Treasury, lends credence to this idea. Table 1 shows the growth of Treasury expenditures and revenues from prohibition enforcement from 1920 to 1932. These figures include both alcohol and narcotics enforcement, since alcohol prohibition under the Eighteenth amendment came into effect in 1920 and its repeal by the twenty-first amendment did not occur until 1933. Expenditures were larger and grew faster than the revenues raised over this entire period. Revenues reflected in table 1 include fines, taxes, and penalties collected from enforcing prohibition, and the expenditures are the outlays from the Treasury to cover the enforcement costs (Holcombe 1996).

As indicated by the figures in table 1, once a bureaucracy is created, incentives arise to ensure its continued existence (make bureaucrats' jobs secure) by expanding its size and scope (Benson 1995). Not surprisingly, Lindesmith (1965, 3) contends that the nation's program for handling the "drug problem" is one "which, to all intents and purposes, was established by the decisions of administrative officials of the Treasury Department." For instance, because

Table 1. Treasury Revenues and Expenditures from Enforcement
(Adjusted for Inflation)

Year	Revenues ($ millions)	Expenditures ($ millions)
1920	1.7	3.1
1921	6.9	9.5
1922	6.6	9.9
1923	7.7	12.3
1924	9.9	11.3
1925	8.9	13.9
1926	8.5	14.5
1927	78.0	17.7
1928	93.4	17.5
1929	82.7	18.6
1930	80.9	20.4
1931	62.5	14.5
1932	59.7	16.7

Source: Wooddy (1934, 101) as cited in Holcombe (1996).

of pressure from the Treasury Department's Bureau of Prohibition, the
Marijuana Tax Act was passed in 1937 (Becker 1963; Lindesmith 1965; Oteri
and Silvergate 1967; Dickson 1968; Hill 1971; Bonnie and Whitebread 1974).
With the end of alcohol prohibition, the bureau needed a new raison d'être
for continued funding through the budgetary process in 1937, and it faced
stiff competition from the FBI for the attention of the public and of Congress
(King 1978), so bureaucratic survival was a probable motivation. Self-interest
likely played a role, as supported by the fact that the campaign leading to this
legislation "included remarkable distortions of the evidence of harm caused
by marijuana, ignoring the findings of empirical inquiries" (Richards 1982,
164; for details, see Lindesmith 1965, 25–34, and Kaplan 1970, 88–136). As
with its predecessor, the Harrison Act, the Marijuana Tax Act was nominally
a revenue-producing act that imposed taxes on physicians who prescribed
marijuana, pharmacists who dispensed it, and others who might deal in the
drug. The Marijuana Tax Act made nonmedical possession and sale of the drug
illegal, however, and all those in the production and distribution chain for
medical purposes were required to keep detailed records and pay annual fees.
These onerous record-keeping requirements, taxes, and fees effectively ended
the legal use of the drug for medical purposes as well.[3]

An excise tax or high regulatory compliance costs (or both), such as those
established by the Marijuana Tax Act, may reduce the legal level of the sin
being taxed,[4] but it simultaneously induces new kinds of sin that are often

much more costly for society. High sin taxes and compliance costs inevitably lead to crime, as individuals attempt to avoid the taxes and compliance costs by means of black markets, smuggling, and violent forms of competition and contract enforcement that accompany such activities. This occurred with both narcotics and marijuana. However, rather than recognize the source of the crime and eliminate the sin taxes and compliance costs, full-blown criminalization of possession and sale of narcotics and marijuana evolved as bureaucrats who were given the authority to police these markets and collect the taxes propagated the belief that it was the "sin" of drug consumption that produced the crime, rather than the incentives to avoid the taxes imposed on the sin. To establish the incentives and issues that have resulted in developing additional implicit taxes through prohibition, we first discuss this criminalization process and related bureaucratic actions, including interbureau competition.

That the Harrison Act and the Marijuana Tax Act did not generate net revenues through taxes, fees, and fines for Congress to allocate does not mean that revenue-seeking was irrelevant. The Bureau of Prohibition (and other departments and agencies that would attempt to become involved in drug policy) did not have the power to actually retain revenues taken directly from narcotics markets through taxes, fees, and fines (as shown in table 1), but they manipulated policy to justify bureaucratic expansion in order to enforce prohibition. Enforcement has focused on suppression (prohibition) for almost a century, as interbureau competition for jurisdiction and budget has become increasingly intense.

It did not take many years before the Bureau of Prohibition and the Treasury Department faced competition from other federal agencies for jurisdiction over drug policy, but they generally retained substantial control for several more decades. For instance, the Federal Narcotics Control Board, consisting of the secretaries of Treasury, State, and Commerce, was created by the 1922 Narcotic Drugs Import and Export Act to develop regulations prohibiting international narcotics trade. This involvement of two additional cabinet-level departments lasted until 1930, when the new Bureau of Narcotics in Treasury consolidated the Bureau of Prohibition and the Federal Narcotics Control Board. This did not end the interbureau competition for drug-control budgets, however, as illustrated by creation of the Bureau of Drug Abuse Control in the FDA.

Ultimately, in 1968, the Bureau of Narcotics and the Bureau of Drug Abuse Control were also merged to form the Bureau of Narcotics and Dangerous Drugs, but this Bureau was placed in the Department of Justice. Thus, the Justice Department gained primary control from the Treasury. The Drug

Enforcement Administration (DEA) replaced this bureau in 1973 in another effort to consolidate and coordinate federal drug control, as several other departments obtained shares of the drug control budget over the 1968–1973 period. The DEA has grown from 2,775 employees at its inception to more than 11,000 in 2015, and this agency's budget has grown from $65 million ($369 million adjusted for inflation) to $2.98 billion over the same period (www.dea.gov).

The shift from Treasury (and other agencies) to Justice reflects the interbureau competition for budget and the efforts on the part of Congress to limit such competition. Law enforcement bureaucracies continued to compete with one another for jurisdiction, however, and other bureaucracies continue to develop and advocate policy initiatives in an effort to capture parts of the drug-control budgetary pie. As Reuter (1994, 145) stresses, "The most visible political battle in drug policy in recent years has been over the allocation of the federal drug control budget. Discussions about what priority to assign to different ways of reducing drug problems have begun and ended with how the federal government spends its money on drug control." Reuter goes on to explain that the estimated federal drug budget in 1993, the year before publication of his article, was $12.2 billion, but only $1.81 billion actually went directly to drug control agencies (the DEA, the Organized Crime Drug Enforcement Task Forces, National Institute of Drug Abuse, the Office of National Drug Control Policy, and the State Department's Bureau of International Narcotics Matters), while the remainder, more than $10 billion, "was hidden in agency budgets," including the Veterans Administration (drug treatment for veterans), the Immigration and Naturalization Service (border patrol interdiction, as well as drug-related investigation, detention, and deportation), the Coast Guard (interdiction), the Department of Education (drug use prevention through education and treatment through rehabilitation), and the Health Care Financing Administration (treatment) (Reuter 1994, 148–51). The Department of Education had also proposed a new "Safe and Drug-Free Schools and Community" program with a request of $660 million in new funding from the 1995 drug control budget (Reuter 1994, 149). This proposal reflects the relatively new emphasis in the debate about the allocation of drug control funding. As Murphy (1994, 2) explains, the debate over the drug budget began shifting in the early 1990s from one focusing on "is the federal government doing enough?" as arguments were made to expand budgets, to "is the federal government doing the right thing?" as various non–law enforcement agencies stressed prevention and treatment rather than enforcement: "The distribution of resources as measured in the federal drug budget—the supply/demand split—became the metric for the debate."[5] By fiscal year (FY) 2011–2012, explicitly budgeted spending for federal illicit drug policy (more than $25 billion) was split among twelve cabinet-level departments (Agriculture, Defense, Health and Human Services, Homeland Security, Housing and Urban Development, Interior, Justice, Labor, State, Transportation, Treasury, and Veteran's Affairs), two court systems (Court Services and Offender Supervision Agency of the District of Columbia, Federal Judiciary), the Small Business Administration, and the Office of National Drug Control Policy and Administration. Drug policy activities in cabinet departments also were spread across several agencies, bureaus, administrations, offices, services, programs, centers, divisions, and institutes (Smith 2012).

The competition for budget resources plays out within agencies as well as across them. Bureaucrats must compete for support and attention from sponsors or superiors, because control of resources is necessary for bureaucrats to achieve most of their goals. Competition leads bureaucrats to develop new policies that allow them to expand the scope of their authority, power, jurisdiction, or agency; to obtain promotions; and to pursue similar purposes (Breton and Wintrobe 1982). Actual documentation of such behavior without rhetorical justifications disguising personal objectives is rare, but one is provided by a former DEA agent, Robert Stutmann.

While Stutmann was involved in various entrepreneurial policy changes over his career,[6] his most significant efforts occurred after he became head of the New York DEA office in 1985. This was about the time that crack cocaine first appeared in the city (Johnson 1987): the federal government had increased its efforts to interdict marijuana in 1984, and the resulting reduction in supply led sellers and users to look for an alternative relatively low-priced drug. Crack began to appear in Miami, Los Angeles, and New York sometime in 1985, as sellers adopted technology already in use in the Bahamas. Stutmann saw crack as a new opportunity to attract attention from his superiors and budget-allocation decision makers. He immediately began changing his office's priorities to focus on crack and set the stage for a "fullblown media campaign" (Stutmann and Esposito 1992, 148) along with a "lobbying effort" to quickly make crack a "national issue" (Stutmann and Esposito 1992, 217). The first article on crack appeared in the *New York Times* on November 29, 1985. DEA headquarters did not think that crack was important enough to warrant more attention, however, so Stutmann and his assistant developed a plan that would simultaneously generate crack arrests and attract attention in Washington. They targeted the Washington Heights area of New York, in part because it was located at the end of the George Washington Bridge, a favorite route for drug buyers from New Jersey and Westchester County, buyers who were pre-dominantly middle-class suburbanites and their children. The plan was to seize their cars (see discussion of asset seizures below), essentially imposing an implicit tax on this specific population.

Before the campaign started, a bulletin was issued to other law enforce-ment officials and the press on May 26, 1986, asserting, among other things, that crack has a "very high addictive potential and that it causes medical and psychological problems" leading to random acts of violence. In June, Stutmann gave DEA administrator Jack Lawn a full-blown presentation focusing on claims that: (1) the overwhelming majority of crack users were middle-income working people and their high-school- or college-student children and (2) that crack was a significant new cause of crime, because the ghetto dwellers who also used it had to steal to buy it while sellers also protected their turf with violence. In this context, Stutmann suggests,

> the timing was perfect, although University of Maryland
> basketball star Len Bias might not have seen it that way.
> On June 19, the day Lawn arrived, we got the call that Bias
> had died. . . . The drug death of a young athlete . . . capped
> the groundwork that had been carefully laid through press
> accounts and [Stutmann's] public appearances. . . . From
> [Stutmann's] perspective, Len Bias had not died in vain.
> (Stutmann and Esposito 1992, 219)

Lawn asked Stutmann to hold off on the plan's implementation while he lob-bied for a $10 million budget enhancement to expand the DEA by creating a new twenty-four agent crack task force. His requested budget increase was denied, so Lawn told Stutmann to implement the plan. On August 14, 1986, the DEA and the New York Police Department announced initiation of an anticrack campaign and seized forty-seven cars. By that time, Stutmann's media campaign had already put the issue before the public. He had a 199-page bound volume of New York and New Jersey news articles reporting that crack was causing a rise in cocaine deaths, along with rising murder rates and virtually all other crime rates (national media also began reporting on the issue beginning with *Newsweek* in June). Before the campaign ended, more than 1,000 cars were seized.

The crack-cocaine scare is like many other scares that came before it and that have occurred since. Innovations in the illicit drug market inevitably fol-low successful campaigns by law enforcement, offsetting and often completely negating the campaign's consequences (Rasmussen and Benson 1994, 76–92). The market innovations in turn provide bureaucratic entrepreneurs with new opportunities to pursue new policies in an effort to justify expansions of their budgets and jurisdictions. The increased interdiction of marijuana in 1984–1985 actually led to crack's introduction (as well as dramatic increases in domestic production), for instance, and that offered Stutmann the entrepreneurial opportunity to create the "crack crisis." In fact, as Zimring and Hawkins (1992, 50–51) explain, when a new drug variant is introduced, it is portrayed by drug enforcement officials as a major new policy problem because of the unique chemical, physiological, or psychological characteristics of the new drug. This argument has been applied over and over again, to opium, heroin, marijuana, LSD, cocaine, crack-cocaine, amphetamines, various prescription drugs that are used for recreational purposes, and so on. Evidence of this process is demonstrated by the recent episode involving synthetic drugs, sometimes referred to as "bath salts." In May 2012, Rudy Eugene was shot and killed after he attacked and bit off part of the face of another man. An ABC News media report stated that police indicated that Eugene "showed behavior consistent with ingesting the synthetic cocaine substance known as bath salts" (ABC News 2012). Days after the incident, CNN (2012) linked the crime to trending "Zombie apocalypse" rumors. Less than 2 months after the attack and amid nationwide hysteria over the event, on July 10, 2012, President Obama signed a law that banned these synthetic drugs at the federal level, and subsequently on July 26, the DEA arrested ninety people in a nationwide bust of these synthetic drugs and seized 5 million packets of the drugs. In an interesting twist, when Eugene's toxicology reports came back, they indicated that he was not under the influence of bath salts or "any other exotic street drug" at the time of the incident (CBS Miami 2012).[7]

Each new drug or drug variant is declared to be "the greatest drug menace" that has ever been introduced. Zimring and Hawkins (1992, 51) note that this occurs because "allegations of a drug's uniqueness can be used as a rhetorical device to shield proponents of a prohibitory policy from counterarguments based on the history of earlier efforts at the state regulation of other substances or of the same substance in different forms or settings." Drugs do vary in their chemical, physiological, and psychological properties, of course, and all drugs can and do have negative consequences on some users, but when such a drug is first introduced, it provides entrepreneurial bureaucrats with an opportunity to heighten the perceived need for a strong prohibition effort by exaggerating the negative effects of the drug before any evidence is available to counter those exaggerations, and even to make up some effects that are ultimately refuted by scientific evidence. For the entrepreneurial bureaucrat, uniqueness "represents the end point of the analysis. . . . [It] entails a corresponding distinctiveness in the social and law enforcement problems it generates, which make irrelevant any reference to past experience with any other drug" (Zimring and Hawkins 1992, 51). Not surprisingly, many early and often repeated claims about crack have since been disproven (Rasmussen and Benson 1994, 145–46).

THE DEVELOPMENT AND CONSEQUENCES OF EARMARKED SIN TAXES FOR PROHIBITION-ENFORCEMENT BUREAUCRACIES

Bureaucratic revenue-seeking can involve more than just competition for budgets allocated by legislatures. If a policy can be successfully justified that allows bureaucrats to retain sin taxes they collect by earmarking them for use by the agency, agency personnel clearly have incentives to pursue the innovation. In this context, one of the most dramatic escalations in the war on drugs in the United States presumably was initiated by President Reagan in October 1982 (Wisotsky 1991). Federal agencies responded to Reagan's declaration, but such an offensive in the United States had to be waged by state and local "troops," and state and local law enforcement agencies generally did not begin to increase their relative efforts against drugs in a dramatic fashion before late 1984, when a substantial reallocation of state and local criminal justice system resources to drug enforcement began. In fact, although drug arrests relative to arrests for reported crimes against persons and property (Part I offenses of murder, manslaughter, sexual assault, assault, robbery, burglary, larceny, and auto theft) remained relatively constant at one to four from 1970 to 1984, the relative effort against drugs increased by roughly 45 percent over the next 5 years. By 1989, criminal justice resources were being allocated to make only about 2.2 Part I arrests for each drug arrest.[8] Drug arrests as a percentage of total arrests (Part I and Part 2, which includes drug arrests) show similar trends, rising from 5.17 percent in 1981 to a temporary peak of 9.56 percent in 1989 (see table 2). The number of drug arrests and drug arrests as a percentage of total arrests has trended upward since 1981 (modest increases occurred after Reagan's speech, and then sharper increases began after 1984 for reasons explained below), with only a few brief periods of reversal (see table 2).[9] Law enforcement groups are the source of demands for the legislation, creating incentives for the significant reallocation of policing resources suggested by table 2.

Table 2. Estimated US Drug Arrests, 1980–2013

Year	Estimated Total Drug Arrests	Estimated Drug Arrests as a Percentage of Estimated Total Arrests	Year	Estimated Total Drug Arrests	Estimated Drug Arrests as a Percentage of Estimated Total Arrests
1980	580,900	5.56	1997	1,586,900	10.36
1981	559,900	5.17	1998	1,559,100	10.73
1982	676,000	5.47	1999	1,532,200	10.67
1983	661,400	5.67	2000	1,579,600	11.30
1984	708,400	6.13	2001	1,586,900	11.56
1985	811,400	6.79	2002	1,538,800	11.20
1986	824,100	6.60	2003	1,678,200	12.30
1987	937,400	7.37	2004	1,745,700	12.52
1988	1,155,200	8.36	2005	1,846,400	13.10
1989	1,361,700	9.56	2006	1,889,800	13.14
1990	1,089,500	7.60	2007	1,841,200	12.96
1991	1,101,000	7.11	2008	1,702,500	12.16
1992	1,066,400	7.57	2009	1,663,600	12.15
1993	1,126,300	8.02	2010	1,538,800	12.49
1994	1,351,400	9.23	2011	1,531,300	12.34
1995	1,476,100	9.76	2012	1,552,400	12.74
1996	1,506,200	9.93	2013	1,501,000	13.28

Source: Table 4.45.2006 from the Sourcebook of Criminal Justice Statistics Online, http://www.albany.edu/sourcebook/pdf/t4452010.pdf.

Earmarking the Proceeds from the Implicit Tax and Resulting Police Behavior

Government seizure of property used in criminal activity has a very long history. It was one stimulus for the King's involvement in law enforcement as early as the ninth century (Benson 1990) and was first used in the United States to combat smugglers avoiding import duties in the early nineteenth century. The justification generally is that the risk of paying the resulting implicit tax on criminal activity is a deterrent, a form of punishment, and a means of imposing at least part of the cost of crime control on criminals (see discussion below)— essentially, a sin tax. Policing agencies are now pursuing property seizures in drug prohibition efforts, and seizures have increased dramatically since 1984. Federal forfeitures (seizures) alone reached $285 million in 1989, fluctuated between $281 million and $597 million from 1990 to 2005, jumped to more than $841 million in 2006, and continued this expansion to more than $1.78 billion in 2010.[10] After adjusting for inflation, this represents a more than 800 percent increase in the dollar amount of federal seizures from 1983 to 2010. Combined federal assets seized from 1989 to 2010 total well over $12.5 billion.[11]

Seizures continue to be common, some of which are very large. For instance, in a 2013 episode of civil seizure based on drug-crime accusations, the FBI seized substantial monetary assets from Ross Ulbricht. Ulbricht was accused of creating and running the online anonymous Internet marketplace called the "Silk Road" under the pseudonym "Dread Pirate Roberts." This marketplace allowed buyers and sellers to transact anonymously using Bitcoin currency. The marketplace was often used by sellers and consumers of illegal drugs. Prior to conviction, the federal government seized more than 700,000 bitcoins from Ulbricht. On May 29, 2015, these bitcoins had an estimated value of $166,124,000 (Paul 2015b). Ulbricht was eventually convicted of seven charges relating to his oversight of the illegal drug marketplace,[12] sentenced to life in prison, and fined $183,961,921[13] (Paul 2015a), most of which was to be paid for by the seized bitcoins.[14] Note, however, that this criminal conviction is not necessarily the norm when assets are seized. As explained below, under so-called civil seizures, assets can be seized without arresting or charging the assets' owners.

Importantly (and in part encouraged and assisted by federal agencies), state and local law enforcement have also increased asset seizure activities since 1984. State asset seizure laws vary considerably, and they varied even more in 1984 than they do now. Many states did not allow state and local police to keep seized assets, for instance, and the standard of proof required for successful seizures also varied.[15] As a consequence, a key piece of federal legislation affecting the incentives of state and local police was a section of the Comprehensive Crime Act of 1984. It required "equitable sharing" by the Justice Department, as shares of federal drug-related property seizures are to be given to the state and local agencies participating in the investigations. In other words, state and local law enforcement agencies were given an opportunity to directly collect and retain sin taxes earmarked for their own use, in the form of asset seizures, even if their states' laws did not allow them to do so (the federal burden of proof was also much easier to meet than many states required, as explained below).

The 1984 Comprehensive Crime Act change in the federal asset forfeiture law relating to drug investigations was a bureaucratically demanded legislative action allegedly justified as policy innovation that would provide a means to expand interbureau cooperation.[16] As an indication of the dominant bureaucratic interests, note that during hearings before the Subcommittee on Crime of the Committee on the Judiciary of the US House of Representatives, held June 23 and October 14, 1983, much of the testimony focused exclusively on seizure and forfeitures issues (Subcommittee on Crime of the Committee on the Judiciary 1983). Among the organizations testifying in support of the forfeitures-sharing arrangement were the US Customs Service, various police departments and sheriffs, the US Attorney's Office from the Southern District of Florida, and the DEA. There was no representation of local government oversight authorities (mayors, city councils, or county commissions) who approve police budgets, either supporting or opposing such legislation; nor were any corrections groups or victims' organizations represented that often have a substantial impact on crime legislation (Benson 1990, 1998).[17] When the change was first introduced, it appears that most non–law enforcement interests did not anticipate its earmarking implications, probably due to the poor quality of information selectively released by law enforcement bureau-cracies and their congressional supporters.[18] Drugs allegedly cause crime, so in addition to stimulating interagency cooperation, supporters of dedicating forfeitures to law enforcement contend that it is justified as a means of recoup-ing the costs of enforcing drug-induced crime.[19] This practical aspect of asset seizures—treating the proceeds as something akin to a crime-fighting tax on criminals—was emphasized in a manual designed to help local jurisdic-tions develop forfeiture capabilities (National Criminal Justice Association 1988, 40). While suggesting that less tangible law enforcement effects (such as deterrence) should be counted as benefits, the manual emphasized that the determining factor for pursuit of forfeitures is "the *jurisdiction's* best interest" (emphasis added). This interest reflects the perspective of law enforcement agencies, a view that is likely to put somewhat more weight on benefits for bureaucrats and somewhat less weight on communitywide (and uncertain) deterrence effects. After all, as Stumpf (1988, 316) notes, we must "look past the external political and social determinants of criminal justice procedures and policies to understand the system in operation. The process is staffed by professionals and quasi-professionals who have their own agenda . . . [and] largely internal imperatives may be of even greater importance in explain-ing their outcomes" (also see Blumberg 1979; Benson 1990; Rasmussen and Benson 1994; Miller 2004). If forfeitures are in the "public interest" because of their deterrent impacts, and if police are exclusively motivated by a desire to serve the public interest, then policing agencies should willingly cooperate in seizure efforts no matter what government agency's budget is enhanced by these seizures. The fact is that the equitable-sharing revenues from drug-related seizures create the potential for law enforcement agencies to expand their discretionary budgets (Benson et al. 1995), thereby enhancing their own well-being, directly and indirectly rewarding supporters with various benefits and privileges (Breton and Wintrobe 1982, 137).

Although not mandated by the 1984 legislation, the Department of Justice (DOJ) offered, in 1986, to treat seizures by state or local agencies as if they involved a cooperating federal agency by "adopting" such seizures and then passing them back to the state or local agency, minus a 20 percent handling charge, thereby allowing the agency to circumvent state laws requiring that some or all of the seizure proceeds go to some specific use (e.g., education) or into general revenues.[20] For example, North Carolina law requires that all proceeds from the sale of confiscated assets go to the County School Fund. Law enforcement agencies in North Carolina have routinely used the 1984 federal legislation and 1986 DOJ adoption program to circumvent the restrictions, so the seized assets could be repatriated to law enforcement agencies rather than going to schools.[21] The same has occurred in many other states, although several states have modified their state forfeiture laws so adoptions are not required for police to retain revenues.[22] Adoptions can be attractive for other reasons, too. Several states do not allow seizures of real property under some circumstance that are allowed under federal law.[23] Perhaps more importantly, the burden of proof required to make seizures under some states' laws is stricter than under federal law (see table 3). The burden of proof for a federal seizure—and therefore, for an adopted seizure—was "probable cause" during much of the period of increasing drug enforcement.[24] Both circumstantial and hearsay evidence is allowed to establish probable cause. In contrast, state laws vary from probable-cause through preponderance-of-evidence to clear-and-convincing-evidence, and even beyond-a-reasonable doubt (Edgeworth 2004, 113–18; Williams et al. 2011). Only ten states (Williams et al. 2011) allow seizures by probable cause, while the other states' burden of proof standards are more difficult to meet, and when a state standard is stricter than the federal requirement, the police have been relatively strongly motivated to use the federal procedures. If state laws allow police to keep asset forfeitures and have other characteristics that encourage seizures, however, then police do not have to turn to federal Equitable Sharing Program.

"With local, state and federal law enforcement agencies suddenly able to keep all the proceeds under federal forfeiture standards, the value of assets confiscated surged from over $100 million in 1983 (the year before the institution of Equitable Sharing) to $460 million in 1990" (Drug Policy Alliance 2015, 9).[25] By 1990, over 90 percent of the police departments with jurisdictions containing populations of 50,000 or more and over 90 percent of the sheriffs' departments serving populations of 250,000 or more were obtaining money or goods through drug asset forfeiture programs (Reaves 1992, 1). The DOJ has been an important conduit for many of these seizures.[26] DOJ only approved the transfer of about $2.5 million to state and local agencies in 1985, but this jumped almost tenfold in a year, as FY 1986 saw transfers of $24.4 million. The Drug Policy Alliance (2015, 11) reports that "revenue to state and local police from the Justice Department forfeiture fund is up 467 percent in inflation adjusted dollars" for the quarter century between 1987 and 2013, from a total of $56.5 million in FY 1987 ($116 million in 2013 dollars) to a total of $657 million in FY 2013. The Treasury Department also instituted its own forfeiture fund in 1993, so law enforcement agencies supervised by Treasury could facilitate the seizure-forfeiture process. O'Harrow et al. (2014) found that about 5,400 departments and drug task forces have participated in the Equitable Sharing Programs between 2008 and 2014. Figure 1 shows the equitable-sharing payments from both the DOJ and Treasury programs from 2001 to 2013.

Asset seizures have become important sources of state and local police budgets. In fact, "Hundreds of state and local departments and drug task forces appear to rely on seized cash, despite a federal ban on the money to pay salaries or otherwise support budgets. The *Washington Post* found that 298 departments and 210 task forces have seized the equivalent of 20 percent or more of their annual budgets since 2008" (Sallah et al. 2014).[27] In fact, almost all these

Table 3. Standard of Proof in State Forfeiture Laws, 2011

Standard of Proof	States
Prima facie/probable cause	Alabama, Alaska, Delaware, Illinois, Massachusetts, Missouri, Montana, Rhode Island, South Carolina, Wyoming
Probable cause and preponderance of the evidence	Georgia, North Dakota, South Dakota, Washington
Preponderance of the evidence	Arizona, Arkansas, Hawaii, Idaho, Indiana, Iowa, Kansas, Louisiana, Maine, Maryland, Michigan, Mississippi, New Hampshire, New Jersey, Oklahoma, Pennsylvania, Tennessee, Texas, Virginia, West Virginia
Preponderance of the evidence and clear and convincing	Kentucky, New York, Oregon
Clear and convincing	Colorado, Connecticut, Florida, Minnesota, Nevada, New Mexico, Ohio, Utah, Vermont
Clear and convincing and beyond a reasonable doubt	California
Beyond a reasonable doubt	Nebraska, North Carolina,** Wisconsin

(Left margin, vertical text with downward arrow:) More difficult to forfeit assets

Source: Williams et al. (2011, table 2).
Notes: * In states with two forfeiture standards, most commonly the higher one is for forfeiture of real property.
** State law effectively does not allow for civil forfeiture.

Figure 1. Federal Equitable Sharing Payments from the Department of Justice and Treasury Department Forfeiture Programs to State and Local Law Enforcement Agencies, FY 2001–2013

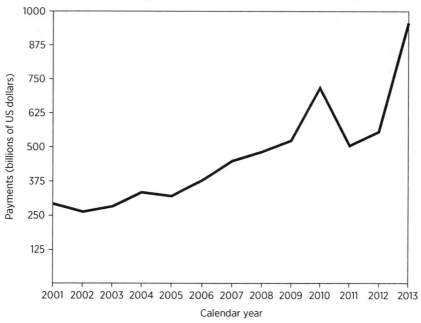

Source: Drug Policy Alliance (2015, 11).

departments and task forces have produced at least 20 percent of their annual budgets through seizure at least three times over the 6 years examined in the *Post* study.

Sallah et al. (2014) cited a former DEA agent, Steven Peterson, who reported that although patrol officers used to try to make their names with large drug busts, this changed when police agency leaders realized that cash seizures could provide funding for their departments. While the intent of the seizure laws allegedly are to attack large drug organizations, they have been "used as a routine source of funding for law enforcement at every level" (O'Harrow et al. 2014). Indeed, as Gary Schons, a former California deputy attorney general observed, "Much like a drug addict becomes addicted to drugs, law enforcement agencies have become dependent on asset forfeitures. They have to have it" (Ehlers 1999, 3). Brad Cates, a former director of asset forfeiture programs at the DOJ, has been cited as saying that Equitable Sharing provides police with "a free floating slush fund" and limits elected officials' ability to influence law enforcement priorities through traditional budget processes (O'Harrow et al. 2014). He now advocates ending the program.

The opportunity to process seizures under federal law clearly offered several reasons for seizures associated with drug investigations to be more attractive than they are under many state seizure laws, and as a result, the federal program increased the incentives for many policing agencies to allocate more effort to drug enforcement.[28] In fact, according to the Heritage Foundation (2015, 4), "42 states shifted their law enforcement priorities toward the pursuit of profit." In addition, the federal authorities will only adopt relatively large seizures, so state laws govern small seizures and, importantly, a large portion of seizures are small. In California, for instance, local prosecutors conducted more than 6,000 forfeiture cases in 1992, and over 94 percent involved seizures of $5,000 or less.[29] Therefore, Mast et al. (2000) hypothesized that states where police keep some portion of seizures under state law should be engaged in greater drug enforcement efforts than states where police cannot keep seizures under state law.[30]

Drug arrests per 100,000 population in states with significant limits on police retention of forfeitures averaged 363 during 1989, whereas states in which police kept seizure proceeds under state law averaged 606 drug arrests per 100,000 during the same year. Other factors, such as the level of drug use or property crime, may explain these interstate differences in drug enforcement, of course, so Mast et al. (2000) tested the hypothesis empirically, controlling for other factors, such as the levels of drug use and of police resources available in a community, alternative demands on those police resources represented by property and violent crime rates, and various socioeconomic characteristics of the community that might influence community demands for drug enforcement.[31] With respect to the impact of asset seizure laws, their results were robust across model specification and alternative samples of cities: police focus relatively more effort on drug control when they can enhance their budgets by retaining seized assets under state laws. State legislation permitting police to keep a portion of seized assets raises drug arrests as a portion of total arrests by about 20 percent and drug arrest per capita by about 18 percent. It appears that local police respond to incentives created by state-level seizure laws. This finding in turn provides indirect support for the contention that the upsurge in drug enforcement that started in 1984–1986 is a result of the incentives created by federal seizure legislation that altered incentives for state and local police. The federal legislation presumably has the largest impact in states where state law does not allow police to keep forfeitures, since they can circumvent such state laws by working through the federal equitable-sharing process.[32] Indeed, Williams et al. (2011) find that when state forfeiture laws allow smaller percentages of takings to be returned to police budgets, police departments respond. The departments that get relatively small portions of seizures under state law tend to be more likely to engage in federal level Equitable Sharing, and thus substitute the more profitable federal forfeiture rules for less profitable state laws. Similar to the studies mentioned above, Williams et al. also find that standards of proof influence the choice to use the federal procedures. Specifically, in states where property owners are presumed innocent and the burden of guilt falls on the arresting agency, these agencies are more likely to pursue federal procedures.

Expanding the Tax Base: Civil Seizures from Innocent Victims

Civil forfeitures can be successful from the police's perspective even if arrest and prosecution are not. Forfeiture laws are supposedly designed to protect lien holders and owners whose property is used without their knowledge or consent, but property owners must bring their claims in civil forfeiture hearings. Furthermore, civil seizures also can be made without filing criminal charges against or arresting the person from whom property is seized, let alone convicting the person of a crime.[33] These facts mean that there really is no way to know with any degree of confidence that criminals and not innocent victims are providing this source of law enforcement revenues.

Generally, owners whose property is alleged to have been used in a drug offense or purchased with the proceeds from drug trafficking have the burden of establishing that they merit relief from the proceeding (National Criminal Justice Association 1988, 41). Not only must the owners prove that they are innocent of the alleged crime, they must also prove lack of both knowledge of and control over any unlawful use of the property. This can be very costly, often prohibitively costly, for many citizens. For instance, in 2009, local law enforcement in Tewksbury, Massachusetts, joined forces with the DOJ to seize The Motel Caswell owned by local resident Russ Caswell and his family. This seizure occurred even though the motel owners were not involved with any criminal activity.[34] The seizure was based on fifteen arrests over a 14-year period (out of an estimated 200,000 guests who stayed at the hotel over the same period) who had been arrested for drug related crimes (Institute for Justice 2013). The government argued that this hotel had facilitated illegal drug transactions throughout this period (Crawford 2015).

The Tewksbury case illustrates one way in which individuals who are not involved in or accused of any drug crimes are still subject to asset seizure, and it also shows that incentives created by civil seizure laws may result in regressive taxes on private property owners. As described by Crawford (2015, 273),

The Motel Caswell was just one of the many commercial properties in Tewksbury with crimes committed on its premises. Police in Tewksbury had made drug-related arrests at both nearby Motel 6 and a Fairfield Inn, as well as in Wal-Mart and Home Depot parking lots. Mr. Caswell's attorneys pointed out that those businesses are corporate entities backed by powerful lawyers and other substantial resources that would enable them to contest a potential seizure; this is in stark contrast to the family-owned Motel Caswell.

In fact, Mr. Caswell spent all his savings (more than $100,000) fighting the ruling before the Institute for Justice (IJ) picked up the case pro bono (Crawford 2015). In January 2013, after IJ had fought for Caswell for 16 months, the case was dismissed, and Caswell regained ownership. The federal judge presiding over the case claimed that the federal government's evidence was exaggerated (Institute for Justice 2013). If IJ did not provide these pro bono services, Caswell may not have been able to pay for continuing the legal battle, and the property (valued at more than $1,000,000) would have provided the local law enforcement agency with a good deal of revenue. The IJ cannot go to the aid of most innocent victims of asset seizures, however, so many of these victims end up negotiating with the policing agency or district attorney and agreeing to accept something less than full reimbursement.

Reliable information on the level of civil asset forfeiture activity is not available. When Williams et al. (2011) attempted to put together data for the Institute of Justice they found that only twenty-nine states had requirements to record the use of civil asset forfeiture and that most of them do not have requirements to share that information. It took 2 years of Freedom of Information Act requests to obtain data from twenty-one of these states, two of which provided unusable data. Double counting and other problems also exist in the available data.[35] Some information from the data obtained is suggestive, however. For instance, local forfeitures were growing rapidly in the states from which Williams et al. (2011) were able to obtain usable data, and the majority of the funds were not obtained through Equitable Sharing.

There appear to be reasons for law enforcement to be reluctant to report on civil forfeiture activity. One of the first major asset-seizure scandals occurred in Volusia County, Florida, during a 41-month period between 1989 and 1992. The county sheriff created a drug squad that seized more than $8 million (an average of $5,000 per day) from motorists on Interstate 95.[36] These seizures were justified by the police as part of the war on drugs. Nonetheless, most Volusia County seizures involved southbound rather than northbound travelers, suggesting that the drug squad was more interested in seizing money than in stopping the flow of drugs. No criminal charges were filed in more than 75 percent of the county's seizure cases. Responses by victims of many of these seizures also suggest that a substantial amount of money was seized from innocent victims. Three-fourths (199) of Volusia County's seizures were contested. Seizures were not returned even when the seizure was challenged, no proof of wrongdoing or criminal record could be found, and the victim presented proof that the money was legitimately earned. Instead, the sheriff's forfeiture attorney handled settlement negotiations. Victims of seizures had to hire attorneys to represent them in the negotiations. Only four people obtained all their money, and presumably, part of the returned funds was paid to lawyers. The rest settled for 50–90 percent of their money after promising not to sue the sheriff's department.[37]

The Volusia County scandal did not end the problematic practice. In fact, the same procedures have been followed many times since then in many more jurisdictions:

> In case after case, highway interdictors appeared to follow a similar script. Police set up what amounted to rolling checkpoints on busy highways and pulled over motorists for minor violations, such as following too closely or improper signaling. They quickly issued warnings or tickets. They studied drivers for signs of nervousness, including pulsing carotid arteries, clenched jaws and perspiration. They also looked for supposed "indicators" of criminal activity, which can include such things as trash on the floor of a vehicle, abundant energy drinks or air fresheners hanging from rearview mirrors. (Sallah et al. 2014)

Increasing numbers of stories about new examples of seizures from innocent victims continued to appear in media outlets and policy studies. One that attracted considerable attention was the shocking story presented in CBS's *60 Minutes* about Donald Scott, killed during a drug raid by local, state, and federal police, who intentionally targeted him to seize his $5 million ranch (no drugs were found). There are far more examples than could be discussed here. The steady stream of such stories has caused a political backlash. For instance, "the attention prompted Congress to reform federal seizure laws in

2000, allowing owners to be reimbursed for their legal fees after successful lawsuits" (Sallah et al. 2014).

An attempt was also made in Congress to end Equitable Sharing, but it failed in the face of the "voracious lobbying" campaign by police and prosecutors, according to former representative Barney Frank (Sallah et al. 2014). In this same context, shortly before he resigned, Attorney General Eric Holder announced a reduction in the adoption program at DOJ. Federal agencies were supposed to stop adopting assets seized by local and state law enforcement agencies unless the property includes firearms, ammunitions, explosives, child pornography, or other materials concerning public safety. These new rules were relatively limited in their effect, as seizures made through joint federal and state or local investigations were still subject to equitable sharing,[38] but as discussed above, they did not last.[39] Given the political power of law enforcement agencies, there clearly is no guarantee that reforms will last.

Political backlash against the misuse of asset seizures has also led to discussion and even change in several state laws.[40] For instance, 69 percent of Utah voters approved an initiative in 2000 that gave much greater protection to property owners caught up in forfeiture proceedings.[41] Most significantly, the law redirected forfeiture funds that had previously been given to law enforcement, by mandating that all forfeiture funds go to the state's education fund. This was a voter approved referendum, however, not state legislation. Police and prosecutor lobbying would have, in all likelihood, prevented passage of such a sweeping change through the state legislature. Law enforcement officials adamantly opposed the forfeiture initiative during the campaign. Furthermore, since it passed, actions have been taken by law enforcement to challenge the change in allocation. The Salt Lake County sheriff and seven other law enforcement officials challenged it in federal court, but the US district court rejected the challenge (Vigh 2002). After that, the state attorney general led a 2002 legislative campaign to overturn the initiative. Legislation was introduced to redirect forfeited revenue back to law enforcement agencies, but angry voters forced the sponsor to withdraw the proposal (Institute for Justice 2003). In January 2003, the state auditor reported that the district attorneys in three counties were actually violating the law, allowing law enforcement agencies to keep at least $237,000 in forfeitures (Stewart 2003). On June 24, 2003, the Institute for Justice, on behalf of Utahns for Property Protection and a group of Utah citizens, filed a "notice of claim" with the attorney general of Utah, demanding immediate action against the three district attorneys to see that the funds were redirected to education. After that the prosecutors returned the money. Law enforcement resistance was not over, however.

In 2013, the Utah attorney general's office presented a fifty-page bill to the Utah House of Representatives majority leader, and told him "that the bill was just minor tweaks that we would call recodifications of that law" in part to bring together scattered laws governing asset forfeitures (Sturgeon 2014). This occurred during the last week of the session, when demands on legislators were at their height. Given the majority leader's assurance that no significant changes were in the bill, as he had been informed by the attorney general's office, the bill passed unanimously without any serious examination of its content. There actually was a significant change in the seizure law, however, as "the new bill substituted the word 'may' for the existing word 'shall' throughout," including in the language of the 2000 referendum (Sturgeon 2014). Legislators were not aware of the change until the Libertas Institute released a paper pointing it out. A new bill overturning the 2013 changes to the original referendum was passed unanimously during the 2014 session.[42]

The evidence provided here suggests that the wide use of civil asset forfeiture in the United States over many decades has created what is somewhat akin to Gordon Tullock's (1975) "Transitional Gains Trap." Even though the "increased value" (to the police) of the use of civil asset forfeiture is obviously not capitalized in any specific resource (real or artificial) belonging to a police department the way rents usually are, it does lead to budget expansion, and presumably to benefits captured by the police or their employers. These beneficiaries have an incentive to continue the practices. Any plans to limit the power of authorities to seize assets has been met by resistance from vested interests that push back or find alternative ways to capture this revenue. A key aspect of this situation, however, is that the vested interest consists of public officials and employees.

Fungible Earmarked Taxes

A frequent consequence of earmarked taxes, particularly when the activity for which the earmark applies also is funded by sources of revenues that are not earmarked (e.g., from the general fund), is that increases in earmarked taxes result in reductions in other funds. Revenues are fungible, so funds generated through earmarked taxes replace (crowd out)[43] other funds. Many states have earmarked revenues from state lotteries by dedicating all these revenues to education, for instance, but this frequently results in reductions in spending on education from state general funds. When this reduction occurs, the activity for which funds are earmarked (e.g., education) does not obtain the anticipated increase in revenues that earmarking presumably was to generate. Total budgets remain roughly the same, with the earmarked funds simply replacing revenues that would come from general funds in the absence of the earmarked tax. Instead of the earmarked taxes providing extra revenues to improve the good or service being provided, they become essential just to maintain the same level and quality that was provided prior to the earmark. Proceeds from asset forfeiture are similarly fungible. They do not necessarily represent a net gain to the local police even when the monies are given directly to the law enforcement agencies, because pressure from other local bureaucrats who are competitors for scarce budgetary resources may cause administrators and politicians with whom bureaucrats bargain to view the flow of money from asset seizures as a substitute for regular appropriations. Police agencies that make substantial forfeitures may see budget allocations reduced to offset expected confiscations.

The extent to which police agencies can increase their budgets through forfeiture activity is explored in Benson et al. (1995) and Baicker and Jacobson (2007). Using data from Florida's local policing jurisdictions, Benson et al. (1995) find that confiscations have a positive and significant impact on police agencies' budgets after accounting for demand and local government budget constraint factors. The estimated elasticity of noncapital expenditures in a given year with respect to confiscations in that year is a very modest .04 for all jurisdictions and .07 for large jurisdictions.[44] Baicker and Jacobson (2007) obtain county-level data from parts of California, Pennsylvania, Arizona, Florida, and New York to test the same hypothesis, and they include additional control variables that were unavailable for Benson et al. (1995). Their empirical results imply that counties reduce police budgets by an average of 82 cents for each dollar seized during the previous year, so police retain about 18 cents per dollar of seizures. Given the lag in budget reductions found by Baicker and Jacobson (2007), police could actually be motivated to pursue seizures even if they expect local governments to reduce budgets by the full amount of the seizures. If police agencies seize assets one year and do not fully anticipate the reduced budget that will follow, they may pursue more seizures the next year to make up for that year's budget shortfall. As this cycle of increased seizures followed by budget reductions repeats, the local government decision makers may begin to assume that seizures will continue and permanently reallocate to other uses a portion of what would be police budgets in the absence of seizures. As a result, the police become dependent on seizures just to maintain their expenditure levels. This is consistent with Worrall's (2001) findings. His survey of a large number of city and county law enforcement executives indicates that many, including almost 40 percent of the large agencies, claim dependence on forfeitures as budgetary supplements. This view is also consistent with Bullock and Carpenter (2010), who examine civil forfeiture from 2001 to 2007 in Texas. For the average agency in Texas, the forfeiture take was 14 percent of their annual budget, but for the top ten forfeiture agencies, it represents on average 37 percent of their budgets, with about 17 percent of these forfeiture funds used for salary and overtime. Pursuit of forfeitures becomes an imperative in such cases, and Worrall (2001, 171) concludes that "the primary implication tied to these findings is that a conflict of interest between effective crime control and creative fiscal management will persist so long as law enforcement agencies remain dependent on civil asset forfeitures."

CONCLUSION

The evolution of the war on drugs is an example of a particularly destructive mechanism of public finance, first through revenue raising "sin taxes" on opium and cocaine, then morphing into budget-maximizing practices of competing bureaucratic agencies that result in prohibition efforts. This process eventually spawned a new earmarked tax in the form of civil asset forfeitures with many of the revenues going to the law enforcement agencies associated in various ways with prohibited drugs. This tax can be applied at the discretion of police, so they, in effect, determine the "tax rate" imposed on each individual who is subjected to the tax. In many states and at the federal level, a civil asset forfeiture need not be accompanied by any type of arrest or formal charge, and the burden of proof is placed on the party whose assets are seized—they must show that the seized assets are not proceeds from criminal activities (or purchased with such proceeds). This provides local authorities with perverse incentives to impose this tax on an ever-expanding tax base. This tax base now includes both criminals and innocent parties who police allegedly suspect of wrongdoing (having assets worth seizing, particularly cash, is apparently a reason to suspect a person of drug dealing).

The rise in the misuse of civil asset seizure earmarked for police use has been met with growing resistance as people increasingly see it as a threat to private property, but this resistance has also been accompanied by push-back from the primary vested interests—the policing agencies. In addition to supporting political pressure against this resistance, vested interests are able to skirt state laws regarding forfeiture. In states where asset forfeiture laws constrain the imposition of such earmarked taxes by state and local police, these policing agencies tend to use federal asset seizure equitable-sharing procedures, established in 1984 as a result of lobbying by law enforcement agencies, to seize property and avoid the more constraining state policies.

It should not come as a surprise that drug prohibition has led to predatory tax mechanisms that extract resources from those supposedly engaged in the drug trade. Substances that alter perceptions, feelings, behavior, or decision-making have been widely targeted as a source of tax revenues. Indeed, the laws that initiated federal involvement with markets in narcotics and marijuana were both tax acts (the Harrison Act of 1914 and the Marijuana Tax Act of 1937), and federal policy implementation was assigned to the Treasury Department. In Treasury, the bureaucratic apparatus engaged in collections was not able to retain the revenues collected, so the agency had to compete for budgets. Their ability to do so was substantially enhanced following the agency's initiatives that criminalized prescriptions for drug addicts. The resulting prohibition policy reduced tax revenues taken directly from narcotics (and later marijuana) markets, but it increased the budgets (portion of other tax revenues) for the policing bureaucracy in Treasury and created incentives for other agencies, federal as well as state and local, to engage in enforcement in order to capture larger budgets.

The rhetoric advanced by public officials and local police departments is inevitably self-serving and thus budget maximizing. This rhetoric has led to more power and increased revenues through predatory public finance in the interbureau competition for budgets, but it has also been used to justify earmarking of a relatively new source of tax revenues—those arising from asset seizures.

NOTES

1. This competition generally involves the pursuit of new policy initiatives (Breton and Wintrobe 1982) that can be used to justify budget increases, much as legislators do when they justify new taxes.

2. Prohibition, monopolization, taxation, and licensing are not mutually exclusive: policy can include combinations of prohibition for some parts of a market (e.g., underage alcohol consumption), monopolization of some parts of the process (e.g., wholesale liquor in some US states), and taxation/licensing (e.g., retail liquor in several states).

3. Interestingly, while several states have passed legislation legalizing medical uses of marijuana, and more recently, the recreational use of marijuana, some of these states are imposing such stringent regulations and high taxes on these legal markets that the illegal markets are still flourishing (Elliott 2014; Ross 2014). In addition, the government itself apparently is beginning to enter the retail marijuana market. On March 7, 2015, a new store was opened in North Bonneville, Washington: The Cannabis Corner. The mayor of the town convinced the city council to form "a Public Development Authority for the sole purpose of selling pot, pipes and marijuana-infused edibles. All the business profits from The Cannabis Corner will now be kicked back to City Hall" (Springer 2015). Thus, the full range of revenue-seeking possibilities for marijuana can now be observed in the United States: market provision

with taxation, licenses, and fees; government provision and implicit taxes from the difference between revenues and costs; and prohibition accompanied by interbureau competition for revenues and asset seizures as an earmarked tax. Now an argument is being made that selling marijuana is an "essential government function" warranted under police powers, just as state liquor stores are (Leff 2016, 12): "The case that marijuana selling is an essential governmental function, however, is stronger than merely the fact that it makes money for the state. Rather, marijuana use has significant negative health and social costs, and so the state's interest in controlling these negative effects, especially among youth, is strong. Just as it is with liquor sales, it is well within the state's police power to seek to control a market in dangerous substances. Protecting the public from the negative effects of such markets is at the heart of what states do."

4.   Given that demand for these products is generally inelastic over a substantial range, large increases in tax rates need not result in equally large reductions in the use of these products.

5.   Murphy (1994, 5) also notes the potential conflict between agencies seeking drug-control funding and agencies seeking funding for other purposes. An illustration is discussed later in the text. Another involves the Office of National Drug Control Policy (ONDCP) and the Department of Health and Human Services (HHS) during the first Bush administration. ONDCP was collecting budget requests from more than fifty agencies at the time to put together the president's budget request. Many of these agencies engage in a large number of activities beyond their drug-control efforts. While these diversified agencies also want to capture part of the drug-control budget, they may see tradeoffs: gaining more of the drug budget could lead Congress to reduce other types of funding. ONDCP does not consider these tradeoffs, however, so "As a result, ONDCP can become an advocate for funding increases that the potential recipient opposes" (Murphy 1994, 5). In this case, ONDCP advocated increased drug treatment funding for HHS, even though HHS objected, because the Department was concerned about lost funding for what they considered to be higher priorities. Given ONDCP's supervisory role over the drug-control process, its incentives to expand drug-control spending dominates its budget requests both for itself and for the programs in other agencies. How important this might be is unclear, however, because the drug budget approval process in Congress is highly fragmented, "falling under the jurisdiction of nine different appropriation bills. Most funding decisions are made at the subcommittee level" (Murphy 1994, 5).

6.   One example occurred in 1966 when Stutmann was stationed in Washington, DC (Stutmann and Esposito 1992, 65–73). His primary focus at the time was on heroin, but he arrested an American University student for selling marijuana, resulting in a *Washington Post* front-page story. Because of the publicity, Stutmann's superior ordered him to drop heroin investigations to focus on marijuana on college campuses. When he arrested a congressman's daughter, the local DEA office increased its focus on marijuana even more, because "all of a sudden lawmakers were reading about their kids. Now they wanted marijuana stopped" (Stutmann and Esposito 1992, 66).

7.   The toxicology reports did indicate that Eugene had marijuana in his system. Apparently, Miami CBS News did not include this in their definition of exotic street drugs.

8.   This trend apparently has continued. In 2013, only 1.31 Part I arrests occurred per drug arrest. Considering such statistics over a very long time period is problematic, however, because many factors could be changing that could also cause these relative values to change rather than (or in addition to) the allocation decisions of police. There could be a decrease in Part 1 arrests, for instance, due to fewer Part I crimes, an increase in drug use, or both. Part 1 arrests were higher in 2013 (2,049,644) than in 1989 (1,432,554), however, even though reported crimes have fallen over the same years (from about 13.25 million to about 9.8 million). The drop in reported crimes could help explain the relative reduction in emphasis on property and violent crimes, of course, even though there has been more than a 43 percent increase in the number of such arrests (total drug and Part 1 arrests both rose, in part due to growing numbers of police, improved policing technology, and other related factors since 1989). If drug crimes were increasing, of course, that could be another causal factor. There is no way to estimate drug crime levels, but there is some information on trends

in drug use obtained from surveys and other sources. Consider, for instance, the national Youth Risk Behavior Survey (YRBS), which monitors priority health risk behaviors that contribute to the leading causes of death, disability, and social problems among youth and adults in the United States (Centers for Disease Control 2015). The national YRBS is conducted every 2 years during the spring semester and provides data representative of ninth and twelfth grade students in both public and private schools. The implications from this survey are mixed. Data on marijuana, cocaine, and steroid use reported in 1991 can be compared to 2013 data (the report includes 2014 and 2015 as well). These data suggest substantial increased use of marijuana, from 31.3 (14.7) percent reporting ever using (currently using) in 1991 to 38.6 (23.4) percent in 2013. Cocaine use apparently has fallen, however, from 5.9 percent reporting ever using in 1991 to 5.5 percent in 2013 (current use estimates are not reported in this document). However, ever having used a steroid without a doctor's permission went from 2.7 percent in 1991 to 3.2 percent in 2013. All information on other drugs indicate falling use, although generally for shorter data periods: reports of ever using heroin fell from 2.4 percent in 1999 (3.1 percent in 2001) to 2.2 percent in 2013; ever using methamphetamines changed from 9.1 percent in 1999 to 3.2 percent in 2013; the percentage reporting ever using ecstasy dropped from 11.1 in 2001 to 6.6 in 2013; use of prescription drugs without a doctor's permission fell from 20.2 percent in 2009 to 17.8 percent in 2013; 13.3 percent reported that they had used hallucinogenic drugs in 2001, but this was down to 7.1 percent in 2013; and ever injecting any illegal drug declined from a 1995 percentage of 2.1 to 1.7 in 2013. Thus, only marijuana and steroid use appear to be rising over this period, while the use of all other drugs apparently has declined, at least relative to the high school population. Interestingly, the percentage reporting use of all drugs except steroids apparently fell from 2013 to 2015, including marijuana.

9. A drop in these figures occurred from 1989 to 1993, for instance, but that was followed by a rapid increase, surpassing the temporary 1989 peak by 1995. Drug arrests as a percentage of total arrests has not fallen below 12 percent since 2003, although the percentage fell again after another temporary 2006 peak of 13.1 percent, before starting upward again in 2010–2011 and surpassing the 2006 peak in 2013.

10. Federal forfeiture actions in drug enforcement started much earlier than 1984, however. The forfeiture provision of the Comprehensive Drug Abuse Prevention and Control Act of 1970 authorizes federal agencies to seize and forfeit illicit drugs, manufacturing and storage equipment, and conveyances used to transport drugs. The Psychotropic Substances Act of 1978 followed, and then the 1980s produced several more changes, all of which expand federal law-enforcement powers to seize property.

11. The outlier of $199 million in 2001 is due to the Civil Asset Forfeiture Act in 2000, which added some procedural requirements that delayed recording of seizures in the following year.

12. These charges included trafficking drugs on the Internet, narcotics-trafficking conspiracy, running a continuing criminal enterprise, computer-hacking conspiracy and money-laundering conspiracy (Van Voris and Hurtado 2015).

13. According to Paul (2015b), this figure is based on transaction records gathered by the FBI that show $182,960,285 in illegal drug sales and transactions for fake identification equaling $1,001,636. As Paul (2015b) claims: "The government contends Ulbricht is liable for all transactions on Silk Road because of the structure of the site."

14. FBI press release of accusations, which at the time of Ulbricht's arrest only included four charges, http://www.fbi.gov/newyork/press-releases/2014/manhattan-u.s.-attorney-announces -the-indictment-of-rossulbricht-the-creator-and-owner-of-the-silk-road-website.

15. There are various possible explanations beyond the one stressed here for the upsurge in drug enforcement that started in the 1980s, but they are not supported by actual evidence (Rasmussen and Benson 1994, 122–27; Benson and Rasmussen 1996, 1997). Many law enforcement personnel stress the introduction of crack cocaine, but as Johnson (1987) reports, crack was not introduced into the United States until October or November 1985, and then only in Miami, Los Angeles, and New York. Another possibility is that the public

was becoming increasingly concerned about drug use, so local public officials, responding to political pressures, were demanding that their police departments increase drug enforcement. However, 1985 public opinion surveys actually suggest that the public did not consider drugs to be a particularly important problem (Rasmussen and Benson 1994, 122–27). In fact, there is evidence that changes in enforcement efforts lead to changes in public opinion. Recall the discussion above about DEA agent Robert Stutmann's manipulation of the media to create the perception that a crack crisis was developing.

16. This was not the first congressional action dealing with drug-related civil asset forfeiture—see note 10. It was not the last either. For instance, in addition to the Comprehensive Crime Act of 1984, Congress passed the Comprehensive Forfeiture Act of 1984, the Anti-Drug Abuse Act of 1986, the Money Laundering Control Act of 1986, and the Anti-Drug Abuse Act of 1988; all contain sections dealing with asset seizures and expanding the power of criminal justice officials to seize assets. Additional legislation dealing with seizure policy has also continued to be produced since the 1980s. Furthermore, the forfeiture power is not limited to drug enforcement. It has grown to include a wide array of both federal and state crimes. There were more than 200 forfeiture statutes at the federal level in 1992, allowing confiscation of private property for various federal crimes (Copeland 1992).

17. As Chambliss and Seidman (1971, 73) explained, "every detailed study of the emergence of legal norms has consistently shown the immense importance of interest-group activity, not the public interest, as the critical variable." Similarly, Rhodes (1977, 13) pointed out that "as far as crime policy and legislation are concerned, public opinion and attitudes are generally irrelevant. The same is not true, however, of specifically interested criminal justice publics." Additional research implies similar conclusions (e.g., Stuntz 2001, Gainer 2011) but also makes it clear that one of the most important "specifically interested criminal justice publics" consists of law enforcement bureaucracies and their employees (e.g., Berk et al. 1977; Rasmussen and Benson 1994, 119–73; Benson et al. 1995; Benson and Rasmussen 1996, 1997). Bureaucrats often try to influence the demand side of the political process (Berk et al. 1977; Breton and Wintrobe 1982; Benson 1990), and in the context of this presentation, it is widely recognized that policing agencies have been and are a major source of demand for much of the relevant legislation. Recall the discussion of the Marijuana Tax Act, for instance.

18. The only group suggesting problems with the legislation in the hearing was the Criminal Justice Section of the American Bar Association. Two drug-therapy organizations (The Therapy Committees of America, and the Alcohol and Drug Problems Association) also advocated forfeiture sharing, but proposed that a share also go to therapy programs. Law enforcement lobbies prevailed, as the statute mandated that shared assets go directly to law enforcement agencies rather than into general funds, education funds, or other recipients that various state laws mandated at the time.

19. This claim has been challenged by academic research. While some drugs may lead to non-drug crime, most of the crime associated with drug markets is systemic. It arises because the market is illegal, so violence is used to enforce contracts, protect property, and compete for market shares. Market participants are also attractive targets for robbery and other crimes, because they generally have cash or drugs and they are not likely to report the crime. See for example, Rasmussen and Benson (1994), Resignato (2000), and Benson (2009).

20. Attorney General Eric Holder announced various limitations to the adoption program in January 2015, but he did not eliminate the entire adoption program or end Equitable Sharing (O'Harrow et al. 2014). Even this partial elimination did not last, however, as Holder's replacement, Attorney General Loretta Lynch, quietly reinstituted the DOJ's Equitable Sharing Program in April 2016 (Glass 2016). See additional discussion below. Under the adoption program, state and local law enforcement agencies ask the DOJ to adopt asset seizure when the conduct giving rise to the seizure violates a federal law and the property is forfeitable under one of the federal forfeiture provisions that the DOJ enforces (with some recently created limitations discussed below). This is the case with drug offenses. A civil burden of proof is also required under federal law, not the criminal burden of proof required in many states. The DEA provided an outline of seizure and forfeiture

procedures for local police applying for adoption through the agency at http://www.cass .net/~wdogs/lfed.htm (a much more detailed specification of the "General Adoption Policy and Procedure" is available in the *United States Attorneys' Manual*, Chapter 9-116, found at http://www.usdoj.gov/usao/eousa/foia_reading_room/usam/title9/116mcrm.htm#9-116 .100). The DEA applies certain conditions when considering the acceptance of a seizure for adoption. A valid prosecutorial purpose must exist when requesting the adoption of a seizure for forfeiture. An example of a valid prosecutorial purpose might be that the state's forfeiture laws require a more stringent standard of proof than does federal law, and the police cannot obtain sufficient evidence to meet the state standard. In addition, the property referred for adoption cannot be appraised below specified minimum monetary values, which vary according to the nature of the property. After the property is delivered to the DOJ, the DOJ can transfer back 90 percent (initially 80 percent) to the law enforcement agency responsible for the seizure. Forfeited property can either be credited directly to the budget of the requesting law enforcement agency or "passed through" an otherwise ineligible entity, such as a district attorney's office, to be used for a law enforcement purpose. The local agency can request return of the forfeited property or the proceeds from its sale. While states are beginning to reconsider and even constrain asset seizure, Attorney General Lynch's actions mean that local agencies can still capture revenues through equitable sharing. This "means that while states have been making real progress on reforming asset forfeiture laws that have led to decades of abuse, the Department of Justice is securing the ability for state and local authorities to continue business-as-usual" (Glass 2016).

21. As education bureaucrats and others affected by the diversion of revenues to law enforcement recognized what was going on, they begin to advocate for a change in the federal law. They were successful, at least initially: the Anti-Drug Abuse Act (passed on November 18, 1988) changed the asset-forfeiture provisions that had been established in 1984.
Section 6077 of the 1988 statute stated that the attorney general had to assure that any seized asset transferred to a state or local law enforcement agency "is not so transferred to circumvent any requirement of state law that prohibits forfeiture or limits the use or disposition of property forfeited to state or local agencies." This provision was designated to go into effect on October 1, 1989, and the DOJ interpreted it to mandate an end to all adoptive forfeitures (Subcommittee on Crime of the Committee on the Judiciary 1990, 166). State and local law enforcement officials immediately began advocating repeal of Section 6077, however. For example, the Subcommittee on Crime heard testimony on April 24, 1989, advocating repeal of Section 6077 from such groups as the International Association of Chiefs of Police, the Florida Department of Law Enforcement, the North Carolina Department of Crime Control and Public Safety, and the US Attorney General's Office. The police lobbies won the battle over federal legislation, as Section 6077 of the Anti-Drug Abuse Act of 1988 never went into effect. Its repeal, hidden in the 1990 Defense Appropriations bill, applied retroactively to October 1, 1989.

22. Edgeworth (2004, 175–83) provides state-law requirements for the distribution of seizure forfeitures as of 2004. Although many state laws have changed since 1984, using the federal statute "as a template . . . in drafting their own civil narcotic forfeiture statutes" (Edgeworth 2004, 28), this 2004 publication reveals that considerable incentives for many law enforcement agencies to circumvent state distributional requirements remain. North Carolina, Missouri, and Utah (see below) direct proceeds to education. Sixteen states allocate a defined portion of forfeitures to law enforcement while also allocating various portions to other purposes. Five states allocate a portion of seizure proceeds to the prosecutor, with the remainder going to the seizing agency without requiring a portion to be spent on specific activities such as education or prevention activities. Other states direct forfeitures to law enforcement but require that some portion be used for specified purposes. Twelve states direct all seizure proceeds to the agencies that make them without specifying that some be used for education or prevention programs. Some of these states actually mandate that the proceeds be deposited in the state or local general fund while requiring that they be spent on law enforcement, but others allow the agency to retain the seizures. Three states direct all proceeds into a state fund for law enforcement (South Dakota's state fund is exclusively for drug control). Five states deposit such proceeds in state or local general (or revolving) funds, although law enforcement agencies presumably can bargain

to get all or some of these funds added to their budgets (in fact, Texas and Oklahoma make this explicit). Several states have recently begun to consider and actually impose limitations on asset seizure activity, however, including Utah, as explained below. In fact, in 2014, 2015, and early 2016, Minnesota, Nevada, Montana, New Mexico, New Hampshire, Maryland, and Nebraska passed legislation requiring criminal conviction before assets can by seized (Meyer 2016; Snead 2016), although police in New Mexico continue to make such seizures (Kaste 2016). Some of these same states, as well as others, raised the standard of proof required for seizures, shifted the burden of proof from the property owner to law enforcement, or redirected some (or all) seizures away from law enforcement. Others imposed transparency reporting requirements on police regarding seizures or took other actions related to seizures. See Institute for Justice (2016) for details. Given the power of the police lobby, of course, such legislation could easily be repealed. Kaste (2016) suggests that the "police chiefs and sheriffs, meanwhile, are still puzzling over how this new state law even happened. Law enforcement's usually pretty good at defending civil forfeiture at state capitols. But somehow, this legislation got past them." Even if the legislation is not repealed, Snead (2016) notes, the "impact of state-level forfeiture reforms is often blunted thanks to a federal program known as 'equitable sharing.'" See note 20 in this context, as well as additional discussion below of other state-level political actions regarding seizures.

23. This was true for more states in 1986, but by 2004, five states still did not have any statutory authority to seize real property used or intended to be used to facilitate a crime: Alaska, Nebraska, New Mexico, North Carolina, and Vermont. All states do allow seizures of real property if that property is obtained as part of the proceeds from the illegal activity. The burden of proof required to make real property seizures may be stricter than it is for other seizures, and stricter than it is for federal seizures. Similarly, many states accept more defenses in the case of real property seizures than they do for other seizures (Edgeworth 2004, 187–98).

24. The federal standard changed in 2000 with passage of the Civil Asset Forfeiture Reform Act. Although this act "substantially enhanced the property subject to forfeiture under the federal system" (Edgeworth 2004, 25), it also changed the burden-of-proof requirement from probable cause to "preponderance of evidence" (Edgeworth 2004, 113).

25. These statistics are originally reported in Miller and Selva (1994).

26. Equitable Sharing clearly has been widely used, but it should be noted that the adoption program actually only accounts for about 10 percent of total equitable-sharing transfers from federal to state and local law enforcement (Drug Policy Alliance 2015, 9).

27. Federal agencies did a lot more to facilitate and encourage this seizure activity. Some of the increase was driven by Operation Pipeline, for instance, a nationwide DEA program launched in 1986 that promotes highway interdiction training for state and local police (Sallah et al. 2014). At least $1 million in Justice and Homeland Security grants to police in Florida, Indiana, Oklahoma, Tennessee, and Wisconsin over the past decade was used to pay for training in seizure methods by Desert Snow, the leading firm in the industry that has developed to teach aggressive methods for highway interdiction and asset seizure. Another $2.5 million was also spent by other federal agencies, such as the DEA, Customs and Border Protection, and Immigration and Customs Enforcement in contracts on Desert Snow training for police. Two million dollars from the DEA also paid for training by another member of the industry, the 4:20 Group. Estimates suggest that more than 50,000 police officers have been taught aggressive techniques by such firms over the past decade (in addition to federal funding, state and local police agencies have spent millions of dollars on training). Sallah et al. (2014) provide a lengthy discussion of such programs, with a focus on Desert Snow (also see O'Harrow et al. 2014). The federal government also has encouraged state and local police to share information about drivers through the private intelligence system, Black Asphalt, started by Desert Snow. Police participating in Black Asphalt or trained by Desert Snow (or both) reportedly seized more than $427 million over 5 years.

28. Many other differences between state and federal seizure laws can influence police incentives. See Edgeworth (2004) and CCIM Institute (2008).

29. "In that regard, little has changed: the average value of a state forfeiture in California in 2013 in constant dollars was $5,145" (Drug Policy Alliance 2015, 16).

30. Many state laws now allow seizures of property arising from investigations of non-drug crimes (federal law does too), but drug enforcement is virtually always the most lucrative source of seizures because of the huge amount of cash involved in the market, along with many transportation, storage, and production assets that are attractive targets for property seizures (e.g., cars, boats, airplanes, land used to grow marijuana). Most other crimes also do not generate as many opportunities for seizures. Drug markets are virtually ubiquitous, and seizures through drug enforcement efforts are relatively easy to make.

31. Mast et al. (2000) use two different samples of cities to test the model, recognizing that one determinant of drug enforcement may be the level of drug market activity. A fully specified model is not possible for a large sample, because there are no reliable estimates of the prevalence of drug market activity in most political jurisdictions. However, annual jurisdiction-level data on drug use for a limited sample of twenty-four cities is provided by the National Institute of Justice's Drug Use Forecasting program. To obtain the measure of drug use in each of the twenty-four cities, urine samples are collected from arrestees in jail. These data provided a good measure of drug use in the arrestee population, but not necessarily for the entire drug market in a city. It does indicate the level of drug use among that part of the population that police deal with, however, and therefore presumably the population that is likely to influence police decision makers' perception of the magnitude of the "drug problem." Use of this sample carries a high price in terms of degrees of freedom in the statistical analysis, but the ability to control for drug use makes it very attractive, particularly when supplemented by an analysis of a substantially larger sample of cities that do not have a direct measure of drug use. The results regarding state seizure laws are robust across both samples.

32. Baicker and Jacobson (2007) reach similar conclusions, finding that a 1 percent increase in the "sharing rate" (a variable that combines information on the sharing percentages going to police as established by state law and a measure of the extent to which counties reduce budgets following seizures to compensate for the increased amount of resources due to forfeitures) results in a 0.1 percent increase in total drug arrests. They find a larger impact on possession arrests than on sales arrests, and on opiate and cocaine arrests than on marijuana arrests (in fact, their marijuana arrest coefficient is not significant). However, some of these estimates may be problematic because of their use of the constructed sharing rate. This variable implies an assumption that police fully anticipate the reductions in budget by the budgeting authority, but perhaps more importantly, it rules out the dependency implications of seizures suggested by Worrall's (2001) findings. The fact that budgets are reduced with a lag may actually imply that the entire amount of the seizure is important for police, either as a net gain or to cover reductions in budget allocations.

33. Information about procedures and strategies for civil forfeiture is provided to policing agencies through continuing education seminars for local prosecutors and law enforcement officials. "Officials share tips on maximizing profits, defeating the objections of so-called 'innocent owners' who were not present when the suspected offense occurred, and keeping the proceeds in the hands of law enforcement and out of general fund budgets" (Dewan 2014).

34. United States v. 434 Main Street, Tewksbury, Mass.

35. This explains why virtually every study and media story about asset seizures focuses on Equitable Sharing. Data from both the DOJ and Treasury are provided in annual reports.

36. See the Pulitzer Prize–winning series of *Orlando Sentinel* articles during June 1992 by Jeff Brazil and Steve Berry that describes, in vivid detail, the asset seizure program in Volusia County, Florida.

37. A 21-year-old naval reservist suffered a $3,989 seizure in 1990, for instance, and even though he produced Navy pay stubs to show the source of the money, he ultimately settled for the return of $2,989, with 25 percent of that going to his lawyer. In similar cases the sheriff's department kept $4,750 out of $19,000 (the lawyer got another $1,000); $3,750

out of $31,000 (the attorney got about 33 percent of the $27,250 returned); $4,000 of $19,000 ($1,000 to the attorney); $6,000 out of $36,990 (the attorney's fee was 25 percent of the rest); and $10,000 out of $38,923 (the attorney got one-third of the recovery). Note that the fact that 25 percent of the seizures are not challenged does not mean that they are "legitimate." The cost of making a challenge may be too high for it to be worthwhile. One Louisiana county sheriff recognized this, for instance, and focused seizure actions on out-of-state cars, realizing that these drivers were less likely to challenge than were state residents (reported on NBC's *Dateline* on January 3, 1997). Many additional "shocking examples of unjust civil forfeitures" are provided in Hyde (1995) and Ehlers (1999). The Heritage Foundation (2015, 13–16) also discusses a few recent examples, and for more, see Braiser (2015) and the six-part *Washington Post* series that includes O'Harrow and Rich (2014), O'Harrow (2014), O'Harrow et al. (2014), and Sallah et al. (2014).

38. "[E]xceptions swallow the new rules. Local and state police departments will no longer be able to "adopt" seized property when they're working completely alone and without any federal aid, but they can still get deputized by a federal agent, work through a federal task force, or cite a vague public safety exemption to tap into forfeiture powers and continue seizing people's stuff for cash" (Lopez 2015). Furthermore, as the DOJ reports in its announcement of Holder's actions, "adoptions currently constitute a very small slice of the federal asset forfeiture program. Over the last six years, adoptions accounted for roughly three percent of the value of forfeitures in the Department of Justice Asset Forfeiture Program" (Department of Justice, Office of Public Affairs 2015). (This may suggest that adoptions did not provide the stimulus for state and local involvement in Reagan's drug war, as contended above, but adoptions are much more important early in the period and they, along with Equitable Sharing, stimulate police interest in seizures and demand for changes in state laws to allow local police to keep seizures without adoption.) More importantly, as Pilon (2015) notes, "the reform does not limit the ability of state and local officials to seize assets under their state laws. Regrettably, many if not most of the abuses today take place at the state level, yet changes in federal law, which often serves as a model for state law, can affect state law as well."

39. See note 20.

40. See note 22.

41. The following paragraph draws on the Institute for Justice (2003) report, where more details can be found.

42. There are many other examples of law enforcement political actions to thwart changes in forfeiture laws that reduce their ability to seize assets and keep the assets seized. See, for instance, O'Harrow and Rich (2014).

43. See Crowley and Hoffer (chapter 6, this volume).

44. Some models of bureaucratic behavior assume that bureau decision makers' utility can be maximized through bureau size maximization or through budget maximization (e.g., Niskanen 1968, 1971). Others contend that discretion also may be a major source of satisfaction (Parker 1992), and in this context, Migué and Belanger (1974) and other theorists propose that bureaucrats seek discretion reflected by a budget with excess revenues over actual costs (discretionary budget) rather than total budget (an argument Niskanen accepted [1975]; a large literature now expands on and tests this Niskanen/Migué and Bélanger model [Benson 1995]). If this is the case then the seemingly modest gains in total budget through seizures does not necessarily mean that it is unimportant to police-agency decision makers, even if they recognize that the revenues they collect will be largely offset by reductions in their general budgets. The apparently small budgetary impact of seizures is potentially large in terms of discretionary budget expansion, since only a small fraction of noncapital expenditures are likely to be discretionary. On the other hand, bureaucrats might be budget maximizers but not recognize that the budget authorities will reduce total budgets due to seizure revenues, and, as a result, they fall into a dependency trap as explained in Worrall (2001) that is discussed below.

REFERENCES

ABC News. 2012. "Face-Eating Cannibal Attack May Be Latest in String of 'Bath Salts' Incidents." June 1. http://abcnews.go.com/Blotter/face-eating-cannibal-attack-latest-bath-saltsincident /story?id=16470389.

Associated Press. 2015. "Holder Announces Changes to Asset Forfeiture Program." January 16. http://www.foxnews.com/politics/2015/01/16/holder-announces-changes-to-assetforfeiture -program/.

Baicker, Katherine, and Mirreille Jacobson. 2007. "Finders Keepers: Forfeiture Laws, Policing Incentives, and Local Budgets." *Journal of Public Economics* 91 (11–12): 2113–34.

Becker, Howard. 1963. *Outsiders: Studies in Sociological Deviance*. New York: Free Press.

Benson, Bruce L. 1990. *The Enterprise of Law: Justice without the State*. San Francisco: Pacific Research Institute for Public Policy.

———. 1995. "Understanding Bureaucratic Behavior: Implications from the Public Choice Literature." *Journal of Public Finance and Public Choice* 8 (2–3): 89–117.

———. 1998. *To Serve and Protect: Privatization and Community in Criminal Justice*. New York: New York University Press.

———. 2009. "Escalating the War on Drugs: Causes and Consequences." *Stanford Law and Policy Review* 20 (2): 293–357.

Benson, Bruce L., and David W. Rasmussen. 1996. "Predatory Public Finance and the Origins of the War on Drugs: 1984–1989." *Independent Review: A Journal of Political Economy* 1 (2): 163–89.

———. 1997. "Predatory Public Finance and the Origins of the War on Drugs: 1984–1989." In *Taxing Choice: The Predatory Politics of Fiscal Discrimination*, edited by William F. Shughart II, 197–225. New Brunswick, NJ: Transaction.

Benson, Bruce L., David W. Rasmussen, and David L. Sollars. 1995. "Police Bureaucracies, Their Incentives, and the War on Drugs." *Public Choice* 83 (1–2): 21–45.

Benson, Bruce L., David W. Rasmussen, and Paul R. Zimmerman. 2003. "Implicit Taxes Collected by State Liquor Monopolies." *Public Choice* 115 (5): 313–31.

Berk, Richard, Harold Brackman, and Selma Lesser. 1977. *A Measure of Justice: An Empirical Study of Changes in the California Penal Code, 1955–1971*. New York: Academic Press.

Blumberg, Abraham. 1979. *Criminal Justice: Issues and Ironies*, 2nd ed. New York: New Viewpoints.

Bonnie, Richard J., and Charles Whitebread II. 1974. *The Marijuana Conviction: A History of Marijuana Prohibition in the United States*. Charlottesville: University of Virginia Press.

Brasier, L. L. 2015. "Police Seized More than $24 Million in Assets from Michiganders in 2013, under Asset Forfeiture Laws." *Detroit Free Press*, February 22. http://www.freep.com/story /news/local/michigan/2015/02/22/civil-asset-forfeiture-michiganseizures-aclu-heritage -foundation-institute-justice/23737663/.

Breton, Albert, and Ronald Wintrobe. 1982. *The Logic of Bureaucratic Control*. Cambridge: Cambridge University Press.

Bullock, Scott, and Dick M. Carpenter II. 2010. *Forfeiting Justice: How Texas Police & Prosecutors Cash in on Seized Property*. Arlington, VA: Institute for Justice. http://www.ij.org/forfeiting -justice.

CBS Miami. 2012. "Medical Examiner: Causeway Cannibal Not High on Bath Salts." June 27. http://miami.cbslocal.com/2012/06/27/medical-examiner-causeway-cannibal-not-high-on -bath-salts/.

CCIM Institute. 2008. *Civil Asset Forfeiture*. Chicago.

Centers for Disease Control. 2015. *Trends in the Prevalence of Marijuana, Cocaine, and Other Illegal Drug Use National YRBS: 1991–2015*. Washington, DC: Division of Adolescent and Youth

Health. http://www.cdc.gov/healthyyouth/data/yrbs/pdf/trends/2015_us_drug_trend _yrbs.pdf.

Chambliss, William, and Robert Seidman. 1971. *Law, Order, and Power*. Reading, MA: Addison-Wesley.

Copeland, Cary H. 1992. *Civil Forfeiture for the Non-Lawyer*. Washington, DC: US Department of Justice, Bureau of Justice Assistance Forfeiture Project.

CNN. 2012. "'Zombie Apocalypse' Trending as Bad News Spreads Quickly." June 1. http://news .blogs.cnn.com/2012/06/01/zombie-apocalypse-trending-as-bad-news-spreads-quickly/.

Crawford, Andrew. 2015. "Civil Asset Forfeiture in Massachusetts: A Flawed Incentive Structure and Its Impact on Indigent Property Owners." *Boston College Journal of Law & Social Justice* 35: 257–84.

Department of Justice, Office of Public Affairs. 2015. "Attorney General Prohibits Federal Agency Adoptions of Assets Seized by State and Local Law Enforcement Agencies Except Where Needed to Protect Public Safety." January 16. http://www.justice.gov/opa/pr/attorney-general -prohibitsfederal-agency-adoptions-assets-seized-state-and-local-law.

Dewan, Shaila. 2014. "Police Use Department Wish List When Deciding Which Assets to Seize." *New York Times*, November 9. http://www.nytimes.com/2014/11/10/us/police-use -department-wishlist-when-deciding-which-assets-to-seize.html.

Dickson, Donald. 1968. "Bureaucracy and Morality: An Organizational Perspective on a Moral Crusade." *Social Problems* 16 (2): 142–56.

Drug Policy Alliance. 2015. *Above the Law: An Investigation of Civil Asset Forfeiture in California*. Los Angeles.

Edgeworth, Dee R. 2004. *Asset Forfeiture: Practice and Procedure in State and Federal Courts*. Chicago: American Bar Association.

Ehlers, Scott. 1999. "Asset Forfeiture." *Drug Policy Foundation Policy Brief*. Washington, DC: Drug Policy Foundation.

Elliot, Steve. 2014. "Washington: Legal Marijuana Stores Having Trouble Matching Black Market Prices." *HempNews*, December. http://hemp.org/news/node/4404#sthash .SARZlO0e.dpuf.

Gainer, Ronald L. 2011. "Remarks on the Introduction of Criminal Law Reform Initiatives." *Journal of Law, Economics and Policy* 7 (4): 587–96.

Glass, Kevin. 2016. "A Setback for Justice: Obama's DOJ Is Doing Criminal Justice Reform No Favors by Propping Up Unfair Asset Forfeiture Laws." *U.S. News and World Report*, April 11. http://www.usnews.com/opinion/articles/2016-04-11/obamas-doj-sets-back-justice-with -asset-forfeiture-program.

Heritage Foundation. 2015. *Arresting Your Property: How Civil Asset Forfeitures Turn Police into Profiteers*. Washington, DC: Heritage Foundation.

Hill, Stuart. 1971. *Crime, Power and Morality: The Criminal Law Process in the United States*. Scranton, PA: Chandler Publishing.

Holcombe, R. G. 1996. "Growth of the Federal Government in the 1920s." *Cato Journal* 16 (2): 175–99.

Hyde, Henry. 1995. *Forfeiting Our Property Rights: Is Your Property Safe from Seizure?* Washington, DC: Cato Institute.

Institute for Justice. 2003. *Utah Asset Forfeiture—Background*. Arlington, VA. http://www.ij.org /utah-asset-forfeiture-background.

———. 2013. *Massachusetts Civil Forfeiture*. Arlington, VA. https://www.ij.org/massachusetts-civil -forfeiture.

———. 2016. *End Civil Forfeitures*. Arlington, VA. http://endforfeiture.com/#legislation.

Johnson, Elaine M. 1987. "Cocaine: The American Experience." In *The Cocaine Crisis*, edited by David F. Allen, 33–44. New York: Plenum.

Kaplan, John. 1970. *Marijuana: The New Prohibition*. New York: World Publishing.

Kaste, Martin. 2016. "New Mexico Ended Civil Asset Forfeiture. Why Then Is It Still Happening?" National Public Radio, June 7. http://www.npr.org/2016/06/07/481058641/new-mexico -ended-civil-asset-forfeiture-why-then-is-it-still-happening.

King, R. 1957. "Narcotic Drug Laws and Enforcement Policies." *Law and Contemporary Problems* 22 (1): 113–31.

———. 1978. "Drug Abuse Problems and the Idioms of War." *Journal of Drug Issues* 8 (2): 221–31.

Klein, Dorie. 1983. "Ill and Against the Law: The Social and Medical Control of Heroin Users." *Journal of Drug Issues* 13 (1): 31–55.

Leff, Benjamin M. 2016. "Tax Benefits of Government-Owned Marijuana Stores." *U.C. Davis Law Review* (2): 659–88.

Lindesmith, Alfred. 1965. *The Addict and the Law*. New York: Vintage.

Lopez, German. 2015. "Police Seized His Life Savings without Charging Him for a Crime. Now He's Fighting Back." Arlington, VA: Institute for Justice. http://www.vox.com/2015/6/17 /8792623/civil-forfeiturecharles-clarke.

Mast, Brent D., Bruce L. Benson, and David W. Rasmussen. 2000. "Entrepreneurial Police and Drug Enforcement Policy." *Public Choice* 104 (3/4): 285–308.

Meyer, Jared. 2016. "Maryland Restricts Cops Stealing from Innocent People: The State Puts the Brakes on 'Policing for Profit.'" *FEE.org*, May 23. https://fee.org/articles/maryland-restricts -cops-stealing-from-innocent-people/.

Migué, J.-L., and G. Bélanger. 1974. "Towards a General Theory of Managerial Discretion." *Public Choice* 17:27–43.

Miller, Lisa L. 2004. "Rethinking Bureaucrats in the Policy Process: Criminal Justice Agents and the National Crime Agenda." *Policy Studies Journal* 32 (4): 569–88.

Miller, Mitchell, and Lance Selva. 1994. "Drug Enforcement's Doubled-Edged Sword: An Assessment of Asset Forfeiture Programs," *Justice Quarterly* 11: 313–35.

Murphy, Patrick. 1994. "Keeping Score: The Frailties of the Federal Drug Budget." Rand Drug Policy Research Center Issue Paper 138, 1–5. Santa Monica, CA: Rand Drug Policy Research Center.

National Criminal Justice Association. 1988. *Asset Seizure and Forfeiture: Developing and Maintaining a State Capability*. Washington, DC.

Niskanen, William. 1968. "The Peculiar Economics of Bureaucracy." *American Economic Review* 58:293–305.

———. 1971. *Bureaucracy and Representative Government*. Chicago, IL: Aldine-Atherton.

———. 1975. "Bureaucrats and Politicians." *Journal of Law and Economics* 18:617–43.

O'Harrow, Robert Jr. 2014. "Highway Seizure in Iowa Fuels Debate about Asset-Forfeiture Laws." *Washington Post*, November 10. http://www.washingtonpost.com/investigations/highway -seizure-in-iowa-fuels-debate-about-asset-forfeiture-laws/2014/11/10/10f725fc-5ec3-11e4 -8b9e-2ccdac31a031_story.html.

O'Harrow, Robert Jr., and Steven Rich. 2014. "D.C. Police Plan for Future Seizure Proceeds Years in Advance in City Budget Documents." *Washington Post*, November 15. http://www.washing tonpost.com/investigations/dc-police-plan-for-future-seizure-proceeds-years-in-advance-in -city-budget-documents/2014/11/15/7025edd2-6b76-11e4-b053-65cea7903f2e-story_html.

O'Harrow, Robert Jr., Steven Rich, Alberto Cuadra, Ted Mellnik, and Shelly Tan. 2014. "Asset Seizures Fuel Police Spending." *Washington Post*, October 11. http://www.washingtonpost .com/sf/investigative/2014/10/11/asset-seizures-fuel-police-spending/.

Oteri, Joseph, and Harvey Silvergate. 1967. "In the Marketplace of Free Ideas: A Look at the Passage of the Marihuana Tax Act." In *Marihuana: Myths and Realities*, edited by J. L. Simmons. North Hollywood, CA: Brandon House.

Parker, Glenn R. 1992. *Institutional Change, Discretion, and the Making of the Modern Congress.* Ann Arbor: University of Michigan Press.

Paul, Kari. 2015a. "Ross Ulbricht Sentenced to Life in Prison for Running Silk Road." *Vice*, May. http://motherboard.vice.com/read/ross-ulbricht-sentenced-to-life-in-prison-for-running -silk-road?trk.

———. 2015b. "The Government Tells Ross Ulbricht He Owes It $183,961,921." *Vice*, May. http:// motherboard.vice.com/read/the-government-tells-ross-ulbricht-he-owes-them-183961921.

Pilon, Roger. 2015. "America's Frightening 'Policing for Profit' Nightmare." *National Interest*, January 23. http://nationalinterest.org/feature/americas-frightening-policing-profit -nightmare-12094.

Rasmussen, David W., and Bruce L. Benson. 1994. *The Economic Anatomy of a Drug War: Criminal Justice in the Commons.* Lanham, MD: Rowman & Littlefield.

Reaves, Brian A. 1992. "Drug Enforcement by Police and Sheriffs' Departments, 1990." In *Bureau of Justice Statistics: Special Report.* Washington, DC: US Department of Justice, Bureau of Justice Statistics.

Reinarman, Craig. 1983. "Constraint, Autonomy, and State Policy: Notes toward a Theory of Controls on Consciousness Alteration." *Journal of Drug Issues* 13 (1): 9–30.

Resignato, Andrew J. 2000. "Violent Crime: A Function of Drug Use or Drug Enforcement." *Applied Economics* 32 (6): 681–88.

Reuter, Peter. 1994. "Setting Priorities: Budget and Program Choices for Drug Control." *University of Chicago Legal Forum* 1994: 145–73.

Rhodes, Robert. 1977. *The Insoluble Problems of Crime.* New York: John Wiley and Sons.

Richards, David A. J. 1982. *Sex, Drugs, Death, and the Law: An Essay on Human Rights and Overcriminalization.* Ottawa, NJ: Rowman & Littlefield.

Ross, Phillip. 2014. "Marijuana Costs in the US: Black Market, Retail, and Medical Pot Prices Compared." *International Business Times*, June. http://www.ibtimes.com/marijuana-costs-us -how-blackmarket-retail-medical-pot-prices-compare-1622362.

Sallah, Michael, Robert O'Harrow Jr., and Steven Rich. 2014. "Stop and Seize: Aggressive Police Take Hundreds of Millions of Dollars from Motorists Not Charged with Crimes." *Washington Post*, September 6. http://www.washingtonpost.com/sf/investigative/2014/09/06/stop-and-seize/.

Smith, P. 2012. "What's in Obama's New Drug War Budget? (Hint: Same, Old Broken Policies)." *Drug War Chronicle*, February.

Snead, Jason. 2016. "Nebraska Abolishes Civil Forfeiture: Police Can No Longer Arbitrarily Confiscate Innocent People's Property." *FEE*, April 27. https://fee.org/articles/nebraska -abolishes-civil-forfeiture/?utm_source=newsletter&utm_medium=email&utm_campaign =fee_daily&mkt.

Springer, Dan. 2015. "First Government-Owned Pot Store Opens in Washington State." *Fox News*, March 18. http://www.foxnews.com/politics/2015/03/18/washington-state-pot-store-brings -revenue-to-local-town.html.

Stewart, Kirsten. 2003. "Seized Assets Are Pocketed." *Salt Lake Tribune*, January 25.

Stumpf, Harry P. 1988. *American Judicial Politics.* San Diego: Harcourt Brace Jovanovich.

Stuntz, William J. 2001. "The Pathological Politics of Criminal Law." *Michigan Law Review* 100 (3): 505–600.

Sturgeon, Wina. 2014. "Civil Asset Forfeiture." *Utah Stories*, October 10. http://www.utahstories .com/2014/10/civil-asset-forfeiture/.

Stutmann, Robert M., and Richard Esposito. 1992. *Dead on Delivery: Inside the Drug War, Straight from the Streets*. New York: Warner Books.

Subcommittee on Crime of the Committee on the Judiciary, House of Representatives. 1990. *Hearing on Federal Drug Forfeiture Activities*, 101st Congress, 1st Session, Serial no. 55. Washington, DC: US Government Printing Office.

US Drug Enforcement Administration. 2015. *DEA Staffing and Budget*. Washington, DC. https://www.dea.gov/about/history/staffing.shtml.

Van Voris, Bob, and Patricia Hurtado. 2015. "Ross Ulbricht Convicted of Running Silk Road as Dread Pirate Roberts." *Bloomberg*, February 4. http://www.bloomberg.com/news/articles/2015-02-04/rossulbricht-convicted-of-running-silk-road-as-dread-pirate.

Vigh, Michael. 2002. "Judge Rules on Forfeiture Statute." *Salt Lake Tribune*, August 3, B3.

Williams, Marian R., Jefferson E. Holcomb, Tomislav V. Kovandzic, and Scott Bullock. 2011. *Policing for Profit: The Abuse of Civil Asset Forfeiture*. Arlington, VA: Institute for Justice. http://www. http://ij.org/wp-content/uploads/2015/03/assetforfeituretoemail.pdf.

Wisotsky, Steven. 1991. "Zero Tolerance/Zero Freedom." Paper presented at the Seventh Annual Critical Issues Symposium, Policy Sciences Program, Florida State University, Tallahassee.

Worrall, John L. 2001. "Addicted to the Drug War: The Role of Civil Asset Forfeiture as a Budgetary Necessity in Contemporary Law Enforcement." *Journal of Criminal Justice* 29 (3): 171–87.

Zimring, Franklin E., and Gordon Hawkins. 1992. *The Search for Rational Drug Control*. Cambridge, MA: Cambridge University Press.

CHAPTER 9
The Economics of Gross Receipts Taxes:
A Case Study of Ohio

ROBERT LAWSON

Cox School of Business, Southern Methodist University

G ross receipts taxes (GRTs) tax firms on the full value of the revenue they earn. Unlike income taxes, GRTs do not allow the firm to deduct for costs of production, except perhaps for a standard deduction. Gross receipts taxes are not new; Adam Smith ([1776] 1937) wrote of a version known as the alcavala, which operated from the fourteenth through the eighteenth centuries in Spain. In the first half of the twentieth century, many European countries relied on gross receipts or "turnover" taxes until later replacing them with value added taxes. In modern times, several American states levy GRTs (see table 1).

This chapter uses Ohio's commercial activity tax (CAT) as a case study. On July 1, 2005, Ohio implemented a new tax on the gross receipts of Ohio businesses. The new CAT is levied on

> gross receipts, which is defined as the total amount realized, without deduction for the cost of goods sold or other expenses incurred, from activities that contribute to the production of gross income. Examples are

Table 1. Selected States with Gross Receipts Taxes

State	Tax	Base	Rate(s)
Alabama	Utilities gross receipts tax	Electricity, water, and natural gas firms' gross receipts	4% on first $40,000; $1,600 plus 3% on $40,000–$60,000; $2,200 plus 2% over $60,000
Delaware	Gross receipts tax	All business' gross receipts (minus varying standard exclusions depending on the business activity)	0.1006% to 0.7543%, depending on the business activity
Florida	Gross receipts tax on utility services	Gross receipts from the sale, delivery, or transportation of natural gas, manufactured gas, or electricity	2.5%
New Mexico	Gross receipts tax	Gross receipts received by selling property in New Mexico; leasing or licensing property employed in New Mexico; granting a right to use a franchise employed in New Mexico; performing services in New Mexico, and selling research and development services performed outside New Mexico, the product of which is initially used in New Mexico	5.125% to 8.6875% depending on the location of the business
Ohio	Commercial activity tax	Businesses with Ohio taxable gross receipts of $150,000 or more per calendar year	0.26% on gross receipts above $150,000
Pennsylvania	Gross receipts tax	Pipeline, conduit, steamboat, canal, slack water navigation, and transportation companies; telephone, telegraph, and mobile telecommunications companies; electric light, water power, and hydroelectric companies; managed care organizations; express companies; palace car and sleeping car companies; and freight and oil transportation companies	4.4% for electric utilities; 5.0% for others

(continued)

Table 1. (*continued*)

State	Tax	Base	Rate(s)
Texas	Franchise tax[a]	The lowest tax liability from among the following: Total revenue minus 30% of total revenue; total revenue minus cost of goods sold; total revenue minus compensation; total revenue minus $1 million.	0.5% for a wholesaler or retailer or 1% for all other types (e.g., construction, mining, financial services, agriculture)
Washington	Business and occupation tax	The value of products, gross proceeds of sale, or gross income of the business.	0.471–1.5%, depending on business type

Sources:
Alabama: Findlaw. "Alabama Code Title 40. Revenue and Taxation." http://codes.lp.findlaw.com/alcode/40/21/3.
Delaware: State of Delaware, Department of Finance, Division of Revenue. "Gross Receipts Tax Frequently Asked Questions." http://revenue.delaware.gov/information/faqs_gr.shtml.
Florida: Florida Department of Revenue. "Florida Gross Receipts Tax on Utility Services." http://dor.myflorida.com/dor/taxes/grt_utility.html.
New Mexico: Department of Taxation and Revenue. "Gross Receipts Overview." http://www.tax.newmexico.gov/Businesses/gross-receipts.aspx.
Ohio: Department of Taxation. "Commercial Activity Tax." http://www.tax.ohio.gov/commercial_activities.aspx.
Pennsylvania: Department of Revenue. "The Tax Compendium, December 2014." http://www.revenue.pa.gov/GeneralTaxInformation/News%20and%20Statistics/Documents/Tax%20Compendium/2014_tax_compendium.pdf.
Texas: Ginn, Vance, and Hon. Talmadge Heflin. 2015. "Economic Effects of Eliminating Texas' Business Margin Tax." Center for Fiscal Policy, Texas Public Policy Foundation, Austin, Texas. http://www.texaspolicy.com/library/doclib/MarginTax-CFP.pdf.
Washington: Department of Revenue. "Business & Occupation Tax." http://dor.wa.gov/find-taxes-rates/business-occupation-tax.
[a] The Texas franchise tax is a hybrid gross receipts tax and income tax.

> sales; performance of services; and rentals or leases. The calculation for gross receipts is based on what the taxpayer is required to use for federal income tax purposes, i.e., accrual or cash basis. The tax is being phased in over a five-year period in approximately equal increments beginning July 1, 2005. Businesses with annual gross receipts of $150,000 or less are not subject to the CAT. . . . On Jan. 1, 2010, the permanent rate of the CAT will be 0.26 percent. (Ohio Department of Taxation 2008)

The purpose of this chapter is to briefly compare a GRT to a sales or excise tax. After showing that there is no relevant economic distinction between these types of taxes, I turn to a legal challenge to Ohio's CAT on grounds that it violates the state constitution's ban on sales taxation of food. I conclude with a discussion of other pros and cons, from a traditional public finance point of view, about GRTs.

THE INCIDENCE OF SALES AND GROSS RECEIPTS TAXES

"Tax incidence" refers to the analysis of who actually bears the burden of a tax. It is important to note the difference between how economists and tax authorities approach tax incidence. Legislators and tax administrators are interested in the legal or statutory burden of a tax. That is, governing statutes specify who is legally liable for a tax. In contrast, economists are interested in who bears the burden of the tax rather than who writes the check to the government. Legal incidence is rarely, if ever, the same as economic incidence. The reason for this divergence is straightforward—the party bearing the legal incidence of a tax may change his or her behavior in ways that result in some, or even all, of the burden of the tax being shifted to other parties.[1] For example, taxing the seller of an item may lead to part of or all the tax being shifted to buyers of the product in the form of higher prices. The widely understood price-increasing consequences of cigarette taxes levied on tobacco firms or alcohol taxes levied on beer and spirits producers are examples of this phenomenon (Li et al. 2014).

Ultimately, all taxes levied on businesses are paid by either consumers, in the form of higher prices; employees, in the form of lower wages; suppliers, in the form of lower prices for their goods and services; or owners, in the form of lower profits. Hence, economic incidence, not legal incidence, provides the true measure of the burden of a tax.

One interesting and, to many noneconomists, surprising fact about the economic incidence of a tax is that the sharing of the tax burden among these various stakeholders is invariant to the legal incidence. Suppose the state levied a 5 percent tax on a product or group of products and required the tax be legally paid by the seller. Now suppose instead that the state levied a 5 percent tax on a product or group of products but required the tax be legally paid by the buyer. In both cases, the result would be some kind of sharing of the burden among these stakeholders dependent on the relative elasticities of supply and demand in the market. The interesting result is that this economic incidence would be the same in either case. Hence, for the purposes of determining economic incidence, the standard conclusion is that legal incidence does not affect the distribution of the burden of the tax between the buyer and seller.

Tax authorities also draw a distinction between the entity legally liable for the tax according to the statute and the one legally responsible for remitting the tax. In the case of the Ohio sales tax, for example, the law states that although the buyer is legally liable for the tax, it is typically, though not in all cases, the seller who must remit it to the state.[2] In the case of the Ohio CAT, however, the seller is liable under the statute and is also required to remit the tax. Thus, both the Ohio sales tax and the CAT require the seller to remit the tax; they differ in that the Ohio sales tax assigns statutory liability to the buyer, while the Ohio CAT specifies that the seller is liable.

There may be important differences between requiring the seller versus the buyer to remit a tax in terms of administration, compliance, and enforcement costs (see Slemrod 2008). Such concerns are an important part of determining tax policy, but they do not alter the underlying point that the manner in which the burden of a tax is shared between buyer and seller is independent of the statutory point of tax collection.

THE FORMAL ECONOMICS OF AN AD VALOREM SALES TAX

The following analysis is a standard economic approach to understanding how a tax impacts a given market. Consumers and sellers are responsive to prices as described by demand $f(\cdot)$ (equation 1a) and supply $g(\cdot)$ (equation 1b) functions:

$$Q_d = f(P_d), \qquad (1a)$$
$$Q_s = g(P_s), \qquad (1b)$$

where Q_d is the quantity of the good purchased by the buyer, P_d is the price paid by the buyer, Q_s is the quantity sold by the seller, and P_s is the price received by the seller.

Buyers respond to higher prices by decreasing the amount they want to purchase, so

$$\Delta Q_d / \Delta P_d < 0. \qquad (2a)$$

Sellers respond to higher prices by increasing the amount they want to sell; thus,

$$\Delta Q_s / \Delta P_s > 0. \qquad (2b)$$

The market is in equilibrium when the buyers and sellers want to buy and sell the same quantity of the good:

$$Q_d = Q_s. \qquad (3)$$

In the absence of taxation, it is easy to solve for the price that equilibrates the market. However, if an ad valorem tax, t_s, is introduced, then a wedge is driven between the price the buyer pays and the price the seller receives,[3] so

$$P_d = (1 + t_s) P_s, \tag{4a}$$
$$P_s = P_d / (1 + t_s). \tag{4b}$$

The tax increases the price paid by buyers:

$$\Delta P_d / \Delta t_s > 0. \tag{5a}$$

Likewise, the tax decreases the price received by sellers:

$$\Delta P_s / \Delta t_s < 0. \tag{5b}$$

The quantity purchased and sold decreases:

$$\Delta Q_d / \Delta t_s < 0, \tag{6a}$$

because of equations 2a and 5a, and

$$\Delta Q_s / \Delta t_s < 0, \tag{6b}$$

because of equations 2b and 5b.

THE FORMAL ECONOMICS OF A GROSS RECEIPTS TAX

Like a sales tax, the GRT drives a wedge between buyers and sellers but in an apparently different way. The existence of a sales tax means that buyers will pay a higher price for the product than the sellers receive (as in equation 4a above). In contrast, the gross receipts, t_g, is levied on gross receipts such that the total amount paid by the buyers, R_d, is greater than the gross amount received by the sellers, R_s:

$$R_d = (1 + t_g) R_s. \tag{7}$$

Gross receipts are simply the multiplication of price and quantity:

$$R_d = P_d Q_d, \tag{8a}$$
$$R_s = P_s Q_s. \tag{8b}$$

Rearranging terms from equations 3, 7, 8a, and 8b, we find

$$P_d = (1 + t_g) P_s, \tag{9}$$

which, for $t_g = t_s$, is identical to equation 4a.

Thus, a GRT of a given percentage rate is literally identical to a general sales tax of the same rate facing any given market.

DIFFERENCES BETWEEN THE APPLICATION OF SALES AND GROSS RECEIPTS TAXES IN PRACTICE

Just as there are subtle but important administrative, compliance, and enforcement differences between general retail sales taxes and other types of sales taxes (e.g., value added taxes), there are important administrative and economic differences between GRTs and general sales taxes in practice. The biggest difference between the two taxes is the manner in which GRTs "cascade" or "pyramid" as products are sold from firm to firm in the intermediate stages of production.

The analysis in the foregoing sections assumed only a single stage of production in order to show the equivalence of a retail sales tax and the GRT in the simplest way possible. That conclusion is still valid: A GRT and a sales/excise tax are identical when applied to any given market.

Recognizing that the GRT applies at all stages of production complicates matters, but it does not change the fundamental result that a GRT is a sales tax. For every GRT that pyramids, there is an equivalent noncascading retail sales tax that could be applied to that product. Consider table 2, illustrating the production of bread.

In this example, a 0.82 percent retail sales tax rate is exactly equivalent to a 0.26 percent GRT rate. In the case of the GRT, the 0.26 percent tax would generate a total of $1.72 in tax revenue from the various stages of production. In the case of the sales tax, the government simply waits until the end of production and applies the 0.82 percent sales tax to the final product value.[4] In either case, the government collects the same $1.72 from the sale of this product, though the tax is administratively collected at different stages of the production process.

It would complicate matters still further once we recognize that there are differences in the stages of production for different goods. One would have to

Table 2. The Tax Incidence of Bread Production—A Hypothetical Example

Agent	Valued Added ($)	Gross Value ($)	Sales Tax[a] ($)	Gross Receipts Tax[b] ($)
Wheat farmer	100.00	100.00	0.00	0.26
Miller	50.00	150.00	0.00	0.39
Baker	50.00	200.00	0.00	0.52
Retail grocer	10.00	210.00	1.72	0.55
Total	210.00	210.00	1.72	1.72

[a] Sales tax rate is 0.82%.
[b] Gross receipts tax rate is 0.26%.

recalculate the figures in the table to determine a different retail sales tax rate for each good that would be equivalent to the GRT rate.

Thus, in the aggregate, the GRT should be viewed as the equivalent of a series of selective sales or excise taxes on goods and services that apply at different rates, depending on the differences in the stages of production across goods and services markets.

Additionally, note that even retail sales taxes pyramid in many instances. Holcombe (1996, 273) notes that sales taxes often tax "construction materials such as lumber and concrete, even when those materials are sold as inputs into the production process, such as to construct a factory or warehouse." In addition, he notes that "to the extent that nonretail transactions are taxed, a general sales tax has the inefficiencies associated with the turnover tax." Quick and McKee (1988) highlight this cascading by noting that retail sales tax laws do not allow firms to fully exempt intermediate goods, and thus these goods can be taxed repeatedly by the retail sales tax. Likewise, Ring (1989) provides an extensive discussion of nonretail, business-to-business transactions that are subject to retail sales taxes. He estimates that 30 percent of Ohio's sales tax is paid on business-to-business transactions. A follow-up study (Ring 1999) finds similar results.

The phenomenon of pyramiding means only that the effective sales tax rate on the final product is higher than the published statutory GRT rate; it does not mean that it is not a sales tax. To conclude that the double taxation of a good as it moves from one stage of production to another is not a sales tax would be to reach the strange conclusion that taxing the sale of an item once is a sales tax but taxing the sale of that item twice is not. Instead, the real meaning of pyramiding is that items with multistage production processes face higher effective taxes. If pyramiding disqualifies a tax from being a sales tax, then there is no such thing as a sales tax.

Furthermore, it is the academic consensus that GRTs that apply to all stages of production are still theoretically sales taxes. Holcombe (1996, 267) remarks: "A turnover [gross receipts] tax is like a sales tax in that it is a tax paid as a fixed percentage of the value of a transaction, but a turnover tax taxes all transactions, not just retail sales." Likewise, the authoritative Musgrave and Musgrave (1984, 434–35) cover turnover taxes in their textbook chapter on sales taxes.

OHIO GROCERS ASSOCIATION ET AL. V. WILKINS

The discussion above indicates that no important economic distinction can be made between sales/excise taxes and GRTs. The sensible conclusion then would be that the Ohio CAT, inasmuch as it is clearly a GRT, is in fact economically identical to a sales or excise tax. The Ohio Grocers Association, along with three food retailers and one food wholesaler, filed suit on February 17, 2006, against William Wilkins in his official capacity as Ohio's tax commissioner, arguing that the Ohio CAT violated Ohio's constitutional ban on applying sales or excise taxes to food.[5]

The plaintiffs sought (1) a declaration that the CAT, when applied to receipts from the sale of food for human consumption off the premises where sold, violates Article XII, Section 3(C) of the Ohio Constitution; (2) an order invalidating the CAT when applied to receipts from the sale of food for human consumption off the premises where sold; (3) an order enjoining Tax Commissioner Wilkins, his agents, and successors to refrain from levying or enforcing the CAT; and (4) an order requiring Tax Commissioner Wilkins to refund any amounts paid under the CAT with regard to receipts from the sale of food for human consumption off the premises where sold.

In a second count, the Ohio Grocers Association and co-plaintiffs sought similar relief on the grounds that the CAT also violated the Ohio Constitution's provision (Article XII, Section 13) that "no sales or other excise taxes shall be levied or collected (1) upon any wholesale sale or wholesale purchase of food for human consumption, its ingredients or its packaging; . . . or (3) in any retail transaction, on any packaging that contains food for human consumption on or off the premises where sold."

Although the State of Ohio pursued some other arguments, its primary defense was that the Ohio "CAT is a franchise and privilege tax imposed on doing business in Ohio. It is not a transactional tax, which is the kind of tax prohibited in Section 3(C), Article XII, and Section 13, Article XII of the Constitution."[6] That is, the state holds that since the statutory incidence of the CAT falls on the seller and is calculated after the point of sale, the CAT is not a sales tax. In contrast, sales taxes (according to the state) assign statutory liability to the buyer (though they are remitted by the seller in most cases) and are calculated at the point of sale. This argument emphasizing the statutory liability of the tax and its administrative timing as being critical determinants of whether the tax is a sales tax is odd, to say the least, from the standpoint of standard public finance principles.

On August 24, 2007, the trial court ruled summarily in favor of the State of Ohio, making quite explicit the importance of legal incidence and timing in the court's judgment:

> The Court further finds that the CAT is imposed directly
> on the business for the privilege of doing business in Ohio,

and therefore the "incidence" of the tax rests upon the
business not the consumer. While the tax may ultimately
be passed on to the consumers in the form of higher prices,
it cannot be directly billed to and paid by the purchaser. As
such, the Court finds that the CAT is significantly different
from a sales tax.[7]

The court also found the administrative timing of the collection of the tax to
be important:

In addition, the Court finds that unlike a sales tax, the very
terms of the CAT tie the obligation to pay the CAT to a
time or date, not a specific transaction or sale.

However, on September 2, 2008, the appellate court ruled in favor of the
plaintiffs, echoing the economic logic presented above:

Though appellee suggests the CAT is a franchise tax and
is not equivalent to a sales or transactional tax, by its very
operation when applied to gross receipts derived from the
sales of food, a transactional tax is precisely what the CAT
becomes. This is so because the tax is measured *solely* by
gross receipts and is based on aggregate sales, including those
from the sales of food. Because the CAT is not based on
each transaction or each individual sale, appellee contends
the CAT is constitutional. However, though not based
on individual sales at the time they are made, the CAT is
merely based on the aggregate of all sales within a specified
time frame. If the legislature is prohibited from collecting a
tax on the individual sale, it logically follows the legislature
would be prohibited from collecting a tax on the aggregate
of those same sales.[8]

The State of Ohio appealed the case to the Ohio Supreme Court, which
ruled in September 2009.[9] The case was closely watched. Aside from the interesting legal and economic issues at stake, if the state lost, it faced the daunting
prospect of having to refund hundreds of millions of dollars to food sellers.
In the end, the Ohio Supreme Court, placing a high burden of proof on the
plaintiffs, ruled that the CAT would be constitutional "if it may plausibly be

interpreted as permissible"[10] and then, notwithstanding the economic arguments made by the plaintiffs and the appellate court, merely accepted the state's assertion that the CAT was a tax on "the privilege of doing business" instead of an excise tax. Hence the court effectively rendered Ohio's constitutional prohibition on taxing the sale of food economically nugatory.

OTHER ECONOMIC EFFECTS OF GROSS RECEIPTS TAXES

It might be argued that GRTs, which tend to have broader tax bases than retail sales or excise taxes, would be preferred on public finance grounds. Leaving aside the constitutional issue, states without constitutional prohibitions on taxing food might find other taxes to be sounder policy options. Here I explore five reasons for this.

First, since the tax base is gross receipts rather than net receipts, the tax is effectively larger on low profit margin firms (e.g., grocers) than on higher profit margin firms. Moreover, the taxation of gross receipts rather than net receipts means that firms incurring losses are still subject to the tax.[11] Hence, the tax bears no relation to firms' ability to pay, one of the widely accepted normative criteria for tax equity.

Second, the tax also violates the benefit principle, another commonly accepted normative criterion for taxation. Under this criterion, tax burdens should be related to the benefits received from the government services funded by the taxation. Since the GRT makes no adjustments for the intensity of firms' use of government funded services (e.g., roads), it is not consistent with the benefit principle of tax equity.

Third, the taxation of gross receipts rather than net receipts means that the tax falls more heavily on goods with multifirm production processes. To the extent that the tax is shifted forward, the tax pyramids or cascades with each subsequent stage of production. Chamberlain and Fleenor (2006) examine the degree of tax pyramiding under Washington State's GRT for approximately three dozen industries. They find that the tax pyramids 2.5 times for the average industry examined, but is greatest (6.7 times) in the food manufacturing industry. Such compounding of the tax with each business-to-business transaction in the production process belies the GRT advocates' claim that it is a low rate tax applied evenly to all goods and services produced. Consequently, GRTs create an artificial incentive for firms to vertically integrate (Chamberlain and Fleenor 2006).

Fourth, the tax burden on goods can be affected by the timing of the value added in a multistage production process. Value added that occurs earlier in the production process will be subject to more pyramiding and ultimately lead to a higher final price for the consumer. Consider, for example, a three-stage production process that begins when Firm A sells $10 of material to Firm B. Firm B then adds $170 of value to the product and sells it for $180 to Firm C. Firm C finishes the product and sells it to a consumer for $200. Adding a 10 percent GRT, assumed to be fully shifted to consumers, to this production process results in sales prices of $11.00 from Firm A to Firm B, $199.10 (=$181 × 1.1) from Firm B to Firm C, and $241.01 (=$219.10 × 1.1) from Firm C to the consumer.

Suppose instead that more of the value added occurs earlier in the production process: Firm A sells $170 of material to Firm B. Firm B refines the product and sells it for $180 to Firm C. Firm C finishes the product and sells it to the consumer for $200. Applying a 10 percent GRT to this process yields prices of $187.00, $216.70, and $260.37 at the respective stages of the production process. These simple examples illustrate that production processes with the same number of stages and the same value added will be taxed differently based on the timing of the value added in the production process.

Fifth, the application of a GRT to business-to-business sales means that, to the extent the tax is shifted forward, suppliers located in the state have higher prices than do suppliers located outside the state. The GRT, then, creates an incentive for in-state firms to find suppliers located outside the state; obviously, this incentive is mitigated by any accompanying increase in transportation costs. Not surprisingly, however, Ohio has adopted an economic nexus rationale for subjecting out-of-state firms to the CAT for their sales in Ohio.

CONCLUSION

Gross receipts taxes, such as Ohio's CAT, are economically identical to sales or excise taxes in any given market in which they are applied. As such, it would seem that such taxes, when applied to gross receipts derived from food, contradict applicable legal provisions exempting food from sales or excise taxation. In deeming the Ohio CAT to be constitutional, the Ohio Supreme Court has confused statutory incidence for economic incidence and in the process undermined the Ohio Constitution's ban on the sales taxation of food. More generally, all but six of the forty-five states with sales taxes exempt groceries from sales taxes or subject them to a reduced rate (Kasprak 2012). Hence understanding that GRTs are equivalent to sales taxes is important for states that wish to reduce the sales tax on groceries.

Independent of the CAT's constitutionality, the inequities and inefficiencies of GRTs make them poor tax instruments compared to available alternatives, such as either conventional sales taxes or value-added taxes.

NOTES

1. In certain market environments, it may also be possible to observe overshifting or price increases greater than the amount of the tax imposed. See Kenkel (2005).

2. This is similar to income tax withholding, where employers must withhold and send tax payments to the government on behalf of their employees. It is still the employee, however, who is legally liable for the tax.

3. An ad valorem tax is expressed as a percentage of the sales price. All sales and many excise taxes are ad valorem in nature. However, some excise taxes, such as the gasoline tax, are fixed unit taxes expressed as a certain amount of money per unit. Unit taxes still drive a wedge between buyers and sellers: $P_d = P_s + t$.

4. The results in table 2 assume that the full economic burden of the tax falls on the seller and that none of the tax is passed on to the buyer in the form of a higher price. This assumption is made purely for simplicity.

5. Ohio Grocers Assn. v. Wilkins, Complaint for Declaratory and Injunctive Relief. Court of Common Pleas, Franklin County, OH. Case No. 06CVH-02-2278. Full disclosure: The author was the expert witness hired on behalf of the plaintiffs.

6. Ohio Grocers Assn. v. Wilkins, Defendant's Memorandum Opposing Plaintiff's Motion for Summary Judgment and Cross-Motion for Summary Judgment. Court of Common Pleas, Franklin County, OH. Case No. 06CVH-02-2278.

7. Ohio Grocers Assn. v. Wilkins, Franklin County Court of Common Pleas Case No. 06CVH-02-2278.

8. Ohio Grocers Assn. v. Wilkins, 178 Ohio App.3d 145, 2008-Ohio-4420.

9. Ohio Grocers Assn. v. Levin, 123 Ohio St.3d 303, 2009-Ohio-4872. Note that the named defendant changed because there was a new tax commissioner in Ohio following the 2008 election.

10. Ohio Grocers Assn. v. Levin, Ohio Supreme Court, No. 2008-2018.

11. Note, too, that taxing firms experiencing losses may serve as an impediment for start-up firms, since such firms often require some time before becoming profitable.

REFERENCES

Chamberlain, Andrew, and Patrick Fleenor. 2006. "Tax Pyramiding: The Economic Consequences of Gross Receipts Taxes." Tax Foundation Special Report 147. Washington, DC: Tax Foundation.

Holcombe, Randall G. 1996. *Public Finance: Government Revenues and Expenditures in the United States Economy*. Eagan, MN: West Group.

Kasprak, Nick. 2012. "Monday Map: Sales Tax Exemptions for Groceries." Tax Foundation blog, February 6. http://taxfoundation.org/blog/monday-map-sales-tax-exemptions-groceries.

Kenkel, Donald S. 2005. "Are Alcohol Tax Hikes Fully Passed through to Prices? Evidence from Alaska." *American Economic Review* 95 (2): 273–77.

Li, Shanjun, Joshua Linn, and Erich Muehlegger. 2014. "Gasoline Taxes and Consumer Behavior." *American Economic Journal* 6 (4): 302–42.

Musgrave, Richard A., and Peggy B. Musgrave. 1984. *Public Finance in Theory and Practice*, 4th ed. New York: McGraw-Hill.

Ohio Department of Taxation. 2008. *2008 Business Tax Guide* 19. http://www.tax.ohio.gov/portals/0/communications/publications/ohio_business_tax_guide_2008.pdf.

Quick, Perry D., and Michael McKee. 1988. "Sales Tax on Services: Revenue or Reform?" *National Tax Journal* 41 (3): 395–409.

Ring, Raymond J. 1989. "The Proportion of Consumers' and Producers' Goods in the General Sales Tax." *National Tax Journal* 42 (2): 167–79.

———. 1999. "Consumers' Share and Producers' Share of the General Sales Tax." *National Tax Journal* 52 (1): 79–90.

Slemrod, Joel. 2008. "Does It Matter Who Writes the Check to the Government? The Economics of Tax Remittance." *National Tax Journal* 61 (2): 251–75.

Smith, Adam. [1776] 1937. *An Inquiry into the Nature and Causes of the Wealth of Nations*, book V, chapter 2, edited by Edwin Cannan, 769–858. New York: Modern Library.

PART III

FISCAL FEDERALISM AND SELECTIVE TAXATION

CHAPTER 10
Economic Development Tax Incentives: A Review of the Perverse, Ineffective, and Unintended Consequences

PETER T. CALCAGNO
Department of Economics, College of Charleston

FRANK HEFNER
Department of Economics, College of Charleston

S tate and local governments use targeted tax incentives in an attempt to create jobs and stimulate economic growth. According to Poole et al. (1999, 1), "governors, mayors, legislators, and council members justify these public investments on the grounds that private-sector decisions to invest in a community result in jobs, income, and tax revenues that are essential to the economic and social well-being of a community or state." Targeted tax incentives take many forms, including job development and retraining tax credits; tax abatements; infrastructure financing; or in some cases, outright grants and loans of public funds. State and local officials use these fiscal tools to attract a private firm to a new location, help support or expand an existing business, or prevent a company from relocating to another city or state. While these policies are common among state and local governments, many scholars and policymakers have repeatedly questioned the efficacy of these policies.

Besides not achieving the stated goals, these incentive programs may encourage behavior that can lead to a host of perverse and unintended consequences.

If the efficacy associated with these types of policies is in serious doubt, why are they so popular with state governments? The answer is that businesses engage in rent-seeking behavior, employing resources to lobby for tax breaks and other subsidies that add to owners' profits. This lobbying often creates a bidding war between two or more state and or local governments that can increase the value of the incentives and rents the firm can extract from these government agencies. Economist William Baumol (1990) notes that entrepreneurial individuals have a choice to devote their labor efforts toward either creating private-sector wealth or securing wealth redistribution through political and legal processes (e.g., lobbying and lawsuits).

Numerous studies point out that there are clear political benefits for using targeted financial incentives (Bennet and DiLorenzo 1983; Esinger 1989; Buss 1999a, 2001; Ellis and Rogers 2000; Saiz 2001; Calcagno and Hefner 2007). Hinkley et al. (2000) claim that economic development agencies are not providing enough information to either legislators or the public about the economic incentives being offered and call for an increase in audits of these agencies. While several authors do concede that targeting has a political component to it, they fail to recognize that targeting industries may well be an inefficient allocation of resources (Dewar 1998; Buss 1999a,b; Finkle 1999; Wiewel 1999; Calcagno and Hefner 2009; Coyne and Moberg 2014).

Industries seeking preferential treatment dominate the political process, because voter-taxpayers have very little incentive to be well informed about the costs associated with these tax incentive programs and to create any means of organized opposition. The jobs created at a new plant are plainly visible to the state or local community; the community will not see the jobs that are lost elsewhere in the economy due to the higher tax burdens imposed on other businesses and consumers. Nor do taxpayers see the scarce resources that this political process is allocating away from ventures that could instead produce real output and growth. In addition, taxpayers may be unable to see that their future tax bills will be higher in order to amortize and service the public debt issued to finance the subsidies diverted toward the owners of politically influential private companies (Hicks and Shughart 2007).

The purpose of this chapter is to review the consequences of tax incentives to provide the reader with a better understanding of the role targeted tax incentives may play in state and local economic development. Earlier research has typically focused on the efficacy of these incentives: are jobs actually created? A different branch of research has focused on other outcomes, such as the possibility that such incentives may lead to rent-seeking by the firm and politicians and the possibility of political corruption. We begin by discussing the possible economic distortions and unintended consequences that these policies create. Then we examine the efficacy of targeted tax incentives by presenting a summary of research findings. We then provide some specific cases of state and industry experiences that demonstrate how these perverse incentives lead to ineffective policies and unintended consequences. We conclude with a summary and policy recommendations.

UNINTENDED CONSEQUENCES OF TAX INCENTIVES

Incentives Cannot Turn a Moose into a Camel

Site location consultants are fully aware that they must first meet certain fundamental criteria for their industry for a successful location decision. This often places tax incentives at the bottom of the list of criteria. For example, a report by CBRE (2013), a commercial real estate services company, discussed the site location criteria for data centers. What are driving these choices are four primary considerations: power, telecommunications, geography, and climate:

- Power: Cost per kilowatt hour, carbon footprint, fuel mix, and infrastructure;

- Telecommunications: Fiber providers, latency;

- Geography: Proximity to headquarters or airport locations, population size, labor force, and water; and

- Climate: Environmental risk (e.g., hurricanes, tornadoes, earthquakes), free cooling.

After identifying locations based on these primary drivers, communities will remain on the short list based on real estate availability and cost. This holds true for existing co-location facilities or greenfield sites for new construction. Taxes and incentives are the last criteria. The report observes that taxes and incentives are the tools that governments have control over in order to attract a data center. As of 2013, seventeen states have customized incentive programs for this industry. In 2012 and 2013, eight states either created or modified existing programs to lure these centers. To be "competitive," many states are simply mirroring the others' incentive programs. For example, Georgia, Virginia, South Carolina, Alabama, Nebraska, Arizona, Texas, and Ohio all offer 100 percent exemption from the sales tax. At some point, as these states equalize their tax rates, any advantage gained by the exemptions will evaporate, so that the ability of any state to attract additional employers is largely unchanged from before any states offered such tax exemptions. Not only would development be largely unchanged, but also tax burdens would arguably be more evenly distributed across taxpayers without these exemptions. Thus, firms identify location sites considering industry-specific resource needs and availability. Tax incentives cannot create these criteria for these industries. Incentives will not overcome the lack of necessary resource considerations, such as environmental risk or access to a port.

Strategic Rent-Seeking

Rent-seeking firms would certainly take advantage of the possibility of playing states against one another where discretionary incentives are available. Patrick (2016) analyzed BMW's decision to locate in South Carolina. In 1992, BMW announced that it would locate a plant in Greenville County, SC, after a site selection process that ended in a bidding war between Greenville and Omaha, NE. Earlier we noted that the fundamental characteristics of a region are the primary drivers of the site selection process and that incentives, if they matter at all, only matter at the margin. The chairman of BMW stated the critical factors in the site selection were proximity to an international airport, *port* (our emphasis added), rail, union presence, and the number of time zones between Bonn, Germany, and the site. How Nebraska became a potential site is astounding, given the absence of a port, among other issues. Fundamentally, the absence of a port is a characteristic that would be difficult to overcome with tax incentives. The initial incentive package from South Carolina was valued at $35 million (Kurylko 1992a). However, Nebraska offered a package valued at $240 million. South Carolina countered with a package that was estimated to be $150 million (Kurylko1992b). Patrick concludes that, "Nebraska's lucrative incentive package served a useful purpose for the company—raising South Carolina's bid from $35 million to $150 million" (Patrick 2016, 9). As with any other rent-seeking activity, this process does more than simply transfer wealth from consumers to producers. The process of acquiring the rents results in the whole transaction being a welfare loss to society.

Continued Rent-Seeking: Receiving Incentives after Location Selection

If the purpose of tax incentives is to induce a company to locate in a region, then what justification could there be for providing more incentives after the location decision has been made? Consider the example from the municipality of North Charleston, SC, whose city council voted to reduce business license fees for four companies that were already in the region: Boeing, Daimler Vans Manufacturing, Select Health of SC, and Trident Regional Medical Center (Slade 2013). These additional incentives demonstrate Buchanan's (1986) point that once state government policymakers open the door to incentives, these businesses are motivated to try to influence the policy to continue to work in their favor. According to Coyne and Moberg (2014), this continued rent-seeking opportunity can create a system of cronyism, giving these firms access to public resources to extract these rents.

Good Jobs First tracks incentives offered to industries across the United States (Morgan et al. 2013). One subset of their list is "megadeals." They define a mega-deal when the subsidy award totals more than $75 million from state and local governments. Table 1 lists repeat megadeals made in the same state. If the goal of incentives is to recruit industry, then clearly there is no need to offer larger packages to firms already in place. One could argue that this piling on of incentives is a form of job blackmail, whereby the firm threatens to leave unless additional incentives are offered. These repeated deals make it clear that this behavior is simply rent-seeking by these firms. Recently, Kennametal, a firm that had been located in Latrobe, PA, for more than 70 years was awarded $1 million in incentives by the state of Pennsylvania to move its headquarters to Pittsburgh. The reason for offering these incentives to move the firm's headquarters from one county to another was to keep the company in the state (Gannon and Belko 2015; Sheehan 2015). In 1996, South Carolina passed legislation allowing "all qualified tire manufacturers" in the state to take a jobs tax credit for all jobs transferred from one plant to another as if they were newly created jobs.[1]

Incentives Crowd Out Public Expenditures

The counterfactual of how one would allocate these resources if government officials were not using them to target firms is a difficult (if not impossible) task. However, it is still important to think about alternative uses of these funds not only remaining in the private sector, but also how else these funds may have been allocated in the public sector. Wang (2016) examines whether

Table 1. Repeat Megadeals by State

State	Year	Company	Subsidy ($ millions)	State	Year	Company	Subsidy ($ millions)
Alaska	1990	Teck Resources	180.0	New Mexico	1993	Intel	645.0
	1999	Teck Resources	870.0		2004	Intel	2,000.0
Alabama	1993	Mercedes	238.0	New York	2002	Sematech	210.0
	2000	Mercedes	119.3		2008	Sematech	300.0
	2009	Mercedes	100.0		2000	IBM	660.0
	1999	Honda	158.0		2008	IBM	140.0
	2002	Honda	89.7	Ohio	2009	General Electric	121.0
Illinois	1989	Sears	242.0		2014	General Electric	98.0
	2011	Sears	275.0		2002	General Motors	63.0
Kansas	2006	General Motors	156.0		2008	General Motors	82.1
	1985	General Motors	136.0	Oregon	1993	Intel	121.5
	2012	General Motors	120.0		1999	Intel	200.0
Kentucky	1985	Toyota	147.0		2005	Intel	579.0
	2013	Toyota	146.5		2014	Intel	2,000.0
Michigan	1999	General Motors	98.9	South Carolina	2009	Boeing	900.0
	2000	General Motors	284.6		2013	Boeing	120.0
	2001	General Motors	76.5		1992	BMW	150.0
	2008	General Motors	268.5		2002	BMW	103.5
	2009	General Motors	1,015.5	Tennessee	2008	Volkswagen	554.0
	2009	General Motors	166.8		2014	Volkswagen	263.3
	2000	Ford Motors	222.0		2000	Nissan	200.0
	2003	Ford Motors	90.3		2005	Nissan	230.0
	2009	Ford Motors	174.7		2009	Nissan	98.0
	2010	Ford Motors	909.0	Texas	2006	Samsung	233.4
Minnesota	1988	Triple Five	108.0		2012	Samsung	83.6
	2013	Triple Five	250.0	Washington	2003	Boeing	3,244.0
					2013	Boeing	8,700.0

Source: Good Jobs First, http://www.goodjobsfirst.org.

economic development incentives crowd out or reduce public expenditures. Her research finds that incentive expenditures reduce spending on what is often called productive public goods, such as education, health and human services, sanitation, and utilities. She finds a 2-year lag in per capita public goods expenditures of approximately $18.60 for every $100 spent per capita on incentives. These findings suggest that, even if the tax revenues funding these targeted incentives were to remain in the public sector, state governments could spend it on producing the core functions of government that even advocates of limited government recognize. Thus, state governments are misdirecting this tax revenue, and as a result, they produce less of the public goods they are responsible for and fewer of the services that firms require.

Incentives Lead to Corruption

Glaeser and Saks (2006) investigate the determinants of corruption at the state level. Corruption is of course nothing new in America's history. However, we tend to associate it more with underdeveloped countries. These authors note that between 1990 and 2002, "federal prosecutors convicted more than 10,000 government officials of acts of official corruption, such as conflict of interest, fraud, campaign-finance violations, and obstruction of justice" (Glaeser and Saks 2006, 1053). Indeed, it is not rare that governors of several states have had to resign amidst allegations of corrupt practices. Glaeser and Saks found a weak negative relationship between corruption and economic development in a state. Utilizing the same data as Glaeser and Saks, Felix and Hines (2013) investigate the connection between tax incentives (in the form of tax abatements, tax credits, and tax incremental financing arrangements) and corruption. They find a positive and statistically significant correlation between offering incentives and corruption. Felix and Hines also find that communities in states with less of a culture of corruption tend to avoid offering businesses incentive packages. They hypothesize that communities with less corruption tend to prefer to structure their general tax levels, spending programs, and other business recruitment policies instead of designing specific deals for specific firms.

We do not maintain that tax incentives are structured to promote corruption. However, the manner in which these deals are structured opens the door to corruption. In the case of tax incentives for the film industry, a state audit in Iowa found $26 million in improperly issued tax credits. The state's former film office director was convicted of falsifying public records. State prosecutors charged five independent filmmakers and a tax credit broker. The tax incentive program was suspended in 2009 (Verrier 2015). Even though these incentives resulted in political corruption, the state of Iowa reestablished the film office in 2013 but did not provide funding at that time.

The High Cost of Optics

"Commentators generally agree that incentives violate the most basic principles of sound tax policy. Incentives result in tax systems that are less accountable, less efficient, and less fair. Moreover, there is more than ample evidence that incentives do not work" (Zelinsky 2008, 1151). In addition, as Richard Pomp (1998) notes, "tax incentives probably reward corporations for doing what they would have done anyway." So why are targeted incentives so prevalent an economic development tool for state and local governments, and why does their use continue to grow? Pomp observes that legislators "fear that being perceived as anti-business or anti-jobs is worse than being seen as promoting highly visible, albeit ineffective, incentives" (Zelinsky 2008, 1151).

Morgan (2009) maintains that, from the view of policymakers, thinking that they are winning some of the time in the incentive game is better than always losing. Bartik (2005) claims that public officials might be willing to tolerate the inefficiency of incentives if they provide an edge, *no matter how slight* (emphasis added). Taking a public choice approach, Calcagno and Hefner (2007) find evidence of a Leviathan theory of government. They argue that government officials offer these types of targeted incentives to maximize corporate tax revenue. Whether higher corporate tax revenue results in economic growth is uncertain, but Calcagno and Hefner offer one possible explanation of why state governments continue to offer a tax incentive that otherwise offers no obvious economic benefit to the state. Even if corporate tax revenues increase, the net effects to the tax burden and overall tax revenue are less clear. Regardless of the net effects, this result suggests that politicians have a motivation different from the stated objective. If politicians are willing to trade off the misallocation and inefficiencies of resources to maximize revenue and have constituents perceive them as business friendly, these actions can be to their political benefit.

BACKGROUND: THE EFFICACY OF TAX INCENTIVES

Economists and policymakers have argued that competition among states to entice companies through targeted incentives provides no net gain to the US economy:[2] "From the states' point of view each may appear better off competing for particular businesses, but the overall economy ends up with less of both private and public goods than if such competition was prohibited" (Burstein and Rolnick 1995, 7).[3] So what effects do these policies have on a state's economic growth?

The subject of state governments targeting industries through tax policy raises important questions regarding economic growth and development, which requires us to examine whether the economic benefits of these tax policies are worth the economic costs. Whether state development incentives lead to real job creation and economic growth has been the subject of much debate among economic scholars. The economics literature abounds with research studies that have examined a variety of programs across the United States at both the state and local levels. These studies suggest that economists have long doubted the efficacy of using state tax policy to induce mobile firms (Esinger 1989). Economists have found the evidence associated with the issue of tax and other development incentives generating economic growth unconvincing (Buss 1999a,b, 2001).

For instance, several of the Federal Reserve District Banks have published articles investigating the role of tax incentives on state economic growth.[4] The evidence in these studies suggests that state governments should eliminate, abolish, or refine tax incentives policy and thereby remove the competition for investment that is occurring among states.

Ultimately, all these targeted incentives claim to have one major goal: to create jobs in the state. Gabe and Kraybill (1998), in a study that examines which firms in Ohio receive targeted incentives, find that the number of new jobs promised by the targeted business is the major factor in deciding who receives the incentive. One could argue that this is a result of political versus market decision-making. Examining more than 2,000 programs across all states, Saiz (2001) finds no evidence of overall growth in state gross domestic product or employment levels associated with offering financial incentives and finds negative impacts in certain industries. A 2008 report analyzing the impact of state government incentives to attract businesses across Kentucky counties examines the actual incentives claimed by these businesses and found weak positive effects associated with tax incentives, but only in border counties. The report found no evidence of spillover effects in adjacent counties. The authors argue that since Kentucky's incentive packages are similar to those of most states, they could generalize their findings to other states (Hoyt et al. 2008). Hicks and Shughart (2007) provide a summary of the literature, which has consistently found that targeted tax incentives have little effect anywhere in the United States. Using a meta-analysis of the most commonly cited reviews of this literature, Peters and Fisher (2004, 35) arrive at the same conclusion:

"the most fundamental problem is that many public officials appear to believe that they can influence the course of their state or local economies through incentives and subsidies to a degree far beyond anything supported by even the most optimistic evidence." Coyne and Moberg (2014) illustrate a variety of cases to demonstrate that targeted tax incentives are less than desirable policy. They present several justifications that state governments offer for providing these incentives but note that if firms would have located to an area without the economic incentives, then state governments cannot really claim that they have created these jobs. Instead they argue, as we noted above, that these types of targeted incentives create a culture of cronyism and rent-seeking.

Not only does recent academic research question the efficacy of tax incentives, but also, as far back as the 1940s, research in South Carolina pointed to the same conclusion. During the Second World War, the Preparedness for Peace Commission noted that tax rates were not the sole reason that industries chose to locate in a state (Stone 2003). An earlier report by the State Planning Board questioned the effectiveness of granting special tax exemptions to new industries. Although many Southern states were employing exemptions to be competitive, a survey of these states found that nearly all of them found the practice undesirable. Furthermore, as states competed with one another, tax rates equalized, thus destroying any advantage gained by the exemptions. Even in the face of longstanding research that questions the value of targeted incentives, legislatures persist in making them available. This is especially the case in the film industry, where research has found the incentives to be wasteful (Hefner 2008; Luther 2010). Several states have responded by reducing or terminating these incentives, only to reenact them subsequently.

Buss (1999a, 2001) claims that the research shows that state development agencies' conduct has little economic value and that state governments should not meddle with private location decisions. According to Poole et al. (1999), the actual impact of development strategies is often unknown, because these economic developers lack the necessary skills to identify the appropriate method and have limited data for analysis.[5]

The tool most often used by economic development agencies is the economic impact study. These studies often contain serious flaws. As a result, they may overstate the employment and economic gains associated with a new or expanded plant. One should note several issues here. First, no single methodology is universally accepted for counting jobs and income. While the targeted firm may create new jobs, the local labor force will likely be reshuffled in an effort to fill the new jobs. In 2001, Nissan opened a facility in Canton,

MS, where 90 percent of the workers employed lived and previously worked in the five counties surrounding the plant (Peavy 2007). Thus, only 10 percent of the jobs at the new Nissan plant were either taken by individuals who were unemployed prior to opening the plant or moved to Madison County, MS, from more distant locations, including out of state (Hicks and Shughart 2007). The economic impact studies do not indicate whether the jobs that workers leave are filled, remain vacant, or are eliminated when they move to the new job openings. Thus, economic impact studies cannot determine whether the overall change in employment is merely a redistribution of existing employees from one firm to another. Second, the benefit of these jobs to the state can be mitigated, depending on whether labor migrates from out of state to fill these positions. Third, the benefits of new jobs are subject to overstatement and double counting when the studies evaluate the indirect or ripple effects. The indirect effects attempt to measure the economic benefits that the new jobs create throughout the economy. Coyne and Moberg (2014) argue that even sophisticated statistical methods have difficulty determining whether the investment by a firm in a location, or the hiring of new workers was the direct result of specific benefits provided. And while the benefits and costs of these policies are difficult to determine, the necessary counterfactual case of how the resources would have been allocated is also unknowable. It is the fact that we cannot easily demonstrate these unseen effects of how else consumers and producers would allocate these resources that, in part, allows politicians to continue these policies.

Often firms that receive these targeted incentives are subject to little or no accountability and rarely create the number of jobs or the hourly wage rates they promise. According to the *New York Times*, in 2009, General Motors, after receiving a federal bailout, closed fifty properties where incentives were awarded, leaving the taxpayers to pay for the incentives promised (Story 2012). These firms will often move their operations elsewhere when the tax incentives or subsidies end. In particular, call centers and high-tech companies that employ few specialized physical assets will relocate, because they can easily abandon one site in favor of another in search of a more attractive incentive package (LeRoy 2005).

When these targeted incentives attract individuals from other states or cities to the local labor force, state and local governments may have to provide additional public goods to accommodate them. If the state government is granting the new company in the area relief from state and local taxes, and if the tax revenue generated from the new firm does not cover these additional costs, the increased government spending will fall on other existing businesses. This shifting tax burden may destroy as many jobs as the incentives provided to the new firm might create.

ECONOMIC COSTS: EXAMPLES FROM INDUSTRY

Although tax incentives have long been endorsed as the highway to prosperity, with promises of attracting businesses, providing jobs, and enriching the state, most public finance experts consider them bad policy. These incentives can shrink the tax base, thus shifting the burden of taxes and reducing tax revenue available for the basic functions of state government. Furthermore, they open the door to rent-seeking and corruption. Finally, there is little evidence that targeted incentives result in economic growth in the form of good paying jobs.

Firms that receive incentives to locate in states do create jobs, but at what cost? When FedEx created a new hub in North Carolina, the state effectively paid $77,000 per job (LeRoy 2005).[6] The automobile industry generates a lot of attention when companies relocate or build new plants in areas after receiving state incentive packages. Table 2 reports the average cost per job to attract automobile factories to the various states that offered incentives to attract automobile producers. Are employees at these plants earning a salary comparable to what the state is paying to attract these jobs, and is what they are adding to the state economic growth providing a return for the state's "investment"? Finally, are these jobs reducing the unemployment rate in these areas?

Efficacy Revisited

In 1984, 10 years before the first major auto plant investment in Alabama by Mercedes, the unemployment rate in the state was consistently higher than the national average. Alabama then attracted Honda in 1998, Toyota in 2001, and Hyundai in 2002. In 10 of the 18 years after the Mercedes expansion, the state unemployment rate was higher than the national average. In only 8 of the post-Mercedes years did the state unemployment rate drop below the national average (we exclude the year of the announcement).

Michigan incentivized General Motors in 1998. In 6 out of the 10 years prior to that subsidy, the state's unemployment rate was higher than the national rate. In 8 out of 10 years after the event, it was still higher. South Carolina entered the automotive industry incentive game in 1992 with BMW. In only 2 out of the 10 years prior to that event was the state's unemployment rate higher than the national rate. After BMW's arrival, that changed to 6 out of 10 years. Kentucky attracted Toyota in 1986. In six out of ten years before the

Table 2. US Auto Plant Investments

Company	State	Announcement Date	Initial Employment Estimate	Nominal Announced State and Local Incentives ($ millions)	Real Announced State and Local Incentives[a] ($ millions)	Real Incentive Cost per Job[a] ($)
Hyundai	Alabama	2002	2,000	118	118[b]	59,000[b]
Toyota	Alabama	2001	350	29	29	82,857
Nissan	Mississippi	2000	4,000	295	299	74,835
Honda	Alabama	1999	1,500	158	165	110,290
GM	Michigan	1998	700	107	114	162,287
Mercedes	Alabama	1994	1,500	253	289	192,730
BMW	South Carolina	1992	1,900	130	155	81,479
Toyota	Kentucky	1986	3,000	147	214	71,404

Source: Division of Research, University of South Carolina (2002).
Note: Inflation adjustments are made using GDP deflator series 2001 as the base year.
[a]Includes only initial incentives in real terms, not additional or ongoing incentives.
[b]2002 dollars, assumed equal to 2001 dollars.

plant and six out of ten years after Toyota's arrival, the state's unemployment rate was higher than the national rate.

We have investigated the statistical relationship between a state's unemployment rate compared to the national rate before and after the advent of an automotive plant expansion. We find that the state unemployment rate is highly correlated with the national rate and not related to the expansion of an automotive plant.

When using the unemployment rate as a pre- versus post-measure, like many researchers, we find a weak to nonexistent relationship with incentives. In addition, we investigated the connection between the tax burden in these automotive-incentive states by comparing the effective tax rates before and after the event of landing an automotive facility. If attracting these plants and creating these jobs is an effective economic policy, it should be generating higher tax revenues, which could lower the effective tax burden. Using data from the Tax Foundation, we found a positive statistically significant relationship: the effective tax burden increased afterward, but not by much.[7]

Highlighting the Film Industry Once Again

The film industry is very aggressive in seeking incentives from state governments, and states seem eager to offer these incentives. The state film incentive offices provide relevant data which illustrate our point further. What is so unique about the film industry that warrants special types of incentives? And why not provide similar incentives to other industries?

What makes the film industry special? The industry has desirable features: it is creative, entertaining, and environmentally clean, to name a few. The answer perhaps was best summarized in a Federal Reserve Bank of Minneapolis publication: "Call it a movie trailer for economic development: A film production company comes to town with its director and stars, spends a lot of money on lodging and food, hires locals as crew and extras. Residents run into their favorite stars at the local coffee shop, and the location is seen by millions of viewers on the big screen—a great boost for tourism" (Cobb 2006, 14). In an effort to capture this economic development, almost every state in the country has a film office. More importantly, almost every state offers a very favorable incentive package to the film industry. Indeed, if each state is attempting to create a competitive advantage in the film industry using tax incentives, then there should be no surprise that each state "ups the ante" each time another state raises the stakes. Since so many states are competing with one another for a limited number of films, these subsidies encourage a race to the bottom, as each state raises the ante in their generosity. As one New York producer noted about Connecticut's increase in their subsidies: "The good news is that Connecticut could spur the New York credit higher" (Foderaro 2008).

Calcagno and Hefner (2009) discussed the inefficiencies of film incentives in South Carolina from a public finance perspective. One interesting aspect of the film industry is that in many states, it is the most transparent in terms of identifying the costs of the incentives. For example, film offices often report these incentives. In addition, various revenue departments also report the incentives. It is relatively easier to analyze and thus criticize this type of corporate welfare. In 2002, only five states offered film incentives. By 2009, forty-four states had jumped on the bandwagon.

In 2013, South Carolina passed the Film Rebates Bill. This bill resurrected a set of film subsidies, making them permanent. South Carolina once again offers a cash rebate of up to 30 percent for supplies purchased from South Carolina vendors. The film companies can also receive rebates for wages up to 25 percent for South Carolina residents and 20 percent for out-of-state residents. Previously the supply and wage rebates were 15 percent, which is a decrease from where they were in 2004. Also under the new law, the incentives are permanent and are not subject to the General Assembly's annual budget process (Knich 2013).

Button (2015) estimates the impacts of state-level motion picture production incentives on filming location, establishments, and employment and found that most incentives have a moderate effect on filming location but almost no effects on employment or establishments.

Michigan is another case study of incentives gone amok (Skorup 2015). Michigan joined the film incentive scene in 2008, developing a program that reimbursed filmmakers for up to 42 percent of costs. Since then, Michigan has spent $450 million on film incentives, but the state has fewer film jobs in 2015 than it did in 2008. Thom (2015) reports that in 2013, film incentives created zero full-time jobs. In 2010, Michigan's nonpartisan Senate Fiscal Agency found that the program returned $0.11 for every taxpayer dollar spent. Similar findings exist for other states: $0.23 on the dollar in Louisiana, and $0.14 on the dollar in Massachusetts. Connecticut came in at a $0.07 return, Pennsylvania at $0.24, Arizona at $0.28, and New Mexico at $0.14 (Hudson and Bryson 2015). The poor return on incentives in the film industry demonstrates that continuing to offer these targeted incentives only leads to further rent-seeking behavior and the corruption that comes from engaging in it, as noted above.

CONCLUSION

It is not the proper function of government to decide which businesses should receive favor, nor do they have the unique ability to identify which of these businesses will succeed. This is the role of the private sector and the profit-and-loss system. As noted above, Hayek's (1945) idea of the division of knowledge explains why these types of targeted economic incentive cannot succeed.

The vast literature on the ineffectiveness of incentives bears out this point, as does the evidence presented in this chapter. So why do policymakers persist in asking for legislation to provide more incentives? The literature argues that there clearly is a political benefit to offering these incentives, even if no economic benefit accrues to the state. Calcagno and Hefner (2007) find that offering incentives can increase a state's corporate tax revenue, which might provide political motivation.[8] Regardless of whether tax revenues increase, providing targeted incentives gives the appearance that legislatures and policymakers are doing something concrete to generate economic development and solve the problems of the state. In addition, Buss (2001) notes that politicians face little risk from offering these types of incentives. If the firm fails, they can blame it on economic conditions; if it is successful, they can take all the credit. Public choice economics argues that politicians are often shortsighted in their policy judgments, not looking beyond the next election cycle. Furthermore, the state government culture of offering targeted incentives creates opportunities for selected firms to capture the rents and leads to either further rent-seeking activity or cronyism. This type of rent-seeking activity, like all rent-seeking activity, leads to a waste of resources and reduces economic activity.

The political economy of taxing citizens to favor select firms is one that clearly produces political benefit while not delivering on economic growth, jobs, and overall tax revenue. Politicians, by taxing consumers to generate "business friendly" policies, are taxing away choice from consumers and entrepreneurs regarding what business they would otherwise patronize, invest in, or develop. Every state offers some type of targeted tax incentives that create distortions in the economy and limits the ability of the private sector to generate economic growth. These incentives simply create unnecessary competition among states, increasing the incentives offered with little benefit to the state. State governments need to reform their economic development policies to be market friendly and attempt to attract any and all firms by offering greater overall economic freedom. By eliminating targeted tax incentives, states can reduce rent-seeking opportunities and potential political corruption, while competing based on real market conditions that firms actually use to make their decisions.

A tax system that is competitive between states and that attracts businesses and protects property across the board (as opposed to being targeted or discriminatory) will do more to reduce unemployment and generate economic growth than any targeted incentive (Blankart 2002; Hines 2010; Coyne and Moberg 2014).

As a first-choice policy solution, our preference and recommendation is that states cease to offer any type of targeted economic incentives and instead focus on general tax reform and pro-growth public expenditures. Our view mirrors that of Zelinsky (2008): state and local governments play a constructive role in economic development by providing good public services, which make them desirable places to live and invest. The elimination of all targeted tax incentives is a difficult political proposal, as states fear they will lose in this economic development arms race. A second-best proposal would be that state governments engage in a true cost-benefit analysis of the economic incentives they offer. The current economic impact proposals evaluated do not account for the costs of the economic incentives offered, and so they overstate the benefits. In addition, state governments need to offer their citizens a fully transparent accounting of the actual costs of the economic incentives offered to businesses. Few states fully disclose all aspects of their incentive packages. The aspects of the incentive packages that the state discloses are often estimates and not the actual costs of the package. Finally, as a palatable move in the right direction, we recommend full transparency with an actual accounting of the costs of the incentive package over the life of the agreement with the state.

State governments that adopt these policy recommendations would create greater economic investment opportunities for entrepreneurs and firms in their states. These policies would provide greater information to citizens about the true costs of these "business friendly" policies, by revealing the costs associated with firms receiving these targeted incentives. Movements in these directions by state governments would reduce the unintended and perverse existing incentive structure and create more market friendly policies that should generate greater economic growth.

NOTES

1. See Act 231 of 1996, South Carolina Legislature. At the time there was only one tire manufacturer in the state. http://www.scstatehouse.gov/billsearch.php?billnumbers=4397&session=111&summary=B.

2. We need to make a distinction here between competition among states that is related to tax competition or fiscal federalism as discussed in the literature (Tiebout 1956; Brennan and Buchanan 1980; Oates 2011) and the political competition to attract firms using tax incentives that are targeted only to a specific firm. The former is a desirable form of competition

thought to harmonize tax policy and restrain governments, whereas we argue that the latter is wasteful and ineffective.

3. Mauey and Spiegel (1995) and Bartik (2002) question whether benefits outweigh these costs. Bartik (1994) argues that development incentives provide the greatest benefit to high unemployment areas. However, he notes that state governments often attract firms to areas that have low unemployment, limiting the benefits that a state may receive from these types of incentives. Calcagno and Thompson (2004) find that targeted incentives merely reallocate resources rather than generate real economic growth.

4. Articles from regional Federal Reserve Bank publications include Burstein and Rolnick (1995), Cunningham (1995), Mauey and Spiegel (1995), and Becsi (1996).

5. At the core of this issue is a knowledge problem, as illustrated by F. A. Hayek (1945). Along with a division of labor there is a division of knowledge, and no one entity or small group of individuals has all the knowledge necessary, much of which is relevant to time and place, to plan these kinds of economic development incentives.

6. According to careerbliss.com, the average FedEx employee earns $35,000 annually. https://www.careerbliss.com/fedex/salaries/.

7. Statistical results available from the authors (Calcagno and Hefner 2016a,b).

8. As noted above, potential increases in corporate tax revenue do not equate to overall increases in tax revenue. However, if politicians are tax revenue maximizers they may see these policies as a way to gain some additional tax revenue while promising economic prosperity.

REFERENCES

Bartik, Timothy J. 1994. "Jobs, Productivity, and Local Development: What Implications Does Economic Research Have for the Role of Government?" *National Tax Journal* 47 (4): 847–61.

———. 2002. "Evaluating the Impacts of Local Economic Development Policies on Local Economic Outcomes: What Has Been Done and What Is Doable?" Upjohn Institute Staff Working Paper 03-89. W. E. Upjohn Institute for Employment Research, Kalamazoo, MI.

———. 2005. "Solving the Problems of Economic Development Incentives." *Growth and Change* 36 (2): 139–66.

Baumol, William, J. 1990. "Entrepreneurship: Productive, Unproductive and Destructive." *Journal of Political Economy* 98 (5): 893–921.

Becsi, Zsolt. 1996. "Have State and Local Taxes Contributed to the South's Economic Rise?" *Federal Reserve Bank of Atlanta Regional Update* 9 (3): 6–7.

Bennett, James, and Thomas DiLorenzo. 1983. *Underground Government: The Off-Budget Public Sector.* Washington, DC: Cato Institute.

Blankart, Charles B. 2002. "A Public Choice View of Tax Competition." *Public Finance Review* 30 (5): 366–76.

Brennan, Geoffrey, and James M. Buchanan. 1980. *The Power to Tax: Analytical Foundations of a Fiscal Constitution.* Cambridge: Cambridge University Press.

Buchanan, James M. 1986. "The Constitution of Economic Policy." In *Nobel Lectures: Economic Sciences 1981–1990*, edited by Karl-Göran Mäller, 180–89. Singapore: World Science.

Burstein, M. L., and A. J. Rolnick. 1995. "Congress Should End the Economic War among the States." *Federal Reserve Bank of Minneapolis 1994 Annual Report* 9 (1): 3–19.

Buss, Terry F. 1999a. "The Case against Targeted Industry Strategies." *Economic Development Quarterly* 13 (4): 339–56.

———. 1999b. "To Target or Not to Target, That's the Question: A Response to Wiewel and Finkle." *Economic Development Quarterly* 13 (4): 365–70.

———. 2001. "The Effect of State Tax Incentives on Economic Growth and Firm Location Decisions: An Overview of the Literature." *Economic Development Quarterly* 15 (11): 90–105.

Button, Patrick. 2015. "Do Tax Incentives Affect Business Location? Evidence from Motion Picture Production Incentives." Working Paper, University of California, Irvine. http://www.economics .uci.edu/files/docs/phdcandidates/13-14/pbuttonfilmincentives15oct14-1.pdf.

Calcagno, Peter T., and Frank Hefner. 2007. "State Targeting of Business Investment: Does Targeting Increase Corporate Tax Revenue?" *Journal of Regional Analysis and Policy* 37 (2): 90–102.

———. 2009. "South Carolina's Tax Incentives: Costly, Inefficient and Distortionary." In *Unleashing Capitalism: A Prescription for Economic Prosperity in South Carolina*, edited by Peter T. Calcagno, 131–47. Columbia, SC: South Carolina Policy Council.

———. 2016a. "Tax Incentives for Industrial Recruitment: A Critical Review." Presented at the 55th Annual Meeting of the Southern Regional Science Association, March 31–April 2, Washington, DC.

———. 2016b. "Tax Incentives: Market vs Business Friendly." Presented at the 53rd Annual Meeting of the Public Choice Society, March 10–12, Ft. Lauderdale, FL.

Calcagno, Peter T., and Henry Thompson. 2004. "State Economic Incentives: Stimulus or Reallocation?" *Public Finance Review* 35 (5): 1–15.

CBRE. 2013. "Impact of Taxes & Incentives on Data Center Locations." July. www.cbre.us/services /office/ . . . /Data-Center-Taxes-Incentives-2013.pdf.

Cobb, Kathy. 2006. "Roll the Credits . . . and the Tax Incentives." Federal Reserve Bank of Minneapolis. *Fedgazette,* September: 14–15.

Coyne, Christopher J., and Lotta Moberg. 2014. "The Political Economy of State-Provided Targeted Benefits." Working Paper 13-14, Mercatus Center at George Mason University, Arlington, VA.

Cunningham, Thomas. 1995. "Development Incentives—Good or Bad?" *Federal Reserve Bank of Atlanta Regional Update* 8 (1): 8–9.

Dewar, Margaret E. 1998. "Why State and Local Economic Development Programs Cause So Little Economic Development." *Economic Development Quarterly* 12 (1): 68–87.

Division of Research. 2002. "The Economic Impact of BMW on South Carolina." Columbia, SC: University of South Carolina.

Ellis, Stephen, and Cynthia Rogers. 2000. "Local Economic Development as a Prisoners' Dilemma: The Role of Business Climate." *Review of Regional Studies* 30 (3): 315–30.

Esinger, Peter K. 1989. *The Rise of the Entrepreneurial State: State and Local Development Policy in the United States.* Madison: University of Wisconsin Press.

Felix, Alison R., and James Hines. 2013. "Who Offers Tax-Based Business Development Incentives?" *Journal of Urban Economics* 75: 80–91.

Finkle, Jeffery A. 1999. "The Case against Targeting Might Have Been More . . . Targeted." *Economic Development Quarterly* 13 (4): 361–64.

Foderaro, L.W. 2008. "Gone with the Cash: Films Go for the Best Tax Breaks." *New York Times,* March 29. http://www.nytimes.com/2008/03/29/nyregion/29film.html.

Gabe, Todd M., and David S. Kraybill. 1998. "Tax Incentive Requests and Offers in a State Economic Development Program." *Review of Regional Studies* 28 (3): 1–14.

Gannon, Joyce, and Mark Belko. 2015. "Latrobe-Based Kennametal to Move Headquarters to Pittsburgh." *Pittsburgh Post-Gazette,* September 18. http://www.post-gazette.com/business /pittsburgh-company-news/2015/09/18/Latrobe-based-Kennametal-to-move-headquarters -to-Pittsburgh/stories/201509180314.

Glaeser, E. L., and R. E. Saks. 2006. "Corruption in America." *Journal of Public Economics* 90: 1053–72.

Hayek, F. A. 1945. "The Use of Knowledge in Society." *American Economic Review* 35 (4): 519–30.

Hefner, Frank. 2008. "Impact Analysis for Film Production in South Carolina." S.C. Coordinating Council for Economic Development. http://www.sccommerce.com/docdirectory/.

Hicks, Michael J., and William F. Shughart II. 2007. "Quit Playing Favorites: Why Business Subsidies Hurt Our Economy." In *Unleashing Capitalism: Why Prosperity Stops at the West Virginia Border and How to Fix It*, edited by Russell S. Sobel, 119–30. Morgantown, WV: Center for Economic Growth, Public Policy Foundation of West Virginia.

Hines, James R., Jr. 2010. "Treasure Islands." *Journal of Economic Perspectives* 24 (4): 103–26.

Hinkley, Sara, Fiona Hsu, Greg Leroy, and Katie Tallman. 2000. "Minding the Candy Store: State Audits of Economic Development." *Good Jobs First*, 1–84. Washington, DC: Institute on Taxation and Economic Policy.

Hoyt, William, Christopher Jepsen, and Kenneth Troske. 2008 "Business Incentives and Employment: What Incentives Work and Where?" Working Paper Series 2009-02, Institute for Federalism and Intergovernmental Relations, University of Kentucky, Lexington.

Hudson, Chris, and Donald Bryson. 2015. "Yelling 'Cut!' for Moviemaking Tax Breaks." *Wall Street Journal*, September 19–20.

Knich, Diane. 2013. "Incentives Give S.C. Star Quality." *Post and Courier*, May 17.

Kurylko, Diana. 1992a. "BMW Narrows Site Selection to S. Carolina, Nebraska." *Automotive News*, May 18.

———. 1992b. "BMW Plant in Review." *Automotive News*, June 15.

LeRoy, Greg. 2005. *The Great American Jobs Scam: Corporate Tax Dodging and the Myth of Job Creation*. San Francisco: Berrett-Koehler.

Luther, William. 2010. "Movie Production Incentives: Blockbuster Support for Lackluster Policy." Washinton DC: Tax Foundation.

Mauey, Joe, and Mark M. Spiegel. 1995. "Is State and Local Competition for Firms Harmful?" *Federal Reserve Bank of San Francisco Weekly Letter*, 95–26.

Morgan, Jonathon. 2009. "Using Economic Development Incentives: For Better or for Worse." *Popular Government* Winter: 16–29.

Morgan, Philip, Kasia Traczynka, and Greg LeRoy. 2013. "The Largest Economic Development Subsidy Packages Ever Awarded by State and Local Governments in the United States." Washington, DC: Good Jobs First.

Oates, Wallace E. 2011. *Fiscal Federalism*. Cheltenham, UK: Edward Elgar.

Patrick, Carlianne. 2016. "Identifying the Local Economic Impact Development Effects of Million Dollar Facilities." *Economic Inquiry*. doi: 10.1111/ecin.12339.

Peavy, John Patrick. 2007. "A Comparison of Two Alternative Models of Economic Impact: A Case Study of the Mississippi Nissan Plant." PhD dissertation, University of Mississippi, University.

Peters, Alan, and Peter Fisher. 2004. "The Failures of Economic Development Incentives." *Journal of the American Planning Association* 70 (1): 27–37.

Pomp, Richard D. 1998. "The Future of the State Corporate Income Tax: Reflections (and Confessions) of a Tax Lawyer. " Future of State Taxation 49: 49–72.

Poole, Kenneth E., George A. Erickcek, Donald T. Iannone, Nancy McCrea, and Pofen Salem. 1999. *Evaluating Business Development Incentives*. Washington, DC: US Department of Commerce Economic Development Administration, National Association of State Development Agencies.

Saiz, Martin. 2001. "Using Program Attributes to Measure and Evaluate State Economic Development Strategies." *Economic Development Quarterly* 15 (1): 45–57.

Sheehan, Andy. 2015. "Kennametal Moving from Westmoreland Co. to Hazelwood." CBS Pittsburgh KDKA, October 15.

Skorup, Jarett. 2015. "Film Subsidies Fade to Black." *Wall Street Journal*, July 1.

Slade, David. 2013. "Tax Break for Big Business." *Post and Courier*, July 6.

Stone, Richard. 2003. "Making a Modern State: The Politics of Economic Development in South Carolina, 1938–1962." PhD diss., University of South Carolina, Columbia.

Story, Louise. 2012. "As Companies Seek Tax Deals, Governments Pay High Price." *New York Times*, December 1. http://www.nytimes.com/2012/12/02/us/how-local-taxpayers-bankroll -corporations.html?pagewanted=all&r=0.

Thom, Michael. 2015. "Film Tax Credits Don't Grow the Economy." *Viewpoint on Public Issues*. Mackinac Center for Public Policy. https://www.mackinac.org/21400.

Tiebout, Charles M. 1956. "A Pure Theory of Local Expenditures." *Journal of Political Economy* 64 (5): 416–24.

Verrier, Richard. 2015. "Iowa Film Tax Credit Program Wracked by Scandal." *Los Angeles Times*, January 19. http://articles.latimes.com/2011/jan/19/business/la-fi-ct-onlocation-20110119.

Wang, Jai. 2016. "Do Economic Development Incentives Crowd Out Public Expenditures in U.S. States?" *BE Journal of Economic Analysis & Policy* 16 (1): 513–38.

Wiewel, Wim. 1999. "Policy Research in an Imperfect World: Response to Terry F. Buss, 'The Case Against Targeted Industry Strategies.'" *Economic Development Quarterly* 13 (4): 357–60.

Zelinsky, Edward. 2008. "Tax Incentives for Economic Development: Personal (and Pessimistic) Reflections." *Case Western Reserve Law Review* 58 (4): 1145–55.

CHAPTER 11
Tax Schemes for Sports Venues

DENNIS COATES
University of Maryland, Baltimore County

CRAIG A. DEPKEN II
University of North Carolina at Charlotte

S ince 1990, the United States has experienced a boom in the construction of new facilities for professional sports franchises. Overall, 20 new hockey arenas, 24 new basketball arenas, 22 new football stadiums, and 26 new baseball stadiums have been constructed, many with substantial public subsidies. This construction frenzy has occurred despite what appears to be an increased skepticism about the promised net benefits of stadiums since the previous building period of the 1960s.

While economists have been studying the impact of new stadiums, franchise (re)locations, and hosting events on various measures of economic interest, the public discourse surrounding a new stadium has remained remarkably static over time. Generally, the main justification for contributing public dollars to the construction of stadiums and arenas centers on the impact on the local economy of the stadium, the franchise housed there, and the events that take place there. Some of these impacts are temporary, such as jobs in the construction sector during the building phase; other impacts are thought to be more permanent, such as permanent jobs associated with the events in the stadium or with indirect and induced effects of the stadium and its events. Still other effects are more ephemeral, including a sense of civic pride and the advertising effects that a new stadium generates for local tourism and business location.

Balanced against these hoped-for benefits are often several hundred millions of public dollars that help fund the construction of the new stadium or arena. These public dollars are rarely paid for out of surplus at the city or state level but rather are generated through combinations of special purpose sales, excise, and property taxes. Many times the taxes are intentionally levied on activities associated with tourism, such as hotel taxes, food and beverage taxes, and car rental taxes, with the intention of having out-of-towners pay for the stadium costs and ostensibly allowing the locals to pay less. However, such tax schemes often have a larger than predicted impact on local citizens and on the hospitality industry.

Proposed stadium projects are often presented with a cost-benefit study that is generated long before stadium construction begins and even longer before the stadium opens. The nature of the ex ante analysis is that it is predictive in nature and suffers from the same prediction bias that accompanies cost-benefit analysis of other public projects and regulation. The information required for an accurate prediction is often lacking, as is any accountability for being incorrect. This results in rosy predictions of millions of dollars in direct, indirect, induced, and implicit benefits to the local economy and citizens, hundreds if not thousands of jobs associated with the new venue, and relatively little emphasis on the direct, indirect, and opportunity costs associated with the public's contribution to the project.

These ex ante studies stand in stark contrast to the hundreds of ex post studies of venues, franchise (re)locations, and event hosting. Such studies often find small, and often negative, impacts on many economic variables of interest, such as income, wages, jobs, tourism spending, hotel registration, business relocation, and tax revenues, to name a few (a good summary of the literature is Coates and Humphreys 2008). The ex post studies have the advantage of utilizing actual data generated after a new stadium opens, of being developed over a longer period of time without looming deadlines associated with referendum dates, and of being generally apolitical in the methodology and results obtained.

This chapter describes the range of taxes used to finance stadium and arena construction, presents information on the prevalence of the various taxes, highlights their characteristics, and offers some insight into the incidence of these taxes. Finally, we discuss the evidence concerning who benefits from stadium and arena projects.

TAX INSTITUTIONS AND THEIR FREQUENCY OF USE

The typical stadium construction project is financed in whole or in part by some amount of government borrowing via issuing bonds. While some previous projects have been funded at the state and county level, most often they are funded at the city or metropolitan level. Subsidies by the host city can be justified on economic grounds if there are substantial benefits that redound to the local economy. By issuing debt, the borrowing entity promises to make principal and interest payments on the bonds over a set period of time, typically 30 years. The higher the interest rate, the more expensive a given level of debt is to service, and interest rates have been shown to be highly correlated with debt ratings, which are, in turn, related to many such things as existing debt levels, corruption, economic and population growth, and governance structures, to name a few.[1] As the interest rate charged to a municipality is highly correlated with the expected ability for the borrowing government to repay on a timely basis, it is important that the borrowing government be able to clearly signal how it will service the debt and whether the debt might be retired early.

The most generic means of financing a stadium project would be for the borrowing government to issue general obligation bonds that are serviced using general tax revenues from all sources, including income taxes, property taxes, excise taxes, lottery proceeds, and business taxes. However, it is relatively rare for a borrowing government to use general obligation bonds. One reason might be the perception that having separate stadium debt increases transparency about how the debt is being serviced, which might reduce the interest rate such debts carry. Furthermore, separating the stadium debt allows for specifically enumerated sources of funds—such as sales taxes, excise taxes, hotel occupancy taxes, car rental taxes, and ticket surcharges—to be negotiated. Finally, separating stadium debt might yield a political advantage in the case of a public referendum on the proposed stadium project if voters feel that dedicating general revenues carries too high an opportunity cost.

How the money is raised to service public stadium debt is strongly connected to the theory of political economy and public choice. Logic suggests that franchises prefer financing schemes with the smallest impact on their ability to generate revenue from the franchise and the events held in the stadium and that obligate them for the smallest possible share of the financing and operating costs of the stadium, holding other things constant. Because of these incentives, franchises, leagues, and private-citizen supporters apply pressure on city, county, and state officials to provide public-sector financial and other support for a new stadium. This pressure can include economic impact studies that purport to show how much value the team offers the local economy, testimonials about how much fans are affected by the existence and location of the team, or threats to relocate if a new stadium is not forthcoming. If a team is able to secure partial or full public funding for a new stadium, the question of how the debt will be financed is also negotiated. Clearly the team seeks to retain as much as possible of the revenue generated by events in the stadium, money to be made through advertising in and outside the stadium, and all other revenue streams that the team generates. For example, if a fan is willing to spend $100 on a ticket, the team would clearly prefer to retain the full $100 rather than share any of that money with the government that provides the public subsidy for the stadium. To this end, teams and leagues often push for any public debt to be serviced using revenues generated outside the sphere of the team. Doing so serves the dual purpose of retaining as much revenue for the team as possible and making the incidence of taxes used to finance the subsidies as opaque as possible.

Tables 1 and 2 present information on the relative usage of the various revenue sources states and local governments use to fund stadium and arena subsidies. Table 1 reflects the 99 North American professional sports facilities operating in 2001. Table 2 presents similar information for 112 professional sports facilities operating in 2015. Table 1 shows that many facilities in 2001 were subsidized using different taxes but that the majority included some general revenue funding. While the *Sports Facility Reports* (National Sports Law Institute, Marquette University Law School 2015) do not indicate when general government revenue or lease revenue is used to help finance stadium

Table 1. Number of Sports Facilities Using Different Revenue Sources, 2001

League	Total Number of Facilities	Number of Facilities Using Revenue Source					
		General Revenue	Facility Lease	Sales Tax	Hotel and Car Rental Taxes	Alcohol, Tobacco, and Lottery Taxes	Other
MLB	25	16	9	6	6	3	5
MLB/NFL	5	5	0	0	0	0	0
NFL	24	16	5	6	4	3	0
NBA	15	10	2	2	1	1	2
NBA/NHL	13	7	4	0	2	0	1
NHL	17	11	3	2	3	0	0
Total	99	65	23	16	16	7	8

Source: Derived from Long (2002), table 4.30.

Table 2. Number of Sports Facilities Using Different Revenue Sources, 2015

League	Total Number of Facilities	Number of Facilities Using Revenue Source			
		Sales Tax	Hotel and Car Rental Taxes	Alcohol, Tobacco, and Lottery Taxes	Other
MLB	29	10	7	1	1
MLB/NFL	1	0	0	0	0
NFL	31	8	11	1	0
NBA	21	2	6	1	0
NBA/NHL	9	3	2	0	3
NHL	21	1	1	0	0
Total	112	24	27	3	4

Source: Derived from National Sports Law Institute, Marquette University Law School (2015).

subsidies, table 2 suggests that many subsidies are still financed with general revenue at some level.

Table 1 shows that, in sixty-five out of ninety-nine cases, state and local governments were paying for sports facilities at least in part out of general revenues. In other words, at least two-thirds of the facilities being subsidized by local and state governments did so directly at the expense of other state and local government services. The proportion is lower to the extent that sales, hotel and car rental, and excise and lottery taxes were enhanced or specifically created to help finance the sports facilities.

Comparing tables 1 and 2, it becomes clear that the financing of newer facilities has evolved. Greater use is made of both sales tax and hotel and car rental taxes as funding sources in 2015 compared to 2001. The so-called sin taxes (on alcohol, tobacco, and lottery sales) have become less common over time. In addition, tax increment financing (TIF) and the use of property taxes are more explicit in 2015. Finally, the stadium for the Washington (DC) Nationals is financed in part by a tax on utilities and by a gross receipts tax on businesses with gross receipts of more than $5 million.[2]

One method of financing stadium debt is the introduction of a temporary increase in the local sales tax. Of the thirty-two NFL stadiums currently in operation, eight use some form of sales tax as part of their financing for construction or renovation; ten of thirty MLB teams do so, while five of thirty NBA teams and four of thirty NHL teams use some form of sales tax (see table 2). A sales tax is, generally speaking, imposed by law on the purchase of a good or service in a specific geographic area, such as a city, county, or state. Operationally, the sales tax is added to the price of the good or service at the point of sale by the seller, but the burden of the sales tax is shared by both the buyer and the seller. The more elastic the demand for the product, the less the burden falls on consumers, whereas the more elastic is supply, the less the burden falls on sellers. As supply and demand are rarely at the extremes of perfect elasticity, a sales tax usually raises the price of the taxed item for the buyer, lowers the net-of-tax revenue for the seller, and reduces the quantity of the taxed item traded in the market.

An important issue with this sort of taxation is the nature of the tax base, or the range of final goods and services to which the tax applies. In the case of NFL stadiums, five are financed with add-ons to the general sales tax rate, while three utilize a sales tax increase only on stadium-related purchases. The narrower the set of goods and services subject to the sales tax, the higher the tax rate must be to raise the necessary revenues. Because taxing some goods but not others makes the untaxed goods more attractive, changes in the sales tax can alter consumption patterns, which can affect the amount of revenue generated by the increased tax. This ability to influence consumption is important, because different states define the tax base differently. In other words, two states can both finance their stadium debt via a sales tax, yet those taxes can have quite different impacts, because the states apply the sales tax to different sets of goods and services.

Consider a tax on tickets for events held in the stadium. The tax could be a percentage of the ticket's face value or it could be a fixed fee per ticket.[3] One advantage of such a tax, from the point of view of economists, is that it follows the benefit principle: those who gain the most by the new stadium—fans in attendance and the teams that play there—bear much of the cost of financing the new stadium.[4] Because fans and the teams both have the incentive to avoid paying for the new stadium in this way, such surcharges are not often utilized. For example, only three of the thirty-two NFL stadiums use ticket surcharges as a form of finance, no MLB stadium finances involve ticket surcharges, and only three NBA and four NHL facilities do so.

Other special sales taxes often used to finance stadiums are additions to the local hotel, lodging, or accommodations tax, and increased taxes imposed on car rentals. These taxes are imposed at some percentage rate in addition to whatever tax rates applied to these expenditures prior to stadium finance. Eleven NFL facilities, five MLB stadiums, three NBA arenas, and one NHL arena are partially funded by hotel taxes. Four NFL stadiums, four MLB stadiums, four NBA arenas, and one NHL arena are funded in part with car rental taxes. Although use of such a tax for the University of Phoenix Stadium in Phoenix was declared unconstitutional by the Maricopa County

Superior Court in 2014, the tax is still being collected while the ruling is appealed.

Property taxes are a very common method of funding local public services, especially education, in the United States. Practices vary across states, but generally real property (e.g., cars), residential, commercial, industrial, and agricultural land and structures are taxed at a fixed percentage of their assessed value. Tax rates vary across types of property, and most states have exemptions for some portion of the value, especially in the case of residential and agricultural property. No current NFL, MLB, or NBA stadium is explicitly financed by special provisions of property taxes, and only two NHL arenas involve financing from property taxation. The more common manipulation of property taxes in the case of new stadiums is to partially or fully exempt the new stadium from local or state property taxes. For example, the Pepsi Center in Denver is exempt from property taxes, saving the arena, and indirectly its two primary occupants (the NBA Denver Nuggets and the NHL Colorado Avalanche), more than $2 million a year.

Tax increment financing is a common method of encouraging local economic development expenditures. First used in California in the early 1950s, the theory behind a TIF is that an initial public subsidy is provided for a specific development project in a particular narrow geographic area and is repaid with increased real estate tax revenues from the TIF district. The increase in real estate tax revenues is expected to flow from increased economic activity and higher property values attributed to the presence of the development project. While TIFs have been very popular in the United States throughout the past four decades, at present no NFL, one MLB, and one NBA/NHL facility is financed using TIF.

Some facilities have been partly financed by dedicating some or all revenues from the state lottery to paying principal and interest on the state and local government debt incurred to fund stadium construction. For example, in Washington, specially developed sports-themed lottery games have been created and are expected to produce $127 million for Century Link Field (home of the NFL Seahawks) and $3 million a year toward Safeco Field (home of the MLB Mariners), both located in Seattle. Baltimore's Oriole Park at Camden Yards is also funded with state lottery revenues; indeed, the Maryland Lottery was created to fund stadium construction. No current NBA or NHL facilities are explicitly funded via lottery revenues.

Two additional means of financing stadiums and arenas are described despite not being, strictly speaking, taxation. Despite this, they do involve use of public resources and are akin to tax expenditures, that is, the forgoing of tax collections rather than direct spending of taxes collected. The first of these methods is Payments in Lieu of Taxes (PiLoTs), the second is facility naming rights.

PiLoTs are traditionally used in the context of not-for-profit institutions whose property is exempted from property taxes. Since the not-for-profit receives local public services, such as fire and police protection and garbage collection, yet pays no property taxes, it gets the services for free. Local governments, particularly those experiencing financial difficulties, negotiate with the not-for-profits for some payment for these services, in lieu of taxes.[5] Even though most professional sports franchises in North America are for-profit entities, they are often exempted from property tax payments. A PiLoT arrangement was used in the financing of the new Yankee Stadium in 2006, projected to save the Yankees $786 million over a 40-year period, and Matheson and Humphreys (2009) suggest this approach could spread in financing sports facilities. The primary benefit for the Yankees lies in lower costs of borrowing to cover their portion of construction costs. Under the terms of the agreement between the New York Yankees and the New York City Industrial Development Agency, the agency borrows hundreds of millions of dollars that are used to construct the new Yankee Stadium. Instead of paying property taxes, revenues from which would be used to pay interest and principle on the bonds, the Yankees pay interest on the bonds out of its regular revenues. The Agency borrows at the interest rate on state and local bonds, so the PiLot saves the Yankees money, because the club incurs lower costs than if it borrowed the money directly.

The sale of naming rights could be a common source of stadium financing. However, in nearly all cases, the tenant teams are allowed to sell the name of the stadium and retain the revenue themselves, with no explicit revenue sharing arrangement with the host city or any explicit requirement to dedicate the naming rights revenue to servicing the stadium debt. In the case of naming rights, local government allows the club or franchise to sell the rights, with those funds often being counted toward the club's contribution to paying for the facility. Carl Lindner became majority owner of the Cincinnati Reds in 1999, and his company Great American Insurance purchased naming rights to the Cincinnati baseball stadium. Delaney and Eckstein (2003, 213) write that "the money goes to the team and is counted as part of the team's contribution toward stadium costs." PNC Park, home of the Pittsburgh Pirates, opened in 2001 at a cost of $262 million. The cost of the stadium to state and local taxpayers was $75 and $137 million, respectively, and the Pirates contributed $50 million, of which $30 million was covered by the naming rights (Panyard 2010).

GEOGRAPHIC AND TEMPORAL REACH

Taxes to finance stadium and arena construction have both a geographic and a temporal aspect that may differ from other taxes. The geographic aspect is best exemplified by comparing those cases in which a sales tax applies only to purchases inside the stadium with those where the sales tax applies to all sales in the jurisdiction. Clearly, taxes to finance stadium debt can be narrowly focused or more broadly based. In Wisconsin, voters in Brown County, home to the Green Bay Packers, approved a sales tax add-on to fund renovations to Lambeau Field. A regional sales tax was imposed in Milwaukee, Ozaukee, Racine, Washington, and Waukesha Counties to fund the baseball stadium for the Milwaukee Brewers. In terms of geographical reach, the farthest point from Lambeau Field in Brown County is approximately 19 miles, whereas the farthest geographic distance from Miller Park in Milwaukee's multicounty tax jurisdiction is 42.3 miles.

Most common, however, is the case in which the state has committed to paying the debt from general revenues. (See tables 1 and 2.) In other words, stadium debt repayment is not tied to either the users of the facility or the communities where most of the users will come from. For example, New Jersey's legislature obligated itself to paying off the bonds of the New Jersey Sports and Exposition Authority, if that organization were unable to do so, by backing those bonds with its moral authority. As another example, initially some funds for paying the stadium-related debt linked to construction of Oriole Park at Camden Yards, in Baltimore, were to come from the state lottery with new games created for that purpose (Miller 2012). Of course, players of the state lottery reside in all parts of the state. This spreads the cost of the stadium across a wide geographic area, including many people who will never view an event in the new stadium.

Finally, the federal exemption from income tax of interest from state and local government debt means that US taxpayers from states without professional sport franchises are paying for some of the stadium and arena subsidies for those that have teams. This form of tax exemption was dropped in President Barack Obama's proposed federal budget for fiscal year 2016/2017. The temporal aspect of the taxes has two dimensions. First, legal authorization for the tax may expire when the bonds are paid off. The alternative is, of course, that once the tax is authorized for the purpose of funding the stadium, the politicians find alternative purposes for the funds after the stadium financing is complete. So the tax, once enacted, may never be repealed. In Seattle, a 2011 bill proposed extending the taxes used to pay off the Kingdome and its replacement, Qwest Field, as well as Safeco Field. Proposed uses of the funds included an expansion of the convention center and funding arts programs. Naturally, opponents of the extension contended that when the taxes were enacted in 1995, the legislature committed to the taxes expiring when the stadium debt was retired. In Wisconsin, the special tax to fund the Lambeau Field renovations had raised enough money to pay off the associated debt in 2011. The tax continued on, generating revenues dedicated to covering maintenance costs for the field through the end of the Packers' lease in 2031. Funds for that obligation were met in March 2015, yet the tax continued until September 30, 2015. Now there is a debate on how to distribute the excess revenues collected via the tax. In the Milwaukee area, the five-county taxing district that has financed the MLB Miller Park is anxious that the tax might be extended to help finance a new arena for the NBA Bucks; state legislation was proposed in 2013 that would sunset the sales tax used to finance the baseball stadium.

The second temporal dimension of the taxes concerns retirement of the debt. Some stadium and arena debt is paid off before the term of the initial bonds. Taxes and other revenue sources are such that the local government is able to retire the bonds before they reach maturity. For example, debt used to construct the ballpark in Arlington in the early 1990s for the Texas Rangers, was paid off 10 years early. In contrast, some debt exists beyond the life of the facility whose construction it funded. Giants Stadium, in New Jersey, was demolished to make way for a new stadium while $110 million in debt incurred for it remained outstanding. The Kingdome in Seattle was demolished in 2000, yet in 2010 there was still $80 million in debt to be paid. Looking at Wisconsin again, in 2014 the Milwaukee Bucks began pushing for a new arena while $20 million of debt on their existing arena was still outstanding.

TAX INCIDENCE

So far, the discussion has focused on the types of taxes used to finance a new stadium and the geographic and temporal reach of these taxes. In this section, the analysis turns to the incidence of the taxes. We can discuss this either philosophically or empirically. Philosophically, the issue is who should pay, a normative question. Empirically, the question is who does pay.

The normative question often focuses on whether the tax should be designed based on the ability-to-pay principle or on the benefit principle. According to the former principle, the tax system should levy greater taxes on individuals with greater income or wealth. Unfortunately, the ability-to-pay principle does not offer guidance on the precise relationship between an increased ability to pay and the actual level of a tax. For example, if income rises by 10 percent, the principle is silent on whether taxes paid should rise by less than, exactly, or more than 10 percent. In each case, taxes rise with income, satisfying the definition of ability to pay.[6] A tax designed under the benefit principle will collect tax payments that increase with the size of the benefits generated for the taxpayer by a publicly provided good or service.[7]

Consider an individual wealthy taxpayer who is uninterested in sports but is a devotee of the theater. Under the ability-to-pay principle, the wealthy theater-lover would pay a high level of taxes to support construction of a new stadium, even though he or she may never set foot in the venue. The same individual would pay nothing toward the stadium under the benefit principle of taxation. By contrast, a low-income sports fan will pay little under the ability to pay principle but may pay a large sum under the benefit principle, though that will depend upon how the taxes are collected. Given the normative nature of this debate, different people can reasonably come to different judgments on this issue.

The empirical question about who actually pays the tax centers not on who "writes the check" for the taxes but instead on who is made worse off by the taxes used to finance the facility and how much worse off those individuals are. Our focus here is on taxation, but it is also important to consider the incidence of any benefits from the public-sector funding of stadium construction. Siegfried and Peterson (2000) find that individuals who purchased season or single game sports tickets have income on average 59 percent larger than individuals who do not purchase tickets. The benefits of the stadium subsidies thus seem to redound more so to wealthier individuals. If the taxes fall on the same people, the situation is similar to taxation under the benefit principle. Of course, the individuals in the stands and those who pay the taxes may not be the same people.

The incidence of the taxes used to finance sport facility construction is difficult to determine in a general way because of the variety of methods of raising the revenues. What is clear is that the extent to which it is fans, the general population, franchise owners, or players is determined entirely by the price elasticities of supply and demand. The more elastic demand is, for a given elasticity of supply, the smaller is the share of the burden on consumers. The less elastic is demand, the more the tax falls on the consumers.

The general sales tax is regressive, meaning that those with lower incomes pay a larger share of their income in sales tax than do those with higher incomes. For example, the Institute for Tax and Economic Policy (2015) reports that the share of income paid in sales taxes by the bottom 20 percent of the income distribution is nearly 8 times the share paid by the wealthiest 1 percent. Families in the middle of the income distribution pay about 5 times the share of their income compared to the wealthy. Consequently, to the extent that the new stadium financing comes from sales taxes, the burden of financing the subsidies falls more heavily on the poor than on the wealthy. The degree to which this is true depends significantly on the sales tax base. For example, some states exempt food purchases from the sales tax. If food makes up a larger share of the budget of the relatively poor than of the relatively wealthy, then this exemption means the burden of the sales tax on the poor will be smaller than under a general sales tax.

Taxes that apply only to tickets or to merchandise purchased inside the stadium clearly burden the relatively wealthy more than the poor, since the evidence is that the wealthy are the individuals who attend the stadium events. However, if in-stadium purchases are price elastic, meaning that fans at the games choose not to purchase souvenirs or refreshments at the games, then it is also possible that the burden falls on the concessionaires and their employees.[8] If the employees are low-wage workers, then perhaps even the tax that hits only purchases inside the stadium will hit hardest on the relatively poor.

Even when taxes are targeted to a specific place, they are unlikely to do so. For example, the gross receipts tax used in Washington is, by law, imposed on firms with sales revenue over a specific level. This tax is very much like a general sales tax, but because of the exemption it has complicated incidence and distributional effects. As shown by Lawson (chapter 9, this volume) such a tax creates a wedge between the price that the consumer pays and the amount of money that the seller retains after paying the tax, with the former greater than the latter.

The gross receipts tax applies a specific tax rate to the gross receipts of the firm, which is ultimately no different than a sales tax on each individual transaction. Therefore, just as under a sales tax, the gross receipts tax creates a wedge between the price paid and the price kept by the seller. It is straightforward to show that a sales tax and a gross receipts tax have identical incidence effects if $T = t/(1-t)$, where T is the sales tax, and t is the gross receipts tax. If a gross receipts tax was 4 percent, then the incidence would be the same as a sales tax of 4.1 percent. Thus, if a gross receipts tax was chosen somewhere close to the previously prevailing sales tax, lawmakers might think they are taxing business under the gross receipts tax, but they are likely taxing both business owners and consumers.

The last issue we consider regarding the incidence of the taxes used to finance stadium subsidies is what is often termed "tax exporting." Tax exporting occurs when those who bear the burden of a tax live or work outside the jurisdiction imposing the tax. The use of hotel and rental car taxes to finance stadium construction is an example of exporting the tax burden to nonresidents who choose to stay at local hotels or rent cars. It is likely that nearly all people who rent rooms in hotels or who rent cars are visitors to the city. If these travelers cannot change anything about their travel, including consuming in the so-called sharing economy by renting housing or transportation from individuals who do not pay taxes, then these individuals rather than local citizens bear the burden of the hotel and rental car taxes. If the travelers simply choose some other city as their destination, then the burden of the taxes falls on all local businesses and their employees, and the lost revenues could potentially require the borrowing government to shift resources from elsewhere to service the stadium debt.

TAX REVENUES

Knowing precisely how much revenue each of the taxes generates is difficult. It is possible to identify how much each was intended to collect, as these amounts are often part of the legislation enabling the taxes or establishing the stadium subsidy. Based on the data from Long (2002), we have generated histograms depicting the distribution of tax revenue obligations created by various stadium funding agreements. Revenue totals were classified as 0 if the plan did not include revenues from a specific tax, 1 for revenues less than $10 million (all figures are in 2001 dollars), 2 if between $10 and $50 million, 3 if between $50 and $100 million, 4 if between $100 and $150 million, 5 if between $150 and $200 million, 6 if between $200 and $250 million, 7 if between $250 million and $300 million, and 8 if more than $300 million. Many stadium financing plans omit one or more of the taxes enumerated above, resulting in many categories with totals of 0; the histograms omit these categories.

Figure 1 shows the distribution of revenue intentions for general revenues. Of the ninety-nine facilities in operation in 2001, thirty-two of them had no plan to rely on state or local government general revenues for financing. Half, forty-nine, had general revenue expectations above $10 million but below

Figure 1. Distribution of General Revenue Obligations

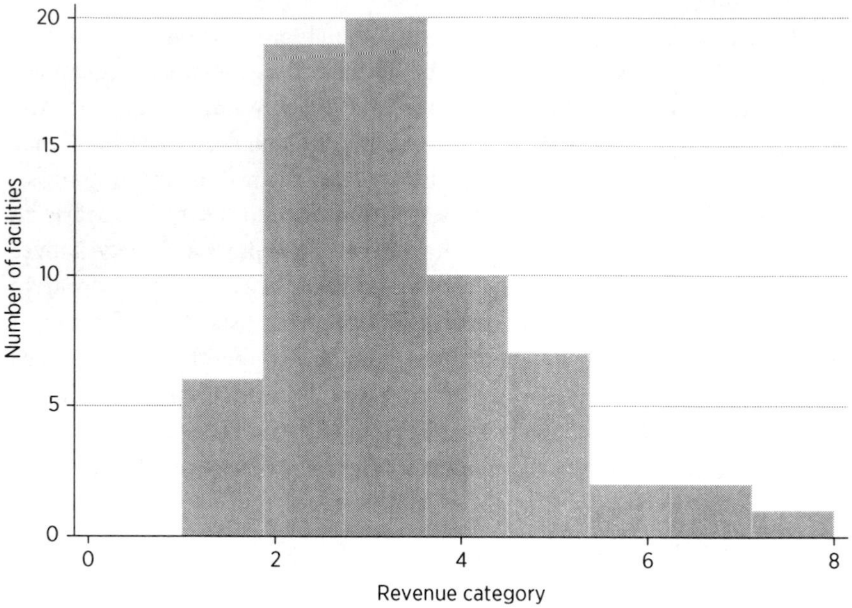

Source: Derived from Long (2002).

Notes:
1 = less than $10 million
2 = between $10 and $50 million
3 = between $50 and $100 million
4 = between $100 and $150 million
5 = between $150 and $200 million
6 = between $200 and $250 million
7 = between $250 and $300 million
8 = more than $300 million

$150 million. Figure 2 reports the distribution for lease revenues. Only twenty-two of the ninety-nine financing arrangements required the tenant teams to pay rent to the city for the privilege to play in the venue. All expected lease revenues covered less than $200 million of stadium debt.

The distribution of expected sales tax revenues is reported in figure 3. Only fifteen of the ninety-nine stadium financing agreements included sales tax revenues. Hotel and car rental taxes are in figure 4. As can be seen, seventeen of the ninety-nine financing agreements included hotel and car rental taxes. This number is somewhat surprising, given the predilection of public officials (and taxpayers) to express the desire to export the funding of stadiums (and other projects) to nonlocals. Figure 5 shows that only nine of the 99 financing agreements implemented a so-called sin tax on alcohol, tobacco, or lottery sales. It appears that the actual financing agreements are somewhat different

Figure 2. Distribution of Lease Revenue Obligations

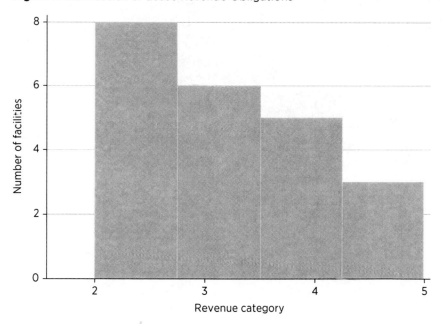

Source: Derived from Long (2002).

Notes:
1 = less than $10 million
2 = between $10 and $50 million
3 = between $50 and $100 million
4 = between $100 and $150 million
5 = between $150 and $200 million
6 = between $200 and $250 million
7 = between $250 and $300 million
8 = more than $300 million

from the rhetoric used by local politicians and team owners when pitching the agreement. This might reflect the hesitancy to implement taxes that are dedicated to the specific stadium project.

CONCLUSION

Taxes used to service debt incurred to publicly subsidize stadium and arena construction in the United States take a number of forms. Some taxes are quite explicit, like an increase in the local sales tax, whereas others might be less obvious, such as taxes on gross business receipts. Furthermore, property tax exemptions are most often not explicit budget items and therefore can be easily hidden from the general public. Public subsidies for stadium construction are almost always financed with the broadest tax base possible, including those

Figure 3. Distribution of Sales Tax Revenue Obligations

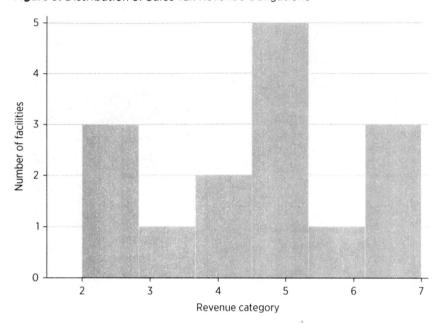

Source: Derived from Long (2002).

Notes:
1 = less than $10 million
2 = between $10 and $50 million
3 = between $50 and $100 million
4 = between $100 and $150 million
5 = between $150 and $200 million
6 = between $200 and $250 million
7 = between $250 and $300 million
8 = more than $300 million

who live and work in the city or state that is financing the subsidies and those who visit the city or state for business or leisure.

While the nature of the subsidies has evolved somewhat over the past 15 years, the wealth transfer they represent has not changed. Economists have searched for the combination of subsidies and taxes, stadium and city characteristics, and event and team characteristics that lead to a net positive present-value payoff for the local economies that support the subsidies. To date, although almost all stadium projects promise a net positive impact before the stadium is built, very few in reality have provided positive economic outcomes (see Coates and Humphreys 2008).

The incidence of any tax is difficult to determine, but it is likely that both consumers and businesses bear some of each tax that is imposed. To the layperson, the direct impact might seem obvious: tax payments are made to the

Figure 4. Distribution of Hotel and Car Rental Tax Obligations

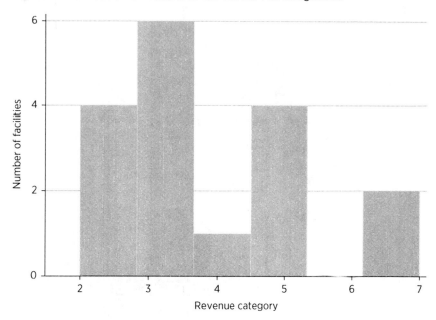

Source: Derived from Long (2002).

Notes:
1 = less than $10 million
2 = between $10 and $50 million
3 = between $50 and $100 million
4 = between $100 and $150 million
5 = between $150 and $200 million
6 = between $200 and $250 million
7 = between $250 and $300 million
8 = more than $300 million

local government to help service the stadium debt. However, economists point out that the true incidence of a tax is more nuanced. For example, if an increased hotel occupancy tax causes a multiday conference to choose another city in which to convene, the loss of money from the reduction of hotel room occupancy would reflect a cost of the tax that would not be obvious to the casual observer.[9] Additionally, the decision to subsidize stadium or arena construction carries with it implicit or explicit decisions about the fairness of the chosen sources of revenue.

Given these complications and assuming the stadium or arena will be built, principles for the design of a system of financing stadium construction are largely the same as those for the design of any tax system. The approach should seek to minimize the excess burden of the tax while simultaneously carefully considering the equity of the system of finance. For a general tax system that

Figure 5. Distribution of Alcohol, Tobacco, and Lottery Tax Revenue Obligations

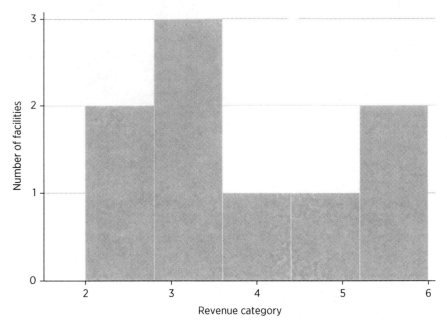

Source: Derived from Long (2002).

Notes:
1 = less than $10 million
2 = between $10 and $50 million
3 = between $50 and $100 million
4 = between $100 and $150 million
5 = between $150 and $200 million
6 = between $200 and $250 million
7 = between $250 and $300 million
8 = more than $300 million

will finance a broad array of public services, it is perhaps sufficient to think about equity independent of the distribution of benefits from spending. After all, everyone receives benefits from government generally. But in the case of the stadium or arena, the beneficiaries from the subsidies are identifiable. Team owners, players, sports fans, and game attendees benefit; owners of other entertainment and leisure activity businesses and non-sports fans do not. In this case, designing the tax system along the lines of the benefit principle is natural both from an equity and an efficiency point of view.

An additional principle of tax system design is to minimize the administrative cost of collecting the revenue. This is not another way of describing the excess burden but is instead an issue of the cost of compliance with the law and its enforcement. The more complicated the tax (with exemptions, deductions, and exclusions), the more costly for consumers and firms to comply and the more resources government must expend to verify and enforce the tax law. Closely related to minimizing the administrative cost is the consideration of transparency of the tax system. In a transparent system, people are better able to determine how much they are paying for the services they get. A sales tax surcharge on tickets to sports events is highly transparent and connects the tax payment to consumption. A general sales tax add-on is far less transparent; as a consequence, consumer decisions regarding public services are distorted.

Finally, the issue of taxation to subsidize stadium and arena construction must carefully consider all the costs and benefits of the facilities. For example, it is often argued that professional sports franchises provide significant community benefits in the form of civic pride and status of the city. Such benefits are public goods from which everyone in the city benefits and, consequently, everyone should share in the cost of provision. Leaving aside the possibility that such arguments overstate the size, and even existence, of such benefits, the presumption is that the marginal benefit of these public goods is positive to all citizens. That need not be the case, as many citizens may derive no happiness and feel no pride from having a professional sports team playing in a beautiful stadium. Efficiency requires that the marginal value to the community be equal to the marginal cost to the community, but fairness requires that individuals for whom marginal benefits are zero pay nothing, while those for whom marginal benefits are positive pay their marginal benefit value. To do otherwise is simply to forcibly redistribute income from those who would choose not to utilize the stadium in any way to those for whom the choice is the opposite.

NOTES

1. For example, Depken and LaFountain (2006) show that interest rates of US state bonds are positively related to existing debt level in the state, negatively related to state economic and population growth, and positively correlated with public corruption.

2. See chap. 9 in this volume by Robert Lawson for a specific discussion on the tax incidence of gross receipt taxes.

3. In chap. 7 of this volume, Todd Nesbit discusses the incentive to substitute for items of higher quality in the case of per unit taxes, whereas ad valorem (percentage of the price) taxes are argued to impose no such substitution in quality.

4. In chap. 2 of this volume, Justin Ross discusses various tax principles, including the benefit principle.

5. See Kenyon and Langley (2010) for more detail on PiLoTs in the context of not-for-profits.

6. In the first instance, the tax is regressive; in the second, it is proportional; in the third, it is progressive.

7. The benefit principle is agnostic about whether the increased taxes are regressive or progressive. It is possible for those who pay higher taxes based on the benefit principle to actually have lower incomes than those who would not pay based on this principle. For example, if a low-income family buys tickets to the football game on which a tax surcharge is placed while a high-income family watches the game at home, the former will pay more taxes than the latter.

8. Unfortunately, detailed data on concession sales are not available, and therefore any discussion about the price elasticity of demand for in-stadium purchases is purely speculative.

9. Ultimately, much of the tax incidence occurs in what Frederic Bastiat referred to as the "unseen" rather than in the "seen" (Bastiat [1848] 1995).

REFERENCES

Bastiat, F. [1848] 1995. "What Is Seen and What Is Not Seen." In *Selected Essays on Political Economy*, edited by G. B. de Huszar. Irvington-on-Hudson, NY: Foundation for Economic Education.

Coates, D., and B. R. Humphreys. 2008. "Do Economists Reach a Conclusion on Subsidies for Sports Franchises, Stadiums, and Mega-Events?" *Economic Journal Watch* 5 (3): 294–315.

Delaney, K. J., and R. Eckstein. 2003. *Public Dollars, Private Stadiums: The Battle over Building Sports Stadiums*. New Brunswick, NJ: Rutgers University Press.

Depken, C. A., and C. LaFountain. 2006. "Fiscal Consequences of Public Corruption: Empirical Evidence from State Bond Ratings." *Public Choice* 126 (1): 775–85.

Kenyon, D. A., and A. H. Langley. 2010. *Payments in Lieu of Taxes: Balancing Municipal and Nonprofit Interests*. Policy Focus Report. Cambridge, MA: Lincoln Institute of Land Policy.

Long, J. G. 2002. "Full Count: The Real Cost of Public Subsidies for Major League Sports Facilities." PhD thesis, Harvard University, Cambridge, MA.

Matheson, V., and B. R. Humphreys. 2009. "Pilots and Public Policy: Steering through the Economic Ramifications." *Villanova Sports and Entertainment Law Journal* 16 (2): 273–89.

Miller, W. S. 2012. "US Gaming and Sports Facility Financing." In *Sports Betting: Law and Policy*, edited by Paul M. Anderson, Ian S. Blackshaw, Robert C. R. Siekmann, and Janwillem Soek, 910–35. Netherlands: T. M. C. Asser.

National Sports Law Institute, Marquette University Law School. 2015. *Sports Facility Reports* 16, appendices 1–4. https://law.marquette.edu/national-sports-law-institute/sports-facility -reports.

Panyard, J. 2010. "$1 Billion and Counting for State's Taxpayer-Funded Stadiums." *Philadelphia Free Press*, September 22. http://weeklypress.com/billion-and-counting-for-states -taxpayerfunded-stadiums-p2168-1.html.

Siegfried, J. J., and T. Peterson. 2000. "Who Is Sitting in the Stands? The Income Levels of Sports Fans." In *The Economics of Sports*, edited by W. S. Kern. Kalamazoo, MI: W. E. Upjohn Institute for Labor Research.

Wisconsin Department of Revenue. N.d. "Stadium Sales and Use Tax." https://www.revenue.wi.gov /faqs/pcs/stad.html. Accessed 10/10/15.

CHAPTER 12
The Use of Locally Imposed Selective Taxes to Fund Public Pension Liabilities

THAD CALABRESE
Robert F. Wagner Graduate School of Public Service, New York University

Personnel costs are the single largest spending category for state and local governments. In fiscal year 2013, state and local governments spent more than $857 billion on employee salaries and wages, and an additional $338 billion on personnel benefits. These numbers represent more than 37 percent of direct spending by these governments and more than half of spending when considering current (i.e., noncapital) operations alone.[1] Approximately 90 percent of all state and local employees have access to retirement benefits, and 89 percent of these workers actually participate in the benefit programs offered (Bureau of Labor Statistics 2015). The primary form of retirement benefit for public employees is a defined benefit pension system, in which all employer and employee contributions are aggregated and deposited into a pension fund for investing purposes. The contributions typically are prefunded—that is, made over the course of employees' working lives. Benefits paid out to retirees also come from the pension fund. These pension benefits are the primary source of retirement income for millions of public retirees, including about 27 percent of public employees who are not part of the federal Social Security system (Nuschler et al. 2011).

In the private sector, defined benefit pension plans are insured by the Pension Benefit Guaranty Corporation (PBGC) to ensure that beneficiaries do not lose all pension benefits in the event a corporation or its pension fund becomes insolvent. Government pension plans, however, are not insured by the PBGC. If a public pension plan exhausts its resources, it will either cease to pay benefits (as happened in Prichard, AL; see Cooper and Walsh 2010) or the plan sponsor will need to provide additional money to keep benefits flowing to retirees. This chapter examines a growing phenomenon in pension funding in which a jurisdiction enacts a new selective tax or fee, or increases an existing one, to fund its unfunded pension liabilities. Given the relatively recent enactment of this practice in a few jurisdictions, the trend is described and commonalities between those jurisdictions are detailed. In addition, this chapter frames the importance of public pensions to the finances of state and local governments, and it highlights other potential changes that might influence the use of locally imposed selective taxes by governments to address unfunded liabilities (pensions as well as others).

IMPORTANCE OF PUBLIC PENSIONS TO PUBLIC FINANCES

In 1993, state and local governments spent nearly $2 trillion in total (in inflation-adjusted dollars), $86 billion of which were pension expenditures paid into pension funds, representing 4.3 percent of total state and local spending.[2] By 2012, state and local spending had grown to more than $3.2 trillion in total; pension contributions grew to $248 billion—or 7.6 percent of total spending. Whereas total expenditures by state and local governments grew 63 percent in real terms between 1993 and 2012, pension expenditures increased 187 percent—nearly three times as much. On average, while state and local government spending has increased nearly 3 percent in real terms every year, pension expenditures have increased at almost double the rate of all spending (see table 1). This increased spending is not only the result of the economic troubles governments faced from stock market declines in 2008. Excluding 2008–2014, pension expenditures still grew nearly 7 percent annually.

Furthermore, these expenditures reflect only spending actually paid into public pension systems and do not include contributions deferred by governments. Novy-Marx and Rauh (2014) estimate that contributions to public pension systems would have to exceed 14 percent of state and local government revenues for public pensions to reach full funding (in which assets matched actuarial accrued liabilities) over 30 years.

Table 1. Public Pensions and Public Budgets, 1993–2014

Year	Total State and Local Pension Expenditures ($ thousands)	Annual Change (%)	Total State and Local Expenditures ($ thousands)	Annual Change (%)	Public Pensions as Share of Total State and Local Expenditures (%)
1993	86,173,052		1,988,456,407		4.3
1994	93,543,266	8.6	2,019,586,835	1.6	4.6
1995	98,848,408	5.7	2,099,304,490	3.9	4.7
1996	107,127,319	8.4	2,108,797,926	0.5	5.1
1997	112,483,107	5.0	2,154,590,504	2.2	5.2
1998	122,018,715	8.5	2,221,117,707	3.1	5.5
1999	127,961,273	4.9	2,310,433,282	4.0	5.5
2000	138,106,837	7.9	2,401,650,562	3.9	5.8
2001	150,059,331	8.7	2,538,662,797	5.7	5.9
2002	161,504,669	7.6	2,699,681,446	6.3	6.0
2003	173,492,641	7.4	2,784,447,842	3.1	6.2
2004	182,281,796	5.1	2,840,640,409	2.0	6.4
2005	189,159,379	3.8	2,870,792,148	1.1	6.6
2006	195,409,964	3.3	2,938,372,703	2.4	6.7
2007	210,737,977	7.8	3,041,449,309	3.5	6.9
2008	213,824,545	1.5	3,119,254,658	2.6	6.9
2009	226,365,027	5.9	3,273,581,348	4.9	6.9
2010	235,090,873	3.9	3,383,268,617	3.4	6.9
2011	246,172,916	4.7	3,328,493,356	−1.6	7.4
2012	247,723,000	0.6	3,249,742,998	−2.4	7.6
2013	262,498,990	6.0	N/A		
2014	272,862,247	3.9	N/A		
Cumulative change, 1993–2012	187.47%		63.43%		
Average annual change, 1993–2012	5.74%		2.64%		
Average annual change, 1993–2007	6.61%		3.09%		

Sources: US Census Bureau (1993–2014) and US Census Bureau (1993–2012).
Note: All data are inflation adjusted to 2014 levels using the Bureau of Labor Statistics Consumer Price Index All Urban Consumers (CPI-U) table. N/A = data are not yet publicly available.

Table 1 shows that public pension expenditures are an increasing share of state and local government spending, increasing from just over 4 percent in 1993 to nearly 8 percent in 2012. In addition, because pension expenditures consume general fund revenues of governments, other programs that are also funded from governments' operating budgets must compete with these growing pension expenditures for resources (Peng 2014). Some states and municipalities have issued taxable pension obligation bonds, in which debt substitutes for other current budgetary resources; empirical analyses of this technique have found little budgetary relief resulting from this strategy (e.g., see Calabrese and Ely 2013). State and local governments, then, face the need to either reduce spending on nonpension items or increase taxes. Another option is deferral of required pension contributions, causing the government to fall even further behind in the long term.

LINKING THE BUDGET TO THE BALANCE SHEET—UNFUNDED PENSION LIABILITIES

Unfunded pension liabilities occur because governments deliberately underfund their annual pension contributions or because results (including investment returns) do not meet expectations. When discussing the unfunded levels of government pension systems, this chapter relies on data reported by governments, which do not report liabilities calculated in a common method with common actuarial assumptions. Government systems tend to use discount rates that are much higher compared to private pension systems (GAO 2014),[3] and government liabilities are lower as a result. Furthermore, existing analyses find government decision makers may alter actuarial inputs to reduce required pension contributions or reported liabilities (Barro 2012; Biggs 2009; Stalebrink 2012).[4]

Most state and local governments operate under balanced budget requirements, which vary in stringency. Nevertheless, Poterba (1994) argues that altering expenditures in one fiscal year to achieve a balanced budget merely reflects a timing issue; that is, an expenditure deferred in the current fiscal year is recognized instead in the next fiscal year. Chaney et al. (2002) note this is generally true, but not in the case of pension contributions—because deferred pension contributions are not recognized until paid in the future, and many governments do not make the full contribution to their pension plans annually (implying a long-term deferral of these costs).[5] Chaney et al. (2002) find that states defer pension contributions to achieve budget balance, implying that tax revenues are insufficient to achieve economic budget balance. Pension underfunding is a form of debt financing, and Buchanan and Wagner (1977) extend fiscal illusion theory to argue that debt financing increases government spending, because immediate taxes are not required from the citizenry. As a result, decision makers perceive the costs of public employees' pension benefits as lower than they actually are, leading to increased public spending and employee benefits. Johnson (1997) finds that pension generosity increases as governments contribute less to pension funds currently than required, and Sneed and Sneed (1997) find underfunded pensions result in greater state government spending overall. Hence, the beneficiaries of this fiscal illusion are public employees and labor representatives.[6] Elected officials who support these expanded employee pensions may also benefit from campaign contributions from this key voter constituency.

In 2001, state and local pension plans were generally fully funded in the aggregate; that is, governments had assets in pension funds that equaled the accrued liabilities of workers and retirees. Importantly, this was not due to adequate pension funding by plan sponsors; rather, Giertz (2003) finds most chronic underfunding of liabilities disappeared because of strong equity returns that were in excess of actuarial assumptions during the 1990s. As investment gains slowed or turned to losses and employee benefits were enhanced,[7] these plans were approximately $155 billion underfunded collectively by 2002 (see table 2), meaning liabilities exceeded assets.

Even in 2001, when the collective systems were fully funded, 55 percent of the individual pension plans reported an unfunded liability (called the "unfunded actuarially accrued liability," or UAAL), meaning these plans were not fully funded. Using a less stringent but arbitrary standard defining 80 percent funded as "healthy," only about 19 percent of pension plans were not healthy.[8] Therefore, public pension systems at the beginning of the century were relatively well funded, and even those not fully funded were not significantly underfunded on average. In 2002, the total UAAL of combined pension systems would have required only 6 percent of total spending to make up the accumulated shortfall to date. Table 2, however, shows that the combined UAAL has grown significantly since 2001, when pensions were fully funded collectively. The combined UAAL has grown more than 646 percent, and annual increases have averaged over 23 percent; further, it would now require nearly 35 percent of total state and local government spending (in 2014 dollars) to top off pension plans and return them to full funding. While this one-shot scenario is obviously unrealistic, it illustrates the increasing burden

Table 2. Size and Growth of Public Pension Unfunded Actuarially Accrued
Liabilities (UAAL), 2002–2013

Year	Combined UAAL All Pension Plans ($ thousands)	Annual Change (%)	Ratio of UAAL to Total Annual Expenditures (%)	Percentage of Plans with UAAL >$0	Percentage of Plans Funded Less than 80%
2002	155,279,867		5.8	70	19
2003	348,670,957	124.5	12.5	81	27
2004	421,086,797	20.8	14.8	84	29
2005	482,442,028	14.6	16.8	89	37
2006	502,594,286	4.2	17.1	87	39
2007	482,966,924	-3.9	15.9	86	37
2008	562,968,616	16.6	18.0	89	45
2009	830,915,917	47.6	25.4	92	57
2010	958,643,138	15.4	28.3	94	62
2011	1,026,134,196	7.0	30.8	95	63
2012	1,123,906,722	9.5	34.6	97	69
2013	1,158,492,941	3.1	N/A	96	68
Change from 2002 to 2013	646.07%				
Annual change, 2002–2013	23.58%				

Sources: Center for Retirement Research at Boston College (2002–2013); and US Census Bureau (1993–2012).
Note: All data are inflation adjusted to 2014 levels using the Bureau of Labor Statistics Consumer Price Index All Urban Consumers (CPI-U) table. N/A = data are not yet publicly available.

that accumulated pension liabilities have on government operations and overall fiscal health (see the third column in table 2).

The funded ratio for all pension systems combined in 2012 was approximately 72 percent,[9] and the data in table 2 indicate a cumulative shortfall of
more than $1 trillion in assets to cover pension obligations. As pension costs
consume an increasing amount of public budgets while unfunded liabilities
continue to grow, calls for reforms have become more vocal.

Pension contributions are composed of two parts: (1) a portion for the present value of future benefits earned by current employees in the current fiscal
year (which is known as the "normal cost"), and (2) a portion for the amortized
part of the unfunded liability. As a result of this amortized part, the larger the
unfunded actuarial accrued liability is, the larger becomes the required annual
pension contribution. Efforts to improve the funded status of these pension
trusts are aimed at reducing this amortized portion of the annual contribution

Table 3. Number of States Enacting Public Pension Reform Legislation by Type of Reform, 2012–2015

| Year Enacted | Type of Reform Effort Enacted | | |
	Contribution Rates and Funding	Cost-of-Living Adjustments	Change to Plan
2012	12	4	21
2013	22	8	31
2014	36	9	34
2015	27	4	26

Source: National Conference of State Legislatures, "Pensions and Retirement State Legislation Database, 2012–2015."

either gradually and systematically over time or all at once, which reduces the required annual contribution to the pension fund.

As shown in table 3, some states have enacted changes in contribution rates and funding schedules over the past several years, usually increasing required contributions from employers. This action is arguably not even a reform and is simply a budgetary increase. Limiting cost of living adjustments is another way to control the growth in liabilities—especially since some beneficiaries have already retired and are receiving pension benefits. The "Change to Plan" category includes such efforts as creating new tiers of pension benefits that lower pension benefits for future employees, thereby lowering the normal cost associated with new hires.

Constitutional or statutory limitations exist in many states that prohibit changing pension benefits for current employees or retirees, so many reform efforts do not address accumulated unfunded pension liabilities at all (see Munnell and Quinby 2012). Most actions included under "Change to Plan" reforms fall into this category. Some states (e.g., Illinois and New York) have constitutional provisions that protect not just employee benefits at the time of hire (meaning that current employees cannot see their benefits reduced), but also future cost-of-living adjustments. Other states (e.g., California, Massachusetts, Pennsylvania, and Washington) have similar protections via state law. Hence, reform efforts like some of those outlined in table 3 may be unavailable to some governments without significant institutional changes, such as constitutional amendments. Some states (e.g., Michigan, Florida, and Virginia) only protect prior benefits and exclude future cost-of-living adjustments, so that reform efforts like those listed in table 3 can be used to limit the growth in unfunded pension liabilities.

SELECTIVE TAXES, TAX INCREASES, AND PENSION FUNDING

As pension expenditures and unfunded liabilities continue to increase (even with periodic and limited reforms), some governments have turned to increased taxes and fees to fund these retirement benefits. Sometimes these taxes and fees are explicitly earmarked or tied to pension expenditures, at other times they are merely alluded to in legislation or referenda language. To date, the primary users of these select taxes and fees have largely been municipalities in Pennsylvania and Illinois. Both states are examined here as case studies, and both have strong protections for public pension benefits. However, municipalities in other states have begun exploring this option as well and are also discussed.

Pennsylvania

Of the nearly 3,200 pension plans established for local government employees, more than 44 percent are in Pennsylvania alone.[10] In other words, pension management in Pennsylvania is largely a local government concern. In 1895, the state implemented a 2 percent tax on foreign (that is, out-of-state) fire and casualty insurance companies' premiums on in-state property and earmarked this revenue for distribution to local governments to pay for pensions. The law's stated goal was to provide fiscal relief for municipalities' paid and volunteer fire departments by distributing tax revenue collected by the state to the political subdivisions in which the insured property was located. The 2 percent tax on all fire and casualty insurance gross premiums for personal and business property sold in the state by corporations incorporated in a state other than Pennsylvania is not unique to Pennsylvania. Most states tax insurance premiums of out-of-state insurers (Casey and Conlin 2009), but Pennsylvania explicitly dedicates this tax to municipal pension benefits. Other states, such as Colorado, Florida, Idaho, Illinois, Oklahoma, and Washington, similarly dedicate some or all insurance premium taxes to fire or police pension funds (Civic Federation 2007). What makes Pennsylvania unique, however, is that the state funds are then distributed to municipal pension systems.

Public pensions became a public policy concern in the 1970s, when what was then called the US General Accounting Office (1979) estimated that public pension systems were only about 50 percent funded. In 1984, Pennsylvania Act 205 was implemented, which required municipalities to make pension contributions on a schedule that would address any underfunding in 30 years. Municipalities that were found to be distressed could extend this to a 40-year schedule. The 1984 Act also replaced the original act of 1895 in which the state of Pennsylvania allocated pension aid based on where the insured property was located; instead the new allocation was essentially based on the number of public employees in a locality. Each public employee was considered a "unit," and uniformed employees (such as police and fire) each represented two units. The pool of insurance tax revenue collected by the state was then divided by the sum of municipal units to arrive at a unit value. This distribution could subsidize local governments' pension expenditures up to 100 percent of the annual cost. In 1985, this tax generated $62.3 million in revenues; as a result, each unit value was worth $1,146—meaning that local governments received $1,146 for pension funding for each public employee and an additional $1,146 for pension funding for each uniformed public employee. Importantly, 75 percent of municipalities received enough funding from this revenue in 1985 to fully offset their pension costs.

This dedicated revenue stream from the state led some local government decision makers to increase pension benefits. For example, if a municipality had to contribute less than the $1,146 annually for a regular employee or $2,292 for a uniformed employee, the municipality was effectively incentivized to increase benefits to public employees up to this limit, because local public employees would receive increased benefits at no direct budgetary cost to the municipality. Perhaps more correctly, the tax likely increased insurance costs for residents and businesses (and then only a small fraction of the cost), but not directly for the government employer. Further, this system privileged pension benefits relative to other compensation, because these payments (borne at least statutorily by out-of-state companies) could only be used for financing pensions and not other forms of compensation. Overall, then, an attempt to support pension costs statewide led to a system that encouraged increased benefits.

By the late 1980s, nearly all municipalities in Pennsylvania had their pension costs fully covered by this dedicated state tax, with fairly significant increases in subsidies per employee. By 1989, for example, 96 percent of municipalities received money from the state to fully cover their annual pension costs, even as the value per unit had increased from $1,146 to $3,269—a nominal increase of more than 185 percent and a real increase of nearly 150 percent in just 5 years. By 2014, each unit value had increased to $3,873 as tax revenues to the state had increased to $248.3 million. Despite increased subsidies, only 38 percent of municipalities received enough allocation from the pool to offset the full costs of pensions. The subsidy from the state insurance tax was growing, but not as fast as annual pension contributions. Municipalities needed even more revenues or less spending to compensate.

Because of the significant fiscal stress governments experienced following the Great Recession, Act 44 became law and provided plan sponsors pension funding relief, largely by allowing sponsors to alter actuarial assumptions and thereby reduce required pension contributions. Hence, state law further encouraged pension benefit growth, which contributed to fiscal stress for plan sponsors. Subsequently, a new law was implemented that provided pension funding relief to distressed municipalities. This relief, however, merely delayed funding (primarily by manipulating how the required contribution was calculated) rather than providing any permanent fix, such as reforming the structure of the pension plan or the level of benefits provided to current or future employees.

As part of Act 205 of 1984, pension plans had to report to the state on their funded status. Plans with funded ratios at or above 90 percent did not need to implement any changes. For those plans below this 90 percent threshold, sponsors had to implement voluntary and mandatory remedies (depending on the funded status reported) that were nominally designed to improve the funded status of the plan. Many municipalities in Pennsylvania had pension systems that were below the 90 percent threshold and therefore, required remedies; many chose to impose selective taxes to address pension shortfalls as voluntary remedies. The history of municipal pension funding in Pennsylvania can thus be summarized as follows:

- Implementation of a public financing system that encourages pension benefit growth by financing local pensions with a state tax;

- Passage of additional laws requiring certain pension funding levels;

- Passage of even more laws that provide temporary pension funding relief when unsubsidized expenditures are deemed too costly, which further grew liabilities for distressed municipalities (because the relief is just a deferral); and

- Passage of additional regulation that requires remedies when pension systems are underfunded significantly, largely as a result from prior years' deferrals brought about by prior legislation.

To further illustrate, the city of York has three major pension plans: one for fire fighters, another for police officers, and a third for nonuniformed city workers. As of 2012, the fire fighter pension system was 58 percent funded, the police system was 53 percent funded, and the nonuniformed system was

76 percent funded.[11] In 2014, the city passed a 0.25 percent "Public Safety Pension Tax" on income earned in York as one of its voluntary remedies to address the poor funding of its pension systems. Although the new tax was frequently referred to as a commuter tax, city residents were also taxed. However, it is noteworthy that the city did initially seek to tax only the incomes of workers who commuted to the city. The new money was expected to cover the city's increased pension contributions.

Similarly, Scranton manages three pension systems defined as severely distressed. In 2012, its fire fighters pension plan was 17 percent funded, the police system was 29 percent funded, and the nonuniformed system had only 23 percent of assets compared to liabilities. To begin addressing these shortfalls as part of its voluntary remedies, Scranton passed a 0.75 percent tax on commuters' earned income in the city; however, a judge blocked the new tax, because it exempted residents. As a result, Scranton passed a local services tax in 2015 on both commuters and residents.

By 2012, Philadelphia also had severely distressed pension plans. The fire fighter pension plan was only 45 percent funded, the police plan was 49 percent funded, and the nonuniformed pension plan was 47 percent funded. Facing chronic budgetary problems, the city council passed a temporary 1 percentage point sales tax increase in 2009; when the temporary rate was renewed in 2014, any revenue in excess of $120 million was dedicated to the city's pension plans (Coen 2014). The state permitted the city to pass a $2 per pack cigarette tax to fund a planned budget deficit for the school system. Much of the system's increased costs were caused by rapidly increasing mandatory pension contributions (Costrell and Maloney 2013).

Whereas York and Scranton used income taxes to fund pensions and also expand their tax bases beyond city limits, Philadelphia already had a high income tax for both residents (3.924 percent in fiscal year 2014) as well as commuters (3.495 percent in fiscal year 2014).[12] Philadelphia likely turned to cigarette taxes because its income tax capacity was largely exhausted.

In addition to these municipal examples, many school districts in Pennsylvania increased property taxes as a voluntary measure specifically to fund increased teacher pension costs. Pennsylvania law (Act 1) caps annual property tax increases, and districts must seek rates higher than these caps through voter referenda.[13] However, Act 1 explicitly permits districts to file for exemptions from the referendum requirement because of costs resulting from special education, debt, and pensions. In fiscal year 2015, 164 school districts (out of nearly 500 statewide districts) applied for exemptions from the state Department of Education, and 163 cited pension contributions as

Table 4. School District Referendum Exceptions from Pension Obligations, Pennsylvania, 2007–2015

Fiscal Year	Statewide SDs Requesting Exemptions	SDs Requesting Exemptions because of Pension Obligations	Percentage of Exemptions because of Pension Obligations	Percentage of Statewide SDs Requesting Exemptions because of Pension Obligations	Percentage of Approved Expenditures Over Limits
2007–2008	210	188	89.5	37.6	6.9
2008–2009	102	27	26.5	5.4	3.6
2009–2010	61	6	9.8	1.2	0.5
2010–2011	133	128	96.2	25.6	32.4
2011–2012	228	221	96.9	44.2	29.3
2012–2013	197	194	98.5	38.8	49.3
2013–2014	171	169	98.8	33.8	68.5
2014–2015	164	163	99.4	32.6	61.2

Source: Pennsylvania Department of Education. "Report on Referendum Exceptions," various years. http://www.education.pa.gov/Teachers%20-%20Administrators/Property%20Tax%20Relief/Pages/Referendum-Exceptions.aspx.

the reason for the exemption request.[14] In other words, nearly one-third of Pennsylvania school districts chose to increase property tax rates in excess of statutory limits as a result of pension costs. As shown in table 4, these exemptions brought about from pension obligations remain a significant cause of exemptions from property tax limits, and the amount of expenditures financed by these exemptions has grown significantly over the past few years. Pension obligations remain a significant financial hurdle for Pennsylvania school districts despite the state-dedicated revenue for local pension systems.

One major hurdle for reforming public pension costs in Pennsylvania is that the courts have rejected reform efforts as impairments to existing contracts. The protection extends to past accruals (i.e., benefits earned to date) but also to future adjustments as well (so that even altering cost-of-living adjustments may not be possible; see Munnell and Quinby 2012). Absent major structural changes from elected officials to alter these protections—at great political cost to themselves—reforms that might actually shrink liabilities are not realistic options.

Illinois

Chicago participates in six pension plans for its employees, and all plans are generally less than one-half funded (i.e., the funded ratio is less than 50 percent for all plans). As of 2012, Chicago's pension UAAL reached nearly $27 billion, and the city (or related agencies) contributed nearly $700 million to the funds,[15] compared to total governmental fund expenditures of less than $7 billion (City of Chicago 2012). Chicago's pension systems were so poorly funded that the state required the city to make mandated payments to reduce the UAALs. Wanting to avoid a property tax increase in 2014 (an election year), Chicago policymakers chose instead to pass a tax increase on telephones, increasing the 911 tax from $2.50 per telephone per month to $3.90. Although the revenue from the tax was earmarked for 911 services, the goal of the tax increase was to fully fund the emergency service from this monthly fee and not require additional public subsidy, thereby freeing up millions of dollars for pension payments. This tax increase was simply an expedient, as the mayor and city council increased the property tax rate one year later in 2015 (Peters 2015). Increasing pension funding to begin paying down the UAALs of the police and fire pension systems was an explicit reason given for the property tax increase, estimated to be $550 million annually (Dardick and Ruthhart 2015). In addition, the mayor also proposed a garbage fee for homeowners to free up additional public dollars for pensions.

Cook County (where Chicago is located) itself increased the county portion of the sales tax in 2015 from 0.75 percent to 1.75 percent to fund its own public pensions. By 2014, the county faced a pension system only about one-half funded and annual pension costs that were growing rapidly. For example, in 2014, the annual pension contribution was approximately $200 million and was expected to increase to $350 million by 2016. In raising the tax rate, the combined sales tax rate in the area became the nation's highest for a major city at 10.25 percent, effective 2016 (Dardick 2015).

Selective taxation for pension funding is not limited to the Chicago area in Illinois. The municipality of Normal, IL, saw its pension costs growing significantly for its three pension funds. The UAALs for these systems had reached nearly $50 million by 2015, compared to annual budgeted expenditures of just over $57 million.[16] To begin paying down this UAAL, the city increased garbage collection fees on residents and imposed a new 4¢ per gallon gasoline tax (VanMetre 2015). In 2014, Peoria, IL, increased water and natural gas utility taxes and doubled its garbage fees on residents to address its growing pension problem. The city's pension systems were all funded below 63 percent in 2012 (Dabrowski et al. 2014).

In Illinois, municipalities may sponsor their own pension systems—650 such systems are managed through the Illinois Municipal Retirement Fund (IMRF)—but the state legislature sets municipal pension laws that outline cost of living adjustments, benefit formulas, retirement ages, and so forth (Illinois

Municipal Retirement Fund 2014, 25). Therefore, the costs of municipal pension systems are determined separately from the taxpayers in jurisdictions who ultimately must pay for these costs. This decoupling of costs and financing has left much of the state's governments managing pension payments that eat up increasing shares of public budgets with no direct mechanisms to reduce the costs. Recently, the Illinois Supreme Court affirmed that the retirement benefits offered a government employee on his or her first day or employment can never be reduced,[17] so that reform efforts are necessarily limited to changing benefits for future workers only. Governments cannot directly change the pension liabilities accrued to date, which also increase current required pension contributions from these governments. Most importantly perhaps, government employers in the IMRF are required by state statute to pay their full contribution. If full payment is not made, the IMRF can sue the government and have state funds diverted to pay for the pension contribution (Peng and Boivie 2011). As a result, an increasing number of participating governments are turning to new or additional revenue sources as the only option available to them.

The state of Illinois itself adopted a tax in part to pay for its own pension contributions. In 2011, Illinois passed a temporary income tax increase to pay down its accumulated unpaid bills, which explicitly included unpaid pension contributions. The state is currently looking to extend this temporary measure. Importantly, this measure was not intended to reduce the state's UAALs with its pension systems (i.e., begin paying off the accumulated debt from the past). Instead this tax increase was simply meant to help the state meet the normal cost of its pension obligations.[18]

Other Municipalities

Although the examples of municipalities selectively imposing or increasing taxes and fees to fund pensions largely have been drawn from two states, recent activity suggests this municipal finance technique is spreading. Charleston, WV, increased its sales tax rate from 0.5 percentage points to 1 percentage point (which is levied in addition to the state rate of 6 percent), with the proceeds placed in a reserve account dedicated to pensions.[19] Elected officials opted for this increased sales tax rate to begin addressing its woefully underfunded pension system, which was only 24 percent funded in 2014 (Pew Charitable Trusts 2013).

Facing a $200 million UAAL and a 36 percent funded ratio, voters in Springfield, MO, passed a sales tax increase of 0.75 percentage points in 2009 to fund police and fire pensions. The original referendum was intended to sunset after 5 years (to counter taxpayer concerns that this tax increase was permanent). In 2014, the voters reauthorized the increased sales tax rate, and the funded ratio had reportedly improved to 67 percent since the 2009 initiative.[20]

In August 2015, the city of Prescott, AZ, presented city voters a ballot initiative to adopt an additional 0.55 percentage point sales tax rate for 20 years with the revenue restricted to paying the UAAL of the Arizona Public Safety Personnel Retirement Systems (estimated to be approximately $70 million, or about 50 percent funded). The voters rejected the ballot measure, with most opponents arguing that the additional revenue—absent any significant reforms to the benefits in place for current or future workers—would not improve the situation and solve the fiscal problems caused by the unfunded pension liabilities.

WHAT DOES THE FUTURE HOLD FOR SELECTIVE TAXES AND PENSION FUNDING?

The use of selective taxes to specifically fund pensions is fairly limited at this time. Nevertheless, we can find some basic similarities among these various cases. Most obviously, the governments or voters who have approved selective taxes are the ones with significantly below average funding for their pension plans (the average pension system is 72 percent funded). In some extreme cases, the pension systems are predicted to run out of money to pay benefits in only a few years. Of course, a natural question for future empirical research is whether this poor funding resulted in the adoption of selective and dedicated taxes, or whether these taxes led to reduced funding of pensions.

Most governments using selective taxes also have been either unable or unwilling to implement pension reforms that would require employees to fund more of their own pension benefits or reduce current and future retirees' benefits. In many cases, state statutes or constitutions prevent localities from changing future benefits. Therefore, if pension reform efforts fail (as they have in Illinois) or are avoided, it seems probable that governments will seek additional revenues to fund growing pension expenditures. Because most municipalities face balanced budget requirements, these increased pension expenditures necessarily require increased revenues, reductions in other non-pension expenditures, or some combination of both. In fiscal year 2015, no state reported using cuts to state employee benefits as a strategy for managing its budget, and only two states reported this as a strategy for fiscal year 2016 (NASBO 2015). Instead, targeted spending cuts (twenty-six states in 2015 and twenty-four in 2016)—reductions in other public spending—and increased sales and other consumption tax rates (e.g., on alcohol and tobacco; twelve states in 2016) are currently the preferred budget strategies rather than reducing pension costs. Debt issuances can fill budget gaps temporarily, and several hundred local governments have issued pension obligation bonds nationally,[21] but it is neither fiscally sustainable nor justifiable to issue debt to balance operating budgets.

Additional revenues, though, will not improve pension funding if this new revenue simply replaces the funding already in place. If a government replaces general fund revenue with a dedicated sales tax for pensions, for example, the unfunded liability is unlikely to improve: the new revenue stream simply replaces another instead of augmenting the flow of funds to the pension system. Ultimately, unless these selective taxes are not used to substitute for current funding streams, these new taxes are unlikely to improve the fiscal health of pension systems. They will, however, permit public decision makers to claim they are addressing the fiscal problems associated with unfunded pension liabilities.

Many states do not tax the pension income received by retirees. Ten states fully exclude pension income from their income tax base, and an additional eleven states partially exempt pension income.[22] Perhaps unsurprisingly, all the examples in this chapter come from states that fall into the full or partial exclusion states. Notably, both Illinois and Pennsylvania completely exclude pension income from their income tax bases. The tax base is reduced for the benefit of retirees, and selective income tax increases effectively shift the burden to current workers. In the case of increasing sales tax rates or increasing user fees, the reduced tax base for beneficiaries is paid for by expanding other tax bases or increasing rates on existing bases. Currently, Illinois is considering a sales tax on services to help fund its pensions (Galland 2015), and Pennsylvania is considering increasing fishing license fees for more pension funding (Staub 2015).

Governments with tax bases that are smaller because of other policy or political goals are more likely to turn to selective taxes to fund pensions compared to those with broader tax bases with fewer exclusions, even though the same amount of revenue must be raised, all else being equal. These narrower tax bases not only reduce income taxes owed to these states for public expenditures but also may lead to other distortionary behavior. For example, public employees may prefer larger pension benefits rather than more current income, because the benefits are not taxed when they are earned while working nor taxed as income when received in retirement.

The selective taxes used to fund unfunded pension liabilities are not limited to one particular type of tax. Consumption and income taxes do seem particularly attractive for these purposes, perhaps because the mechanics are simple—simply adjust an existing tax rate upward. The transaction costs of the selective tax are thus minimized. In addition, because of progressive income taxation systems, income tax increases can be sold as tax increases on higher income taxpayers. And as mentioned, new fees or increases in existing fees may be implemented. These revenue sources may be popular with municipalities because they may have more ability to impose or raise fee rates than taxes due to home rule limits in some states.[23]

Most of the examples in this chapter are of governments that sponsor their own pension plans. Many governments, however, do not; many belong instead to cost-sharing pension systems in which employees of all participating governments are aggregated into a common pool.[24] Governments participating in cost-sharing plans are generally legally required to fully fund their annual pension contributions (Ives et al. 2009), because governments otherwise could effectively be financing other governments' pension obligations to workers. Therefore, cost-sharing systems try to minimize the free riding of one government on other plan participants. Local government participants in cost-sharing plans have "no control over actuarial or funding decisions" (Fitch Ratings 2011). For example, CalPERS requires 90 percent of the member contributions during the fiscal year or it assesses interest costs on the unpaid portion at the actuarial interest rate (currently 7.5 percent; see CalPERS 2015); any amount not paid within 30 days of the fiscal year end is also assessed interest costs.[25] The city of Stockton, CA, chose to borrow money in 2007 rather than not pay its CalPERS contributions, because the cost of borrowing (5.81 percent) was lower than the cost of deferring its payment to CalPERS (7.75 percent at the time; Long 2012). In New York State, participating governments are required under state law to contribute to the New York State and Local Employee Retirement System and the New York State and Local Police and Fire Retirement System, or else accrue interest at the applicable interest rate for that year as set by statute.[26] Governments participating in these cost-sharing pension plans may thus be more likely in the future to impose selective taxes to make growing pension contributions because they are not only unable to alter benefits to current employees because of constitutional and statutory limits, but also because they cannot defer contributions to these cost-sharing systems without incurring significant penalties and costs. In other words, deferring pension contributions in these cost-sharing arrangements is not a budget strategy. Further reform efforts for these pension systems will require the political efforts of elected state officials as well as pension fund board members.

Furthermore, multi-employer public pension systems generally set benefits for employees, but government employers must pay for these benefits. These multi-employer public pension systems are common. Hence, many governments belong to pension systems in which the benefit cost and funding decisions reside in two separate bodies. This decoupling of pension benefits and the resources needed to fund them suggests that government employers may find selective taxation increasingly appealing to meet pension obligations they have little direct control over.

Finally, even extreme fiscal distress or bankruptcy may not be enough to reduce pension costs. CalPERS, for example, threatened to sue San Bernardino for missing pension payments after the city formally entered Chapter 9 bankruptcy in 2012 (Reid 2012); when Stockton sought bankruptcy protection in 2012, CalPERS argued (and a federal judge ultimately agreed) that pension costs still needed to be paid by the city (Hecht 2013).

OTHER ISSUES TO WATCH THAT ARE RELATED TO ADDITIONAL SELECTIVE TAXATION

A growing number of jurisdictions has used selective taxes and fees as an attempt to improve the funding of their public pension plans without reforming their systems or to avoid budget cuts in other public spending priorities. Governments in the United States have other large unfunded liabilities as well, such as retiree health insurance benefits (colloquially referred to as "other postemployment benefits," or OPEB). Because many public employees can retire before they are eligible for Medicare, many governments offer retirees health insurance benefits. When individuals become Medicare eligible, they pay a monthly premium for health insurance coverage (for example, in 2015, most Medicare recipients paid between $105 and $210 monthly for insurance coverage, depending on income).[27] As part of OPEB benefits for public retirees, some governments also reimburse retirees for their out-of-pocket Medicare medical insurance premiums (referred to as "Medicare Part B premiums").

Importantly, while most governments have prefunded pensions for decades (although perhaps insufficiently), OPEB liabilities were not even recorded in government financial statements until 2007, and governments have largely funded these retiree benefits on a pay-as-you-go basis (i.e., they are not prefunded). The sizes of these liabilities are very large. For example, New York City recognized its entire OPEB liability in 2007, reporting a $57.8 billion liability on its government-wide statement of net position (City of New York 2007, 38). By way of comparison, the city's bonds and notes payable in 2007 totaled $56.2 billion (City of New York 2007). Nationally, state governments alone have outstanding OPEB liabilities of nearly $600 billion. While state governments have accumulated more than $700 billion in assets to pay for pension benefits for current and future retirees, they have only accumulated approximately $35 billion in assets for OPEB benefits, implying a funded ratio of just 6 percent nationally (Pew Center on the States 2011). Table 5 compares pension and OPEB obligations of state governments, and clearly demonstrates the lack of funding OPEB obligations have received. OPEB liabilities are still being amortized onto balance sheets, so these obligations are still underreported. Further, the data only report state obligations and not local obligations. OPEB obligations tend to be focused at the local government level rather than the state level because police, fire, and teachers— who have earned the bulk of accumulated OPEB benefits—tend to be local government employees.

In 2010, state governments paid more than $17 billion for OPEB, even though actuaries estimated the annual cost at nearly $51 billion (Pew Center on the States 2012), indicating that governments were deferring nearly two-thirds of annual OPEB cost to the future. If actual OPEB spending begins to increase, governments could face the same situation as they do with pensions: spending on current programs is crowded out by spending on unfunded liabilities incurred for past programs. In Minnesota, some local governments even issued OPEB obligation bonds in an attempt to manage this fiscal stress. This increase in budgetary pressure could lead to selective taxation efforts in some jurisdictions to pay for OPEB obligations, and the unfunded gap for these liabilities are far worse than for pensions. OPEB liabilities are potentially more open to reform efforts compared to pensions. Although many states have constitutional or statutory protections for pensions, OPEB protections are more ambiguous (for more details, see Peng 2008, chapter 8).

In addition to potential pressures from OPEB liabilities, the Governmental Accounting Standards Board (GASB) changed financial reporting standards for public pension plans, effective 2013 (GASB 2012). Prior to this change, pension liabilities and funding were found in the notes to the financial statements. Now governments must report their net pension liabilities (i.e., the difference between total assets) and total liabilities on the balance sheets of their government-wide financial statements. Because these unfunded pension liabilities are now more visible (because they are now reported directly

Table 5. Comparison of State Pension to Retiree Health Insurance Obligations, Fiscal Year 2012

State	Unfunded Pension Obligations ($ thousands)	Unfunded Retiree Health Obligations ($ thousands)	Per Capita Pension Unfunded Obligation ($)	Per Capita OPEB Unfunded Obligations ($)	Funded Ratio: Pensions (%)	Funded Ratio: OPEB (%)
Alabama	14,379,973	11,116,162	2,982	2,305	66	9
Alaska	8,190,013	7,924,700	11,197	10,834	55	47
Arizona	14,374,813	737,480	2,194	113	72	68
Arkansas	7,509,607	2,150,165	2,546	729	71	0
California	131,318,184	79,392,286	3,452	2,087	77	0
Colorado	22,711,123	1,944,182	4,378	375	63	13
Connecticut	24,545,994	20,953,000	6,837	5,836	49	0
Delaware	1,037,497	5,642,000	1,131	6,152	88	3
Florida	28,955,936	6,782,210	1,499	351	82	0
Georgia	16,775,839	18,238,921	1,691	1,839	81	5
Hawaii	8,440,900	13,566,837	6,063	9,744	59	0
Idaho	2,077,557	124,788	1,302	78	85	15
Illinois	94,581,645	54,221,394	7,346	4,211	40	0
Indiana	16,354,957	314,737	2,502	48	61	18
Iowa	6,156,310	648,233	2,003	211	80	0
Kansas	10,252,933	532,115	3,553	184	56	3
Kentucky	21,355,447	6,182,103	4,875	1,411	47	19
Louisiana	19,305,848	8,543,177	4,195	1,856	56	0
Maine	2,935,200	1,975,942	2,208	1,487	79	4
Maryland	20,867,630	9,898,976	3,546	1,682	64	2
Massachusetts	28,104,234	15,377,400	4,229	2,314	61	3
Michigan	31,159,292	23,564,300	3,153	2,384	61	7
Minnesota	15,608,624	1,029,771	2,902	191	75	0
Mississippi	14,860,423	664,738	4,978	223	58	0

Missouri	12,522,783	3,282,845	2,080	545	78	4
Montana	4,302,807	447,105	4,281	445	54	0
Nebraska	2,426,073	N/A	1,307	N/A	79	N/A
Nevada	11,236,871	1,181,488	4,073	428	71	0
New Hampshire	4,573,477	2,585,155	3,463	1,957	56	1
New Jersey	47,209,474	63,880,700	5,326	7,206	65	0
New Mexico	12,489,369	3,687,626	5,989	1,768	63	6
New York	21,457,000	73,103,000	1,096	3,735	87	0
North Carolina	3,880,079	23,187,804	398	2,378	95	5
North Dakota	2,014,300	124,873	2,879	178	63	32
Ohio	63,143,558	8,433,170	5,470	731	67	65
Oklahoma	11,602,379	4,457	3,041	1	65	0
Oregon	5,621,100	390,800	1,442	100	91	43
Pennsylvania	47,286,100	17,535,850	3,705	1,374	64	1
Rhode Island	4,521,245	858,737	4,305	818	58	2
South Carolina	15,646,868	9,724,138	3,312	2,059	65	6
South Dakota	638,207	67,774	766	81	93	0
Tennessee	3,388,550	1,623,943	525	252	92	0
Texas	31,636,460	55,435,898	1,214	2,127	82	1
Utah	6,569,173	270,711	2,301	95	76	37
Vermont	1,418,457	1,825,584	2,266	2,916	70	1
Virginia	28,138,000	5,358,000	3,437	655	65	18
Washington	3,256,200	7,381,134	472	1,070	95	0
West Virginia	6,020,234	3,369,165	3,245	1,816	63	12
Wisconsin	69,700	1,210,176	12	211	100	47
Wyoming	1,691,194	243,197	2,934	422	80	0
National	914,653,163	576,738,947	2,920	1,841	72	6

Source: Data are from Pew Center on the States, "Size of Long-Term Obligations Varies across States," August 19, 2014, available at http://www.pewtrusts.org/en/research-and-analysis/analysis/2014/08/size-of-long-term-obligations-varies-across-states.

Note: OPEB = other postemployment benefits.

in financial statements instead of in notes only), governments may feel more pressure from creditors or bond raters to increase funding for their liabilities and reduce net pension liabilities. If so, more governments may increasingly turn to selective taxes as one potential tool to reduce these liabilities and manage their balance sheets.

CONCLUSION

The use of selective taxes and fees to fund pensions is still rather rare. However, as pension and OPEB costs continue to place stress on many public budgets, public decision makers may increasingly turn to these taxes and fees to help manage growing unfunded liabilities. This chapter draws on the experiences in Pennsylvania and Illinois to examine how these taxes have operated where used, how the decoupling of setting and financing employee benefits tends to lead to these taxes, and how the use of these taxes is associated with significantly underfunded pension systems. As government financial reporting standards increase the visibility of unfunded pension liabilities in the future, state and local governments may increasingly turn to selective taxes for sources of pension funding rather than renegotiating and making employee benefits less expensive.

NOTES

1. Data and calculations derived from table 1: "State and Local Government Finances by Level of Government and by State: 2012–2013" (US Census Bureau 2013). https://www.census .gov//govs/local/historical_data_2013.html.

2. All data in this discussion are derived from table 1.

3. As of 2013, public-sector pension plans used an average discount rate of 7.7 percent based on expected investment returns, while private-sector single-employer plans use a lower rate (between 1.3 percent and nearly 6.8 percent, depending on funding levels) based on high-quality bond yields. See US Government Accountability Office (2014).

4. Barro (2012) notes that some governments increased pension amortizations following 2008 to reduce pension contributions, and Stalebrink (2012) finds empirical support that political considerations lead to higher discount rates—which reduce required pension contributions. Biggs (2009) details how actuaries are pressured by public officials to use specific actuarial assumptions that reduce required pension contributions.

5. Governmental Accounting Standards Board (GASB) standards recognize a pension expenditure in the governmental funds financial statements only when the amount is actually contributed to the pension fund, not when it is legally owed. See chap. 10 of Granof et al. (2015).

6. In the public sector, 39 percent of all workers are represented by a labor union, compared to 7 percent in the private sector. Bureau of Labor Statistics (2017).

7. As an example, in 1999, the California Public Employees Retirement System (CalPERS) proposed and the state legislature passed a bill that (1) allowed workers hired since 1991, who were in a less expensive pension tier, to be moved into the more expensive older tier; (2) reduced retirement ages; and (3) increased benefits for uniformed members. In 2001, elected

leaders passed a law allowing local government employees not in CalPERS to bargain for similar benefits. See Malanga (2013).

8. The discussion in this section is derived from the data in table 2.

9. From Pew (2014).

10. Based on US Census Bureau (2014).

11. All funded ratios in this section are from Pennsylvania Public Employee Retirement Commission, Commission of Pennsylvania (2014).

12. Rates are from "Summary Schedule of Tax Rates since 1952, City and School District of Philadelphia," http://www.phila.gov/Revenue/Documents/Tax%20Summary%20 Schedule%20rev%207.1.pdf, and reflect when the cigarette tax was initially proposed. Rates were slightly lower in fiscal year 2015, when the cigarette tax was approved and implemented.

13. See "Taxpayer Relief Act, Special Session Act 1 of 2006, Frequently Asked Questions for Taxpayers," http://www.education.pa.gov/Documents/Teachers-Administrators/ Property%20Tax%20Relief/Frequently%20Asked%20Questions%20for%20Taxpayers.pdf.

14. See "Taxpayer Relief Act, Special Session Act 1 of 2006, Report on Referendum Exceptions for School Year 2013–2014," http://www.education.pa.gov/Documents/Teachers -Administrators/Property%20Tax%20Relief/2014-15%20Report%20on%20Referendum%20 Exceptions.pdf.

15. See "Just the Facts: Answers to Frequent City Pension Questions," http://www.cityofchicago .org/city/en/depts/mayor/iframe/just_the_facts.html.

16. Town of Normal, IL. 2015, "Comprehensive Annual Financial Report for the Fiscal Year April 1, 2014 to March 31, 2015," https://www.normal.org/DocumentCenter/View/6661.

17. See Rickert (2015) and also Munnell and Quinby (2012). The IMRF is a multi-agent employer pension system in which each participating government employer maintains its own accounts for assets and liabilities. The plan provides administrative and investment services, and, in the case of the IMRF, the state limits the benefit offerings available and potential changes to these offerings. The same holds true for CalPERS (see CalPERS 2015, primary benefits offered).

18. The Taxpayer Accountability and Budget Stabilization Act (P. A. 96-1496).

19. See http://www.tristateupdate.com/story/27262324/sales-tax-increase-approved-by-the-city -of-charleston-west-virginia and http://www.taxrates.com/blog/2015/05/01/west-virginia -sales-tax-changes-july-2015/.

20. See https://ballotpedia.org/Voters_in_Springfield,_Missouri,_renew_sales_tax_to_support _old_pension_fund.

21. More than 90 percent of all pension obligation bond issuers are cities, counties, towns, or school districts. See Calabrese and Ely (2013).

22. Information derived from the National Conference of State Legislatures (2015).

23. "Home rule" refers to the legislative authority granted to local governments by states. This authority varies by state, so that municipalities in different states have different abilities to impose or increase taxes.

24. Nearly 70 percent of pension plans in the CRR Pension Plan Database, one of the only detailed national databases of state and local pension plans, are cost-sharing systems.

25. From the CalPERS Payroll Reporting Procedures, http://d3n8a8pro7vhmx.cloudfront.net /friendsoftorrance/pages/14/attachments/original/1376189442/pasrg-payroll-reporting.pdf ?1376189442, p. 95.

26. See New York State and Local Retirement System Comprehensive Annual Financial Report (2015), https://www.osc.state.ny.us/retire/word_and_pdf_documents/publications/cafr/cafr _15.pdf, p. 46.

27. See https://www.medicare.gov/your-medicare-costs/costs-at-a-glance/costs-at-glance
.html#collapse-4809.

REFERENCES

Barro, Josh. 2012. "How Congress Can Help State Pension Reform." *National Affairs*. http://www
.nationalaffairs.com/publications/detail/how-congress-can-help-state-pension-reform.

Biggs, Andrew G. 2009. "Public Pensions Cook the Books: Some Plans Want to Hide the Truth
from Taxpayers." *Wall Street Journal*, July 6, A13.

Buchanan, James M., and Richard E. Wagner. 1977. *Democracy in Deficit: The Political Legacy of
Lord Keynes*. Indianapolis, IN: Liberty Fund.

Bureau of Labor Statistics. 2015. *National Compensation Survey, Retirement Benefits: Access,
Participation, and Take-Up Rates*. Washington, DC.

———. 2017. "Table 3: Union Affiliation of Employed Wage and Salary Workers by Occupation and
Industry." http://www.bls.gov/news.release/union2.t03.htm.

Calabrese, Thad D., and Todd L. Ely. 2013. "Pension Obligation Bonds and Government Spending."
Public Budgeting and Finance 33 (4): 43–65.

CalPERS (California Public Employees Retirement System). 2015. *Comprehensive Annual Financial
Report, 2014–2015*. https://www.calpers.ca.gov/docs/forms-publications/cafr-2015.pdf.

Casey, B. T., and R. D. Conlin. 2009. "State Insurance Premium and Other Insurance Taxes."
In *New Appleman on Insurance Law Library Volume 2*, edited by Jeffrey E. Thomas and
Nathaniel S. Shapo. New Providence, NJ: LexisNexis.

Center for Retirement Research at Boston College. 2002–2012. *Public Plans Data*. http://crr.bc.edu
/data/public-plans-database/.

Chaney, Barbara A., Paul A. Copley, and Mary S. Stone. 2002. "The Effect of Fiscal Stress and
Balanced Budget Requirements on the Funding and Measurement of State Pension
Obligations." *Journal of Accounting and Public Policy* 21: 287–313.

City of Chicago. 2012. *Comprehensive Annual Financial Report for Fiscal Year 2012*. https://www
.cityofchicago.org/city/en/depts/fin/supp_info/comprehensive_annualfinancialstatements
/2012_financial_statements.html.

City of New York. 2007. *Comprehensive Annual Financial Report of the Comptroller for the Fiscal
Year Ended June 30, 2007*. https://comptroller.nyc.gov/wp-content/uploads/documents
/cafr2007.pdf.

Civic Federation. 2007. "Dedicated Revenue Sources for State Pension Funds." http://www.nasra
.org/files/Topical%20Reports/Funding%20Policies/dedicated%20funding.pdf.

Coen, A. 2014. "Treasurer: Sales Tax Extension to Aid Philadelphia Pensions." *Bond Buyer*,
December 11.

Cooper, Michael, and Mary Williams Walsh. 2010. "In Town That Stopped Checks, a Warning on
Public Pensions." *New York Times*, December 22, A1.

Costrell, R., and L. Maloney. 2013. "The Big Squeeze: Retirement Costs and School District
Budgets. Paying the Pension Price in Philadelphia." Washington, DC: Thomas B. Fordham
Institute. http://edex.s3-us-west-2.amazonaws.com/publication/pdfs/20130606-paying-the
-pension-price-in-philadelphia-FINAL_7.pdf.

Dabrowski, T., K. Woodruff, and J. Hegy. 2014. "The Crisis Hits Home: Illinois' Local Pension
Problem." *Illinois Policy*, February. https://d2dv7hze646xr.cloudfront.net/wp-content
/uploads/2014/12/The-Crisis-Hits-Home-Illinois-Local-Pension-Problem.pdf.

Dardick, H. 2015. "Preckwinkle Sales Tax Hike Plays Well on Wall Street." *Chicago Tribune*,
July 23.

Dardick, H., and B. Ruthhart. 2015. "Emanuel's Tax Hike Tab: $755 Million." *Chicago Tribune,* October 28.

Fitch Ratings. 2011. "Enhancing the Analysis of U.S. State and Local Government Pension Obligations." http://www.nasra.org/resources/Fitch1102.pdf.

Galland, Z. 2015. "Issue Brief: Expanding the Base of Illinois' Sales Tax to Consumer Services Will Both Modernize State Tax Policy and Help Stabilize Revenues." Center for Tax and Budget Accountability and Taxpayers Federation of Illinois. http://www.ctbaonline.org/reports /issue-brief-expanding-base-illinois%E2%80%99-sales-tax-consumer-services

GASB (Governmental Accounting Standards Board). 2012. *Accounting and Financial Reporting for Pensions.* Statement 68. Norwalk, CT.

Giertz, J. Fred. 2003. "The Impact of Pension Funding on State Government Finances." *State Tax Notes* 29 (7): 507–13.

Granof, Michael H., Saleha B. Khumawala, Thad D. Calabrese, and Daniel L. Smith. 2015. *Government and Not-for-Profit Accounting: Concepts and Practices,* 7th ed. Hoboken, NJ: Wiley.

Hecht, Peter. 2013. "Judge Rejects Bid to Halt Stockton Bankruptcy." *Sacramento Bee,* April 2.

Illinois Municipal Retirement Fund. 2014. *2014 Annual Comprehensive Annual Financial Report.* https://www.imrf.org/en/publications-and-archive/annual-financial-reports.

Ives, Martin, Laurence Johnson, Joseph A. Razek, and Gordon A. Hosch. 2009. *Introduction to Governmental and Not-for-Profit Accounting,* 6th ed. Upper Saddle River, NJ: Pearson.

Johnson, Richard W. 1997. "Pension Underfunding and Liberal Retirement Benefits of State and Local Government Workers." *National Tax Journal* 50 (1): 113–42.

Long, Cate. 2012. "How Bankrupt Stockton, CA, Was Sold Pension Obligation Bonds." Reuters, September 7. http://blogs.reuters.com/muniland/2012/09/07/how-bankrupt-stockton-ca -was-sold-pension-obligation-bonds/.

Malanga, Steven. 2013. "The Pension Fund That Ate California." *City Journal.* http://www.city -journal.org/html/pension-fund-ate-california-13528.html.

Munnell, A. H., and L. Quinby. 2012. *Legal Constraints on Changes in State and Local Pensions.* State and Local Pension Plans 25. Chestnut Hill, MA: Center for Retirement Research at Boston College, State and Local Pension Plans. http://crr.bc.edu/wp-content/uploads/2012 /08/slp_25.pdf.

NASBO (National Association of State Budget Officers). 2015. *Fiscal Survey of the States, Fall 2015: An Update of State Fiscal Conditions.* https://www.nasbo.org/sites/default/files/Fall%20 2015%20Fiscal%20Survey%20of%20States%20%28S%29.pdf.

National Conference of State Legislatures. 2012–2015. *Pensions and Retirement State Legislation Database.* Denver, CO: National Conference of State Legislatures. http://www.ncsl.org /research/fiscal-policy/pension-legislation-database.aspx.

———. 2015. *State Personal Income Taxes on Pensions and Retirement Income: Tax Year 2014.* Denver, CO: National Conference of State Legislatures.

New York State and Local Retirement System. 2015. "Comprehensive Annual Financial Report." https://www.osc.state.ny.us/retire/word_and_pdf_documents/publications/cafr/cafr_15.pdf.

Novy-Marx, Robert, and Joshua Rauh. 2014. "The Revenue Demands of Public Employee Pension Promises." *American Economic Journal: Economic Policy* 6 (1): 193–229.

Nuschler, Dawn, Alison M. Shelton, and John J. Topoleski. 2011. *Social Security: Mandatory Coverage of New State and Local Government Employees.* Washington, DC: US Congressional Research Service.

Peng, Jun. 2008. *State and Local Pension Fund Management.* Boca Raton, FL: CRC.

———. 2014. "Public Pension Funds and Operating Budgets: A Tale of Three States." *Public Budgeting and Finance* 24 (2): 59–73.

Peng, Jun, and Ilana Boivie. 2011. "Lessons from Well-Funded Public Pensions: An Analysis of Six Plans that Weathered the Financial Storm." Washington, DC: National Institute on Retirement Security. http://www.nirsonline.org/storage/nirs/documents/Lessons%20 Learned/final_june_29_report_lessonsfromwellfundedpublicpensions1.pdf.

Peters, M. 2015. "Chicago City Council Passes Largest Tax Increase in City History." *Wall Street Journal*, October 28.

Pew Center on the States. 2011. "The Widening Gap: The Great Recession's Impact on State Pension and Retiree Health Care Costs." http://www.pewtrusts.org/~/media/legacy/upload edfiles/pcs_assets/2011/pewpensionsretireebenefitspdf.pdf.

———. 2012. "The Widening Gap Update." http://www.pewstates.org/uploadedFiles/PCS _Assets/2012/Pew_Pensions_Update.pdf.

Pew Charitable Trusts. 2013. "A Widening Gap in Cities: Shortfalls in Funding for Pensions and Retiree Healthcare Care." http://www.pewtrusts.org/~/media/legacy/uploadedfiles/pcs _assets/2013/pewcitypensionsreportpdf.pdf.

———. 2014. "The Fiscal Health of State Pension Plans." http://www.pewtrusts.org/en/research -and-analysis/analysis/2014/04/08/the-fiscal-health-of-state-pension-plans-funding-gap -continues-to-grow.

Poterba, James. 1994. "State Responses to Fiscal Crises: The Effects of Budgetary Institutions and Politics." *Journal of Political Economy* 102 (4): 799–821.

Public Employee Retirement Commission, Commission of Pennsylvania. 2014. "Status Report on Local Government Pension Plans." December. Harrisburg, PA. http://www.paauditor.gov /media/default/MunPenReporting/2014StatusReport.pdf.

Reid, Tim. 2012. "CalPERS Threatens San Bernardino over Pension Debt." Reuters, October 19. http://www.reuters.com/article/us-usa-debt-calpers-idUSBRE89I1FG20121019.

Rickert, D. S. 2015. "Commentary: First, Lay Off All the State Workers." *Chicago Tribune*, May 11. http://www.chicagotribune.com/ct-illinois-pension-reform-workforce-perspec-0512 -20150511-story.html.

Sneed, Cynthia, and John E. Sneed. 1997. "Unfunded Pension Obligations as a Source of Fiscal Illusion for State Governments." *Journal of Public Budgeting, Accounting, and Financial Management* 9 (1): 5–20.

Stalebrink, Odd J. 2012. "Public Pension Funds and Assumed Rates of Return: An Empirical Examination of Public Sector Defined Benefit Pension Plans." *American Review of Public Administration.* doi: 10.1177/0275074012458826.

Staub, A. 2015. "Anglers Could Be on the Hook for Pennsylvania's Public Pensions." *Pennsylvania Watchdog*, September 3. http://watchdog.org/236624/fishing-license-pension-pennsylvania/.

US Census Bureau. 1993–2012. *Annual Surveys of State and Local Government Finances.* Washington, DC.

———. 1993–2014. *Survey of Public Pensions: State and Local Data.* Washington, DC.

US General Accounting Office. 1979. *Funding of State and Local Government Pension Plans: A National Problem.* Report to the Congress of the United States. Washington, DC.

US Government Accountability Office. 2014. "Pension Plan Valuation: Views on Using Multiple Measures to Offer a More Complete Financial Picture." GAO-14-264. http://www.gao.gov /assets/670/666287.pdf.

VanMetre, Benjamin. 2015. "Another Illinois Town Hikes Taxes Amid Skyrocketing Pension Costs." *Illinois Policy*, March 5. https://www.illinoispolicy.org/another-illinois-town-hikes -taxes-amid-skyrocketing-pension-costs/.

CHAPTER 13
Tax Reform as a Discovery Process

J. R. CLARK
Probasco Distinguished Chair of Free Enterprise,
University of Tennessee at Chattanooga

DWIGHT R. LEE
William J. O'Neil Center for Global Markets and Freedom,
Southern Methodist University

W hat is the best tax structure? Neither pundits, politicians, nor economists know. Many have good suggestions for changes that would improve the tax structures we have now. But there is no best tax structure, since what is best depends on circumstances and preferences that vary over time and place. The best tax structure can only be discovered by responding to the decisions of taxpayers when they have choices among alternative tax structures. While taxpayers currently have such choices at the state and local levels, the motivation to make them, and the political response to the information they provide, are greatly moderated by the fact that the power to tax is concentrated in the federal government. With this in mind, we recommend a radical change in the fiscal environment in which taxes and spending policies that best serve the interests of those subject to them can more effectively emerge through a discovery process.

THE PROBLEM

America's fiscal problems cannot be easily dismissed. The federal and state governments impose taxes that unnecessarily burden taxpayers and distort economic decisions so politicians can cater to organized interest groups at the expense of the general public. The growth in federal spending appears to be unsustainable, given expectations of productivity growth, while it likely contributes to productivity growth falling to historically low levels. State and local governments have become increasingly compliant to the federal government to secure transfers that come with federal demands for more spending at state and local levels.

Increasingly, politicians are promising to make tough choices to restore fiscal responsibility by reforming taxes and controlling spending. They claim these reforms have to wait, however, until the weak economy strengthens, at which point the promised reforms will be largely forgotten. As Saint Augustine asked, "Lord, give me chastity and restraint, but not yet" (see Dyson 2006, 18). Until prevailing political incentives are changed, politicians will keep promising fiscal responsibility while their actions are saying, "but not yet."

We argue in this chapter that the above problems are aggravated by perverse political incentives that have resulted from the increased concentration of taxing and spending decisions in Washington. Until well into the twentieth century, peacetime federal tax receipts never exceeded 4 percent of GDP, nor were they greater than total state and local tax receipts; and in 1930, federal receipts were close to 35 percent of total government receipts. Furthermore, during peacetime, the federal budget was in surplus except during rather short recessions, when the budget deficits resulted from revenue declines, not spending increases. Since the Second World War, however, federal tax revenues have consistently exceeded state and local tax revenues, with the federal share reaching over 57 percent of total government receipts in 2009 and approximately 18 percent of GDP.[1] Peacetime federal deficits became common during the Great Depression of the 1930s and through the 1950s. They have been chronic since 1960.

A RADICAL PROPOSAL

The shift in the power to tax and spend from the state and local governments to the federal government explains much of the fiscal irresponsibility just discussed. That shift has made political rent-seeking for economically wasteful privileges and transfers easier and more profitable. These privileges and transfers take many forms, but certainly the insertion of provisions in tax codes that provide tax breaks to influential groups, industries, and even particular firms are of critical importance.[2] It is difficult to believe that tax codes full of loopholes or tax breaks do not reduce productivity by distorting economic decisions and diverting wealth-producing activities into activities to capture existing wealth. Wasteful rent-seeking is not confined to those in the private sector. State and local governments spend significant amounts to capture more money from the federal government for projects that are attractive to the recipients largely as a means of recapturing some of the federal dollars they sent to Washington and more likely than not are worth less than they cost (see Munger 2006).

That the above problems, and others, are largely the result of centralizing taxing and spending power in the federal government can be seen by considering how a radical proposal to decentralize that power would greatly reduce them. Our proposal is to move to an arrangement we call Tiebout taxation, which we believe would promote the type of fiscal federalism that Tiebout (1956) had in mind.[3] Under Tiebout taxation, federal taxation would be eliminated entirely. All tax revenue would be raised in the states, with each state required to transfer a uniform percentage of its revenue—say, 35 percent—to the federal government.[4] This fiscal arrangement is similar to that established by the Articles of Confederation, the original constitution of the thirteen United States, which was submitted for ratification in 1777, ratified in 1781, and established the rules under which the Revolutionary War was fought and won. The biggest complaint with the Articles was that the central government, being dependent on the states' voluntary contributions for revenue, was chronically underfunded.[5] Although a strong argument has been made by Sobel (1999) that the collection rate under the Articles of Confederation was as high or higher than existed under the new US Constitution, our proposal requires a specified percentage of the tax revenue raised in each state be transferred to the federal government, with this percentage being the same for all states.[6] How local tax revenue is raised would be determined in each state, and henceforth we will use the term "state" to refer to state or local (or both).

We next consider how our proposal would establish a fiscal environment that would facilitate the discovery of the tax structures most suitable for each state.

DISCOVERING BETTER TAX STRUCTURES

The most important feature of Tiebout taxation is that it would intensify competition among states. Competition among states already exists, of course. But with most tax revenue being raised by the federal government, differences in tax burdens across the states only modestly affect decisions on where to live, invest, and do business. This changes dramatically when the only tax burden comes from state taxes. Tiebout taxation would create a tax environment in which tax-base movements between states become very sensitive to relative differences in state tax burdens. Few things would concentrate politicians' minds on reforming taxes as much as significant reductions in their state's tax base as that base moves to other states. In this section, we argue that Tiebout taxation, by intensifying tax competition among the states, would motivate serious tax reform that would reduce the social cost of raising tax dollars and create a political environment that facilitates the discovery of the most appropriate reforms.

The federal tax code is riddled with thousands of special-interest complications and confusions that make it a horribly wasteful way of raising tax revenue (see chapter 19, this volume, by Matt Mitchell for more on special interests and the tax code). State tax codes are not much better, but for obvious reasons, most tax reform discussions concentrate on federal taxes.[7] The most obvious advantage of Tiebout taxation is that it reforms federal taxation by eliminating it and the over 74,000 pages of convoluted details needed to describe it (see figure 1).

Tiebout taxation greatly increases the prospects for reforming state taxation in three ways. First, it increases the political motivation in the states to reform taxes. Second, it reduces some difficulties facing serious state tax reform. And third, it facilitates a process by which a better tax arrangement can be discovered in each state.

While no one knows what the best tax system is for a state, it is not difficult to think of better tax structures than now exist at the state level. The main problem facing state tax reform is motivating politicians to consider it seriously. By intensifying competition among the states, Tiebout taxation would provide this motivation.

Tiebout taxation not only increases political incentives for states to reform their tax codes, it also reduces the difficulty of doing so. The elimination of federal taxes automatically removes an important tax distortion in all states. The federal deduction of state taxes reduces the taxpayers' cost of paying higher state taxes, which creates an obvious distortion. This deduction artificially lowers the state tax cost of services best provided privately (or not provided at all), thus making it more likely that states will provide them publicly. Consider such things as trash collection, tennis courts, golf courses, swimming pools, sports stadiums, and diversity specialists, which state governments would less likely fund without the federal government subsidizing state taxes. And education should not be overlooked. Good education at a low social cost is clearly not an advantage realized from public schools, but being able to pay for those schools

Figure 1. Income Tax Code Growth, Title 26 Restrictions, 1930–2016

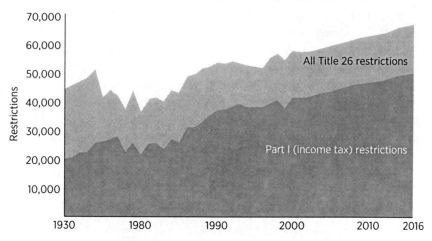

Source. RegData 3.0. All data from the RegData project are available at RegData.org and the related site, QuantGov.org. Figure produced by Patrick A. McLaughlin.

Note: The RegData project quantifies numerous features of government regulation and policy and parses regulations published in the *Code of Federal Regulations* (CFR). Title 26 of the CFR contains the regulations of the Internal Revenue Service (IRS). Part 1 of Title 26 comprises IRS regulations pertaining to federal income taxes. These rules concern individuals, trusts, estates, and various types of corporations and partnerships. Part 1 details IRS treatment of these taxable entities, including the procedures for the collection of revenue, the rates at which the entities will be taxed, and the tax credits allowed under current law. Part 1 of Title 26 is the longest and most restrictive single part in the entire CFR, with nearly 9 million words and over 50,000 restrictions.

with dollars exempt from the federal income tax artificially lowers that cost. Without this tax distortion, public schools would face more competition from private schools, and the political ability of public school unions to resist school choice would be weakened.

Tiebout taxation would increase the political motivation to eliminate wasteful state tax breaks that remain after federal taxation is eliminated. Of course, interest groups would strongly oppose eliminating their tax breaks, but let us consider the costs of those tax breaks and how Tiebout taxation would intensify those costs and increase the motivation for politicians to respond to them.

A major cost of imposing taxes is what economists call the excess burden of taxation (sometimes called the dead-weight loss of taxation), which is a cost in excess of the amount of money raised. The tendency is for politicians to ignore the excess burden of the taxes and think that the cost of raising tax revenue is given by the amount raised. For example, if a dam is worth $1.1 million and it takes $1 million in tax revenue to build it, politicians will claim it is worth $100,000 more than it costs. But the burden of raising another $1 million in taxes is in excess of $1 million, because people respond to increased taxes by making investment, consumption, and labor supply and demand decisions that create less value than those that would be made without the tax increases. The marginal excess burden of a tax depends on (among other things) the type of tax, how many ways it can be legally avoided (think tax breaks), and how much tax competition the taxing jurisdiction faces. Raising another dollar with the federal income tax has been estimated to cost society between $1.30 and $1.50—a marginal excess burden of between $.30 and $.50.[8] By increasing the intensity of competition among states, Tiebout taxation would increase the excess burden of taxation and make reducing that excess burden a more salient concern of state politicians.[9]

But even if this did not motivate much political action, we can be sure the requirement that each state has to transfer 35 cents to the federal government for every tax dollar it raises to support state spending would. Each state would need to increase taxes by $1.54 (that is, $1.00 ÷ .65) for every dollar it could spend. This "excess burden" of 54 percent would be impossible for politicians to ignore, since it would represent a very visible 54 percent tax increase on every taxpayer unless serious tax reform was undertaken.[10]

Serious tax reform is not possible without expanding the tax base (reducing the number of the tax breaks) and lowering tax rates. Eliminating tax breaks and lowering tax rates work together to reduce the real excess burden of taxes in three ways. First, fewer tax breaks would result in fewer opportunities to capture tax advantages by making socially inefficient investment and consumption decisions. Second, the lower tax rates are, the less the benefit would be from taking advantage of tax breaks that remain. Third, the lower the tax rates are, the lower real excess burdens of taxation would be.[11] Also, interest groups would be more agreeable to give up their tax breaks in return for the lower tax rates if other groups were willing to give up theirs. So instead of attempting to eliminate tax breaks one by one, Tiebout taxation would likely motivate state politicians to package a large number of tax breaks for consideration, with no one break being eliminated unless all are. This creates the reciprocity needed to reduce political opposition. In other words, it is easier to eliminate the alligators by draining the swamp than by fighting one alligator at a time.

Of course, the details of the best tax structure depend on a number of considerations, such as the preferences of citizens and economic circumstances that vary from state to state. And no matter how well informed and dedicated a state's politicians and their advisors are, they have nowhere near enough information to know the tax structure that best serves the general interest of the state's citizens. Maybe the biggest advantage of Tiebout taxation over the highly centralized tax structure we have currently is that it would provide more information to decision makers on whether changes in a state's tax code are improvements and would create strong incentives for them to respond appropriately to that information. The information would come in the form of directional flows in the tax base, which would be far more responsive to tax rates and the burdens they impose on taxpayers under Tiebout taxation than they are currently. In other words, Tiebout taxation would create a discovery process that helps guide tax reform with more information and stronger incentives than exist in the present tax arrangements.

Consider, for example, federal taxes on corporate profits. The federal tax rate on corporate profits is higher than the national corporate tax rate in any other industrialized country in the world, far higher in many cases.[12] This creates incentives for American corporations to relocate to other countries and keep their profits in those countries, even though they incur a productivity loss by doing so. However, this locational distortion has not been sufficient to motivate federal politicians to make such an obvious adjustment as reducing the corporate tax rate. There can be little doubt that, under Tiebout taxation, if a state imposed the same taxes on corporate profits that the federal government does now, its politicians would quickly consider corporate tax reform seriously as their state's tax base shifted to other states.

Obviously, a move to Tiebout taxation, and the resulting tax reform, would cause significant changes in the states' tax structures. One could object to this by pointing out that a stable tax environment is desirable, because it is better to maintain an existing tax rather than constantly change it, even when the changes are to a better tax system. Changing taxes does make it harder to know what future taxes will be, which hampers making sound economic decisions. But taxes are constantly changing now, and the changes are seldom improvements. And when significant improvements are made, they are typically eroded quickly in response to political incentives. For example, the Reagan tax reforms of 1986 replaced eight tax brackets in the personal income tax with two, dropped the highest bracket from 50 to 28 percent, and significantly broadened the tax base by eliminating a large number of tax loopholes.[13] But the lower rates and broader tax base created a tax-revenue-enhancing opportunity too tempting for Congress to resist. With the elimination of a lot of tax loopholes, a tax rate increase raised more revenue than before, when ways to exempt income from taxation were plentiful. So the number of tax brackets started increasing as higher rates were added to the income tax. But, as tax rates increased, the value of tax loopholes also increased, and interest groups were willing to pay more for those tax loopholes in terms of campaign contributions and promises of support from large voting blocs. And this is exactly what happened, as predicted by Lee (1985a). Within 20 years of the 1986 reforms going into effect, the number of tax brackets had increased from two to seven and the highest tax rate had increased from 28 to 39.6 percent.[14]

The tax improvements made in response to the incentives created under Tiebout taxation could be expected to be more permanent than they would be now. Taxpayers, and tax bases, would be more responsive to the cost of taxation in their locational decisions, including the cost of changes in tax codes. Since the changes that would be made under Tiebout taxation are more likely to be agreeable to taxpayers, the changes that are made would be influenced more by changes in the circumstances and concerns of taxpayers than by the whims of politicians.

BETTER SERVICE AT LOWER COSTS IN THE STATES

We have so far emphasized the importance of tax competition among states. But neither taxing nor spending can be adequately examined without considering the other. For example, part of the motivation for tax reform under Tiebout taxation is that more efficient taxation would make it possible for a state to improve its competitive position with respect to other states by providing government services more cheaply. In this section, by focusing on spending competition among the states, we consider how intensified interstate competition motivated by Tiebout taxation would create another interaction between spending efficiency and taxing reform.

Much of the current competition among states involves each trying to free ride on the tax contributions of others by fighting over federal transfers. This competition requires (1) hiring lots of people who, instead of producing new wealth, fight over existing wealth by lobbying for federal money to subsidize costly public projects that commonly do more to promote political agendas of federal authorities than to generally benefit the state's citizens, and (2) being willing to accept federal regulations and mandates that increase the cost, and often the value, of the projects. This negative-sum competition destroys wealth in all states. If a state drops out of this competition, however, its citizens would still have to send the same amount of tax dollars to the federal government, with those dollars being spent in other states. It is understandable why each state's politicians and interest groups believe that even when the federal government is wasting taxpayer dollars, it is better to waste them in their state than somewhere else. Our current tax environment puts us all in a prisoner's dilemma in which cooperating by reducing our demand for wasteful government spending would be in the interest of all if everyone did so, but demanding more wasteful government spending is in the interest of each, no matter what others do.

Tiebout taxation reduces this prisoner's dilemma not only by intensifying competition among the states, but also by changing the competition in a way that generates positive-sum outcomes. The altered competition would still be motivated by each state's attempt to free ride on the tax contributions of other states, but with an important difference. As discussed in the next section, Tiebout taxation would create a strong incentive for the federal government to restrict its spending to providing public goods that benefit most, if not all, states. Thus, each state would have an incentive to free ride on other states by reducing its contribution for the general benefits it receives from spending by the federal government. The most effective way for a state to get such a free ride from other states would be by reducing the amount it raises in taxes, and the best way of doing this is by eliminating expenditures on state services that are not worth what they cost and providing the services that are as efficiently as possible. Of course, the free-rider advantage of more efficient spending is enhanced by the previously discussed competitive advantage achieved by reducing the cost of spending with tax reform.[15]

So under Tiebout taxation, we could expect tax reform and spending reform to reinforce each other. Of course, with all taxation taking place at the state level, and supporting both state and federal services, state taxes would increase under Tiebout taxation. But the overall tax burden would decrease, as all tax revenue would be raised and spent more efficiently than is currently the case. There is little hope for such fiscal improvement given the federal government's current power to tax and spend—a power that suppresses the tax competition among states and provides a steady stream of transfers to the states for the purpose of sustaining wasteful spending while encouraging them to increase their own tax revenues. One can reasonably think of our current fiscal arrangement as a tax cartel between the federal and state governments, making it possible for all levels of government to squeeze more money out of taxpayers and spend it with little regard to the long-run interest of their citizens.

INCREASED FEDERAL FISCAL RESPONSIBILITY

Tiebout taxation would improve the federal government's fiscal responsibility if for no other reason than the government would have less money to spend irresponsibly. In addition, it would create incentives for federal authorities to spend money more efficiently than is currently the case.

First, the incentive to avoid spending federal money to pay for services best provided by state governments or left to private provision would be palpable. If state services are worth providing, the more the federal government paid for them, the less money states would have to raise, thereby reducing the federal government's only source of revenue. If the services are not worth paying for, anything the federal government paid for them would reduce the amount it could spend on projects that would increase its revenue, which leads to the second reason for expecting more responsible federal spending under Tiebout taxation. The only way the federal government could increase its revenue, short of changing the percentage of state revenue it receives (which would require a supermajority of Congress) would be by limiting its expenditures to those services that increase general economic productivity but that are not in the interest of any one state or consortium of states to fund. In other words, the political incentives facing federal authorities would shift in favor of funding national public goods and providing them efficiently.

The US Congress would quickly recognize that providing federal money to assist state governments to pay for such things as bike paths, community swimming pools, public schools, street repairs, bullet trains, and light-rail systems would reduce its income while reducing opportunities to increase its income with expenditures that increased the prosperity of the general public. Federal politicians would also begin paying serious attention to the fact that a lot of corporate welfare reduces national prosperity and their own revenues. Fiscally irresponsible activities, such as paying farmers to grow cotton in the desert; subsidizing the production of ethanol and so-called green energy projects that often go bankrupt even with the subsidies; and bailing out failing automobile companies and their unionized workers, along with banks considered too big to fail, would lose much of their political appeal under Tiebout taxation.

When the massive federal transfer programs—such as Social Security, Medicare, and Medicaid, along with anti-poverty programs—are considered, over 60 percent of the federal budget is now devoted to transfer programs, with the largest being unsustainable as currently structured.[16] These federal transfer programs have created a growing sense of entitlement and growing dependency on government for an increasing number of things that were considered to be personal responsibilities in the past. The result is that we are moving toward a situation described by the nineteenth-century French economist, Frederic Bastiat (2012, 97), in which *the state is the great fiction by which everyone endeavors to live at the expense of everyone else* (emphasis in original). One does not have to believe we are about to reach such an economically destructive situation to recognize that once we are on such a path, it is easier to keep traveling down it than to make the tough decisions required for a U-turn. The longer we wait before such proposals as Tiebout taxation are considered seriously, the more difficult turning back will be.

Admittedly, making such a U-turn will require major reforms in the largest of the transfer programs (Social Security, Medicare, and Medicaid), which have grown to include far more recipients, and cost far more, than initially anticipated (or admitted) when they were enacted. This will be difficult, in large measure because of the transitional problem caused by the fact that current beneficiaries (and those workers who expect to be future beneficiaries) of the first two programs (and to a far lesser degree for Medicaid) have already earned much of their benefits by paying for the benefits received by past beneficiaries. Discussing possible ways of dealing with this transition, or other difficulties in reforming (and in some cases eliminating) other transfer programs is beyond the scope of this chapter. What we can say is that under Tiebout taxation, much of the reform would take place in the states, and politicians would be motivated to give serious attention to reforming transfer programs and spending reforms more generally. Furthermore, their reform would be aided by a discovery process making use of feedback generated by interstate competition.

Tiebout taxation has another advantage, at least from the perspective of many economists. Without going into a detailed discussion of the economic flaws and political misuse of Keynesian economics (see Lee 2012), Tiebout taxation would, for reasons that should be clear from the previous discussion, greatly reduce (if not eliminate altogether) political enthusiasm for using fiscal policy to fine-tune the economy.

CONCLUSION

Tiebout taxation is a radical proposal that will be dismissed by many as too drastic to be taken seriously. Yet we present it with the seriousness that should be given to what we see as shortsighted irresponsibility that has long characterized government taxing and spending. The fiscal incentives created by the centralization of the power to tax and spend are motivating taxing and spending decisions that are slowing, and could reverse, the growth in economic productivity necessary to sustain that power. Unless something is done, a serious fiscal crisis is inevitable.

We would be naive to believe Tiebout taxation would eliminate perverse economic policies. Taxing and spending are not the only ways the federal government can pursue political objectives that harm economic productivity. By influencing monetary policy, imposing regulations, and criminalizing economic activity, the federal government could continue attempting to fine-tune the economy, imposing inflationary taxation, transferring wealth and income, and raising funds through fines. No tax reform eliminates these problems, but this is hardly an argument for dismissing the importance of tax reform.

Also, we think putting forth the arguments for eliminating federal taxation and replacing it with Tiebout taxation is a useful exercise, even if the hope for enactment is slim. By considering our proposal, the perverse pattern of fiscal incentives that currently exists is clearly illuminated. And the reason for the harmful economic result of those incentives is seen to be the direct result of the power to tax being heavily centralized in the federal government. Other approaches to tax reform are certainly worthy of consideration. But we are convinced that for a proposed reform to be most effective it has to (1) consider the problem of discovering and motivating better tax structures, (2) recognize the importance of decentralizing taxing power, and (3) be considered seriously before a crisis is unavoidable.

We recognize, however, the tendency for politicians to continue either denying fiscal problems, or making empty promises about bringing them under control, as long as possible. This leaves the second-best hope, which is to have some reasonable options available when the problems finally have to be confronted. Friedman (2002, xiii–xiv) recognized the importance of this second-best response with the observation:

> There is enormous inertia—a tyranny of the status quo—in private and especially government arrangements. Only a crisis—actual or perceived—produces real change. When that crisis occurs, the actions that are taken depend on the ideas that are lying around. That, I believe, is our basic function: to develop alternatives to existing policies, to keep them alive and available until the politically impossible becomes politically inevitable.

We believe Tiebout taxation is an alternative that should be available for consideration when the fiscal trajectory we are currently on leads to an inevitable, and very real, crisis.

NOTES

1. Federal spending is an ever larger percentage of GDP than state and local spending, because deficits finance a larger percentage of federal spending than they do of state and local spending.

2. These tax breaks often go directly to the customers of those who lobbied, or organized the lobbying effort, with the latter receiving the benefits indirectly. Tax advantages to homeowners and the exemption of the value of employer-provided medical insurance from taxable income are examples.

3. Tiebout's (1956) theory assumes that local governments are more aware of, and sensitive to, the preferences of their citizens for type and cost of public services provided than is the federal government. Given the differences in these preferences, and the relative ease with which people can move from one local jurisdiction to another, Tiebout argues that competition among local governments will facilitate the ability of people to sort themselves into communities that best accommodate their preferences for local public services.

4. With the exception of allowing the federal government to impose a tax in case of war (with a declaration of war requiring a supermajority of both chambers of Congress), the elimination of federal taxation means no income taxes, no corporate taxes, no excise or sales taxes, and no tariffs on imports. States could not impose tariffs on imports from other states. However, if a state wanted to burden its citizens with a tariff on foreign imports, that would be allowed. Earlier versions of this idea were first developed by one of the authors: see Lee (1985b, 1996) and Buchanan and Lee (1994). This chapter has been extensively rewritten to focus attention on tax reform.

5. A detailed examination of the free-rider incentives that hampered the federal government's ability to raise revenue under the Articles of Confederation is given by Dougherty (2001). While Dougherty argues that the federal government was woefully underfunded under the Articles, he points out that funding was greater than implied by the standard model of voluntary payments for collective (or public) goods.

6. As indicated above, the federal government accounted for approximately 35 percent of total government revenues in 1929. Specifying the same percentage for all states eliminates the rent-seeking that would be the inevitable result of allowing states to transfer different percentages to the federal government. This includes tax revenues raised by local governments in each state. Although we use 35 percent in the discussion in this chapter, the actual number would be determined through a process of amending the Constitution. Also, the argument for it being the same for every state does not rule out the rate being changed a by supermajority of both chambers of Congress.

7. When state taxes are considered, it is often done to examine how they are affected by federal taxes. For example, see Bartlett (2012, chapter 13). We defer to other chapters in this volume to discuss the distortions and inefficiencies in existing tax codes in more detail than we do here.

8. See Browning (2008, 156). So the cost of the dam, once the marginal excess burden is considered, would be $1.3 million ($200,000 more than the dam is worth, even using the lowest estimate for the marginal excess burden of taxation).

9. See Laffer et al. (2014), especially chapter 1 for evidence that state tax bases are sensitive to taxpayer burdens now, where the taxpayer burden includes how much taxpayers have to pay as well as the excess burden.

10. We have put quotation marks around "excess burden," since it is not really an excess burden but a transfer to the federal government. Politicians will consider it the same as a real excess burden, however, and might overestimate the real excess burden. But since no tax reform will eliminate all political tendencies for excessive taxing and spending, it is highly unlikely that overestimating the tax cost of government programs will result in too little government spending. But even if it did, there is no reason to believe too little spending is more harmful than too much, which is surely what we have currently, with so much of the social cost of taxation being ignored by politicians.

11. The "excess burden" created by the 35 percent transfer requirement would be unaffected by tax reform. But as we shall see in the next section, this transfer requirement and the intensified competition among the states would motivate politicians to reduce spending by making more efficient spending decisions.

12. See http://www2.deloitte.com/content/dam/Deloitte/global/Documents/Tax/dttl-tax-corporate-tax-rates-2015.pdf.

13. However, it should be noted that after the reform, a rate of 33 percent applied to a taxable income level somewhat above the level at which the 28 percent rate kicked in and then

dropped back to 28 percent at a somewhat higher income level. Also, the reform still left plenty of loopholes in the personal income tax code.

14. See http://taxfoundation.org/blog/twenty-years-later-tax-reform-act-1986.

15. There is an elasticity issue here, since by reducing the cost of spending through tax reform, it could be efficient for a state to raise more tax dollars to spend. In this situation, the state would not be free riding on other states but taking advantage of its improved efficiency by adding to the net value of public services provided.

16. One can argue that Social Security and Medicare are not transfer programs, since a rough connection exists between the benefits a person receives and the amount he or she paid into the program. Yet there is a clear transfer element in them, since the amount paid in by beneficiaries has long been less than the amount paid out to them.

REFERENCES

Bartlett, Bruce. 2012. *The Benefit and the Burden: Tax Reform, Why We Need It and What It Will Take*. New York: Simon and Schuster.

Bastiat, Frederic. 2012. "The State." In *Frederic Bastiat: "The Law," "The State," and Other Political Writings, 1843–1850*, edited by J. de Guerin, 97. Vol. 2 of *The Collected Works of Frederic Bastiat*. Indianapolis, IN: Liberty Fund.

Browning, Edgar K. 2008. *Stealing from Each Other: How the Welfare State Robs Americans of Money and Spirit*. Westport, CT: Praeger.

Buchanan, James M., and Dwight R. Lee. 1994. "On a Fiscal Constitution for the European Union." *Journal des Economistes et des Etudes Humaines* 5 (2/3): 219–32.

Dougherty, Keith L. 2001. *Collective Action under the Articles of Confederation*. Cambridge: Cambridge University Press.

Dyson, R. W. 2006. *St. Augustine of Hippo: The Christian Transformation of Political Philosophy*. London: Continuum International Publishing Group.

Friedman, Milton. 2002. *Capitalism and Freedom*. Chicago: University of Chicago Press.

Laffer, Arthur B., Stephen Moore, Rex A. Sinquefield, and Travis H. Brown. 2014. *An Inquiry into the Nature and Causes of the Wealth of States*. Hoboken, NJ: John Wiley and Sons.

Lee, Dwight R. 1985a. "Real Flat Rate is the Only Durable Reform." *Wall Street Journal*, August 22, op. ed. page.

———. 1985b. "Reverse Revenue Sharing: A Modest Proposal." *Public Choice* 45 (3): 279–89.

———. 1996. "A Case for Fiscal Federalism." *Intercollegiate Review* 31 (1): 37–45.

———. 2012. "The Keynesian Path to Fiscal Irresponsibility." *Cato Journal* 32 (3): 473–91.

Munger, Michael. 2006. "Rent-Seek and You Will Find." Featured article, *Library of Economics and Liberty*, July 3. http://www.econlib.org/library/Columns/y2006/Mungerrentseeking.html.

Sobel, Russel S. 1999. "In Defense of the Articles of Confederation and the Contribution Mechanism as a Means of Government Finance: A General Comment on the Literature." *Public Choice* 99 (3/4): 347–56.

Tiebout, Charles M. 1956. "A Pure Theory of Local Taxation." *Journal of Political Economy* 64 (5): 416–24.

PART IV

THE ECONOMICS OF THE FAILING NANNY STATE

CHAPTER 14
Taxation as Nudge:
The Failure of Anti-obesity Paternalism

MICHAEL MARLOW
Department of Economics, California Polytechnic State University

SHERZOD ABDUKADIROV
Mercatus Center at George Mason University

Paternalistic policymakers intend to improve social welfare by implementing a set of prescriptive policies designed to remedy systematic mistakes individuals make. In recent years, some paternalists[1] have relied increasingly on findings of behavioral economics research—a rapidly growing discipline that studies individuals' systematic biases—to justify paternalistic policies. The paternalists focus on devising "nudges" (soft paternalism) or "shoves" (hard paternalism) that steer individuals toward choices more in sync with the individuals' best interests. In effect, paternalists argue that policymakers can exploit individuals' departures from rationality in ways that correct what paternalists see as irrational individual mistakes. The paternalists aim to fix individual failures by introducing interventions devised by better-informed, benevolent policymakers.

Proponents of paternalistic policies attempt to use findings from behavioral economics research to demonstrate how cognitive biases and bounded self-control prevent individuals from maximizing their welfare (Rizzo and

Whitman 2009). Paternalists argue that individuals know what they want but too often fail to achieve their goals. Hence, paternalists advocate government policies that help individuals overcome their biases to achieve self-defined well-being.

Paternalists believe that the evidence supporting behavioral economics justifies expanding the scope of government intervention beyond regulating market failure and into regulating individual failure. The implications of this broader regulatory scope could be far reaching. If individual failure becomes an accepted motive for government intervention, policies are likely to become more intrusive and restrictive than present regulatory policies are. Paternalistic policies motivated by behavioral economics thus warrant a close examination. In this chapter, we examine the growing use of behavioral economics to justify government intervention regarding obesity. Public health advocates often view the growing prevalence of obesity as proof that many individuals pursue behaviors that are out of sync with their own best interests. That is, obesity is not attributed to choices based on personal preferences but rather to irrational behavior that can be successfully amended via government policy. Paternalistic policies believed to steer individuals toward improved lives via leaner bodies include taxes on so-called unhealthy food, regulations requiring calorie counts on restaurant menus and vending machines, bans on children's toys at fast food restaurants, bans on soda and unhealthy food at schools, and moratoriums on new fast food restaurants.

We argue that the growing use of paternalism to justify government intervention in individual food and lifestyle choices is often misguided and that policies are too easily justified on the assumption that government officials are better informed than the individuals they seek to guide.[2] Our examination demonstrates that government intervention is often ineffective in remedying individual failures and that, in some cases, policies are counterproductive for society. Our arguments are also supported by our examination of the recent tax on sugary drinks adopted in Berkeley, California.

RISING PREVALENCE OF OBESITY

The rising prevalence of obesity in the United States is often referred to as a public health epidemic, because it is associated with so many health problems, including diabetes, hypertension, high cholesterol, heart disease, stroke, sleep apnea, some cancers, gallstones, gout, asthma, and osteoarthritis (Dixon 2010). In the United States, annual medical spending on treating obesity was estimated at $168 billion (in 2005 dollars), roughly 16.5 percent of all medical spending (Cawley and Meyerhoefer 2010).

Researchers hypothesize many causes for excessive weight gain, including increased consumption of sugar-sweetened beverages (Malik et al. 2006; Vartanian et al. 2007; Bleich et al. 2009); falling food prices (Chou et al. 2004; Courtamanche and Carden 2008; Cawley 2010); urban sprawl (Zhao and Kaestner 2010); increase in calories consumed away from home (Chou et al. 2004; Larson et al. 2009); food engineering that encourages food addiction (Ruhm 2010); sedentary lifestyles fostered by technology (Philipson and Posner 2003; Lakdawalla and Philipson 2009); increased availability of restaurants (Chou et al. 2004; Larson et al. 2009); fewer grocery stores selling healthy foods (Larson et al. 2009); and agricultural policies that encourage production of unhealthy foods (Wallinga 2010).

Whether directly or indirectly, most of these studies point to individual failures—biased reasoning or lack of self-control—as the main causes of obesity. A recent *New England Journal of Medicine* article argues that

> Many persons do not fully appreciate the links between consumption of these beverages and health consequences, they make consumption decisions with imperfect information. These decisions are likely to be further distorted by the extensive marketing campaigns that advertise the benefits of consumption. A second failure results from time-inconsistent preferences (i.e., decisions that provide short-term gratification but long-term harm). This problem is exacerbated in the case of children and adolescents, who place a higher value on present satisfaction while more heavily discounting future consequences. (Brownell et al. 2009, 1601)

Traditional economic theories assume that people are rational, that they know exactly what they want, and that they choose the best way to increase their own welfare within the limits of the information at their disposal. As long as people are free to choose, they are believed to achieve the best outcomes for themselves given their circumstances and information. They will also learn from their mistakes. The traditional paradigm is simply to let people manage their own lives, because they are best able to determine their own welfare.

A discipline at the intersection of psychology and economics, behavioral economics examines whether people make rational choices under various economic scenarios. Behavioral economists challenge the traditional view by documenting numerous instances in which individual actions demonstrate *bounded rationality* (see Ariely 2008 and McKenzie 2009 for numerous examples). Not only do individuals make mistakes in their decision-making, but they are also believed to repeat the same mistakes under similar conditions. Behavioral economists assert that, rather than some people making random irrational choices, individuals frequently deviate from rational decisions in consistent and predictable manners. In other words, choices are systematically biased.

Systematic bias in human behavior falls into two broad categories (Buckley 2009). First, *cognitive biases* prevent people from pursuing actions that improve their welfare. Individuals rely on heuristics or rules of thumb when making decisions, which may lead them to less optimal decisions. For example, patients are more likely to opt for a surgery if the outcome probability is framed in terms of success rate rather than failure (Tversky and Kahneman 1981).

In the second category, behavioral economists question individuals' willpower to choose rational courses of action. In economic jargon, such individuals are said to suffer from *hyperbolic discounting* that leads them to exhibit time inconsistency. For example, while individuals might strive toward quitting smoking, an inconsistency exists between this long-term objective and their short-term behavior that results in time-inconsistent choices. A smoker may find it hard to quit today, but may decide to quit tomorrow when the benefits of better health outweigh the costs of quitting. Yet, when tomorrow arrives, the individual reverses this decision when he believes the costs of quitting outweigh benefits. Consequently, the individual finds it exceedingly difficult to quit smoking. The same logic applies to an obese person trying to stick to a diet or an exercise program. In effect, individuals are believed to suffer from persistent difficulties in self-control.

Seemingly irrational behavior prompts many public health advocates to call for government intervention on behalf of obese citizens. Local, state, and federal governments have responded by issuing policies aimed at curbing individual failures. Policies range from highly stringent (e.g., bans or taxes on unhealthy foods) to less intrusive (e.g., food labeling requirements and public service announcements that exercise is helpful). As discussed below, these measures have achieved little to no success.

GOVERNMENT INTERVENTION IS INEFFECTIVE

For most of the twentieth century, regulation was used to correct market failures. Consequently, a standard government regulatory toolkit was developed to deal with these types of market failure. This toolkit contains two approaches to deal with market failure. The first approach requires information disclosure to counter information asymmetry. The second approach increases the cost of "bad" behavior to deal with negative externalities.

Paternalistic policymakers have used both approaches in attempts to deal with obesity. Federal, state, and local governments have required food producers and servers to disclose calorie counts, sugar and fat contents, and other information to steer consumers toward healthier choices. Regulations are based on the assumption that consumers are poorly informed about the negative effects of their choices and that fuller disclosure will remedy the problem of information asymmetry. Some governments press even further by imposing higher taxes on or banning various unhealthy foods altogether. This heavy-handed approach presumes consumers lack sufficient incentives to watch what they eat or exercise to maintain healthy weight. Paternalists thus attempt to selectively punish such behavior by increasing the cost of unhealthy choices— not unlike policies aimed at correcting such negative externalities as pollution. However, government policies designed to remedy market failures are ineffective in mitigating the consequences of individual failures.

Obese People Do Not Suffer from a Lack of Information

Obesity may be a widespread problem, but it does not necessarily result from a lack of information. Studies indicate that adults recognize various personal health risks associated with obesity. Finkelstein et al. (2008) conducted a survey of 1,130 adults in the United States to test whether overweight and obese individuals believe they are at greater risk of obesity-related diseases and premature mortality. They found that overweight and obese adults forecast life expectancies that are 2.4 and 3.9 years, respectively, shorter than those of normal-weight adults. Excess weight was associated with greater self-perceived risk of developing diabetes, cancer, heart disease, and stroke. The authors concluded that mortality predictions generated from the survey were reasonably close to those generated from actual life tables for adults in the United States. These results are consistent with the findings of Falba and Busch (2005) that overweight and obese adults predict they will have shorter life expectancies. Examining data on 9,035 individuals aged 51 to 61, they found that overweight and obese adults believe their weight will reduce their life expectancy by an average 2.5 years and 4 years, respectively.

Thus, recent interventions are relatively ineffective when they simply repeat information individuals already know. A study of New York City's 2008 law requiring restaurant chains to post calorie counts examined how menu calorie labels influenced fast food choices. Information provided by patrons of fast food restaurants in New York City was compared with information provided by patrons in Newark, New Jersey, a city without labeling laws. While 28 percent of New York patrons said the information influenced their choices, researchers could not detect a change in calories purchased after the law (Elbel et al. 2009). Finkelstein et al. (2011) reached a similar conclusion in a study of a mandatory menu-labeling regulation requiring all restaurant chains with fifteen or more locations to disclose calorie information in King County, Washington. No effect on purchasing behavior—measured by transaction trends and calories per transaction at one fast food restaurant chain—was found.

Obese People Do Not Suffer from Lack of Motivation

The obese do not lack economic motivation to watch their weight. Individuals making poor food choices have strong incentives to correct them. Obese individuals generally want to lose weight for reasons that may include better health, longer life span, and higher wages. For example, it is well known that the obese earn less than the nonobese. Baum and Ford (2004) conclude that both men and women experience a persistent obesity wage penalty during the first two decades of their careers. After controlling for various socioeconomic and familial variables, they also find that standard covariates do not explain why obese workers continue to experience persistent wage penalties. They suggest that job discrimination, health-related factors, or obese workers' behavior patterns may explain why obesity continues to adversely affect wages.

Obese individuals' income loss can be substantial. Cawley (2004) found that obese white females earned 11.2 percent less than their nonobese counterparts. A difference in weight of two standard deviations (roughly 65 pounds) was associated with a 9 percent difference in wages—an effect equivalent to the wage effect of roughly 1.5 years of education or 3 years of work experience. Bhattacharya and Bundorf (2009) find that cash wages for obese workers are lower than those for nonobese workers, because the employers' costs for providing health insurance to obese workers is higher. Obese workers who receive employer-sponsored health insurance pay for their higher medical costs by receiving lower cash wages than nonobese workers.

Recent evidence also calls into question interventions aimed at steering obese individuals away from junk and fast food. Van Hook and Altman (2012) recently concluded that children with access to junk food (e.g., soft drinks, candy bars, potato chips) were no heavier than those without. The study followed nearly 20,000 students from kindergarten through the eighth grade in 1,000 public and private schools and found that in the eighth grade, 35.5 percent of children in schools with junk food were overweight, while 34.8 percent of those in schools without it were overweight. The authors suggest that children's food preferences and dietary patterns may be firmly established before adolescence. The evidence thus offers little support for anti-obesity interventions aimed at stopping junk food consumption in middle school. The authors conclude that food sales in schools are, on average, unrelated to obesity; this result supports other research that school-based interventions to reduce childhood obesity are often unsuccessful (Sharma 2006; Kropski et al. 2008).

Anderson and Matsa (2011) found that the causal link between the consumption of restaurant foods and obesity is minimal at best, based on an examination of data collected between 1990 and 2005. Analyses of food intake data revealed that, although restaurant meals were associated with greater caloric intake, additional calories were mostly offset by reductions in eating during the rest of the day. They concluded that efforts to reduce fast food consumption might be ineffective in lowering obesity, because consumers may overturn such efforts by substituting other foods or simply eating more food at home. In other words, unhealthy food or even overindulgence of healthy food does not require ready access to fast food restaurants when grocery stores and full service restaurants are available.

GOVERNMENT INTERVENTION IS COUNTERPRODUCTIVE

Paternalistic policymakers often possess insufficient information required for effective policymaking (Rizzo and Whitman 2009). Advocates of government paternalism often assume that a government official is not only fully rational but also fully informed and committed to improving the welfare of others. Yet dealing with individual failures requires not just general knowledge (e.g., health impact of trans fats) but also very specific knowledge of individual circumstances and preferences dispersed across society (e.g., when individuals are more likely to consume unhealthy foods, how a government policy would interfere with their private weight loss initiatives). Absent such information, policies initiated by paternalists are likely to be misguided and ineffective.

Paternalistic policies may also lead to unintended consequences, which may, on balance, hurt the people such policies were meant to help. And even if paternalists proposed policies that could remedy individual failures, it is unlikely those policies would survive the policymaking process intact.

Unintended Consequences

The burdens of government policies are borne not only by those citizens who are believed to lack sufficient information or self-control. Research demonstrates that tax hikes on alcohol and tobacco serve primarily to decrease consumption by light, not heavy, users. In other words, raising taxes causes those without problems to reduce consumption, leaving those with problems to simply pay higher taxes (Ayyagari et al. 2009). There is little reason to suspect anything different when taxes are imposed on individuals believed to eat too much and exercise too little. Taxes more heavily steer elastic, not inelastic, consumers away from taxed products, exerting little to no effect on those citizens regulations actually target. Such interventions are also often regressive in nature, placing higher burdens on the poor rather than the non-poor (Hoffer et al. 2015).

Interventions may also impose adverse unintended consequences on public health. Tax hikes on cigarettes harm smokers, for example, who switch to higher tar and nicotine brands to smoke fewer, but more addictive, cigarettes (Farrelly et al. 2004; Adda and Cornaglia 2006). Epidemiological research indicates that outcomes of such smoking patterns are more detrimental to health (Thun et al. 1997). One study found that teen marijuana consumption rose following state tax increases on beer, indicating that policies targeted at one problem (excessive alcohol consumption) may also affect other problems (youth marijuana consumption; DiNardo and Lemieux 2001). Chou et al. (2004) found that higher cigarette prices stemming from tax hikes reduce smoking but also are associated with higher rates of obesity—again suggesting that policies aimed at correcting some individual failures (smoking) can unintentionally promote other individual failures (obesity).

Rent-Seeking

Beyond unintended consequences, paternalistic policies open up a new area of private activity to special interest and lobbying influence in the legislative context. When policymakers decide which products or technologies should dominate a market, they boost some industries at the expense of others. Consequently, industries affected by paternalistic policies have a strong incentive to shape policies to their own benefit. Yet paternalists often forget that policymaking itself is a political process. Paternalistic policies are not crafted by benevolent, perfectly rational, fully informed bureaucrats. Rather, they are the product of highly contentious political processes in which competing interests collide on a range of issues. The final compromise may be far from the most efficient course of action.

For example, the federal school-lunch program classified pizza as a vegetable, because it contained tomato paste (Tomson 2011). Attempts by the Department of Agriculture to replace pizza with more vegetables were blocked in Congress by legislation attached to a 2012 appropriations bill.[3] The same bill proposed to block the USDA from implementing new guidelines that would require more whole grains in school food while cutting sodium and starchy vegetables like potatoes.

SODA TAXES AS NUDGES

Berkeley's tax on sugary drinks demonstrates the various concerns with the paternalistic government policies aimed at changing consumer behavior. When economists discuss the use of taxes to change behavior, they typically focus on the traditional economic mechanisms: taxes increase the price of a product and consumers react to the higher prices by reducing consumption of that product (see, e.g., Wang et al. 2012). Proponents of taxing "bad" foods like sodas or snacks often justify their policies using this traditional economic argument after complaining that food companies entice consumers to eat unhealthy food by making junk food too cheap (Thompson 2010). Moreover, some health advocates also argue for soda or junk food taxes to raise consumer awareness about the harmful nature of sugary drinks (Oatman 2012).

More recently, some health advocates have begun to argue for taxing "bad" foods by appealing to behavioral economics (Clark 2014). There are several ways in which a soda tax might work as a nudge.[4] First, taxes may act as a reminder to consumers who are often believed to be overwhelmed by the many attributes of food—quality, price, expiration dates, discounts—that they should be choosing healthier options. Most consumers' shopping behavior is believed to be driven by habit, and this automatic behavior can override explicit plans to choose healthier options (Marteau et al. 2012).

Second, taxes may act as a micro-incentive. One of the most striking findings in behavioral economics is that assigning even small costs to particular choices can have extraordinarily large impacts on overall outcomes. For example, one study found that placing junk food in the back of the school cafeteria considerably reduces consumption of junk food (Hanks et al. 2012). Thus, imposing a trivial cost on a particular choice—walking a few extra steps to reach the junk food—may result in a substantial impact on consumers' food choices.

Third, taxation may change consumer behavior by appealing to social norms. For example, the energy analytics company Opower teams up with utility companies to provide feedback to customers on their energy usage and the energy usage of their neighbors (Schultz et al. 2007; Allcott 2011). Efficient customers receive an approval message—a smiley face—on their bill. This social comparison combined with an approval message proved to be effective at nudging utility customers to reduce their energy consumption. The tax may act in a similar fashion by conveying an injunctive norm—the public disapproval of soda consumption.

Ironically, behavioral economics also suggests that appealing to social norms may actually backfire. Consumers who perceive being manipulated or forced into specific choices may react by increasing the undesirable behavior. This is what psychologists call reactance (Brehm and Brehm 1981). For example, Opower had discontinued the use of a frowny face as a disapproval message for the least efficient users after receiving numerous customer complaints (Stern 2013).

The public backlash to New York City's attempt to ban large soda containers is another example of reactance that might also increase soda consumption rather than decrease it (Wansink and Just 2012). For example, one behavioral simulation study examined whether a sugary drink limit would still be effective if larger-sized drinks were converted into bundles of smaller-sized drinks (Wilson et al. 2013). Study participants were offered varying food and drink menus. One menu offered 16 oz, 24 oz, or 32 oz drinks for sale. A second menu offered 16 oz drinks, a bundle of two 12 oz drinks, or a bundle of two 16 oz drinks. A third menu offered only 16 oz drinks for sale. The method involved repeated elicitation of choices, and the instructions did not mention a limit on drink size. Participants bought significantly more ounces of soda with bundles than with varying-sized drinks. Total business revenue was also higher when bundles rather than only small drinks were sold.

Discussion: Berkeley's Sugary Drink Tax

On November 2014, Berkeley, CA, became the first city in the United States to impose a specific tax on sugary drinks (Mandaro 2014). Tax proponents argued for the measure using a mix of traditional and behavioral economic rationales.[5] For example, proponents cited various studies that used the traditional economic framework to estimate how much soda consumption would decrease in response to a higher price. But advocates also viewed the tax and its associated media campaign as instruments to raise public awareness of soda's adverse impact on health.

Specific implementation of the tax is notable for three reasons.[6] First, the tax is imposed on the distributors of sugary drinks and not directly on consumers, though most media outlets referred to it as a sales tax. Under California's constitution, local government cannot impose sales taxes on food on top of taxes already imposed by the state. However, local jurisdictions have the power to impose business license taxes on businesses operating within their limits.[7] Consequently, the city of Berkeley imposed the tax on soda distributors with expectations that they would pass the tax on to consumers (Brockett and Rose 2014).

Second, tax revenues accrue to Berkeley's general fund and are not earmarked for health programs. The designation of the tax revenues was an important issue during the campaign for the tax; tax proponents wanted all revenues to be used by health programs in the city (see Crowley and Hoffer, chapter 6, this volume, for a further discussion of earmarking tax revenue). However, earmarking tax revenues in this manner would have turned it into a special tax as opposed to a general tax whose revenues can be used for any purpose. While both special and general taxes have to be approved by voters, a special tax requires a two-thirds majority approval, whereas the general tax requires only a simple majority. Concerned with a higher approval threshold, the city council proposed the soda tax as a general tax while promising to use all revenues for health programs (Siler 2014). Interestingly, these concerns proved to be groundless, as voters approved the tax by an overwhelming 76 percent majority.

Finally, the sugary drink tax contains numerous exceptions that include exemptions for various drinks, such as fruit juices and milk, that may also have high sugar content. The council justified its exemptions on the grounds that these exceptions provide substantial nutritional value. The tax also exempts small businesses; it only applies to soda deliveries to stores with more than $100,000 in annual revenues.[8]

MICHAEL MARLOW AND SHERZOD ABDUKADIROV

The Unclear Connection between Sugar and Obesity

Proposals for taxing soda presume that soda consumption is a leading source of sugar in the United States. But the Centers for Disease Control and Prevention (CDC) state that the majority of our sugar calories come from food, not beverages. Moreover, the CDC concludes that consumption of added sugars in the United States decreased from 1999–2000 to 2007–2008, primarily because of a reduction in soda consumption (Welsh et al. 2011). The authors state that, although the driving force behind the reversal in the trends in added-sugar consumption is unknown, it is undoubtedly multifactorial and may include rational changes in consumer preferences as well as government efforts to promote healthier diets.

Other research also indicates that sales of full-calorie soft drinks have been declining in part because soda makers are meeting growing consumer demands for more no-calorie and low-calorie options. Evidence on youth consumption trends is particularly enlightening. Between the 2004 and 2009 school years, the beverage industry reduced calories shipped to schools by 90 percent; on a total ounces basis, shipments of full-calorie soft drinks to schools decreased by 97 percent (Wescott et al. 2012). Availability of beverages sold from vending machines and student access to sugar-sweetened beverages has steadily decreased since the 2006–2007 school year (Turner and Chaloupka 2012). Again, it is likely that reasons for this shift are multifactorial.

A recent systematic review of the evidence for an association between sugar-sweetened beverages and risk of obesity also indicates room for caution when it comes to assigning blame for obesity prevalence to soda (Trumbo and Rivers 2014). Sugar-sweetened beverages are the fourth-highest contributor of calories in the diets of the general US population, with grain-based desserts, yeast breads, and chicken and chicken-mixed dishes being the top three contributors. The authors conclude that it remains unclear how sugar-sweetened beverages contribute to caloric intake and, possibly, obesity in a manner that would be different from these top three contributors.

Another study examined whether fructose consumption in the United States has increased sufficiently to be a causal factor in the rise in obesity prevalence (Carden and Carr 2013). Data indicate that total fructose availability in the United States did not increase between 1970 and 2009, and thus, was unlikely to have been a unique causal factor in the increased obesity prevalence. The authors concluded that increased total energy intake due to increased availability of foods providing glucose (primarily as starch in grains) and fat was a significant contributor to increased obesity.

316

Moreover, the connection between sugar and obesity is also not so clear. Nutritionists have recently argued that the evidence is not yet convincing that fructose-containing sugars contribute to weight gain more so than other sources of energy in the diet (Choo et al. 2015). In addition to those fructose-containing sugars, other highly palatable aspects of a Western dietary pattern (refined grains, processed meat, red meat, French fries, etc.) also deserve our attention when it comes to theorizing about what foods are causally related to rising obesity prevalence.

Evidence on Soda Taxes

It is not surprising that the effectiveness of soda taxes remains speculative rather than factual, given the lack of evidence of a causal connection between soda and obesity. Tax proponents widely cite Mexico's experience as evidence that taxation causes a substantial reduction in soda consumption (Colchero et al. 2016). In 2014, Mexico imposed a tax of approximately 10 percent that applied to nondairy and non-alcoholic beverages with added sugar. One study reports a 6 percent average decline in purchases of taxed beverages over 2014 compared to pre-tax trends (Colchero et al. 2016). However, even if soda consumption fell by 6 percent, we do not know what Mexicans consumed instead. The authors admit that they cannot quantify any potential changes in calories and other nutrients purchased or their potential health implications. Given the tenuous causal connection between soda consumption and obesity, it remains unlikely that obesity prevalence will be significantly affected.

Many other studies cast doubt on the effectiveness of soda taxes. One study based on state soft drink sales and excise taxes between 1989 and 2006 finds that increases in soda tax rates moderately decrease soda consumption among children, but have no effect on total caloric intake. Children increased their consumption of other high-calorie beverages in ways that completely offset decreased soda consumption (Fletcher et al. 2010b). A recent study using scanner data at grocery stores looked at the effect of two tax events on soft drink consumption: a 5.5 percent sales tax on soft drinks imposed by the state of Maine in 1991, and a 5 percent sales tax on soft drinks levied in Ohio in 2003 (Colantuoni and Rojas 2015). The authors concluded that neither sales tax had a statistically significant impact on the consumption of soft drinks.

Another study estimates the effects of current soft drink taxes on weight outcomes for the U.S. population. The authors find that a one percentage point increase in soft drink taxes decreases adult BMI by 0.003. The authors concluded that even a 58 percent tax on soda would drop the average BMI by only a trivial 0.16 points (Fletcher et al. 2010a). Another study by the same authors found no evidence that larger tax hikes were any different than smaller tax hikes, reconfirming studies showing little to no effects of current sales tax rates on consumption or obesity (Fletcher et al. 2015).

There is little reason to predict that the Berkeley tax will fare any differently. The tax relies on soda distributors to pass it on to consumers. However, Cawley and Frisvold examined the impact of Berkeley's measure on soda prices and found that only a small fraction of stores passed the tax on to consumers in the manner intended by the city council (Cawley and Frisvold 2015). The vast majority of stores either absorbed the cost of the tax or increased the prices for both diet and regular sodas. Their actions effectively defeat the purpose of the tax to make regular sodas more expensive and to push consumers towards less caloric drinks.

Rent-Seeking

Beyond the questions regarding the effectiveness of soda taxes, there are concerns over the misaligned incentives that policymakers face in using taxes as nudges (Hoffer et al. 2014). Specifically, the incentive to raise revenues lies in direct contradiction with its goal to reduce soda consumption. The goal of the soda tax is to give consumers an additional incentive to choose healthier drinks.

However in its first month, the tax already netted more than $116,000 in revenues.[9] The city expected the measure to bring in around $1.2 million in its first year. In fact, the city council already began apportioning the tax revenues.[10] The city has advanced $500,000 to a newly appointed panel of experts to apportion the revenues to the various health programs. Effectively, the city treats the tax as a source of revenues to finance a variety of programs. Consequently, Berkeley's policymakers have a financial incentive to maintain these tax revenues, despite its purported goal of reducing soda consumption.

The logic of nudges inevitably runs counter to the logic of politics in this case. For the soda tax to work as a nudge, either as a reminder or as a micro-incentive, the tax should be highly visible and cut through the noise of a typical supermarket environment to grab consumers' attention. That is required to make the drink choice salient. Yet, to "reap" the tax revenues, the very same behavioral economic literature suggests the tax should be mostly invisible, based on predictions that consumers underreact to such taxes, thus leading to higher revenues (Chetty et al. 2009).

Berkeley's soda tax is designed to raise revenues. The city imposed the tax on soda distributors, who ultimately decide the degree to which they pass it on to the consumers. Even if the distributors raise soda prices, the increase will be indistinguishable from the usual price volatility of food items. Nothing on the price tag of soda or on a consumer's receipt would indicate that a set part of the cost comes from the tax. One could argue that the less salient tax design is a by-product of constitutional limitations placed by the state on the taxation powers of local governments. Yet the city could easily go around the limitation by posting a sign next to the soda aisle informing consumers of the soda tax. The fact that they chose not to do so suggests their interest is in raising tax revenues rather than improving consumers' choices.

Two other aspects of the soda tax implementation point to it being driven by politics rather than public health. First, the city exempted a number of drinks with high sugar content from the tax. Specifically, the city exempted fruit juices and milk, the drinks that are commonly perceived as "natural," even though sugar has the same impact on weight regardless of its source. The exemptions open the door for political lobbying over what drinks should be considered healthy and which should be exempt from taxation. One need only look at the recent congressional decision to declare pizza a vegetable to see the potential for abuse (Winstead 2011).

Second, the city imposed the tax only on larger stores; the stores with revenues under $100,000 were exempt from the tax. While sparing small businesses is good politics, it hardly serves the needs of consumers who, according to tax advocates, should reduce their soda consumption. There is no theoretical difference in the health impact of sodas purchased from a large store or a small one. If a soda tax were effective in changing consumers' behavior, the small business exemption could have considerably undermined its impact.

Unintended Consequences

Attempts by government to change consumer behavior often backfire. For example, a field study shows that a soda tax led to an initial drop in consumption that was followed by a return to original consumption levels (Wansink et al. 2014). Unexpectedly, the tax also led some consumers to switch to beer—hardly the healthier choice that tax proponents envisioned. Soda taxes have also been shown to steer consumers into consumption of a wide array (twenty-three categories) of other food and beverages (Zhen et al. 2013). A price increase of one half-cent per ounce for sugary drinks reduced caloric intake of those beverages, but subjects quickly compensated by consuming almost half of those calories in substitutes that were often laden with sodium and fat.

Studies in behavioral economics point to several potential unintended consequences. Consumers who reduced their soda consumption as a result of the tax may reward themselves for the "good" choice by indulging in other caloric foods. For example, a study demonstrates that consumers who purchased a meal at Subway, which is perceived as a healthier fast food restaurant, were less likely to select diet soda with their meal compared to consumers who ate at McDonald's (Chandon and Wansink 2007). Similarly, the mere presence of healthier items on the menu leads consumers to purchase more caloric items (Wilcox et al. 2009).

In addition, the nontaxed status of fruit juices and milk may confer a so-called health halo on these drinks, similar to the effect of "low sugar" or "low fat" health claims (Williams 2005; Wansink and Chandon 2006). Consumers tend to interpret such health claims to mean that the food item is healthy and consequently can be consumed in large quantities. As a result, they tend to overconsume such foods, leading to a higher caloric intake. Since fruit juices are frequently as high in sugar as soda drinks, overconsumption of fruit juice may actually increase consumers' caloric intake.

CONCLUSION

Obesity is a serious health problem. But advocates of paternalistic policies overstate the benefits of intervention, even as they understate the costs. Paternalistic policymakers justify policies all too easily on the assumption that they are better informed than the individuals they seek to guide. Government intervention regarding obesity stems from good intentions; as one recent paper puts it, "after all who can question actions intended to improve health?" (Craven et al. 2012, 39). In this chapter, however, we demonstrate that paternalism, no matter how well intentioned, is a poor guide for policy making and can adversely affect obese and nonobese citizens alike.

It is difficult to argue that obesity results from lack of information. Research indicates that the obese understand the health implications of obesity and its link to poor health and lower incomes. Research also demonstrates that employers have incentives to push employees to lose weight; there is no market failure that requires government intervention. The obese hardly need the government to give additional incentives to lose weight, since lack of motivation does not appear to cause obesity. Interventions focusing on steering them away from particular foods or toward more exercise are thus unlikely to provide new information or result in much weight loss. These predictions are consistent with research that shows government interventions have little to no effect on obesity. Unfortunately, on realizing that softer interventions are ineffective, regulators are likely to be tempted to turn to harder paternalism.

Somewhat lost in the public health debate is the reality that people who know they are overweight also experience strong personal incentives to lose weight. Individuals' growing demand for weight reduction is evidenced by the market for diet books, health foods, weight-loss centers, exercise equipment, athletic clubs, and other independent weight-control methods. Paternalists appear to disregard market attempts to deal with obesity, since its prevalence offers them latitude to overstate the effectiveness of interventions. Furthermore, this disregard coheres with the paternalistic belief that reduction of obesity prevalence is unlikely sans government intervention.

The case of Berkeley's soda tax is illuminating. The city council advanced the tax as a way to nudge consumers toward less caloric beverages. However, the policy's effectiveness is questionable. The policy is justified based on two assertions. The first assertion is that consumption of sugary drinks causes obesity. The second is that taxing sugary drinks will reduce obesity. Both assertions are unfounded. Little conclusive evidence links sugary drink consumption to obesity. Furthermore, taxing sugary drinks may not reduce soda consumption. Even when it does, consumers frequently switch from soda to other highly caloric foods and drinks. Consequently, a soda tax is unlikely to reduce caloric intake or have any impact on obesity.

Another important issue is the government's misalignment of incentives when it attempts to use taxes to manipulate consumers' choices. The primary goal of the tax as a nudge is to ensure that people switch to other, less caloric drinks, and in doing so, citizens will not actually pay the tax. Yet the tax represents a substantial source of revenue, which the city council has already begun to apportion to finance various programs. As constituencies build up around these programs, the city may experience increasing incentives or pressures to protect soda tax revenues, to the possible detriment of reducing soda consumption.

The way that the city implemented the tax reveals which incentive wins out in the end. For the tax to work as a nudge and incentivize consumers to change their soda consumption habits, it should be highly visible and salient. Yet the city council imposed the tax on soda distributors rather than on consumers and took no steps to make the tax visible and salient to consumers at the point of purchase. Consequently, the tax seems designed to raise revenues rather than change consumer behavior. The tax's numerous exemptions for certain businesses and categories of drinks also open the door for further political manipulation of the intended goal of the tax—reduced consumption of sugar—and again supports our view that the use of taxes as nudges is not only ineffective but may in fact be counterproductive to public health.

NOTES

1. See, for example, Camerer et al. (2003), O'Donoghue and Rabin (2003), Thaler and Sunstein (2008), Congdon (2011).

2. This is in fact a crucial assumption on the part of paternalists. The paternalist assumes that he or she is better positioned than the subject to evaluate what is good for the subject. Hence, the paternalist substitutes his or her own judgment for the subject's.

3. Consolidated and Further Continuing Appropriations Act of 2012, H.R. 2112, 112th Cong. (2012).

4. For a review of behavioral intervention mechanisms, see Lashawn Richburg-Hayes et al. (2014a,b).

5. The website of tax proponents lists the various reasons to support the tax. See "Frequently Asked Questions," *Berkeley vs. Big Soda*, n.d., http://www.berkeleyvsbigsoda.com/faq.

6. City of Berkeley (2014).

7. Public Health Law & Policy (2011).

8. City of Berkeley (2014).

9. See http://www.mercurynews.com/my-town/ci_28141086/berkeley-soda-tax-first-months -take-116-000.

10. See http://www.berkeleyside.com/2015/05/18/berkeley-soda-tax-raises-116000-revenue-in -first-month/.

REFERENCES

Adda, Jerome, and Francesca Cornaglia. 2006. "Taxes, Cigarette Consumption, and Smoking Intensity." *American Economic Review* 96 (4): 1013–28.

Allcott, Hunt. 2011. "Social Norms and Energy Conservation." *Journal of Public Economics* 95 (9–10): 1082–95.

Anderson, Michael L., and David A. Matsa. 2011. "Are Restaurants Really Supersizing America?" *American Economic Journal: Applied Economics* 3 (1): 152–88.

Ariely, Dan. 2008. *Predictably Irrational: The Hidden Forces That Shape Our Decisions*. New York: HarperCollins.

Ayyagari, Padmaja, Partha Deb, Jason Fletcher, William T. Gallo, and Jody L. Sindelar. 2009. "Sin Taxes: Do Heterogeneous Responses Undercut Their Value?" NBER Working Paper 15124, National Bureau of Economic Research, Cambridge, MA.

Baum, Charles L., II, and William F. Ford. 2004. "The Wage Effects of Obesity: A Longitudinal Study." *Health Economics* 13 (9): 885–99.

Bhattacharya, Jay, and M. Kate Bundorf. 2009. "The Incidence of the Healthcare Costs of Obesity." *Journal of Health Economics* 28 (3): 649–58.

Bleich, Sara N., Y. Claire Wang, Youfa Wang, and Steven L. Gormaker. 2009. "Increasing Consumption of Sugar-Sweetened Beverages among US Adults: 1988–1994 to 1999–2004." *American Journal of Clinical Nutrition* 89 (1): 372–81.

Brehm, Sharon S., and Jack W. Brehm. 1981. *Psychological Reactance: A Theory of Freedom and Control.* New York: Academic.

Brockett, Jennifer, and Loring Rose. 2014. "Berkeley's Measure D: What Distributors, Restaurants and Retailers Need to Know about the Berkeley 'Sugar Tax.'" *Hospitality Law Blog,* November 21. http://www.dwthospitalitylaw.com/2014/11/articles/food-beverage/berkeleys-measure-d-what-distributors-restaurants-and-retailers-need-to-know-about-the-berkeley-sugar-tax/.

Brownell, Kelly D., Thomas Farley, Walter Willett, Barry Popkin, Frank Chaloupka, Joseph Thompson, and David S. Ludwig. 2009. "The Public Health and Economic Benefits of Taxing Sugar-Sweetened Beverages." *New England Journal of Medicine* 361 (16): 1601.

Buckley, Francis. H. 2009. *Fair Governance: Paternalism and Perfectionism.* New York: Oxford University Press.

Camerer, Colin, Samuel Issacharoff, George Loewenstein, Ted O'Donoghue, and Matthew Rabin. 2003. "Regulation for Conservatives: Behavioral Economics and the Case for 'Asymmetric Paternalism.'" *University of Pennsylvania Law Review* 151 (3): 1211–54.

Carden, Trevor J., and Timothy P. Carr. 2013. "Food Availability of Glucose and Fat, but Not Fructose, Increased in the US between 1970 and 2009: Analysis of the USDA Food Availability Data System." *Nutrition Journal* 12: 1–8.

Cawley, John. 2004. "The Impact of Obesity on Wages." *Journal of Human Resources* 39 (2): 451–74.

——. 2010. "The Economics of Childhood Obesity." *Health Affairs* 29 (3): 364–71.

Cawley, John, and David Frisvold. 2015. "The Incidence of Taxes on Sugar-Sweetened Beverages: The Case of Berkeley, California." NBER Working Paper 21465, National Bureau of Economic Research, Cambridge, MA.

Cawley, John, and Chad Meyerhoefer. 2010. "The Medical Care Costs of Obesity: An Instrumental Variables Approach." NBER Working Paper 16467, National Bureau of Economic Research, Cambridge, MA.

Chandon, Pierre, and Brian Wansink. 2007. "The Biasing Health Halos of Fast-Food Restaurant Health Claims: Lower Calorie Estimates and Higher Side-Dish Consumption Intentions." *Journal of Consumer Research* 34 (3): 301–14.

Chetty, Raj, Adam Looney, and Kory Kroft. 2009. "Salience and Taxation: Theory and Evidence." *American Economic Review* 99 (4): 1145–77.

Choo, V. L., V. Ha, and J. L. Sievenpiper. 2015. "Sugars and Obesity: Is It the Sugars or the Calories?" *Nutrition Bulletin* 40 (2): 88–96.

Chou, Shin-Yi, Michael Grossman, and Henry Saffer. 2004. "An Economic Analysis of Adult Obesity: Results from the Behavioral Risk Factor Surveillance System." *Journal of Health Economics* 23 (3): 565–87.

City of Berkeley. 2014. "Measure D—Impose a General Tax on Distributors of Sugar-Sweetened Beverages." *Election Information: 2014 Ballot Measures,* September 2. http://www.cityof berkeley.info/Clerk/Elections/Election__2014_Ballot_Measure_Page.aspx.

Clark, Christopher James. 2014. "Sugar Taxation: A Healthy Nudge in the Right Direction?" *Huffington Post UK,* July 28. http://www.huffingtonpost.co.uk/christopher-james-clark /sugar-taxation_b_5624785.html.

Colantuoni, Francesca, and Christian Rojas. 2015. "The Impact of Soda Sales Taxes on Consumption: Evidence from Scanner Data." *Contemporary Economic Policy* 33 (4): 714–34.

Colchero, M. Arantxa, Barry M. Popkin, Juan A. Rivera, and Shu Wen Ng. 2016. "Beverage Purchases from Stores in Mexico under the Excise Tax on Sugar Sweetened Beverages: Observational Study." *BMJ* 352: h6704.

Congdon, William J. 2011. *Policy and Choice: Public Finance through the Lens of Behavioral Economics.* Washington, DC: Brookings Institution Press.

Courtamanche, Charles, and Art Carden. 2008. "The Skinny on Big Box Retailing: Wal-Mart, Warehouse Clubs, and Obesity." Mimeo, October 31, Department of Economics, University of North Carolina, Greensboro. http://www.unc.edu/the/archives/courtemanche.pdf.

Craven, Barrie M., Michael L. Marlow, and Alden F. Shiers. 2012. "Fat Taxes and Other Interventions Won't Cure Obesity." *Economic Affairs* 32 (2): 36–40.

DiNardo, John, and Thomas Lemieux. 2001. "Alcohol, Marijuana, and American Youth: The Unintended Consequences of Government Regulation." *Journal of Health Economics* 20 (6): 991–1010.

Dixon, John B. 2010. "The Effect of Obesity on Health Outcomes." *Molecular and Cellular Endocrinology* 316: 104–8.

Elbel, Brian, Rogan Kersh, Vicotria L. Brescoll, and L. Beth Dixon. 2009. "Calorie Labeling and Food Choices: A First Look at the Effects on Low-Income People in New York City." *Health Affairs* 28 (6): 1110–21.

Falba, Tracy A., and Susan H. Busch. 2005. "Survival Expectations of the Obese: Is Excess Mortality Reflected in Perceptions?" *Obesity Research* 13 (4): 754–61.

Farrelly, Matthew C., Christina T. Nimsch, Andrew Hyland, and Michael Cummings. 2004. "The Effects of Higher Cigarette Prices on Tar and Nicotine Consumption in a Cohort of Adult Smokers." *Health Economics* 13 (1): 49–58.

Finkelstein, Eric A., Derek S. Brown, and W. Douglas Eva. 2008. "Do Obese Persons Comprehend Their Personal Health Risks?" *American Journal of Health Behavior* 32 (5): 508–16.

Finkelstein, Eric A., Kiersten L. Strombot, Nadine L. Chan, and James Krieger. 2011. "Mandatory Menu Labeling in One Fast-Food Chain in King County, Washington." *American Journal of Preventive Medicine* 40 (2): 122–27.

Fletcher, Jason M., David E. Frisvold and Nathan Tefft. 2010a. "Can Soft Drink Taxes Reduce Population Weight?" *Contemporary Economic Policy* 28 (1): 23–35.

———. 2010b. "The Effects of Soft Drink Taxes on Child and Adolescent Consumption and Weight Outcomes." *Journal of Public Economics* 94 (11–12): 967–74.

———. 2015. "Non-Linear Effects of Soda Taxes on Consumption and Weight Outomes." *Health Economics* 34 (5): 566–82.

Hanks, Andrew S., David Just, Laura Smith, and Brian Wansink. 2012. "Healthy Convenience: Nudging Students toward Healthier Choices in the Lunchroom." *Journal of Public Health* 34 (3): 370–76.

Hoffer, Adam J., Rejeana Gvillo, William F. Shughart II, and Michael D. Thomas. 2015. "Regressive Effects: Causes and Consequences of Selective Consumption Taxation." Working Paper, Mercatus Center at George Mason University, Arlington, VA.

Hoffer, Adam J., William F. Shughart, and Michael D. Thomas. 2014. "Sin Taxes and Sindustry: Revenue, Paternalism, and Political Interest." *Independent Review* 19 (1): 47–64.

Kropski, Jonathan A., Paul H. Keckley, and Gordon L. Jensen. 2008. "School-Based Obesity Prevention Programs: An Evidence-Based Review." *Obesity* 16 (2008): 1009–18.

Lakdawalla, Darius, and Tomas Philipson. 2009. "The Growth of Obesity and Technological Change." *Economics and Human Biology* 7 (3): 283–93.

Larson, Nicole I., Mary T. Storey, and Melissa C. Nelson. 2009. "Neighborhood Environments: Disparities in Access to Healthy Foods in the US." *American Journal of Preventive Medicine* 36 (1): 74–81.

Malik, Vasanti S., Matthias B. Schulze, and Frank B. Hu. 2006. "Intake of Sugar-Sweetened Beverages and Weight Gain: A Systematic Review." *American Journal of Clinical Nutrition* 84 (2): 274–88.

Mandaro, Laura. 2014. "Nation's First Soda Tax Is Passed." *USA Today*, November 5. http://www.usatoday.com/story/news/nation-now/2014/11/05/berkeley-passes-soda-tax/18521923/.

Marteau, Theresa M., Gareth J. Hollands, and Paul C. Fletcher. 2012. "Changing Human Behavior to Prevent Disease: The Importance of Targeting Automatic Processes." *Science* 337: 1492–95.

McKenzie, Richard B. 2009. *Predictably Rational? In Search of Defenses for Rational Behavior in Economics.* London: Springer.

Oatman, Maddie. 2012. "Soda: Ban It? Nah. Tax It? Yep." *Mother Jones,* June 18. http://www.mother jones.com/environment/2012/06/soda-sugar-tax-richmond.

O'Donoghue, Ted, and Matthew Rabin. 2003. "Studying Optimal Paternalism, Illustrated by a Model of Sin Taxes." *American Economic Review* 93 (2): 186–91.

Philipson, Tomas J., and Richard A. Posner. 2003. "The Long-Run Growth in Obesity as a Function of Technological Change." *Perspectives in Biology and Medicine* 46 (3): 87–107.

Public Health Law & Policy. 2011. "Local Taxes on Sugar-Sweetened Beverages in California: Legal Considerations and Procedural Requirements." Oakland, CA. http://changelabsolutions.org /sites/default/files/Local-Taxes-SSBs-CA_Legal_Memo-20130513.pdf.

Richburg-Hayes, Lashawn, Caitlin Anzelone, Nadine Dechausay, Saugato Datta, Alexandra Fiorillo, Louis Potok, and Matthew Darling, John Balz. 2014a. *Behavioral Economics and Social Policy: Designing Innovative Solutions for Programs Supported by the Administration for Children and Families.* Report 2014-16a. Washington, DC: Office of Planning, Research and Evaluation. http://www.acf.hhs.gov/sites/default/files/opre/bias_final_full_report _rev4_15_14.pdf.

———. 2014b. *Behavioral Economics and Social Policy: Designing Innovative Solutions for Programs Supported by the Administration for Children and Families, Technical Supplement: Commonly Applied Behavioral Interventions.* Report 2014-16b. Washington, DC: Office of Planning, Research and Evaluation http://www.acf.hhs.gov/sites/default/files/opre/bias_2014_report _technical_supplement.pdf.

Rizzo, Mario J., and Douglas G. Whitman. 2009. "The Knowledge Problem of New Paternalism." *Brigham Young University Law Review* 4: 905–68.

Ruhm, Christopher. 2010. "Understanding Overeating and Obesity." NBER Working Paper 16149, National Bureau of Economic Research, Cambridge, MA.

Schultz, P. Wesley, Jessica M. Nolan, Robert B. Cialdini, Noah J. Goldstein, and Vladas Griskevicius. 2007. "The Constructive, Destructive, and Reconstructive Power of Social Norms." *Psychological Science* 18 (5): 429–34.

Sharma, M. 2006. "School-Based Interventions for Childhood and Adolescent Obesity." *Obesity Reviews* 7 (3): 261–69.

Siler, Charles. 2014. "Berkeley Puts Sugar Tax on November Ballot; Could Be First City in Country to Take on Big Soda." *Berkeleyside,* July 2. http://www.berkeleyside.com/2014/07/02 /berkeley-puts-sugar-tax-on-november-ballot-could-be-first-in-country-to-take-on-big -soda/.

Stern, Mark Joseph. 2013. "A Little Guilt, a Lot of Energy Savings." *Slate,* March 1. http://www.slate .com/articles/technology/the_efficient_planet/2013/03/opower_using_smiley_faces_and _peer_pressure_to_save_the_planet.html.

Thaler, Richard H., and Cass R. Sunstein. 2008. *Nudge: Improving Decisions about Health, Wealth, and Happiness.* New Haven, CT: Yale University Press.

Thompson, Derek. 2010. "Why Is American Food So Cheap?" *Atlantic,* January 11. http://www .theatlantic.com/business/archive/2010/01/why-is-american-food-so-cheap/33259/.

Thun, Michael J., Cathy A. Lally, John T. Flannery, Eugenia E. Calle, W. Dana Flanders, and Clark W. Heath Jr. 1997. "Cigarette Smoking and Changes in the Histopathology of Lung Cancer." *Journal of the National Cancer Institute* 89 (21): 1580–86.

Tomson, Bill. 2011. "Lawmakers Step into Food Fight over Pizza." *Wall Street Journal*, November 18. https://www.wsj.com/articles/SB10001424052970204517204577044533506200916.

Trumbo, Paula R., and Crystal R. Rivers. 2014. "Systematic Review of the Evidence for an Association between Sugar-Sweetened Beverage Consumption and Risk of Obesity." *Nutrition Reviews* 72 (9): 566–74.

Turner, Lindsey, and Frank J. Chaloupka. 2012. "Encouraging Trends in Student Access to Competitive Beverages in U.S. Public Elementary Schools, 2006–2007 to 2010–2011." *Archives of Pediatrics and Adolescent Medicine* 166 (7): 673–75.

Tversky, Amos, and Daniel Kahneman. 1981. "The Framing of Decisions and the Psychology of Choice." *Science* 211: 453–58.

Van Hook, Jennifer, and Claire E. Altman. 2012. "Competitive Food Sales in Schools and Childhood Obesity: A Longitudinal Study." *Sociology of Education* 85 (1) 23–39.

Vartanian, Lenny R., Marlene B. Schartz, and Kelly D. Brownell. 2007. "Effects of Soft Drink Consumption on Nutrition and Health: A Systematic Review and Meta-Analysis." *American Journal of Public Health* 97 (4): 667–75.

Wallinga, David. 2010. "Agricultural Policy and Childhood Obesity: A Food Systems and Public Health Commentary." *Health Affairs* 29 (3): 405–10.

Wang, Y. Claire, Pamela Coxson, Yu-Ming Shen, Lee Goldman, and Kirsten Bibbins-Domingo. 2012. "A Penny-per-Ounce Tax on Sugar-Sweetened Beverages Would Cut Health and Cost Burdens of Diabetes." *Health Affairs* 31 (1): 199–207.

Wansink, Brian, and Pierre Chandon. 2006. "Can 'Low-Fat' Nutrition Labels Lead to Obesity?" *Journal of Marketing Research* 43 (4): 605–17.

Wansink, Brian, Andrew S. Hanks, and David R. Just. 2014. "From Coke to Coors: A Field Study of a Fat Tax and Its Unintended Consequences." Scholarly Paper, SSRN, Rochester, NY. http://papers.ssrn.com/abstract=2473623.

Wansink, Brian, and David Just. 2012. "How Bloomberg's Soft Drink Ban Will Backfire on NYC Public Health." *Atlantic*, June 14. http://www.theatlantic.com/health/archive/2012/06/how-bloombergs-soft-drink-ban-will-backfire-on-nyc-public-health/258501/.

Welsh, J. A., A. J. Sharma, L. Grellinger, and M. B. Vos. 2011. "Consumption of Added Sugars Is Decreasing in the United States." *American Journal of Clinical Nutrition* 94 (3): 726–34.

Wescott, R.F., B. M. Fitzpatrick, and E. Phillips. 2012. "Industry Self-Regulation to Improve Student Health: Quantifying Changes in Beverage Shipments to Schools." *American Journal of Public Health* 103 (10): 1928–35.

Wilcox, Keith, Beth Vallen, Lauren Block, Gavan J. Fitzsimmons. 2009. "Vicarious Goal Fulfillment: When the Mere Presence of a Healthy Option Leads to an Ironically Indulgent Decision." *Journal of Consumer Research* 36 (3): 380–93.

Williams, Peter. 2005. "Consumer Understanding and Use of Health Claims for Foods." *Nutrition Reviews* 63 (7): 256–64.

Wilson, Brent M., Stephanie Stolarz-Fantino, and Edmund Fantino. 2013. "Regulating the Way to Obesity: Unintended Consequences of Limiting Sugary Drink Sizes." *PLoS ONE* 8 (4): e61081. doi:10.1371/journal.pone.0061081.

Winstead, Lizz. 2011. "Is Pizza a Vegetable? Well, Congress Says So." *Guardian*, November 18. http://www.theguardian.com/commentisfree/cifamerica/2011/nov/18/pizza-vegetable-congress-says-so.

Zhao, Zhenxiang, and Robert Kaestner. 2010. "Effects of Urban Sprawl on Obesity." *Journal of Health Economics* 29 (6): 779–87.

Zhen, C., E. A. Finkelstein., J. M. Nonnemaker, S. A. Karns, and J. E. Todd. 2013. "Predicting the Effects of Sugar-Sweetened Beverage Taxes on Food and Beverage Demand in a Large Demand System." *American Journal of Agricultural Economics* 96 (4): 1070–83.

CHAPTER 15
Prohibition by Price: Cigarette Taxes and Unintended Consequences

MICHAEL LAFAIVE
Morey Fiscal Policy Initiative, Mackinac Center for Public Policy

T he reader would be hard pressed today to find many souls in the United States willing to defend the country's "noble experiment" in alcohol prohibition. Ratification of the Eighteenth Amendment, which took effect in 1920, was supposed to mean that "Hell will be forever for rent," as the Rev. Billy Sunday once famously preached at a fake funeral for John Barleycorn, a fictional representation of alcohol. It was not to be.

People still had a strong preference for alcohol consumption despite a national edict against its manufacture and distribution. Consumers were willing to break the law to obtain the product, and crime syndicates—large and small—were happy to provide it for a profit. Individuals made their own alcohol, visited underground businesses known as speakeasies that would sell alcohol to them, or made more creative arrangements to obtain the product. The Twenty-first Amendment repealed Prohibition in 1933.

Policymakers were taught an important lesson but a limited one. Prohibition of popular products will lead to a raft of unintended consequences that may undermine laudable health and economic goals. Governments around the country no longer work to prevent the manufacture and distribution of alcohol. They do, however, work to reduce the negative consequences associated with certain products by imposing so-called sin taxes. In fact, they did so even before the alcohol prohibition experiment. Imposing excise taxes raises the price of consumption (the sin), which—as both theory and evidence tell us— reduces consumption. This is the logic behind high taxes on tobacco products, particularly cigarettes.

Between January 1, 2005, and December 31, 2013, state governments and Washington, DC, raised excise taxes on cigarettes seventy-two times (Orzechowski and Walker 2014). These increases do not include the 61¢ increase (to $1.00) imposed by the federal government in 2009[1] or those imposed by cities, townships, counties, or other taxing jurisdictions (US Department of the Treasury, Alcohol and Tobacco Tax and Trade Bureau 2010). Nationwide, 602 local units imposed some sort of excise tax on cigarettes through fiscal year 2014 (Orzechowski and Walker 2014).

To be clear, the number and size of such tax increases does not constitute prohibition. They do not prevent the legal purchase of cigarettes. The title of this chapter is intended to underscore the fact that taxes help facilitate illegal activity in much the same way that actual prohibition does. In fact, prohibition is merely "the ultimate tax," as Gary Anderson (1997, 171) wrote in *Taxing Choice,* the predecessor to this book:

> The sin is first subjected to a tax; sometime later this tax is increased to prohibitive levels; and finally, the same government institutes an outright prohibition directed against the activity in question.

Due in large part to tax-induced price increases, an illicit trade in cigarettes has developed, which significantly parallels the problems of the Prohibition era. Today's cigarette market features massive amounts of tax evasion through illegal distribution (smuggling); high risks of theft and violence; adulterated products, such as "loosies" and "roll-your-own;" and corruption, among other issues.

In effect, the nation's cigarette market is experiencing prohibition by price, whereby the product remains legal, but the legal purchase of it is increasingly difficult. Likewise, cigarettes are growing in profit-earning potential for dealers of illicit goods.

Because different units of government—especially the states—choose different cigarette excise tax levels, opportunities exist to arbitrage price differences for profit. That is, individuals may buy cigarettes in low-tax states and then transport them to high-tax states for personal use or for sale and distribution. The tax-induced difference between the cigarettes, minus transportation and other costs of doing business (including taking steps to avoid detection), represent profit (or savings) to those who smuggle or transport cigarettes across such taxing jurisdictions.

Not all tax avoidance is evasion. Such states as Minnesota permit their citizens to acquire a small number of cigarettes from other taxing jurisdictions for personal consumption. Moving a carton of cigarettes from North Dakota to Minnesota represents legal avoidance until the number of cigarettes moved into the state violates Minnesota's de minimis limits of one carton per month (State of Minnesota, Department of Revenue 2013, 2).

Michigan, in contrast, has a zero tolerance policy. One cigarette brought in from Indiana, Ohio, Wisconsin, or Canada is illegal and would qualify as a smuggled product. The evasion-avoidance description is one reason the term "diversion" is used periodically in the literature to describe cross-border flows of cigarettes.

To what extent are cigarettes in the United States diverted from legal channels? To what degree do consumers knowingly engage in tax evasion or avoidance, and how do they do it? Scholars have tried to answer such questions, and they have come up with a range of answers depending on the techniques they use and the political entities they study.

PAST RESEARCH SHOWS SUBSTANTIAL TAX AVOIDANCE

For the most part, scholars have used three methods of estimating the pervasiveness of tax avoidance and smuggling: ask people about their behavior, observe their behavior, and look at evidence of tax avoidance in the legal marketplace.

Regardless of method used, however, the conclusions point to three general facts (table 1). First, smuggling and avoidance does occur. Second, cigarettes are transported over distances short and long in the pursuit of avoiding higher taxes. And third, anywhere from 4 percent to 76.2 percent of cigarettes are bought and sold with the goal of avoiding higher taxes or profiting from providing lower-taxed cigarettes.

Population Surveys

The most straightforward way to estimate tax avoidance is to ask people about their habits. For example, 19 percent of respondents in a study involving the state of New York confessed to always buying their smokes on Indian reservations,

Table 1. Estimates of Cigarette Tax Avoidance, Expressed in Percentages of Tax Stamps, Cigarettes, Packages of Cigarettes, or Consumers

Estimates of Avoidance	Methods Used to Make Estimate	Reference
4.5 percent of stamps showed tax stamp from Virginia; 10.6 percent were counterfeit	Examine tax stamps on 830 cigarette purchases made in New York, looking for counterfeit or out-of-state stamps	Silver et al. (2015)
8.5 percent of cigarettes smoked (net) were purchased in another jurisdiction.	Determine market share of avoidance and evasion by comparing the difference between reported smoking rates and legal sales	National Research Council (2015)
19 percent of consumers surveyed sought tax avoidance	Ask survey respondents in New York State how often they purchase from Indian reservations	DeCicca et al. (2014)
20–21 percent of packs owned by subjects may have been acquired outside participants' home state	Classify unopened packs sent in by smokers as taxed or untaxed by smokers' home jurisdiction	Fix et al. (2013)
4.1–18.7 percent of smokers acknowledged buying cigarettes in other jurisdictions	Examine smokers' acknowledgments of cross-border purchases in US Census Bureau surveys	DeCicca et al. (2010)
13–25 percent of smokers (nationally) and up to 63 percent in Washington, DC, buy in other jurisdictions	Determine percentage of smokers in metropolitan areas who buy cigarettes across taxing jurisdictions based on estimates of cigarette demand	Lovenheim (2008)
4 percent of smokers will cross a state border to purchase cigarettes	Estimate casual smuggling based on surveys of purchasing behavior reveal that smokers will travel 2.7 miles to save a dollar	Chiou and Muehlegger (2008)
34 percent of smokers shop in untaxed/low tax venue	Survey smokers by telephone to explore patterns for purchases	Hyland et al. (2005)
30.5–42.1 percent of packs are trafficked across a jurisdiction	Examine discarded packs in five northeastern cities	Davis et al. (2013)
76.2 percent of packs avoided state and local tax through an absent or counterfeit stamp	Examine discarded packs in South Bronx to calculate number of cigarettes that avoided city and state tax	Kurti et al. (2012)
15 percent of packs were without a stamp; went up to 24 percent after tax increase	Examine discarded packs in New York, before and after a tax increase, looking for packs without a stamp	Chernick and Merriman (2011)

Table 1. (*continued*)

Estimates of Avoidance	Methods Used to Make Estimate	Reference
29 percent of packs in Chicago area bore the Indiana tax stamp; only 25 percent carried the city tax stamp	Examine discarded packs in Chicago for evidence of out-of-jurisdiction stamps	Merriman (2010)
12.7 percent of cigarettes in 2001 obtained through avoidance and evasion	Compute difference between reported smoking rates and sales	Stehr (2005)

Source: Author's compilation.

which do not levy state taxes (DeCicca et al. 2014). Another group of researchers, who asked smokers to mail them a package of their unopened cigarettes, found that 20 percent of the packs returned to them in 2009 "were classified as untaxed by the participants," while the number for 2010 was 21 percent (Fix et al. 2013). In a working paper published by the National Bureau of Economic Research, DeCicca et al. (2010, table 2) drew on data from the 2003 and 2006–2007 "Tobacco Use Supplement to the Current U.S. Population Survey." They found that in 2006–2007, some 18.7 percent of respondents in Vermont and 18.5 percent of them in Washington, DC, admitted to cross-border purchases. The figures are 13.7 percent for Maryland and 4.1 percent for New York for this period.

Finally, yet another survey, this one of 3,602 smokers in the United States in 2001, determined that 34 percent of respondents "regularly purchase from a low or untaxed venue" (Hyland et al. 2005, 86). A "venue" could mean an Indian reservation or another state or country. The study's authors also noted that one of "the strongest predictors of purchasing less expensive cigarettes" was "living within 40 miles of a place with a lower cigarette excise tax." (Hyland et al. 2005, 90). Of those responding to the survey from Binghamton and Johnson City in New York State, 66 percent (240) said they purchased lower-priced cigarettes elsewhere—most likely in Pennsylvania, which is only miles away (Hyland et al. 2005, 89).

Examining Discarded Cigarette Packs

Since people are not always trustworthy or reliable when talking about their habits, a second approach of estimating tax avoidance is to examine their behavior. One way of doing this is to collect and analyze discarded cigarette packs.

In one report, Davis et al. (2013) collected and examined discarded cigarette packages in Boston, New York, Philadelphia, Providence, RI, and Washington, DC. By looking at each package, the researchers identified tax stamps that specify the origin of the cigarettes.

The authors determined that among the five cities, 30.5–42.1 percent of the discarded packs were moved through illegal trafficking. The authors also estimate that these cities lose between $680 million and $729 million annually as a result of illicit trafficking (Davis et al. 2013, 1).

Of the study's city-specific numbers, two stand out. More than 75 percent of discarded packs collected in Providence, RI, originated from Massachusetts. The dataset used by the authors includes 2011 excise tax rates. At that time, Massachusetts maintained a tax rate of $2.51 per pack, while Rhode Island's rate was $3.46 per pack. Of those packs collected in Washington, DC, 50 percent came from Virginia, and 32 percent from Maryland (Davis et al. 2013, 3).

A more narrowly focused study looked at New York City, using discarded cigarette packs to measure smuggling rates in the city. Merriman and Chernick (2013, 8) collected discarded packs in thirty city Census tracts—once before a 2008 state excise tax increase of $1.25 and then three times after it.

They found that before the hike, 15 percent of discarded packs had no tax stamp, but afterward, this number leapt to 24 percent. The authors also argue that "tax avoidance may be higher in poorer areas of NYC neighborhoods." The degree to which a relationship exists between poverty and smuggling is quantified this way: "a one standard deviation increase in poverty rates impl[ies] a five percentage point increase in avoidance rates" (Merriman and Chernick 2013, 11, 20; quote is from p. 27).

An even more focused study looked at the South Bronx, a poor area in the city. This study collected discarded cigarette packs throughout the area to estimate the percentage that had been taxed. Kurti et al. (2012, 138) found that "76.2 percent of cigarette packs collected avoided the combined New York City and State tax." Almost 58 percent were not taxed at all. The authors' conclusion was that poor areas of the United States may have higher tax evasion and avoidance rates compared to other locations.

Moving away from the Northeast, a 2010 study used discarded packs collected from Chicago's streets in 2007. It concluded that 29 percent of the packs collected in the city bore the tax stamp of Indiana (Merriman 2010, 69). The report also found that only 36 percent of those discarded cigarette packages bore the tax stamp of Cook County, while only 25 percent bore the tax stamp of the city of Chicago. (Both the county and the city impose additional excise taxes on cigarettes.) In other words, "Chicago littered packs were slightly more likely to have an Indiana stamp than a Chicago stamp" (Merriman 2010, 69–70).

Note that these discarded packages in Chicago were collected before the most recent cigarette excise tax increases by state, county, and city governments. Cook County hiked its cigarette excise tax in 2013 by $1 to $3 per pack,[2] and Chicago hiked its cigarette tax in 2014 by 50 cents.[3] Also raising its cigarette excise tax was the state of Illinois, which had lifted its excise tax in 2012, by $1 (Orzechowski and Walker 2014, 10). In addition, two cities in Cook County also mandate municipal-level taxes: Evanston and Cicero imposed excise taxes on cigarettes of 50¢ and 16¢, respectively (Boonn 2016).

Examining Retail Shops

Another approach to estimating tax avoidance, also measuring behavior, is to look at the prevalence of counterfeit tax stamps in retail settings.

In an attempt to quantify how many cigarette packs are sold illegally in retail stores, an investigative team made 830 purchases of cigarettes in 92 neighborhoods, at 80 subway stops (across five boroughs of New York City) and in twelve retail areas with bus or train access to Staten Island (Silver et al. 2015, 1). The team found that more than 15 percent of cigarette packs bought had either out-of-state or counterfeit stamps, the latter comprising 10.6 percent of the total. Of the 125 packs with out-of-state or counterfeit stamps, 29.6 percent had a tax stamp from Virginia, while the other 70.4 percent bore counterfeit stamps designed to replicate those used by the city or state of New York (Silver et al. 2015, 2).

Statistical Techniques Comparing Smoking Rates to Legal Paid Sales

Last, there are statistical estimates that scholars make using different measuring techniques. One of the most recent—published by the National Research Council and Institute for Medicine in 2015—involved comparing estimated smoking rates to legal paid sales. The difference between the two must be explained, and the authors attributed the difference to tax avoidance and evasion. Their estimate found that 8.5 percent of cigarettes nationwide are diverted (National Research Council 2015, 3).

My colleague, Ball State University economist Todd Nesbit, and I have used the same technique in a larger statistical model to measure smuggling rates since 2008. The Institute for Medicine and National Research Council used our Mackinac Center research estimates to calculate a national smuggling rate of 13.5 percent (National Research Council 2015).

A third study using a residual method was published in 2005 and concluded that that between 59 and 85 percent of declines in legal paid sales of cigarettes may be explained by tax avoidance and evasion. It also estimated that by 2001, 12.7 percent of cigarettes were being purchased without payment of state taxes (Stehr 2005, 294, 295).

In 2008, a Stanford professor used micro-data on consumption of cigarettes from the Current Population Survey Tobacco Supplement to estimate cigarette demand, from which he determined the estimated percentage of smokers in metropolitan areas who purchase cigarettes across jurisdictional boundaries. His estimates suggested that nationwide, the percentage of cigarette consumers who smuggle ranges between 13 percent and 25 percent.

PARALLELS WITH PROHIBITION

In 2002, Michael Bloomberg, then mayor of New York, signed into law a measure increasing the city's excise tax to $1.50 a pack. He said at the time, "This may be the most important measure my administration takes to save people's lives." He added that he viewed the hike not as a revenue initiative so much as a public health one. "If it were totally up to me, I would raise the cigarette tax so high the revenues from it would go to zero" (quoted in Cooper 2002, n.p.).

As Bloomberg's comments suggest, excise taxes may for practical purposes make cigarettes cost prohibitive. The results include many of the attendant consequences of the alcohol prohibition experiment of the Progressive Era.

In simple theoretical terms, a tax-induced price increase should move buyers upward on the demand curve, reducing the quantity of cigarettes demanded. This theory is supported by empirical evidence, which shows that people reduce or eliminate consumption of cigarettes as a direct result of price increases (Callison and Kaestner 2014).

Prices act as signals, however, and as the relative price of one product rises, it leads people to substitute one product for another—sometimes one of inferior quality or greater potency. They also signal to producers and distributors that profits can be made and to consumers that money can be saved. In the case of high cigarette taxes, individual consumers and distributors face powerful incentives to arbitrage the difference between the tax-induced prices of cigarettes of various jurisdictions.

The result is large-scale tax evasion and avoidance, the majority of which is probably the result of diversion (much of which is illegal smuggling). This is the largest and most obvious parallel between today's rampant cigarette smuggling and the era of alcohol prohibition.

The state of Michigan seems to be at a crossroads in the parallels between prohibition of alcohol by statute and prohibition of cigarettes by price. In his popular book, *Last Call: The Rise and Fall of Prohibition*, Daniel Okrent (2010, 124) writes that some "900,000 cases of liquor found their way from Canadian distilleries to the border city of Windsor, Ontario," across from Detroit.

That liquor often passed through Michigan first on its way to other US destinations. During Prohibition, more than 75 percent of the hard liquor entering the country came across the Detroit River, the St. Clair River, and Lake St. Clair (Nolan 1999). At one point along the Detroit River, only 1 mile separates Canada from Michigan. Illegal booze flowed southward into Michigan on boats, biplanes, and at least one underwater sled. In the winter, ice skiffs were used. Trains and trucks also delivered illegal liquor. Smuggling was so rampant that at one point, 27 percent of the federal government's Prohibition enforcement budget for the country was spent fighting the illicit trade in Michigan (Engelmann 1979, xiv).

The smuggling of alcohol was not limited to international borders. Canadian whiskey, for example, transited a number of states before reaching its destinations. But Michigan went "dry" in 1918, before the rest of the country, and interstate smuggling of alcohol began almost immediately.

There was so much illegal alcohol flowing north from Ohio that one stretch of highway—US 25 (also known as the "Dixie Highway")—was dubbed "The Avenue de Booze." Years later, the freeway constructed nearby could easily be called "The Avenue de Smokes" for all of the illegal cigarettes flowing northward into southeast Michigan.

Today smuggling still occurs between the United States and Canada—and Michigan still plays a role, given its proximity to the border. But the smuggling now involves exports of tobacco instead of alcohol, and it flows in the opposite direction. In 2013, I along with co-researcher Todd Nesbit estimated that for every 100 smokes consumed in Michigan, an additional 3 were smuggled out to Canada. While smokers in Detroit pay a state excise tax of $2.00, those across the Detroit River in Windsor are taxed at CA$3.300 per pack.[4] Michigan is not the only source state for Canadian consumers.

Loose tobacco is trafficked northward, too. In January 2013, 30,000 pounds of loose tobacco was confiscated by the Canadian government at the Ambassador Bridge, which connects Canada to the United States (LaFaive and Nesbit 2013). This bridge, which opened in 1929, once helped facilitate liquor smuggling into the United States.

In 1994, Michigan voters adopted Proposal A, a public school funding package designed to revolutionize the way schools are financed. One component involved a cigarette tax increase of 50¢, a 200 percent increase. This large increase was passed without a corresponding mandate for tax stamps, which provide evidence on each package of cigarettes that the appropriate taxes had been paid.

So a smuggler could purchase vanloads of cigarettes in North Carolina, which had very low excise taxes of 5¢ per pack—and also had no tax stamp requirement—and shuttle them up to Michigan for distribution and sale, where taxes had increased to 75¢ per pack. Smugglers would thus arbitrage the 1,400 percent tax-induced price difference between the states. Authorities were unable to tell the difference between the two states' cigarettes, which made illicit trafficking all the more attractive. This created an opportunity for high profits at low cost, including the low probability of getting caught.

Cigarette smuggling continued to grow in Michigan and in 2007, I—along with scholars Todd Nesbit and Patrick Fleenor—measured its growth. The result was an exhaustive study about the degree to which cigarette taxes are diverted, usually by being smuggled illegally from low-tax to high-tax jurisdictions. The study contained smuggling rates by year, from 1990 through 2006 for forty-seven of the forty-eight contiguous states (LaFaive et al. 2008; LaFaive, Nesbit, and Drenkard 2015).[5]

The average smuggling rate for calendar year 1993—the year before the adoption of Proposal A—was just 8.67 percent of all Michigan-specific consumption. In the first full calendar year after adoption of Proposal A (1995), the smuggling rate was 20.5 percent, a 136.4 percent increase in illicit activity. Given the theoretical underpinnings and supportive empirical research, it would be incredible if this huge increase in smuggling after a big jump in excise taxes was just a coincidence or an anomaly. It is instead likely that illicit trafficking increased as a direct result of a law that had the unintended consequence of encouraging lawlessness, much like what happened during Prohibition.

To estimate diversion rates we used a two-stage residual econometric model that examined the difference between per capita legally paid sales and reported smoking rates by state.[6] The difference between official sales and what sales would have been without diversion is the total diversion rate. Our model cannot distinguish between evasion and avoidance, but we believe that legal avoidance by individual consumers represents a small part of the total.

The model also generated "percentages of diversion" in two major categories: casual and commercial. The former involves individuals who cross into another taxing jurisdiction to acquire cheaper cigarettes or purchase them on the Internet for personal consumption. The latter involves long-haul, large shipments, typically from a "tobacco state" like North Carolina to a higher-taxed state like Michigan or Illinois.

The results of our model complement the findings from the existing literature cited earlier. Recall that this literature generally concludes that legal cigarettes are diverted to a significant degree through tax avoidance and evasion strategies.

In the 2015 update to the study (LaFaive, Nesbit, and Drenkard 2015), we noted that through 2013, New York State stands out as a perennial leader in cigarette diversion percentages. We found that 58 percent of the Empire State's total market was diverted, most of which likely involved smuggling. The highest rate was followed by Arizona (49.3 percent),[7] Washington State (46.1 percent), New Mexico (46.1 percent), and Rhode Island (32 percent) (see table 2).

The top five exporting states include New Hampshire (28.7 percent), Idaho (24.2 percent), Delaware (22.6 percent), Virginia (22.6 percent), and Wyoming (21 percent). That is, for every 100 cigarettes consumed in, say, New Hampshire, an additional 28.7 percent were diverted to other states.

According to our estimate using 2013 data, the net revenues lost to cigarette tax avoidance and evasion in the continental United States is $5.1 billion. To obtain this number, we added up revenue gains to states that export cigarettes and subtracted revenue losses from state's that import diverted smokes.

INCIDENCE OF VIOLENCE

Violence was part and parcel of Prohibition. It was used by organized crime syndicates to enforce territorial agreements and intimidate unwilling participants or witnesses to the trade. The artificially high price of alcohol at this time also encouraged criminals to use violence to steal the product. Indeed, violent acts were an omnipresent feature of Prohibition.

Professor Mark Thornton (1991, 6), writing for the Cato Institute, noted that serious crime had been trending downward until Prohibition, when trends did a U-turn. He noted among other changes that occurred with Prohibition that

Table 2. State Cigarette Smuggling as a Percentage of Total State Cigarette Consumption (Legal and Illegal), 2013

State	Per Capita Legal Sales (packs)	Tax Rate (cents per pack)	Commercial (Interstate) Percentage	Casual (Interstate) Percentage	Smuggling Involving Canada or Mexico Percentage	Total Percentage	2013 Rank	2012 Rank	Rank Change
AL	64.6	42.5	0.28	6.85	0.00	7.11	37	39	–2
AR	57.5	115.0	–8.56	0.06	0.00	–8.50	25	25	0
AZ	24.4	200.0	–7.56	–12.06	–18.04	–49.28	2	2	0
CA	23.9	87.0	–3.24	–7.44	–17.70	–31.50	6	6	0
CO	38.3	84.0	–3.99	–9.17	0.00	–13.55	20	20	0
CT	31.4	340.0	–28.14	2.42	0.00	–24.82	11	12	–1
DE	77.1	160.0	–13.94	32.27	0.00	22.58	44	43	1
FL	44.3	133.9	–6.72	–9.43	0.00	–17.10	17	16	1
GA	49.9	37.0	0.93	3.29	0.00	4.20	36	37	–1
IA	48.5	136.0	–7.50	–8.31	0.00	–16.66	18	17	1
ID	43.1	57.0	–2.03	22.92	3.49	24.20	46	45	1
IL	31.7	198.0	–17.68	–2.75	0.00	–20.92	14	30	–16
IN	66.9	99.5	–7.14	21.40	0.00	15.55	40	36	4
KS	41.0	79.0	–3.58	–10.96	0.00	–14.95	19	19	0
KY	93.5	60.0	–1.56	8.97	0.00	7.56	38	38	0
LA	73.3	36.0	0.80	–3.62	0.00	–2.78	30	27	3
MA	32.2	251.0	–27.12	12.09	0.00	–12.04	22	21	1
MD	32.6	200.0	–15.86	–3.66	0.00	–20.19	15	15	0
ME	48.5	200.0	–16.18	0.97	3.75	–10.65	24	23	1
MI	45.4	200.0	–12.83	–13.84	2.98	–24.97	10	10	0

MN	43.1	160.0	-9.67	-10.40	2.69	-17.96	16	14	2
MO	87.4	17.0	2.73	11.30	0.00	13.70	39	40	-1
MS	63.9	68.0	-2.29	-5.97	0.00	-8.42	26	24	2
MT	44.3	170.0	-9.17	-15.68	2.42	-23.66	12	13	-1
ND	72.5	44.0	0.09	1.93	1.76	3.74	35	33	2
NE	51.2	64.0	-1.87	-0.93	0.00	-2.83	29	28	1
NH	89.6	168.0	-12.88	34.24	3.43	28.65	47	47	0
NJ	30.6	270.0	-29.43	12.98	0.00	-12.90	21	18	3
NM	26.4	166.0	-8.06	-8.45	-21.81	-46.13	4	3	1
NV	43.2	80.0	-6.19	24.03	0.00	18.76	41	41	0
NY	16.6	435.0	-28.41	-25.34	4.02	-57.99	1	1	0
OH	54.6	125.0	-9.25	2.02	0.00	-7.05	27	26	1
OK	67.2	103.0	-5.92	2.78	0.00	-2.95	28	29	-1
OR	43.3	118.0	-6.89	-3.64	0.00	-10.82	23	22	1
PA	52.8	160.0	-14.15	12.61	0.00	0.12	31	31	0
RI	35.3	350.0	-22.34	-6.95	0.00	-31.98	5	7	-2
SC	62.0	57.0	-1.31	3.68	0.00	2.41	32	34	-2
SD	42.7	153.0	-9.01	-11.83	0.00	-22.29	13	11	2
TN	66.2	62.0	-2.00	4.78	0.00	2.87	33	35	-2
TX	36.2	141.0	-6.36	0.49	-19.61	-27.38	8	8	0
UT	21.4	170.0	-11.42	-13.92	0.00	-27.34	9	9	0
VA	69.4	30.0	1.79	21.13	0.00	22.58	45	44	1
VT	42.1	262.0	-29.41	21.15	5.65	3.08	34	32	2
WA	19.5	302.5	-23.16	-22.95	4.07	-46.37	3	4	-1
WI	39.8	252.0	-13.71	-14.04	0.00	-31.24	7	5	2
WV	103.1	55.0	-1.21	20.49	0.00	19.50	42	42	0
WY	60.8	60.0	-2.13	22.74	0.00	20.98	43	46	-3

Source: LaFaive, Nesbit, and Drenkard (2015), using 2013 data.

the "homicide rate increased to 10 per 100,000 population during the 1920s, a 78 percent increase over the pre-Prohibition period."

In his paper "Violence and the U.S. Prohibitions of Drugs and Alcohol," Jeffrey Miron (1999, 3) writes that there exists a "demand for violence" designed to resolve disagreements. The private sector, asserts Miron, has several dispute resolution mechanisms that can be deployed—"negotiations, lawsuits, arbitrations"—that peacefully resolve disagreements over commercial transactions. When a product is prohibited and parties are working in an illegal environment, however, they more easily turn to violence "in lieu of lawyers" as a solution.

Miron is not the only observer to note that extralegal activities often come with extralegal solutions. In his book, *Last Call: The Rise and Fall of Prohibition*, Daniel Okrent (2010, 276) describes how famed attorney Clarence Darrow—an enemy of Prohibition—explained the "bootleggers' dilemma:"

> The business pays very well, Darrow said, but it is outside the law and they can't go to court, like shoe dealers or real-estate men or grocers when they think an injustice has been done them, or unfair competition has arisen in their territory. So, Darrow concluded, they naturally shoot.

During Prohibition, the St. Valentine's Day Massacre of six organized crime participants was one of the highest-profile uses of violence to end a dispute—this one involving control of Chicago's liquor traffic. But it was hardly the only one. Violence is still used in the illicit cigarette market for many of the same reasons it was employed during Prohibition. Consider a few examples.

- In October 2014, a convenience store clerk in Frankfort Township, Illinois (East of Joliet), was forcibly zip-tied and left in a bathroom while a team of four thieves stole cigarettes, cash, and other items.[8] Stealing cigarettes is not an uncommon phenomenon. Each pack in high-tax states represents a little gold bar to criminals, a secondary currency of sorts.

- In June 2013, a shooting death involving three gunmen may have been related to cigarette smuggling in Virginia. Frank Green, a reporter with the *Richmond Times-Dispatch* noted that "a law enforcement source said the slaying is believed to have been related to cigarette trafficking" (Green 2015a). In a September 2015 interview, the detective assigned to the case told this author that the victim was "heavily involved in cigarette trafficking." The detective, citing an ongoing police investigation, could not confirm that the murder was directly tied to smuggling.[9]

- In September 2013, police in Warren, Michigan, were forced to shoot at cigarette thieves in self-defense. In their attempt to escape capture, the thieves swerved their getaway van directly toward officers (Gantert 2015).

One of the greatest costs associated with trade in any prohibited arena is the costs associated with getting caught. Traffickers will go to great lengths to avoid capture, and that includes putting others' lives at risk:

- In October 2013, two men were indicted in a murder-for-hire scheme against witnesses scheduled to testify in a cigarette smuggling operation. A press release from the New York attorney general indicates that these were just two of sixteen members in a smuggling operation that purportedly avoided $80 million in taxes on their contraband smokes. Police Commissioner Raymond Kelly said in a press statement: "This indictment shows the scope of intent of these two individuals was not limited to generating profits through illegal cigarettes; it now includes a murder plot" (New York State Office of the Attorney General 2013). This is not the only hired gun story involving illicit smokes.

- In 2010, a Fairfax, Virginia man named Xing Xiao pleaded guilty in a conspiracy to hire someone to kill a man whom he thought had stolen 15,000 cartons of his contraband cigarettes, according to the US Department of Justice. Xing Xiao was one of fourteen people who were working to purchase and resell 77 million cigarettes in New York.[10]

- In 2008 in Cornwall in the Canadian province of Ontario, an American couple died when a suspected smuggler slammed into their automobile while trying to flee the police.[11]

Violence is also sometimes used to acquire a product, particularly one that is prohibited by law or price. Arguably the most brazen acts of theft involve the hijacking of both legal and illegal shipments.

During Prohibition, the "Gustin Gang" was known for hijacking the illicit shipments of delivery vehicles at street intersections, among other crimes. The leader of the gang, Frankie Wallace, was ultimately murdered by a rival crime syndicate.[12]

In his book on Prohibition, *Last Call*, Daniel Okrent (2010, 278) noted the constant "threat of hijackers looking to commandeer a boat and seize its cargo." There were "auxillaries of the violent urban gangs" on the ocean, robbing "rum runners" of cash and liquor in acts that also included extreme violence.

The irony is rich and repeated in the prohibition by price of cigarettes: one group of lawbreakers robs another group of lawbreakers. The headline of an April 2015 news story borders on the humorous: "Robbery Victim Arrested, Charged in Cigarette Trafficking." As it turned out, the victim was robbed by at least one employee of his own cigarette outlet store, a store that was apparently a legal front for an illegal cigarette distribution system. The news article reports that "New York authorities complain traffickers there have been robbing each other of cash and valuable, readily disposable cigarettes." In this case, the victim had made ninety cash deposits in the business's bank account worth more than $14 million (Green 2015b).

In January 2015, two men who were loading a van with cigarettes were hijacked before they could finish the job. The hijackers stole products valued at $90,000, according to the *Richmond Times-Dispatch* (Green 2015a). In 2011, a cigarette delivery truck was hijacked by an armed robber in Hitchcock, Texas (Weisman 2011). In 2010, in East Peoria, Illinois, cigarette delivery trucks were stolen before drivers had a chance to move their cargo (Ori 2010). A 2012 news report in the *Journal Star* indicated that the stolen cigarettes had a value of about $8 million and that the theft was carried out by a crime syndicate working out of Florida. The syndicate was responsible for stealing more than cigarettes and worked in other states, too (Renken 2012).

While these recent stories are dramatic in their own right, earlier stories out of Michigan also deserve mention. In 2005, two separate hijackings of cigarette delivery trucks operated by wholesaler Martin & Snyder of Detroit left management and employees shaken. The drivers of the trucks were tied up and eventually freed unharmed, but all parties wanted to avoid the future risk of injury or death (LaFaive et al. 2008, 47).

As mentioned above, one cost to illicit traffickers is the risk of getting caught. But there is another cost that is often borne by legal distributors of the product that is prohibited by price, including Martin & Snyder. Its cost was that of being victimized by a robbery, being subjected to physical violence, and then having to pay for tighter security.

Martin & Snyder hired Threat Management Group to help protect its employees and shipments as they moved through the Detroit area. The work not only included the use of twelve armed guards but also an empty decoy truck, a security dog, a live camera from a security vehicle to Martin & Snyder headquarters, and a rotating delivery schedule to avoid shipment predict-ability.[13] The plan minimized the company's risk of being subject to theft and violence, but it came at great expense to the wholesaler of a legal product.

The same business owner also suffered brazen violence to his property when thieves smashed their way through the brick exterior of his business to steal cigarettes. Others businesses have similarly suffered. In July 2015, thieves broke through the brick wall of a Detroit retailer to steal cigarettes, alcohol, and lottery tickets (Herrera 2015). In September 2012, a Columbus, Ohio, retail store was robbed of 120 cartons of cigarettes after a car smashed through a large door.[14]

The list of damage done to people and property is long. They are distin-guished by the costs associated with it and the incentive from which it was born: prohibition by price. The list above involves mainly examples of explicit violence, but countless stories exist of robberies where the threat of violence is either simply implied or not made at all.

CORRUPTION

Corruption of public officials also appears to be routine under both prohibi-tion scenarios, although the extent of corruption under Prohibition was much larger than it is today.

Mark Thornton (1991, 8) quotes Commissioner of Prohibition Henry Anderson: "The fruitless efforts at enforcement are creating public disregard not only for this law [but also] for all laws. Public corruption through the pur-chase of official protection for this illegal traffic is widespread and notorious." That is more than mere speculation. Almost 9 percent of federal prohibition agents between 1920 and 1931 were fired over issues related to corruption (Comte 2010, 170).

According to Daniel Okrent (2010, 274–75), "political corruption had been baked into the system almost from the beginning." One "dry" congressman from Kentucky arranged for 1 million gallons of liquor—dubbed "medicinal"—to be released to bootleggers in New York.

Excise taxes on cigarettes can be profitable for modern lawmakers, too. In June 2015, Tennessee state Rep. Joe Armstrong was indicted on tax fraud and other charges stemming from profits he made arbitraging cigarette excise taxes on which he voted. As for most states, Tennessee imposes a tax stamp on each pack of cigarettes sold as evidence that the taxes it levies have been paid. In this case, Armstrong purchased a large quantity of cigarette tax stamps the day before he and his colleagues voted to more than triple the excise tax on cigarettes, from 20¢ to 62¢ per pack.

According to news reports, he later sold those stamps at a profit, tried to cover up the transaction, and failed to report income from the deal. Armstrong pleaded not guilty.[15]

- In 2012, an official in Cook County's revenue office was caught taking payments from retailers for advanced warnings of raids on their businesses (LaFaive and Nesbit 2014–2015).

- In 2013, a sheriff with decades of experience in law enforcement was sent to prison in Illinois for taking part in a cigarette smuggling scheme for which he was paid thousands of dollars. In a secret recording made in 2011, a smuggler named Mustafa Mohd Shaikh endorses the sheriff: "Anything happens to you in Chicago, this guy will get you out," he said. "This guy is willing to protect. Nobody will touch you or come by you" (LaFaive and Nesbit 2014–2015, 17).

In 2012, a police officer in Maryland's Prince George's County was sentenced for helping run illegal cigarettes while in uniform, firearm at the ready, and with his police vehicle (LaFaive 2015).

Corruption does not stop at the thin blue line. It is all too easy to find stories about prison and jail guards smuggling cigarettes—among other items—into federal, state and local corrections facilities. Police officers have also been impersonated by the criminal class during alcohol Prohibition and today's prohibition by price with cigarettes.

- The Gustin Gang posed as federal agents to confiscate the illegal liquor of other bootleggers and then resell it.[16]

- In November 2013, Charles Watson was sentenced to prison for stealing cigarettes from a retail store while pretending to be a cop (LaFaive and Nesbit 2014–2015).

BATHTUB GIN

Prohibition saw its share of injury and death from adulterated liquor products, often made by those who had little knowledge of alcohol production. Purveyors of cheaply made liquor produced their goods in innumerable—but usually discreet—locales. Their work included acquiring genuine, safer liquor and cutting it with chemicals to increase the volume of alcohol (and hence, their revenues). Today, counterfeit cigarettes have been found to carry all manner of materials that do not belong there.

The UK *Daily Mail* reported in 2012 on similar findings from an investigation of discarded packs of cigarettes in the city of Birmingham. Some cigarettes contained "human excrement, asbestos and dead flies" (Preece 2012). Counterfeit cigarettes are often sold to unsuspecting customers and may include dangerous chemicals, such as sulphur and carbamide (Shen et al. 2010, 245).

THE IRON LAW OF PROHIBITION

In addition to counterfeit cigarettes, today smokers may seek out packages and cartons bearing lower tax rates. But they have also substituted cigarettes produced by licensed manufacturers with those they roll themselves with loose tobacco. This need not be a more dangerous route, but it can be if consumers increase their nicotine intake by forgoing the use of filters—getting more bang for their nicotine buck. This practice has parallels to the era of alcohol Prohibition.

In his analysis, Mark Thornton (1991, 3) details how beer became more expensive relative to liquor "because of its bulk." In other words, it cost more to illicitly move that product than its more potent alternatives. "The typical beer, wine, or whiskey contained a higher percentage of alcohol by volume during Prohibition than it did before or after." Likewise, people have substituted other products for cigarettes to get their nicotine fix; such substitutions are not necessarily healthier or safer (CDC 2012).

A 2012 report from the Centers for Disease Control (CDC 2012) notes that certain smokers changed tobacco types to avoid higher cigarette taxes. Specifically, the CDC reported that while cigarette use declined by 32.8 percent between 2000 and 2011, the use of loose tobacco and cigars leapt by 123.1 percent during the same period. The change came most notably—according to the CDC—after the 2009 federal cigarette excise tax increase (CDC 2012).[17]

Despite the good intentions of reformers, prohibition—either by mandate or by price—undermines the goals often used to justify proposed policies. The public health improvements sought by champions of the excise tax are frustrated by tax evasion and avoidance as well as the substitution effect.

LOOSIES

One of the more interesting parallels between Prohibition and today's high cigarette prices and illicit trade are "loosies," or loose cigarettes sold one or two at a time for 25–50¢ or more. The term loosie is not a new one, but it took on particular prominence after the tragic death of Eric Garner. His death was caused by a confrontation with police officers in New York City and aggravated by his own poor health, according to a New York City official. The reason Garner was confronted by the police in the first place, however, was his sale of cigarettes. Garner was apparently selling loosies in Staten Island.

According to the *Wall Street Journal,* arrests associated with the sale of loosies in New York dropped 33 percent after Garner's death, to 295 through July 5, 2015, from 439 through the same time frame in 2014 (Francescani 2015). An October 2015 report indicated that Chicago arrested 800 people in 2013 for selling loosies and issued 490 citations costing $1,000 per recipient. The problem is so pervasive that one alderman has publicly remarked that gang wars over loosie turf might erupt in the city.[18]

During Prohibition, some men sold single shots of whiskey to others as they left the factory for the day. In *Last Call,* Daniel Okrent (2010, 283) writes: "In some cities they [cars] were mobile taverns, their proprietors parking outside factory gates, peddling shots of liquor for twenty cents apiece and speeding off at the first scent of an honest Prohibition Agent." Today those cars are simply backpacks worn on the backs of street sellers or perhaps a simple box underneath the counter of some retailer.

CONCLUSION

Cigarette excise taxes have increased in the past decade at all levels of government, some to a much greater degree than others. The tax-induced price differences of cigarettes have led to a raft of unintended consequences that mimic those of Prohibition. It is easy to see why.

The extraordinary profits associated with prohibiting a popular product have given criminals and even law-abiding citizens lucrative incentives to engage in trade in often illicit or legal but expensive products. Some do it to save money; some do it to make money. In some instances, those products are less expensive substitutes that may also provide a more potent shot of nicotine than might otherwise be ingested.

The first and most obvious unintended consequence of prohibition by price is rampant smuggling. The academic literature on the subject points to illicit trafficking on a large scale. Nationwide, one 2015 study pegged the average tax evasion and avoidance rate in the United States at as low as 8 percent and as high as 21 percent.

Of course, this is just the national average. States that have some of the highest excise taxes typically have higher rates of tax evasion and avoidance.

Fifty-eight percent of New York State's total cigarette market may be illicit. The state's smuggling rate is high due in part to its proximity to low-tax Virginia, much as Michigan's Prohibition-era alcohol smuggling was due first to its proximity to wet Ohio and ultimately to Canada.

This unintended consequence, however, is only the largest and most obvious parallel with the era of Prohibition. Others—including the creation of crime syndicates, violence against people and property, corruption of elected officials and police, adulterated and increasingly potent product substitutes, and the sale of loosies—are all reflected in a quasi-prohibition, that of a tax-induced prohibition by price.

NOTES

1. "Children's Health Insurance Program Reauthorization Act of 2009" (Washington, DC: Government Printing Office, February 4, 2009), (Sec. 701), https://www.gpo.gov/fdsys/pkg /PLAW 111publ3/pdf/PLAW-111publ3.pdf (accessed September 10, 2015).

2. "Cook County Department of Revenue Tobacco Tax Ordinance: Notice of 2013 Tax Rate and Definition Changes," https://perma.cc/2UHA-BBL8 (accessed July 25, 2017).

3. City of Chicago "Cigarette Tax Delinquency Notices," https://www.cityofchicago.org/city /en/depts/fin/provdrs/tax_division/alerts/2013/dec/notice-of-cigarette-tax-increase.html (accessed July 25, 2017).

4. "Tobacco Tax," 2017 (Ontario: Ontario Ministry of Finance), http://www.fin.gov.on.ca/en/tax /tt/. We also estimated that Vermont, Washington State, New York, New Hampshire, North Dakota, Montana, Minnesota, Maine, and Idaho act as source states for illicit exports to Canada. For every 100 cigarettes consumed in these states, between 1.8 and 5.7 cigarettes are smuggled to Canada. Of course, US states are not the only source of illicit importation. Both Canadian and American authorities must also consider other nations (for example, China) or the tribal nations in each country as sources of illicit product. American Indian reservations have been a major source of low-tax cigarettes in the United States and in Canada (LaFaive et al. 2015).

5. The LaFaive et al. (2008) smuggling study was first published in 2008 using 2006 data and was updated in LaFaive and Nesbit (2015) with data through 2013.

6. We also estimated a single-stage model including prevalence of smoking, a time trend, and the same variables as appear in our two-stage model. When our study was first published in 2008, this was an approach adopted by other scholars. The results were similar to those for the two-stage model, for which we have a great preference.

7. Our model attributes much of this smuggling to cross-border activities with Mexico. However, it is possible that a large portion may actually be coming through bonded warehouses instead. We are unable at this time to include a measure of this traffic due to the dearth of available data.

8. "Frankfort Township Tobacco Store Robbed," *Herald-News* (Joliet, IL), October 6, 2014, http:// www.theherald-news.com/2014/10/06/frankfort-township-tobacco-store-robbed/asewmp4/.

9. Telephone conversation between Detective Johnny Capocelli of the Chesterfield Police Department and Michael LaFaive, Director of the Morey Fiscal Policy Initiative with the Mackinac Center for Public Policy, September 29, 2015.

10. US Department of Justice, US Attorney's Office, Eastern District of Virginia, "Fairfax Man Pleads Guilty to Murder-for-Hire Scheme as Payback for Stolen Cigarettes" (news release, 2010), https://www.staffordsheriff.com/apps/public/news/newsView.cfm?News_ID=184.

11. "Suspected Cigarette Smuggler Kills Couple in Crash." *Ottawa Citizen*, 2008, http://www
    .canada.com/ottawacitizen/story.html?id=a73ac247-4ede-4db4-b12a-9e53fcb8ef7d.

12. Wikipedia Foundation, "Gustin Gang," March 29, 2015, https://en.wikipedia.org/wiki
    /Gustin_Gang.

13. And this is only part of the story. A Martin & Snyder cash-and-carry customer was hijacked
    of his cigarettes and car and was shot in the process. He lived but lost a kidney. These are just
    some of the costs imposed on this one wholesaler in association with high cigarette excise
    taxes (Lafaive et al. 2008, 47).

14. WBNS-10TV, Columbus, OH, "Thieves Crash Car into Carry Out to Steal 100 Boxes of
    Cigarettes," September 24, 2012, http://www.10tv.com/article/thieves-crash-car-carry-out
    -steal-100-boxes-cigarettes.

15. Mike Donila and Jim Matheny, "Armstrong Pleads Not Guilty to Tax Fraud; Governor
    Reacts to Charges," WBIR, Knoxville, TN, June 19, 2015, http://www.wbir.com/story
    /news/2015/06/19/representative-joe-armstrong/28976805/.

16. Wikipedia Foundation, "Gustin Gang."

17. The percentages reported here may exaggerate the substitution effect taking place. Without
    absolute volumes, it is difficult to determine just how much cigarette consumption was offset
    by loose tobacco and cigars.

18. Stephanie Cox and Ted Lulay, "'Loosies' Cigarette Sales Could Spark Gang Conflict, Alderman
    Says." DNAinfo.com (Chicago), October 7, 2015, https://www.dnainfo.com/chicago/20151007
    /near-west-side/loosies-cigarette-sales-could-spark-gang-conflict-alderman-says.

REFERENCES

Anderson, Gary. 1997. "Bureaucratic Incentives and the Transition from Taxes to Prohibition." In
    Taxing Choice: The Predatory Politics of Fiscal Discrimination, edited by William F. Shughart
    II, 139–67. Oakland, CA: Independent Institute.

Boonn, Ann. 2016. "Top Combined State-Local Cigarette Tax Rates (State plus County plus City)."
    Washington, DC: Campaign for Tobacco-Free Kids, July 27. http://www.tobaccofreekids.org
    /research/factsheets/pdf/0267.pdf.

Callison, K., and R. Kaestner. 2014. "Do Higher Tobacco Taxes Reduce Adult Smoking? New
    Evidence of the Effect of Recent Cigarette Tax Increases on Adult Smoking." *Economic
    Inquiry* 52 (1): 155–72.

CDC (Centers for Disease Control and Prevention). 2012. "Consumption of Cigarettes and
    Combustible Tobacco—United States, 2000–2001." Morbidity and Mortality Weekly Report,
    August 3. Atlanta, GA. https://www.cdc.gov/mmwr/pdf/wk/mm6130.pdf.

Chernick, H., and Merriman, D. 2011. "Using Littered Pack Data to Estimate Cigarette Tax
    Avoidance in NYC." Working Paper. http://papers.ssrn.com/sol3/papers.cfm?abstract_id
    =2192169 (accessed July 27, 2017).

Chiou, Lesley, and Erich Muehlegger. 2008. "Crossing the Line: Direct Estimation of Cross-Border
    Cigarette Sales and the Effect on Tax Revenue." *B.E. Journal of Economic Analysis & Policy* 8
    (48): 1–41.

Comte, Julien. 2010. "Let the Federal Men Raid." *Pennsylvania History: A Journal of Mid-Atlantic
    Studies* 77 (2): 166–92.

Cooper, Michael. 2002. "Cigarettes Up to $7 a Pack with New Tax." *New York Times*, July 1. http://
    www.nytimes.com/2002/07/01/nyregion/cigarettes-up-to-7-a-pack-with-new-tax.html.

Davis, Kevin C., Victoria Grimshaw, David Merriman, Matthew C. Farrelly, Howard Chernick,
    Micaela H. Coady, Kelsey Campbell, and Susan M. Kansagra. 2013. "Cigarette Trafficking in

Five Northeastern US Cities." *Tobacco Control*, December 11: 1–7. https://www.tobaccocon trol.bmj.com.

DeCicca, Philip, Donald S. Kenkel, and Feng Liu. 2010. "Excise Tax Avoidance: The Case of State Cigarette Taxes." NBER Working Paper 15941. National Bureau of Economic Research, Cambridge, MA. http://www.nber.org/papers/w15941.

———. 2014. "Reservation Prices: An Economic Analysis of Cigarette Purchases on Indian Reservations." NBER Working Paper 20778. National Bureau of Economic Research, Cambridge, MA. http://www.nber.org/papers/w20778.

Engelmann, Larry. 1979. *Intemperance*. New York: Free Press.

Fix, Brian V., Andrew Hyland, Richard J. O'Connor, K. Michael Cummings, Geoffry T. Font, Frank J. Chaloupka, and Andrew S. Licht. 2013. "A Novel Approach to Estimating the Prevalence of Untaxed Cigarettes in the USA: Findings from the 2009 and 2010 International Tobacco Control Surveys." *Tobacco Control* 23: Abstract i61–i66.

Francescani, Chris. 2015. "Loose Cigarette Arrests in NYC Drop in Year after Eric Garner's Death." *Wall Street Journal*, July 15. https://www.wsj.com/articles/loose-cigarette-arrests-in-nyc-drop -in-year-after-eric-garners-death-1436992014.

Gantert, Tom. 2015. "High Taxes Make Cigarettes 'Gold Bars' for Thieves." *Capitol Confidential* (Midland, MI), September 7. http://www.michigancapitolconfidential.com/cigarette-taxes -encourage-thieves.

Green, Frank. 2015a. "Cigarette Trafficking Spawning Other Crimes, and Possibly Violence." *Richmond Times-Dispatch*, March 28. http://www.richmond.com/news/local/crime/article _e101477f-1c3d-5117-bcce-f8839f52485c.html.

———. 2015b. "Robbery Victim Arrested Charged in Cigarette Trafficking." *Richmond Times-Dispatch*, April 20. http://www.richmond.com/news/local/crime/article_d0b7c28c-b7d7 -513b-b55a-5bace65a6b3a.html.

Herrera, Halston. 2015. "Thieves Smash through Brick Wall to Steal from Detroit Store." *WDIV: Click on Detroit*, July 15. https://www.clickondetroit.com/news/thieves-smash-through-brick -wall-to-steal-from-detroit-store.

Hyland, A., J. F. Bauer, Q. Li, S. M. Abrams, C. Higbee, L. Peppone, and K. M. Cummings. 2005. "Higher Cigarette Prices Influence Cigarette Purchase Patterns." *Tobacco Control* 14: 86–92. http://tobaccocontrol.bmj.com/content/14/2/86.

Kurti, M. K., K. von Lampe, and D. E. Thompkins. 2012. "The Illegal Cigarette Market in a Socioeconomically Deprived Inner-City Area: The Case of the South Bronx." *Tobacco Control* 22 (2): 138–40. http://tobaccocontrol.bmj.com/content/22/2/138.

LaFaive, Michael. 2015. "Smuggling Undermines Tobacco Tax Hike Goals." Midland, MI: Mackinac Center for Public Policy, February 4. http://www.mackinac.org/18254.

LaFaive, Michael, and Todd Nesbit. 2013. "Cigarette Smuggling Study Explained." Midland, MI: Mackinac Center for Public Policy, February 1. http://www.mackinac.org/18238.

———. 2014–2015. "An Academic's View." *Trafficked: The Illicit Trade in Tobacco* (Winter): 16–17.

LaFaive, Michael, Patrick Fleenor, and Todd Nesbit. 2008. "Cigarette Taxes and Smuggling: A Statistical Analysis and Historical Review." Midland, MI: Mackinac Center for Public Policy, December 24. http://www.mackinac.org/archives/2008/s2008-12.pdf.

LaFaive, Michael, Todd Nesbit, and Scott Drenkard. 2015. "Cigarette Smugglers Still Love New York and Michigan but Illinois Closing In." Midland, MI: Mackinac Center for Public Policy, January 14. www.mackinac.org/20900.

Lovenheim, Michael. 2008. "How Far to the Border? The Extent and Impact of Cross-Border Casual Cigarette Smuggling." *National Tax Journal* 61 (1): 7–33.

Merriman, David. 2010. "The Micro-Geography of Tax Avoidance: Evidence from Littered
Cigarette Packs in Chicago." *American Economic Journal: Economic Policy* 2 (2): 61–84.
https://www.aeaweb.org/articles?id=10.1257/pol.2.2.61.

Merriman, David, and Howard Chernick. 2013. "Using Littered Pack Data to Estimate Cigarette
Tax Avoidance in New York City." *National Tax Journal* 66 (2): 635–68. https://www.ntanet
.org/NTJ/66/3/ntj-v66n03p635-668-littered-pack-data-cigarette-tax.pdf.

Miron, Jeffrey A. 1999. "Violence and U.S. Prohibitions of Drugs and Alcohol." NBER Working
Paper 6950. National Bureau of Economic Research, Cambridge, MA. http://www.nber.org
/papers/w6950.pdf.

National Research Council. 2015. *Understanding the U.S. Illicit Tobacco Market: Characteristics,
Policy Context, and Lessons from International Experiences.* Washington, DC: National
Academies. doi:10.17226/19016.

New York State Office of the Attorney General. 2013. "A. G. Schneiderman Announces New
Charges after Foiled Murder-for-Hire Plot in Massive Eastern Seaboard Cigarette Trafficking
Case," October 17. Albany, NY. https://ag.ny.gov/press-release/ag-schneiderman-announces
-new-charges-after-foiled-murder-hire-plot-massive-eastern.

Nolan, Jenny. 1999. "How Prohibition Made Detroit a Bootlegger's Dream Town." *Detroit News,*
June 14. http://blogs.detroitnews.com/history/1999/06/14/how-prohibition-made-detroit-a
-bootleggers-dream-town/.

Okrent, Daniel. 2010. *Last Call: The Rise and Fall of Prohibition.* New York: Scribner.

Ori, Ryan. 2010. "Police Say EP Warehouse Burglary Was a Coordinated Operation." *Journal Star*
(Peoria, IL), January 25. http://www.pjstar.com/article/20100125/NEWS/301259877.

Orzechowski, William, and Robert Walker. 2014. "The Tax Burden on Tobacco: Historical Compilation,
Volume 49." Arlington, VA: Orzechowski and Walker, 10–11. http://goo.gl/M2ttwg.

Preece, Rob. 2012. "Human Excrement, Asbestos, and Dead Flies: The Ingredients Found in
Fake Cigarettes That Cost the Taxpayer Billions." *Daily Mail* (London), September 9. http://
www.dailymail.co.uk/news/article-2200633/Human-excrement-asbestos-dead-flies-The
-ingredients-fake-cigarettes-Britain.html.

Renken, Leslie. 2012. "Miami Arrests Linked to Major Cigarette Theft in East Peoria." *Journal Star*
(Peoria, IL), May 3. http://www.pjstar.com/article/20100125/NEWS/301259877.

Shen, Anqi, Georgios A. Antonopoulos, and Klaus Von Lampe. 2010. "The Dragon Breathes Smoke:
Cigarette Counterfeiting in the People's Republic of China." *British Journal of Criminology* 50
(2): 239–58. http://bjc.oxfordjournals.org/content/early/2009/11/11/bjc.azp069.abstract.

Silver, Diana, Margaret M. Giorgio, Jin Yung Bae, Geronimo Jimenez, and James Macinko. 2015.
"Over-the-Counter Sales of Out-of-State and Counterfeit Tax Stamp Cigarettes in New
York City." *Tobacco Control* 25: 584–86. http://tobaccocontrol.bmj.com/lookup/doi/10.1136
/tobaccocontrol-2015-052355.

State of Minnesota, Department of Revenue. 2013. "Cigarette and Tobacco Products Customs
Declaration." Minneapolis, MN. http://www.revenue.state.mn.us/Forms_and_Instructions
/ct207.pdf.

Stehr, Mark. 2005. "Cigarette Tax Avoidance and Evasion." *Journal of Health Economics* 24: 277–97.

Thornton, Mark. 1991. "Alcohol Prohibition Was a Failure." Cato Institute Policy Analysis 157.
Washington, DC: Cato Institute. https://object.cato.org/sites/cato.org/files/pubs/pdf/pa157.pdf.

US Department of the Treasury, Alcohol and Tobacco Tax and Trade Bureau. 2010. "Tobacco:
Federal Excise Tax Increase and Related Provisions." Washington, DC.

Weisman, Laura. 2011. "Police Look for Cigarette-Truck Thief in League City." *Houston Chronicle,*
August 31. http://blog.chron.com/newswatch/2011/08/police-look-for-cigarette-truck-thief
-in-league-city-%E2%80%94-daily-news/.

CHAPTER 16
Persecuting Plastic Bags

E. FRANK STEPHENSON
Department of Economics, Berry College

I n his preface to *Taxing Choice*, William Shughart noted the growing tendency toward "taxing all manner of products and regulating all types of remotely objectionable behavior." He added that "the list of the traditional sins of smoking, drinking, and gambling is relentlessly being expanded to include cooking outdoors, wearing perfume, eating snack foods, buying expensive cars or yachts, bearing arms, and on and on" (Shughart 1997a, xiii). That ongoing spread of regulating individual choice has continued unabated in the subsequent two decades and today includes an ever-widening array of targeted taxes, subsidies, and behavioral regulations. This chapter focuses on the plastic grocery sack, an item that had not yet drawn regulatory attention at the time that *Taxing Choice* was published in 1997 but has since become subject to taxes and bans in all or part of more than a dozen countries, including the United States.[1] As we shall see, the bag bans and taxes that have popped up in the past dozen years have many similarities to the selective commodity taxation described in *Taxing Choice*.

High-density polyethelene (henceforth, "plastic") grocery bags were invented in Sweden in the 1960s. Their use in the United States was rare until the Kroger and Safeway grocery chains started offering them to customers in 1982. Consumer opinions about the new bags were mixed—bags with handles were appealing to urban consumers, but shoppers taking their purchases home in their cars tended to prefer the sturdier paper bags that were less likely to spill in moving vehicles. Since plastic bags were substantially cheaper than the commonly used paper bags, their use spread rapidly. By 1985, three-fourths of grocery and convenience stores were offering plastic bags. By the early 2000s, plastic bags accounted for 80 percent of all grocery bags used (Petru 2014).

Most early restrictions on plastic bags were imposed outside the United States.[2] In 2002, Bangladesh banned bags out of concern that bag litter was clogging drains and causing flooding. Likewise, in 2002, Ireland enacted a tax of 0.15 euro per bag (later increased to 0.22 euro) as a deterrent to littering.[3] Since that time, China, Italy, and South Africa have joined approximately one dozen countries banning or taxing plastic bags at the national or subnational level. Others include parts of Australia, Pakistan, and the Philippines.

In the United States, municipal governments took the lead in restricting or taxing plastic grocery bags. The first tax or prohibition imposed in a large jurisdiction was San Francisco's 2007 ban of single-use plastic bags by supermarkets and chain pharmacies.[4] Bag bans or taxes were subsequently adopted by more than seventy-five cities, including Oakland, Long Beach, San Jose, and Los Angeles; municipal bag ordinances came to cover more than one-third of Californians. Bag bans and taxes are less prevalent outside California, but cities restricting or taxing plastic bags include Portland, OR; Santa Fe, NM; Cambridge, MA; and Austin, TX. One of the most publicized actions was Washington, DC's 2010 adoption of a 5¢ per bag tax.[5]

Legislation at the state level has been fairly sparse, but a few states have required that retailers using plastic bags offer in-store collection points for recycling. The first statewide legislative action banning or taxing plastic bags was passed in California in 2014. California's legislation would have imposed a statewide ban effective on July 1, 2015, but the legislation was put on hold when bag ban opponents gathered enough signatures to trigger a 2016 referendum on the ban (Miller 2015). Although Hawaii has not enacted statewide legislation, Honolulu's July 1, 2015, implementation of a bag ban means that the state has a de facto ban, because all its municipalities prohibit single-use plastic bags.[6]

RATIONALES FOR BAG BANS AND TAXES

Environmental activists advocate banning or taxing single-use plastic grocery sacks because of external harms supposedly associated with their use. Plastic grocery bags are claimed to increase carbon emissions and to increase litter and associated harm to wildlife (particularly marine life).

It is certainly true that plastic bags are a petroleum derivative and would therefore exacerbate any environmental harms associated with carbon usage. However, plastic grocery sacks are extremely thin and lightweight. A bag weighing 5 grams can carry some 1,000 times its weight (Mangu-Ward 2015). Goodyear (2007) reports that 430,000 gallons of oil are required to produce 100 million plastic bags, figures that imply 0.0043 gallons of oil used per bag. Even allowing that hundreds of millions of bags are produced each year, the carbon emissions associated with their production would be very small compared to emissions from electricity generation or automobile use. Moreover, discouraging plastic bag use via bans or taxes may well lead to the use of more carbon-intensive alternatives, a topic taken up in the next section.

Proponents of plastic bag bans and taxes also cite bag litter as a rationale for discouraging or eliminating bag use. As with bag production increasing carbon emissions, there is a kernel of truth in this claim. Plastic bags are sometimes among the litter found along streets and highways. In extreme cases, the litter has been associated with flooding caused by blocked drains (Bangladesh's motivation for banning bags)[7] or harm to marine wildlife from bags that make their way into waterways (the rationale for a ban on bags in eastern North Carolina). Again, however, bag bans and taxes seem to have been implemented reflexively rather than based on estimates of actual harm caused by bags. For example, little consideration seems to have been given to bags' share of the overall litter problem or to the overall harm done to marine wildlife. Indeed, Minter (2015) cites a Fort Worth, TX, study that finds that plastic bags were 0.12 percent (by weight) of the city's litter. Similarly, Mangu-Ward (2015) reports that the 2009 Keep America Beautiful survey found that bags were 0.6 percent of all visible litter nationwide.[8] Given bags' small contribution to litter, it is hard to rationalize singling them out for bans or taxation without applying similar treatment to other litter sources, such as fast food packaging or snacks from convenience stores.

As for wildlife harm associated with plastic bags, Mangu-Ward (2015) reports that plastic bag opponents claim "more than 1 million birds and 100,000 marine mammals and sea turtles die each year from eating or getting entangled in plastic." She then proceeds to explain that these figures come from a Canadian study on incidental harm from fishing off Newfoundland, not from an assessment of plastic bag damages. Moreover, she notes that the Canadian study was conducted from 1981 to 1984, thereby predating the widespread use of plastic shopping bags.

Another rationale offered for bag bans or taxes is their use of landfill space. Minter (2015) cites an Environmental Protection Agency study finding that plastic bags were only 0.28 percent (by weight) of total municipal solid waste. Of course, something lightweight but bulky could consume landfill space, but bags compact easily, so this concern should be minimal. Municipalities concerned about rapidly filling landfills have many, more reasonable, options, such as increasing tipping fees for all trash.

Even if, relative to available alternatives, plastic shopping bags do increase carbon emissions, increase litter, harm wildlife, or consume landfill space, efficient policy requires setting the per bag fee equal to the marginal damage associated with each bag. Determining the marginal harm would be difficult and would likely vary from place to place (e.g., bags would be more likely to clog drains in Bangladesh than in an arid location). Nonetheless, there appears to have been little effort by the jurisdictions banning or taxing bags to determine the actual harm caused per bag. Instead, the idea that bags cause harm is assumed without any questions about the marginal damage associated with each bag or any comparison to other sources of carbon emissions.[9] Indeed, the marginal contribution of each bag to increased carbon emissions (or to the aggregate waste people generate) is likely very small since bags are so lightweight, so choosing to single out bags for taxation or prohibition is arbitrary.

To summarize, bag bans and taxes seem to be arbitrary and based on a general, albeit vague, sense that bags are environmentally harmful.[10] However, little critical analysis has been done on the actual harm caused by plastic bags and particularly how that harm compares to any damages associated with other products or on people's behavioral responses to bag bans and taxes.

UNINTENDED CONSEQUENCES

Unlike groceries, books, or clothing, people do not shop directly for plastic bags. Instead, plastic bags are useful for taking purchases from a store to a home or other location. Banning or taxing plastic bags does not reduce people's need to get their goods home from the store. Yet bag ban and tax advocates seem to ignore the important question: "compared to what?"

Consider the argument for banning plastic bags based on their contribution to carbon emissions. It is important to think about what people would use instead of plastic bags and the effect that those alternatives would have on carbon emissions. One possibility is that people will transport their purchases without using any bag, as is currently the practice at Costco and Sam's Club warehouse stores. If bag bans lead people to transport their purchases without bags, then bag bans reduce the level of carbon emissions. However, there are other possibilities, all of which lead to carbon emissions. For example, people might use the thicker, reusable plastic bags that are allowed in some jurisdictions. In this case, one must compare the amount of carbon used in the thicker reusable bags against the carbon content of single-use bags. Since the reusable plastic bags are thicker than the single-use bags, the reusable bags must be used many times for them to lead to a reduction in carbon emissions. Mangu-Ward (2015) cites a UK Environmental Agency study finding that reusable plastic tote sacks must be used at least eleven times to be more carbon efficient than single-use bags. That the heavier duty bags might actually increase carbon emissions is borne out by Austin, TX, which found that its ban on single-use bags was almost completely offset by an increase in thicker multiuse bags in its municipal waste stream (Minter 2015).

Alternatively, people might substitute single-use paper bags for single-use plastic bags. Indeed, Taylor and Villas-Boas (2016) find that plastic bag bans lead the proportion of customers choosing paper bags to increase from 5 percent to 40 percent. The production of single-use paper bags also emits carbon from cutting trees, milling the pulp into bags, and transporting the bags (which are heavier than plastic bags) to stores. That using paper instead of plastic might actually increase carbon emissions is apparently a possibility that has not been considered by bag ban and tax proponents. Roach (2003) reports plastics industry figures that "compared to paper grocery bags, plastic grocery bags consume 40 percent less energy, generate 80 percent less solid waste, produce 70 percent fewer atmospheric emissions, and release up to 94 percent fewer waterborne wastes." Interestingly, many of the municipalities imposing plastic bag bans levy taxes on single-use paper bags, a policy that implicitly assumes paper bags are less harmful than plastic bags. Again, public policy toward plastic bags seems arbitrary.

People faced with plastic bag bans might also switch to the reusable cloth bags that are popular among eco-conscious consumers. Perhaps this is the desired outcome of bag bans and taxes. However, manufacturing reusable cloth bags requires much more carbon than single-use plastic bags. The reusable bags need to be used about 130 times to be carbon equivalent with single-use plastic bags (Mangu-Ward 2015; Minter 2015). Consumers who, perhaps out of forgetfulness or losing their bags, do not obtain such a usage level from their cloth bags would actually increase carbon emissions.

Another important consideration is that cloth bags require washing to keep them clean and sanitary. This is yet another behavioral response that could increase rather than decrease carbon emissions. A more significant concern might be if people do not wash their reusable bags. Since food sometimes leaks or spills while being transported from the store, bags can become contaminated with harmful bacteria, such as *E. coli*. Wallop (2010) reports that a study of reusable bags in the United Kingdom found that half contained traces of *E. coli* and many contained evidence of salmonella. Moreover, Wallop (2010) reports that a poll found a whopping 97 percent of reusable bag users reported that they never washed or bleached their bags. To analyze the potential health effects of banning single-use bags, Klick and Wright (2012) examined San Francisco's 2007 bag ban. They found that San Francisco's emergency room admissions for *E. coli* illnesses increased by about one-fourth relative to other counties when the county imposed its bag ban in October 2007. They also document increases in *E. coli*–related emergency department visits following bag bans in the cities of Palo Alto, Malibu, and Fairfax, and a 46 percent increase in deaths attributable to foodborne illnesses.[11] Needless to say, an upsurge in severe illnesses and fatalities is an expensive tradeoff for—even in the best case scenario—small reductions in litter or carbon emissions.

Saying that plastic grocery sacks are "single-use" also hides another possible unintended consequence. Many people actually do reuse plastic bags for such purposes as lining a cat litter box, disposing of soiled diapers, or bringing workout clothing to or from a gym. A bag ban would cause these consumers to find other ways to fill the needs now being filled by reused grocery bags. It is possible that grocery bags would be replaced with heavier plastic bags, thereby increasing carbon emissions and energy use. Indeed, reports indicate that can liner sales increased by 77 percent after Ireland's grocery sack ("carrier bag") tax was implemented.[12]

Yet another possible unintended consequence is an increase in stolen merchandise from grocery stores. Since plastic bags are no longer common, it is more difficult to determine which customers have paid for their goods and apparently some people skip the checkout line and take unbagged groceries out of stores. Systematic data on increased prevalence of theft are not available but anecdotal evidence suggests increased theft is not rare. Thompson (2013) reports that 21.1 percent of Seattle business owners surveyed indicated that the city's bag ban had increased shoplifting. Other news reports point to increased shoplifting following bans in Hawaii, California, and the United Kingdom.

In short, regardless of a consumer's reaction to a ban on plastic grocery sacks, it is entirely possible that he or she will choose an alternative that results in more rather than less carbon emissions. It is also possible that the unintended consequences of bag bans and taxes will include illnesses transmitted by reusable bags that have not been properly cleaned. While bag ban and tax advocates may feel good about restricting bag use, it is far from clear that they are actually achieving their stated policy goals.

THE POLITICAL ECONOMY OF BAG BANS AND TAXES

Up to this point, this chapter has ignored one of the central arguments of *Taxing Choice* and of this volume, namely, that discriminatory taxation is not just the result of naive or misguided policy but rather that it is the deliberate outcome of some people trying to use the political system to their advantage. Shughart (1997b, 2) notes that "while 'social cost' rhetoric has come to dominate the public-policy debate, ordinary political forces are frequently at work." This section considers the political economy of bag taxes and bans in the context of California's legislation banning plastic bags statewide.

The impetus behind passing regulatory legislation is often a "bootleggers and Baptists" alliance of morally earnest advocates and rent-seekers (Yandle 1983; Smith and Yandle 2014). It comes as no surprise, therefore, to see such a coalition pushing for California's statewide plastic bag ban (or pushing to avoid having it overturned by the 2016 referendum). The Baptists part of the coalition is obvious—environmentalists such as the Surfrider Foundation and the Sierra Club favor plastic bag bans even though, for reasons explained above, they are probably misguided.[13]

The bootleggers are the more interesting part of the coalition. In the case of California's bag ban, the obvious beneficiaries are producers of alternative bags. Hence it is no surprise that such companies as Earthwise Bag Company and Green Bag Company are among the supporters of the referendum upholding a statewide ban.

California grocers stand to reap a windfall from the ban and are part of the bootlegger coalition.[14] First, they will no longer supply plastic bags as part of the purchase price of their grocery sales. For firms facing downward-sloping demand curves, a decrease in production costs is only partially passed along to consumers in the form of lower prices. Nash (2014) reports that Californians use 14 billion plastic bags per year, and Mangu-Ward (2015) indicates that bags cost $0.01 apiece, so a bag ban would reduce retailer costs by $140 million, with some portion of this amount being captured as higher profits.

Second, California's plastic bag ban allows for paper bags, but retailers must charge at least 10¢ for them, with retailers pocketing the proceeds.[15] Since paper bags cost retailers less than 10¢ each, selling paper bags to shoppers becomes a new profit source for grocers. This is where the real money lies for retailers. Markay (2015) states that the paper bag provision is worth hundreds of millions of dollars; Nash (2014) claims that the windfall could approach $1 billion. Hence, it is not surprising that the California Grocers Association is leading the charge against the referendum that would overturn the plastic bag ban and has, according to Markay (2015), donated $100,000 in its effort to preserve the plastic bag ban.

With plastic bags banned and paper bags subject to the 10¢ fee, California's policy should also be supported by makers of reusable bags. Not surprisingly, Markay (2015) also reports that three reusable bag makers who would benefit from the ban have collectively contributed $10,000 to California vs. Big Plastic, an umbrella group advocating for maintaining California's bag ban.

Aspects of public choice other than bootleggers and Baptists are also evident in the California plastic bag ban. Legislators can glean support from their constituents by targeting benefits to their districts if the costs are dispersed across the state. What might cost a typical Californian a few dollars might provide a large benefit if transferred to a small number of beneficiaries. To this end, Skelton (2014) reports that California Senator Kevin de León of Los Angeles, whose district is home to two plastic bag makers, had a $2 million loan fund included in the plastic bag ban legislation to help existing bag makers retool to make reusable bags.

CONCLUSION

Plastic grocery bag bans and taxes are becoming increasingly common, but the rationalizations that they will reduce carbon emissions and litter do not withstand critical scrutiny. Instead, the restrictions appear to be victories of symbolism over sound policy, especially when their unintended consequences are considered. As with other instances of fiscal discrimination, predatory politics may often be found lurking beneath the green veneer of plastic bag bans and taxes.

NOTES

1. To be clear, this chapter focuses on the plastic bags with handles that are used at the checkouts of supermarkets and other retailers and are used by consumers to transport purchases from stores to their desired locations. It does not cover plastic garbage bags or the handleless plastic bags used for purchasing loose fruits or vegetables.

2. Actually, Nantucket banned plastic bags in 1990, but its ban drew little attention and the issue of bag bans and taxes was dormant for the subsequent decade.

3. Convery et al. (2007) report that Ireland's bag tax reduced bag use by 90 percent.

4. Applying the ban only to chain establishments is, of course, also a form of selective taxation. After all, whatever external costs might be imposed by plastic bags does not depend on whether the bag originated at a chain establishment or at a "mom and pop" business. However, exempting small businesses might be justified if the costs of enforcing a bag tax or ban are proportionately larger for small firms.

5. Unless otherwise noted, much of the information in this paragraph was obtained from a list of bans and taxes compiled by the Surfrider Foundation, an organization that advocates banning plastic bags. http://www.surfrider.org/pages/plastic-bag-bans-fees.

6. This paragraph is based on the National Conference of State Legislatures summary of state plastic bag legislation. http://www.ncsl.org/research/environment-and-natural-resources /plastic-bag-legislation.aspx.

7. Presumably bag-clogged storm drains would be less common in more developed countries, such as the United States, where trash disposal is more sophisticated. So even if Bangladesh's policy is the best choice among its available alternatives, a ban might not be the best alternative in other places.

8. Mangu-Ward also cites two California studies finding that plastic bags are 3.8 percent and 8 percent of coastal trash but notes that these studies are based on 1-day surveys and are not representative samples.

9. Convery et al. (2007, 3) write that Ireland's bag "tax implemented in March 2002 is not Pigouvian; there was no attempt to identify the marginal external costs and determine the optimum level of tax."

10. While clinging to questionable rationales of banning or taxing plastic bags, ban and tax proponents overlook one of the genuine harms associated with plastic bags—their tendency to get caught up in the mechanical workings of capital-intensive recycling systems (Minter 2015). It is hard to imagine, however, that a large percentage of bags produce such results, so this harm, while genuine, would be a weak basis for a bag ban or tax

11. Klick and Wright (2012) report that twelve individuals died from foodborne illnesses in San Francisco in the year before the bag ban; thus, their estimates imply the bag ban is associated with about five or six additional deaths from foodborne ailments.

12. See Frisman (2008), "The Effect of Plastic Bag Taxes."

13. The Sierra Club and the Surfrider Foundation are listed as supporters of California's ban on the referendum's Ballotpedia page. http://ballotpedia.org/California_Plastic_Bag_Ban _Referendum_(2016).

14. Although California grocers strongly support the ban, evidence of how bans affect retailers is mixed. Convery et al. (2007) survey seven retailers (some large chains) and conclude that the Irish bag tax had a neutral or positive effect on the retailers, but Taylor (n.d.) finds that Washington, DC's bag tax reduced retailer productivity by 5 percent in the short run. Dallas imposed a tax for the first 5 months of 2015, but it was repealed in part because of widespread confusion among retailers about which bags were subject to the tax and which were exempt (Benning 2015). The need to count the bags at the end of transactions also created confusion and slowed checkout lanes (McCarthy 2015).

15. This provision was necessary because California requires two-thirds legislative support for tax increases. Since California's Republican legislators controlled more than one-third of the seats and were not supportive of bag bans or taxes, the Democratic majority had to let retailers keep the 10¢ per bag fee rather than remit it to Sacramento as a tax.

REFERENCES

Benning, Tom. 2015. "Few Stores Are Found to Be Following Dallas Bag Law." *Dallas News*, January 16. http://www.dallasnews.com/news/community-news/park-cities/headlines/2015 0116-few-stores-are-found-to-be-following-dallas-bag-law.ece.

Convery, Frank, Simon McDonnell, and Susana Ferreira. 2007. "The Most Popular Tax in Europe? Lessons from the Irish Plastic Bags Levy." *Environmental and Resource Economics* 38 (1): 1–11.

Frisman, Paul. 2008. "The Effect of Plastic Bag Taxes and Bans on Garbage Bag Sales." OLR Research Report 2008-R-0685, Connecticut General Assembly, Office of Legislative Research, Hartford. https://www.cga.ct.gov/2008/rpt/2008-R-0685.htm.

Goodyear, Charlie. 2007. "S.F. First City to Ban Plastic Shopping Bags." *SF Gate*, March 27. http://www.sfgate.com/green/article/S-F-FIRST-CITY-TO-BAN-PLASTIC-SHOPPING -BAGS-2606833.php.

Klick, Jonathan, and Joshua D. Wright. 2012. "Grocery Bag Bans and Foodborne Illness." Research Paper 13-2, University of Pennsylvania, Institute for Law and Economics, Philadelphia. http://ssrn.com/abstract=2196481 or http://dx.doi.org/10.2139/ssrn.2196481.

Mangu-Ward, Katherine. 2015. "Plastic Bags Are Good for You." *Reason*, September 1. https:// reason.com/archives/2015/09/01/plastic-bags-are-good-for-you.

Markay, Lachlan. 2015. "California Grocers Gear Up to Protect Plastic Bag Ban Windfall." *Washington Free Beacon*, June 1. http://freebeacon.com/issues/california-grocers-gear-up-to -protect-plastic-bag-ban-windfall/.

McCarthy, Amy. 2015. "At Grocery Stores, Dallas' Paper and Plastic Ban Confuses Customers and Store Clerks Alike." *Dallas Observer*, January 5. http://www.dallasobserver.com/restaurants /at-grocery-stores-dallas-paper-and-plastic-bag-ban-confuses-customers-and-store-clerks -alike-7039532.

Miller. Jim. 2015. "California Plastic Bag Ban On Hold Pending 2016 Vote." *Sacramento Bee*, February 24. http://www.sacbee.com/news/politics-government/capitol-alert/article 11084876.html.

Minter, Adam. 2015. "How a Ban on Plastic Bags Can Go Wrong." *Bloomberg View*, August 18. http:// www.bloombergview.com/articles/2015-08-18/how-a-ban-on-plastic-bags-can-go-wrong.

Nash, James. 2014. "California Grocers Lobby for First State Plastic Bag Ban." *Bloomberg*, June 30. http://www.bloomberg.com/news/articles/2014-06-30/california-grocers-lobby-for-first -state-plastic-bag-ban.

Petru, Alexis. 2014. "A Brief History of the Plastic Bag." *Triple Pundit*, November 5. http://www .triplepundit.com/2014/11/brief-history-plastic-bag/.

Roach, John. 2003. "Are Plastic Grocery Bags Sacking the Environment?" *National Geographic News*, September 2. http://news.nationalgeographic.com/news/2003/09/0902_030902 _plasticbags.html.

Shughart, William F. II. 1997a. "Preface." In *Taxing Choice: The Predatory Politics of Fiscal Discrimination*, edited by William F. Shughart II, xiii–xv. New Brunswick, NJ: Transaction.

———. 1997b. "Introduction and Overview." In *Taxing Choice: The Predatory Politics of Fiscal Discrimination*, edited by William F. Shughart II, 1–9. New Brunswick, NJ: Transaction.

Skelton, George. 2014. "Charging for Paper Bags Isn't Justified." *Los Angeles Times*, August 24. http://www.latimes.com/local/politics/la-me-cap-plastic-bags-20140825-column.html.

Smith, Adam, and Bruce Yandle. 2014. *Bootleggers and Baptists: How Economic Forces and Moral Persuasion Interact to Shape Regulatory Politics*. Washington, DC: Cato Institute.

Taylor, Rebecca. n.d. "Paper or Plastic . . . or Reusable? An Analysis of the D.C. Disposable Bag Tax on Worker Productivity & Learning." Working Paper, University of California, Berkeley.

Taylor, Rebecca, and Sofia B. Villas-Boas. 2016. "Bans vs. Fees: Disposable Carryout Bag Policies and Bag Usage." *Applied Economic Perspectives and Policy* 38 (2): 351–72.

Thompson, Richard. 2013. "Plastic Bag Ban Leads to Nationwide Increase in Shoplifting Rates." *Daily Caller*, July.

Wallop, Harry. 2010. "Bags for Life Could Have *E.coli*." *Telegraph*, June 10. http://www.telegraph .co.uk/finance/newsbysector/retailandconsumer/7863807/Bags-for-life-could-have-E.coli .html.

Yandle, Bruce. 1983. "Bootleggers and Baptists—The Education of a Regulatory Economist." *Regulation*, May/June, 12–16.

CHAPTER 17
Gambling Taxes

DOUGLAS M. WALKER
Department of Economics, College of Charleston

COLLIN D. HODGES
Division of Resource Economics and Management,
West Virginia University

M ost politicians have an interest in increasing government tax revenues to support ever-growing government spending. This is one of the key motivations for the legalization and expansion of commercial gambling. Gambling is generally a state-level issue, with state governments being responsible for what types of gambling are legal in their respective states. The federal government is involved in regulating certain forms of gambling, for example, online betting, casinos, and poker.[1] Nevertheless, the great majority of industry revenue and tax revenue from legal gambling comes from state lotteries and commercial brick-and-mortar casinos.

What makes the gambling industry somewhat unique is that in many states, gambling is specifically banned either in the state's constitution, or through long-standing legislation. For example, the anti-gambling law in South Carolina dates back to 1802, and the police selectively enforce these laws.[2] Thus, an act of state government is usually required for the industry to exist legally in a state. With the existence of the gambling industry squarely in their hands, politicians may be expected to extract high rents from the industry.

This chapter discusses the expansion of legal gambling in the United States, with a focus on the taxes derived from lotteries and commercial casinos.

BACKGROUND

Legalized gambling began its modern expansion outside Nevada beginning with the introduction of the New Hampshire state lottery in 1964. Over the next few decades, other states would follow, and in 2016, all but five states operated a lottery.[3] The expansion of state lotteries was controversial, with a key argument against them being their regressive nature. Clotfelter and Cook (1991) provide a comprehensive discussion of the different issues surrounding lottery expansion, while Alm et al. (1993) and Jackson et al. (1994) provide econometric evidence on the factors explaining lottery expansion. Despite longstanding controversy over lotteries and state-sanctioned gambling in general, most state governments have apparently judged that the benefits from the lottery revenues outweigh the social costs of having the games. In many states that have more recently introduced lotteries, revenues have been earmarked for "good causes," such as scholarships for college students. Examples include the lotteries in Georgia and South Carolina. This earmarking has likely made lotteries more palatable for voters.

The present-day casino industry traces its roots back to 1931, when casinos were introduced in Nevada. Casinos were then legalized and opened in Atlantic City, NJ, in 1978. It was not until the 1987 *California v. Cabazon Band of Indians* (480 U.S. 202 (1987)) case in the US Supreme Court and the 1988 Indian Gaming Regulatory Act, which effectively relegated casino regulation to state governments, that tribal and commercial casinos began to spread across the United States. Currently more than 1,000 casinos operate in the United States.[4] The expansion of the casino industry has been the subject of much more controversy than lottery expansion was. This is likely because many people used to consider casino gambling "sinful" or a vice. During the early 1990s, concerns over the potential negative impacts of casinos were expressed with little or no supporting evidence by its staunchest opponents (e.g., see Goodman 1994). At the same time, empirical evidence in support of the positive economic impacts of casinos outside Nevada was limited. The lack of empirical evidence, combined with moral concerns about state-sponsored gambling, has fueled a long debate over the economic and social impacts of casinos.

Roughly half of US casinos are owned by sovereign Indian tribes. Tribal casinos come about after a process through which tribal lands are taken into trust by the Bureau of Indian Affairs (Department of the Interior) and a compact is signed between the tribe and the relevant state government.[5] Although tribal casinos do not pay taxes per se, in many states, tribes pay significant fees to maintain a monopoly in the state. For example, in Connecticut, the Mohegan Sun and Foxwoods casinos have agreed to pay 25 percent of their slot machine revenues to the state government in exchange for a guarantee that no commercial casinos will be approved in the state (Light and Rand 2005, 70). In some states, such as Alabama, Georgia, and South Carolina, Las Vegas–style table and slot machine games (Class III games) are not allowed. However, machine game manufacturers have been very clever in designing bingo games (Class II games), which are, from the customer's perspective, almost identical to Class III slot machines.[6] As a result, tribal casinos can effectively offer slot machines even in states where such machines are illegal. In the remainder of this chapter, discussion about casinos is limited to commercial casinos. This is because data on tribal casinos is generally not publicly available.[7]

Commercial casinos are those sanctioned and regulated by state governments. Such casinos have been legalized in more than fifteen states, beginning with South Dakota in 1989. Many Midwestern states adjacent to the Mississippi River legalized casinos in the early 1990s. The most recent wave of expansion has been in the Mid-Atlantic and Northeast, where Maryland, New York, and Massachusetts have recently legalized commercial casinos. As of early 2016, expansion is being considered in New Hampshire, Rhode Island, Connecticut, and New Jersey.

Although the expansion of lotteries and casino gambling could be attributed to an expanding appreciation for individual liberty or deference to consumer choice, empirical evidence suggests that fiscal stress has been a key determinant of lottery and casino legalization (Alm et al. 1993; Jackson et al. 1994; Calcagno et al. 2010). Interestingly, fiscal stress was not found to be a key determinant outside the United States (Richard 2010). However, it is clear that, in the United States, the potential revenues to governments remain a key catalyst for the expansion of legalized gambling.

TAX REVENUES

Although different states have legalized a variety of types of gambling— including pari-mutuel betting on horse and greyhound races—lotteries and casinos provide the vast majority of gambling tax revenues for state governments. For each $1 lottery ticket, approximately 20 percent goes to administrative costs and commissions to retailers, about 50 percent is returned to players in the form of prizes, and the remaining 30 percent is kept by the sponsoring state. This third allotment is called the "lottery tax." Empirical analysis has suggested that lotteries are generally designed to maximize revenues for the state (Garrett 2001).

Taxes on casino revenues vary greatly, from a low of around 6.75 percent in Nevada to 50 percent or more in such states as Illinois, New York, and Delaware. It is interesting to note that the casino tax rate is lower in larger, more established markets, including Nevada; Atlantic City, New Jersey; and Mississippi. Typically, taxes on casino revenues are applied to gross receipts, and most states have implemented complicated graduated tax schemes, so that larger casino properties with higher revenues will pay a higher percentage of their revenues than smaller casinos will. Even though taxes on commercial casinos and lottery sales are higher than on most other industries, legal gambling still contributes only a modest amount to state coffers. Walker and Jackson (2011) calculate state revenues due to gambling taxes to be less than 5 percent in most states. Recent evidence suggests that government revenues from the gambling industry have flattened, despite casino industry expansion (see Povich 2015).

Figures 1–4 present aggregate revenues from lotteries and casinos across all US states and the take by government, again aggregating across all states.[8]

Figures 1 and 2 illustrate lottery sales and state revenues over the past 15 years. Sales have continued to climb at a healthy rate since 2000, with the exception of flat sales during the Great Recession. Lottery sales in fiscal year 2013 were more than $64 billion, with state governments retaining about $21 billion from lottery sales in that year.

Casino revenues in the United States have increased dramatically since 2001, to about $38 billion in 2014. (This amount does not include tribal casinos, which are probably about another $30 billion.) The government tax revenue in all states amounted to about $8 billion in 2011.

INTERINDUSTRY RELATIONSHIPS

One common concern about the expansion of casino gambling has been that the industry may lead to the demise of other types of gambling or other nongambling industries. Such interindustry relationships are commonly called "industry cannibalization" in the gambling literature (Walker 2013, 26–28). Several studies have examined the relationships among different types of gambling. Most evidence suggests that casinos and lotteries are substitutes, and that these forms of gambling harm one another's revenues (see, e.g.,

Figure 1. Total Lottery Sales, All States, 2000–2013

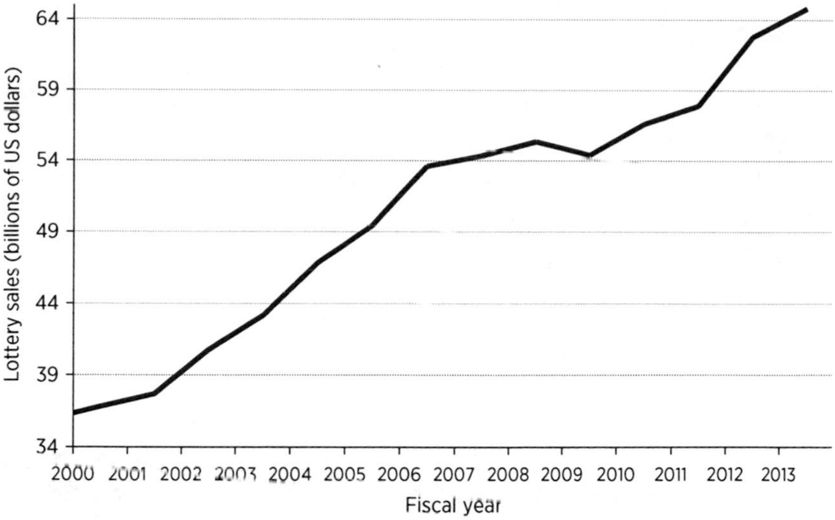

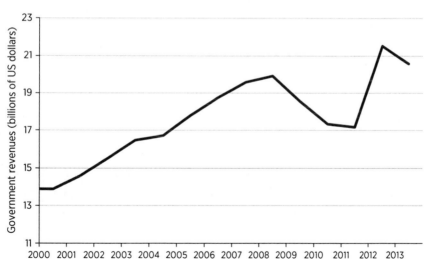

Source: *LaFleur's Magazine*, 2009–2013; *LaFleur's World Lottery Almanac* 17e, 1993–2008.

Figure 2. Total Government "Tax" Revenues from Lottery Sales, All States, 2000–2013

Source: *LaFleur's Magazine*, 2009–2013; *LaFleur's World Lottery Almanac* 17e, 1993–2008.

Figure 3. Total Casino Revenues, All States, 2001–2014

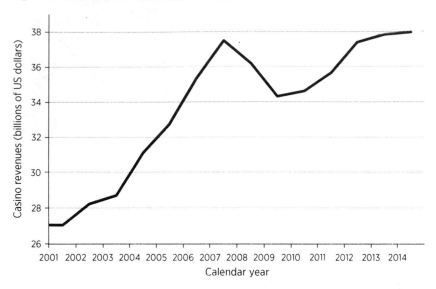

Source: University of Nevada, Las Vegas, Center for Gaming Research, Las Vegas, NV. http://gaming.unlv.edu/.

Note: Tribal casino revenues are not included in this figure.

Mobilia 1992; Anders et al. 1998; Ray 2001; Siegel and Anders 2001; Elliott and Navin 2002; Popp and Stehwien 2002; Kearney 2005).[9] However, there is no conclusive evidence from the literature that all types of gambling act as substitutes for one another. One comprehensive US study has found that certain types of gambling are complementary (Walker and Jackson 2008). For example, horse racing gambling revenues and casino revenues have been found to be complements, but this may stem from the development of "racinos" (racetrack casinos).

The relationships among different types of gambling are clearly important as a matter of politics. In some states, incumbent gambling industries staunchly oppose casinos. An example is the horse racing industry's opposition to casinos in Kentucky (see Hall 2014). In many states, the effect of casinos on lotteries has been an important concern. If casinos and lotteries are substitutes, for example, then the net benefit from casino taxes will be less than their gross tax receipts, as lottery tax receipts are likely to fall as a result of casino expansion. However, a recent study found that casinos had a negative impact on the lottery of only about 5 percent. This suggests that the net impact of casinos on aggregate gambling taxes are still overwhelmingly positive (Cummings et al. 2017).

Figure 4. Total State Government Revenues from Casino Taxes, All States, 1998–2011

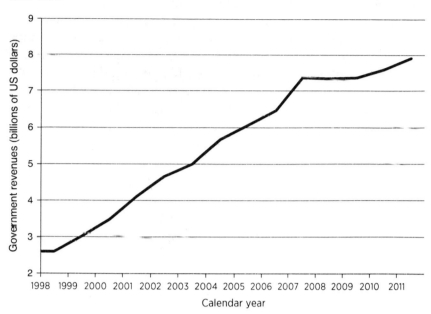

Source: University of Nevada, Las Vegas, Center for Gaming Research, Las Vegas, NV. http://gaming .unlv.edu/.

Note: Tribal casino revenues are not included in this figure.

Much less is known about the relationship between gambling and non-gambling industries and whether casinos significantly "cannibalize" other industries. Cannibalization might occur, for example, if people divert much of their entertainment spending away from sporting events or movies and concerts, for example, in order to gamble at casinos. The limited available evidence on property values in areas surrounding casinos suggests that the effect of casinos is probably positive on net (Phipps 2004; Wenz 2007; Wiley and Walker 2011). Cotti (2008) examines county-level employment and wage data in the United States, finding that casinos have had a modestly positive impact on employment, with a very slight positive effect on local wages. This evidence suggests that, at least at the county level, casinos likely have not hurt other industries. Even if they did, however, the tax rate applied to gambling is much higher than the tax rate typically applied to nongambling goods and services. Therefore, it seems safe to conclude that even considering interindustry relationships, casinos and lotteries have tended to increase net state revenues.

MARKET SATURATION

During the past few years there has been increasing concern, particularly among politicians in the northeastern United States, that the casino industry may be becoming saturated. The primary example of this is in Atlantic City, where four of the twelve casinos there closed during 2014.[10] Although the term "saturation" has not yet been clearly defined in the context of the casino industry, it loosely means that there are too many casinos for the market. Various stakeholders may adopt differing perspectives. For example, casino patrons may not think a market is saturated until there is at least one casino within a 15-minute drive from their house. Politicians may view market saturation to mean that a new casino opening does not increase overall casino tax revenues. The casino industry might define saturation as the point at which a new casino causes a decline in existing casinos' revenues or profits. Or it might simply be the point at which consumer spending at casinos reaches its maximum, regardless of new or additional supply of casino capacity. Almost no academic research has been done in this area.[11]

Only three published studies have focused on the saturation issue, with an emphasis on the impact of new casinos in the Northeast (McGowan 2009; Condliffe 2012; Barrow et al. 2016). Condliffe and McGowan focus on whether the introduction of casinos in Pennsylvania led to an increase or decrease in regional aggregate casino revenues. Findings from the studies are in conflict and use simplistic empirical analyses, limiting both the impact and generalizability of their results. Barrow et al. (2016) provides a framework for analyzing the degree to which the casino industry might be saturated. However one limitation of the proposed metrics is that they do not effectively deal with how tourism might affect the saturation measures. Despite the recent papers in this area, it remains one of the most seriously neglected areas of research on the economic impacts of gambling, as the issue has important implications for the stability of casino tax revenue streams.

SOCIAL ISSUES

Gambling can be thought of as a form of entertainment. Casino games and lotteries are entertaining to many people because of the rush of excitement they may create. For example, the consumption value of lottery tickets may simply be the enjoyment people have imagining what they would do if they won a multimillion dollar jackpot. Casino games can be exciting both because of the potential to win large sums of money and the social nature of the games. Similarly, playing daily fantasy sports games may be enjoyable largely because players have friends who are also playing, and they enjoy comparing their results.

Regardless of the consumer benefits from gambling, most politicians believe that the government has a role in regulating gambling. This perspective may have its roots in a moral concern over gambling, or the view that gambling is a vice that should be controlled. However, in recent decades the debate over lotteries and casinos has raised other concerns about the effects of legal gambling. As noted earlier, a key concern with lotteries has been their regressive nature. Nevertheless, state governments have expanded lotteries. Because lottery revenues are often earmarked for positive purposes, such as subsidizing college tuition, the regressive nature of lotteries has apparently not quelled their popularity.

Concerns over casino gambling center around social cost issues. The social costs of gambling have been debated in the literature and are still controversial (Walker 2013). The potential harms that stem from gambling are generally associated with problem gambling, which is akin to drug or alcohol addiction. Problem gambling is gambling to an extent that it negatively affects a person's professional or personal life.[12] Such problems are commonly manifest as financial problems and are thought to lead to increased rates of crime, divorce, and bankruptcy (Walker 2013). However, the degree to which gambling alone can be blamed for such problems is debatable, because most problem gamblers have other disorders, often involving excessive drug and alcohol use (for a discussion, see Petry et al. 2005; Kessler et al. 2008).

The fact that gambling has been linked to a variety of social problems has likely led to its unique status among industries. It is one of the most strictly regulated and highest taxed industries in the United States. Despite the potential for large tax revenues, many observers argue that the state should not be offering, sponsoring, or promoting gambling because of the potential public health harms. Such concerns seem to have been overwhelmed by the arguments in favor of expanded gambling, as no movement has succeeded in repealing casino or lottery legalization in any state.

PUBLIC CHOICE ISSUES

As already noted, empirical evidence suggests that state lotteries are designed to maximize the revenues of the sponsoring state governments. Casino legislation, too, seems to be drafted with an aim toward maximizing tax revenues. However, state governments do little to analyze the tax rates that should be applied to casino revenues to maximize government revenues. That the casino industry is allowed to exist by an act of government raises the potential for enormous rents to be captured by state governments.

Most states do not allow a free market in casinos, although Nevada is close. Typically, a strict limit is placed on the number of casinos allowed, as well as the number of gambling machines and table games (i.e., gambling positions) allowed in each casino. States do vary on the degree to which they control the sizes and number of casinos. States that have more recently legalized gambling commonly use a regional model, in which a single casino is allowed in each region of the state. Examples of this model appear in Kansas, Ohio, and Massachusetts. Obviously, when the state restricts the number of casinos, rent-seeking is likely to occur. This situation creates an opportunity for corrupt activities (Walker and Calcagno 2013).

One result of the special status of casinos is that the casino industry itself has a large hand in helping develop the regulations that will control it. This has resulted in regulatory changes over time that appear to be favorable to the casino industry (Calcagno and Walker 2016). For example, states such as Missouri that initially had regulated maximum bets no longer do. States that once allowed only riverboat casinos, such as Mississippi, now allow land-based casinos. Regardless of a trend toward more favorable regulations, the industry is still heavily taxed. However, given that casino taxes represent a relatively small part of state governments' budgets, why are casinos so hotly debated and promoted by politicians?

One answer to this question is that, although casinos do not make a big difference in most states' finances, casinos can help politically—at the margin (Walker 2013). Consider that many states have seen growing fiscal crises, particularly since the Great Recession. Politically, it is difficult to cut spending on popular (and even unpopular) government programs. It is also unpalatable to raise sales, property, or income taxes at the state level. This may help explain why politicians are so willing to consider the legalization and expansion of the gambling industry. This explanation is also consistent with the findings from the literature that fiscal stress is a key determinant of lottery and casino legalization.

TECHNOLOGY AND THE FUTURE OF GAMBLING

The landscape of legal gambling in the United States has changed dramatically since 1990. State lotteries exist in the majority of states, casino gambling is available in most states, and only two states currently ban all forms of gambling. Already widespread, lotteries and casinos are unlikely to see dramatic change in the near future. The key determinant of how the gambling industry will develop is technology. The ability of people to gamble over the Internet using their home computers or smartphones presents unimaginable possibilities for the expansion of gambling. For example, the popularity of daily fantasy sports, exemplified by Draft Kings and Fan Duel, exploded during the fall of 2015, along with a constant barrage of advertising. Both potential customers and regulators have taken note. A variety of state governments and the federal government are now studying this new activity. There is some debate over whether these activities constitute gambling and how the current laws will treat daily fantasy sports. Online poker and online lotteries have seen similar developments over the past few years, although they developed somewhat more slowly than daily fantasy sports (see Rose 2016).

It would be surprising if state governments and perhaps even the federal government did not decide to step in to regulate all forms of online gambling.[13] Although such regulations will be sold under the guise of consumer protection, it is likely that regulated online gambling would also come with heavy taxes.

CONCLUSION

Despite the view of some that gambling is a vice and should not be sanctioned or allowed by government, most US states have legalized gambling in one form or another. Lotteries have expanded to forty-five states since they were introduced in New Hampshire in 1964. Casinos began their spread outside Nevada and Atlantic City, New Jersey, beginning in 1989. Now more than 1,000 casinos operate in the United States, and gambling plays an important public finance function in many states. The overall contribution of the gambling industry to state budgets is still somewhat small, even though states impose higher taxes on gambling revenues than on many other goods or services.

Increased competition in the gambling industry across state lines has been a catalyst for reconsidering gambling policy in some markets. Some states, for example, have begun to consider lowering their casino tax rates. Other states have expanded the number of casinos allowed beyond what they allowed when casinos were first legalized. In still other states, completely new ideas are gaining attention. For example, some politicians in New Hampshire have even suggested that a free market in gambling might be the best model. It would certainly be unique and could operate better than highly regulated markets.

The most interesting developments in the gambling industry are certainly technology related. Little is known about the relationships between online forms of gambling and traditional lottery and brick-and-mortar casinos. Certainly, continuous technological advances pose a potential threat to the traditional gambling sectors, and, in turn, to state gambling tax revenues. As a result, we should not be surprised to see state governments, and even the federal government, taking aggressive steps to control and tax new types of gambling as technology allows their development. As a result, the US gambling industry will likely be very different 10 years from now.

NOTES

1. Online poker, sports betting, and daily fantasy sports are examples of games that the federal government has a role in defining and regulating. The legality and regulation of these industries have been controversial and are not settled matters at the time of this writing. As a result, and because revenues from these components of the gambling industry still represent a very small proportion of overall revenues, these issues are not addressed in this chapter.

2. See http://www.scstatehouse.gov/code/t16c019.php for the anti-gambling law in South Carolina, and Town of Mt. Pleasant v. Chimento et al., South Carolina Supreme Court Opinion No. 27197, November 21, 2012, for an example of a case near Charleston in which a home poker game was raided by police.

3. The exceptions are Alabama, Alaska, Hawaii, Nevada, and Mississippi.

4. The number includes tribal and commercial casinos, as well as racetrack casinos and card rooms. See www.casinocity.com for a list of casinos and other gambling venues in each state.

5. For more information, see http://www.indianaffairs.gov/WhatWeDo/ServiceOverview/Gaming/index.htm.

6. For example, at the Poarch Creek Indian tribe's Wind Creek Casino in Wetumpka, AL, the machines are identical to Class III slot machines with one minor detail. At one corner of the display screen, there is a small bingo card. Once the player hits the "play" button, a new bingo card appears, along with winning numbers. Then the slot machine display begins and shows the result of the slot machine play. This entire process takes about 2 seconds. Although it looks just like a Class III slot machine, it is technically and legally considered to be a bingo (Class II) machine.

7. Some aggregated tribal casino data are available in Meister (2015).

8. The data presented in figures 1–4 are the most recent publicly available data as of this writing. As mentioned earlier, tribal casino revenues are excluded, as are any so-called fees paid by tribal governments to state governments in which tribal casinos are located.

9. In this discussion, the terms "substitutes" and "complements" refer only to the relationship between revenues in different industries, not to the economic relationship between the demand for one product and changes in the price of another.

10. Recent data showing higher profits for the remaining Atlantic City casinos suggest that the closures in 2014 may have simply been a normal market correction. See Wayne Perry, Associated Press, "Atlantic Casino Profits Up 31 Percent," May 23, 2016, https://www.indystar.com/story/news/2016/05/23/ac-casino-profits-increase/32621749/.

11. The study by Walker and Nesbit (2014) examined the effect a new casino in Missouri would have on existing casinos' revenues, but this was not a direct test for industry saturation.

12. A growing literature in psychology and medicine is dedicated to understanding and treating gambling problems. Such problems are estimated to affect about 1 percent of the general population and a higher percentage of the adolescent population.

13. As of July 2017, it is unclear how the federal government may act toward expanded online gambling. This issue has become more complicated as US Attorney General Jeff Sessions has reportedly recused himself from making any decisions regarding online gambling (see Brody 2017).

REFERENCES

Alm, James M., Michael McKee, and Mark Skidmore. 1993. "Fiscal Pressure, Tax Competition, and the Introduction of State Lotteries." *National Tax Journal* 46: 463–76.

Anders, Gary C., Donald Siegel, and Munther Yacoub. 1998. "Does Indian Casino Gambling Reduce State Revenues? Evidence from Arizona." *Contemporary Economic Policy* 16: 347–55.

Barrow, Clyde W., David R. Borges, and Alan P. Meister. 2016. "An Empirical Framework for Assessing Market Saturation in the U.S. Casino Industry." *Gaming Law Review and Economics* 20 (5): 397–411.

Brody, Ben. 2017. "Adelson-Backed Lobbying against Web Gaming Makes Sessions Fold." *Bloomberg*, June 30. www.bloomberg.com.

Calcagno, Peter T,, and Douglas M. Walker. 2016. "A Review of Regulatory Theory and the U.S. Casino Industry." *Journal of Gambling Business and Economics* 10 (1): 14–39.

Calcagno, Peter T., Douglas M. Walker, and John D. Jackson. 2010. "Determinants of the Probability and Timing of Commercial Casino Legalization in the United States." *Public Choice* 142: 69–90.

Clotfelter, Charles T., and Philip J. Cook. 1991. *Selling Hope: State Lotteries in America*. Cambridge, MA: Harvard University Press.

Condliffe, Simon. 2012. "Pennsylvania Casinos' Cannibalization of Regional Gambling Revenues." *UNLV Gaming Research & Review Journal* 16 (1): 45–58.

Cotti, Chad D. 2008. "The Effect of Casinos on Local Labor Markets: A County Level Analysis." *Journal of Gambling Business and Economics* 2 (2): 17–41.

Cummings, Will E., Douglas M. Walker, and Chad D. Cotti. 2017. "The Effect of Casino Proximity on Lottery Sales: Evidence from Maryland." *Contemporary Economic Policy* 35(4): 654–99.

Elliott, Donald S., and John C. Navin. 2002. "Has Riverboat Gambling Reduced State Lottery Revenue?" *Public Finance Review* 30 (3): 235–47.

Garrett, Thomas A. 2001. "The Leviathan Lottery: Testing the Revenue Maximization Objective of State Lotteries as Evidence for Leviathan." *Public Choice* 109: 101–17.

Goodman, Robert. 1994. *Legalized Gambling as a Strategy for Economic Development*. Northampton, MA: United States Gambling Study.

Hall, Gregory. 2014. "Horse Group Now Opposes Kentucky Casinos." *Courier-Journal*, December 5. www.courier-journal.com.

Jackson, John D., David S. Saurman, and William F. Shughart II. 1994. "Instant Winners: Legal Change in Transition and the Diffusion of State Lotteries." *Public Choice* 80: 245–63.

Kearney, Melissa S. 2005. "State Lotteries and Consumer Behavior." *Journal of Public Economics* 89: 2269–99.

Kessler, R. C., I. Hwang, R. LaBrie, M. Petukhova, N. A. Sampson, K. C. Winters, and H. J. Shaffer. 2008. "DSM-IV Pathological Gambling in the National Comorbidity Survey Replication." *Psychological Medicine* 38: 1351–60.

Light, Steven, and Kathryn Rand. 2005. *Indian Gaming & Tribal Sovereignty: The Casino Compromise*. Lawrence: University Press of Kansas.

McGowan, Richard. 2009. "The Competition for Gambling Revenue: Pennsylvania v. New Jersey." *Gaming Law Review and Economics* 13 (2): 145–55.

Meister, Alan. 2015. *Casino City's Indian Gaming Industry Report*. Newton, MA: Casino City.

Mobilia, Pamela. 1992. "Trends in Gambling: The Pari-Mutuel Racing Industry and Effect of State Lotteries, a New Market Definition." *Journal of Cultural Economics* 16: 51–62.

Petry, Nandy M., Frederick S. Stinson, and Bridget F. Grant. 2005. "Comorbidity of DSM-IV Pathological Gambling and Other Psychiatric Disorders: Results from the National Epidemiological Surveys on Alcohol and Related Conditions." *Journal of Clinical Psychiatry* 66 (5): 564–74.

Phipps, Alan G. 2004. "Crime and Disorder, and House Sales and Prices around the Casino Sites in Windsor, Ontario, Canada." *Canadian Geographer* 48 (December): 403–32.

Popp, Anthony V., and Charles Stehwien. 2002. "Indian Casino Gambling and State Revenue: Some Further Evidence." *Public Finance Review* 30 (4): 320–30.

Povich, Elaine. 2015. "State Gambling Revenue Takes Hit as Millennials Bring New Habits to Casinos." *Stateline*, September 15. http://www.pewtrusts.org/en/research-and-analysis/blogs/stateline/2015/09/15/state-gambling-revenue-takes-hit-as-millennials-bring-new-habits-to-casinos.

Ray, Margaret A. 2001. "How Much on That Doggie at the Window? An Analysis of the Decline in Greyhound Racing Handle." *Review of Regional Studies* 31: 165–76.

Richard, Brian. 2010. "Diffusion of an Economic Development Policy Innovation: Explaining the International Spread of Casino Gambling." *Journal of Gambling Studies* 26 (2): 287–300. doi: 10.1007/s10899-009-9166-4.

Rose, I. Nelson. 2016. "Daily Fantasy Sports & Internet Poker: Winning Battles, but Losing War." *Gaming Law Review and Economics* 20 (4): 308–12.

Siegel, Donald, and Gary C. Anders. 2001. "The Impact of Indian Casinos on State Lotteries: A Case Study of Arizona." *Public Finance Review* 29: 139–47.

Walker, Douglas M. 2013. *Casinonomics: The Socioeconomic Impacts of the Casino Industry*. New York: Springer.

Walker, Douglas M., and Peter T. Calcagno. 2013. "Casinos and Political Corruption in the United States: A Granger Causality Analysis." *Applied Economics* 45 (34): 4781–95.

Walker, Douglas M., and John D. Jackson. 2008. "Do U.S. Gambling Industries Cannibalize Each Other?" *Public Finance Review* 36 (3): 308–33.

———. 2011. "The Effect of Legalized Gambling on State Government Revenue." *Contemporary Economic Policy* 29 (1): 101–14.

Walker, Douglas M., and Todd M. Nesbit. 2014. "Casino Revenue Sensitivity to Competing Casinos: A Spatial Analysis of Missouri." *Growth and Change* 45 (1): 21–40. doi: 10.1111/grow.12035.

Wenz, Mike. 2007. "The Impact of Casino Gambling on Housing Markets: A Hedonic Approach." *Journal of Gambling Business and Economics* 1 (2): 101–20.

Wiley, Jonathan A., and Douglas M. Walker. 2011. "Casino Revenues and Retail Property Values: The Detroit Case." *Journal of Real Estate Finance and Economics* 42: 99–114.

PART V

EVALUATING AND PRESCRIBING BETTER TAX POLICY

CHAPTER 18
In Loco Parentis: A Paternalism
Ranking of the States

RUSSELL S. SOBEL

Baker School of Business, The Citadel

JOSHUA C. HALL

College of Business and Economics, West Virginia University

T he Latin term *in loco parentis*, originally from English common law,
translates to "in place of a parent" and is used to refer to cases where an
organization or individual takes on the functions or responsibilities of
a parent over someone else. The chapters in this volume, *For Your Own Good*,
and its predecessor, *Taxing Choice* (Shughart 1997), discuss some of the many
ways governments use their policies to distort the choices that would normally
be made by individuals in a free society. Rather than allowing choices based
on unregulated markets and market prices, governments attempt to alter these
choices in certain directions. In this chapter, we rank the states in terms of
their degree of policy paternalism. That is, we attempt to measure the extent to
which the policies of each state are consistent with paternalistic public policy.[1]

At the outset, we acknowledge that there are two sides to the debate over
the extent to which governments should engage in paternalistic policies.
On one side are people who tend to favor less government paternalism and
prefer to leave these choices up to individuals acting on their own free will.

377

The policies preferred by this side are broadly based and minimize the distortions in the relative prices and choices faced by individuals. There are generally two categories of arguments, one a normative (i.e., subjective) view that people should in principle be free to decide, act, and trade without interference; and that government's main role is to protect the rights and liberties of otherwise free individuals.[2] The second category of arguments is positive (i.e., objective), arguing that the government policies often create secondary effects (unintended consequences) that result in those policies either exacerbating the problem they were trying to solve or creating problems in other dimensions to a point where the total costs exceed the total benefits from having the policy.[3] That is, the policies may have positive effects that are easy to see, but the negative ones that are not so obvious may swamp the more easily visible benefits.[4] The chapters in this volume, and its predecessor, fall on the side of minimizing government distortions of free choice.

On the other side of this argument are people who believe paternalistic government policies can steer individuals toward making "better" choices. At the root of this argument is the belief that if left to their own accord, individuals have biases or tendencies that may lead them to make bad decisions in the absence of a governmental "nudge."[5] The policies preferred by proponents of this side restrict the availability of certain goods deemed harmful (e.g., the war on drugs), increase the prices of undesirable behaviors or lower the prices of desirable ones (e.g., tax cigarettes and subsidize recycling), and mandate individuals do certain things (e.g., mandated retirement savings and mandatory flood insurance).

While we acknowledge this debate, we seek to create an unbiased index of the extent to which states engage in policies consistent with the paternalistic view. The only possible bias we introduce is which end of the spectrum is ranked first versus fiftieth. As economists in agreement with the arguments made by economists in general, and illustrated in this volume, we rank the state with the *least* paternalistic policies as being first, the highest rated state. So, our index ranks are not really a ranking of paternalism, but of the *freedom from* paternalism. The fiftieth ranked state in our index would be the most paternalistic. This index would be equally useful to someone who was on the opposite side of this argument, but their preference would be to give the fiftieth ranked state instead a ranking of "first," with that term's connotation of "best." Therefore, while individual views of the relative merit of moving up or down in this index may be different, the rankings are not affected by the position we take on the underlying issue. Our job is simply to try to measure, with data, the extent to which states engage (or fail to engage) in policies consistent with paternalism.[6]

We begin by looking specifically at the relative extent to which states use selective taxes (primarily on gluttonous or so-called sinful activities, e.g., drinking or smoking) versus broad-based tax policies. We then more narrowly consider the specific areas of "saint subsidies," and then finally other miscellaneous restrictions and bans consistent with paternalism. Each state is rated in each area, and then an overall index is provided that incorporates information from all areas. That final index is used to rank the states against one another.

GENERAL METHODOLOGY

While there is no single, perfect way to create an index, we follow the well-established methodology used to create the Economic Freedom of the World (EFW) index (Gwartney et al. 2015). This methodology is proven in the literature on index creation; it allows for a method of translating a variety of data into an index score that ranges from 0 to 10 for each variable and that can be aggregated both into subcategories and an overall index. The EFW index is a widely used political economy indicator that has been cited in hundreds of studies across business and social science disciplines (Hall and Lawson 2014). Gwartney and Lawson (2003) provide an overview of the history and philosophical foundations of the EFW index; the tradeoffs involved in constructing any political economy indicator such as the EFW can be found in Lawson (2008).

We are creating a single cross-sectional index that ranks the states, so we must pick a particular year for collecting our data. Based on current data availability, we have chosen to use data for 2013, as it has the most abundant data for our variables of interest. If a variable is not available for 2013, however, we use data available from the year that is closest to 2013. Like the EFW, we break our index into conceptual areas and average ratings across the areas. We have chosen to break the index down into three conceptual areas: use of selective taxes that are often sin taxes (Area 1), use of "saint" subsidies that reward behavior viewed as beneficial (Area 2), and use of miscellaneous bans and regulations (Area 3). With this first attempt to evaluate the extent to which state policies may be consistent with paternalism, we realize that we may be missing particular taxes, subsidies, or policies that are paternalistic and for which comparable data are available across all fifty states. However, we have identified all the major tax, subsidy, and regulatory policies consistent with paternalism.[7] These three conceptual areas are described in more detail below.

Each of the three areas can be described using variables that reflect the analytical concept of each area. For example, for Area 1, we use state excise taxes on beer to capture the degree of paternalism toward the consumption of alcohol. For most variables, we use the following formula to calculate the area ratings from 0 to 10:

$$\text{Rating}_i = 10 \times (V_i - V_{min})/(V_{max} - V_{min}),\qquad(1)$$

where the index i is the state being rated on the specific variable, V_{min} is the minimum value the variable takes on across all states, and V_{max} is the maximum value the variable takes on across all states. We again remind the reader that since we are measuring freedom from paternalism that V_{max} is frequently a small number and V_{min} a large number. Since most states also collect the normal sales tax on beer in addition to excise taxes, the maximum freedom from paternalism was set to 0, and the minimum (or most paternalistic) value for this variable was set to the highest beer excise tax rate in the country— that of Tennessee at $1.17 per gallon. Tennessee therefore receives a 0 on that component of the index and the state with the highest rating on the index with a 9.8 is Wyoming, which only has a $0.02 per gallon excise tax on beer. The 0–10 ratings are averaged over each area and then each of the areas is summed to make a final rating and ranking of the states of the extent to which they are free from paternalism.

AREA 1: USE OF SELECTIVE TAXES

In this section, we examine the extent to which tax policy at the state level is consistent with paternalism in the sense that it does not rely on a broad-based sales tax. A broad-based tax would be, for example, a 5 percent sales tax on all goods. Such a tax does not alter the relative prices of goods, but rather applies equally to all goods. In contrast, selective taxes set rates differently for different goods (e.g., special individual taxes on soda drinks, gasoline, or alcohol) and thus alter relative prices and distort consumer choice regarding those goods relative to all other goods.[8] This change in the relative prices alters the choices made by individuals, lessening the quantity purchased of the now relatively higher cost item (and increasing the quantity purchased of the relatively lower cost item). The result of the tax is a reduction in total consumer welfare or utility, assuming that consumers can and do know what is in their own best interests.[9]

However, the use of selective taxes over broad-based taxes in general has even more detrimental impacts on economic growth and prosperity than simply affecting consumption choices.[10] Government policies are set and influenced by the efforts of individuals through lobbying and other means of producing political pressure. These efforts are socially wasteful and have an opportunity cost in terms of taking resources away from the production of goods and services. Just as with a professor who is easy to talk into changing grades if a student came to complain, the line will soon form outside the office. More and more individuals and groups will spend their time and effort to seek favorable tax treatments for themselves and unfavorable tax treatments for their competitors.

The first part of our index attempts to include a general measure of the degree to which a state's sales tax policies are uniform versus selective. Our data for this area come from the US Census Bureau's 2013 Annual Survey of State Government Finances (US Census Bureau 2013). This survey decomposes sales tax revenue into two categories: (1) "General Sales and Gross Receipts Taxes," and (2) "Selective Sales and Gross Receipts Taxes." The first category is revenue from the state's general retail sales tax (if they have one) that is broadly applied to all goods. The second category is what is relevant for our purposes. It measures the revenue from individual taxes on items ranging from soda to gasoline—the revenue from every consumption-based tax that is independently determined. Arguably, some states are high-tax states while others are low-tax states due to many factors. For our purposes, we want to know not necessarily how high these sales and gross receipt taxes are, but rather how heavily states use selective sales and gross receipt taxes relative to general sales and gross receipts taxes. Thus, we compute what percentage selective tax revenue is of each state's total sales and gross receipts tax revenue as our first component in Area 1.

For each state, the first column in table 1 shows the percentage of total sales and gross receipts tax revenue that is attributable to selective taxes. Column 2 shows the index value we assign, on a scale of 0–10, where 0 represents all taxes being selective sales taxes in 2013 and 10 represents no use of selective taxes (which does not actually occur). The formula used to rank states is shown in equation 1 above. The most paternalisitic a state could be (i.e., minimum freedom from paternalism), V_{min}, is set to the highest percentage of sales and gross receipt taxes accounted for by selective sales taxes that exists in 2013: 100 percent. Alaska, Delaware, Montana, New Hampshire, and Oregon all receive 100 percent of their sales and gross receipts revenue from selective sales and gross receipts taxes and thus receive a rating of 0.[11] The least paternalistic state is Wyoming, which receives only 15.0 percent of its sales and gross receipt revenue through the use of selective excise taxes and therefore receives a score of 8.5 [$10 \times (15.0 - 100.0)/(0 - 100.0)$]. Not all the goods and services taxed in this manner are paternalistic, as states tax a wide variety of goods and services, but we think that this variable captures the extent to which a state's policy toward the taxation of goods and services is consistent with paternalism in a manner not captured by the other components in Area 1.

Table 1. Area 1: Selective Taxes

State	Selective Excise Taxes	Score	Soda Taxes	Score	Cigarette Taxes	Score	Beer Taxes	Score	Wine Taxes	Score	Spirit Taxes	Score	Area 1 Overall Score
Alabama	50.5	5.0	6.7	6.7	0.43	9.0	1.05	1.0	1.70	4.6	18.24	4.8	5.2
Alaska	100.0	0.0	10.0	10.0	2.00	5.4	1.07	0.9	2.50	2.1	12.80	6.4	4.1
Arizona	21.1	7.9	10.0	10.0	2.00	5.4	0.16	8.6	0.84	7.3	3.00	9.1	8.1
Arkansas	29.4	7.1	6.7	6.7	1.15	7.4	0.32	7.3	1.42	5.5	6.57	8.1	7.0
California	29.5	7.1	3.3	3.3	0.87	8.0	0.20	8.3	0.20	9.4	3.30	9.1	7.5
Colorado	43.5	5.6	3.3	3.3	0.84	8.1	0.08	9.3	0.32	9.0	2.28	9.4	7.5
Connecticut	43.1	5.7	3.3	3.3	3.40	2.2	0.23	8.0	0.72	7.7	5.40	8.5	5.9
Delaware	100.0	0.0	10.0	10.0	1.60	6.3	0.16	8.6	0.97	6.9	3.75	8.9	6.8
Florida	29.1	7.1	3.3	3.3	1.34	6.9	0.48	5.9	2.25	2.9	6.50	8.2	5.7
Georgia	28.8	7.1	6.7	6.7	0.37	9.1	1.01	1.4	1.51	5.2	3.79	8.9	6.4
Hawaii	25.1	7.5	10.0	10.0	3.20	2.6	0.93	2.1	1.38	5.6	5.98	8.3	6.0
Idaho	25.3	7.5	10.0	10.0	0.57	8.7	0.15	8.7	0.45	8.6	10.92	6.9	8.4
Illinois	44.6	5.5	3.3	3.3	1.98	5.4	0.23	8.0	1.39	5.6	8.55	7.6	5.9
Indiana	34.0	6.6	3.3	3.3	1.00	7.7	0.12	9.0	0.47	8.5	2.68	9.2	7.4
Iowa	30.2	7.0	3.3	3.3	1.36	6.9	0.19	8.4	1.75	4.5	12.99	6.3	6.1
Kansas	22.6	7.7	10.0	10.0	0.79	8.2	0.18	8.5	0.30	9.1	2.50	9.3	8.8
Kentucky	40.9	5.9	3.3	3.3	0.60	8.6	0.76	3.5	3.16	0.0	6.86	8.1	4.9
Louisiana	43.2	5.7	10.0	10.0	0.36	9.2	0.32	7.3	0.11	9.7	2.50	9.3	8.5
Maine	39.8	6.0	3.3	3.3	2.00	5.4	0.35	7.0	0.60	8.1	5.81	8.4	6.4
Maryland	44.0	5.6	3.3	3.3	2.00	5.4	0.45	6.2	1.38	5.6	4.41	8.7	5.8
Massachusetts	30.5	7.0	10.0	10.0	2.51	4.2	0.11	9.1	0.55	8.3	4.05	8.9	7.9
Michigan	31.2	6.9	10.0	10.0	2.00	5.4	0.20	8.3	0.51	8.4	11.92	6.6	7.6
Minnesota	39.6	6.0	3.3	3.3	1.23	7.2	0.48	5.9	1.20	6.2	8.83	7.5	6.0
Mississippi	30.2	7.0	6.7	6.7	0.68	8.4	0.43	6.3			7.10	8.0	7.3
Missouri	34.2	6.6	10.0	10.0	0.17	9.6	0.06	9.5	0.42	8.7	2.00	9.4	9.0
Montana	100.0	0.0	10.0	10.0	1.70	6.1	0.14	8.8	1.06	6.6	9.30	7.4	6.5

State													
Nebraska	24.0	7.6	6.7	6.7	0.64	8.5	0.31	7.4	0.95	7.0	3.75	8.9	7.7
Nevada	33.5	6.7	10.0	10.0	0.80	8.2	0.16	8.6	0.70	7.8	3.60	9.0	8.4
New Hampshire	100.0	0.0	10.0	10.0	1.68	6.1	0.30	7.4			0.00	10.0	6.7
New Jersey	30.7	6.9	3.3	3.3	2.70	3.8	0.12	9.0	0.88	7.2	5.50	8.4	6.4
New Mexico	25.8	7.4	6.7	6.7	1.66	6.2	0.41	6.5	1.70	4.6	6.06	8.3	6.6
New York	47.8	5.2	3.3	3.3	4.35	0.0	0.14	8.8	0.30	9.1	6.44	8.2	5.8
North Carolina	42.4	5.8	3.3	3.3	0.45	9.0	0.62	4.7	0.79	7.5	13.02	6.3	6.1
North Dakota	28.1	7.2	3.3	3.3	0.44	9.0	0.39	6.7	1.06	6.6	4.66	8.7	6.9
Ohio	37.6	6.2	3.3	3.3	1.25	7.1	0.18	8.5	0.32	9.0	9.84	7.2	6.9
Oklahoma	34.6	6.5	10.0	10.0	1.03	7.6	0.40	6.6	0.72	7.7	5.56	8.4	7.8
Oregon	100.0	0.0	10.0	10.0	1.18	7.3	0.08	9.3	0.67	7.9	22.73	3.5	6.3
Pennsylvania	46.0	5.4	3.3	3.3	1.60	6.3	0.08	9.3			7.22	8.0	6.5
Rhode Island	41.9	5.8	0.0	0.0	3.50	2.0	0.11	9.1	0.60	8.1	3.75	8.9	5.6
South Carolina	28.5	7.1	6.7	6.7	0.57	8.7	0.77	3.4	1.08	6.6	5.42	8.5	6.8
South Dakota	30.5	6.9	10.0	10.0	1.53	6.5	0.27	7.7	1.21	6.2	4.68	8.7	7.7
Tennessee	27.4	7.3	6.7	6.7	0.62	8.6	1.17	0.0	1.27	6.0	4.46	8.7	6.2
Texas	33.5	6.7	3.3	3.3	1.41	6.8	0.20	8.3	0.20	9.4	2.40	9.3	7.3
Utah	31.2	6.9	10.0	10.0	1.70	6.1	0.41	6.5			11.26	6.8	7.3
Vermont	64.7	3.5	10.0	10.0	2.62	4.0	0.27	7.7	0.55	8.3	0.00	10.0	7.2
Virginia	40.1	6.0	3.3	3.3	0.30	9.3	0.26	7.8	1.51	5.2	20.56	4.2	6.0
Washington	24.1	7.6	0.0	0.0	3.03	3.0	0.76	3.5	0.87	7.2	35.22	0.0	3.6
West Virginia	51.3	4.9	0.0	0.0	0.55	8.7	0.18	8.5	1.00	6.8	2.82	9.2	6.3
Wisconsin	37.8	6.2	3.3	3.3	2.52	4.2	0.06	9.5	0.25	9.2	3.25	9.1	6.9
Wyoming	15.0	8.5	6.7	6.7	0.60	8.6	0.02	9.8			0.49	9.9	8.7

Source: Authors' calculations based on data from US Census Bureau (2013), Chriqui et al. (2014), Tax Foundation (http://taxfoundation.org/data).

Notes: Column 1: Selective excise taxes as a percentage of total general sales and gross receipts taxes.

Column 3: Authors created index based on three criteria: (1) Is soda taxed higher than food? (2) Are vending machines taxed higher than food? (3) Does the state have a unique tax on soda at the retailer, wholesale, or distributor level? In all cases, deviations from the equal treatment of soda received lower scores.

Column 5: Cigarette excise tax rate.

Column 7: Beer excise taxes measured in dollars per gallon.

Column 9: Wine excise tax rates measured in dollars per gallon.

Column 11: Spirits excise tax rates measured in dollars per gallon.

As can be seen in table 1, the states relying least on selective sales and gross receipt taxes as a proportion of sales and gross receipt tax revenue are Wyoming (15.0 percent), Arizona (21.1 percent), Kansas (22.6 percent), Nebraska (24.0 percent), and Washington (24.1 percent). At the other end of the spectrum, the states most extensively using selective sales and gross receipt taxes are Alaska, Delaware, Montana, New Hampshire, and Oregon (all rely 100 percent on selective taxes and do not use a general sales tax). The highest use of selective sales and gross receipt taxation by a state with a general sales tax is Vermont, with 64.7 percent of its total sales and gross receipt revenue coming from selective sales taxes. West Virginia is the next closest, with 51.3 percent of its sales and gross receipt revenue coming from selective taxation, followed by Alabama, New York, and Pennsylvania.

Not all selective sales taxation is paternalistic in nature. To better capture the extent to which selective sales taxation is selective, in the remainder of this section we break down the selective taxes to consider the categories of taxes on soda, cigarettes, beer, wine, and spirits. These are sometimes referred to as "sumptuary" taxes or "sin" taxes. These types of specific taxes are intended to decrease the consumption of these goods by increasing the cost of purchasing them. They are perhaps the most obvious area of state paternalistic policy practiced by taxing choice.[12]

The second component we consider is soda taxes. Unlike selective excise taxes, we do not calculate these scores using a max-min approach. We do this because regular, sugar-sweetened soda is taxed in a variety of ways beyond the normal sales tax. Using data from Chriqui et al. (2014), we identify three ways that states treat soda differently through the tax code. First, some states have a higher sales tax on regular soda than on general food products sold at stores. If this is the case, we give the state a 0; otherwise it receives a 10. Second, some states tax soda sold through vending machines at a higher rate than the tax on food. Again, if this is the case, we give the state a 0 and otherwise a 10. Finally, seven states impose additional taxes or fees on soda at the manufacturer, wholesaler, distributor, or retailer level.[13] These 0s and 10s for each state are then averaged to produce a soda tax score for each state, which is the number in column 4 of table 1. States like New Hampshire, Alaska, and Delaware that treat soda the same as all other foods at stores and in vending machines and do not levy taxes at an intermediate level on soda production receive scores of 10. In contrast, states like Ohio, which tax soda at a higher rate than food at stores and in vending machines but not at the wholesale level, receive a score of 3.33. Rhode Island, Washington, and West Virginia are the only three states to receive a 0 in this category.

For the remainder of the sin taxes in this area, we convert the data into an index number and then arrive at an overall Area 1 score by averaging the index scores for each item. The underlying data are the tax per unit (in dollars) for each good consistently measured (dollars per 20-pack for cigarettes; dollars per gallon for beer, wine, and spirits).[14] These data are from the Tax Foundation and are the rates as of January 1, 2013.[15] Several states have government-run liquor stores, and their data impute the implied tax rate for spirits, but not for wine, so several states are without data on their wine tax rates.[16] Following the procedure used in the EFW for missing variables in an area, we simply do not include that variable in the area score for states without a rating for a component.

Columns 5–12 of table 1 show the tax rates, the scores each state is given on each tax, and column 13 presents the overall score for Area 1 (selective taxes). In the overall Area 1 scores, the states with the highest scores (least paternalistic) are Missouri (9.0), Kansas (8.8), Wyoming (8.7), Louisiana (8.5), and Idaho (8.4). These states generally have the lowest use of selective sales taxes, especially ones that are widely considered to be sin taxes. At the other end of the spectrum, the lowest rated state (most paternalistic) was Washington, followed by Alaska, Kentucky, Alabama, and Rhode Island. These states have the highest overall use of selective sales and gross receipt taxes.[17]

AREA 2: SAINT SUBSIDIES

The sumptuary or sin taxes examined in the previous section are only one side of the paternalistic policy coin. Relative prices can just as easily be influenced by government subsidies or tax deductions in favor of the consumption of goods that are viewed as being paternalistically "good" choices. We term these "saint subsidies." Examples include bottle bills that require refundable deposits on drink bottles, sales tax exemptions for healthy items and medicines, and tax credits or subsidies for energy efficiency purchases or uses.

Our data for bottle bills come from the National Conference of State Legislatures.[18] State beverage container deposit laws, commonly known as "bottle bills," attempt to encourage recycling. These deposits are imposed by having retailers pay a deposit to distributors, this cost is then passed on to consumers, who can receive the refund when the empty container is returned, and the redemption center is then reimbursed by the distributor. States that have no laws receive a 10 and states with a law, such as Hawaii, receive a score of zero.

Our data on sales tax exemptions is from the Federation of Tax Administrators.[19] States are almost all uniform in their exemptions (or a subsidy for lower income families in lieu of the tax) for food and prescription drugs from the state general sales tax. Therefore, there is no reason to include these exemptions, as they do not vary enough across states to contribute to the index. However, the states do vary in applying the general sales tax to other nonprescription, over-the-counter drugs. Thus we include this as one of our measures and again assign states without such an exemption a 10 and those that do have an exemption, like Florida, a 0.

Our data on state energy incentives are from the North Carolina Clean Energy Technology Center's Database of State Incentives for Renewables & Efficiency (DSIRE).[20] West Virginia, one of the two states tied for the lowest number, has eleven such incentives, while California has the most (197). To give a sampling, West Virginia has a property tax incentive for wind energy systems, a business lighting rebate incentive program, and a residential energy efficiency rebate program. There is no obvious way to weight these different schemes, so we simply count them. The data reflect the number of state programs listed, and we make no allowance for the unmeasurable size or nature of the programs. The maximum is set to 197 and the minimum to 0, and states are placed on the 0–10 scale according to equation 1, described earlier.

Table 2 shows these data, the scores on each variable, and the overall score for Area 2: Saint Subsidy. Clearly, the higher variation in the energy variable drives most of the ranking. Two states are tied as the states with the fewest such saint subsidies: Kansas and West Virginia. At the other end of the spectrum, New York has the highest number (and thus the lowest rank), followed by Vermont, California, Minnesota, and Texas.

AREA 3: MISCELLANEOUS BANS AND REGULATIONS

The final area attempts to pick up bans and regulations. While not obviously policies that change relative prices, they clearly restrict choices in a manner consistent with paternalism. Also to the extent that black markets may still exist with higher prices, the policy functions much like a very high tax, creating a risk premium in the cost of supply and consumption. As discussed at the start of this chapter (see the notes there for sources), such bans drive these activities into the underground economy (as in the case with gambling) or often create secondary effects that work against the original intent of the policy.

Area 3 includes ten different rules or bans, mostly measured as a yes/no (sometimes allowing a half credit for partial policies). Our data for these variables come from the Mercatus Center publication *Freedom in the 50 States* (Ruger and Sorens 2013), and *Disposal Bans & Mandatory Recycling in the United States* (published by the Northeast Recycling Council).[21] These variables include a mea-

Table 2. Area 2: State Saint Taxes

State	Bottle Bill Refund	Score	Nonprescription Drug Exemption	Score	Number of Energy Subsidies or Credits	Score	Area 2 Overall Score
Alabama	0	10.0	0	10.0	19	9.0	9.7
Alaska	0	10.0	0	10.0	18	9.1	9.7
Arizona	0	10.0	0	10.0	61	6.9	9.0
Arkansas	0	10.0	0	10.0	30	8.5	9.5
California	1	0.0	0	10.0	197	0.0	3.3
Colorado	0	10.0	0	10.0	103	4.8	8.3
Connecticut	1	0.0	0	10.0	51	7.4	5.8
Delaware	0	10.0	0	10.0	25	8.7	9.6
Florida	0	10.0	1	0.0	75	6.2	5.4
Georgia	0	10.0	0	10.0	46	7.7	9.2
Hawaii	1	0.0	0	10.0	29	8.5	6.2
Idaho	0	10.0	0	10.0	32	8.4	9.5
Illinois	0	10.0	1	0.0	71	6.4	5.5
Indiana	0	10.0	0	10.0	66	6.6	8.9
Iowa	1	0.0	0	10.0	60	7.0	5.7
Kansas	0	10.0	0	10.0	11	9.4	9.8
Kentucky	0	10.0	0	10.0	55	7.2	9.1
Louisiana	0	10.0	0	10.0	19	9.0	9.7
Maine	1	0.0	0	10.0	23	8.8	6.3
Maryland	0	10.0	1	0.0	70	6.4	5.5
Massachusetts	1	0.0	0	10.0	79	6.0	5.3
Michigan	1	0.0	0	10.0	49	7.5	5.8
Minnesota	0	10.0	1	0.0	143	2.7	4.2
Mississippi	0	10.0	0	10.0	22	8.9	9.6
Missouri	0	10.0	0	10.0	63	6.8	8.9

(continued)

Table 2. (*continued*)

State	Bottle Bill Refund	Score	Nonprescription Drug Exemption	Score	Number of Energy Subsidies or Credits	Score	Area 2 Overall Score
Montana	0	10.0	0	10.0	36	8.2	9.4
Nebraska	0	10.0	0	10.0	18	9.1	9.7
Nevada	0	10.0	0	10.0	31	8.4	9.5
New Hampshire	0	10.0	0	10.0	43	7.8	9.3
New Jersey	0	10.0	1	0.0	44	7.8	5.9
New Mexico	0	10.0	0	10.0	44	7.8	9.3
New York	1	0.0	1	0.0	91	5.4	1.8
North Carolina	0	10.0	0	10.0	83	5.8	8.6
North Dakota	0	10.0	0	10.0	18	9.1	9.7
Ohio	0	10.0	0	10.0	50	7.5	9.2
Oklahoma	0	10.0	0	10.0	33	8.3	9.4
Oregon	1	0.0	0	10.0	110	4.4	4.8
Pennsylvania	0	10.0	1	0.0	52	7.4	5.8
Rhode Island	0	10.0	0	10.0	28	8.6	9.5
South Carolina	0	10.0	0	10.0	52	7.4	9.1
South Dakota	0	10.0	0	10.0	29	8.5	9.5
Tennessee	0	10.0	0	10.0	20	9.0	9.7
Texas	0	10.0	1	0.0	124	3.7	4.6
Utah	0	10.0	0	10.0	29	8.5	9.5
Vermont	1	0.0	1	0.0	40	8.0	2.7
Virginia	0	10.0	1	0.0	44	7.8	5.9
Washington	0	10.0	0	10.0	104	4.7	8.2
West Virginia	0	10.0	0	10.0	11	9.4	9.8
Wisconsin	0	10.0	0	10.0	63	6.8	8.9
Wyoming	0	10.0	0	10.0	20	9.0	9.7

Source: Bottle bill refund, National Council of State Legislatures (2017); nonprescription drug exemption; Federation of Tax Administrators (2017); energy subsidies or credits, DSIRE (database).
Notes:
Column 1: A state receives a 1 if it has a bottle bill refund law, 0 otherwise.
Column 3: A state receives a 1 if it has a nonprescription drum exemption law, 0 otherwise.
Column 5: The total number of state energy subsidies or credits.

sure of whether the state has mandated recycling of at least one good, a plastic bag ban in any of the major cities or statewide, fireworks bans, beer keg rules, happy hour laws, helmet laws for motorcycles or bicycles, bans on social gambling, bans on Internet gambling, and blood testing required for marriage.[22]

To conserve space, for the variables in table 3 we present only our index scores and not the underlying data, because the transformation from the underlying source to the score is self-evident. The variables are almost entirely yes/no, so the index score data are 0s and 10s, which reveal directly the underlying 0/1 data.[23] In some cases (e.g., fireworks), the underlying data assigned a 0.5 for a partial ban or restriction, which results in a score of 5. The scores across the ten rules or bans are then summed and divided by 10 to get the overall score for each state for Area 3.

At the top of our list for the least paternalistic (highest scoring) state in Area 3 is Kentucky (10.0), followed by Wyoming, Colorado, Arizona, and Alaska (tied with a score of 9.0). At the bottom, the most paternalistic state (lowest score) in Area 3 is Massachusetts (3.0), followed by New York and Washington (4.0), and then a number of states like California and New Jersey tied with a score of 5.0.

THE OVERALL INDEX: FREEDOM FROM PATERNALISM

The final index is the average of the scores in the three individual areas. Because we have scored states higher if they allow more choice and freedom and lower if they have paternalistic policies, our index is best titled a "freedom from paternalism" index. Table 4 presents each area score and the overall score and rank for each state in alphabetical order, while table 5 sorts the states from least paternalistic to most paternalistic.[24]

Table 5 shows that the state scoring as least paternalistic (highest score) overall is Wyoming (9.1), followed by Arizona (8.7), Nevada (8.6), Kansas (8.5), and Missouri (8.3). These are the states we judge as having tax and spending policies, laws, and regulations most consistent with the idea of individual freedom of action without interference in the name of protecting individuals from themselves. At the other end of the spectrum, the state scoring as most paternalistic (lowest score) is New York (3.9), followed by Vermont, Washington, California, and Oregon. These are the states we judge as having policies most consistent with paternalism, and taxing choice—allowing citizens and policymakers to substitute their collective judgment for that of free individuals. The map in figure 1 portrays each state's freedom from paternalism score.

Table 3. Area 3: Bans and Restrictions (Scores Only)

State	Plastic Bag Ban	Beer Keg Law Score	Happy Hour Law Score	Mandated Recycling Score	Fireworks Law Score	Motorcycle Helmet Score	Bicycle Helmet Score	Social Gambling Score	Internet Gambling Score	Blood Test Score	Area 3 Overall Score
Alabama	10.0	10.0	0.0	10.0	10.0	0.0	0.0	10.0	10.0	10.0	7.0
Alaska	10.0	10.0	0.0	10.0	10.0	10.0	10.0	10.0	10.0	10.0	9.0
Arizona	10.0	10.0	0.0	10.0	10.0	10.0	10.0	10.0	10.0	10.0	9.0
Arkansas	10.0	0.0	10.0	10.0	10.0	10.0	10.0	0.0	10.0	10.0	8.0
California	0.0	0.0	10.0	0.0	10.0	0.0	0.0	10.0	10.0	10.0	5.0
Colorado	0.0	10.0	10.0	10.0	10.0	10.0	10.0	10.0	10.0	10.0	9.0
Connecticut	10.0	0.0	0.0	0.0	10.0	10.0	0.0	10.0	10.0	10.0	6.0
Delaware	10.0	10.0	0.0	10.0	0.0	10.0	0.0	10.0	10.0	10.0	7.0
Florida	10.0	10.0	10.0	10.0	10.0	10.0	0.0	10.0	10.0	10.0	8.5
Georgia	10.0	0.0	10.0	0.0	10.0	0.0	0.0	5.0	10.0	10.0	5.0
Hawaii	0.0	10.0	10.0	10.0	10.0	10.0	0.0	0.0	10.0	10.0	8.0
Idaho	10.0	0.0	10.0	0.0	10.0	10.0	10.0	0.0	10.0	10.0	7.0
Illinois	10.0	10.0	0.0	0.0	5.0	10.0	10.0	0.0	0.0	10.0	5.5
Indiana	10.0	0.0	0.0	0.0	10.0	10.0	10.0	0.0	0.0	10.0	5.0
Iowa	10.0	0.0	10.0	0.0	5.0	10.0	10.0	5.0	10.0	10.0	7.0
Kansas	10.0	0.0	0.0	10.0	10.0	10.0	10.0	0.0	10.0	10.0	7.0
Kentucky	10.0	10.0	10.0	10.0	10.0	10.0	0.0	10.0	10.0	10.0	10.0
Louisiana	10.0	0.0	0.0	10.0	10.0	0.0	0.0	10.0	0.0	10.0	5.0
Maine	0.0	0.0	0.0	0.0	10.0	10.0	0.0	10.0	10.0	10.0	5.0
Maryland	10.0	0.0	10.0	10.0	10.0	0.0	0.0	10.0	10.0	10.0	6.0
Massachusetts	0.0	0.0	0.0	10.0	0.0	0.0	0.0	0.0	10.0	10.0	3.0
Michigan	10.0	0.0	0.0	10.0	10.0	0.0	10.0	0.0	10.0	10.0	6.0
Minnesota	10.0	0.0	10.0	0.0	10.0	10.0	10.0	10.0	10.0	10.0	8.0

Mississippi	10.0	10.0	10.0	10.0	0.0	10.0	0.0	10.0	0.0	7.0
Missouri	10.0	0.0	10.0	10.0	0.0	10.0	0.0	10.0	10.0	7.0
Montana	10.0	0.0	10.0	10.0	10.0	0.0	10.0	0.0	0.0	7.0
Nebraska	10.0	0.0	10.0	10.0	0.0	10.0	0.0	10.0	10.0	6.0
Nevada	10.0	10.0	10.0	10.0	0.0	10.0	0.0	0.0	10.0	8.0
New Hampshire	10.0	0.0	10.0	10.0	10.0	0.0	0.0	10.0	10.0	7.0
New Jersey	10.0	10.0	0.0	0.0	0.0	10.0	0.0	10.0	10.0	5.0
New Mexico	0.0	0.0	0.0	10.0	10.0	0.0	0.0	10.0	10.0	5.0
New York	0.0	10.0	10.0	0.0	0.0	10.0	0.0	10.0	0.0	4.0
North Carolina	10.0	0.0	10.0	10.0	0.0	0.0	0.0	10.0	10.0	5.0
North Dakota	10.0	0.0	0.0	0.0	10.0	10.0	5.0	10.0	10.0	7.5
Ohio	10.0	10.0	0.0	5.0	10.0	10.0	10.0	0.0	10.0	7.5
Oklahoma	10.0	0.0	0.0	10.0	10.0	10.0	0.0	10.0	10.0	7.0
Oregon	0.0	0.0	10.0	10.0	0.0	0.0	10.0	0.0	10.0	5.0
Pennsylvania	10.0	10.0	0.0	0.0	10.0	0.0	0.0	10.0	10.0	6.0
Rhode Island	10.0	0.0	0.0	0.0	10.0	0.0	0.0	10.0	10.0	5.0
South Carolina	10.0	0.0	10.0	10.0	10.0	10.0	10.0	10.0	10.0	8.0
South Dakota	10.0	0.0	0.0	10.0	10.0	0.0	0.0	10.0	10.0	6.0
Tennessee	10.0	10.0	10.0	10.0	0.0	10.0	0.0	10.0	10.0	6.0
Texas	0.0	10.0	10.0	10.0	10.0	10.0	10.0	10.0	10.0	8.0
Utah	10.0	10.0	10.0	10.0	0.0	10.0	0.0	10.0	10.0	7.0
Vermont	10.0	0.0	10.0	5.0	0.0	0.0	0.0	10.0	10.0	5.5
Virginia	10.0	0.0	0.0	10.0	0.0	0.0	0.0	10.0	10.0	6.0
Washington	0.0	0.0	0.0	0.0	0.0	10.0	10.0	0.0	10.0	4.0
West Virginia	10.0	10.0	10.0	10.0	0.0	0.0	0.0	10.0	10.0	7.0
Wisconsin	10.0	10.0	0.0	0.0	10.0	0.0	10.0	0.0	10.0	7.0
Wyoming	10.0	0.0	10.0	10.0	10.0	10.0	10.0	10.0	10.0	9.0

Source: Ruger and Sorens (2013); Northeast Recycling Council (2017).

Table 4. Overall State Scores for Freedom from Paternalism

State	Area 1 Score	Area 2 Score	Area 3 Score	State Overall Score	State Overall Rank
Alabama	5.2	9.8	7.0	7.3	25
Alaska	4.1	9.8	9.0	7.6	24
Arizona	8.1	9.5	9.0	8.7	2
Arkansas	7.0	9.7	8.0	8.2	8
California	7.5	3.3	5.0	5.3	47
Colorado	7.5	7.5	9.0	8.2	7
Connecticut	5.9	6.2	6.0	5.9	40
Delaware	6.8	8.1	7.0	7.8	16
Florida	5.7	7.7	8.5	6.5	34
Georgia	6.4	7.9	5.0	6.9	29
Hawaii	6.0	6.4	8.0	6.7	30
Idaho	8.4	8.1	7.0	8.3	6
Illinois	5.9	5.2	5.5	5.6	44
Indiana	7.4	7.8	5.0	7.1	27
Iowa	6.1	5.3	7.0	6.2	36
Kansas	8.8	9.9	7.0	8.5	4
Kentucky	4.9	9.5	10.0	8.0	11
Louisiana	8.5	9.8	5.0	7.7	18
Maine	6.4	4.8	5.0	5.9	41
Maryland	5.8	7.7	6.0	5.8	43
Massachusetts	7.9	4.3	3.0	5.4	45
Michigan	7.6	7.9	6.0	6.5	35
Minnesota	6.0	5.5	8.0	6.1	37
Mississippi	7.3	9.8	7.0	8.0	13
Missouri	9.0	9.5	7.0	8.3	5
Montana	6.5	9.7	7.0	7.6	22
Nebraska	7.7	9.8	6.0	7.8	17
Nevada	8.4	9.7	8.0	8.6	3
New Hampshire	6.7	9.6	7.0	7.7	21
New Jersey	6.4	4.6	5.0	5.8	42
New Mexico	6.6	6.3	5.0	7.0	28
New York	5.8	2.6	4.0	3.9	50
North Carolina	6.1	9.3	5.0	6.6	33
North Dakota	6.9	8.2	7.5	8.0	10
Ohio	6.9	7.1	7.5	7.8	15
Oklahoma	7.8	9.7	7.0	8.1	9
Oregon	6.3	5.7	5.0	5.4	46
Pennsylvania	6.5	6.2	6.0	6.1	38
Rhode Island	5.6	8.1	5.0	6.7	31
South Carolina	6.8	9.6	8.0	8.0	12
South Dakota	7.7	8.1	6.0	7.7	19
Tennessee	6.2	9.8	6.0	7.3	25
Texas	7.3	5.6	8.0	6.6	32
Utah	7.3	9.8	7.0	7.9	14
Vermont	7.2	5.5	5.5	5.1	49
Virginia	6.0	6.3	6.0	6.0	39
Washington	3.6	5.8	4.0	5.3	48
West Virginia	6.3	9.9	7.0	7.7	20
Wisconsin	6.9	7.8	7.0	7.6	23
Wyoming	8.7	9.8	9.0	9.1	1

Source: Authors' calculations.

Table 5. Overall State Scores for Freedom from Paternalism, by Rank

State	Area 1 Score	Area 2 Score	Area 3 Score	State Overall Score	State Overall Rank
Wyoming	8.7	9.8	9.0	9.1	1
Arizona	8.1	9.5	9.0	8.7	2
Nevada	8.4	9.7	8.0	8.6	3
Kansas	8.8	9.9	7.0	8.5	4
Missouri	9.0	9.5	7.0	8.3	5
Idaho	8.4	8.1	7.0	8.3	6
Colorado	7.5	7.5	9.0	8.2	7
Arkansas	7.0	9.7	8.0	8.2	8
Oklahoma	7.8	9.7	7.0	8.1	9
North Dakota	6.9	8.2	7.5	8.0	10
Kentucky	4.9	9.5	10.0	8.0	11
South Carolina	6.8	9.6	8.0	8.0	12
Mississippi	7.3	9.8	7.0	8.0	13
Utah	7.3	9.8	7.0	7.9	14
Ohio	6.9	7.1	7.5	7.8	15
Delaware	6.8	8.1	7.0	7.8	16
Nebraska	7.7	9.8	6.0	7.8	17
Louisiana	8.5	9.8	5.0	7.7	18
South Dakota	7.7	8.1	6.0	7.7	19
West Virginia	6.3	9.9	7.0	7.7	20
New Hampshire	6.7	9.6	7.0	7.7	21
Montana	6.5	9.7	7.0	7.6	22
Wisconsin	6.9	7.8	7.0	7.6	23
Alaska	4.1	9.8	9.0	7.6	24
Tennessee	6.2	9.8	6.0	7.3	25
Alabama	5.2	9.8	7.0	7.3	25
Indiana	7.4	7.8	5.0	7.1	27
New Mexico	6.6	6.3	5.0	7.0	28
Georgia	6.4	7.9	5.0	6.9	29
Hawaii	6.0	6.4	8.0	6.7	30
Rhode Island	5.6	8.1	5.0	6.7	31
Texas	7.3	5.6	8.0	6.6	32
North Carolina	6.1	9.3	5.0	6.6	33
Florida	5.7	7.7	8.5	6.5	34
Michigan	7.6	7.9	6.0	6.5	35
Iowa	6.1	5.3	7.0	6.2	36
Minnesota	6.0	5.5	8.0	6.1	37
Pennsylvania	6.5	6.2	6.0	6.1	38
Virginia	6.0	6.3	6.0	6.0	39
Connecticut	5.9	6.2	6.0	5.9	40
Maine	6.4	4.8	5.0	5.9	41
New Jersey	6.4	4.6	5.0	5.8	42
Maryland	5.8	7.7	6.0	5.8	43
Illinois	5.9	5.2	5.5	5.6	44
Massachusetts	7.9	4.3	3.0	5.4	45
Oregon	6.3	5.7	5.0	5.4	46
California	7.5	3.3	5.0	5.3	47
Washington	3.6	5.8	4.0	5.3	48
Vermont	7.2	5.5	5.5	5.1	49
New York	5.8	2.6	4.0	3.9	50

Source: Authors' calculations.

Table 6. Correlation Matrix of Area Scores

	Area 1	Area 2	Area 3
Area 1	1.00		
Area 2	0.24	1.00	
Area 3	0.08	0.51	1.00

Source: Authors' calculations.

Each of the three areas considered here contributes independent information to the overall index, as can be seen in the correlation table across areas presented in table 6. The correlations across areas are generally small, with Areas 2 and 3 having the highest correlation coefficient of 0.51. Looking across areas, the scores highlight that each of the areas captures something different regarding paternalism. For example, Alaska finds it relatively easy not to use selective excise taxes given the state's other sources of revenue. Alternatively, Tennessee's decision to not have an income tax on normal income almost certainly plays a role in the state's use of sin taxes. Similarly, saint subsidies appear to be a normal good, with more paternalism manifesting with higher state income. While we do not go more into the determinants of paternalism (or the lack of paternalism), as it is beyond the scope of this chapter, one of the advantages to creating an index is that it creates the opportunity for other scholars to use the index to explain cross-state variations in paternalism.

CONCLUSION

In this chapter, we have provided a first attempt at a "freedom from paternalism" index. Measuring paternalism in three areas, we find that Wyoming is the state that had the most freedom from paternalism in its state policies in 2013. Conversely, New York was the most paternalistic state, scoring very poorly in two of the three areas of our index. The Northeast and the West Coast appear to be the most paternalistic regions.

We have created this index in the hope that it can be useful for further study by other researchers. We have attempted to construct it in an unbiased fashion, with the only subjective component being which state is ranked first versus last. Obvious questions that could be addressed with our index include both questions about why some states have these policies to a greater extent than others (e.g., public choice and political economy factors), as well as seeing the impact that having these policies has on measures of economic or personal well-being. We leave these questions to future researchers, as our interest here is producing an index of freedom from paternalism.

Figure 1. Overall State "Freedom from Paternalism" Scores

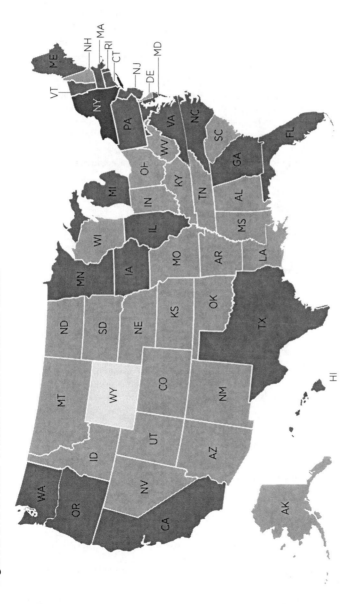

Lowest 5 State Scores
New York
Vermont
Washington
California
Oregon

Highest 5 State Scores
Wyoming
Arizona
Nevada
Kansas
Missouri

worst score 0–2 3–4 5–6 7–8 9–10 best score

Source: Authors' calculations.

NOTES

1. We say "consistent with," because some policies we highlight as being paternalistic are also consistent with other normative views about what policy should be trying to do. For example, high taxes on tobacco and alcohol might be part of a tax system designed to minimize the excess burden of taxation by taxing goods with an inelastic demand curve (Grossman et al. 1993). Inferring why voters, legislators, and bureaucrats passed specific legislation is an impossible task. We are merely identifying the policies that are consistent with paternalism, even though the raison d'être for a policy in a particular state might be something besides paternalism.

2. For examples, see Hayek and Bartley (1989), Boaz (1998), and Bastiat ([1850] 2007).

3. Miron and Zwiebel (1995) and chapter 10 of Holcombe (1995) discuss the secondary effects of the war on drugs, Walker (2007) discusses how bicycle helmet laws may do harm by causing drivers to drive closer to cyclists, and Klick and Wright (2012) show how plastic bag bans may increase foodborne illness rates.

4. For classic statements of this argument, see Bastiat's ([1850] 1995, 1–50) essay "That Which Is Seen, and That Which Is Not Seen," and Hazlitt (1946, 3), who refers to the "persistent tendency of men to see only the immediate effects of a given policy, or its effects only on a special group, and to neglect to inquire what the long-run effects of that policy will be not only on that special group but on all groups. It is the fallacy of overlooking secondary consequences."

5. The book *Nudge* (Thaler and Sunstein 2009) vividly illustrates this argument.

6. Note that we are merely trying to categorize the extent to which a state's policies are consistent with paternalism. We are not trying to explain why some states are more paternalistic than others. Instead we are just attempting to quantify the degree of paternalistic policies across states in the most straightforward manner possible, so other researchers might be able to better understand paternalism. In this regard, our approach is very similar to that employed in the *Economic Freedom of the World* index. On this point, see Bologna and Hall (2014).

7. Some policies, such as plastic bag bans, are emerging paternalistic policies. Thus we include them so as to possibly capture the extent to which certain policies are growing over time.

8. Microeconomic consumer theory illustrates how consumers choose optimally to maximize their utility among goods using indifference curves to reflect preferences and a budget line whose slope depends on the relative prices of the two goods to reflect constraints. In this context, a free, unregulated choice between good A and good B would be influenced by the relative prices of the two goods, that is, $(P_A \div P_B)$. Ad valorem (or percentage) based taxes on the two goods, at rates t_A and t_B, respectively, would result in an after-tax relative price ratio of $[P_A \times (1 + t_A)] \div [P_B \times (1 + t_B)]$. Only in the case where $t_A = t_B$ would this fraction equal the original fraction. That is, the only way the taxes do not distort the relative price ratio is if the two goods are taxed at the same rate.

9. The expenditures undertaken with the tax revenue, however, are a separate factor to consider and would impact how the consumer's welfare was influenced in total.

10. For in-depth arguments, see Tullock (1967), Baumol (1990), Holcombe (1998), and Sobel (2008).

11. Again, we are not trying to explain why states score high or low, just to measure the extent to which state tax policies are consistent with paternalism. Oregon, for example, does not have a general sales tax. It thus heavily uses selective sales taxes compared to general sales taxes. Whether this is a good idea or not is a matter for others to decide. For our purposes, it just means that Oregon levies selective sales and gross receipts taxes in a manner consistent with paternalism.

12. However, this does not necessarily imply the rates are purely set out of paternalistic, benevolent interests. Political influences also play a role. See Britton et al. (2001) for a discussion of the political influences on wine taxes, and Holcombe (1997) for a similar analysis in general and on cigarette taxes.

13. The seven states are Alabama, Arkansas, Rhode Island, Tennessee, Virginia, Washington, and West Virginia.

14. Note that this includes only the state tax rate, thus any local option sales taxes are not included.

15. See Tax Foundation website, http://taxfoundation.org/data.

16. A footnote in the Tax Foundation data explains that for the control states, the spirit excise tax rate is calculated using methodology designed by the Distilled Spirits Council of the United States.

17. Of the five states listed here, only Alaska does not have a statewide general sales tax.

18. See http://www.ncsl.org/research/environment-and-natural-resources/state-beverage -container-laws.aspx.

19. See http://www.taxadmin.org/fta/rate/sales.pdf.

20. The database can be found at http://www.dsireusa.org/.

21. For the Mercatus Center publication, see http://freedominthe50states.org/download/print -edition.pdf. The Northwest Recycling Council document can be found at https://nerc.org /documents/disposal_bans_mandatory_recycling_united_states.pdf.

22. Our variables are generally measured only at the state level except for the plastic bag ban variable. We made an exception in this case, to better monitor this trend, given the recent rise in localities banning plastic bags.

23. In the original data, however, not all the variables have the same sense (e.g., in some, 1 indicates "yes," while in others it indicates "no," yet some are phrased as bans and others phrased as whether the activity in question is allowed). We have indexed them all such that the index score is higher (10) when it implies more freedom and less interference, while a lower score implies more paternalism (0).

24. Freedom from paternalism scores in tables 4 and 5 are presented only to one decimal point for ease of discussion. In ranking states, however, all information was used. As a result, two states that appeared to be tied in their rounded scores will have different rankings if two or three decimal points are used.

REFERENCES

Bastiat, Frederic. [1850] 1995. *Selected Essays on Political Economy*. Irvington-on-Hudson, NY: Foundation for Economic Education.

———. [1850] 2007. *The Law*. Auburn, AL: Ludwig von Mises Institute.

Baumol, William J. 1990. "Entrepreneurship: Productive, Unproductive and Destructive." *Journal of Political Economy* 98 (5): 893–921.

Boaz, David. 1998. *Libertarianism: A Primer*. New York: Free Press.

Bologna, Jamie, and Joshua Hall. 2014. "Economic Freedom Research: Some Comments and Suggestions." In *Economic Freedom and Economic Education, Ideas and Influence of James Gwartney*, edited by Joshua Hall, 123–35. Volume VI in *The Annual Proceedings of the Wealth and Well-Being of Nations*. Beloit, WI: Beloit College Press.

Britton, Charles R., Richard K. Ford, and David E. R. Gay. 2001. "The United States Wine Industry: Restraint of Trade and the Religious Right." *International Journal of Wine Marketing* 13 (2): 43–58.

Chriqui, Jamie F., Shelby S. Eidson, and Frank J. Chaloupka. 2014. "State Sales Taxes on Regular Soda (as of January 1, 2014)." Bridging the Gap Program, Health Policy Center, Institute for Health Policy Research and Policy, University of Illinois at Chicago.

DSIRE (Database of State Incentives for Renewables & Efficiency). North Carolina Clean Energy Technology Center. http://www.dsireusa.org/.

Federation of Tax Administrators. 2017. "State Sales Tax Rates and Food & Drug Exemptions." https://www.taxadmin.org/assets/docs/Research/Rates/sales.pdf.

Grossman, Michael, Jody L. Sindelar, John Mullahy, and Richard Anderson. 1993. "Policy Watch: Alcohol and Cigarette Taxes." *Journal of Economic Perspectives* 7 (4): 211–22.

Gwartney, James D., and Robert A. Lawson. 2003. "The Concept and Measurement of Economic Freedom." *European Journal of Political Economy* 19 (3): 405–30.

Gwartney, James D., Robert A. Lawson, and Joshua C. Hall. 2015. *Economic Freedom of the World 2015 Annual Report*. Vancouver, BC: Fraser Institute.

Hall, Joshua C., and Robert A. Lawson. 2014. "Economic Freedom of the World: An Accounting of the Literature." *Contemporary Economic Policy* 32 (1): 1–19.

Hayek, Friedrich A, and William W. Bartley. 1989. *The Fatal Conceit: The Errors of Socialism*. Chicago: University of Chicago Press.

Hazlitt, Henry. 1946. *Economics in One Lesson*. New York: Harper & Brothers.

Holcombe, Randall G. 1995. *Public Policy and the Quality of Life*. Westport, CT: Greenwood.

———. 1997. "Selective Excise Taxation from an Interest-Group Perspective." In *Taxing Choice: The Predatory Politics of Fiscal Discrimination*, edited by William F. Shughart II, 81–103. New Brunswick, NJ: Transaction.

———. 1998. "Tax Policy from a Public Choice Perspective." *National Tax Journal* 51 (2): 359–71.

Klick, Jonathan, and Joshua D. Wright. 2012. "Grocery Bag Bans and Foodborne Illness." Institute for Law and Economics Research Paper 13-2. University of Pennsylvania Law School, Philadelphia.

Lawson, R. 2008. "On the Methodology of the Economic Freedom of the World Index." In *The Design and Use of Political Economy Indicators*, edited by King Banaian and Bryan Roberts. New York: Palgrave Macmillan.

Miron, Jeffrey A., and Jeffrey Zwiebel. 1995. "The Economic Case against Drug Prohibition." *Journal of Economic Perspectives* 9 (4): 175–92.

National Conference of State Legislatures. 2017. "State Beverage Container Deposit Laws." http://www.ncsl.org/research/environment-and-natural-resources/state-beverage-container-laws.aspx.

Northeast Recycling Council. 2017. "Disposal Bans & Mandatory Recycling in the United States." NERC, Brattleboro, VT. https://nerc.org/documents/disposal_bans_mandatory_recycling_united_states.pdf.

Ruger, William P., and Jason Sorens. 2013. *Freedom in the 50 States: An Index of Personal and Economic Freedom, 2013 Edition*. Arlington, VA: Mercatus Center at George Mason University.

Shughart, William F. II, ed. 1997. *Taxing Choice: The Predatory Politics of Fiscal Discrimination*. New Brunswick, NJ: Transaction.

Sobel, Russell S. 2008. "Testing Baumol: Institutional Quality and the Productivity of Entrepreneurship." *Journal of Business Venturing* 23 (6): 641–55.

Thaler, Richard H., and Cass R. Sunstein. 2009. *Nudge: Improving Decisions about Health, Wealth, and Happiness*. New York: Penguin.

Tullock, Gordon. 1967. "The Welfare Cost of Tariffs, Monopolies, and Theft." *Western Economic Journal* 5 (3): 224–32.

US Census Bureau. 2013. "2013 Annual Survey of State Government Finances Tables." https://www.census.gov/data/tables/2013/econ/state/historical-tables.html.

Walker, Ian. 2007. "Drivers Overtaking Bicyclists: Objective Data on the Effects of Riding Position, Helmet Use, Vehicle Type and Apparent Gender." *Accident Analysis & Prevention* 39 (2): 417–25.

CHAPTER 19
Overcoming the Special Interests That Have Ruined Our Tax Code

MATTHEW MITCHELL

Mercatus Center at George Mason University

THE TAX CODE IS A MESS. THIS IS NOT AN ACCIDENT

Federal, state, and local tax policy is a mess. The tax code is unjustly arbitrary, maddeningly complex, and unnecessarily inefficient. Since tax law has been written by human beings, one is tempted to wonder what motivated these misanthropes to design the system as they did. But such musings misunderstand the origins of our tax law. The tax code was not written by a single mind. Instead, it has emerged over the centuries as countless voters, politicians, and bureaucrats made public choices—large and small—that tweaked and changed the system, eventually resulting in the patchwork of tax policies we see today. To paraphrase the great Scottish Enlightenment economist Adam Ferguson, the tax code is the product of human action but not of human design (Ferguson 1782, 205).

If there is a tragic character to tax law, this is no coincidence. As the political economist Richard Wagner (2012) has noted, fiscal policy often suffers from a tragedy of the commons. The public purse is a common pool resource subject to the sort of misuse that often characterizes common property (Hardin 1968). But so too is the system of tax laws that dictate how revenue is generated.[1] If we are to overcome this tragedy, we must understand its origins. In this chapter, I outline the public choice processes that gave rise to the tax code we see today.

As the title of the chapter indicates, special interests played an outsized role in these public choices. But though special interests often dominate public policy, their perpetual hegemony is not ensured. At times, special interests can and do lose out to more general or diffuse interests. And we can learn from these episodes. Once I have sketched the various explanations for special interest domination over the tax code, I then discuss the important elements that seem to be present when special interests have lost. The goal is to give reformers hope—and direction—as they develop strategies to overcome the tragedy of our tax code.[2]

HOW DID WE GET HERE?

No one would sit down and design the tax code we currently have. It is frustratingly complex, costing us somewhere between $218 and $987 billion each year in compliance costs.[3] It is ruinously inefficient, creating an excess burden over and above compliance costs that is perhaps as much as 75 percent of the revenue it generates (Hines 2007). And it is littered with inequitable provisions that disproportionately benefit arbitrary groups.[4]

Examples of the tax code's inequity abound. And many readers no doubt have their (least) favorite illustrations. A brief tour through one aspect of the tax code—its treatment of the obscure notion of "depreciation"—will serve to make the case. When businesses incur expenses to make their products or offer their services, they are allowed to "write off" the cost of these purchases. This makes sense; if you must spend $20 to earn $100, then your income is really only $80 and only that $80 should be taxed. But what about capital purchases that wear out over time? Some economists think that firms should only be allowed to write off the cost of these purchases as the equipment depreciates or breaks down.[5] Others disagree. In their famous "flat tax" proposal, Robert Hall and Alvin Rabushka (1995) would have allowed all firms to write off the cost of long-lived purchases at the time of purchase.[6]

Both sides, however, agree that the rules ought to apply equally to all firms.[7] But the tax code's current treatment of business purchases is far from equitable. Most businesses must follow the IRS's "depreciation schedules," writing off the cost of each piece of equipment as it is believed to wear out. But a few favored industries are allowed to write off the cost of equipment faster than it depreciates, and some may even write it off immediately. Among the favored purchases are racehorses, motorsports complexes, film and television production costs, green energy property and equipment, magazine circulation expenditures, and intangible drilling costs (there are, of course, many more examples; see Joint Committee on Taxation Staff 2015, 2016; de Rugy and Michel, 2016). Because of the time value of money, these firms benefit handsomely from these accelerated depreciation rules. And because for many, accelerated depreciation is an obscure and strange concept, these privileges largely escape notice, let alone debate.

But arbitrary gains such as these come at the expense of everyone else. Tax privileges add complexity to the tax code, necessitate higher tax rates to make up for lost revenue, and cause labor and capital to be misallocated across the economy. These privileges also undermine the public's trust in the system. More than two-thirds of Americans say they are bothered "a lot" by the feeling that some corporations are not paying their fair share in taxes (Motel 2015).

Yet every arbitrary privilege and inefficient provision, every unjust imposition and time-wasting complexity was duly enacted through the democratic process. Why?

IDEAS MATTER. BUT SO DO INTERESTS

There are a lot of normative ideas about what constitutes good tax policy and sometimes differing conceptions of the public good conflict. When efficiency conflicts with equity, simplicity, or some other normative goal (e.g., paternalism), genuine disagreements arise about how to make the appropriate tradeoff in the name of the general welfare. These normative disagreements, in turn, are informed by genuine scientific disagreements about the magnitude of these tradeoffs. How much would inequality be reduced, for example, if the top personal income tax rate were raised to 50 percent and all the resultant revenue transferred to the bottom quintile of citizens?[8] And how much efficiency would be lost by such a move (Okun 1975)? Different models yield different answers. In short, there are different conceptions of the public good and different ideas about how to achieve it. What I consider to be inefficient, unjust, or overly complex, another might judge to be appropriate for the public good.

In this chapter, however, I focus on another source of bad tax law: special interests. While there is genuine debate about how to serve the public good, many provisions of tax policy only serve a narrow subset of the population.[9]

Consider the host of tax privileges, found in both federal and state law, that attend home ownership.[10] These provisions fail to serve just about every normative conception of the common good. They add complexity. They are inefficient (Horpedahl and Searles 2013). They fail to achieve their purpose.[11]

And they are regressive (Brown 2009). Those whom these rules purport to serve, homeowners, earn higher incomes and have higher stocks of wealth than the average taxpayer. But it turns out that these rules don't even serve them. Consider the mortgage interest deduction. Because the value of this deduction is capitalized into the price of homes, it simply makes home sales prices higher. Thus, it fails to help homeowners and it fails to encourage home ownership (Hilber and Turner, 2014). And yet this provision of federal and state tax policy—and many others like it—persists. Why? I offer eight explanations:

1. Rent-seeking
2. Concentrated benefits and diffused costs
3. Increasing returns to political activity
4. Logrolling
5. Bootleggers and Baptists
6. Agenda control
7. Rational ignorance and rational irrationality
8. The transitional gains trap

I discuss each in turn.

Rent-Seeking

While homeowners are not served by the mortgage interest deduction, another group is (at least for a time; see the "transitional gains trap" section below). Realtors, home builders, and financiers all gain from higher home prices. Economists call the above-normal profits that these groups earn as a result of this provision "rent." The rent is a transfer in the sense that it comes at the expense of home buyers and other taxpayers. In other words, the gain to realtors, home builders, and financiers is exactly offset by the losses of home buyers and taxpayers. But there is another cost. Those who gain from this provision invest considerable time, money, and effort in persuading policymakers to maintain it. They lobby, they donate to political action committees, and they adjust their services to satisfy policymakers. Economists call these efforts "rent-seeking."[12] And though the rent itself is a wash (one group's gains are offset by another's losses), rent-seeking is socially costly. In fact, rent-seeking societies are systematically poorer societies.[13]

Concentrated Benefits and Diffused Costs

The theory of rent-seeking predicts that those who stand to profit from special privileges will invest scarce resources in an attempt to gain and maintain those privileges. It does not necessarily predict that their efforts will be successful (indeed, rent-seeking is socially costly, in part, because many ultimately disappointed rent-seekers will nevertheless try; Tullock 1980).

Who, then, can we expect to prevail in the political struggle to obtain rent? Note that the benefits of the mortgage interest deduction are concentrated on a relatively small group, while its costs are diffused across the broader population. As a number of political scientists and economists have observed, this pattern—of concentrated benefits and diffused costs—is characteristic of much public policy (Olson 1965; Lowi 1969; Wilson 1991). The economist Mancur Olson explained why in his classic text, *The Logic of Collective Action*. All collective action, he observed, is difficult. It takes time, money, and effort for a group of like-minded or like-interested people to persuade policymakers to pursue a particular course of action. What's more, each member of the group has an incentive to free ride on the efforts of others. This incentive discourages everyone from acting. For this reason, most of us who stand to gain by banding together and lobbying for a particular policy never get very far.

Olson observed, however, that small groups have an easier time overcoming these problems than do large ones. First, being fewer in number, the per-person benefit of collective action is greater in small groups than in large groups. Second, it is easier to coordinate the activities of a small number of people than it is to coordinate those of a large number.[14]

For these reasons, small, concentrated groups like realtors, developers, and lenders often have an organizational advantage over large, diffuse groups like consumers, borrowers, and taxpayers. This tends to result in such policies as the mortgage interest deduction, which concentrate benefits on the few while diffusing costs across the many.

Increasing Returns to Political Activity

The organizational advantages that small concentrated interests enjoy tend to grow with use. In a penetrating analysis of corporate political activity, Lee Drutman (2015) has found that once firms decide to engage in politics, they tend to stay engaged and often expand their activities. The marginal costs of lobbying fall, while the marginal benefits increase; in other words, there are economies of scale in political activity.[15] In the case of tax law, the returns to political activity can be extraordinary. One study examined the lobbying activity surrounding a provision in the American Jobs Creation Act of 2004, which permitted a tax holiday on repatriated earnings (Alexander et al. 2009). The researchers found that for every $1 spent on lobbying, firms reaped a $220 tax benefit. This is equivalent to a 22,000 percent rate of return. In a more general study of the relationship between lobbying expenditures and tax liability, researchers found that a 1 percent increase in lobbying expenditures was associated with a 0.5–1.6 percentage point reduction in a firm's effective tax rate (Richter et al. 2009).

Once the tax laws have been written, some firms are better than others at taking advantage of its loopholes. In 2010, for example, General Electric filed a 57,000-page federal tax return that enabled it to pay $0 in taxes on $14 billion in profits (McCormack 2011). Only a wealthy and sophisticated company with an army of accountants could pull off such a feat.

Logrolling

Though small groups have some political advantages compared with large groups (especially if they have been at it for some time), they must still gain the assent of a majority of state or federal legislators to achieve their public policy goals. The practice of "logrolling," or vote-swapping, facilitates this.[16] When legislators logroll, each agrees to vote for the other's interests. In this way, a majority coalition can be assembled whereby each member agrees to support the (concentrated) interests of every other member of the coalition (Tullock 1959; Riker and Brams 1973; Riker 1984). Costs may then be externalized onto the minority, much as a polluting factory externalizes part of its production costs onto its neighbors.

Though anecdotal accounts of logrolling are as old as democracy, it has also been documented in more formal analyses. Professor Thomas Stratmann (1992, 1995), for example, has found that members representing dairy and sugar interests tend to vote for peanut interests, and vice versa. Logrolling is also evident in large bills that tie together multiple interests. Consider, again, the 2004 American Jobs Creation Act. This sprawling 650-page bill contained targeted tax benefits for NASCAR track owners, tobacco growers, Native Alaskan whaling captains, film producers, and manufacturers of everything from archery equipment to sonar fish finders to tackle boxes (Drutman 2015, 127).[17]

Bootleggers and Baptists

Superior organizational ability and well-constructed legislative logrolls are helpful. But it also helps to have a good story. Thus, it is quite common for those seeking special tax, spending, or regulatory privileges to claim that these special favors serve the general welfare. In some cases, these groups even form strange bedfellow coalitions with publicly spirited groups. Regulatory economist Bruce Yandle coined a term for this phenomenon, calling it the "Bootleggers and Baptists" theory of regulation (Yandle 1983; Smith and Yandle 2014). The term gets its name from the strange bedfellow coalition of bootleggers and religious groups who advocate for laws banning the sale of alcohol on Sundays. Bootleggers value these laws because they offer relief from legal competition one day a week. And religious groups value them because they promote abstention on the Lord's Day.

Thus, the mortgage interest deduction is not sold as a way to pad the pockets of realtors. Instead, it is said to promote "an ownership society." Film tax credits are not a wasteful privilege to a flashy industry. They are a smart way to promote "economic development." And tax exemptions for bonds issued to finance sports arenas are not giveaways to wealthy and well-connected team owners. They are a means to "redevelop" urban corridors.

Agenda Control

An important but rarely discussed quirk of democratic decision-making helps special interests dominate the political process. First discovered by an eighteenth-century French aristocrat, the Marquis de Condorcet, the idea was also explored in the nineteenth century by Charles Dodgson, better known as Lewis Carroll (Condorcet 1785; Dodgson [1876] 1958). The modern iteration of the problem was explained by economists Duncan Black and Kenneth Arrow in the middle of the twentieth century (Black 1948; Arrow 1951). Here is the problem: When two policies are considered at once or when one policy has multiple dimensions to it (and just about every issue in politics is multi-faceted), those who control the order in which votes are taken can determine the outcome.[18] In most modern legislatures, party leaders and committee chairs determine the order in which votes are taken (which is one among many reasons these positions are so coveted by members). By controlling the agenda, these leaders are able to ensure the victory of their most-preferred outcome (McKelvey 1976).

As the political scientists Peter Bachrach and Morton Baratz (1962) have argued, agenda control is as much about keeping certain items *off* of the agenda as it is about putting items on it. In other words, those who wield true power in politics use it to ensure that certain items, such as removal of tax privileges, are simply never brought up for discussion. And that is the way special interests want it.

Rational Ignorance and Rational Irrationality

In many cases, those with political power do not have to work hard to make sure that removal of special interest privileges remains off the agenda. That is because most of the public is "rationally ignorant" about these policies. Rational ignorance may at first sound like an oxymoron, but it is not. It takes time, money, and effort to become informed on any subject. And given that each of these commodities is scarce, rational humans will be selective in how they choose to inform themselves. Most of us will choose to become informed on a topic only when the benefits of gathering information exceed the costs. This is why most of us know very little about the anatomy of the mongoose.

In a typical election, the probability that any one vote will sway the outcome is minuscule (Gelman et al. 2009). Given this, little is to be gained by becoming informed on the issue. Hence, as the political economist Anthony Downs (1957) explained many years ago, most voters are rationally ignorant on most matters of public policy.

Even when voters do have an incentive to gather information about an issue, they often have little incentive to process that information. Consider, again, the mortgage interest deduction. Homeowners have a strong incentive to know about the existence of this provision, because it can save them thousands of dollars on their tax bills. Few, however, take the time to study the economic theory of tax capitalization and therefore do not realize that this provision also raises the price that they paid for their home in the first place. Economist Bryan Caplan (2008) coined the term "rational irrationality" to describe this failure to think through the implications of policy.

The special interests who benefit from privileges, of course, do not suffer from either rational ignorance or rational irrationality. They have every incentive to know about and think critically about the policies from which they benefit. They even have an incentive to purposely obfuscate policy in order to keep large and diffuse interests in the dark (Zingales 2011, 203). This explains why they prefer obscure privileges, such as accelerated depreciation, to more conspicuous privileges, such as cash subsidies.

The Transitional Gains Trap

There is an irony to the market for political privilege. Privileged firms only seem to reap extraordinary profits during the transition period in which they gain the privilege. Over the long run, though, these privileged firms and industries tend to fare no better than others. Gordon Tullock (1975), who was the first to observe this phenomenon, offered a compelling explanation for it. He suggested that firms often need certain assets to obtain privilege. For example, taxi operators must have a medallion to enjoy the regulatory privilege of operating with limited competition. Similarly, farmers must have land to obtain farm subsidies. And other rent-seekers must have a well-connected lobbying team to access politicians dispensing favors. Tullock noted that, over time, the value of the rent tends to get capitalized into the value of these assets, driving up the cost of medallions, farmland, and lobbyists. Thus, to obtain above-normal profits, firms must undertake above-normal expenses. Net of these expenses, the long-run return to rent-seeking is no greater than a normal rate of return. In the words of David Friedman, "the government can't even give anything away."[19]

This insight has important—and depressing—implications for the elimination of privilege. Because privileged firms are no better off for their privileges, the elimination of their special treatment threatens to impose a significant loss on them. This makes them willing to fight tooth and nail to avoid these losses (McCormick et al. 1984; Shughart 1999).

HOW CAN WE OVERCOME SPECIAL INTERESTS?

Special interests clearly play an outsized role in the formation of public policy. Their mark on the tax code—which features special privileges for agribusinesses, film producers, sports teams, relocating firms, and many more—can hardly be denied.

And yet sometimes special interests lose. Consider just a few examples:

For centuries, an elite group of white slaveholders benefited from the "peculiar institution" of slavery. The Civil War and the Constitutional amendments that followed put an end to the worst of these privileges, liberating approximately 3.9 million slaves. It would take another century, but the last legal privileges of southern whites eventually were eliminated as well.

Under the Articles of Confederation, state governments could protect local merchants from competition by imposing discriminatory duties on interstate trade. When it was adopted in 1789, the new Constitution outlawed such protectionist measures, eventually allowing the United States to become the largest free trade zone in the world, much to the benefit of American consumers.

In the early years of the Republic, certain merchants profited from discriminatory regulatory measures imposed by state and local governments. But eventually these were struck down in a US Supreme Court case that one historian would call the "Emancipation Proclamation of American Commerce."[20]

For much of the nineteenth century, the patronage system ensured that federal jobs were dispensed on the basis of personal connection and political corruption. But a series of civil service reforms ended the worst of these practices.

For most of US history, American consumers paid an exorbitant price for the protectionist privileges afforded domestic manufacturers. In 1932, the average tariff on dutiable imports was over 59 percent. Today it is less than 5 percent, and global trade is freer than ever (US International Trade Commission 2011).

In the 1970s, airlines, freight railroads, and truckers benefited from a wall of regulations that protected them from competition. But deregulation opened these industries up to competition, vastly improving the consumer experience (Morrison and Winston 1986, 1989).

In the latter half of the twentieth century, communities with strategically obsolete military installations were able to apply pressure to maintain these bases, even when military leaders said they were unnecessary. But through the Base Realignment and Closure (BRAC) process, 350 bases have been closed, saving taxpayers millions of dollars (Brito 2011).

These episodes do not disprove the public choice lesson that special interests often dominate political processes. But they suggest that there are exceptions to the rule. Moreover, on closer examination, we find that these exceptions display certain patterns. While no one is likely to wage a civil war over the mortgage interest deduction, those who are interested in eliminating the special interest privileges in our tax code—and elsewhere in policy—can learn from these episodes. Seven lessons stand out:

1. Ideas matter, especially in the long run.

2. Institutions matter, too.

3. Go for the "grand bargain."

4. Reform requires good leaders.

5. Sometimes it takes a special interest to beat a special interest.

6. Never let a crisis go to waste.

7. Embrace permissionless innovation.

Drawing on historical case studies, I briefly touch on each of these in turn.

Ideas Matter, Especially in the Long Run

I began this chapter by noting that bad ideas are not the sole source of bad tax law. Sometimes, inefficient and inequitable policies are enacted because special interests favor them.

But this is not to say that ideas are unimportant. In their insightful study of social change, Edward López and Wayne Leighton (2012) note that John Maynard Keynes and F. A. Hayek—intellectual antagonists on so many issues—agreed on at least one point: over the long run, ideas shape history. Keynes (1937, 328) wrote of the "academic scribblers" whose ideas eventually influence kings and world leaders, even though the latter are "practical men who believe themselves quite exempt from any intellectual influence." Hayek (1949, 417) described the mechanism by which the ideas of academic scribblers are turned into social change, emphasizing "intellectuals," those "secondhand dealers in ideas" who refine, distill, and ultimately sell the ideas of the academic scribblers to their fellow citizens.

The abolitionist movement, the free trade movement, and the (short-lived) deregulatory movement of the late 1970s were intellectual ideas before they were anything else. Their origins, which predated policy change by years and sometimes decades, are in the writings of such scribblers as William Lloyd Garrison, Frederick Douglass, Harriet Beecher Stowe, Sojourner Truth, David Ricardo, Adam Smith, J. S. Mill, John Bright, Richard Cobden, Milton Friedman, F. A. Hayek, Ronald Coase, James Buchanan, George Stigler, George Douglas, James Miller III, and Alfred Kahn. The arguments that these men and women put forth eventually overcame the array of advantages enjoyed by the special interests who opposed them.

But it is important to note the *sorts* of ideas that seem to take hold. As Alex Tabarrok (2002, 3) has observed, "no one goes to the barricades for efficiency. For liberty, equality or fraternity, perhaps, but never for efficiency." Tax reformers should take note that equity, in particular, is a powerful idea. Despite what you may remember from seventh grade, colonial anger over the Tea Act of 1773 erupted not because it was a tax increase (it was not), but because it was a tax cut for one and only one company, the East India Tea Company. Similarly, while the inefficiencies of airline regulation had long been discussed by economists (Douglas and Miller 1975; Jordan 1979), the political impetus for deregulation in the late 1970s was driven by a series of congressional hearings that exposed the inequitable and anticompetitive effects of regulation (McCraw 1984, 267). Of particular relevance for tax reformers, the Tax Reform Act of 1986 (TRA-86) was spurred in part by reports that 128 major corporations availed themselves of tax loopholes to avoid paying any federal corporate income tax at all (Murray and Birnbaum 1988, 12). Thus, the idea of lowering rates and closing loopholes took hold, appealing to such ideologically diverse "practical men" as Dan Rostenkowski, Bill Bradley, and Ronald Reagan.

Institutions Matter, Too

The Tax Reform Act of 1986 (TRA-86) was an impressive feat on many levels. It closed scores of loopholes and exemptions, each of which had a powerful constituency defending it. But within a few years, most of these special interest provisions (and many more) were back. That is because TRA-86 had no mechanism to prevent backsliding. It did nothing to change the incentives of politicians to dispense targeted privileges to concentrated interests, and so they kept on doing so. The 1986 winner of the Nobel Prize in economics, James Buchanan, theorized that some policymakers may have even voted for TRA-86 to wipe the slate clean and then offer to "renegotiate" new loopholes. "In one fell swoop," he wrote in 1987, "the political agents may have created for themselves the potential for substantially increased rents. This rent-seeking hypothesis will clearly be tested by the fiscal politics of the post-1986 years. To the extent that agents do possess discretionary authority, the tax structure established in 1986 will not be left in place for decades or even years" (Buchanan 1987, 33–34).

This sort of backsliding is not inevitable, however. And institutions, which Douglass North (1990, 3) defined as "the humanly devised constraints that shape human interaction," are one reason why not.

As I noted earlier, the average US tariff on dutiable imports fell from more than 59 percent in 1932 to under 5 percent today, and, with few exceptions, these rates have remained low. Much of this decline can be credited to the institutional changes wrought by fast-track trade negotiation and the World Trade Organization.

Franklin Roosevelt's Secretary of State, Cordell Hull, was an early champion of fast-track trade negotiation. Like most southern Democrats at the time, Hull was a free trader (Zeiler 1999, 7). But as a former member of Congress, he believed that the problem with trade policy was that it was in the hands of Congress. The typical member of Congress, he reasoned, was moderately in favor of more liberalized trade but wanted an exception for whatever product happened to be made in his or her district. This meant that any free trade deal struck by a president was liable to be picked apart by representatives and senators seeking to protect their hometown companies. Hull's idea was for Congress to give the president the authority to negotiate a tariff reduction agreement with other countries while Congress would bind itself to an up-or-down vote on the deal and not amend any part of it. The institutional innovation was known as the Reciprocal Tariff Agreement Act (RTAA). Over time, the idea came to be known as "fast-track trade negotiation."

This achieved two things. First, in voting for fast-track trade negotiation, the typical member of Congress was able to cast a conspicuous vote in favor of the general interest. Second, in pushing the details of the deal off on to the president, the typical congressman was able to obtain some cover in voting against his or her hometown special interests. Presidents, of course, are susceptible to special interest pressures, too (Stratmann and Wojnilower 2015). But because a president represents the entire nation, it is not as easy for him or her to externalize the costs of special interest privileges on to others (Lohmann and O'Halloran 1994).

Similar institutional incentives have facilitated other special interest clawbacks. BRAC commissions work the same way (Brito 2011). When an individual member of Congress votes for BRAC, he or she is able to cast a conspicuous vote in favor of cutting unnecessary military spending. But the commission itself decides which particular bases to close, allowing the member whose hometown base is closed to tell constituents that her hands were tied. In fact, congressional members with bases in their districts are invited to come before the commission and plead their cases, giving them extra cover before their constituents. The key, as former Representative Dick Armey told me in an interview, was that individual members were spared the blame: "When you fail to save your base, your failure won't be held against you."[21]

While some institutions such as fast-track trade negotiation and BRAC offer policymakers an incentive to serve the general interest (and cover when taking away privileges from special interests), other institutions "lock in" changes once they have been made, reducing the incidence of backsliding. The World Trade Organization, for example, polices free trade agreements by allowing members to file formal complaints when other signatories renege on the promises they have made. Thus, when the United States is found guilty of subsidizing its domestic cotton producers (to the detriment of US taxpayers and international producers) or of protecting domestic steel, tire, magnet, paper, chemicals, flooring, wind turbine, and kitchen fitting manufacturers (to the detriment of US consumers and foreign producers), it must either pay a fine or reverse policy course (Pelc 2014).[22]

The US Constitution itself is an institutional device that mitigates the power of special interests and prevents backsliding into special interest privilege. Article I, Section 10's provision that "No State shall, without the Consent of Congress, lay any Imposts or Duties on Imports or Exports" has, in effect, created the world's largest free trade zone (Riker 1964). Similarly, for more than half a century, the General Welfare Clause was understood to limit Congress's ability to appropriate funds for the benefit of special interests (Eastman 2001).

Ideas and institutions interact in complex ways. As many institutional theorists have noted, some of our most important and enduring institutions are informal norms, ideas, and practices (Boettke et al. 2008; Williamson 2009). And even formal institutions can be ignored if they are not widely seen as legitimate (Ferejohn et al. 2001).

But the historical lesson is clear for tax reformers: if they wish to make the tax code more general and less particularistic and if they wish to prevent backsliding into particularism, they will need to bind the hands of future policy makers through constitutional or institutional constraints (Buchanan 1990, 2000).

Go for the "Grand Bargain"

The prisoners' dilemma of game theory is an apt description of special interest politics.[23] Consider table 1. Imagine that two special interests each have an option to seek a privilege through the tax code. If neither seeks a privilege, each has a net tax burden of $0.00. If one seeks a privilege while the other abstains, then the privilege-seeker obtains a net tax benefit of $2.00 while the abstainer pays a net burden of −$1.00. If both seek privileges, however, then each bears a burden of −$0.50 (not $0.00, because taxation involves deadweight loss and privileges entail a host of economic costs; Mitchell 2012). In this scenario, privilege seeking is a dominant strategy. That is because no matter what B does, A always has an incentive to seek privileges and vice versa (if B seeks no privileges, A has an incentive to seek privileges, because $2.00 is greater

Table 1. Special-Interest Politics

		Special Interest B			
		Seeks No Privileges		Seeks Privileges	
Special Interest A	Seeks No Privileges	A gets:	B gets:	A gets:	B gets:
		$0.00	$0.00	−$1.00	$2.00
	Seeks Privileges	A gets:	B gets:	A gets:	B gets:
		$2.00	−$1.00	−$0.50	−$0.50

than $0.00; and if B does seek privileges, then A still has an incentive to do so, because losing $0.50 is better than losing $1.00).

Acting independently, both A and B are doomed to seek privileges, and both will end up losing $0.50. It is the anti-Adam Smith theorem: in seeking his own interest, each is impelled as if by an invisible hand to undermine the public interest.

But if the two special interests could somehow cooperate, they could avoid this fate. Institutions—rules—can facilitate such cooperation. In a fascinating study called *Politics by Principle*, James Buchanan and Roger Congleton (1998) examine the consequences of a simple and normatively intuitive rule: the generality norm. This rule states that public policy can take any form so long as it is nondiscriminatory. No individual or group may be singled out for either special privilege or special punishment. In terms of the game-theoretic model described above (see table 1), the generality norm would constrain the participants to the shaded diagonal cells; either both may have their privilege or neither may. Thus constrained, the rational course is for neither to seek a privilege, which happens to be the most efficient outcome.

The practical lesson for reformers hoping to eliminate special interest privileges is to "go for the grand bargain." If you take away any one group's special privilege, they are sure to put up a strenuous fight. But people may not mind having their ox gored so long as everyone else's ox is gored as well, thus reducing one's share of ox-upkeep costs. This is not just theory. TRA-86 eliminated special interest loopholes and used the tax savings to reduce tax rates across the board. Special interests were willing to give up some of their favors so long as others did so as well, allowing the rates everyone paid to fall. Similarly, multilateral tariff reduction agreements, such as NAFTA, are able to achieve freer trade because all interested parties are willing to give up their protections.

Reform Requires Good Leaders

Grand bargains align incentives so that it is in everyone's interest to eliminate privilege. But they are extraordinarily difficult to achieve. This is because bargains involving multiple parties have extraordinarily high "transaction costs." Not to be confused with the terms of trade—the price one pays in an exchange—transaction costs are the cost of finding a willing party with whom to exchange, striking a bargain with him or her, and enforcing that agreement (Coase 1937; Williamson 1979). Transaction costs tend to rise as the number of parties to an agreement rise. And they tend to be higher in political settings than in commercial settings, because there is typically no one to enforce a political agreement (Dixit 1998; Acemoglu 2003).

This is why leadership matters. Leaders are coalition builders who set the agenda and assemble the grand bargainers (Douglas 1990). Often, their efforts prod others to contribute to the public good (Houser et al. 2014). And in so doing leaders are also institutional entrepreneurs who create and modify the institutional framework (North 1990, 83–84).

In every instance I can find where a special interest has lost its privilege, a leader has played a key role. Madison proposed the institutional change and assembled the grand bargain ensuring that the Constitution prohibited interstate barriers to trade (e.g., see Madison 2000). Cordell Hull developed the idea of fast-track trade negotiation but sold it to Franklin Roosevelt, who then saw it into law (Zeiler 1999, 7). Alfred Kahn (with an assist from Ted Kennedy) led the effort to deregulate airlines (McCraw 1984). Representative Dick Armey and Senator Phil Gramm led the creation of BRAC. Senator Bill Bradley, Representative Dan Rostenkowski, and President Ronald Reagan championed the effort to reform taxes in 1986. It is difficult to imagine these efforts succeeding without the work of those leaders.

Sometimes It Takes a Special Interest to Beat a Special Interest

A charismatic leader with the right idea can assemble a coalition and urge his or her followers to take collective action to support the cause. He or she can also appeal to the better angels of their nature the way "Baptists" do in the "Bootleggers and Baptists" model.

But what leaders have in charisma and moral high ground they often lack in organizational and financial resources. Even the most charismatic leader could use the help of a bootlegger. And that is where other special interests come in. While Olson's theory predicts that concentrated interests often will prevail over diffuse interests, a concentrated interest sometimes exists whose motives happen to align with those of more diffuse interests. And this can be very helpful in overcoming other special interests.

Consider the slave trade. Politically powerless, American slaves had no way to exert direct influence on public policy. Yet as soon as the Constitution permitted it (in 1808), Congress outlawed the importation of slaves. Humanitarian organizations, such as the Pennsylvania Abolition Society, played an important role. But these "Baptists" (they were actually Quakers) were aided and abetted by a highly organized and politically potent group of "bootleggers": mid-Atlantic slaveholders (Anderson et al. 1988). As net exporters of slaves to other colonies, the large slaveholders of the mid-Atlantic could command a higher price for the slaves they sold once the overseas supply was eliminated. This made these politically powerful men important advocates for the elimination of the overseas slave trade. It was a happy coincidence that slaves who would have otherwise been imported as well as American slaves, who were likely treated somewhat better since they could not be as easily replaced by new imports, also benefited.

Decades earlier, when James Madison won his victory for consumers by ensuring that the Constitution outlawed duties on interstate trade, he too had assistance from a concentrated interest group. Farmers who exported their surplus crops across state lines (Madison himself was one of them) were often a powerful voice for free trade among the states, and they proved to be powerful advocates for this provision in the Constitution (McGillivray et al. 2001).

In general, exporters have often been advocates of free trade, as reciprocal free trade agreements give them access to new and larger markets. In the years after the RTAA passed, exporters became important advocates for free trade (Hiscox 1999). Typically, their interests are aligned with those of consumers, but being fewer in number and more concentrated, they are not as hamstrung by the collective action problem.

Decades later, when exporters found themselves defending their own privilege, another concentrated interest group sided with the general interest to oppose them. In 2015, the long-ignored Export-Import Bank (Ex-Im) came up for congressional reauthorization. This federal agency risks taxpayer dollars to help finance exports for foreign buyers (de Rugy and Castillo 2014). Only about 2 percent of all US exports receive aid from the agency, and a majority of the assistance goes to just ten large firms (over 35 percent goes to Boeing alone; de Rugy 2015a,b). The agency shifts risk on to taxpayers, siphons capital from other projects, and raises the prices of some goods (Ikenson 2014; Mitchell 2014). The costs of the bank exceed its benefits (Beekman and Kench 2015). But since taxpayers, borrowers, and consumers are far more numerous and diffuse than the handful of exporters who benefit from Ex-Im, the agency has outlasted thirteen presidents and thirty-nine Congresses.

The year 2015, however, was different. For the first time in its 80-year history, the bank's congressional charter lapsed. Those whom Keynes would call scribblers and Hayek would call intellectuals, such as my colleague Veronique de Rugy and journalist Tim Carney deserve a great deal of credit for this achievement.[24] But they were aided by a concentrated interest, Delta Airlines. Delta, it turns out, is harmed by Ex-Im in two ways. First, because Ex-Im's subsidies increase the demand for wide-body aircraft, the agency raises the cost of airplanes. Second, because it subsidizes foreign airlines, such as Air India, Delta has more difficulty competing along some foreign routes. Thus, Delta was a highly organized and effective advocate for the elimination of the bank.[25]

The lesson for tax reformers is that they will have an easier time serving the general interest if they can find some concentrated interests who might gain from tax reform. Who might this be? One suggestion is any group that is currently singled out for particularly harsh tax treatment. This includes the purveyors of inelastically demanded goods, politically incorrect goods, goods that are taxed by multiple overlapping jurisdictions, or goods that are primarily sold to nonvoters, such as out-of-town tourists.

Never Let a Crisis Go to Waste

As has been noted many times by many different and disparate voices, radical institutional change is sometimes advanced by external forces. This is what Milton Friedman (1962, xiv) meant when he asserted that "Only a crisis—actual or perceived—produces real change. When that crisis occurs, the actions that are taken depend on the ideas that are lying around." Years later, President Obama's chief of staff, Rahm Emanuel, would echo this sentiment, asserting in the midst of the financial crisis of 2009 that "you never want a serious crisis to go to waste. And what I mean by that is [that it's] an opportunity to do things you think you could not do before."[26]

The political economist Robert Higgs (1987) wrote an insightful and revealing book detailing the role that crises have played in the growth of American government. But crises and other external events have also played a role in the elimination of special interest privilege.

Regardless of how it began, the smartest of the abolitionists—including, in the end, President Lincoln—understood that the Civil War had to conclude as a war to end slavery. And though slavery might have ended in other ways, the abhorrent institution and the extraordinary privilege it afforded southern slaveholders was ended by a crisis.[27]

A generation later, a different crisis furnished a reason to do away with a different privilege. For much of the nineteenth century, political parties overcame their collective action problem by offering selective benefits to those who contributed to their cause. The most common of these benefits was public office. Long detested, this patronage or "spoils system" had withstood countless reform efforts. Then, in 1881, President James Garfield was assassinated by a disappointed office seeker who felt slighted that his campaigning for the president had not bought him a high profile position in the Garfield administration. The event galvanized support for civil service reform and prompted Garfield's successor, Chester A. Arthur, to become an unlikely champion of the cause (Millard 2012, 289). Civil service reform was accomplished through an institutional innovation, civil service exams, which introduced a measure of competition in federal hiring.

The Second World War was the crisis that abetted free trade. The war had decimated foreign exporters, giving a boost to American exporters, who, as already discussed, tended to favor free trade. It so happened that these exporters largely were located in northern, mostly Republican, districts. This is important because, for the better part of a century, the Republican Party had been held together by the high tariff plank of its platform. With exporters suddenly emboldened in Republican-leaning districts, the party's longstanding opposition to free trade began to whither (Hiscox 1999).

In the 1970s, a macroeconomic crisis aided the cause of deregulation. For decades, the Civil Aeronautics Board had shielded air carriers from interstate competition (Jordan 1979). Unable to compete over price, airlines resorted to nonprice competition, which tended to raise costs (Douglas and Miller III 1975). Consumers were stuck with the bill for this regulatory protection, but as previously noted, it typically is difficult to organize a large and diffuse group, such as consumers, for collective action. The 1970s, however, were not typical times. The Federal Reserve's expansion of the monetary base by 25 percent between 1974 and 1976 had yielded double-digit inflation (Smiley 1993, 218). This meant that voters and politicians were unusually interested in price levels. Unpersuaded by Milton Friedman's (1970, 11) assertion that inflation was "always and everywhere a monetary phenomenon," policymakers took a keen interest in eliminating any policy that might be causing high prices. President Ford created the Council on Wage and Price Stability, and Senator Kennedy began holding hearings investigating the role of the Civil Aeronautics

Board in fixing airline prices. Alfred Kahn parlayed this interest in prices into sweeping deregulation of the airlines (McCraw 1984).

From 1980 to 1988, the national debt nearly tripled. Though it seems quaint to say it now (with federal debt more than six times 1988 levels) many policymakers and pundits worried at the time that the national debt had reached crisis proportions. Thus, when Senator Phil Gramm and Congressman Dick Armey proposed BRAC as a way to reduce unnecessary military spending, their proposal was well tuned to the crisis du jour.

Embrace Permissionless Innovation

The economist David Henderson has observed that "competition is a hardy weed, not a delicate flower." (Henderson 2012) Try as they might to shield themselves from the gales of competition through government privilege, firms must always be wary of competitors. As Bruce Benson (2002, 248) has observed, entrepreneurs in highly regulated industries have "incentives to explore all uncontrolled or ineffectively enforced margins."

This can push institutions in one of two directions. The first—and apparently most common—is toward ever-expanding intervention. Alfred Kahn described it in the context of airline regulation:

> Control price, and the result will be artificial stimulus
> to entry. Control entry as well, and the result will be an
> artificial stimulus to compete by offering larger com-
> missions to travel agents, advertising, scheduling, free
> meals, and bigger seats. The response of the complete
> regulator, then, is to limit advertising, control scheduling,
> and travel agents' commissions, specify the size of the
> sandwiches and seats and the charge for inflight movies.
> (quoted in McCraw 1984, 272)

The dynamic can also lead to regulation of additional industries. In this way, regulation of railroads begot regulation of trucking, which begot regulation of airlines (Hilton 1966).

Institutions might respond to dynamic competition in a second way. They might become more liberalized, especially if dynamic competition is strong enough. Sam Peltzman (1989), for example, showed that technological change (the widespread adoption of jet-powered aircraft) altered the composition of the political coalition behind airline regulation, leading the regulator to permit more service competition. Similarly, Diana Thomas (2009) documents the way disruptive technology in the fifteenth-century German beer industry—they began using hops instead of *grut*—created an end-run around existing regulatory privileges. This was possible because the older technology had been central to the way the regulatory privileges worked: "During the eleventh century, the Holy Roman Emperor awarded local monopoly privileges in the production and sale of *grut*" (Thomas 2009, 333). Once that ingredient was no longer needed, the regulatory privilege crumbled.

A similar dynamic is occurring today in urban transportation markets. Uber, Lyft, and other sharing economy firms have developed business models that are so different from the existing taxi models that many regulations protecting taxi operators from competition simply do not apply (and when regulators assert that they do apply, the ride-sharing firms often have ignored them).

There are two lessons here. First, disruptive technologies and a culture that embraces what Adam Thierer (2014) has termed "permissionless innovation" can challenge existing privileges. Second, the opportunity for such a challenge is ironically greatest when regulatory privileges are most stifling, locking in particularly inefficient and outdated technologies.

CONCLUSION

Ever since Madison warned about the power of "faction" in Federalist 10—and probably well before then—people have been complaining about the outsized influence of special interests. Public choice theory and data suggest that these concerns are well founded. Small, well-heeled, and well-organized interests are often able to win public policies that concentrate benefits on themselves and foist the costs on others. Federal, state, and local tax policy provides numerous examples.

And yet there are exceptions to the rule. Occasionally, diffused and general interests prevail over concentrated and special interests. Moreover, certain patterns seem to mark these exceptions. These patterns suggest some rules of thumb for reformers hoping to overcome the special interests who have carved up our tax code.

But it is prudent to end on a note of caution. Every pattern I identify here could be used by special interests to obtain privilege, just as it could be used by reformers to serve the general interest. There is no guarantee that ideas will be good ones (think of the human misery wrought by Marx's ideas). Nor can we be certain that institutional change will always be for the better. Some of the institutions I have discussed, such as BRAC and fast-track trade negotiating authority, concentrate power in the executive, since the executive's constituency is typically more diffuse than that of individual legislators. But executives, too, are susceptible to special interest suasion, and too much power in the executive can be dangerous. A "grand bargain" may untie the Gordian knot of the tax code if every special interest agrees to give up its privilege in exchange for every other interest doing the same. But large, multifaceted bills are also a good way to facilitate special-interest-serving logrolls. Leaders can rally the public around the general interest, assemble grand coalitions, and improve institutions. But charismatic leaders with great power can, of course, do great harm. It goes without saying that working with special interests to defeat other special interests can sometimes backfire.[28] And, of course, crises can lead to bad as well as to good social change.

Nevertheless, the historical record should give some hope and direction to tax reformers.

NOTES

1. When multiple overlapping jurisdictions tax the same base, it leads to a different sort of tragedy, a tragedy of the anticommons. For more details, see Mitchell and Stratmann (2015).

2. This chapter offers a short preview of a book I am currently writing on the subject of overcoming special interests.

3. For the costs of federal tax complexity from a market-oriented perspective, see Fichtner and Feldman (2013). For the costs of state tax complexity from a progressive perspective, see Weinstein (2014).

4. Married homeowners with children, for example, are privileged (Harris and Parker 2014).

5. As the economists Leonard Burman and Joel Slemrod (2013, 72) put it, "only a small fraction of the cost of a factory that will last twenty years is really a cost of earning income this year."

6. See chap. 3 of their book. Note that this, along with other aspects of their proposal, make it a flat consumption tax.

7. My own view is that Hall and Rabushka have it right. See Mitchell (2013).

8. According to one model, the effect on income inequality would be "exceedingly modest." Gale et al. (2015).

9. For a broader overview of policies that privilege particular interest groups, see Mitchell (2012).

10. These include the mortgage interest deduction, the exclusion of principal residences from capital gains taxation, the tax free status of imputed rental income from owner-occupied residences, and various rules that keep state property taxes low. For details, see Hasen (2015). To be more precise, many of these provisions attend "home borrowship" rather than ownership (Kling 2008).

11. Gale et al. (2007, 1171): "Evidence suggests, however, that the mortgage interest deduction . . . does little if anything to encourage homeownership. Instead, it serves mainly to raise the price of housing and land and to encourage people who do buy homes to borrow more and to buy larger homes than they otherwise would." Glaeser and Shapiro (2003, 39): "While the deduction appears to increase the amount spent on housing, it also appears

to have almost no effect on the homeownership rate." Mann (2000, 1391): "None of the evidence from economists or from other countries suggests that the repeal of the home mortgage interest deduction would reduce demand for owner occupied housing or home ownership rates."

12. The concept was first developed by Tullock (1967), though the term was coined by Krueger (1974).

13. For an overview of the literature, see Congleton et al. (2008).

14. Olson identified other ways that groups might overcome their collective action problems. For example, a group might offer selective benefits to those who contribute to their collective goals.

15. Drutman's findings are particularly depressing when one considers the fact that formal models of rent-seeking contests demonstrate that rent-seeking losses are greatest when no barriers to rent-seeking exist and when there are economies of scale in rent-seeking. For more, see Mitchell (2015).

16. Though it appears to refer to the practice of rolling logs, the term's origins are unclear.

17. "Lobbyists' Delight," *Economist*, October 14, 2004, http://www.economist.com/node/3291288.

18. Agenda manipulation can also occur in single-issue space if some portion of the electorate has what are known as "multi-peaked preferences." The proofs are somewhat technical. For an overview, I refer the curious reader to Mueller (2003, 84–103).

19. Quoted in Tullock (1975, 671).

20. Charles Warren (1926, 616). The "Dormant Commerce Clause" doctrine took some time to materialize. But it is generally considered to have begun with Gibbons v. Ogden, 22 U.S. (Wheat.) 1 (1824).

21. Dick Armey, author's interview with Representative Dick Armey, March 15, 2013.

22. "US Loses to China in WTO Trade Dispute," *DW.COM*, July 14, 2014, http://www.dw.com/en/us-loses-to-china-in-wto-trade-dispute/a-17785657.

23. The prisoners' dilemma is perhaps the most celebrated game in game theory. Originally developed by Merrill Flood and Melvin Dresher, Albert Tucker formalized it in 1950 and used the example of prisoners to illustrate it (Tucker 1983). Models of special interest politics often take this form. See, for example, Tullock (1959) and Buchanan and Tullock (1962).

24. "The POLITICO 50: 2015—Timothy P. Carney, Veronique de Rugy—Washington Examiner Columnist; Mercatus Center Researcher," *POLITICO Magazine*, 2015, http://www.politico.com/magazine/politico50/2015/timothy-p-carney-veronique-de-rugy.

25. As of this writing, the bank's fate is uncertain. After bank boosters employed a rare procedural maneuver to bring reauthorization up on the House floor, it was reauthorized. Since its board lacks a quorum, however, the bank cannot make large loans.

26. *Rahm Emanuel: You Never Want a Serious Crisis to Go to Waste*, 2009, https://www.youtube.com/watch?v=1yeA_kHHLow.

27. Lincoln's own commitment to the cause was clearly shaped by external forces. His famous Emancipation Proclamation was only issued after the Union had won at Antietam and at any rate only freed those slaves held in the Confederacy.

28. Lord Acton warned: "At all times sincere friends of freedom have been rare, and its triumphs have been due to minorities, that have prevailed by associating themselves with auxiliaries whose objects often differed from their own; and this association, which is always dangerous, has been sometimes disastrous, by giving to opponents just grounds of opposition, and by kindling dispute over the spoils in the hour of success" (Dalberg-Acton 1907, n.p.).

REFERENCES

Acemoglu, Daron. 2003. "Why Not a Political Coase Theorem? Social Conflict, Commitment, and Politics." *Journal of Comparative Economics* 31 (4): 620–52.

Alexander, Raquel, Stephen W. Mazza, and Susan Scholz. 2009. "Measuring Rates of Return on Lobbying Expenditures: An Empirical Case Study of Tax Breaks for Multinational Corporations." *Journal of Law and Politics* 25 (4): 401.

Anderson, Gary M., Charles K. Rowley, and Robert D. Tollison. 1988. "Rent Seeking and the Restriction of Human Exchange." *Journal of Legal Studies* 17 (1): 83–100.

Arrow, Kenneth Joseph. 1951. *Social Choice and Individual Values*. New Haven, CT: Yale University Press.

Bachrach, Peter, and Morton S. Baratz. 1962. "Two Faces of Power." *American Political Science Review* 56 (4): 947–52. doi:10.2307/1952796.

Beekman, Robert L., and Brian T. Kench. 2015. "Basic Economics of the Export-Import Bank of the United States." Mercatus Research, Mercatus Center at George Mason University, Arlington, VA. http://mercatus.org/publication/basic-economics-export-import-bank-united-states.

Benson, Bruce L. 2002. "Regulatory Disequilibrium and Inefficiency: The Case of Interstate Trucking." *Review of Austrian Economics* 15 (2–3): 248. doi: 10.1023/A:1015722906781.

Black, Duncan. 1948. "The Decisions of a Committee Using a Special Majority." *Econometrica* 16 (3): 245–61. doi:10.2307/1907278.

Boettke, Peter J., Christopher J. Coyne, and Peter T. Leeson. 2008. "Institutional Stickiness and the New Development Economics." *American Journal of Economics and Sociology* 67 (2): 331–58. doi: 10.1111/j.1536-7150.2008.00573.x.

Brito, Jerry. 2011. "Running for Cover: The BRAC Commission as a Model for Federal Spending Reform." *Georgetown Journal of Law & Public Policy* 9: 131–56.

Brown, Dorothy A. 2009. "Shades of the American Dream." *Washington University Law Review* 87 (2): 329–78.

Buchanan, James M. 1987. "Tax Reform as Political Choice." *Journal of Economic Perspectives* 1 (1): 33–34.

———. 1990. "The Domain of Constitutional Economics." *Constitutional Political Economy* 1 (1): 1–18. doi: 10.1007/BF02393031.

———. 2000. *The Reason of Rules*. Indianapolis, IN: Liberty Fund.

Buchanan, James M., and Roger D. Congleton. 1998. *Politics by Principle, Not Interest: Toward Nondiscriminatory Democracy*. Cambridge: Cambridge University Press.

Buchanan, James M., and Gordon Tullock. 1962. *The Calculus of Consent: Logical Foundations of Constitutional Democracy*. Ann Arbor: University of Michigan Press.

Burman, Leonard, and Joel Slemrod. 2013. *Taxes in America: What Everyone Needs to Know*. New York: Oxford University Press. http://www.amazon.com/Taxes-America-What-Everyone-Needs/dp/0199890269/ref=sr_1_1?ie=UTF8&qid=1364226212&sr=8-1&keywords=slemrod.

Caplan, Bryan. 2008. *The Myth of the Rational Voter: Why Democracies Choose Bad Policies*, new ed. Princeton, NJ: Princeton University Press.

Coase, Ronald H. 1937. "The Nature of the Firm." *Economica* 4 (16): 386–405.

Condorcet, Marie Jean Antoine Nicolas de Caritat, marquis de. 1785. *Essai Sur L'application de L'analyse á La Probabilité Des Décisions Rendues á La Pluralité Des Voix* [*Essay on the Application of Analysis to the Probability of Majority Decisions*]. Paris. http://gallica.bnf.fr/ark:/12148/bpt6k417181.

Congleton, Roger, Arye Hillman, and Kai Konrad (eds.). 2008. *40 Years of Research on Rent Seeking 1—Theory of Rent Seeking.* New York: Springer. http://www.springer.com/economics /public+finance/book/978-3-540-79181-2.

Dalberg-Acton, John Emerich Edward. 1907. "The History of Freedom in Antiquity." In *The History of Freedom and Other Essays,* edited by John Neville Figgis and Reginald Vere Laurence. London: Macmillan, n.p. http://oll.libertyfund.org/titles/acton-the-history-of -freedom-and-other-essays.

de Rugy, Veronique. 2015a. "Export Jobs Won't Disappear Absent Ex-Im Bank." Mercatus Chart, Mercatus Center at George Mason University, Arlington, VA. http://mercatus.org /publication/export-jobs-won-t-disappear-absent-ex-im-bank.

———. 2015b. "White House Confirms Negligible Impact of the Ex-Im Bank on Exports." Mercatus Chart, Mercatus Center at George Mason University, Arlington, VA. http://mercatus.org /publication/white-house-confirms-negligible-impact-ex-im-bank-exports.

de Rugy, Veronique, and Andrea Castillo. 2014. "The US Export-Import Bank: A Review of the Debate over Reauthorization." Mercatus Research Report, Mercatus Center at George Mason University, Arlington, VA. http://mercatus.org/publication/us-export-import-bank-review -debate-over-reauthorization.

de Rugy, Veronique, and Adam Michel. 2016. "A Review of Selected Corporate Tax Privileges." Mercatus Research, Mercatus Center at George Mason University, Arlington, VA.

Dixit, Avinash K. 1998. *The Making of Economic Policy: A Transaction-Cost Politics Perspective,* 48–49. Cambridge, MA: MIT Press.

Dodgson, Charles. [1876] 1958. "A Method of Taking Votes on More than Two Issues." In *The Theory of Committees and Elections,* edited by Duncan Black, 214–33, reissue ed. Cambridge: Cambridge University Press.

Douglas, Arnold R. 1990. *The Logic of Congressional Action.* New Haven, CT: Yale University Press.

Douglas, George W., and James C. Miller III. 1975. *Economic Regulation of Domestic Air Transport: Theory and Policy.* Washington, DC: Brookings Institution.

Downs, Anthony. 1957. *An Economic Theory of Democracy.* New York: Harper & Row.

Drutman, Lee. 2015. *The Business of America Is Lobbying: How Corporations Became Politicized and Politics Became More Corporate.* New York: Oxford University Press.

Eastman, John C. 2001. "Restoring the General to the General Welfare Clause." *Chapman Law Review* 4 (63): 63–87. http://papers.ssrn.com/abstract=906063.

Ferejohn, John, Jack Rakove, and Jonathan Riley, eds. 2001. *Constitutional Culture and Democratic Rule,* 1st ed. Cambridge: Cambridge University Press.

Ferguson, Adam. 1782. *An Essay on the History of Civil Society,* 5th ed. London: T. Cadell.

Fichtner, Jason, and Jacob Feldman. 2013. "The Hidden Costs of Tax Compliance." Research Paper, Mercatus Center at George Mason University, Arlington, VA. http://mercatus.org /publication/hidden-costs-tax-compliance.

Friedman, Milton. 1962. *Capitalism and Freedom,* 40th anniversary ed. Chicago: University of Chicago Press.

———. 1970. *The Counter-Revolution in Monetary Theory.* London: Transatlantic Arts.

Gale, William G., Jonathan Gruber, and Seth I. Stephens-Davidowitz. 2007. "Encouraging Homeownership through the Tax Code," *Tax Notes* 115 (12): 1171. http://papers.ssrn.com /abstract=1758888.

Gale, William G., Melissa S. Kearney, and Peter R. Orszag. 2015. "Would a Significant Increase in the Top Income Tax Rate Substantially Alter Income Inequality?" Washington, DC: Brookings Institution. http://www.brookings.edu/~/media/research

/files/papers/2015/09/28-taxes-inequality/would-top-income-tax-alter-income
-inequality.pdf.

Gelman, Andrew, Nate Silver, and Aaron Edlin. 2009. "What Is the Probability Your Vote Will
Make a Difference?" NBER Working Paper 15220, National Bureau of Economic Research,
Cambridge, MA. http://www.nber.org/papers/w15220.

Glaeser, Edward L., and Jesse M. Shapiro. 2003. "The Benefits of the Home Mortgage Interest
Deduction." In *Tax Policy and the Economy*, edited by James Poterba, 37–82. NBER Book
Series Tax Policy and the Economy, volume 17. Cambridge, MA: MIT Press. http://www
.nber.org/chapters/c11534.

Hall, Robert E., and Alvin Rabushka. 1995. *The Flat Tax: Updated Revised Edition*, 2nd ed.
Stanford, CA: Hoover Institution.

Hardin, Garrett. 1968. "The Tragedy of the Commons." *Science* 162: 1243–48.

Harris, Benjamin H., and Lucie Parker. 2014. "The Mortgage Interest Deduction across Zip
Codes." Research Paper, Brookings Institution, Washington, DC. http://www.brookings.edu
/research/papers/2014/12/mortgage-interest-deductions-across-zip-codes-harris.

Hasen, David. 2015. "How I Learned to Stop Worrying and Love Our Homeowner Tax Rules." *State
Tax Notes*, October 19. https://papers.ssrn.com/sol3/papers.cfm?abstract_id=2622300.

Hayek, Friedrich A. 1949. "The Intellectuals and Socialism." *University of Chicago Law Review* 16
(3): 417–33.

Henderson, David. 2012. "The Ten Pillars of Economic Wisdom." *EconLog*, Library of Economics
and Liberty, April 12. http://econlog.econlib.org/archives/2012/04/the_ten_pillars.html.

Higgs, Robert. 1987. *Crisis and Leviathan: Critical Episodes in the Growth of American Government*,
25th anniversary ed. Oakland, CA: Independent Institute.

Hilber, Christian, and Tracy Turner. 2014. "The Mortgage Interest Deduction and Its Impact on
Homeownership Decisions." *Review of Economics and Statistics* 96 (4): 618–37.

Hilton, George W. 1966. "The Consistency of the Interstate Commerce Act." *Journal of Law and
Economics* 9: 111.

Hines, James R. 2007. "Excess Burden of Taxation." In *New Palgrave Dictionary of Economics*,
edited by Lawrence E. Blume and Steven N. Durlauf. http://www.bus.umich.edu/otpr
/WP2007-1.pdf.

Hiscox, Michael J. 1999. "The Magic Bullet? The RTAA, Institutional Reform, and Trade
Liberalization." *International Organization* 53 (4): 669–98. doi: 10.2307/2601306.

Horpedahl, Jeremy, and Harrison Searles. 2013. "The Home Mortgage Interest Deduction."
Mercatus on Policy, Mercatus Center at George Mason University, Arlington, VA. http://
mercatus.org/publication/home-mortgage-interest-deduction.

Houser, Daniel, David Levy, Kail Padgitt, Sandra Peart, and Erte Xiao. 2014. "Raising the Price
of Talk: An Experimental Analysis of Transparent Leadership." GMU Working Paper
in Economics, George Mason University, Fairfax, VA. http://papers.ssrn.com/abstract
=2438259.

Ikenson, Daniel J. 2014. "The Export-Import Bank and Its Victims: Which Industries and States
Bear the Brunt?" Policy Analysis. Washington, DC: Cato Institute. http://www.cato.org
/publications/policy-analysis/export-import-bank-its-victims-which-industries-states-bear
-brunt.

Joint Committee on Taxation Staff. 2015. "Estimates of Federal Tax Expenditures for Fiscal Years
2015–2019." Washington, DC. https://www.jct.gov/publications.html?func=startdown&id
=4857.

———. 2016. "List of Expiring Federal Tax Provisions 2016–2025." Washington, DC. https://www
.jct.gov/publications.html?func=startdown&id=4862.

Jordan, William A. 1979. *Airline Regulation in America: Effects and Imperfections*, new ed. Westport, CT: Greenwood.

Keynes, John Maynard. 1937. *The General Theory of Employment, Interest, and Money*. San Diego: Harcourt, Brace & World.

Kling, Arnold. 2008. "Kling on Freddie and Fannie and the Recent History of the U.S. Housing Market." Interview by Russ Roberts, *EconTalk*, September 29. http://www.econtalk.org /archives/2008/09/kling_on_freddi.html.

Krueger, Anne O. 1974. "The Political Economy of the Rent-Seeking Society." *American Economic Review* 64 (3): 291–303.

Lohmann, Susanne, and Sharyn O'Halloran. 1994. "Divided Government and U.S. Trade Policy: Theory and Evidence." *International Organization* 48 (4): 595–632. doi: 10.2307/2706897.

López, Edward, and Wayne Leighton. 2012. *Madmen, Intellectuals, and Academic Scribblers: The Economic Engine of Political Change*. Stanford, CA: Stanford University Press.

Lowi, Theodore J. 1969. *The End of Liberalism: The Second Republic of the United States*, 40th anniversary ed. New York: W. W. Norton.

Madison, James. 2000. "Vices of the Political System of the United States, Apr. 1787." In *The Founders' Constitution* 1: 16, 350–51. Chicago and Indianapolis, IN: University of Chicago Press and Liberty Fund.

Mann, Roberta F. 2000. "The (Not So) Little House on the Prairie: The Hidden Costs of the Home Mortgage Interest Deduction." *Arizona State Law Journal* 32: 1391.

McCormack, John. 2011. "GE Filed 57,000-Page Tax Return, Paid No Taxes on $14 Billion in Profits." *Weekly Standard*, November 17. http://www.weeklystandard.com/ge-filed-57000 -page-tax-return-paid-no-taxes-on-14-billion-in-profits/article/609137.

McCormick, Robert E., William F. Shughart, and Robert D. Tollison. 1984. "The Disinterest in Deregulation." *American Economic Review* 74 (5): 1075–79.

McCraw, Thomas K. 1984. *Prophets of Regulation*. Cambridge, MA: Belknap Press of Harvard University Press.

McGillivray, Fiona, Lain McLean, Robert Pahre, and Cheryl Schonhardt-Bailey. 2001. *International Trade and Political Institutions: Instituting Trade in the Long 19th Century*. Cheltenham, UK: Edward Elgar, 83–91.

McKelvey, Richard D. 1976. "Intransitivities in Multidimensional Voting Models and Some Implications for Agenda Control." *Journal of Economic Theory* 12 (3): 472–82. doi: 10.1016/0022-0531(76)90040-5.

Millard, Candice. 2012. *Destiny of the Republic: A Tale of Madness, Medicine and the Murder of a President*, reprint ed. New York: Anchor.

Mitchell, Matthew. 2012. "The Pathology of Privilege: The Economic Consequences of Government Favoritism." Special Study, Mercatus Center at George Mason University, Arlington, VA.

———. 2013. "What Is a Loophole?" *Neighborhood Effects*, April 3, http://neighborhoodeffects .mercatus.org/2013/04/03/what-is-a-loophole/.

———. 2014. "Ex-Im's Deadweight Loss." *Neighborhood Effects*, August 6. http://neighborhood effects.mercatus.org/2014/08/06/ex-ims-dead-weight-loss/.

———. 2015. "Of Rent-Seekers and Rent-Givers." Book Review of *The Business of America Is Lobbying*, by Lee Drutman (New York: Oxford University Press, 2015). *Library of Law and Liberty*, December 14. http://www.libertylawsite.org/book-review/of-rent-seekers-and-rent-givers/.

Mitchell, Matthew, and Thomas Stratmann. 2015. "A Tragedy of the Anticommons: Local Option Taxation and Cell Phone Tax Bills." *Public Choice* 165 (3–4): 171–91. doi: 10.1007/s11127-015-0302-7.

Morrison, Steven, and Clifford Winston. 1986. *The Economic Effects of Airline Deregulation.* Washington, DC: Brookings Institution.

———. 1989. "Airline Deregulation and Public Policy." *Science* 245: 707–11.

Motel, Seth. 2015. "5 Facts on How Americans View Taxes." *Fact Tank, Pew Research Center,* April 10. http://www.pewresearch.org/fact-tank/2015/04/10/5-facts-on-how-americans -view-taxes/.

Mueller, Dennis C. 2003. *Public Choice III.* Cambridge and New York: Cambridge University Press.

Murray, Alan, and Jeffrey Birnbaum. 1988. *Showdown at Gucci Gulch,* reprint ed. New York: Vintage.

North, Douglass C. 1990. *Institutions, Institutional Change, and Economic Performance.* Cambridge and New York: Cambridge University Press.

Okun, Arthur M. 1975. *Equality and Efficiency: The Big Tradeoff,* expanded and revised ed. Washington, DC: Brookings Institution.

Olson, Mancur. 1965. *The Logic of Collective Action: Public Goods and the Theory of Groups,* 2nd printing with new preface and appendix. Cambridge, MA: Harvard University Press.

Pelc, Krzysztof J. 2014. "Why the Deal to Pay Brazil $300 Million Just to Keep U.S. Cotton Subsidies Is Bad for the WTO, Poor Countries, and U.S. Taxpayers." *Washington Post,* October 12. https://www.washingtonpost.com/blogs/monkey-cage/wp/2014/10/12/why-the-deal-to-pay -brazil-300-million-just-to-keep-u-s-cotton-subsidies-is-bad-for-the-wto-poor-countries -and-u-s-taxpayers/.

Peltzman, Sam. 1989. "The Economic Theory of Regulation after a Decade of Deregulation." *Brookings Papers on Economic Activity: Microeconomics:* 1–59. doi: 10.2307/2534719.

Richter, Brian Kelleher, Krislert Samphantharak, and Jeffrey F. Timmons. 2009. "Lobbying and Taxes." *American Journal of Political Science* 53 (4): 893–909.

Riker, William H. 1984. *The Theory of Political Coalitions.* New Haven, CT: Yale University Press.

———. 1964. *Federalism: Origin, Operation, Significance.* Boston: Little, Brown and Co.

Riker, William H., and Steven J. Brams. 1973. "The Paradox of Vote Trading." *American Political Science Review* 67 (4): 1235–47. doi: 10.2307/1956545.

Shughart, William F. 1999. "The Reformer's Dilemma." *Public Finance Review* 27 (5): 561–65. doi: 10.1177/109114219902700506.

Smiley, Gene. 1993. *The American Economy in the Twentieth Century.* Cincinnati, OH: South-Western Publishing.

Smith, Adam, and Bruce Yandle. 2014. *Bootleggers and Baptists: How Economic Forces and Moral Persuasion Interact to Shape Regulatory Politics.* Washington, DC: Cato Institute.

Stratmann, Thomas. 1992. "The Effects of Logrolling on Congressional Voting." *American Economic Review* 82 (5): 1162–76. doi: 10.2307/2117472.

———. 1995. "Logrolling in the U.S. Congress." *Economic Inquiry* 33 (3): 441–56.

Stratmann, Thomas, and Joshua Wojnilower. 2015. "Presidential Particularism: Distributing Funds between Alternative Objectives and Strategies." Working Paper, Mercatus Center at George Mason University, Arlington, VA. http://mercatus.org/publication/presidential -particularism-distributing-funds-between-alternative-objectives.

Tabarrok, Alexander T., ed. 2002. *Entrepreneurial Economics: Bright Ideas from the Dismal Science.* Oxford: Oxford University Press.

Thierer, Adam. 2014. *Permissionless Innovation: The Continuing Case for Comprehensive Technological Freedom.* Arlington, VA: Mercatus Center at George Mason University.

Thomas, Diana W. 2009. "Deregulation Despite Transitional Gains." *Public Choice* 140 (3–4): 329–40. doi: 10.1007/s11127-009-9420-4.

Tucker, Albert. 1983. "The Mathematics of Tucker: A Sampler." *Two-Year College Mathematics Journal* 14 (3): 228–32.

Tullock, Gordon. 1959. "Problems of Majority Voting," *Journal of Political Economy* 67. http://ideas.repec.org/a/ucp/jpolec/v67y1959p571.html.

———. 1967. "The Welfare Costs of Tariffs, Monopolies, and Theft." *Western Economic Journal (Economic Inquiry)* 5 (3): 224–32. doi:10.1111/j.1465-7295.1967.tb01923.x.

———. 1975. "The Transitional Gains Trap." *Bell Journal of Economics* 6 (2): 671–78. doi: 10.2307/3003249.

———. 1980. "Efficient Rent Seeking." In *Towards a Theory of the Rent-Seeking Society*, edited by Robert D. Tollison and Gordon Tullock, 97–112. College Station: Texas A&M University Press.

US International Trade Commission. 2011. "Value of U.S. Imports for Consumption, Duties Collected, and Ratio of Duties to Values, 1891–2010." Washington, DC: Statistical Services Division, Office of Investigations, Office of Operations, US International Trade Commission. https://dataweb.usitc.gov/scripts/AVE.PDF.

Wagner, Richard E. 2012. *Deficits, Debt, and Democracy: Wrestling with Tragedy on the Fiscal Commons*. Cheltenham, UK: Edward Elgar.

Warren, Charles. 1926. *The Supreme Court in United States History*, revised ed. Boston: Little, Brown.

Weinstein, Paul Jr. 2014. "The State Tax Complexity Index: A New Tool for Tax Reform and Simplification." Policy Memo, Progressive Policy Institute, Washington, DC.

Williamson, Claudia R. 2009. "Informal Institutions Rule: Institutional Arrangements and Economic Performance." *Public Choice* 139 (3–4): 371–87. doi: 10.1007/s11127-009-9399-x.

Williamson, Oliver E. 1979. "Transaction-Cost Economics: The Governance of Contractual Relations." *Journal of Law and Economics* 22 (2): 233–61.

Wilson, James. 1991. *Bureaucracy: What Government Agencies Do and Why They Do It*. New York: Basic Books.

Yandle, Bruce. 1983. "Bootleggers and Baptists: The Education of a Regulatory Economist." *AEI Journal on Government and Society*: 12–16.

Zeiler, Thomas W. 1999. *Free Trade, Free World: The Advent of GATT*. Chapel Hill: University of North Carolina Press.

Zingales, Luigi. 2011. *A Capitalism for the People: Recapturing the Lost Genius of American Prosperity*. New York: Basic Books.

CONCLUSION
Moving Forward: Tax Policy Lessons

ADAM J. HOFFER

Department of Economics, University of Wisconsin–La Crosse

TODD NESBIT

Department of Economics, Ball State University

On July 17, 2014, a plainclothes New York Police Department officer approached a man he believed to be selling untaxed cigarettes in Staten Island. The suspect was unarmed. An hour later, the suspect was pronounced dead at the Richmond University Medical Center.

The rash actions of the New York City Police Department that resulted in the tragic death of Eric Garner were initiated because he was suspected of tax evasion. Excessive cigarette taxation created the environment that ultimately led to Mr. Garner's death. Selective taxation imposes real costs on individuals in our society, and these costs extend far beyond the superficial discussion of dollars paid.

To say that selective taxes are the primary source of society's social and economic problems would certainly be an overstatement, but selective taxes do have real costs. Every day millions of Americans, predominantly from lower-income households, are made worse off because of selective taxes. Life is made unnecessarily more difficult as the government increases prices, makes arrests, and paternalistically makes choices for people who should be free to choose on their own.

Creating effective public policy is difficult. The myriad unintended and secondary consequences of tax and expenditure policy create much confusion regarding both the source of and solutions to social problems. Further adding to the complexity of effective policy making is the fact that policy is enacted through a political process that tends to reinforce discriminatory and inefficient policy solutions. The political system is plagued by imperfect information and unchecked self-interest.

The analytical approach of this book has been to apply fundamental economics to evaluate selective sales and excise tax policy. We examined the expected behavior of self-interested political participants under various institutional rules, incorporating lessons from public choice theory, constitutional economics, law and economics, and behavioral economics, among other fields of study.

In this final chapter of the book, we summarize the common themes gleaned from the contributed chapters. We then conclude the book with a discussion of policy recommendations. We suggest policies that make taxes less burdensome, more efficient, and more transparent.

RESEARCH FINDINGS

The broad conclusions deduced from the earlier chapters suggest that the democratic system is rife with rent-seeking. Without proper restrictions on the actions of policymakers, the system inevitably results in a churning of discriminatory policy.

Tax policy can and should be improved, and the lessons of this book can aid in this process. While each contributed chapter can stand alone in advancing the discussion of improved tax policy, we summarize the common findings in each section of the book.

Part I. Public Finance and Public Choice: Establishing the Foundation

Selective sales and excise taxes do not enhance efficiency. Instead, selective taxation predictably and discriminately benefits elite politically favored groups at the expense of other politically disfavored and disenfranchised groups.

Discriminatory tax policy catering to the special interests of politically favored individuals, firms, and industries is a common concern raised throughout this book. Current tax policy is the result of a long series of small discriminatory modifications to the status quo. Each modification represents the outcome of the influence of special interests who gain political support for tax changes that disadvantage competitors or impose costs on others to fund a concentrated expenditure benefiting the special interest. Each modification to the existing broad tax structure comes at an increasing marginal cost as discriminatory provisions become more and more prevalent, until large-scale tax reform becomes feasible. The sequence of new discriminatory modifications is then restarted until the next large-scale reform is possible.

Part II. The Political Economy of Public Budgeting

Policymakers lie, deceive, and act on incomplete information when creating tax policy. The chapters in this section point out that tax policy can be exceedingly complex. Policy is manipulated to conceal the goal of feeding ever-expanding budgets rather than pursuing the social well-being. Selective taxation is also enacted using strategies that make it difficult for voters to identify and assess the impact of a tax.

Even when policy seems well intentioned and straightforward, such as a lottery tax earmarked to be spent on education, the observed outcomes are complicated and often not what was promised. Tax earmarking is a convenient approach to gain support for tax increases, but it rarely leads to anything resembling the promised increased expenditures in the targeted area. Taxation also leads to a large number of secondary effects that often cause substantial burdens on those most vulnerable in society.

Part III. Fiscal Federalism and Selective Taxation

Under the appropriate institutional rules, intergovernmental competition that exists under fiscal federalism can encourage efficient and equitable tax policy. Unfortunately, it is clear that the existing institutional rules governing state and local tax policy need much improvement to result in the oft-promised economic growth, long-term stability, and overall improved well-being.

State and local government attempts to drive economic growth by selective subsidies have failed to deliver time and time again. Not only have these saint subsidies not led to economic and job growth, but they also necessitate increased taxation, often in the form of selective taxes. However, selective taxes fail to fund large-scale expenditures, such as infrastructure and pensions, and the burden of such taxes generally falls heavily on less-wealthy local residents. Institutional changes are necessary to encourage improved state and local tax policy.

Part IV. The Economics of the Failing Nanny State

As a coercive tool, selective sales and excise taxes fail to improve individual and societal well-being. Whether the goal is to discourage the use of plastic shopping bags, unhealthy eating habits, cigarette smoking, or other undesirable behavior, hard nudges simply fail to improve well-being as promised. In many cases the taxes are counterproductive, leading to worsening health and environmental conditions.

The effects of prohibitive taxation—or, as coined by Michael LaFaive, "prohibition by price"—share more in common with the failures of alcohol and narcotics prohibition than with effective tax policy. While taxation does lead some consumers to avoid the consumption of the good, many others turn to the underground economy for less expensive options. This brings along with it greater exposure to a whole host of undesirable outcomes for the individual, including violence to person and property, a distrust between law enforcement and all citizens, and severe legal repercussions that can also limit future employment prospects.

There are better alternatives than selective taxation to help empower consumers make more informed and better choices.

Part V. Evaluating and Prescribing Better Tax Policy

The tax code reflects the preferences of special interests and paternalistic politicians. Because those preferences vary, we observe different policies across the country. The difference in policies provides an opportunity to study the effects of these discriminatory taxes and from such studies; we can formulate recommendations for better policy.

PRESCRIBING BETTER POLICY

We consider various policy alternatives to the existing system of selective and discriminatory taxation. Our policy recommendations range from the ideal to those serving only to modestly improve the status quo. We recognize the first-best policy prescription is not always politically feasible. It is far better to take even small steps toward improved policy than to simply accept the inadequacies of the status quo.

The following list of policy guidelines should not be viewed as either-or. Instead, policymakers can improve their tax codes by incorporating any number of these prescriptions.

First-Best Policy

1. Eliminate selective taxes. Selective taxes are poor policy tools. Get rid of them. Allow individuals to make their own choices.

If the heavy hand of paternalism cannot be completely removed and government wants to continue to play a role in individual choices, we offer second-best policy recommendations for behavioral programs. If the government simply cannot function without the revenue currently provided by selective taxation, we also provide second-best policy recommendations for revenue generation.

2. Constitutionally limit government's power to tax discriminatorily. As Richard Wagner notes in chapter 4, constitutionally limiting a government's ability to discriminate among taxpayers reduces that government's ability to affect the commercial value of individual enterprises. This, in turn, reduces the return on—and therefore the value of—campaign contributions and engaging in other forms of rent-seeking. The precise language or content of such a constitutional limit is still debated. As has been observed in the debate over the proper balanced budget amendment,[1] walking the line between too little and too much specificity is challenging. This is no easy task.

For example, an effective constraint would need to be specific enough to eliminate the subjective determination of what can be labeled as discriminatory, yet broad enough so as to capture future political innovations in policy-making designed to skirt the constraint. Furthermore, such an amendment limiting politicians' abilities to engage in discriminatory taxation (and expenditure) would certainly face heavy opposition from the very enterprises currently benefiting from the status quo. It is very likely that, as has been the case in many states passing restrictions on eminent domain usage for private gain (Lopez et al. 2009), pressure will mount for the passage of a constraint that is more symbolic than truly effective. Ultimately, the proper content of such a constitutional constraint is likely something that is best discovered through various state-led attempts at restricting discriminatory policy making.

3. Make taxation more transparent by collecting all taxes from consumers and workers.

> Lack of transparency is a huge political advantage. And basically, call it the stupidity of the American voter or whatever, but basically that was really really critical for the [Affordable Care Act] to pass. And it's the second-best

> argument. Look, I wish Mark was right that we could make
> it all transparent, but I'd rather have this law than not.
> (Jonathan Gruber, MIT economist and co-designer of the
> Affordable Care Act)[2]

Can tax policy be more deplorable? Taxes are too often designed to be dis-
guised, hidden from the would-be taxpayer. Gruber's argument in the quote
above succinctly states that if the American voters, Congress members responsible for voting on the Affordable Care Act (ACA), and the Congressional
Budget Office responsible for summarizing the economic impacts of the ACA
accurately understood what the bill would do, the bill would have been voted
down. The implicit argument here is that the architects of the bill clearly knew
what was better for the American people than any of the other parties responsible for making that decision and any of the people that would be affected by
the bill.

We borrowed the above quote from Randall Holcombe's chapter 5.
Holcombe goes on to describe the way in which many taxes are hidden from
taxpayers. The most popular means of disguising a tax is to apply the tax to
producers.

Those absent the knowledge of Economics 101 may believe that the tax
incidence of supply-side tax falls on businesses or producers. That is simply
not the case. Taxes are almost always passed along to consumers in the form
of higher prices.

How, then, to make taxes more transparent? Simplifying the tax code by
eliminating selective taxes would be a great start. Short of that, we recommend
collecting *all* taxes from consumers and workers. Sales, excise, use, and selective taxes are almost exclusively collected by producers. Employers withhold
employee federal income tax, state and local income tax, Medicare tax, Social
Security tax, unemployment insurance tax, and disability insurance tax. Basic
economics tells us that market prices and quantities will not be affected by
which party—consumer or producers; employers or employees—has to hand
the tax money over to the government.

A common argument in favor of producers/employers collecting taxes is
convenience. However, when convenience results in a lack of transparency and
a misunderstanding of the cost of government, convenience becomes a weak
argument. Voters should face head-on the cost of the government we collectively consume, just as we each face the cost of consuming private goods. Costs
of consumption should be transparent; only then can we make more informed
choices in the voting booth.

Second-Best Guidelines

4. Minimize selective taxation—both in scale and scope. Decrease or remove the tax rate on existing selectively taxed goods. Create no new selective taxes.

If completely removing the tax rate on traditionally taxed goods (e.g., cigarettes, alcohol, gasoline, and gambling) is too unpalatable, decreasing the tax rate is a step in the right direction. A gradual phase out may be easier for budget adjustments. However, an immediate, complete elimination of a particular tax may be more politically feasible for areas in which political power oscillates.

We recommend similar policy for the scope of selective taxation. As we mentioned in the introduction, discriminatory taxes have expanded far beyond the scope of cigarettes, alcohol, gasoline, and gambling. In various parts of the country, extra taxes are applied to playing cards, fur clothing, marijuana, sex-related or nude services, candy, soda, chewing gum, potato chips, pretzels, milkshakes, baked goods, ice cream, popsicles, bagel slicing, sporting or entertainment tickets, parking, hotel rooms, medical devices, electric cars, health insurance, *not* purchasing health insurance, and many other goods. Scale back the scope of these taxes and stop the growth of selective taxes on new items.

5. Use more broadly based taxation. For government revenue needs, use broadly based taxes, such as the general sales tax and the income tax. These taxes are more transparent and raise revenue more effectively than do selective taxes.

On a cautionary note, exemptions from broadly based taxes often mirror the effect of distortionary selective taxes. The federal income tax code has been modified over time to selectively encourage the purchase of hybrid vehicles, energy-saving replacement windows, and roofing while also incentivizing the production of ethanol, among many other items.

Likewise, the general sales tax is anything but "general" these days. The list of items exempted from sales taxation in any given state is striking. For instance, the Ohio Department of Taxation provides a sixty-two point list of types of sales that are exempted from sales tax.[3] The list of exempted sales in Ohio has shrunk in recent years. The *Cleveland Plain Dealer* reported that 127 items were exempt from the general sales tax in 2013.[4] Some of the items for which the exemption was removed in the 2013 biannual budget include "bank service charges; overnight trailer parks; bowling alleys and billiard parlors; hunting and fishing guides; pari-mutuel racing events; and admission to museums, amusement parks, circuses, fairs, concerts and sporting events that don't involve an educational institution."[5] The elimination of some sales tax exemptions coincided with a modest sales tax rate reduction.

The State of Ohio's combination of broadening the base while reducing the rate is a step in the right direction for reducing the state's discriminatory influence on market outcomes, although Ohio could go further. Other states are encouraged to follow suit by also broadening the general sales tax base (eliminating exemptions) and lowering the sales tax rate to maintain revenue neutrality. A similar approach could be used in the taxation of income at all levels of government.

6. Limit new expenditure programs and expansions of existing ones. Public programs (e.g., Medicaid and Medicare) as well as new laws (e.g., the ACA) have helped create an environment in which taxpayers believe they should have the right to control how other citizens live and what they consume. The consumption of cigarettes, trans fats, and sugary drinks (among many other items) certainly can lead to various health concerns for the individual consumer, particularly if not consumed in moderation. These are cases of what Adam Hoffer and William Shughart in chapter 3 describe as "internalities," in which consumption choices can harm one's future self. The consumption of too much salt or sugar imposes a personal cost on the individual consumer; it does not naturally produce an externality problem.

However, establishing programs to force taxpayers to pay for medical expenses and enacting tax policy that favors employer-provided group insurance plans does create an environment in which less healthy consumption choices impose greater costs—higher taxes or higher insurance premiums—on others. The end result is an environment in which taxpayers and group insurance plan participants believe they should have a say in the consumption decisions of other individuals. A common policy response is to impose discriminatory excise taxes on politically incorrect consumption. As Randall Holcombe mentions in chapter 5, these taxes fall on a minority of the population, who are argued to be deserving of taxation due to their behavior.

To be clear, the external costs in the form of higher taxes and group insurance premiums is a policy failure rather than some form of market failure. There would be no policy-relevant external costs to speak of in the absence of public funding for health care. In order to reduce voter support for increased discriminatory selective sales and excise taxes to be used as hard nudges, governments would be best to roll back public provision for health care. At the very least, governments should restrict further expansion of existing programs and not support the passage of new expenditure programs.

7. Use more carrots, fewer sticks. Selective taxes are often used as a measure to discourage consumption. Policymakers and industry professionals want to steer consumers toward "better" choices. Smoking is detrimental to an individual's health. Increasing the price will decrease overall cigarette consumption, of course. But most people do not quit, and those who continue to consume shoulder an even heavier financial burden. Plus, as Michael LaFaive detailed in chapter 15, prohibition by price carries tremendous unintended consequences, such as the development of underground markets.

If the goal of public policy truly is to help people, use more carrots and fewer sticks. Reward healthier, more pro-social behavior. Stop punishing individuals with heavy-handed taxation or, in the case of the war on drugs (see Bruce Benson and Brian Meehan's discussion in chapter 8), jail time for their behavior. Economic and psychology research shows again and again that rewards are equal to or better than punishments at influencing behavior. And rewards come with fewer unintended consequences.

If politicians want less smoking, help people quit who want to quit. Use information and support groups to help people quit cold turkey. The Australian government subsidizes nicotine patches, for example.[6]

Worried about too much sugar or fat consumption? Help people purchase fresher, healthier options. Support farmer's markets in urban food deserts. Reward via a tax break or medical subsidy individuals who lose weight.

Rewards are a powerful tool for behavioral change. Public policy should be designed to help people, not to inflict varying degrees of punishment.

8. Localize policymaking where possible. In chapter 13, J. R. Clark and Dwight Lee present an intriguing and innovative approach to the federal tax code. The focus of their proposal is to rely on the competitive pressures present in fiscal federalism to encourage better tax and expenditure policy. What is unique in their proposal is the high effective cost of enacting expenditure programs that benefit special interests. Such a tax structure discourages special interest legislation, including subsidies to encourage firm relocation (see Peter Calcagno and Frank Hefner's chapter 10) and sports subsidies (see Dennis Coates and Craig A. Depken II's chapter 11), areas in which there is substantial competition across cities and states. Overall, Clark and Lee's tax reform proposal discourages wasteful spending while encouraging low and efficient taxation methods.

Despite the potential good than can stem from Clark and Lee's tax reform proposal, such an extreme tax change is unlikely anytime soon. However, the basic idea to encourage a good competitive environment across government units can be applied in other ways. For example, the reduction or elimination of many intergovernmental grants could encourage better tax and expenditure policy. Some of the intergovernmental grant programs are, at least in part, supported by efficiency arguments. For instance, according to Edward Gramlich (1990, 1994), the spillover benefits to nondirect users of interstate highways in California—that is, those of us who do not drive on California highways—justify a federal subsidy to cover 30 percent of the expenditure on highway infrastructure. A similar approach could be used for other expenditure areas, such as education, health care, public housing, and welfare spending. If Gramlich's approach is applied to all intergovernmental grant programs, federal expenditures on such grants is expected to fall substantially, leaving states with increased responsibility to pay for programs that benefit their own constituents and greater incentives to enact only those programs that pass a benefit-cost analysis.

Creating an environment in which inefficient state and local policies are no longer paid for largely by far-away taxpayers, who have little knowledge of the decisions being made and no responsibility for electing those who make the decisions, will put greater pressure on elected officials to support cost-effective policy and keep taxes lower. Barry Weignast, Kenneth Shepsle, and Christopher Johnsen's (1981) model, now commonly referenced as the "Law of 1/N," explains how tax exporting through intergovernmental grants encourages the passage of inefficient policy, potentially greatly increasing the tax liability across all jurisdictions. Restricting the ability of state and local governments to rely on intergovernmental grants would cause both voters and elected officials to be more concerned with the net benefits of proposed expenditures, as those in the jurisdiction would face the full cost of the expenditure rather than just a small percentage of it.

As a second example, the desire to enact numerous selective sales and excise taxes to fund subsidies for professional sports stadiums and other large businesses could be limited by an appropriately constructed federal policy. In fact, former President Obama supported a policy along these lines in his budget proposal in 2015. The then president sought to prohibit the use of tax-exempt bonds to finance professional sports stadiums (Povich 2015), an act that would not prohibit sports subsidies but one that would arguably limit the ability of franchise owners to pit city against city in an effort to extract large subsidies funded by taxpayers.

The goal here is to rely on the benefits of a localized system of government. Local elected officials have a knowledge advantage concerning the needs of their constituents more so than politicians elected for federal office. Local officials may also face greater incentives to act in the interest of their constituents as they are more likely to answer questions when venturing out to the local coffee shop or grocery store. Underperforming local governments may suffer from poor policy choices as residents and businesses are mobile. Without restrictions on intergovernmental grants, which disconnect the funding from those who benefit, and on selectively issued subsidies to attract businesses, local governments may engage in inefficient competition and wasteful expenditures. By reducing wasteful expenditures, the call to employ discriminatory selective sales and excise taxation will also be reduced.

CONCLUSION

Public policy is complex. Outcomes are difficult to measure and the best policies can be politically unpalatable. To the extent economists have identified the effects of selective taxes, the taxes fail to improve the lives of citizens. The combination of misaligned incentives and paternalistic tendencies of policymakers make selective taxes a poor choice for public policy intended to improve well-being. Selective taxation should be eliminated where feasible and otherwise transparent and highly limited by constitutional constraints. In circumstances where the first-best policies cannot currently be implemented, we offer policies that are a step in the right direction, including a focus on broader taxation, more carrots and fewer sticks, and limiting unsustainable government expenditures. By adhering to these guidelines, elected officials will help promote a less discriminatory tax code that also contributes to an institutional environment supportive of a more prosperous society.

NOTES

1. See, for example, McCulloch (2012).
2. The Gruber quote can be found at www.forbes.com /sites/theabothecary/2014/11/10/aca -architect-the-stupidity-of-the-american-voter-led-us-to-hide-obamacares-tax-hikes-and -subsidies-from-the-public/#d008d52779b.
3. See http://www.tax.ohio.gov/faq/tabid/6315/Default.aspx?QuestionID=433&AFMID =11354, accessed May 16, 2017.
4. "The Taxes You Don't Pay: All 127 Exemptions from Ohio State Taxes," *Cleveland Plain Dealer*, February 4, 2013, http://www.cleveland.com/metro/index.ssf/2013/02/the_taxes _you_dont_pay_all_127.html.
5. "State's List of New Things to Tax Is Long," *Columbus Dispatch*, February 7, 2013, http:// www.dispatch.com/content/stories/local/2013/02/07/states-list-of-new-things-to-tax-is -long.html.
6. See http://www.pbs.gov.au/info/publication/factsheets/shared/Extension_of_the_listing_of _nicotine_patches.

REFERENCES

Gramlich, Edward. 1990. *A Guide to Benefit-Cost Analysis*, 2nd ed. Upper Saddle River, NJ: Prentice-Hall.

———. 1994. "Infrastructure Investment: A Review Essay." *Journal of Economic Literature* 32 (3): 1176–96.

Lopez, Edward, R. Todd Jewell, and Noel Campbell. 2009. "Pass a Law, Any Law, Fast! State Legislative Responses to the Kelo Backlash." *Review of Law & Economics* 5 (1): 101–36.

McCulloch, J. Huston. 2012. "An Improved Balanced Budget Amendment." *Independent Review* 17 (2): 219–25.

Povich, Elaine. 2015. "Is Obama Proposal the End of Taxpayer-Subsidized Sports Stadiums?" *USA Today*, March 16. https://www.usatoday.com/story/news/politics/2015/03/16/stateline -obama-proposal-taxpayer-subsidized-sports-stadiums/24845355/.

Weingast, Barry, Kenneth Shepsle, and Christopher Johnsen. 1981. "The Political Economy of Benefits and Costs: A Neoclassical Approach to Distributive Politics." *Journal of Political Economy* 89 (4): 642–64.

ABOUT THE CONTRIBUTORS

Sherzod Abdukadirov has been a research fellow in the Program for Economic Research on Regulation at the Mercatus Center at George Mason University. While at the Mercatus Center, he specialized in the federal regulatory process, institutional reforms, food and health, and social complexity. Abdukadirov received his PhD in public policy from George Mason University and his BS in information technology from Rochester Institute of Technology, Rochester, New York. He has prepared numerous policy briefs on regulatory issues. He has written for *US News & World Report* and also for such scholarly journals as *Regulation, Constitutional Political Economy,* and *Asian Journal of Political Science.*

Bruce Benson is professor emeritus at Florida State University (FSU) and a senior fellow at the Independent Institute. Prior to retiring from FSU, he was DeVoe Moore Professor and Distinguished Research Professor in Economics, a Courtesy Professor in Law, director of the BB&T Center in Private Enterprise, and Economics Department chair. Among his other recent affiliations, he has served as a Templeton Visiting Scholar at Texas Tech's Free Market Institute. He earned his PhD at Texas A&M, College Station. Recent honors include a Liberty in Theory and Practice Award from the Libertarian Alliance in London and a Leavy Award for Excellence in Private Enterprise Education.

Thad Calabrese is an associate professor at the Robert F. Wagner Graduate School of Public Service at New York University. He received his PhD from New York University in public administration and policy. He has authored numerous publications on pension finance and management in the public and not-for-profit sectors, as well as on retiree health benefits for government employees. In addition to his academic work, Thad has provided frequent commentary to the press to explain and analyze issues about public pension finance. He has been quoted or cited in the *New York Times, Wall Street Journal, Bloomberg, Bond Buyer,* and *Atlanta Journal-Constitution,* among others.

Peter T. Calcagno is a professor of economics at the College of Charleston, South Carolina, and is the director of the Center for Public Choice & Market Process, an undergraduate free market center. His primary areas of research are in applied microeconomics specifically public choice economics and political economy. Dr. Calcagno is member of the editorial board of *Journal of Entrepreneurship and Public Policy* and is a board member of the Public Choice Society. He is the author of dozens of journal articles and book chapters, and the editor of *Unleashing Capitalism: A Prescription for Economic Prosperity in South Carolina*. He earned his BS in economics and history from Hillsdale College, Hillsdale, Michigan, and a PhD in economics from Auburn University, Auburn, Alabama.

J. R. Clark holds the Probasco Distinguished Chair at the University of Tennessee at Chattanooga. He earned his PhD in economics from Virginia Polytechnic Institute under Nobel Laureate James Buchanan. He is the author of seven books and more than 100 academic articles dealing with public finance, public choice, and taxation. He is a former president of the Association of Private Enterprise Education (APEE), currently serves as secretary/treasurer of both the Southern Economic Association and APEE, and is treasurer of the Mont Pelerin Society.

Dennis Coates is a professor of economics at University of Maryland, Baltimore County. He received his PhD in economics from the University of Maryland, College Park, and was on the faculty of the University of North Carolina, Chapel Hill, before moving to the University of Maryland. His research focuses on political economy and public policy issues with an emphasis on sports and sports economics topics. He is the editor of the *Journal of Sports Economics* and is on the editorial boards of *International Journal of Sport Finance*, *Journal of Sport Management*, *Public Choice*, and several other journals. He is the founding president of the North American Association of Sports Economics.

George R. Crowley is an associate professor of economics at Troy University in Troy, Alabama. He earned his PhD in economics from West Virginia University. His research focuses on topics in public economics and constitutional political economy, and his articles have appeared in such journals as *Economic Inquiry*, *Southern Economic Journal*, *Public Choice*, and *Constitutional Political Economy*. At Troy, he teaches principles and intermediate microeconomics, public finance, and econometrics.

Craig A. Depken II is a professor of economics at the University of North Carolina at Charlotte. He earned his PhD from the University of Georgia, Athens. Dr. Depken has widely published in areas including sports economics, real estate economics, industrial organization, and applied public choice. His articles include "Salary Disparity and Team Performance in the National Hockey League," with J. Lureman, in *Contemporary Economic Policy*, and "A Favorite-Longshot Bias in Fixed-Odds Betting Markets: Evidence from College Basketball and College Football," with J. Berkowitz and J. Gandar, in *Quarterly Review of Economics and Finance*.

Joshua C. Hall is an associate professor of economics and director of the Center for Free Enterprise in the College of Business and Economics at West Virginia University, Morgantown. He earned his PhD from West Virginia University, and BS and MS degrees in economics from Ohio University, Athens. A coauthor of the widely cited *Economic Freedom of the World* annual report, he is also author or coauthor of more than ninety articles in such journals as *Public Choice, Contemporary Economic Policy, Journal of Economic Behavior and Organization*, and *Public Finance Review*.

Frank Hefner is a professor of economics, director of the Office of Economic Analysis, and former chair of the Department of Economics and Finance at the College of Charleston, South Carolina. He received his BA in economics from Rutgers University, New Brunswick, New Jersey, and his MA and PhD from the University of Kansas, Lawrence. He is a past president of the Southern Regional Science Association. He has published research on measuring economic impacts and policy issues related to industrial recruitment.

Collin D. Hodges is currently a third-year PhD student in economics at West Virginia University. Hodges conducts background research and works with data collection, organization, and analysis for Casinonomics, a small consulting firm focusing on the economic and social impacts of legalized gambling, particularly casino gambling in the United States.

Adam J. Hoffer is an associate professor of economics at the University of Wisconsin–La Crosse. He earned his PhD in economics at West Virginia University, Morgantown, in 2012. At the University of Wisconsin–La Crosse, Dr. Hoffer teaches principles of microeconomics and public policy, sports economics, and modern political economy. His research interests include political economy, public choice, sports economics, experimental economics, and pedagogy. He is the associate editor of the *Journal of Economics and Finance Education* and the director of the Wisconsin Initiative for Economic Research.

His research has been published in many peer-reviewed academic journals, books, and popular media outlets.

Randall G. Holcombe is DeVoe Moore Professor of Economics at Florida State University, Tallahassee. He received his PhD in economics from Virginia Polytechnic Institute and State University, Blacksburg. Dr. Holcombe is also senior fellow at the James Madison Institute, and has served on Florida governor Jeb Bush's Council of Economic Advisors from 2000 to 2006. He is the author of fifteen books, including *From Liberty to Democracy: The Transformation of American Government* and *Producing Prosperity*, and has written more than 150 articles published in academic and professional journals. His primary areas of research are public finance and the economic analysis of public policy issues.

Michael LaFaive is senior director of fiscal policy for the Mackinac Center for Public Policy, a Midland, Michigan–based research institute where he has worked for more than two decades. He has undergraduate and graduate degrees in economics from Central Michigan University, Mount Pleasant. Since 2008 he has coauthored several major studies, including "Cigarette Taxes and Smuggling: A Statistical Analysis and Historical Review," and original research on the impact of cigarette excise tax rates on cigarette smuggling and other unintended consequences. His subsequent research with economist Todd Nesbit has been published in op-eds and articles in publications as varied as *Crain's New York* and *Orange County Register*. LaFaive has also examined the impact of alcohol control laws and rules on the price of alcohol and on public safety.

Robert Lawson holds the Jerome M. Fullinwider Endowed Centennial Chair in Economic Freedom and is director of the O'Neil Center for Global Markets and Freedom at the Southern Methodist University Cox School of Business, Dallas. Lawson is a coauthor of the widely cited *Economic Freedom of the World* annual reports, which present an economic freedom index for more than 150 countries. Lawson has numerous professional publications in journals, including *Public Choice, Journal of Economic Behavior and Organization*, and *Cato Journal*. He earned his PhD and MS in economics from Florida State University, Tallahassee, and his BS in economics from the Honors Tutorial College at Ohio University.

Dwight R. Lee is a senior fellow at the O'Neil Center for Global Markets and Freedom at Southern Methodist University, Dallas. He received his PhD from the University of California, San Diego. He has been president of the Association of Private Enterprise Education and of the Southern Economic Association. His books include *Economics in Our Time* (with R. McNown) and *Common Sense Economics* (coauthored). A contributor to twenty-five other books, he is the author of more than 163 refereed journal articles, and his articles have appeared in the *Washington Times, Chicago Tribune, Wall Street Journal, Christian Science Monitor,* and *Forbes.*

Michael Marlow is a professor of economics at California Polytechnic State University, San Luis Obispo. He has been at Cal Poly since 1988 and was named a University Distinguished Scholar in 2007. He received his PhD in economics from Virginia Polytechnic Institute and State University, Blacksburg. His research focuses on the economic effects of government policies, and his most recent research has focused on public health economics in the areas of obesity, nutrition guidelines, and right-to-know laws. He has published two books and more than seventy-five refereed articles in academic journals.

Brian Meehan is an assistant professor of economics at Berry College, Mount Berry, Georgia. Meehan earned his PhD in economics at Florida State University, Tallahassee, with research interests in law and economics, and public choice. He earned his MA in economics from Central Michigan University, Mount Pleasant, and his BS in economics from Northern Michigan University, Marquette. His research has been featured in the journals *Public Choice, International Review of Law & Economics, Applied Economics,* and *Journal of Private Enterprise.*

Matthew Mitchell is a senior research fellow and director of the Project for the Study of American Capitalism at the Mercatus Center at George Mason University. He is also an adjunct professor of economics at Mason. Mitchell received his PhD and MA in economics from George Mason University and his BA in political science and BS in economics from Arizona State University. He specializes in public choice economics and the economics of government favoritism toward particular businesses, industries, and occupations. His research has been featured in the *New York Times, Wall Street Journal, Washington Post, LA Times, U.S. News & World Report,* NPR, and C-SPAN. Mitchell has testified before the US Congress and has advised several state and local government policymakers on both fiscal and regulatory policy.

Todd Nesbit is an assistant professor of economics at Ball State University, Muncie, Indiana, and is on the Board of Scholars at the Mackinac Center for Public Policy. He earned his PhD in economics at West Virginia University, Morgantown, in 2005. He has authored numerous papers that have appeared in such peer-reviewed professional journals as the *Journal of Economic Behavior and Organization, Southern Economic Journal,* and *Public Budgeting and Finance.* His primary interest is in the secondary and unintended effects of excise taxation.

Justin M. Ross is a public finance economist specializing in state and local tax policy. Ross joined the Indiana University School of Public and Environmental Affairs, Bloomington, in 2008 and teaches public revenue theory, public managerial economics, and benefit-cost analysis. Ross's primary research interests include property tax–related issues, such as assessment and zoning. His articles have appeared in the top public finance, economics, and public administration journals, including *National Tax Journal, Land Economics, Journal of Environmental Economics & Management,* and *Public Finance Review.*

William F. Shughart II is research director and senior fellow at the Independent Institute; the J. Fish Smith Professor in Public Choice in the Jon M. Huntsman School of Business at Utah State University, Logan; and former president of the Southern Economic Association. A former economist at the Federal Trade Commission, Professor Shughart received his PhD in economics from Texas A&M University, College Station, and he has taught at George Mason University, Clemson University, University of Mississippi, and the University of Arizona. He is the editor in chief of *Public Choice* and the editor of *Taxing Choice: The Predatory Politics of Fiscal Discrimination* (Transaction Publishers, 1997).

Russell S. Sobel is a professor of economics and entrepreneurship in the Baker School of Business at The Citadel in Charleston, South Carolina. He earned his BS in business economics from Francis Marion College, and his PhD in economics from Florida State University. Sobel has authored or coauthored more than 150 books and articles, including a nationally best-selling college textbook, *Economics: Private and Public Choice.* His research has been featured in the *New York Times, Wall Street Journal, Washington Post,* and the *Economist,* and he has appeared on CNBC, Fox News, CSPAN, NPR, and the CBS Evening News. His recent research focuses on the areas of state economic policy reform and entrepreneurship.

E. Frank Stephenson is the Henry Gund Professor of Economics at Berry College in Mount Berry, Georgia. He earned his PhD in economics at North Carolina State University, Raleigh, and a BA in economics from Washington and Lee University, Lexington, Virginia. His research interests are public policy and sports economics, and his research has appeared in such journals as *Public Choice, Public Finance Review, Journal of Sports Economics,* and *Contemporary Economic Policy.*

Richard E. Wagner is the Holbert L. Harris Professor of Economics at George Mason University, Fairfax, Virginia. He joined the faculty of George Mason University in 1988. Professor Wagner's fields of interest include public finance, public choice, political economy, and macroeconomics. He has authored more than 200 articles in professional journals and some thirty books and monographs, including *Inheritance and the State; Democracy in Deficit* (with James M. Buchanan); *Public Finance in a Democratic Society;* and *To Promote the General Welfare.*

Douglas M. Walker is a professor in the Department of Economics at the College of Charleston, South Carolina, where he has taught since 2007. His primary research focuses on the socioeconomic impact of gambling, particularly casino gambling, which he has been studying for more than twenty years. Regarded as one of the top experts in the world on this issue, he has published two books and more than fifty articles and book chapters on this subject. He has also served as an advisor or consultant for a variety of industry groups, state governments, and consulting firms, and was a visiting professor at Harvard Medical School and the Cambridge Health Alliance, Division on Addiction, where he began to study "responsible gambling."

INDEX

Figures and tables are noted by *f* and *t* following page numbers.

alcohol bans and taxes (*continued*)
  demand elasticity, 62–63, 65–66
  earmarks, *122t*
  earmarks, stickiness, 129, 131–132, *131t,*
    133t, 135–136, *136t, 137t*
  federal excise tax, 1, 23–25, 27–29, *30t,* 135n2
  history, 23–25, 27, 28–29, 135n2
  quality substitution, 144
  reducing consumption of light users, 312
  revenue generated, *30t,* 135n2, 141n11
  Second World War, 28–29
  stadium financing, *246t,* 247, *247t,* 256, *260f*
  state monopolies, 21, 167–168, 397n16
  Sunday sales, 36n12
  unintended consequences, 312
  as user fees, 31
  Whiskey Rebellion and, 23–25
  See also beer; distilled spirits; Prohibition;
    whiskey tax (1791)
Allen, William, 145–146, 149, 163
  See also Alchian-Allen theorem
allocative efficiency, 42–43, 60, 71n2
Alm, James M., 362
Altman, Claire E., 311
American Bar Association, Criminal Justice
  Section, 195n18
American Beverage Association, 67
American Jobs Creation Act (2004), 404
American Revolution, 21–22, 23
American University, 193n6
Anderson, Gary, 328
Anderson, Henry, 343
Anderson, Michael L., 311
Anderson, William, 149–150, 157
Annual Survey of State Government Finances
  (US Census Bureau), 20, 36n3
Anti-Drug Abuse Act (1986), 195n16
Anti-Drug Abuse Act (1988), 195n16, 196n21
anti-obesity paternalism, 305–326
  behavioral economics, 59–60, 306, 313–314
  consumers' attitudes toward risk, 74n19
  as corrective taxation, 90
  as counterproductive, 306, 311–313
  food labeling, 309
  government as better informed than
    individuals, 306, 309, 311, 320, 322n2
  as ineffective, 35, 70, 309–311, 320–321
  informational programs, 306, 309–310
  introduction, 11–12, 305–306
  junk food as target of, 311
  medical spending on obesity, 306–307
  obese people, information needs, 309–310,
    320
  obese people, motivation, 310–311, 320
  obesity, associated health problems, 306,
    309–310
  obesity, causes of, 307
  obesity, rising prevalence of, 306–308

  rent-seeking, 312–313, 318–319
  school programs, 311
  soda taxes, evidence on, 317–318
  soda taxes as nudges, 313–320
  sugar and obesity, unclear connection
    between, 316–317
  support for, 59
  unintended consequences, 312, 319–320
  See also Berkeley, California, sugary drink
    tax; junk food; soda taxes
arena construction. *See* sports venues
Arizona
  asset seizures, *182t,* 190
  cigarette tax, sales, and smuggling, 337, *338t*
  economic development tax incentives,
    224, 235
  paternalism ranking, *382t,* 384, *387t,* 389,
    390t, 392t, 393t
  pension and retiree health insurance
    obligations, *282t*
  stadium financing, 248–249
Arizona Public Safety Personnel Retirement
  Systems, 277
Arkansas
  asset seizure laws, *182t*
  cigarette tax, sales, and smuggling rate, *338t*
  paternalism ranking, *382t, 387t, 390t, 392t,*
    393t
  pension and retiree health insurance
    obligations, *282t*
  soda taxes, 397n13
Arlington, Texas, 252
Armey, Dick, 411, 414, 418
Armstrong, Joe, 343–344
Arrow, Kenneth, 4–5, 405
arrow shafts, tax rate, *32t*
Arthur, Chester A., 417
Articles of Confederation, 22, 291, 301n5,
  407–408
artificially sweetened beverages, 68
asset seizures
  abuses, 199n38
  adoption policy, 181, 195–196nn20–21,
    197n26, 199n38
  arrests, increase in, 184, 198n32
  burden-of-proof requirement, 197n24
  earmarked for law enforcement, 169, 180–
    185, 195n18
  Equitable Sharing Program, 182–185, *183t,*
    196n20, 197n26, 198n32, 199n38
  federal increase in, 178, 194n11
  fungibility of proceeds, 190
  history, 178
  from innocent victims, 185–189
  introduction, 8–9
  justification, 178
  return of assets, 198n37
  as sin tax, 178

CPSIA information can be obtained
at www.ICGtesting.com
Printed in the USA
FFOW01n0020201217
44119853-43420FF

9 781942 951384